T0374202

The Girl from Rat Row

The Bootlegger's Daughter

Part 1

Evangelist Hazel Singleton

authorHOUSE®

AuthorHouse™
1663 Liberty Drive
Bloomington, IN 47403
www.authorhouse.com
Phone: 1 (800) 839-8640

This book is a work of non-fiction. Unless otherwise noted, the author and the publisher make no explicit guarantees as to the accuracy of the information contained in this book and in some cases, names of people and places have been altered to protect their privacy.

Published by AuthorHouse 09/09/2017

ISBN: 978-1-5462-0810-5 (sc)
ISBN: 978-1-5462-0811-2 (hc)
ISBN: 978-1-5462-0809-9 (e)

Library of Congress Control Number: 2017913931

Print information available on the last page.

This book is printed on acid-free paper.

Contents

Chapter 1: Beginnings

The earliest memory of my life relates to the very first time I had a great encounter with my uncle Cleo. I used my four-year-old imagination to sneak out of the bedroom, captivated by the noises coming from outdoors. The one voice that held my attention on that cold winter night was the voice of my favorite uncle. He had a tone like nobody else in town. If he had been wanted anywhere for anything, and he spoke, his voice would certainly have given him away.

Growing up, I lived in a dysfunctional family. The pain that grew inside of my body each day became more than a hindrance in my life. Life as I encountered it never allowed those memories to disappear. Instead, they stuck to my brain like gum glued to a cavity in a tooth. There is always something lurking about to remind me of those days growing up in a small town—so small it can barely be found on the map.

As a result, I learned that experience is the best teacher. Having to face life without a true identity taught me that one must learn life before appreciating life. You only get out what you put in. See it all, experience it all, walk through it all. Maturity is then birthed out, and deliverance comes from it. Then one can surely say, "But God."

In time, honesty, faithfulness, and believing in myself are what favored me. "Put trust in no man"—I thought on and constantly heard those words ring in my mind. By the time I grasped what I was hearing, time had almost passed me by. I was standing alone. I had been deceived, set up, put down, shut down, let down, and sometimes even made to bow down. I had no pride or haughtiness left in me.

Things can work out when we look to other people as our resource, without the possibility of believing in ourselves. Instead, we think on how others treat us and feel about us. Everyone wants to be treated fairly. No one wants to be lied to or lied about. We want friends, family members, and people generally to be loyal with kindness. We all want these things, but what are we giving in return? It has to do with our upbringing—how we live our lives and how we end up. There is always an "it depends."

I learned the best way to a good life after living beneath the life God had so beautifully ordained for me is to lay down every weight that beset me and run the race for perfection. Having experienced the many heartaches of loving the wrong folk and trusting the wrong people educated me more than any book I could have read. My greatest accomplishment in life was eventually learning what contentment was—certainly not people or things. It was the almighty God.

I was in bondage for so long, like the children of Israel, and it kept leading me into more and more sin. I learned that sin isolates us from all the promises God has in store for us. We can always blame someone else for our failures, troubles, or reasons for the way our lives end up, but until we look at ourselves, the stories we tell just hide the problems deep beneath the surface. Our decisions are within us, no matter how we find someone else to blame. Words have meanings. Words make sentences. Words become truth or words become lies. Therefore, let every man be a liar and God be the truth.

Looking back over my life, it is not a beautiful picture. What captivated my inner spirit were the other people whom God allowed me to meet, learn about, and get to know. Not one person around me was any different than I was, but I found some to be far worse than I ever dreamed of being. Unfortunately, those were the people I learned to love. They taught me what love is all about. I realized what our heavenly Father sees in us. He made us people, all races of people, and he knows every rotten thing about us. But he loves us regardless.

"For God so loved the world that He gave His only begotten son that whosoever believe in Him shall not perish but have everlasting life" (John 3:16 KJV). This was one of the very first verses I learned to quote from the Bible. It grew up with me and in me, and I live by it.

Traveling down the red-dust roads of southwestern Georgia, sitting on the side of the red clay hills, and digging ditches in the red clay dirt somewhat remind me of the Jerusalem, Jericho, and Damascus roads Jesus traveled. He was saving and healing, working miracles in the lives of lost, unhealthy people who were sick in the mind as well as in the body. Living a godly life is never easy. Neither was it easy for Jesus, but he never stopped.

I will never be Jesus, but learning to live again taught me that I am close to being the daughter he is seeking in these last evil days. Gratitude will get anyone farther than ingratitude will. My relationship with the Lord is all the proof I need of what a great God we serve. So often, being encouraged to trust God gave me more strength to press on for the good things that life holds for me. He brought me out of my darkness. The memories get more and more vivid, but I get even more determined to "press toward the mark for the prize of the high calling of God in Christ Jesus" (Phil. 3:14 KJV).

Throughout the better years of my life, I couldn't think beyond my circumstances: a tenth-grade dropout having to work a minimum-wage job and take care of not just my two children but other family members' children also. I was the example that folk made me out to be. But through all the trials, tribulations, and hard times I encountered, it was when I gave my life over to God that I found the peace I didn't think I could ever have.

God is joy, unspeakable joy, and the kind of love that I never felt from my family, friends, or anyone else on this God-given earth. I found that love in Jesus Christ, the Son of the living God. His love is the unconditional love that I sought in all the wrong places. God does not love as the world pretends to, loving you today and hating you tomorrow. No, God's love, as I have encountered personally, is the kind of love that taught me how to really love in return.

Through all the pain, sorrow, misunderstandings, and sin that came within my reach, I learned that I can do all things through Christ who strengthens me. I thank God for being my strength. Truly, with God all things are possible for those who believe.

I spent my childhood carrying adult responsibility. It is not a beautiful memory. I think back on the many times I took care of children though being only a child myself, doing grown-up chores. Being unable to attend school certainly didn't help my situation; it caused me a mental disability unknowingly. That sucks the life right out of a person. It's the kind of damage that cripples righteousness but leaves one holding on to unrighteousness. I was so twisted and blinded by fate that unrighteousness became right to me. It left me scarred almost for life.

I endured the troubles by safeguarding myself, sometimes even by resorting to violence. Fighting for everything becomes a way of life for any person who grows up in a jacked-up environment. It leaves you with nothing to live for. I felt I had to fight with my mind, fight with my heart, fight with my mouth, and fight with my fists. I ended up notorious. Notwithstanding that, in time it made me a strong black woman.

I was born on a late April day back in the nineteen-forties, in a little town full of prejudice and hatred from white folk. I lived with my mother, father, sisters, and brother.

Gemmy BB, my oldest sister, was fourteen years old. I didn't like her very much because she was mean and always antagonized me. Even at four years old, I was smart enough to recognize envy. I was only too young to understand why. I always knew she had an atrocious feeling toward me, which helped me to stay alert. I was instantly cautious of her always, but never figured out why she disliked me so much. Maybe it was jealousy because my father was not her father. I was the oldest of my father's six children.

Two years younger than Gemmy BB was Passy Kate. Lou Anna, my favorite sister, was eight. My grandfather, whom we called Papa, nicknamed her Tise. Even though I was younger than the three of them, I could relate to Tise on her own level. Next after me was my brother Georgie Boy, named after Papa.

It was late one chilly winter night, and we were all gathered about the big oak fire, trying to stay warm. I remember the harsh whistling of the wind, beating vehemently against the old, unpainted, wood-framed house that we lived in. The ceiling was very high, making it nearly impossible to warm the entire house. The cracks in the walls were so big, we had to pack old rags in them to keep the heat in and the cold wind out. Rats were so big in that neighborhood, the street was called Rat Row. I was never able to understand why it was only called Rat Row down on the end where we lived. Midway up the street, there were as many rats as there were on our end, but that part was called Peer Street.

Regardless, we were the family that every other family thought they were better than. They lived in better houses and many of them were better educated; therefore, I suppose, that made them "better." Even though they had more material things, they were still working families. I was a bit young to understand the difference between rich, poor, and middle-class lifestyles. I was certainly a child interested in them all—except old lady Brittney, the schoolteacher. She lived all the way down at the other end of the street, near old Flappy Boots. The rats down there walked among the neighbors more boldly than the ones on our end did. I remember hearing some say the rats were Flappy's regular customers.

Mama always said I was nosy from the day I was born. I didn't know if that was a positive or negative point of view. I was very perceptive of the least little noise, even over the racket of the window shutters whipping against the house. I could hear voices outside. They seemed to be coming from across the road, where all the local folk gathered after work.

I eased out to the kitchen, pretending to get some water. I reached for my red plaid coat that hung on a rusty nail behind the door, hurrying to put it on and exit before anyone caught me. Suddenly, Tise called out, "Haley, bring me a drink!"

"Naw, me ain't! Git it yourself—I got me some by myself!" I responded, knowing I didn't have time to fulfill her request.

Tise entered the kitchen, asking, "Haley, what you doin wit dat coat?"

"Don't talk loud, gurl, you gon wake Mama an er baby up!"

Mama had, not so long before, given birth to a baby girl. She at that time was about three months old. Her name was Annie Dora. "I'll be quiet, but where you gwine wit dat coat, gurl?" she asked.

"I heard noises, so I want to peep outside to see. Come on wit me an us go see who it is?"

She didn't hesitate. She grabbed her coat and we tiptoed out the back door.

The first person we saw was Papa—Mama's father, George Molden. He and some neighbors were standing on the other side of the road, as usual. They had a fire to keep themselves warm as they drank their moonshine. We stood watchful so we wouldn't be seen. I recognized my uncle Cleo and overheard him telling Papa it was time for them to go. It was the same routine with Cleo when the time came for him to leave—he would refused angrily, which was what he did when he was good and drunk.

Uncle Cleo was my uncle by marriage to my mother's baby sister, Aunt Lucy Sue, with whom Papa resided. Uncle Cleo was a terrific father to my cousins.

We could always tell when Papa was drinking his moonshine. Everybody in Rat Row could hear him, and he didn't play the radio. No, no, no, old man Molden didn't play. He was always serious as a heart attack. I would often hear people say, "Don't bother wit Uncle George, chilluns, if you don't want no Molden trouble!"

Grinning, making a joke, he was steady as he shouted out his bold words: "I ain't your g——d—— child!" Folk knew when he used that tone to leave him alone. Uncle Cleo was about the only one who could calm him down when he seemed out of control. My sister Tise was the only grandchild he would listen to also; she could get through to him when no one else could.

The wind was really whistling. The weather was getting colder and colder, and I was shivering. I was holding on to the tail of Tise's coat. I told her, "Let's just go back inside," but she wanted to go down to the other corner of the house so we could see more clearly. "Naw," I protested. "I wanna go back inside, cause we gon git in trouble when Mama wake up an find out we went out de door without askin her permission." I was shivering so hard, my teeth were clicking together. We argued back and forth.

Then I looked, and there was the masked lady everyone in town was talking about. I pointed. "Look, Tise! Dere go dat lady wit de false face. Let's go fore she git us!" The mask looked like a Halloween mask. I commenced to get scared and cry. I cried from natural fear. I was scared stiff of that woman, Ms. Onna, and I wondered what she was hiding underneath that mask. I begged, "Please, Tise! Let's us go! I want to go home. Let's us go, please!"

"Stop cryin. I'll take you back. Come on. You ain't had no business in comin out here in de first place."

Uncle Cleo looked up and spotted us. He came directly over to where we were. I was happy to see him because he was our favorite uncle. I thought he was the best uncle in the whole wide world. He always knew the right words to say that would soothe anybody's spirit. "What y'all gurls doin out dis here door, cold as it is?" he said, smiling. He knew we were out there without permission.

He bent down and lifted me up from the ground, speaking softly. "Don't you know y'all need to be inside de house, cold as it is out here? I bet Jenny Rue don't even know y'all little gals out dis door, do she?" He kissed me on my forehead and lowered me back down. As he walked us back toward the house, Tise made sure to tell him that it was my idea to come out to see what the noise was.

But he reminded her that she was the older one. "Oh! You little gurls just needed to come out an see Ms. Onna wearin her Halloween mask on her face, huh? Well, ain't nothin wrong wit dat, but you know y'all ain't got no business bein out in dis here dark," he said.

We watched as the masked lady begin walking toward the end of the road, down by Pa Jack's café. "Where she goin?" I asked him.

He said politely, "She might be just gon see de little old lady dat moved down by Shelmore's store."

Ms. Onna was one of the sisters who lived directly across the road from where we lived. According to the talk around there, she was mean as any rattlesnake that was in a coil and ready to strike. I asked, "Why in de Lord's world do she want to bother dat old lady? Gee, she just a sweet old lady, don't bother nobody." I had not even seen the old lady they were speaking of. Just talking about her caused something to rattle very heavily inside me that couldn't be explained. Only I could feel it.

"Come along now," Uncle Cleo said, approaching the back steps. He pushed the door open and tiptoed on into the room, looking back at us and saying, "Let's git inside."

Mama was still fast asleep; we hadn't even been missed. We wanted to take full advantage of our time, so we rushed in and took our coats off.

But the slamming of the door woke Mama up. In an angry voice, she yelled, "Who dat got dat door oped on my baby?"

Uncle Cleo, being who he was, said in our defense, "It's your brudder-in-law, Jenny Rue. It's Cleo. Just stoppin by to see how you was gittin long, since I was on dis end."

Mama reached up and pulled down her brown corduroy housecoat from the iron headboard of the bed, saying, "Cleo! Come on up an pull up a chair an warm your hands. I know dey bout done froze out dere in all dat cold."

She took a look at me as she walked slowly over to the fireplace. "Haley, what is you still doin up? Now you go on, little woman, and git your little self in dat bed." By now she was wide awake. "Cleo, who come down here wit you?" Before he could answer, she had two more questions. "Where is Papa? Did he come wit you?"

"Yeah, he come down here wit me. Sittin right outside, shootin de jive."

"Y'all just sat out dere shootin de jive? What else goin on out dere?" she asked suspiciously, as if she knew something else was going on that he hadn't said.

He responded eagerly, "Nothin much else. Like everybody else, just watchin Onna in er devilment, wearin dat mask."

I could hear the tone change in Mama's voice when she asked, "What she out dere doin, Cleo? Is she out dere scarin dem dere chilluns again? Lord, when will she ever stop?"

Uncle Cleo answered, "Naw, Jenny Rue, it ain't dem chilluns. All dem already in for de evenin. I think it's dat little old lady dat just moved in down by Shelmore's grocery store."

Mama took a seat in one of the straw high-back chairs, but she didn't sit long. She got up and walked slowly to the bed where the baby was sleeping. Mama looked down at the baby, rubbing her hand across her face. She made sure the baby was covered securely, and she walked back to the chair and sat down again. In a low tone, she asked, "Lord, when will she ever stop?" Then, angrily, "Dat damn woman gon burn in hell one of dese days!"

She didn't yell, big as her mouth was. But I remember how furious she got when she heard what Ms. Onna was doing.

She went on, "Well, Annie Dora is already three months old. I'mo go down dere to make my quaintance wit er tomorrow. I used to watch er when she first moved down dere, fore I had de baby. She look so lonesome and scared. Cleo, do anybody know what er name is or where she come from?"

"Jenny Rue, I heard some talk dat she is some kind of kin to Sonny Rhimes. Dat's bout all I know, but y'all git it."

She gave me that look, and I trotted on off to bed. But I didn't go off to sleep.

Not long after, I heard Uncle Cleo saying his good-night. He never told Mama about Tise and I being outside. I didn't know if it was right or wrong, but our secret was safe with him.

Tise and I slept together. Gemmy BB and Passy Kate slept together whenever they stayed home. They were all in bed, comfortably sleeping—or so I thought as I lay still. Then I heard the back door squeak, and I knew it was Gemmy BB sneaking out to meet that Jacob dude behind the chimney. After a while, I got up. I tiptoed to the kitchen without being heard and sneaked out the back. Right I was—there they were in the corner of the chimney, kissing.

I stood looking at them with a grin. Then I laughed out loud, which made her notice me. She got so angry! By the look on her face as she started toward me, I could see she was not pleased with me at all.

I started to back away from her, not cautious of the darkness. The only light was the big, beautiful moon shining down on the land. She struck at me, and I fell over a piece of broken glass that drove directly in my right rear end. I screamed out loud in fear, "Oh, I done hurt myself!"

My screaming made Gemmy BB even angrier with me. She put her hand across my mouth to prevent me from waking up the others. As she gripped me, she stated, "Now cause of you, everybody gon know. You see what you done? If you wouldn'ta been so doggone nosy, dis wouldn'ta happened wit yo' little grown self!"

She lifted me up, carrying me back inside quietly. I was bleeding kind of heavy from the wound, and she was nervous, because she had to explain what happen to me to Mama. She cried out in a panicky voice, as if it was my fault, "Haley done got her fast self outside again an fell on a piece of glass an cut herself."

Mama, she got up slowly and went to the kitchen. She took out the old black kettle and put it on to the fire to heat the water. She took a clean white piece of rag and wiped the blood from the wound. I was crying like somebody was killing me, not really knowing if I was crying because of the cut or because she was going to kill me for sure. I had been warned often about sneaking out in the middle of the night, and I just knew I was going to get a good spanking. But I guess the wound prevented my behind from getting tanned. After she finished dressing the wound, she sent me to bed. She didn't have to say it twice.

She said it in an angry tone, yet one filled with deep concern. "Haley, you better go to sleep, cause if you git back outer dat bed one more time, little sister, I'mo tear your little ass up."

I knew she meant every word. I went right off to sleep as soon as I was ordered to. I had to adjust to the discomfort and stay asleep the entire night. Usually I would hear Daddy when he came home from gambling.

Everyone in the house knew when Daddy came home. He would have Mama up cooking or warming food for him. Half the time he would be too intoxicated to even eat it. He had her scared of him. Whatever he wanted her to do, she would do it for him. He felt that to fear a person was to respect a person. Only Gemmy BB and Passy Kate were never frightened by him—not that he never tried, but they were never easily frightened by anyone, especially him.

Mama's morning always started off bright and early. After she was done cooking, she'd call out, "Breakfast is ready! Y'all come on in here an eat!"

I pulled back the covers from over my head, hearing the wind still whipping against those old wooden shutters. As I crawled out of bed, my back end was so sore that it was impossible to sit comfortably on it. Daddy was already at the kitchen table, drinking coffee. He would sometimes take me up in his lap and hold me when he was in a good mood. That morning, he was, and I was unable to sit. I had to explain what was wrong.

Gemmy BB was looking right at me. Before I could open my mouth, she told her version of what happened and then said, "Dat's good for you—you ain't had no business out dere bein nosy."

Everyone got still as a mice. The only noise came from the harsh wind.

After a moment, Daddy said, "Is dat what happen? You got your little nosy ass out in de cold and fell?"

"Yes, sir."

"Den maybe dis'll teach you a lesson." And he pushed me to the side. Hurrying his breakfast, he jumped up from the table and left.

I was calm, but I knew Gemmy BB was still mad as hell at me. The first chance she got, she was going to go upside my head.

It was wash day, and Gemmy BB and Passy Kate did their share. "Go out dere an git de fire round de pot started," Mama demanded. She cleared the dirty dishes from the table. "I'll git the washin started for y'all. Den I'm gwine down dere to see de little lady dat everybody is talkin bout."

"Kin I come too, Mama?" I asked. I was too young to know that everywhere she went, she took me with her. As time went by, I learned she was protecting me from the evil of my older sister's abusiveness. Mama never would leave me alone with Gemmy BB, and the day came when I understood that. Still, whenever I heard her say she was going somewhere, I automatically asked, "Kin I come too, Mama?"

She made sure my sisters were bundled up good against the freezing cold weather. But no matter how cold it was, her wash day continued. She never let cold, rain, or heat stop her. She washed, my sisters washed, and I lay inside, watching the baby—that was my chore.

However, all the other neighbors gathered and joined in to give a helping hand. Before the day ended, they all were washing, cleaning, cooking, and doing whatever chores were needed. That was the way things were—people cared about the welfare of others, their neighbors, meaning the ones who lived on the end where we lived.

Though there were families in the neighborhood who excluded us. It was like we were from across the tracks. We certainly were the black sheep of the neighborhood to some. But we had great neighbors. My mother, whom we all called Mama, was a one-of-a-kind woman, always willing to go far and beyond her call of duty for anyone. She would give the last she had if she felt others needed it more than she did.

As she was getting ready to see the little old lady, I learned that it was the God in Mama to see to the needs of someone else. She loved doing things for other people. Even though she could not read or write very well, she knew what the Good Book said: "Do unto others as you would have them do unto you." She couldn't tell you what chapter or verse that was, but she knew a lot about what the Good Book said. She quoted Scripture often, especially when she was hurting or in need.

She stood in front of the mirror, tying up her head with a baby diaper and putting on her long, red wool coat. She then tied my head up with her red plaid scarf, making sure my ears were securely covered. She gave the instruction that I listen out for the baby while she went and made sure Gemmy BB and Passy Kate had the washing running properly. It wasn't long before she came back inside with Tise and ordered her to watch the baby while we were out. She made sure the work was divided equally.

I recall that as we arrived at the old lady's front yard, we could see her in the backyard. She was standing by a black washpot, pressing around the clothes with a flathead stick. We went around the side of the house and entered the backyard. I could tell instantly from the expression on her face that she was frightened. She looked like she wanted to run. I didn't know why. I thought only that she had been frightened by Ms Onna. She must have thought we were there to bring her some uncomfortableness. It was certain she didn't trust anyone.

After a few minutes of observing us, she slightly smiled and looked from me to Mama. Mama smiled back and held her hand out for a shake. Mama spoke kindly to her, asking, "How you doing? My name is Jenny Rue. Just stopped by to see you and make my quaintance wit you."

The lady looked even more afraid, as if she didn't know what Mama was saying to her. She backed slowly to the door. I stood close behind Mama, who was smiling. I smiled too. The lady stood for a moment. She looked at me again and smiled back. The frightened look upon her face vanished.

Mama stepped up close and reached out again for a handshake. After looking Mama up and down, the lady finally took her hand and led us inside her house. She didn't speak right away, but her facial expression told me that we'd brought happiness into her life that day.

We entered into her kitchen. She led us on through to the bedroom and living room, which were all in one. Today, we'd call it a kitchenette. The first words she said to Mama were, "It's mighty cold out dere dis mornin. Mighty good of you to stop by an see me."

In a few minutes, she was all smiles. She was feeling us out, and I think she was seeking in us. Mama continued to smile at her. The lady took me by my hand and held it. She said sadly, "Poor little thing! Yo hands just like ice. Come on up here by de fire and warm yo hands."

Her room was nice and warm, and it was very clean in there. She had a big, fluffy, brown bedspread on her bed with a multicolor design in the center—as I remember, in a turkey shape. There was a brown-and-white knitted cover on her sofa, and pictures of Jesus were posted all over the walls.

I was fascinated with one picture of Jesus nailed to the cross, the crown of thorns around his head. I had never seen anything like that; we certainly didn't have one. I was interested in knowing what the pictures meant. I could not stop staring at them. I thought the lady was a witch, except she was too nice to be a witch.

I felt something about her that I had never felt from anyone in my four-year-old life. I earnestly believe that that day, I was born in the Spirit through her when she touched me on my cold, cracked cheek. The touch of her hand send chills through my body—not cold chills, but warm chills. The warmth that I felt was spiritual. I really believe she was someone send by God.

She led me over to a chair and insisted that I sit down. I pointed to my backside, hinting that I was hurting and could not sit. She didn't understand what I was saying to her, so I pulled my pants down and showed her my cut.

She placed her ear close to my mouth. I whispered that I had cut myself on a piece of broken glass. She still didn't understand, so I spoke a little louder. That's when Mama said, "De poor old soul can't even hear. She is hard of hearin."

Just like that, we learned how to relate to her. She went over to her bed, picked up a round pillow, and gave it to me. It was the softest pillow I had ever felt; it was made of feathers. "Set on it," she said, looking into my eyes. She had beautiful gray eyes. Her teeth were severely stained from the snuff she dipped. Her hair was white as a sheep and looked like silk.

I sat down on the pillow, and Mama sat on the sofa, beside the old lady. That was the day I found myself a second mother and Mama found herself a true friend. This old lady brought much happiness into our lives, just as we brought it into hers. It was a new start for all of us.

The old lady went into the kitchen and came back with a handful of what I thought were cookies. I was good and hungry. I bit down on one, and it was delicious. I ate them down fast. When I finished, she was still laughing. "You like?" she said. "Dey good, ain't dey?"

"Yeah, ma'am," I answered.

"Dey tea cakes," she replied.

I fell in love with them and after that was never in lack for them.

We learned that day she was in her late seventies or early eighties. Mama was shocked. "Aunt Matilda, you ain't no eighty years old!"

Aunt Matilda really didn't know how old she was, but she proudly smiled and said, "Yes, I is, too. I was twelve years old when de president freed us from slavery in the year of eighteen hunderd an sixty-three." She seemed very sure of the year, and she remembered that day with a tremendous strength of pride.

Listening to her made me feel like I was older than I was. We sat and talked to her as if we had known her all our lives. Before Mama realized it, half the day was gone. "Oh, gosh! I got to go home an nurse my baby."

"What you say? You got to go nurse de baby?" Aunt Matilda looked directly at Mama's mouth, reading every word she spoke.

Mama told her, "Yeah, I got a twelve-week-old baby gurl at home."

Aunt Matilda smiled from ear to ear. Hearing Mama say she had to nurse the baby seemed to tickle her silly.

As we got ready to leave, Aunt Matilda had this look of despair in her eyes, like she was dreading that we had to go. Suddenly that fearful look came back over her face. I told her, "I'll stay wit you if you want me to?"

She lifted me into her arms and hugged me as if I were her own little girl. Mama had to have been feeling what Aunt Matilda and I were feeling; otherwise she never would have left me with a lady she really didn't know. Mama allowed me to stay until dusk.

When Mama came back to get me, it seemed to tear Aunt Matilda's heart out. The look in her deep gray eyes saddened me. She asked softly, "Kin she stay de night?"

I could tell Mama wanted me to stay, but I was not old enough. Mama looked back sorrowfully and said, "Naw. Her daddy ain't home. She too little to stay. But I got another gurl older dan Haley dat I'll let come back an stay wit you, if dat's all right."

Aunt Matilda smiled in a way that said, "I'll take whoever I can git."

Somewhere in the back of my four-year-old mind, I wanted to stay with her all the time. I felt that she needed me day and night. She was all alone in that house, and Ms. Onna put that false face on and frightened her whenever she felt like doing so. I didn't know what I hoped to accomplish by staying with her, but somehow I knew she needed, if not me, then somebody. I was glad she accepted Tise.

There was a dark cloud rising from the back of our street, stirring up in the east. Mama said, "Lord! It's a storm brewin. We got to hurry an beat it or we gon drown."

We left Aunt Matilda sad-faced, although Mama assured her that Tise was coming back to spend the night. She stood on the front porch as we headed back home. I looked back and saw that sadness evaporated—she was smiling all over her face, and her eyes looked somehow brighter. I know that day my mama gained Aunt Matilda's trust like no one else in the whole town.

Mama and I were walking down the highway when suddenly a cold gust of wind struck my face. Instantly, I could no longer see her; my eyes were burning from the windblown sand. Mama was holding on to me with one hand and trying to block the sandy wind from my face with the other. Finally she lifted me up in her arms, and I mean she was practically running down the street. At last we arrived home with a great passion of relief.

Passy Kate was sitting by the fire, holding the baby. "Mama, we had to stop washin," she said. "It was just too cold out dere, an de wind almost blowed the fire from round de pot."

Frustration swept across Mama's face, but she knew it was the truth. Not many people could stand that kind of weather. It was just that she knew Kate herself wasn't true. But she did sympathize with her, and said in annoyance, "Well, den I got to finish washin dem dere clothes, cause ain't nothin else in de house clean."

That's who she was. She would be the only one in the neighborhood washing, whether it was raining or freezing cold or burning hot. She never would let the weather stop her when she was washing her clothes or cleaning her house.

"Y'all clean de house and see bout my baby while I go out an git the washing done. My baby got to have clean diapers."

Passy Kate assured her she had most of the white clothes done. That seemed to give Mama some relief. Passy Kate said urgently, "Dem clothes kin wait, Mama. You can't go out dere in all dat cold, tryin to finish no clothes. Dat wind gon blow you down."

Suddenly there was a big crash, so loud it shook the entire house. Everyone in the house reacted in fear. The strong wind had blown half the tin roof up from the top of the house, and it crashed back so hard it shook the whole building.

Mama took baby Dora from Passy Kate, laid her in the bed, and told me to get in beside her. That was one of my four-year-old chores; I was good at watching her. I played with her fingers and rubbed my hand across her face, as I often saw Mama do. The feel of her was memorable—the softness of her skin and the scent from the baby power and baby oil.

The sound of the wind, whistling like a train, is a sound I will never forget. I wondered about the little old lady and what was she doing alone in her house. Then I remembered Tise was with her, and that made me feel much better. I drifted off to sleep.

Later, I was awakened by loud voices. I looked around the room, but no one was in the room except me. I sat up in the bed. There was no excitement going on; I had awakened from a bad dream. I could hear voices, so I called out to Mama but got no response. I started to cry. My cries got louder and louder.

After I'd been crying for an uncertain amount of time, my sister Gemmy BB came rushing into the room, yelling, "What's wrong wit you, fool?"

I was crying so hard I couldn't even answer her. She was enraged and started yelling. Her yells got louder and so did my screams. She rushed up to the bed and grabbed my arm in a grip so tight I was afraid to scream anymore. I whimpered. She was steady in her shouting, asking me, "What's wrong wit you, gurl? Ain't nothin wrong wit your little grown ass but spoil." She slapped me across my face. "Shut up dat got-durn fuss, gurl! You damn fool, shut dat fuss! I mean it! Shut up right now!"

Just as she was about to give me another slap, we heard footsteps coming toward the room. She quickly let go of my arm, leaving her fingernail prints in my arm. I was afraid to cry out, so I held the tears inside me.

In walked Daddy. He saw right away something was wrong. I ran to him, jumping directly into his arms. I looked back at Gemmy BB, giving her a look that said, "Now you mess wit me."

"What's der matter wit you?" Daddy asked furiously.

Gemmy BB was standing back, unscrupulous, not saying anything. She was waiting to see what I was going to say. I was continuously whimpering; I couldn't seem to control myself. I started to cry again, and Daddy knew for sure something was wrong. He looked at Gemmy

BB with one of his ready-to-strike looks and asked, "What de hell goin on? What did you do to my baby gal?"

She looked angry. She pushed by him, and he followed her. She lied, "Ain't nothin wrong wit dat gurl. She just bein her usual spoil self."

"You look just like you telling a damn lie." He asked me, "What she do to you?"

I looked at her, then back at him and said, "She slapped my face and squeezed my arm real, real tight."

He knew I was not lying. He took my arm and looked at it, seeing the nail prints. Gemmy BB immediately yelled, "Dat ain't de truth! She tellin a story wit her old spoil self!" There was a tremor in her voice, warning me to be even more cautious of her.

So I repeated myself and told Daddy, "She hit me in my face like dis." I wrapped my fingers across his face to demonstrate. Pulling my sleeve up, I again showed him the fingernail marks.

Showing him what she'd done was the only evidence I had to convince him that I wasn't making up a fib on her. She always accused me of being a manipulator, but that time she was the manipulative one. I wasn't trying to get her in trouble, but I needed to be believed. I learned at an early age that adults could and would tell convincing lies, and I learned from the best. If my daddy had doubted me in the least, he would have left me alone with Gemmy BB, and she would have done worse to me. She had me almost terrified of her. I never felt safe around her.

After looking over my arm, he gave her a slap acoss her face, much harder than the one she gave me. She started boo-hoo crying. He put me down on the floor and told her at the same time, "I mean you keep your g——d—— hands off of her, you hear me?"

Daddy never handled a situation intelligently. His way was to curse with every word that came from his mouth. The way she boo-hooed in that room, anyone would have thought he was killing her. I thought she was going to slap him back. She kept lying, saying loudly over and over again, "I ain't did nothin to dat old lyin grown gal! All I did was come in here to see what she was doin all dat screamin for, an for her to come to eat supper."

"Den why in de hell she got all dem dere fingernail marks on er arm? I guess dey just got on dere by dey g——d—— self."

"I was only tryin to make her hush up all dat screamin!"

Mama came through the door, and Gemmy BB screamed, "An I'mo move way from here. Everything dat gal say, y'all believe er. Naw, I can't stand er an old, dirty Mr. Macky neither. I hate em! He slapped me for nothin cause he believe everythin dat old nappy-headed gal say! I won't stand for him puttin his hands on me no damn more!" She ran out of the room before Mama had a chance to comment, fully knowing that an argument would break out between them because of her.

Later she came out through the room with her clothes in a flour sack, saying she was moving out. Mama asked with concern, "Gemmy BB, where in de world you think you goin? You just a child."

"I don't know and I don't care. I'd rather go sleep in the sawmill fore I stay here. I kin find me some work and drop out of school. I ain't gon stay here an take Mr. Macky's mess wit his old, bald-headed, no-good self, all cause of dat old nappy-headed spoil gal. Dat's what wrong wit er now—y'all believe every darn thing she say."

There was a shouting match between her and Mama. I felt bad, but I didn't know if it was because Gemmy BB was so vindictive or because I was old enough to recognize her hatred toward me, a little four-year-old girl.

I went into the kitchen and got my old coat. The wind had calmed down tremendously. I peeked out the door. The breeze was a little high, but not enough that I couldn't ease out without being noticed. I didn't really know where I was going, but I got outside and ran into old Ms. Onna.

There was no misunderstanding that I was afraid of that woman, because she was a cruel one. She was as evil as a coiled snake, ready to strike, or so I thought. I was about to run around the house when someone called out my name. I hesitated answering because I was not supposed to be out. I hadn't noticed the other grown-ups sitting on the side of the road, as they always did. That was where they gathered socially in the early mornings and late evenings to gossip about everything and everybody.

The voice called out my name again: "Little Haley!"

I put my hands over my face. Anxious to know who it was calling me, I slowly turned around. "Who dat call me?" I asked.

"Who you think call you? It's your uncle Martel."

"What you callin me for?"

He wasn't my blood uncle, but he and Sattie Bell always insisted that they were my uncle and aunt. I even felt that they were, for they always treated me as if I were their little niece. But I never could get the right feeling in calling Sattie Bell my aunt, so I called her cousin and him Uncle Martel.

He called me again: "Come here, little Haley, lookin like your daddy."

"What y'all want wit me?"

There was old Mr. Fred playing his guitar. Uncle Martel wanted me to dance and said he'd give me a nickel.

A nickel—wow! I was about to say yeah, when I looked and there stood Ms. Onna. She didn't have a mask on, but I remembered how it looked. Immediately a naw poured out of my mouth. A nickel was a lot of money for a child my age back then. I could have bought ten pieces of two-for-a-penny candy that would have lasted me all day, undoubtedly. But looking at that woman discouraged me in a hurry. I took off running back to the house, where I felt safe.

The moment I pushed open the door, though, I heard Daddy cursing Mama violently over Gemmy BB. Mam was sitting, looking worried. Daddy was pacing to and fro, every horrible word he could use coming from his mouth. It made me mad.

I slammed the door hard got his attention and said, "Uncle Martel said come out dere."

Mama said to him, "Why don't you go out dere where dem dere men at?"

As he started to the door, Daddy saw me looking at him with contempt. His own eyes were bloodshot red. I believe that day my love for my father began to wax cold.

As Daddy was going out, Passy Kate was coming in, saying she had taken all the clothes off the line. She asked if she could go up to her grandma's house to spend the night. Her grandma was Ms. Pancy Suller; she lived up in what was called the pecan orchard. Mama smiled with satisfaction and told her yeah, with stipulations that she come home early the next morning to help with the chores.

Mama and I were alone in the house, sitting at the fire. The baby was asleep. It was times like this, when she was content and Daddy wasn't intimidating her, that I felt at peace with her.

Suddenly someone knocked at the door. I ran to open the door, and it was Mr. Leman, the rent man. He was a kind, quiet white man when he was sober. Unfortunately, the only time I saw him sober was when he came to collect the rent money.

He came into the house and spoke to Mama, warming his hands by the fire as Mama got his money from underneath the bed mattress. He wrote her out a receipt and said, "Jenny Rue, de Johnsons is movin tomorrow. Would you like to move down dere in dat house? Wit de newborn baby an everythin, dat house is a little better dan dis one here. I thought I'd give you first choice if you want it. At least you won't have to walk so far to git your water—de water pump is right in dat backyard, an I just put all new commodes in dat toilet. So if you want it, you can just move on in soon as de three sisters move out. It's all up to you."

She was so happy, she kept telling him over and over again how thankful she was to him. "Yeah, sir, Mr. Leman, yeah, sir. I do thank you," she said, grinning from ear to ear.

He started for the door, then turned and said, "If you know of anybody dat wanter rent dis one, just collect de rent and let them have it. I trust you. I'll just git de money from you next week when I come to collect."

She immediately told him about Aunt Matilda, who needed a bigger house. The one she was living in was much better than ours, but it was not big enough. "Anyhow, Mr. Leman," Mama said, "how come de three sisters is movin?"

"Cause dey is de damn ones keepin all de racket gwine on in de quarters round here, for what I've been told. So I'mo sendin dem back out dere in de damn country where dey belong."

"Well," Mama said sadly, "I guess Onna gonna say I told you dat too."

"I doubt that, cause she's been de one tellin me for months dem dere three sisters is de hellraiser. Well, so long. See y'all next week."

I hurried to shut the door behind him, and he said, "Here, little gal. Here your nickel. Buy you some candy." From then on, when he came to collect the rent, he gave me a nickel.

The day we moved into the new house and Aunt Matilda moved into our old one, we became a family. Tise was already staying nights with Aunt Matilda, so Mama allowed Tise to move in with her permanently. I became Aunt Matilda's bright and shining armor, and she became my second mama and grandma all in one.

The house we moved into was not as big as the one we moved out of. But it didn't have as many cracks as the other one, either, and was more convenient in many ways. Everyone who lived in the quarters used the same toilet, but at least we no longer had to walk as far to use it because it was right out our back door. And we didn't have to carry water so far. The common pump was in our backyard also; others had to come to us to use it.

In a little or no time, Aunt Matilda had covered the walls in both houses with cardboard. What a tremendous difference it made! She also fenced in the backyard, and the day she finished was a whole new beginning for all of us.

She had promised me I could spend some nights with her and Tise. The first night was like staying in a fancy hotel—it was the most peaceful sleep I'd had since I was old enough to remember. The bed was soft and fluffy. So were the pillows, all made out of feathers. Everything in her house was well-kept.

I recall the next morning, waking up to the sweet smell of tea cakes, eggs, bacon, and coffee. I sprang up from the bed to see what was going on. I never had spent the night away from home before, never encountered the kind of treatment she gave us.

I heard voices coming from the kitchen. Everything was peaceful. The only noise aside from the voices was the soothing sizzle of bacon cooking. I rubbed my eyes, trying to focus on whose voices they were and what they was saying. Tise's voice I knew, but the others I had never heard before. I had no earthly idea who they were except one sounded like a boy.

Just then a fair-looking woman came through the door, smiling with a mouth filled with gold teeth. She approached the bed with both arms stretched out, reaching for me. I'd never seen the lady before, but she appeared to know who I was.

"Look at her!" she said joyfully, and proceeded to lift me up from the bed. I know she must have kissed me fifty times without stopping. Standing behind her were two little boys. They looked to be about Gemmy BB's and Passy Kate's ages and stood about the same height as my sisters.

"Look at my little Haley," the lady said softly. "Just look how you done growed."

I as yet did not know who the lady was. Finally, she said to me, "I know you don't know who I is. I'm your aunt Frankie Reese. I'm your great-aunt, and dese here is your kinfolk, Ross Junior and Lenny. All y'all is first cousins."

I had no words for them. I simply held my hand up and waved to them both. They seemed like very friendly boys; I just didn't know how friendly they really were.

They moved in with Mama, which gave me an opportunity to stay with Tise and Aunt Matilda. That was a dream come true. It was for a short time, maybe a couple of weeks. Then they moved into Brake's quarter. But while it lasted, that time with Aunt Matilda was wonderful.

After the fight Gemmy BB had with Daddy, she had already moved round there t the Brake's quarter with a friend named Sarah Rhimes. It was a much nicer neighborhood than Rat Row. From what I understood of the adults' conversation, the neighbors over there all thought they was better than the Rat Row folk.

In some ways it was kinda true, but I learned back in those days that niggers were niggers. Everything that was black—according to the white folk—was all niggers, and poverty was poverty. We all were poor. The neighbors in Brake's quarter were all cotton pickers and maids, just like the other poor blacks. No one was better than anyone else. As

Mama would say, "De kettle can't call de pot black when dey both is black."

Aunt Frankie, whom Mama called "Auntie," looked identical to Aunt Jemima. She wore a head rag tied around her hair the same way. And she was a woman to be reckoned with.

On this day, we all gathered around, warming ourselves at the big oak fire after a long, tiring day. Aunt Frankie asked Mama, "Why did Tise stay wit Aunt Matilda, Jenny Rue? Is she sick or sumnutter?"

I took the words completely from Mama's mouth. "Cause dat mean old Ms. Onna scare her all de time," I answered bravely, as if I were the one Aunt Frankie was talking to. Mama looked disgusted.

Aunt Frankie said, "Is dat so? You seem like you know everythin goin on round here, little lady."

Mama just nodded, saying, "Yeah, she did scare er a few times, but since she moved down here, Onna don't do it now."

"Jenny Rue, where she come from, do anybody know?"

"Dey tell me she come from up dere round dat Damascus plantation."

"Do she got any kinfolk? Atall?" Aunt Frankie asked with concern.

Mama replied, "Well, she's some kin to old man Sonny Rhimes, an she was stayin down dere in one of Rhoda Shepard's houses fore she moved down here by us."

"Dat sure is good of you to let Tise stay wit er. God sure got a mighty good blessing stored up in heaven for you."

Neither one of us knew at the time just why Aunt Matilda was placed in our lives. But from the day we met her, she'd become special to us. It seemed like nobody else wanted anything to do with her. Maybe they all thought she was too old, and nobody wanted or had time for an old lady. That was not the case for us. We recognized love right off the bat, and she became family.

Aunt Frankie sat for a few minutes and then asked Mama, "What kin little Tise do if anything was to happen to er?"

"Well," Mama answered, "she can be dere wit er at night. I think it make er feel good knowin somebody is in de house wit er, an it make me feel good knowin she ain't by herself. Naw, Auntie, don't mine er atall."

The back door opened and we heard Daddy coming in. "Here come

Macky," Mama stated. "Whenever he come home dis soon, he either done won money or lost. Wonder which one it is tonight? I reckon he done gambled up every dime he had. Now he'll heck me all night."

Aunt Frankie looked at Mama with a smile but a serious expression on her face. When the men came in that early, we knew there would be no sleeping in that house. The grown-ups were going to sit up drinking moonshine all night.

They pulled up chairs by the fire, warming their hands for a few seonds. Then Daddy stuck his hand in his pocket and pulled out money—lots of money. He'd finally won. He hadn't come home broke and angry like he usually did.

Mama grinned and I did too. It was about sixty dollars, the most money I'd ever seen at one time. He told Mama to go put it up.

"Gosh, Daddy, kin I have a dollar?" I asked.

"What you gon do wit a big old dollar?" he said. He still hadn't seen Aunt Frankie. He lifted me up from the floor and sat me on his lap. "Is you even worth a dollar?"

I held my hands across my face, feeling bashful, enjoying a pleasant moment. He said, "Take your hands down from your face. You ain't shamefaced."

In walked Aunt Frankie. She'd been putting the boys down for the night. She was just in time to hear Daddy tell Mama to fix him and Cleo something to eat. He said it'd been two whole days since either of them had a home cooked meal. That's when Aunt Frankie made herself known. She said teasingly, "If you stay home sometime, you kin eat a home-cooked meal. Stay home, out de doggone streets, by George."

"Well, I just be damn if it ain't Frankie Reese! Where in de hell you come from, damn your time?" he said, eager to see her.

"A-Lordy Lord, wouldn't you like to know?" she answered jokingly.

"Where is my bro-law? I ain't seen him since I don't know when."

"He round dere workin, tryin to git de house ready to move in for us. Us gittin ready to move back in Brake's quarter."

Daddy and Uncle Cleo both were astounded to see Aunt Frankie. I could see Daddy had a great deal of respect for her. Other than Aunt

Frankie and Aunt Lucy Sue, he didn't have very much respect for women at all.

They forgot all about the food once they heard Uncle Wilson was round in Brake's quarter. They hurried out. When they came back, they had Uncle Wilson with them, and the party began. Old Fred came over with his guitar, and all we could hear the rest of the night was him playing "You Ain't Nothing but a Hound Dog" and "Howling Wolf," popular songs of the day. Old Fred would play day and night for a quarter drink of moonshine. That was all disturbance and no peace. It was their way of juking, especially when he started singing "Blue Suede Shoes" and "Long Tall Sally." I wondered if he was making the song up, changing the name from Laura to Sally. Ms. Laura was a neighbor, and the Lord knows she was long and tall, like a tick on an elephant's back.

The first time I laid my eyes on Uncle Wilson, I was a little leery of him. When he sat down by the fire, he was freezing cold, and his eyes was red as the flames. He looked really rough, almost as rough as Daddy. He was soft-spoken and not as talkative as the others looking on as old man Fred played the guitar. The one thing I sure noticed was that he didn't turn down a single drink that was being passed.

Finally Mama came out. She and Aunt Frankie each had a bottle turned up to their mouths. I was curious as to what they were drinking all of that moonshine for.

Uncle Wilson asked, "Where is my little gal Haley?"

"Here I go right here," I answered.

His eyes were half-closed, and he was smiling. "Well, I just be doggone. Look how she done growed. De last time we seen her, she was just knee-high to a duck." Whatever that meant.

He reached over and took me up, kissing me in my eye. The scent from that moonshine almost knocked me down. I was so outspoken, I said, "Ooh, ooh, you stink."

Everybody got quiet and Mama said, "You git down and go on to Aunt Matilda's. Git ready for bed fore dark. It's gittin late."

Tise was standing in the doorway, ready to take me. I was as ready as she was willing. The expression on Daddy's face said he didn't have any idea I was staying with Aunt Matilda while Aunt Frankie and her family stayed at our house, but for a change he was all right with it. He was so into Uncle Wilson and Aunt Frankie that I could have spent the night anywhere; it wouldn't have mattered to him. He practically pushed me out the door. As Tise and I were leaving, we could hear Daddy saying, "Wilson, you old son of a gun, what storm blowed you back diser way?"

"Well, bro-law, dis here is home, an ain't nothing like home. Baby wanted to come back, so by George, Macky, here we is."

Early the next morning, I was excited that our cousins were staying with us. After Aunt Matilda had finished breaskfast, I dressed in my old coveralls and was out the door before she could stop me.

Mama was up cooking. Everybody else was stretched out dead drunk and asleep. The room smelled just like moonshine. I started to run out and Daddy woke up. He was always an early riser. Money was hanging out of his pocket. He saw me. "Come here, gal. What you doin up so damn early?"

I said, "I want me a dollar."

In came Ross Junior and Lenny. I said to them, "Y'all come on in. Come on in an git y'all a dollar too."

Daddy grinned, saying, "I like your nerve, tellin me to give somebody else a dollar an you ain't almost got none wit your little talkin ass. Just like your mammy, you can't hold water." I took this as a joke.

By then the others had woken up. Old Fred got right back on that guitar. They hadn't washed their faces or brushed their teeth, but they started drinking all over again.

Daddy gave me a quarter and each of the boys a quarter and send us on our way. Mama was hollering for them to come eat. I took the boys to the other side of the room, and we could hear everything was being said.

Fred began playing gospel songs. I guess they had to put the Lord in somewhere, since none of them went to church. They certainly knew how to sing gospel songs.

> Amazing grace! How sweet the sound
> That saved a wretch like me!
> I once was lost, but now am found,

Was blind, but now I see.

It amazed me that they knew the songs and how to sing them, though they lived such sinful lives.

Before long, the whistle at the sawmill blew. That meant all the sawmill workers were getting off for lunch. They would all make straight for my daddy's and drink moonshine for lunch. The whistle blew three times a day: at seven o'clock in the morning to start work, at noon for lunch, and at six for knock-off time. The sawmill was where all the family men worked—except Daddy. He didn't work on any job regularly.

I watched the men drink and sing while old Fred Solomon played. Then came Aunt Matilda. She was holding a bag in her hand and calling me. I learned that day that she didn't take to boys well at all. I invited them to come along, and she quickly said no. I was to let them stay until I came back. And she was not cracking a smile.

I left with her. She had some material she had bought to make Tise and I nightgowns to sleep in. She didn't want us sleeping in long shirts or T-shirts anymore. We'd never had nightgown before. When she finished making them, I didn't want to take mine off.

It didn't take her long to know what we didn't have or what we needed, and she supplied it all—clothes, shoes, and nightclothes. We didn't know about what we didn't have; we were plenty content with what we had. Even though we were poor, we never knew we were poor.

When Mama saw the pretty, colorful nightgowns Aunt Matilda made for us, her eyes welled up with tears. Aunt Frankie looked on as Aunt Matilda took the baby from Mama's arms, so Mama could look at the gowns. She was so impressed.

Aunt Matilda was a guardian angel from heaven. She was sent by the almighty God to be a blessing to us. She was unable to read and she talked very little, but she watched everything and everybody who came and went from my mother's house.

And I was watching her, everything she did and how she did it. I wanted to be like her, so I made a habit of imitating her every move. There was nobody in all of the quarters who could come close to that little five feet, one inch, white-headed woman called Aunt Matilda. The many memories that I have of her will live with me always. I found it amazing that she did not take up with any of the other families. She didn't socialize or mingle with anyone on Rat Row except my mother and her girls. My life changed tremendously after Aunt Matilda came into our lives. Not even the half has been told. I talk of her goodness and the love that she showed us—there aren't enough words in Webster's dictionary to explain this woman. Until the day I die, I'll have a special love for her that will burn in my heart forever.

For some unknown reason on this particular evening, I didn't want to go down to Mama's house. All I wanted was to sit and watch Aunt Matilda quilt. She was making a beautiful quilt.

It was late afternoon when Mama called for me to come and stay in the house with the boys. The grown-ups went out to get more wood for the fire while the boys and I sat in the room. The fire was getting low. When they returned with the wood, I went to the kitchen to get a drink from the bucket. Out from behind the stove jumped the biggest rat! It ran across my foot. I screamed so loud, I believe all of Rat Row heard me. It scared me so bad I peed all down my legs. I couldn't even move my feet; they seemed to be glued to the floor.

Ross and Lenny came to rescue me, but the rat was gone. They asked, "Cuz, what's de matter wit you?" over and over again.

When I got enough energy to breathe, I shouted loudly, "A rat jumped on me!"

My coveralls were soaked with pee. Ross took me by one hand and Lenny took me by the other, and they led me back to the room. Aunt Frankie quickly picked me up. I was shivering from fear. She did all she could to comfort me. "Dey won't hurt you, baby. Dey bout as scared of you as you is dem."

One thing is for certain: I never went into that kitchen alone again. I learned that rats lived and bred in wood. The only place Mama could keep her wood was inside the house. If she left it outside, people would help themselves to it.

Later on, the rats got so brave, we could be sitting around the fire and see one speed across the room. We never were able to see what direction they went in. Daddy put out large rat traps, and when one got trapped, it sounded like someone made a hard stomp. I started having nightmares about rats frequently. I went to bed at night dreading to go to sleep, and when I did, I would wake up screaming.

At long last, Aunt Frankie and her family moved out of Mama's house into their own in Brake's quarter. I knew it wouldn't be long before I had to go back home. I stayed as close to Aunt Matilda's as I possible could. I went to bed at night feeling as if she were my real mama and I was her only little girl. I felt safe with her. Being around her was security.

Sometimes I would be sleeping on her nice, comfortable, cotton mattress and the music from the jukebox down at Pa Jack's café would wake me. Sometime I wouldn't get up. Other times I would just lie there, listen to the music, and make all kind of wishes. My favorite wish was that I would never have to leave her and go back home to live with those big rats. There were little mice in Aunt Matilda's house, but I never saw a big rat at her house. That made a big difference to me. Reliving the times I saw all the big wood rats was the most distressing part of my five-year-old life.

My wish became my fantasy, and my fantasy became reality in my mind. I was determined I was not going back to that house. When Aunt Matilda fell down on her knees to pray, I would kneel alongside her. My prayer was "Lord, let me stay down here wit Aunt Matilda and Tise all the time so I won't have to go back down to my mama's house wit all them dere rats, please."

Then everything I had been fantasizing about started to come true.

Mama got big around her stomach. It was sticking out. I didn't know why she was so fat. Daddy cut a doorway in the outside wall of the house, making a doorway so we could enter through the dining room and kitchen. Not so long after, everyone was making plans for Christmas. This was the first time I understood the word Christmas. I was not really sure what it was, but everyone made it sound really exciting.

And right before Christmas, Mama had another little baby girl.

She was said to be Mama's early Christmas present. They named her after Daddy's older sister, Willa Max. Her birth instilled in me reasons to go to Mama's every day, just to hold and play with my little baby sister. I loved kissing her on her cheeks and smelling the baby powder and baby oil scent when I held her close.

I was told that after the new year, I was going to be six years old and I could go to school. That was something I was looking forward to doing. I thought of nothing else. I asked every day, from Christmas until April, when I was going to be six. I never knew anything about a birthday party; the only person who had birthday parties in our neighborhood was Mrs. Brittney's daughter Dixie Lou. We were never invited because we were from Rat Row. Nobody on our end was good enough for Dixie Lou's parties.

Once Aunt Matilda figured we were old enough to know what having a birthday was, she would make a chocolate cake with much frosting on it and churn us some homemade ice cream. I thought that was the best party anyone could have: just her, me, Tise, Georgie Boy, and Annie Dora. It was the best ever.

The weather was more beautiful to me now, or maybe I was learning to understand the seasons of the year. In early spring, folk were getting ready to plant their gardens and everything was turning green—all the tree leaves and the grass, for yards that had grass in them. There weren't too many black folk who had houses with beautiful yard. The few who did have yards had yards full of dirt.

But springtime made everything beautiful. Flowers bloomed everywhere. All along the roadsides were beautiful flowers, and the aroma from them scented the air in all directions. My favorite scent was honeysuckle. I loved the smell of the honeysuckles and so did Aunt Matilda. She would cut them and place them all over the house, in every room. I got my kicks out of just walking by and breathing the freash scent up my nose. I couldn't have loved my life any better if I had been handed a thousand dollars.

One day, Aunt Matilda and I were walking along the roadside coming from the Shelmore store, picking flowers. I happened to look up at the houses. I could see clearly all the way down the entire quarter.

Across the road sat the Kingsley house with Ms. Onna, Mrs. Angie

Rosa, and her husband Mr. Lance Spike. Directly across from our house as their brother's little house, Mr. Nathaniel. In back of their house sat two other small houses. One was occupied by Mrs. Sara Lee Brimsley and her four boys. John Tate was the oldest; he was Passy Kate's age. Perry was next. His nickname was Tonk, and he was the same age as Tise or maybe closer to my age. The knee-high baby boy was Clevon, nicknamed Nookie, and he was Georgie Boy's age. The baby was Carl, around the same age as Annie Dora. And Mrs. Sara Lee was expecting fifth. The man who lived with them was called Uncle Billy Roliver, the lover of Rat Row.

The house on the left side of Mrs. Sara Lee's was a little house occupied by Mr. Nathaniel's daughter Rothy. She was a huge woman, so dark-skinned she was like the color of Mama's old washpot. Rothy was beautiful. Not too much got past my ears, and word was she was the Rat Row favorite. She had three children. Two were boys: the oldest was Barry and the second oldest was Beon. The girl's name was Jackie. I remember the first time I saw Jackie Lou. She was a pretty little girl about four years old, and she had long, beautiful hair, a snotty nose, and cheeks cracked up from the cold.

We walked slowly past Mr. Nathaniel's house. Sitting on the side of the road was Ms. Onna, along with a few other neighbors. They were mingling around Uncle Martel and Cousin Sattie Bell's front porch. They lived between Aunt Matilda's and our house. Our house and their house were the same, except that two families lived in their house and our house was a one-family house.

On the other side of Uncle Martel's duplex lived Mrs. George Ann. She was about as old as Aunt Matilda, a pretty, tall, light-skinned woman. She was so light she looked white. Her hair was long and streaked in gray, silky like corn silk. Daddy always said she was a slave owner's daughter, gotten by a white man on a black slave woman. They didn't call it rape in those days. Mrs. George Ann never associated with anyone. She walked with a cane, and the only time she was seen out was when the pension checks came on the first of every month. Whenever she sat on the porch, she sat well over on her side and never said to much to anybody.

Every now and then, Uncle Martel got liquored up and made jokes at her. She was never friendly toward him. However, once Aunt Matilda moved into the neighborhood, he had someone to make laugh. He always tantalized her whenever she passed by.

No one could believe that in all her seventy or eighty years, Aunt Matilda had never been with a man. On this day, Uncle Martel teased Aunt Matilda about being her boyfriend. "Matilda, ain't you bout ready for me to move in? I'm ready to leave Sattie Bell now. It's you I want." I had to translate his words to her. She just looked at him, grinning from ear to ear, until she saw Ms. Onna.

Aunt Matilda walked right up to Ms. Onna and said, "I'm an old lady, an I want you to know you hid up under dat false face, but one of dese days you gon burn in hell!"

Ms. Onna sat looking on and never said a word.

Aunt Matilda then looked at Uncle Martel and grinned again. "Jesus love you."

I don't know how Aunt Matilda knew it had been Ms. Onna under the mask. I had all intentions to ask her when we got home.

From then on, Rat Row became the entertainment of the town.

Chapter 2: Wiser and Wiser

It was a lovely, bright Friday night. Aunt Matilda and I usually sat on the front porch until we got ready for bed. Everything was as still as mice. The stars were ever so beautiful, and watching them shine down upon the big earth filled me with laughter. If there was any anger or animosity around, no ne would have recognized it because of the beauty and the peace that were so visible. The sounds of music came from each corner of the town, making the atmosphere even more soothing, along with the humming from Aunt Matilda. We called her kind of hum "moaning." I learned early in life that when we hear the church folk moan, the devil doesn't know what is being said. So I learn how to moan too.

The smell of the fresh breeze every now and then swept across our faces. We sat on the front porch swing, and I really thought the happiness I felt that night would last forever. I felt that the little we had was more than any riches. I didn't know what rich was until that night. I don't mean rich with money—I was rich with pure happiness. I believed that every human being should be happy like I was that night. Sometimes, looking back over that night, I still feel that wonderful feeling penetrate my entire body.

But what appears to be is not always the way it is. We retired around ten o'clock, and it didn't take long after before our heads hit the pillow and we were snoring. Around one or two o'clock in the morning, we were awakened by the siren on old Lund Cabb's Black Maria police van. He was the chief of police and hated blacks with a passion. Folk around town, when they heard the sound of it coming, would take off running for somewhere to hide. My daddy was one of the very few who was not afraid of white folk. He didn't let white or black intimidate him. Many a time I heard him say, "What de hell y'all runnin from dat cracker for? Hell, he put his pants on de same way I put mine on."

The noise was loud so loud that Aunt Matilda was awakened by it, and she was deaf. There was something about the way she got up and went over to the lamp and lit it. I got up with cold chills rushing up and down my little body. She asked me, "Haley, what's dat fuss I hear?"

I heard voices loud and clear coming from the direction of Pa Jack's café. She came over and sat on the bed beside me. The voices grew louder and louder, like they were right in the same room with us. Screams rang out and footsteps ran in all directions.

I went to the old shuttered window and pushed it open to see what all the commotion was. One voice I heard ring clearly: "Oh Lord, have mercy on my poor sister. My sister is dead, y'all. Oh Lord, Lord, have mercy."

I could see the road was full of people headed in our direction. I wasn't old enough to understand what was happening down there, but I was old enough to hear what was said—and that it wasn't anything good. I pushed my head farther out the window, hoping to recognize any of the voices. one sounded like the voice of Gemmy BB's friend Sally Jean. I heard Uncle Fete telling someone a stabbing had happened: two cousins had been fighting, and one was dead. I really didn't know what that meant, but cold chills penetrated my tiny body again and again. It was something horrible, and it made me feel terrible.

"What you doin wit dat window open up, Haley? Shet it back, an come git back here in dis here bed. It's a draft comin in," Aunt Matilda ordered calmly.

I rushed back to the bed, obedient to her command, but my ears was wide open. The screams became louder and the criess became more vivid. I lay listening to the sorrow echoing throughout the neighborhood. Daylight wasn't approaching fast enough.

I looked over at Aunt Matilda. She was sound asleep. I didn't even try to go off to sleep. I tiptoed out of bed again, looking out in time to see the dawn just breaking through the darkness. The voices and cries had not ceased. I was anxious to get down to Mama's house as fast as I could, to find out what had happened.

When it was good and daylight, I shook Aunt Matilda on her shoulder, saying, "Aunt Matilda, I got to go to Mama's house. She keep on callin me." I never lied, but that was the beginning of lying—I never heard Mama call for me. It was my way of getting out of there because I knew in my heart something was wrong.

Aunt Matilda sat up, tilted her head, then got out and fell to her knees at the side of the bed, speaking softly. I never heard a word she was saying but that was her routine. I fell down beside her. When she got up, I asked her, "Who was you talkin to?"

She answered, "Prayin to de good Lord."

"What you do dat for?"

She started to the kitchen. Either she hadn't heard me, or she was just ignoring me. While she was cooking, I left for Mama's house, still wearing my nightgown. The house was full of people; it looked like everybody in the town was in our house. There were always a lot of people in and out, but never that many at one time. Mama and a few of her friends were joking Mrs. Sara Lee about the baby she had not so long ago given birth to.

Cousin Sattie Bell said, "How in de hell Roliver git a baby at his age? Dat de only child he has, an she de spit image of him."

Long Laura Sue stepped into the room in time to butt in, "Abraham was a hundred an Sarah was ninety-five when she gave birth to Isaiah."

Mama's response was, "Well, it's de good Lord's will. He gives an he takes. He took one cousin an gave you an Roliver a pretty little gurl. De Lord gives an de Lord take away. Blessed be de name of de Lord."

Suddenly screams came from the dining room. I could hear folk crying and talking about the stabbing, and how the two were first cousins. I rushed through to the other room. Sitting on Mama's bed was Ms. Hilda, the wife of Aunt Matilda's brother Sonny. With her sister, whom everyone called Long Laura Sue, she was one of Mama's best friends. They were all so busy discussing what had happen down at old Pa Jack's café, no one noticed my presence. Everyone knew Fete Junior was half and half—at least that was what I heard them say about him—but a good friend to everyone he was, and the death of Letrolla was most devastating to him.

Fete Junior was crying and praying. "Lordy, Lordy, Lordy. Why, Lord? Why? Why didn't she take the ass whoppin was put on er like a woman? Now one cousin is in jail and one lying down dere in Bellow's Funeral Home on de coolin board, all for nothin." He was the neighborhood clown. One never could tell when he was serious. But looking at him that morning, I knew he was very serious. He was crying real tears just like a woman.

People were steadily coming in and out of Mama's house. When folk gathered round like that, money was being made. All they did was gossip, tell lies, and drink. For every lie told, half a pint of moonshine was sold.

Before long, Aunt Matilda came in, looking just as confused as all the rest were. I could tell she was wondering why all those people was in my mama's house. She had some clothes in her hand and called to me, "Come here, little Haley. Got you some clothes. Come on here an put em on."

Taking me by my hand, she led me to the other room. As I was putting on the old coveralls and shirt, she said, "You don't need to be down here wit all dese grown people. Come erlong now. Come on out from down here an come back home."

Gathering the other children up from the bed, she led us back to her house. I wanted her to be my mama for real, not play. She knew something was going on but she wasn't quite sure as to what all the commotion was about. Taking us to her house was her way of protecting us from whatever the danger was.

We all stayed there with her for a few days. Mama came down to ask if Aunt Matilda would watch the babies until she got back. "Mama," I yelled, "where you goin?" She first ignored me or maybe didn't hear me, so I yelled out to her again, "Mama, where you goin?"

Not looking at me, she said, "None of your business, little gal. Now git back inside dat house."

I fell out, kicking and hollering, because normally when I did that, I got my way. But that time she kept walking like I didn't exist. I shouted more. The more I yelled, the more I kicked, and the more I was ignored.

Then someone took me up from behind, and the next thing I knew, all my commotion almost turned into a sore rump. Mama reached up and pulled down a branch from a tree. Just as she lunged at me, Fete Junior swept me up, warning me, "Gal, you better stop all dat hollerin cause Jenny Rue fixin to tear you little ass up!" He was doing everything possible to keep that from happening. He begged her not to beat me but to let me go with them. He promised he would carry me so she wouldn't have to. He sat me around his neck, with both my legs hanging down his shoulder.

It was a long walk from our house up to the jail. Everybody walking was a friend to the cousins: Pennena, Mussey Sue, Long Laura, Mrs. Ray Lou, and Pinky Sue along with Mama and a few other Rat Row neighbors. The talk was about the arrest and charges against Katrene.

We arrived at the city hall jail. A beautiful light-skinned lady was sitting high up in a small window that had about six bars. Her words echoed through the air, and everyone heard what she was saying. I couldn't tell if she had a sad look or if that was the way she usually looked. But I do recall that tears blurred her vision when someone from the ground asked her if she was going to make the bail.

Fete Junior always knew the right words to say. As they conversed, I sat comfortably on his shoulder, silent, not fully understanding what was happening. I just knew she was locked up because of something bad. Everyone who came showed much love for her, and before long they had her smiling. No one brought up Letrolla to her.

When the visit was over, she guided a bag tied to a string down, and everybody put some money in it. She thanked everybody for what they gave her. It wasn't much, because it had to go through those narrow bars.

Before everyone left, Katrene asked with concern, "Has de body been put out?"

All looked from one to the other and then up at Katrene through the bars. Fete Junior said with a tremor in his voice, "Yeah, darlin, we gon view er body, and de funeral is at one o'clock. But don't you worry yourself none. We know you didn't mean to do it. But you know dat's de price one have to pay when you keep goin round playin bad. Everybody is hurtin over what done happen."

They headed for the funeral parlor with Fete Junior in the lead, carrying me across his shoulders. It was my first experience viewing a corpse. I won't ever forget the expression on everyone's faces as they entered the room where her body lay. It gave me the most uncomfortable feeling, like my heart was going to beat right out of my chest, pounding at a racing speed.

Letrolla was lying in a pink coffin lined in white. She was wearing pink, what I heard someone say was a negligee, trimmed in ruffles around the sleeves and neck. She looked as if she were only sleeping, as if she would awake when touched. The grown-ups were all rubbing their hands over her face and crying painfully.

Fete Junior lowered me from his shoulder to the floor. I held on to the leg of his pants, crying for him not to let me go. I think I was crying only because I saw the others crying. He lifted me up again, and I saw the tears dropping from his eyes. I gripped his collar. Pennena later said my tiny hands were glued to his shirt, making it impossible for him to get loose.

I wanted to go back home to Aunt Matilda. I cried rubbing my eyes because of whatever it was in the air that was causing everybody's eyes to burn. The stench of it made me feel uneasy. Fete Junior kept saying, "We goin after a while." After a while was not good enough for me. I was ready to go.

Fete Junior made it clear I couldn't go until the adults were ready to go. Then he took my hand. "Here, look, Haley. Feel er face. She can't hurt you. Feel er. I promise if you touch er face, you won't ever be scared of no dead person again. Feel er face."

I was steady about pulling back my hand, but he was more steady about lowering it to the dead woman's face. I started to scream with fear. He pressed my hand down on her face. It was so cold, as cold as ice. I said as much. He continued to rub my hand over her face until I was calm. He looked up at me and down at her, the tears falling, and said, "Now, my little Haley, you won't be scare of no dead person again never."

One thing about black people: they will forever gossip about anything and anybody, no matter where they are or who they are. Folk were pouring in and folk were leaving. Those who stayed helped in any way they could. Everybody knew everybody. Some were crying and some were gossiping; some were sad and some were glad. They were all types of folks having all different ways of showing their feelings.

Ms. Long Laura Sue said emphatically, "Poor soul, her playin bad days done costed her her life. Worst of it is dey was first cousins, one in jail and now one in hell, if I must say so."

Someone replied, "Ah, don't say dat, Laura. You don't know where she is."

"De hell I don't! The Bible say she is. She was drunk when she died, junkin in de café. She done did every dirty thing in de book to git er dere. Tell me where she gone, then. If she went to heaven, den I know all of us gwine."

Speaking the word "hell" was a serious matter then. One way folk were surely different than today is that they had respect for the Lord's house and for preaching. The word "hell" was not disgraceful, but we sure did understand God didn't send anyone to hell. We sent ourselves, according to the lives we lived.

"Y'all know dat little Haley sattin on top of Fete Junior's shoulder, listenin to every word bein said. Y'all know she got old folk sense."

"Don't worry, whatever she heard. If she repeat it, knowin her, she'll tell it just de way she heard it. But she ain't gon tell nothin grown folk said, cause little Haley know Jenny Rue gon tie her butt up."

The death of Letrolla was the talk of the town for months, long after she was dead and buried. Katrene pled guilty and was sentenced to five years on the rock pile in a prison for women. Word was she was sent somewhere near Pensacola, Florida.

Letrolla reminded me of the first time I heard of the first murder in the Bible. Cain killed Abel, his brother. That was the first murder story I heard in my early life. "And Cain talked with Abel his brother: and it came to pass, when they were in the field, that Cain rose up against Abel his brother and slew him" (Gen. 4:8 KJV).

The memory of Letrolla stayed with me for a long, long time. The feel of her face haunted me. But like Fete Junior said, I was no longer afraid of any dead folk.

After a while, talk of her death ceased. Life went on. Uncle Cleo and Aunt Lucy Sue were living up at the pecan orchard where Passy Kate's grandma lived. Before they moved up there, Passy Kate's grandma and her son and his family were the only blacks who lived there except for one other family. The Rockys were Ms. Neddie Bell and her four children: Caddy Mae and Glory Ann were the two girls, and the boys were Darkie Boy and JJ. They all seemed to have a better reputation than our family did, though they were no different.

We were up playing in the orchard with our cousins, Panzy Ann and Polar Boy, when we learned that the Rockys were getting ready to move over into Brake's quarter, and that now Passy Kate was to move in with her grandma and live with her. Nobody liked her grandma, Ms. Pancy Suller, at all. Word was she was the pimp for the white folk. She told them everything that went on among the black folk, because she was old man Lund Cabb's mistress.

We played so hard that day up at the pecan orchard that all we wanted to do was go home and get to bed. I knew Aunt Matilda had a good supper waiting on us. The moment we got home, Daddy was waiting for us to get in the wood. We knew to get the wood without being asked to do so.

Down the road a couple of houses lived Mr. Earnesto and Mrs. Bonnie, his wife. They had as many children as Mama, and like Mama, Mrs. Bonnie was steady in having them. The oldest one was Earnesto Junior, nicknamed Noddie, and you never heard a word out of him. He was what everyone called "her good boy." The second was Bennie, nicknamed Tighteye, and the third one was Jonkey. Now, Jonkey was our good friend. He was the same age as I was, and he was mean—so, so mean. Still, he was our best friend.

Della and Arline was the two oldest girls, and they became our friends too. So did Mrs. Sara Lee's boys John Tate, Tonk, Nookie, and

Carl. Our lives were a roller coaster, jungle gym, and merry-go-round all in one.

There was no other child in the neighborhood like Jonkey. He was a bully, and no one could do anything with him. I don't ever recall their parents spanking or beating their children at all, and maybe that was why Jonkey was the way he was. In our house, we got a whipping for bad behavior, disobedience, overdoing, underdoing—you name it. Our friendship sent us all on a roundabout tour. There was nothing that we couldn't or wouldn't do, and we were not afraid. But best to believe we knew what not to do, right or wrong, just like the average child. We learned how to lie, cheat, pretend, and cover up for each other, and before long we were all bullies.

There was no fear in us and nobody to fear except fear itself. We the girls always kept up with the boys; that's where we learn all tricks and trades. We watched how our parents lived their lives and the things that they did, motivating us to desire to be different.

One thing about my family was we didn't do a lot of visiting. The other neighbors were always over at our house playing; we never went to theirs very much.

Mrs. Bonnie was a very beautiful high-yellow woman with long black hair that hung all the way down her back. She always wore it combed down the sides with a part in the middle and two braids pulled up and crossed atop her head. She was mostly Cherokee Indian. Mr. Earnesto was not a bad-looking man, but he was as dark as the ace of spades and mean as hell. That was one of the reasons why we never visited their house—we felt so unwelcomed by him. Not one time that I remember did Mrs. Bonnie mistreat us or make us feel unwelcome.

I remember noticing the deep, dark marks on each of Mrs. Bonnie's cheeks, like she had been severely burned. She was still beautiful, but anyone could tell she had been much prettier before the scars. I learned through conversations in the backyard with a gossiping neighbor that Mrs. Bonnie's scars came from Mr. Earnesto taking her out into the woods and making her sit out there all day while he worked, because of his jealousy about her.

One torrid summer day, folk were gathered around in the backyard as Mama and the neighbors always did, helping each other with the wash. They were discussing everything and everybody. I went into my special hiding place under the house and behind the chimney corner. I saw Ms. Onna and Mr. Frank Paylor come walking around the corner. They were talking about how Daddy had cleaned up at the gambling table. He won all the money and then sat there until he lost every penny back. Mama laughed out, and she heard her laugh. I swore I heard what she said about my mama.

That night, lying in bed, I could hear those horrible words ring in my ears. I thought of Katrene and Letrolla and how Letrolla's death occurred. I saw Mama's face in the casket instead of Letrolla's. The thought of Mama's death was horrifying.

My nights turned into nightmares. Every time my eyes closed, I saw Letrolla's corpse lying in the casket, and it would turn out to have my mama's face. The nightmares became unbearable, so much so that I was yelling out in my sleep.

Aunt Frankie happened to be in the room one time when I was trying to awaken from a nightmare, and she woke me up from it. She insisted on me telling her what I was dreaming about. I was so fearful for my mama, I almost broke the bed down. I blurted out to her in a panic that Mama was dead in the casket like Ms. Letrolla.

Aunt Frankie looked at me in total shock and said comfortingly, "Baby, dat was only a dream." She looked me over from my head down to my feet, studying my mood. Her look seemed to conquer every hidden secret bubbling inside my mind. I felt she knew exactly what I was thinking before I even thought it.

Though I trusted her, I could never trust anyone as much as I trusted Aunt Matilda—not even my own dear mother. We were eyeball to eyeball. I watched her lips move and all her gold teeth shine as she told me what I said was only a dream.

"No!" I shouted. "Aunt, it's no dream! I did hear her tell Mr. Frank dat her want to hurt Mama!"

"It's a sin to tell a lie. De devil will git you for sure."

"Ask Mr. Frank! I ain't lyin. I was under de house, playin, an I heard her say it."

She stepped away from me and said, "I will ask him. I'mo right now an find Frank an ask him."

Mama had walked in the room and heard the last of what I said. She said to Aunt Frankie, "Pay her no mind. Dat gal done got where she is bout a bigger liar dan any five-year-old could be." It was Mama's voice that I heard speak, but they were Daddy's words of warning. No one knew the awful pain I was experiencing because of her and my daddy, but Aunt Frankie could identify with my pain. She never let on what we had been talking about.

I was soaking wet. I had never wet the bed before, but now every night I was wetting the bed. Aunt Frankie pulled off my wet underpants and gave them to Aunt Matilda, who rinsed them out and put them on the line to dry.

Down the path from Pa Jack's came Mr. Frank Paylor. Aunt Frankie left without saying another word. She cornered Mr. Frank before he entered our house. When she came back, Aunt Matilda was putting me in fresh shorts and a shirt.

When she was finished, Aunt Frankie took me by my hand and led me out by the swing tire. She asked me how old I was. I told her, "Five years old."

She gave me one of my first pep talks. "Haley, you is only five years old, an baby, you got a heap to learn. I'm your great-aunt. I talk to Mr. Frank Paylor, an he told me what Ms. Onna said. Dat was a figure of speech. She didn't mean she was goin to harm your mama for real. She just use de word. Don't you worry your pretty little head atall. Ain't nobody gon do nothin to my niece. You hear me?"

I didn't a bit more know what Aunt Frankie was saying to me than the man on the moon, but it kinda made sense, so I said "Yeah, ma'am."

Aunt Frankie made me promise I wouldn't mention to anybody else what I had told her or about the nightmares I was having. She promised me that she was going to take care of Mama, and I trusted her. She told me to stay outside to play. I didn't go play; I went back to Aunt Matilda's.

Aunt Matilda was sitting on the porch, making another multicolored quilt. She was making it for me. I watched her that day. It wasn't hard to learn from her; all anyone had to do was to watch and it would become natural. I fell asleep watching her stitch and spit snuff. I was surprised, since Aunt Frankie and her family had moved out, that my parents hadn't made me come back home, but they hadn't. I made every minute I spent with Aunt Matilda the best. I thought if Tise wasn't there, I could stay forever and ever.

Waking up to the smell of good old fried chicken, tea cakes, and creamy mashed potatoes took my breath away. I went into the kitchen. Aunt Matilda had the table neatly set for the two of us.

As we sat eating and enjoying the flavor of the food she had made, suddenly there stood two men in the doorway, watching us. I can still see them smiling. One of them was tall and brown-skinned, with a dimple in his cheek and a gold tooth in the corner of his mouth. The other one was medium height and dark-skinned. He looked just like Mr. Sonny Rhimes. For a second I thought he was him.

I touched Aunt Matilda on her shoulder and pointed. She turned and looked suspiciously. Before I could say anything, she was up and over to them, embracing them, with tears flowing down both her cheeks. She was grinning hard. After embracing them for a few minutes, she turned and told me they was her brother Sonny's boys, Lijah and Wesley.

So many surprises! I didn't know if it was a good thing or bad. Lijah stood about six feet tall or so. Wesley was about four inches shorter, and his teeth were white as milk—white like Aunt Matilda's hair was white. The look on Aunt Matilda's face told me that it had been a long time since she had last seem them. They had really made her day; her face literally was glowing. That was the second time I had seen her that happy. It didn't take a whole lot to make her happy. Her real happiness came from making everyone around her happy. If the people she cared about were happy, that made her happy.

Seeing those two young men brought so much joy to her life, the kind of joy she had brought into mine. "How long y'all gon stay wit me dis time?" she asked, as if she knew they would soon be off again.

Lijah answered her first, in a tone in his tenor voice that said he was trying to console her from any other disappointments. "I'm gonna stay wit you until next year." That sounded real good, like a very long time, but even I knew we were only two months away from next year. She was excited to have them for however long.

Hesitantly, he added, "Den I'll be goin into de army."

She didn't respond to what he said; either she didn't hear him or she ignored that statement.

Wesley never said how long he would be staying. I felt an uneasy feeling, like he was hiding or running away from something.

Lijah smiled at me. "Whose pretty little gal dis is, Aunt Matilda?" He lifted me from the floor. I don't think she heard a word he asked her. I started to wonder if Aunt Matilda would respond to only what she wanted to respond to. "Tell me what is your name, little gurl," he ordered me.

"My name is Haley."

"Your name is Haley; Haley what? Do you have a last name?"

"Yes, sir, I got a last name. It's Keath. Haley Keath."

"Wooh! What a pretty name! It is as pretty as your big brown eyes."

I didn't know it at the time, but I was blushing all over. I knew in that instant he was someone who loved Aunt Matilda. He became like a big brother to me, making me even more a part of their family. He immediately asked, "Tell me, do you stay wit Aunt Matilda?"

"Not all de time. My sister Tise stay all de time."

"Den how come you don't stay all de time? And when you gon stay all de time?"

"Don't know. When God tell me I kin stay."

"What do you know bout God?" he asked, startled.

"Aunt Matilda said when you pray to God, den what you ask em to do for you or what you want em to give you, he will do it. So I pray wit Aunt Matilda when her pray, an I ask God to please let me stay wit Aunt Matilda all de time. Now I got to wait till he tell me I could stay." I didn't know who God was, except that Aunt Matilda surely had a strong belief in him. That was good enough for me.

This was the first Thanksgiving I could remember. Everyone was talking about cooking wild turkeys, ducks, baking hens, and dressing. I had no idea what Thanksgiving was; all I knew was that lots of cooking was going on and it was a special day for everybody, a day that all people celebrated.

This Thanksgiving was really special. Both of Aunt Matilda's nephews were home, and she was as happy as I was. The smell of food was coming from all directions, from every house on Rat Row: cakes, pies, turkeys, hens, hams, chitlins, collard greens, peas, and okra.

I rushed down to Mama's house to tell her about Lijah and Wesley. They said I told everything I knew, and they were right. I thought I was supposed to tell everything. As I was standing in front of Mama's house, I could even smell the food coming from the house across the street. I thought it was strange I never saw who lived in that house. No one ever came outside of those four walls. We always knew the man who lived there, Mr. Nathaniel, was inside, but he never came out, summer or winter. I for one was curious to know why that man didn't breathe the fresh air or go for walks or even visit any of the neighbors. If we had met him on the highway or somewhere, we wouldn't have known who he was. I had heard Mama and the others say he was the biggest human being they had ever seen. He was way over four hundred pounds, so big he could hardly walk. Maybe that was his reason for not coming out.

A little later that Thanksgiving morning, I raced over to the Kingsley boys' house. Tonk was already up, sitting on the porch and counting marbles. I had never seen the inside of their house, only the outside. In the back, they had a pond. I asked Tonk if I could see it, and before he could answer me, I was off.

It was nothing like what I expected it to be. It was filthy with all kinds of cans, bottles, bags, and other trash. It smelled terrible. It made me sick.

I ran back around the house. The back door of the mystery house was open, and I got me a glimpse of Mr. Nathaniel himself. He was sitting in a long chair that looked to have been specially made for him. He had a big turkey in front of him and was eating as if it were his last meal.

I could tell Tonk was embarrassed that I had seen his uncle like that. And when I saw the expression on Tonk's face, I was sad for him. His uncle was just as big as folk had described him to be. It was an awful sight to see a human being that size.

Lijah, Aunt Frankie and her boys, and Papa had already gathered around the kitchen when I ran into Mama's house, feeling like I had just got caught with my hands in the cookie jar. I was about to go through the house and Papa called out to me, "Come back here, gal. Where you goin in such a hurry so early dis mornin?"

"Devilment!" Mama yelled. "You know she is up to some kind of devilment." Mama knew me, and when I was up that early, it was for a reason.

Papa sat for a few moments as always. After a while, he got his bottle of moonshine and went out to his private comfort zone under the big pecan tree behind the toilet. I gathered from his movements that he didn't like to be in a crowd of people. He came to Mama's house every day, but after making his presence known, he made his exit out the back door to sit under the tree and drink until there was nothing left to drink.

I was never around Papa too much, although Tise was. On this occasion, I didn't want to stay in there with all those drunks either, so I trotted out back with Papa. He had a special chair he sat in so he took me by my hand and led me to it.

Papa was an old man who sat and drank without a care in the world. Sometimes he had to be carried home, and other times he would just get up and walk all by himself. Those were usually the days when he had no moonshine to drink. Everyone loved and respected him, and his children were his life. I always loved being around him, but I knew Tise was his heart. He loved all of his grandchildren, but Tise was that favorite grandchild.

As the day progressed, people were in and out of our back and front doors. The thought of staying another night in that house made me ill. After eating all the turkey my stomach could hold, I knew it was getting on time for me to either make my way back to Aunt Matilda or crawl into the bedroom there and listen to drunks for the rest of the evening. I heard Lijah and Wesley in the other room, and I knew I had help. Then again, I didn't want to push my luck—Daddy hadn't made Mama bring me back home either. I reckoned they even could have forgotten

I was staying with Aunt Matilda. I thought it was better I kept my big mouth shut and prayed.

I went off to my private praying place inside the house, which was a sheet hanging on a line. I prayed to God, "Please make Mama let me go stay wit Aunt Matilda."

I had just come out from behind the sheet when into the kitchen came Mama. She wasn't feeling any pain; the moonshine was taking its toll. "You better git on down to Aunt Matilda's fore it git dark out dere, little gurl," she warned me happily.

In came Lijah. "So dis your little gal, Jenny Rue? I just be darn when she told me her name was Haley Keath. I never put it together she was you an Macky's gal. I'm sure glad y'all lettin her stay wit Aunt Matilda. God gon bless you for it."

It being a holiday night, we had stayed up later than we usually did, especially with Lijah and Wesley home. I went to bed, but I was awake when they came in that night. I lay quiet as they sat down by the fire, warming themselves. They got into a heated discussion, or what Lijah called "a disagreement," concerning Wesley leaving. I could hardly hear what they were saying because of the low pitch of Lijah's voice, but I did hear him tell Wesley that "he could run but he couldn't hide."

I had known just by looking at him that Wesley had something to hide. He kept looking over his shoulder, and he only went out at night. I guess Lijah was trying to convince him to stay a little longer, as it had been so many years since they had seen Aunt Matilda. But there was more to the conversation than I was able to pick up on.

Shortly afterward, Wesley strolled on over to the other room, leaving Lijah warming at the fire. I crawled out of bed, rubbing my eyes like I had been sleeping. He looked surprised to see me. "Haley, why ain't you sleepin this time of mornin?"

"Dunno," I said, steadily rubbing my eyes as if I had awakened from a long, hard nap.

"You told me yesterday dat you wasn't stayin wit Aunt Matilda for good cause you was waitin on God. Is you heard from God yet?"

"Naw, sir, I ain't, but I know God gon let me cause Aunt Matilda said so."

"Then why ain't God told you dat you kin stay yet, I wonder?" he teased, laughing.

I shook my head, meaning "I don't know," but he insisted that I say what I meant. Shaking my head was not acceptable to him. I said boldly, "Naw, he ain't let me move for good, not yet. But he gon to. Aunt Matilda told me we got to wait on God cause he is a on-time God." I spoke with positiveness because in my mind and my heart, God was the key to my living with Aunt Matilda. He was more than my father figure—God was the big brother I didn't have and my best friend, all in one. At that time I really didn't know what it meant to have God in my life, but it was predestined for someone to enter the Keath children's lives and lay a solid foundation.

Lijah seemed to be amazed at my answer. He picked me up and sat me on his lap. He placed his hand across my head, rubbing my long plaits of hair. "You really believe you is gon stay wit Aunt Matilda all de time, do you?"

I didn't nod my head as I was about to. Instead I said, "Yes, I do believe it, cause God will do just what I ask em to."

"So you asked God already to let you stay wit Aunt Matilda, and now you waitin for God to tell you when you kin stay. Is dat right?"

"Yes, sir."

"Now let me ask you dis. If God tell you you kin stay, an your mama and daddy tell you you can't stay, den what you gon do?"

I scooted down from his lap, stood in front of him, pointed my finger in his face, and said, "I'll do what God say do, cause he rule de whole wide world!"

I didn't know if that was right or wrong, but Aunt Matilda had me so convinced about this God that nothing else mattered. I believed he would do what she'd convinced me he would do. I thik it was at that time I began to build my faith up in God, though I didn't even know what faith was.

Lijah took my hand and hugged me. "You know, you is one smart gurl to be so little. I hope you be dat smart when you grow up. You will be hard to handle. How old is you?"

I counted five fingers and showed them to him. "Five. I'm five years old."

"You just bout ready for school."

"Aunt Matilda said one more year. Den I'll be six, an I kin go to school wit Tise."

"Macky an Jenny Rue just don't know what dey got here. I sure wish I had a smart little gurl like you. Oops, time for bed." He tucked me into bed—something my daddy never did. So many things Daddy didn't do for us, but the good Lord always put somebody in our path to do what Daddy didn't.

I woke up the next morning high-spirited, like I knew that my prayers had been answered somehow, some way. I spent my nights with Aunt Matilda, but after breakfast I was dressed and off to my mama's I would go. That morning, I went just like I knew I had scored big time.

Lijah was there. Aunt Frankie was already up, washing clothes. The smell of the oak wood burning around the washpots came from different directions; it was wash day for everyone in the neighborhood. Laughter filled the air with much happiness. Everything was going as expected. Before long, the backyard was full and the day begun.

For me, it was "watching the children" time. I was not in the mood for babysitting, and I was no more than a baby myself. I was making my way out to see if Tonk wanted to come over to play, but Mama yelled, "Come back here, gal, an help see bout dem chilluns!"

I ran back into the room where Tise sat holding baby Snappy, which was our nickname for Annie Dora. Ross Junior, Lenny, and Georgie Boy were out back, playing marbles. Lijah stood observing everybody. He commented to Mama about how smart I was, and Aunt Frankie agreed with him. "Yeah, Lordy, she sure nough got plenty of sense now. Any little five-year-old dat kin hold a conversation like dat little lady ain't got nothin but old-folk sense."

"Aunt Matilda ain't got no young'uns of er own. I was sittin talkin wit her earlier, fore I come down here, an she told me a thing or two. She know more bout God dan I do. Me an my brother come home to stay wit er for a while, an dis little gal done beat us. But it sure do make us happy she got somebody to help look after er."

Everyone was astonished at how well-mannered the Rhimes boys were. Lijah and Wesley had class. When they spoke, everybody listened. Lijah in particular had a poetic wayof speaking. Standing in the kitchen, he described how the weather was beautiful: "It was cold, but the sun was shining like a bright moon on a hot summer night." I repeated every word to everybody I came in contact with. "The leaves on all the trees were brown, and you couldn't even see a squirrel hopping around." I took that to mean the rats had taken the place of the squirrels; that was why they couldn't be seen.

The day was going well until Ms. Onna made her presence known. She came around the corner and went directly to Cousin Sattie Bell's house, looking like she was mad at the world. Either she had done a bad thing or she was getting ready to do something bad.

It wasn't long before Daddy came from the same direction. He looked like he hadn't slept in days. Everybody knew he was just coming home either from chasing behind his outside women or from over some gambling table. Whatever had happened to him, he wouldn't be Macky if he didn't come home and take his frustration out on Mama.

Thank God for Aunt Frankie and Lijah. Daddy was about to start when he looked at Lijah. Lijah acquainted himself to Daddy so politely, he took Daddy's nerve away.

Mama knew what was next: Daddy was ready to eat. She fixed him food, and he fell asleep in the plate. How disgusting that a human being would do the things that he would do and see no wrong in what he did!

I said to Lijah, "My daddy is a gamblin man."

He just smiled slightly and said, "Don't let me hear you say dat again. Anyhow, where did you hear dat?"

"Daddy said it," I replied confidently. "He said he won a heap of money gamblin."

"Don't tell nobody else dat. Dat ain't nothin to be sayin bout your daddy. Hear me?"

"Yeah, I hear you."

"Den you promise not to tell dat to nobody else." He turned and called out, "Jenny Rue, I'm takin Haley back to Aunt Matilda's. This is somethin she just don't need to be round. Good night to y'all." He lifted me up and we went out.

Folk were gathered outside in the road. There was something different about the crowd of people. They were from everywhere. Again, as they always did, they'd piled up in front of Mama's house like dirty clothes. Lijah said, "Good grief, I didn't know Rat Row had so many Negroes."

Normally we didn't. But something terrible had happened: Mr. Tom Rudolph was dead. Some folk said his wife did it. Others said white folk did it. The fact was he was dead and she was arrested. Lijah carried me inside the house, and the last noise I heard was the sound of the Black Maria taking her off to jail.

She didn't do very much time; she was back on the streets in short order. Word was they worked roots and voodoo, and that's how she got out. Even though she took a life, it was only a down payment on hers. When Funeral Bellow came to take the body away, many said the sheet was covered with blood, and that Mr. Tom's blood would be on her hands until the day Jesus returned. Rat Row had become a living nightmare for many who lived around there. It was like a curse was on that street and landed right at our doorstep.

I stayed inside the house all the next day. I didn't let Aunt Matilda out of my sight. I was afraid to go outside. Everywhere she went, I was right behind her. Every unusual sound I heard, I would jump from fear. I knew dying was not anything good. My fears forced me to think that it was worse than it was.

Shortly after, things had quieted down. We were all playing outside, and Mama came calling for us to come in. The Ku Klux Klan was out.

As we ran inside, several horses came speeding around the corner. The riders were wearing white sheets to hide their true identities. They didn't harm anyone physically, but we were traumatized for many years, Daddy said they were only cowards hiding behind sheets. He swore that if they ever hurt any one of us, "dey might git me, but I damn sure gonna take one of dem wit me—the g——d—— leader, an I know who dat son of a bitch is too."

My worst fears came upon me that day. Around three o'clock that evening, Mama came down to Aunt Matilda's. Daddy was in one of his moods. He hadn't really seen me since Thanksgiving. I guess it was natural for a father to want to see his little girl after being away for days, not knowing what was going on. He stayed around the house a little more after the death of Tom Rudolph and the Klan went out. Mama said, "Your daddy want you to come home."

My entire demeanor changed. I couldn't say the word "please." I begged, "Peese, peese, Lijah, come wit me to Mama an tell him to let me stay. *Peese.*" I put on my old red plaid coat and the hood Aunt Matilda had bought me, and we trotted off to Mama's house. We went in the back door. Old Fred was playing away on that old guitar, singing "Long Tall Sally" and "Good Golly Miss Molly." Daddy was drinking, and I knew I had a great chance of staying at Aunt Matilda's if the right words were said to him. Lijah was the right one to say them.

I could see Daddy looking at me. I didn't know what to make of that look, whether he was mad or in between glad and mad. "You done left home. Old lady Matilda done took you in," he stated. "Well, you kin git ready to bring your little ass right back home. Dis is your house where you live."

I said nothing, but I looked at him big-eyed with not a flicker. I looked at all the drunks in the room, then looked at Lijah. He respected Daddy's authority and struck up a conversation with him. I don't think Daddy remembered who Lijah was. He said, "You Sonny Rhimes's boy, ain't you?"

While he indulged in a conversation with Lijah, I went into the other room with the other children. There, Kate was reading a story about Little Red Riding Hood.

I don't know what Lijah said to my daddy, but by the time the sawmill whistle blew at six o'clock, he let me go back to Aunt Matilda's house. I didn't care if it was only for that night. Tomorrow would take care of itself. When he said, "Now, little Haley, you bout ready to call it a night? You goin to your second home," it was another dream come true for me. The prayer I had prayed was answered, and my worries were over for the moment. I felt safe again. I finally had someone to take up for me and was not afraid to do so. It was a day to remember.

Aunt Matilda and I sat around the fire. She told me Bible stories of her days growing up as a slave and a sharecropper's hand after the president freed them from slavery. She said she was twelve years old when the president freed the slaves. She took a job working for the owners of the plantation where her parents had worked as slaves. They paid her one dollar a month. She never attended school a day in her life; she said she was taught everything she knew by Jesus Christ.

She said her mama died when she was fourteen years old. She had one sister. Her name was Montana. Montana had one daughter, Matilda Ann, and one son, Sonny Rhimes. Montana ran away at the age of seventeen, shortly after the death of their mama. Matilda had never seen or heard from her since that day. Montana left Matilda Ann with Matilda, and Matilda raised the child as if she were her very own little girl.

Sonny took a wife and left. About five years later, Sonny showed up with two boys, Lijah and Wesley. Wesley was the oldest. Sonny intended to work and get a place to live for him and the boys. One morning he left for work. They all sat around the fire on a cold winter night, roasting peanuts, waiting for their father to come home—but he never came. He abandoned the boys without a word.

Ten years passed. They never heard a word from Sonny; they didn't know whether he was living or dead. The same with Montana. Matilda said she raised the boys the best she knew how, with the help of the good Lord. It was the same with me: Aunt Matilda became the mother I stood in need of, the one who taught me spiritual guidance. She became to me what my own mama wasn't.

Matilda and the boys were comfortable in the hut they lived in. She was working from sunup to sundown. One day, an old lady showed up on her doorstep. The stranger was near death. Aunt Matilda took her inside and tried to nurse her back to health, but her ailment was too severe. Her name was Hilda. She lasted only two days, but she was alert enough to explain that she was Matilda's mother's sister. They had been sold apart in slavery. Hilda had learned from some strangers that a Rhimes family lived nearby, and the guidance of the Lord lead her directly to Matilda's doorstep.

The dying aunt made Matilda promise that no matter what she did in life, no matter where she and the boys went, they were to put the Lord first, trust in him, keep praying, and know that God would always take care of them. Then Hilda breathed her last breath.

Aunt Matilda said the time came when she had to take the boys in the middle of the night and leave the Morrison plantation. She took a job on the Sheffield place. She said if she hadn't left in the middle of the night, if she had told Mr. Morrison she wanted to leave, she would have ended up like so many other slaves and sharecroppers—dead.

She stayed with the Sheffields for over fifteen years, until Wesley and Lijah left home went out to fend for themselves. Then she moved off of the Sheffield place to Damascus plantation, where she worked and lived for three years. The moment she started to get her old age pension, she relocated to our town, where she met us Keaths.

As young as I was, I could relate to the pain she had experienced. Somewhere in my heart, I felt the same pain she felt. I was not fully aware of the hardship she had faced. However, my brain registered to my heart, and a connection was made from my heart to her heart. At that moment, we became one.

I grew up that day in my mind. Instead of a five-year-old's mind, it was fifteen. I felt I was ready to enter my first year of school right then. My attachment to Aunt Matilda was motherly. In my heart, I had two mamas.

I waited patiently, minute by minute, for the day to come when I would enter my first year of school. I wondered what people did in school; I had no knowledge. All I ever heard about was going, not being there.

Aunt Matilda began to make me all kinds of dresses. When she bought flour, it came in different-colored sacks. She saved them and made my dresses from them, getting me ready for school.

I decided to ask Lijah about school. I went down to Mama's house, but he was not there and he never came. I got tired of waiting and went back to see what Aunt Matilda was doing. She was out there in her backyard, nailing away. She was putting up a fence. People had been jumping across the old one, and it was all broken down. She was handy with a hammer, hammering and praying. She would break out in prayer anytime or anywhere.

She put that fence up in no time, and about five feet higher than the other one, making it impossible for anyone to get across and smash up her garden. It would keep her new baby chicks in. When she was finished, out she came with a brand new set of chicks. They were the most beautiful yellow chicks I had ever seen in my life. I ran up to see if I could help, knowing she was going to say, "Naw, I got it. But when I git done, you kin helb me feed dem dere rations."

One chick got outside the fence—we never could figure out how—and we had a mighty hard time catching it and getting it back in the coop. We teamed up to chase it. Then out of nowhere, Lijah and Wesley came around the corner, and in no time the chick was caught.

I helped Aunt Matilda feed them, and it was like I was really involved. I was a part in everything she did, just like a family should be. What I was lacking in my parents, I made up for with her.

Once we got the chicks fed and Aunt Matilda was inside, preparing supper, Lijah took me to the store. He said I could get anything I wanted to. Little old me, all I wanted was candy—red hots and long boys. He spent quarters on me and bought what he thought I should have—lots of fruit, like oranges, red delicious apples, and yellow pears, plus cookies and juice. In the store that day, I felt like a little princess. The only time an orange was bought in our house was during the Christmas holiday, and it was just around the corner.

We arrived back to Aunt Matilda's. She was frying chicken. That was a main dish. It could be fixed in so many ways: stewed chicken, baked chicken, fried chicken, barbecued chicken, just to mention some. It smelled good. After supper, Lijah sprung on us that he was getting ready to leave right after Christmas for the United States Army.

I didn't know what the United States Army was. It was something I'd never heard of. I asked him flip-mouthed, "Uncle Lijah, what's de United States Army is?"

"It's where men go off to fight war," he answered me proudly

"How you fight war?"

"With weapons, and weapons consists of guns, bombs, and many other kind."

"You gon shoot somebody wit a gun, Lijah? Dat mean you gon kill em like dat lady killed dat man? Den dat gon make you a killer like she is."

"Naw, Haley, not de way de army is. I won't be killin anybody. If I have to kill somebody, it'll be in self-defense and to save our country one day. You'll understand when you git older."

"You ain't scared to go fight war in de United States Army?"

"Naw, ain't scared."

"When you comin back?"

"I'll be back in six months," he said.

On the same night Lijah left for the army, all my nights turned into nightmares. This time they were different from the nightmares I had previously. I would wake from them not able to remember what they were about.

When it came to carrying news, I was the news carrier. The very first opportunity I had, I spread it to Mama and anybody else who would listen: Lijah and Wesley were going into the United States Army to kill people in defense of their country.

Daddy said jokingly, "Why don't you ask em to take you wit em wit your little talkin-ass self? G—— d—— it, if it got to be told, just tell you!"

The moment I got to Lijah and Wesley I did just as Daddy suggested. My mouth filled with red hots, burning like fire, I blurted out, "Can I go to de United States Army wit you?"

They laughed hard before Lijah said, "If you go wit us, who gon see bout Aunt Matilda?"

He went on to explain to me that females were not allowed to go into the services, only men. And they was expecting me to take real good care of Aunt Matilda while they were gone.

They left two weeks after Christmas. It was a sad day for us. Lijah had packed his clothes in a duffel bag. He gathered Aunt Matilda and me together, put his arm around her shoulder, lifted me up from the floor, and kissed each of us on our cheeks. He stood me down on the floor and reached his hands into both pockets, pulling out fistfuls of change. It was so much, my tiny hand couldn't hold half of it. Aunt Matilda got me a rag and put all of it on the rag. Wesley gave me a dollar bill, and nobody could tell me that I was not rich. I had never seen so much change money at one time. They made my day and night too.

Lijah then pulled out a five-dollar bill from his wallet and gave to Aunt Matilda. She looked at it and started to cry silently. Tears were slowly dropping from her face. I started to cry because she was crying, and before long we were all crying. Lijah patted me and her and told us not to worry, that he'd be back before we knew it. That was my first time witnessing Aunt Matilda being so unhappy since she came into our lives.

The men left, walking down Rat Row for the the bus depot. They waved back as far as we could see them until they turned the corner down by Flappy Boots' café, out of sight.

We went back into the house, sad they were gone. But the happiness they left us with was a story that could always be told. She accepted the fact that her boys were gone off again. It was possible that we might never see them again, but like she always said, "All is well cause de good Lord know all bout it, and he'll take care ob it."

Late in the evening, after she had completed her wash, fed the chicks, and cooked supper, we were eating, and somebody knocked on the front door. I rushed to open it, and there stood a man and woman. "Who you want?" I asked.

"We lookin for Aunt Matilda Rhimes. Do she live here?"

I rushed back to the kitchen, shouting, "Aunt Matilda, dat lady and man want you! Dey ask me do Aunt Matilda live here. Come on! Dey standin on de porch."

Aunt Matilda had just put a big dip of snuff in her lips. I took her by her hand and led her to the front door. The lady stood looking at her and she at the lady. Neither of them said a word.

It was cold, so I said, "Dey kin come inside if dey want to, kin dey, Aunt Matilda?"

She shook her head. I glanced at her face. It seemed like she had a happy look, and then it seemed like she was puzzled about who these people were.

They came in. The lady took her coat off, making herself right at home. Then she grabbed Aunt Matilda and embraced her, crying, "Aunt Matilda, don't you know your niece?"

Aunt Matilda looked her up and down and started to grin. The snuff was running down the corner of her mouth. She said in absolute disbelief, "Marvella, is dat you, baby? Lord hab mercy, it *is* you!"

They hugged for dear life. It was a family reunion. The boys weren't so long left after her not seeing them for many years, and now here was her niece, whom she hadn't seen in thirty or forty years. The expression on her face must have flickered ten times. "My sister's gurl. Thank you, Lord."

Aunt Matilda took Marvella's hand and gently rubbed it over her face. The tears began to roll slowly down both their cheeks. I could see they were tears of happiness. They tenderly embraced with great intent to make up for the lost years. Their relationship was recaptured in five seconds. Aunt Matilda asked the same questions over and over: "Marvella, Marvella, is it really you? Where you come from? Where you been all these years? Lord God hab mercy, I didn't think I would ever see you again. Come on in. Sat down and tell me everythin. Where you been livin? How did you come to find me?"

While they were talking, I ran off to share the good news with Mama. But all of my joy turned quickly into a wide-awake nightmare—Daddy was beating up my mama. I could hear her yelling as I ran through the door. He was beating her like a madman. The other children were crying. I immediately commenced to trying to pull him off of her, shouting, "Leave her alone!"

The instant I said it, he turned and started toward me. His eyes were fiery red. I looked at him with cruel hatred. I disliked him for many reasons, and I wanted to kill him myself. Mama's face was swollen, her lips were busted, and she looked so helpless.

Because he turned toward me, I was able to be a decoy for her. He started after me. I yelled out as loud as I could, "I'mo git de policeman!"

I ran out the back door as others were coming in. I rushed screaming all the way back to Aunt Matilda's house.

She met me at the back door. I knew I was safe. He was not about to come to her house in the condition he was in; he was not positioned to stop me. I warned them what he had done. After they had consoled me, they all took off to see about Mama. Aunt Matilda's niece didn't know anything about my mama but was right with Aunt Matilda every step of the way.

I ran to my hiding place where I normally went when I wanted to cry out and pray to God. It was underneath Mama's house, in the corner of the chimney, quiet and alone. I kept thinking, why would he beat our mama like he did? Why have her face swollen the way it was? Who was he? I didn't fear him; I despised him. In my young life, to have so much despicable feeling rooted in me was beyond my comprehension. A million thoughts were running around in my head.

I heard footsteps. I peeked from under the house so I wouldn't be seen. It was Daddy with some other man I didn't recognize, walking down the road toward Flappy Boots's café. Daddy was cursing, but I was not making any sense of what he was saying. All I knew at that time was I wanted him to go. Just the mention of the police would give us a good three days of rest from him. I wanted him to die or leave us alone.

That night, the nightmare started up again. I dreamed Mama was lying in a coffin again like Ms. Letrolla, and everybody was walking around, looking at her. I awoke terrified, the dream was so real. From then on I dreamed the same dream, until I was afraid to even sleep. Whenever I tried, I would see Mama in that coffin with a bloody face.

Chapter 3: Those Were the Good Old Days

The nightmares didn't stop. They got worse, lessening my chance of emerging out of all that darkness. Somehow I found the way, through the love that I was experiencing from Aunt Matilda. Nobody else knew the strength she possessed to make every day peaceful. I received that strength, using all of my energy to make my mind sane. She was a woman of integrity, a woman with much wisdom and a heart filled with nothing but love, the kind I was able to capture just by watching her. I related to her on her every level, and I learned much from her. Paying attention was all it took.

As time progressed, I grew more and more attached to Aunt Matilda. Everywhere she went, I went. Everything she did, I tried to imitate. I became to her as Ruth was to Naomi.

I was coming up on my sixth birthday, preparing for my first year in school. I had never known what a birthday party was besides tea cakes and Kool-Aid, but it was something I had to look forward to. Then we advanced from tea cakes and Kool-Aid to homemade chocolate cake and ice cream.

For as long as I could remember, Aunt Matilda had gotten her county check. She always spent it wisely. She had bought a basket of baby chicks, which she nourished with much tender loving care. With her handiness, she did everything for herself. She didn't take charity from anyone. She always cautioned me that you could only depend on God and yourself.

Her chicken were multiplying rapidly in the backyard, leading her to put up another chicken coop. It was a hot, beautiful April morning. She had bought more biddies and was changing around what she called "the pullets" from the roosters. She knew the difference between them all. She was the only one in the neighborhood who had poultry like she did. Other neighbors had geese, hens, roosters, and turkeys running around their yards but they were not as professional as she was. Only old man Benny Lee Lang, who lived across from where we lived, was as serious as Aunt Matilda—he had ducks, turkeys, horses, coons, and rabbits. He even had a jackass in his pasture.

Mr. Clerry, who worked up at the bus depot where all farm things were sold, gave Aunt Matilda good instructions on how to care of her baby chicks, and she was excellent in doing so. She taught me how to have the kind of love that was needed to take care of them. Unaware of what I was doing, I became a little farm girl right in her backyard on Rat Row. I never had a complaint from her. She taught me well, and it was fun helping her take care of the chicks.

Lijah returned home on a thirty-day leave. No one knew he was coming; he just showed up like he had that day I first met him. He was full of surprises, and showing up that day really was a surprise.

After a couple weeks, it become noticeable that Lijah was not spending nights at the house. He only spent one night there out of the thirty days. Aunt Matilda somehow had him and Gemmy BB married. Word was out that Gemmy BB was going to get her a soldier man. Little did they know it was not Gemmy BB he wanted.

In June, his time was up. He was getting ready to go back to the service, and this time he was going overseas. He didn't know when he would be returning. But he was not going alone. In behind him walked this short, fat, bow-legged, bald-headed woman wearing the biggest dip of snuff in her lips I had ever seen. She wore hers in one corner, and the juice was running out the other.

Aunt Matilda took one look at her, and I perceived the contempt in her eyes. Her voice instantly transformed. For as long as I had known her, I had never witnessed dislike toward anyone from her, not even old Ms. Onna.

Lijah tried to explain to her that this woman, Essie Lee, was now

Mrs. Lijah. I thought Aunt Matilda was going to collapse from the shock. She was speechless. She looked them both up and down, then walked out of the back door to the chicken coop and started nailing something crazy.

She never came back inside until they were gone. She didn't even say good-bye to either of them. She came and stood in the front door, watching them walk down the alley that led through Mrs. Angie Rosa's backyard on out to the back road that was called Milford Road. By the time they were out on the road, the news had traveled that Lijah was married and had become a family man. Old Long Laura said, "She was old enough to be dat young man's mama." No matter what folk said, she was Lijah's wife for sure.

A letter came every month, and each year brought a new baby picture. Before long, Essie Lee had as many young'uns from him as she'd already had.

Essie Lee returned after five years, and with her the four children she'd had with Lijah. She was the only person other than Ms. Onna whom Aunt Matilda actually despised. Aunt Matilda never had anything to do with Essie Lee or the children. She never accepted Essie Lee as Lijah's wife. We were her only family in all that town. Whatever Aunt Matilda felt, she never spoke a unkind word against Essie Lee, but her facial expression revealed to me everything I needed to know.

We went up to visit with Aunt Lucy Sue. She had given birth to another girl, named Mae Nella. All the grown-ups went inside, helping out with whatever needed to be done. I went outside to play with Tise. She was playing underneath the house; that's where she hid out when she wanted to dodge work.

Tise never wanted anyone else around Papa. From under the house, she had a view of anyone who came near him. If it was someone she didn't want near him, she knew how to prevent them from having any time with him.

As soon as she learned that I was there, she encouraged me to come under the house with her. I never suspected she had a hidden motive, and I loved her. Therefore I would do just about anything she wanted me to do without a second thought. She told me we were going to play barbershop, holding an old pair of rusty scissors in her hand. She insisted on me being the the first one to get a haircut and said she would be second. Only, when she had given me my haircut and left me bald, she then crawled from under the house and got up under Papa, leaning on him for protection. She knew he didn't allow anyone to bother her, whether she was right or wrong.

When Mama called for me, she was getting ready for us to leave for home before time for supper. I came out, hardly understanding the meaning of Tise cutting off my hair. I came through the door, and Mama yelled out loud at the top of her voice, "Who done cut my young'un's hair off her head like dat? Jesus, who done dat?" I was looking like I didn't think anything was wrong. But Mama was devastated over the fact Tise had bald-headed me.

Suddenly she seemed like she was lost for words. Apparently it came to her that nobody else could have done this atrocious thing except Tise. That was proof that every mother knows her own children. Nobody had to tell her. I didn't tell her.

Tise was snuggled under Papa like she normally was when she'd done something she had no business doing. Mama slowly sneaked up on her. Before Papa could get up from the chair, Mama had grabbed Tise by the top of her head. She beat her across the head with her hand. As she hit, she was shouting, "I'll kill your black ass! You done cut all my baby's good hair off her head!"

Papa tried to stop her from hitting Tise, but his strength up against Mama's just didn't match. She almost slung him down to the ground. I'd never seen her that angry before. She was crazy, beating Tise all across the back and head. Tise screamed until she was half out of breath.

There was a lot of conversation after the beating, and the haircut caused big tension between Mama and Papa. It made folk gossip.

Mama made me a paper-sack cap. I believe that was my first experience of hurting because other children made fun of me. It started when we went up to visit Aunt Lucy Sue again after the haircut.

Another outcast family, the Bendersons, lived down at the dead end of that lane. They were the talk of the neighborhood up at the Sawmill quarter. They were as loaded as Ms. Onna, who was the roughest human being ever known.

The Bendersons were a huge family, and they were who you wouldn't want to be. I didn't know how bad folk could hurt one another—I learned from watching one family hurt another, from feeling others hurt. That whole family was big in size: the mother stood about five feet five and weighed three hundred pounds. The five daughters were of similar height but not as big. Mr. Bruce was the smallest of the family, and the kindest. The oldest daughter was Nora. She was the same age as our cousin Nora. There was a set of twins, May and Shay. Dorla, the middle girl, was nonviolent like her daddy. The baby girl, Mary, was like her other sisters—not friendly at all. The two grandchildren of the family, Bonnie and Sole, were taught well by their aunts. Hezekiel, the only son, was an example of "like father, like son"—he was a nice, quiet boy. Old folk said one day he would make some woman a good husband.

Anyone who came across them would know they'd come in contact with trouble. The Bendersons were all alike. As the word goes, the apple don't fall too far from the tree. When anyone went after one member of that family, they had the entire family to deal with. No one in the neighborhood mingled with any of them. That was one of the reasons they was so vindictive. They couldn't stand rejection, and got attention in all the wrong ways.

Cousin Lacy lived down the lane too, about the third house from Aunt Lucy Sue. She had four daughters: Pauline, Salene, Maxine, and a baby girl named Collar. They were like Aunt Lucy Sue's family, very close-knit. They were quiet, and you seldom heard anything negative about them—highly intelligent, soft-spoken, and kept to themselves. But the Bendersons didn't see it that way. They threw rocks at my cousin's family and called them "the stuck-up ones."

There was only one pump in the neighborhood that everybody used. The neighbors were so cautious of the Bendersons that they would get their water early in the evening to keep from coming in contact with any of that family. But one day, Pauline was hot and uncomfortable, so she decided to go out to the pump and draw a foot tub of water to take a cool bath. She was not thinking anything would happen to her at that hour and in such a short time. Little did she know the devil never sleeps.

She was pumping her water when she was attacked by three of the Benderson girls. They beat her awful bad. Her face was like raw meat—they made sure they disfigured her face. If Uncle Cleo hadn't came out when he did to get a bucket of water, there's no telling what they would have done. He saved her life. They had already beaten her unconscious, The doctor said if Uncle Cleo hadn't gotten to her when he did, they probably would have left her out there to bleed to death.

Pauline was in the hospital for over two weeks. The day she regained consciousness, she was able to tell who it was that beat her. Old Lund Cabb arrested all three of the Benderson girls. They tried to lie their way out of it, but Uncle Cleo was Pauline's witness. After their arrest, they went to court. The judge ordered them to pay her hospital bill, and every day she was unable to work, they had to pay her salary.

I learned of violence at an early age. Some things are just plain unavoidable, and some things are meant to happen. But I'm still curious as to why it would take three people to beat one poor, helpless person. Word was Pauline was as scared as any rabbit. She wouldn't have fought if there was only one attacker, because she was a nonviolent human being and too good for those people. Cousin Lacy's family did the right thing by allowing the law to take care of the situation.

Aunt Lucy Sue got caught smack in the middle of their dispute, even though she and Cousin Lacy were the children of different brothers. Aunt Lucy Sue was the type of person who felt your business was yours and hers was hers. She was quick to tell anybody, "Dat ain't none of my business," or "What dat got to do wit me?" The time of day was about all you would get out of her; she said, "It's due to anybody." Because she spoke the same to everybody, she assumed everything was fine.

Ms. Benderson was the best seamstress in the whole town beside Ms. Annie Wilson. Aunt Lucy Sue hired her to do some sewing. She gave her the material, and Ms. Benderson made the dresses just as Aunt Lucy Sue wanted her to. But then Ms. Benderson cut up the dresses into strings and threw them on my aunt's front porch. Aunt Lucy Sue got up in the morning and found the dresses in threads. The devastation she felt, she said, was a memory forever. It was the meanest thing any human could do to another. She took Ms. Benderson to court. The woman was ordered to replace the material, but Aunt Lucy Sue declined to accept anything from her. All she wanted was to be rid of that family.

Shortly after those incidents, folk began to move out from the Sawmill quarter. It was never the same. Cousin Lacy and her family moved all the way up near Korea. Aunt Lucy Sue and Uncle Cleo, with their five children, took a three-room house down in Brake's quarter.

The Darrs family left too. Aunt Lucy Sue and Ms. Dora Darr was the best of friends, and not long after Aunt Lucy Sue moved, Ms. Dora and her husband, Mr. AD, found a little three-room house about two roads over from where Aunt Lucy Sue lived.

The only other family left in the lane was the Crawdads, Mr. Felix and his wife Bonny. She had a sister named Kdella, and they were as thick as thieves, loving as a quarter would spend.

Time passed, and I no longer had to wear the bag on my head. Aunt Matilda made me a bonnet of many colors. It reminded me of the story in the Bible about the brothers who sold their brother Joseph down in slavery. They hated him because their father loved him more and made him a coat of many colors. Each day and night, I prayed that my hair would hurry and grow back before school began, so I wouldn't have to wear that bonnet on my head anymore. I was being picked at enough about my head in the neighborhood; that was more than enough. I dreaded going anywhere.

Now that Aunt Lucy Sue was no longer in the Sawmill quarter, she lived where all the unkind folk lived. Every time I left the house, whether it was with Mama or Aunt Matilda, there was always some evil lurking about and waiting to make my heart pain more.

Aunt Matilda and I went downtown every Saturday just to get out of the house. We would look through the windows and eat a nickel cone of ice cream. On a beautiful, hot, sunny Saturday, we headed out. I had the bonnet on my head. As we passed through Brake's quarter's folk sitting out on their porches, I could hear the children laughing and making fun of my bonnet. Even the grown-ups did. It angered me, but we kept on walking. Aunt Matilda was hard of hearing, so she couldn't hear the ugly remarks.

At the end of Cedar Street sat three ladies: Arketha Horns, Jettey Bellow, and O'Bera Walters. Daddy called them the three slickers. We were about to turn the corner, and loud and clear I heard one of them say, "Little Haley looks like a little old woman wit dat bonnet on her head."

O'Bera said harshly, "She looks damn near old as Aunt Matilda. Hell, if I didn't know no better, I would swear they was damn twins." She was grinning hard, and the tone in her voice told me that lady hated me something terrible. And the way she looked at me corresponded with my belief. From that very day, I was cautious of her always.

I looked up at her, letting her know I heard every harsh word she said. By making eye-to-eye contact, I hoped she would see my pain, even if she didn't feel it. I thought, *One of these old days, I will remember these pains when she is feeling some of her own.* I could see she had no remorse for the things she said. It made me kinda glad for a minute that Aunt Matilda was unable to hear what she said. What else could I expect from a street woman like O'Bera Walters?

Aunt Matilda and I were laughingstocks everywhere we went. What on earth did we do for folk to make fun of us? She walked on her walking stick, and I would sometimes hold on to her dress tail. We didn't bother anybody. She never wronged anyone in the many years I knew her. I concluded that some things were just meant to be.

When we arrived downtown, we both were sweaty, hot, and tired from walking in all that sun, and as thirsty as we were tired. We made our rounds and then sat on the corner of the top step by the dime store. Everything in there was supposed to cost a dime, and sometimes we didn't even have a dime to spend.

We watched the horses and buggies, and the mules and wagons. The country folk somehow could always be known from the town folk. They were wild, like a bird being let out of its cage for the first time. Everybody was running crazy. What amazed me the most was how everyone who passed us made us feel as if we were some show from a zoo.

Aunt Matilda said, "Let's git a ice cream cone."

I didn't know any better. I went in through the front door of the dime store. The smell of hot dogs and hamburgers and popcorn swept across my nose, making me hungry. The first thing that got my attention was all white folk—no blacks or "colored," as they called us. They were all sitting, sipping drinks from straws, laughing as if they were the only race on earth and superior to the world. I didn't sit down. I stood at the counter, waiting to be served. I stood for so long that a stool became empty. I sat down on it to rest my tired feet.

I wasn't sitting long before this red-headed, freckle-faced white woman came over to me and said, "Listen, gal, where do you think you at? Git down off of that stool this here minute!"

This was my first time experiencing being ordered around like some nothing or an inhuman. I was not old enough to know that there was a difference between blacks, coloreds, niggers, or Negroes and the so-called whites. Literally being scolded by the whites piqued my curiosity. Why were we the ones being scolded? I never heard then of any blacks scolding a white person. It was always "Yes, sir, boss," and that was disturbing to me. My introduction that day was just a black and white thing, but to me it was mental cruelty.

I looked at her, but before I could utter a word, Aunt Matilda came in, took me by my hand, and said, "Come on, Haley. What got you in here so long time?"

The woman looked at Aunt Matilda like she was going to smack her, or so I assumed. I took Aunt Matilda's hand and led her toward the door.

The woman said, "Stop. Wait a minute." She looked at Aunt Matilda up and down in dismay. "Matilda—Matilda Rhimes, is that you? My God. Sweet Jesus, it is you. By George, I thought you was dead and rotted."

Aunt Matilda was not hearing a word she said. I translated every word to her, word for word just as the woman spoke it. Aunt Matilda looked at the woman in fear, a look that came over her when she suspected something wasn't right. She was speechless.

The woman asked her, "Matilda, don't you know who I is?"

She really didn't know that woman so she gave her an uncertain grin.

The woman grinned back and touched her on the shoulder. "You cooked many pecan pies for my mama and put many a pair of shoes on my feet, and you mean you don't know me? I'm Rachel Griffin! Member all them times I sat in the kitchen, watchin you bake and cook, and I licked the spoon?"

Something clicked. Aunt Matilda's grin got wider. "Yeah, yeah, you must be Ms. Bertha Wiggler's gurl. Where is Ms. Bertha?" She spoke as if she was not completely sure of her thoughts—as if she knew this woman from somewhere, but wasn't sure of who she really was.

"Mama is at home. Yeah, she still livin, but her health is just bout gone. Matilda Rhimes, I bet she'll know who you are at the door. I'm bout to be gittin off for lunch in a few minutes. Y'all go outside an stand by the window. What y'all want? I'll git it for y'all. My car is right on the corner. Wait for me outside."

She hurriedly gave us each a cone of ice cream, and we did as she ordered us to—walked back outside and waited for her to come out. The car was parked in the front row of the lot, just as she said it was.

Not long after, Ms. Griffin came running out. We had eaten the ice cream. She invited Aunt Matilda to go with her to see her mama. They both were still surprised that Aunt Matilda had accidentally run into somebody she knew from a long-hurting past.

We hopped into the backseat of her nice 1954 Ford, and she drove for about five minutes, pulling right up a driveway into a car shed. The house was beautiful—black and white, with shutters around the windows. The lawn was so manicured, you could fall asleep on it just like a bed.

Ms. Griffin said, "Y'all kin just git on out. I know when Mama hear your voice, it's gonna just take her breath away. I got to prepare you, cause her eyesight is complete gone in both her eyes."

When something good was going to happen, Aunt Matilda would smile broadly. Her voice changed, and that look of fear flickered to a look of blissfulness. Her memories commenced to flow through the depths of her soul. On this day, she stared and grinned repeatedly, saying, "Ms. Bertha is still erlibe."

"Matilda, you was bout the last person I expected to see in the store. I know it's been way over twenty-five years since we saw you. I was married and expectin. You too still alive. You must be pretty much eighty or ninety years old now, ain't you?"

Aunt Matilda looked from Ms. Griffin to me, waiting for me to translate what she was saying. I repeated every word back to her. She laughed, spit running from both corners of her mouth, as if she had come across a million dollars.

Ms. Griffin persisted. "You know we thought you were dead an buried by now."

"No'm, Ms. Griffin, ain't dead yet. De good Lord done been mighty good taking care ob me fur over eighty-five years now."

They stood in the carport, conversing. Aunt Matilda remembered raising Ms. Griffin from a three-month-old baby until she was twenty-four years old. Then Ms. Griffin got married and moved off the plantation. Ms. Griffin looked at me and asked Aunt Matilda suspiciously, "Whose gal is this you got wit you? I know she ain't your young'un."

Ms. Matilda didn't answer. I had learned one thing about Aunt Matilda: if she didn't want to answer, she would pretend she hadn't heard you.

Ms. Griffin's maid placed a mat on the floor off by the carport, reminding us to leave our shoes at the corner of the steps. She was a tall, heavyset, extremely dark-skinned woman. She told us to come on in, and all the while, her eyes were dressing us up and down.

Ms. Griffin said to her, "This here old woman was my nanny for many years. She wanted to come and see Mama. You kin go head an fix my lunch. I'll take them on to Mama's room so she kin visit some while I have my lunch. I'll be back in here in a second."

She led us down a wide hallway. Everything was like what you'd only see in a movie. It was the most beautiful house I had ever seen. As a matter of fact, I had never been inside a white person's house before.

Ms. Griffin called as she was walking us down the hall, "Mama, you awake? She normally is awake at this time of day. Come right on in. Like I told you, Matilda, she is totally blind, but she recognize voices very well. Once she hears you, I know she'll recognize you. How kin anybody forgit your voice, Matilda?"

We entered a room beautifully decorated in blue and gray. A little white-headed white lady was sitting comfortably in a recliner chair by a double window. She wasn't moving, just sitting. Her hair was like shining silk in two braids. She was wearing a long blue grown and matching housecoat with blue house shoes. Ms. Griffin said, "Mama, I'm home. I got somebody with me. You'll never guess who it is."

She led Aunt Matilda over to where Ms. Bertha was sitting. Aunt Matilda stood watching her. Ms. Griffin asked again, "Mama, you awake?"

"Yes, I'm awake," Ms. Bertha stated in a low, weak voice.

Ms. Griffin told Aunt Matilda to say something to her. Aunt Matilda said, as if it were some kind of private code, "Our Father in heaven is gwine swing down, sweet chariot, to come an carry us home."

She got Ms. Bertha's attention. Ms. Bertha held her head up, turning it from side to side. Aunt Matilda laughed out loud, enough for Ms. Bertha to sense that the voice was in front of her. Ms. Bertha giggled a little and asked, "Who's voice is that I hear? It sound so familiar to me, but I just can't quite member whose voice I'm hearing."

Finally Aunt Matilda said, "Ms. Wiggler, I baked your favorite pecan pie, all fur you. I hope you like it."

"Matilda! Matilda Rhimes, dog blasted, is that your voice I'm hearing? Matilda, is that really you?"

Tears commenced to roll down both of their faces. I looked on as Ms. Bertha reached out to Aunt Matilda. When their hands touched, Ms. Griffin left the room.

The most electrifying emotions saturated those two little old ladies. Anyone could see that at one time, they had had something special between them—a bond that could not be broken.

"My God, Matilda, it *is* your voice that I'm hearin. I've prayed for you to come to see me. I've been worried bout you for so many years. I've begged the Lord to let me see you just one more time fore he come an take me home. An just look at this—he done answered my prayer after thirty-odd years."

They hugged each other. They rubbed each other's faces. They kissed each other again and again. Aunt Matilda didn't say very much in the beginning, as if she were searching in the back of her mind for something spontaneous to resurface. Gradually her shocked look changed into a loving, happy look, like somebody had risen from the dead. She pulled up a chair beside Ms. Bertha, and they talked about God for what seemed like hours.

It was really only forty-five minutes before they began to reminisce about past days up on the plantation. They were talking and shedding tears at the same time. Ms. Bertha said, "You know, Matilda, Billy died over twenty-eight years ago. And after he died, I had all the sponsibility on me, havin to take care of all them acres. The farmwork was much more than I could handle. Lord knows I wished many a day that I could just look in your eyes so I could tell you how sorry I was bout everythin, specially bout that mob hangin your sister's boy Tubby. Matilda, I swear to you on my daddy's grave, I have never lived that killin down. Up to this here very day, it haunts me."

I watched how dried-up that elderly white woman was as tears streamed down her face, confessing to Aunt Matilda the awful thing done to her sister's boy. Ms. Bertha was easing her conscience or in need of getting rid of guilt.

I saw it was painful to Aunt Matilda. She made no comment for a long while; she sat watching Ms. Bertha's tears. Then Aunt Matilda took her hands and wiped the tears from her eyes, saying, "God got it."

***

Ms. Griffin came into the room for us. It was time to leave. Aunt Matilda and Ms. Bertha hugged each other, not wanting to let go. As Aunt Matilda let her arms go from around Ms. Bertha's neck, Ms. Bertha started yelling, "Matilda, you ain't leavin, is you? Don't go. Can't you stay just a little while longer? I been waitin so long. Please, Matilda, don't leave me now."

We had to leave. Aunt Matilda promised her she'd be back: "I'mo come back to see your again. Don't fret yourself none, you hear? I'mo come back." When we left that day, Ms. Bertha was unable to see Aunt Matilda, but Aunt Matilda was surely able to see her.

It had been a long, hot day for us. We both were tired. When Ms. Griffin dropped us off home, folk were looking.

Aunt Matilda went directly into the kitchen and started cooking. That was another thing I learned: when there was something heavy weighing on her mind, she kept herself busy. She wouldn't stop moving, no matter how tired she was. But after watching her make the fire in the stove and start preparing the food, I went in for a snooze.

I couldn't have been snoozing long before Aunt Matilda Ann and Uncle Emmet came by. After Aunt Matilda had finished cooking, they convinced us to come back to the farm with them and spend the night. Going to the farm was like going on a long trip that I had never been on before.

Their house sat a ways down from the road. It was like some of the white folks' houses in town—the lawn was well manicured. The chairs were lined up neatly, the barn was stacked with hay, chickens were running around on the grounds, goats were crying, and the cows were mooing. I was amazed. Inside my body, my breath seized. I thought, *This is how I'm going to keep my house when I grow up.* I was motivated by them beyond my wildest dream.

One of my fondest memories is of visiting the Kimball farm the day before Easter Sunday. It was my first time hearing about the resurrection of our Lord Jesus Christ.

It was a beautiful evening when we arrived. I jumped off the back of the wagon and watched Uncle Emmet as he unhitched the mule and put it in the stables. The brightness from the big sun setting was the most fascinating experience I'd seen. Waking up in a different house with the sun shining through the window and the roosters crowing made me think that I was resurrected myself from old to new.

Something happened out there that I couldn't explain. Everything was so different from town life. The Kimballs were hundreds of feet from any of their neighbors. Aside from the animals, everything was still and quiet. I had a different view of the way we lived.

The conversation they had about the coming and resurrection of Jesus Christ was vivid in my mind. I could almost picture him coming back to earth. I practically saw the vision of Christ in his glory. They made it seem so simple.

When I awoke on Easter morning, they were already up and praying and praising God. It was the same in their house as it was in Aunt Matilda's house: prayer came before anything else. It was certainly prayer that was the key to open doors and solve all problems. Prayer could turn any situation around.

As they were praying, I browsed through a picture book. Aunt Matilda Ann had pictures of Christ all over the walls. Other pictures had been cut out of magazines and pasted on sheets of plain paper and sewn into a book. What was so unique about Aunt Matilda and Aunt Matilda Ann was that each of them had the same pictures on their walls, the same pictures pasted on the same kind of paper. They hadn't seen each other for twenty some-odd years, but they had the same mind-set, the same trusting and faithful spirit. Both of them loved the Lord sincerely and taught me how to love him also. Whether he was man or a spirit, he was real in my life. Living around them how could anyone not know who Jesus was? The pictures stared from every wall of the house.

All the pictures showed that Jesus was a white man. It was the only way white folk wanted him to be. To my aunts, there was no color, only Jesus. I didn't know anything about idols or false gods, but I soon learned that they who worship God must worship him in spirit and in truth.

I celebrated Easter morning on the farm, but at eleven o'clock, the three of us were in church. Uncle Emmet didn't attend church, though he had the same type of spirit they did. Aunt Matilda Ann had made me a beautiful yellow dress with puff sleeves, and it was the most beautiful dress I had ever had. No one in that church could have begun to experience the feeling that was inside me, not even my aunts. Sitting in between the two most special women in my life, I felt I could conquer anything in life. They were my inspiration.

Mama was expecting another baby, and I started to think happiness came with a price. Unknown to me, it did—it came with a big price.

The older I got, the more I learned. With it came understanding. I could feel myself maturing. No kindergarten or preschool was yet offered in those days; I was waiting for the day I would enter first grade. Finally, it was my first day. I was to begin school. I was totally excited about it. I must have thanked God about ten times for enabling me to fulfill that desire.

I was up before daylight, waking Aunt Matilda with "It's my school day!" She woke thinking it was time to get up. She crawled out of bed, as happy and excited as I was. She grabbed her long robe and fell down on her knees as she always did, praying. I was right beside her.

When she got to the kitchen, she turned and came directly back, saying, "Haley, it pitch-black dark out dat door. I ain't even muster heard dem dere roosters crawing fur day yet!" Just as she got the last word out of her mouth, the roosters started crowing cock-a-doodle-doo.

She pushed the old shuttered window open to see daylight awakening and darkness retiring. She said, "It's two whole hours 'fore you habe to git to school. You kin go back 'n sleep for ernother hour."

I tried to get back into bed and sleep, but I couldn't. I trotted off to the kitchen and watched as Aunt Matilda made the fire in the stove, preparing to make breakfast. Once the fire started, we both went out to the henhouse to gather the eggs. It was a terrific day. It was exciting that she included me in helping around the house and with chores, especially gathering eggs. The morning of my first day at school finally had arrived.

Time for me to get dressed! I wanted to get dressed all by myself, but Aunt Matilda insisted on helping me, just like I was her own little girl. Knowing me, I probably would have put everything on backward or on the wrong side. That was her main concern—to make sure everything was in place. I hummed me a little tune the whole while she was dressing me.

We looked up and Mama was standing in the front door, watching Aunt Matilda dress me. She was not saying a word, just grinning with happiness painted all over her face. Though Aunt Matilda dressed me, Mama had to take me to school and get me registered.

I couldn't wait to get out of that door. The other children were coming from all directions, and I was included. I waved to everyone as I passed, smiling blissfully. Cousin Sattie Bell, sitting on the porch, paid me a compliment on how pretty I looked, and I was all grins.

Georgie Boy and Snappy were already up and running around the room. Georgie Boy came up to me and whatever he had in his hand, he touched it to my dress, leaving a spot. It upset me so, I pushed him down. It wasn't a hard push, but enough to make him fall back against the side of the bed. He screamed out, so Mama came into the room to learn what I had done. He blew it all out of proportion, but nothing came of it because they didn't want to have to face Aunt Matilda.

She was coming through the door. She could sense something wrong, but she didn't make herself all concerned about it. That day was just too important to me. She wasn't aware that she couldn't sign me in, that Mama had to do it. She went along anyway, and I had two mamas on my first day taking me to school.

Mama took me on into the building and made sure I was signed in. I was assigned to a first grade teacher. Her name was Mrs. Ruthie Crowley. Her room was located in the old gray wooden building next to the old Baptist church, across from the funeral home. The building had four rooms: two first grades and two second grades. They were as ragged as the old houses we lived in.

The other first grade was Mrs. Louisa Greenburg's. The two second grades belonged to Mrs. Susie Funtain, a tall, skinny woman, not at all attractive and as mean as she looked; and to Mrs. Cuties Johnston, who was as white as any white woman that walked, only she was mixed: white daddy and black mama.

Over across the road was where the third and fourth graders attended school, in a building next to Mrs. Rhoda Shepherd's house—the same one that Aunt Matilda had moved out of.

The white folk had a redbrick school with sufficient heating and nice, colorful rooms. We, the black Negroes, had to attend school in ragged buildings with no heat and hardly enough room to move about. The playground was just dirt, no grass.

Once I had been placed in my classroom, I was left on my own, not knowing anyone. No one from our neighborhood was in my classroom. I was brave, sitting in the class, listening to every word the teacher said, but somewhere in my mind I was afraid.

Mrs. Crowley stood in the doorway, greeting each of her students as we entered. She wrote all of the students names on the blackboard, and she showed each of us where our names were. Then she had us, one by one, come up and pick our names out. I believe my name was the shortest name on the board, and when it was my time, I had no problem finding it.

My first day at school was a very exciting day for me. I really thought I was a big girl.

After school was over, Passy Kate and Gemmy BB were waiting for me outside. I was not expecting either of them, but I was certainly expecting Aunt Matilda. I was too excited to allow anyone to spoil what I had experienced that day. The minute I spotted them, I ran up to them, feeling proud. I shouted, "Oh-ho, y'all know what? I mean I got a real pretty teacher, and know what else? I was the only student went up to the board and picked out my name. And I got a book and I gon learn how to read!"

Passy Kate seemed interested in my first day and all I had learned, but Gemmy BB, as always, was her same old self. She had nothing good to say nor made me feel in any way good about myself—but Passy Kate did. I talked about Mrs. Crowley and school all the way home.

When we got to Mama's house, she was sitting on the porch, waiting for me. She laughed and called to me proudly. I knew something was up with her, and it wasn't all concern about my first day. She was as intoxicated as I had ever seen her. "Come on, baby, an tell Mama what you learned in school today."

I was most excited to share with her what my first day at school had been like. The day had been a pleasant experience, a joyous day with much happiness. But I knew when Mama talked with that kind of concern, she been drinking. So I just shouted excitedly, "I learned my name from de blackboard!" Nothing was going to take away what I had experienced. No, no, I was too elated.

Mama came close to me, saying, "You did?"

"Yeah, ma'am, I did. I got me a book cause I'mo learn how to read it."

Passy Kate and Gemmy BB rushed inside the house, leaving me on the porch with Mama. I'd given her all the good news I had, so I went on down to Aunt Matilda's house.

Aunt Matilda was sewing. I tiptoed up to the back of the chair and tapped her on her shoulder, causing her to jump from fear. The needle pricked her finger, causing her some uncomfortableness. That was the first time she ever raised her voice to me. My frightening her made her furious. She spoke in a little angry tone, "Haley, you scared me like dat, look what you made me do!" Her finger was bleeding; just a small amount of blood came out.

I was so uneasy about frightening her, I commenced to cry, saying sincerely, "Cuse me, please, ma'am, Aunt Matilda! Do it hurt? Cuse me! I didn't mean to scare you. I promise I won't scare you never again!"

She looked at the sadness on my face and rubbed her hand across it. I knew I was forgiven. She would never let anything keep her angry. She was very timid about the least little noise or someone touching her from behind. Each day, I learned something new from her, and it always guided me in the right direction.

I asked her again, "Aunt Matilda, do it hurt?"

She nodded her head in a way that meant no, looking up at me with her beautiful gray eyes, smiling. She wasn't hurt, just timid.

Chapter 4: Learning How to Pray

Each morning we were all awakened by the crowing of the roosters in the neighborhood. Everybody knew it was the beginning of a brand-new day. I had been in school for over one month, and I was excited; there was nothing more important to me than residing with Aunt Matilda and attending school. I was a fast learner and catching on real fast.

I was on top of prayer. Aunt Matilda had taught me well, and I was so into it. Prayer in school was mandatory. Once the morning bell rang, the first thing took place was devotion. A song was sung, Scripture was read, and prayer was prayed. We learned to respect prayer, if nothing else. Prayer was the most important factor in school in those days; the whole school was in one accord.

I thought Mrs. Crowley was the prettiest dark-skinned teacher in the whole school. Her skin was as smooth as butter. I just fell in love with her like I did with Aunt Matilda. I loved the way she dressed—she always matched, whatever she wore. Nobody could walk in a pair of high-heeled shoes like she did. She walked like she was the queen of the elementary school. She was fascinating to me. She stood about five feet six inches and weighed about one hundred and ten pounds. Everything she wore hugged her body if the clothes were made especially for her.

Regardless of how good a person tries to be or truly is, the devil is always lurking about, seeking whom he may devour. Mrs. Crowley was to me the best teacher the elementary school ever employed. There was no one who could measure up to her. In her own unique way, she was perfect. Not only was she my first grade teacher, she was also the dance teacher for the sixth through ninth graders. She was an excellent dancer. She had a way with her students like no other teacher.

However, a few people didn't take to her because they were jealous of her. They wanted to be like her but didn't have what it took to be like her. She was who she was, and no one was like her.

One of my very first uncomfortable encounters in school happened when some children from Brake's quarter came out and made fun of me about Aunt Matilda. I really didn't know they were being cruel to me, but I was not comfortable around them. During recess, when they came out from their classes, I wouldn't stay around them. I would just go back inside my classroom, sit in the back, and watch Mrs. Crowley practice dancing with the older students. That made me feel comfortable.

One day she came back after the class was over and inquired why I was there, not outside playing with the other students. I told her they didn't like me and said mean things to me about Aunt Matilda. I could tell by the way she looked at me that she thought there was more to it than what I was telling her. She convinced me that recess was what I needed—being cooped up in the room all day was not good. Sunshine and exercise were good for me. She encouraged me to go over to the other side of the playground, the high school side, where all the play equipment was. She said I would meet other children who would be kind to me. But I didn't want new friends; I just wanted to be near her.

She also assured me that when the new school that was being built was completed, I would be able to be in her dance class. That made me feel so included, I left school all excited and hopeful.

When I got home that evening, Daddy wasn't home and Mama was drinking. Though I looked on Aunt Matilda as a second mama, she was actually more of a mother figure to me than my birth mama. There were times I wanted my mother to listen to me and be there for me, but she was no one I could count on. Aunt Matilda was always there when I needed her—but it was not the same as having my real mother.

The moment I saw Mama drinking with all the drunks around the house, I kept walking on down to Aunt Matilda's house. She was waiting for me with open arms and my favorite snacks prepared in the kitchen. Playclothes were laid out neatly on the bed for me to put on. After I ate my snacks, I sat down beside her and watched as she continued her quilting. Then I went outside to play, holding my news inside me with no one to tell it to. I thought if only Lijah and Wesley were home, I could tell them my good news. I wondered where they were and if they were ever coming back to see us.

Time passed. I spent quiet time alone. Sometimes I would go off to school happy and excited, but after school was over, sadness would set in. I had to pass our house to get to Aunt Matilda's and saw everything going on at Mama's. I learned a lot and had fun at school, but when I got home, I had no one to share it with. Aunt Matilda was deaf and old. She was the sweetest old lady I ever witnessed, and she was unable to read or write.

I recognized it was not her fault. White folk were so mean and evil, they kept black folk working as the slaves whites had turned them into, preventing black folk from learning to read or write. Aunt Matilda never held any kind of animosity in her heart against anyone, not even the white folk. She had more white friends who cared for her than she did black friends, leaving me with the understanding that not all white folk were bad, just as not all blacks were bad either.

Nevertheless, besides Tise and me, there were very few blacks who cared for Aunt Matilda. After we met Ms. Griffin and Ms. Wiggler, white folk started coming around, bringing Aunt Matilda all sorts of nice things that they no longer wanted: lamps, dishes, pots and pans, clothes, shoes, and all sorts of household goods. As long as Aunt Matilda had things to give to her Rat Row neighbors, they poured in like rain. When she had nothing to give, they scattered.

I witnessed the difference between whites and blacks. It was no secret that white folk were prejudiced as hell against us blacks—so strongly that they thought they were superior to blacks. But on the other hand, blacks were just as prejudiced among themselves.

Having a good white friend was like having money in the bank, Aunt Matilda said. She was as giving as she could be.

One day, I went to school feeling despondent and sad. I sat in the classroom with my head down on my desk. Mrs. Crowley came to the back and tapped my head lightly. "Haley, it's recess time. Aren't you going outside to play?"

"Nah, ma'am, I don't wanter go outside."

"Why not? You aren't sick, are you?"

"Nah, ma'am, I ain't sick."

"Well then, you come on outside with me, out of this hot room. Get some of that beautiful sunshine! Come along," she said, taking my hand and pulling me up from the desk. "Come on. Let's go outside and have some fun."

We got outside, and she gathered a few other students who were already on the grounds. She arranged us in a line and said, "I'm going to teach you all some games to play." The first game was called "Simon says." If Simon said it, you did it, but if Mrs. Crowley gave an order without putting "Simon says" first, then anyone who did it got a strike. Three strikes and you were out of the game. The last two standing were another girl and me. I had not yet learned her name; she was from another first grade class.

The next game Mrs. Crowley taught us was the most fun. We called it the "heel-toe, back kick" game. It was just what I needed.

More importantly, Mrs. Crowley gave up her recess to make me and some other students feel better. It is my fondest memory of my school days in her classroom.

After recess was over, Mrs. Crowley gave us instructions: we had to each bring in a bucket of red clay. I went home and explained to Aunt Matilda that I had to take a bucket of clay to school. She didn't hesitate. We went down by the old sawmill and dug it up right away. The next day, I was the only one who brought the clay in—I'd missed the part where she said "in two weeks." But it was a good thing I brought mine in, she said. "That means you won't be late."

I wondered what the clay was for. When the time came, she had us make all sorts of things from it. she taught us how to mix the clay up in water and mold animals. I made an elephant. Other children made chickens, ducks, rabbits, and many more things.

As soon as that project was over, Mrs. Crowley put a program together for us to act out on the stage. It was fascinating to me. I hardly had time to be sad again, not for a very long time.

The program was about playing the parts of nutrients. I was a bottle of milk. I had to say loud and clear, so the sound of each letter could be heard, "Drink plenty of milk and your teeth will be pretty and white." She convinced us that we would do well; all we had to do was learn our parts. She instructed me how I should hold the bottle up in front of me so the audience would be able to see it. She encouraged me to speak up. She said, "The k will sound clearly from the words 'milk' and 'drink,' and the -ty will sound from the words 'plenty' and 'pretty.'"

It was a pleasant day for me, and I had something good I could run home and share with Aunt Matilda. I wanted to stop and share my news with Mama too, but I knew she was going to be drinking. That day, though, she fooled me: she was waiting for me to come by. Full of excitement, I rehearsed my line all the way home, and the moment I saw Mama, my heart rejoiced. "Mama, you know what? I got to be on stage at my school!"

In walked Aunt Matilda. I was able to tell them both my good news, and that I had already learned the words I had to say. For the first time in a long, long time, Mama showed interest. She said, "Let us hear you say de words."

I said them just as they were written on my paper: "Drink plenty of milk and your teeth will be pretty and white."

Aunt Matilda laughed. It made her so proud of me, and she couldn't wait until the night of the play. She asked, "Haley, when you got to tell dis?"

"Mrs. Crowley said we got to say dem next Thursday night, an y'all got to come."

She took the paper out of my hand and looked at it, not able to read a single word. She laughed with joy, because she knew the play would be something that would make her real pleased with me.

I learned the line just as Mrs. Crowley taught it to me. It was as if I thought I was going to be in a movie or something, I was so excited.

That Sunday was one of those Sundays Rev. Huffman preached the roof off the church. I witnessed the members shout unto God as if he were en route to return, I didn't know it then, but I have since learned that it was the Sunday of the anointing of the Holy Ghost.

Rev. Huffman didn't stay for evening service; therefore evening service was canceled. We were on our way home, and I discovered I was old enough to experience shame. Mama's house was full as usual with all the drunks nesting. Uncle Cleo was standing in the doorway. I tried to hide my face, but he recognized me. He called out my name and I waved to him. I speeded my steps as fast as I could before Daddy came out the door, because I knew where Uncle Cleo was, Daddy wasn't far behind. I was not ready to face him yet.

As I made to pass the house, someone lifted me up from behind, saying, "You just gon walk on by your uncle an not give him his sugar?" He tickled me with much love, my favorite Uncle Cleo. "What you got here, your school lesson? Show Uncle what you learned in school."

I felt good when anyone showed me concern. He showed so much interest that I was proud to share my speech with him. He grinned with pride. That was the kind of concern I wanted from my own father and mother. Uncle Cleo was as proud of me going on stage as I was. We sat on the bottom step, and I showed him the paper with my speech on it. He said, "I bet you don't know this."

I shook my head and said, "Yes, me do! I know it! Want me to say it for you?" I stood up directly in front of him and recited word for word, "Drink plenty of milk and your teeth will be pretty and white."

He smiled at me and said, "I knew you could say it. I just wanted to hear it, since I have to work and can't be dere to hear you on stage. Now I heard you fore de rest of dem heard you, and you did good."

The week of the play, there was nothing but excitement all around the school. Everyone was getting ready for the program. Everybody was getting along; no one seemed unhappy. I for one was overjoyed.

Coming home from school that Monday, I saw Daddy sitting on the porch. An uneasy feeling crept up inside me. I wanted to cut around the corner of the house and enter from the back, but the way he was sitting, he would have seen me either way. I went on, holding my head down, pretending I didn't see him. He said, "You just don't come home no more, do you?"

"Cause I stay wit Aunt Matilda. I got to go home an take off my school clothes."

"Come here and let's see what y'got dere in your hand."

"It's my book bout Alice and Jerry on de road to Hill Top Farm."

I went to him as he demanded but stood far off, not wanting to respond at all. He could tell by my reaction I didn't want to come to him. He said, "Come on up here. I can't see de damn book way over dere. Bring it here."

"Yes, sir." I walked up close to him and handed him the paper and the book. I thought just maybe he was interested.

He took the book out of my hand, looked at it for a second, and threw it down on the porch without showing any interest whatsoever. I bent over to pick it up, my heart bleeding. He shouted, "Leave dem damn books down dere! You kin look at dem in school." He propped his leg across the bannister, pulled his shoe from his foot, slid his sock down below his ankle, and said, "Here, rub Daddy's ankle."

I was so filled with anger that I frowned, but I rubbed and rubbed until he fell asleep. The toe jam from his feet had me breathless from the smell. I kept asking him, "Daddy, is dat enough?" He was snoring so hard, he heard nothing I said.

My arm started to get painfully tired. After about an hour, I knew he was good and asleep, so I thought to stop, testing if he was as asleep as I took him to be. He opened his red devil eyes and said, "Who told you to stop rubbin? I didn't tell you to stop. Now rub till I tell you to stop, g—— d—— it!"

I continued rubbing nonstop in the same place. The rubbing must have done some good for his ankle; I didn't know. All I knew was I was dog-tired from rubbing. My shoulder and arm were in pain. I called out a few more times, "Daddy, kin I stop now? Daddy, kin I stop?" He still didn't answer me.

I didn't wait around for him any longer. I picked up my paper and book and struck out running as fast as I could. Aunt Matilda was on her way out the door to see where I was. I just knew he was going to wake up and come calling for me. I stayed closed to Aunt Matilda for dear life. I knew she would protect me from him—she was about the only person around there he did listen to besides Aunt Frankie and Uncle Cleo.

Susie was my little, white, blue-eyed, speckle-faced doll, and when I was in a sort of depressed mood, I'd get Susie and talk to her. She was my make-believe good friend, and she listened to me when I talked to her. Aunt Matilda was busy in the kitchen, making tea cakes. I sat quietly in the room, holding Susie in my arms. I told her, "When I git up and grown and have chilluns, I ain't gon make them rub on my ankle like my old daddy do me." It seemed she would blink her eyes at me, knowing what I was saying to her.

The last three days before the play, we had to stay after school for practice for an hour. When we were finished, Mrs. Crowley would take all her girls home. The last evening she gave us a ride, she asked if our parents were coming to the play. All the other kids said yes. When she got to me, I said yes too, but deep down in my heart I knew Mama might come, and Aunt Matilda for sure, but Daddy? I doubted if he even cared about the play and how special it was to me.

She advised us to be at the auditorum at six thirty. The program began at seven.

She stopped to let me out and said, "Haley, I haven't met your father, only your mama. I'm gonna meet him while I'm down here." She walked up onto the porch and I rushed in front of her. Daddy was sitting in the corner of the porch, and I directed her to him.

Daddy never had any respect for anyone. Every word that came from his mouth was a curse word. She didn't seem surprised—living with Mrs. Brittney, she knew the story of the Keaths' sordid life. She was as cool as they come. She stepped up with her hand stretched out, smiling. "Mr. Keath, I'm Mrs. Ruthie Crowley, Haley's teacher. I gather you are her father."

He looked at her stupidly and said, "Yeah, dat's what dey say. I'm her daddy, so dey say."

"Well, she looks just like you. Where is Mrs. Keath? Is she inside? I stopped by to see if y'all will be bringing Haley to the play tonight?"

I shouted, "Wait, Mrs. Crowley, I'll go git er."

Mama came out looking surprised. "What play? I don't know nothin bout no play."

Mrs. Crowley looked at me suspiciously. "Haley, you mean to tell me you never told your parents erbout you being on stage tonight? You've known about it over two weeks ago."

I stood flat-footed and told her, "I did tell er, but she forgot cause she was drunk."

Daddy said, "I don't know bout er mammy, but I know I won't be coming to no damn play."

Mama looked purely ashamed. "I'll be dere. It just slipped my mind some, but I will be dere."

Mrs. Crowley looked at Daddy and said politely, "It was nice meeting you, Mr. Keath. And Mrs. Keath, I'll be looking forward to seeing you at seven. Good-bye now."

Daddy didn't have intelligence enough to say good-bye to my first grade teacher whom I looked up to so highly.

Mama was not too pleased with me for saying she'd been drunk in front of my teacher. She was about to draw her hand back and hit me. Daddy stopped her and told her she better not put her hands on me for telling the truth. "Hell, I know she tellin the truth cause you been drunk for over two weeks wit dat damn Long Laura and Ruby Ray. Now don't you put you g—— d—— hands on er, and I mean it!"

I was not pleased at what I had done, nor did I have any recognition as to what I had done wrong. But from what Daddy said to Mama, I knew I had caused a disturbance among them and it was going to ruin my night.

But after Aunt Matilda and I got dressed and were leaving, Mama came out of her house and joined us, along with the other parents. The road was full of people—nobody had cars, so we walked everywhere we needed to go.

Mama asked, "Where did you git dat pretty dress?"

Pleased, I held up the tail of my dress and said, "Aunt Matilda made it for me." It was a pretty flour-sack dress.

When we arrived at the auditorium, Mrs. Crowley came out. she was wearing a beautiful beige dress with a matching brown jacket and brown leather pumps. She led her students to the back of the hall and gave us tops to put on over our regular clothes. Each top had the name of what we were written on the front.

It was a lovely evening. The auditorium was full of people. Laughter was coming from all directions. Voices echoed around me. I felt nothing but joy and wished it would last forever.

Mrs. Crowley singled me out and said, "Haley, you look so beautiful. In fact, all of you look beautiful. I know you all are going to do real good." She was happy for me, but she was not nearly as happy as she had made me.

The moment we took our positions on stage and the curtain was pulled open, I saw Aunt Matilda and my mama. They were smiling with joy.

Each one of us remembered our lines just as they were, and we said them loud and clear as Mrs. Crowley had taught us to. A girl I knew, Skitter, was an apple, and she was the first to say her lines: "Apples are fruits and are good to eat. An apple a day will keep the doctors away."

When it was my time, my mouth was bigger than the others. I spoke the loudest and got really loud applause. Mrs. Crowley said the word "plenty" sounded all over the place, just the way she wanted. A few of the others were unable to be heard because they had such low, soft voices, but she never said who they were. She made everybody feel special: we could do anything and nothing could stop us.

We arrived home after the play was over. Aunt Matilda got us some tea cakes and milk. We sat on the porch, watching the stars as they shone down on the night earth, sparkling all around the sky. It was unbelievably magical, yet so far away. Every now and then, one would fall from the sky, and Aunt Matilda would say, "Make a wish." When another star fell, I wished that our lives could be as they were forever.

The next day, there was talk of the play. Everyone was still excited about the way it had turned out. I heard whispering about my big mouth in class, so I didn't go out for recess. I hung around in the classroom as everyone else rushed out, even though it was awonderful day outside.

Mrs. Crowley was grading papers and didn't notice me at first. Then she got up to get a drink and saw me sitting quietly. "Haley, you stayed in again! Why didn't you go outside to play with the other students?"

"I didn't wanter."

"Why? Don't you like to play outside?"

"I don't know," I lied.

"You don't know? I think you just like being in the room with me. Is that right?"

"Yeah, ma'am, I like bein in de room wit you."

"That's good, but you should go out and be with children your own age."

"Dey be mean to me an pick at me."

"Who picks at you? Tell me who they are and I'll put a stop to them picking on you. We won't tolerate any of that."

"Them chilluns on Green Street, they pick on me cause I live on Rat Row."

"That's not good. I live on Rat Row also. What are their names? Are they in this classroom?"

"One of dem is in Ms. Greenburg's room."

She took me outside and went to gather her class together, but they weren't out there—only Skitter Monroe. I joined hands with Mrs. Crowley and Skitter to play. Up came a girl named Soretta, wanting to cut in.

All hell broke loose. For some reason the devil just had to come through somebody standing next to me. I said, "No! I was here first." But Soretta kept on pulling, trying to bogart her way in until she saw she couldn't. She clawed a deep scratch in my hand, and that made me turn Mrs. Crowley's hand loose.

I pushed Soretta down hard to the ground. Mrs. Crowley turned around and asked, "Haley, why did you do that?"

I showed her my hand and said, "Cause she scratched my hand." It was bleeding, and the white was showing in it.

Mrs. Crowley looked at Soretta and asked her why she did it. Soretta looked at me and lied. "I didn't scratch her hand." But my hand was all the proof that was needed.

Skitter spoke up and said, "Yes, you did, cause I saw you." Another classmate said she saw it too.

Since I had retaliated, Mrs. Crowley gave us a warning and threatened to take her strap to both of us if we were physically tough with each other again. She played a couple more games with us before it was time to go into our classrooms.

I went to the toilet, and when I came out, Soretta was waiting with her cousin Baretta. I remembered the trouble everyone had had with them in the quarters before that family moved out, leaving them still up there. I knew she was going to start with me. They threatened that if I came on the other side of the playground to play, they were going to beat me up. Then they ran off. There were no witnesses at the time, but I knew they were mean and evil. I wasn't the least bit afraid; I was just trying to avoid trouble from them. So I went into my classroom as if nothing had happened.

As I was getting out for the evening, I wasn't thinking about anything going wrong. I looked up and they were approaching me. They had been making faces and putting their tongues out at me during class, but I hadn't said anything to Mrs. Crowley. The moment I saw them now, I started swinging and yelling, "You better not hit me, you damn fool."

I ran off and they were right behind me, so I stooped down and grabbed a handful of dirt and threw it in Soretta's eyes. Then I took off running again as fast as I could.

I got home and thought about them getting me when I returned to school on Monday. I was right—from then on, they picked on me every chance they got. They just wouldn't leave me alone. It was two against one and made me feel inferior to them, but I didn't say anything to anyone.

The teachers—Mrs. Crowley, Mrs. Greenburg, Mrs. Johnston, and Mrs. Funtain—took their classes on a field trip to visit what was called "the new colored folk school" that was being built. We walked a long way to the grounds. It was very far from where we lived. Mrs. Crowley said the country children would ride the bus, but undoubtedly the town children would have to walk. Many jobs would be opening up: bus drivers, custodians, kitchen helpers, and groundskeepers, among others.

Gosh, we were delighted to have a new school. It was almost complete. It had indoor toilets and nice sinks. Cool water flowed from a drinking fountain. Each classroom had a beautiful, shining window. Most of all, air would circulate in the summer and there would be heat in the winter. It was nothing like our current school that had old, rotted-out shutters instead of windows and doors, tiny rooms, and no real playground. Things were beginning to look up for the blacks.

When I told Mama of my trip, she suggested to Daddy that he could get one of all those jobs becoming available—driving a bus or groundskeeping or even being a custodian. He cursed her out. He was steady making babies, but had no job. I saw in my father who he was, not what folk said he was. He was a sorry, good-for-nothing, uncaring, inconsiderate human being. I never understood what made him so unfeeling. He was practically inhuman.

Walking back from the trip that evening, Skitter was alongside me and asked me point-blank, "Haley Keath, why you don't like me?"

"I do like you, Skitter. It's dem other gurls I don't like, dat Baretta an Soretta. Dey like to pick at people."

"That's why you don't go to the other side an play on the playground? You scared of em?"

"Naw, I ain't scare of dem. I just don't like em."

"Then when we come back to school, you kin come wit me. I'll come an git you, okay, Haley? Now me an you is friends."

She became my friend. Me, the girl from Rat Row—I became friends with the daughter of the principal of Bethuel Giants Elementary High School. And that spelled trouble for many.

We went over to the high school side together, which was where the playground equipment was located. Those Sawmill girls started to fight me, and Skitter went off and got her father. I was up on the jungle gym when they tried to bully me. I climbed all the way to the top as if I was afraid of them, with the intention that if they followed me up there, I was going to push the first one from the top of that jungle gym to the the ground—and it stood about twenty feet tall.

Then I saw Skitter coming across the campus with a man. I started to climb down. I wasn't worried or afraid of those girls. The man must have seen them do something wrong, because he yelled, "I see you! And if you do that again, I'll strap you with my belt and suspend you."

They climbed down behind me, and he told them they better not bother me anymore. He looked at Skitter and asked, "Are these the girls who're causing trouble?"

"Yes, Daddy. These here girls want to fight my friend, an she ain't botherin them. We were just playin on the jungle gym an here they come, pickin a fight with my friend Haley for nothin."

He warned them off, and they left without uttering a word. Their lips were hanging down, but they weren't giving up. They were a few feet away when Baretta muttered something. He called them back and looked them up and down. "If I hear one more word from y'all, y'all gon be suspended for good. I won't have no fighting in my school. Y'all got that?"

He turned to me and said, "If you have any more trouble out of these girls, you let me know, you hear? Do just what you did today—come tell me. Don't fight them. You tell me and I'll take care of them."

Skitter took me by my hand and said, "Haley, this here is my father, an he's the principal for this school."

He said, "Hey, Haley. Tell me, what did you do to them for them to want to fight you?"

"Nothin. I ain't did nothin to dem chillun." I spoke softly, feeling protected. The school principal himself was defending me, little Haley Keath, the girl from Rat Row.

He left and so did we, leaving those two girls looking odd.

"See, Haley Keath? I told you that my daddy wouldn't let them mess wit you," Skitter said.

I was all excited. She and I walked off, hugged up together. "Skitter," I asked anxiously, "your daddy is a principal like Mr. Brent was?"

"Yes."

"You mean us got two principals at our school?"

"Naw. Mr. Brent and Mrs. Brent moved away. He ain't no principal no more. My daddy is."

"Oh! Den your daddy done been to one of dem big colleges like de white folk."

Skitter looked at me as if it meant absolutely nothing. But to me, even being in the company of the principal's daughter was certainly a big thing. My heart was beating fast from the excitement. I knew I had found myself a dear friend in Assie "Skitter" Monroe.

She said, "You know what? Me an you is like peanut butter and jam."

Whatever that meant, at that moment I felt so special.

Skitter and I played together each day. None of the other kids liked her because she was the principal's daughter. It led from one dispute to another over nothing. How anyone can constantly pick fights with a person "just because," I do not understand. She was nonviolent with a very kind spirit. Each day I spent with her, I got to know her more.

We got out of school for winter break. Two weeks seemed like a long, long time out of school. I was glad we were getting out but but disappointed that I wouldn't be able to see my friend. The good news was she had a phone and gave me her phone number. The bad news was I didn't have a phone to call her.

It all worked out on the last day before break: Skitter's mother came and picked her up, with her younger sister Cindy Faye and her brother Little Teddy. Her mother was as friendly as Skitter was, and she was not prejudiced against me. She welcomed me to come visit Skitter anytime I wanted to—if it was all right with my parents.

She invited me to come home with them after church. They were members at Old First Bethel Church. We attended there on the second Sunday, and on the first Sunday we attended Greater New Salem Baptist Church.

Some days I would walk up to her house and play with them, but I was too young to understand why she was never allowed to come visit with me. It was coming close to the time for our return to school when I asked her why she couldn't come to play at my house. She said, "Because my daddy said your daddy is a bootlegger." It was dangerous for her to come over, but we could always still be friends.

When I arrived at home, I immediately rushed down to Aunt Matilda. She was sitting in her cozy spot on the porch swing. I sat beside her. She was steadily talking, looking up at the stars and smiling. I knew not to interrupt her. It was her time with the good Lord.

I looked up, hoping I would see what she was looking at that made her so happy. I saw nothing but the stars filling the sky. Before long, the sky was covered all over with beautiful stars.

Then she looked down at me and said, "Did you see dat star fall, Haley? You got to make your wish."

"Yes, ma'am, I did," I answered seriously.

I closed my eyes as tight as I could. Without letting her hear what I wished for, I put my hands over my face and said, "I wish Soretta and all her people move a long way far and don't ever come back."

Once I made my wish, I sat listening to Aunt Matilda speak to herself. I knew she was praying on somebody else's behalf. The stars shining down to the earth lit up the entire town. Listening to the crickets crick, I knew I was a very lucky little girl to have such a holy, anointed woman in my life.

Our first day back to school, an announcement was made over the loudspeaker that Mr. Frank James Monroe had officially been made principal over all of Bethuel Giants Elementary High School. It was a joyous day. Mrs. Crowley explained to the class that Mr. and Mrs. Brent had moved away. Before the day was over, the news was all over town. Nobody knew the reason why they moved or where they moved to. The Brents was never heard of again, like they just dropeed off the face of the earth. Folk were hush-hush.

Mrs. Crowley had papers in her hand that she was getting ready to pass out. Suddenly, she took the papers back to her desk, laid them down, and she walked fast over to where Baretta and Soretta were sitting. She demanded that they each sit up in their seats and complete their assignments. Neither of them moved. She asked them why they was being so rude and disrespectful. Neither of them paid her any attention. She asked (with a please) for Baretta to pick up a paper that Baretta had thrown down on the floor. With that, they both jumped up from their seats and ran out, slamming the door behind them as hard as they could.

Later, we had our reading time, which was my favorite time of the day. I loved to read. Reading, writing, and 'rithmatic were the three subjects we were taught. I liked all three, but reading was my favorite.

In came Mrs. Benderson, sliding through the door sideways. The two monsters came in behind her, grinning. They knew what they had done. It was their proudest moment when they went home and filled Mrs. Benderson's head up with all sorts of lies. She'd come running to defend them in their wrongness. The saddest part of the matter was that she didn't even come in decently. She put the classroom in an uproar, shouting, "What de hell do you mean, puttin your hands on my damn gurls? I thought you was here to teach, not to be scratchin up other people chilluns arm!"

Mrs. Crowley said, "Let's take this outside my class, so we can discuss the matter calmly." But Mrs. Benderson refused to budge.

Mrs. Crowley said politely, "What do you mean? I didn't scratch your child's arm or whatever it is they told you. They have fibbed to you. I only tried to stop them from interrupting my class, just as I would with any other student." She went on trying to explain, but Mrs. Benderson didn't want to hear anything she had to say.

"Come around here, Baretta," Mrs. Benderon ordered. "Show her your arm." It was unbelievable the scratches that girl had on her arm. We all knew that Mrs. Crowley had not done that. The only thing anyone could come up with was either she did it herself or she had someone do it to her to do so she could lie on Mrs. Crowley.

Mrs. Crowley was astounded. She said again, "I didn't do that, and I am not going to stand here and listen to no more of these lies."

"You will too!" Mrs. Benderson said.

But as the Word reveals, God always has a ram in the bush. In walked our principal, Mr. Monroe, making his tour of all the classes. Ours was the first one he visited. He stepped through the door in time to hear Mrs. Benderson. He asked sternly in his deep bass voice, "What seems to be the matter in here? Is there a problem, Mrs. Crowley?"

Mrs. Crowley was in tears. She had a handkerchief in her hand and was wiping her eyes as she explained the problem to Mr. Monroe. Mrs. Benderson called her "a damn liar" right in front of the principal's face and had no remorse.

He looked at the two girls and said, "These are the same two girls I had to stop from fighting another student a few week ago. Come over to my office and let's get to the bottom of this problem, because I can see now it is about to get out of hand."

Mrs. Benderson refused to go anywhere. She got very emotional, and it became an ugly scene that got the attention of all the other teachers. They came out of their rooms to help solve the problem those two girls had created.

The bell rang for our last recess of the day. We were allowed to go out the back door. As we went, we could hear Mrs. Benderson cursing.

By the time recess was over, they were gone. Mrs. Crowley let us color for the rest of the day. It was what we mostly did the last few minutes before school was out, but that day she allowed us extra class time. We drew and colored pictures, and she said she was going to put the best ones on the bulletin board. She had been crying and her eyes were red, but she never let on the hurt she was feeling. She didn't deserve that cruel treatment from anyone. I couldn't believe folk were that mean—other than Ms. Onna. As my mama would say, "Dey take de cake."

The Bendersons were the most-discussed family at Bethuel. They made all the teachers' lives a living nightmare.The Benderson name was really popular at school, and there was nothing nice about their popularity. Mrs. Crowley tried to make us understand that some people just need attention, and they will get it any way they can. She wanted the entire class to stay clear of the Bendersons because they was truly one of a kind.

Aunt Matilda always said, "If you will lie, you will steal, an if you will steal, you will kill. Be careful."

It wasn't long after that the talk about the Bendersons became strong. When the name "Mrs. Bigmon" came up, it got everybody's attention. That was the name everybody called Mrs. Benderson outside the school.

Mrs. Brittney lived on the same street I lived on, but she was a middle-class citizen. Mrs. Crowley roomed with her. Mrs. Brittney had a son named Carl, about the same age as Gemmy BB, and a daughter named Dixie Lou, the same age and class as Tise. A niece named Konnie resided with her also. It was a natural thing for any parent to protect her children from distraction when they were being raised in a good, healthy environment, as the Brittneys were.

Doing the school week, one of the Benderson twins got in a dispute with Mrs. Brittney just because she told the girl her slip was hanging down. Carl said it was pretty and had trimming on it. May and Shay attacked Mrs. Brittney's niece Konnie as she came up from the toilet, and beat her like they did our cousin Pauline. They scratched up her face and bit a big plug out of her cheek, causing her beautiful face to be disfigured.

Mrs. Brittney was coming out of her classroom across the street and saw the attack. All the school's faculty was upset. The police were brought into the matter, and May and Shay were kicked out of school for good. I don't recall anyone else ever being expelled from school except them. People were wishing they was dead, wondering who their next victims would be.

Why did they mess up folks' faces as they did? What kind of people were they? And they kept getting into trouble over and over again. Front porch talk was that they were disliked by whites and blacks, but there wasn't too much anybody could do to them because they were grounded in voodoo and witchcraft.

One hot summer night, news came that they had decided to move to South Carolina. It was said somebody else, just as rooted as they were in witchcraft, hexed them up so that they couldn't stay in the town any longer. The Bendersons were the worst root workers around town, and once they moved on, folk got along. There was no hatred among the neighbors, and the children were able to play in peace.

Chapter 5: Things Do Change

The gossip about the Bendersons was dying down, and here comes another family who moved in and took over their reputation. Only these was our own flesh-and-blood folks—the Bakers, on Papa's side of the family. Our cousin, Big C, was Uncle Carl Lee's daughter. Her family moved in on Rat Row across from us and next door to Pa Jack's café. They used the same toilet, pumped water from the same pump, and hung clothes on the same line. I really thought we would get along as family's supposed to.

There was no husband, but seven boys and three girls. Two daughters were twins, Mallie and Pallie Lea. The baby daughter, Belinda, was the same age as I was. The boys ranged in age from nineteen on down. The oldest was Chip. Eddie D was second, then Dean. Next came Poor Dog, Jacob, Buddy, and finally the baby of them all, Teddy.

The mother of the clan we called Cousin Big C or Big C Lottie. She was a pretty, light-skinned woman, tall and strict. Mama said with that many boys, she had to be tough, and she was as protective as she was tough. The family was no different from the Benderson, though some different from the Kingsleys. But God up above knows the heart of every man.

Chip and Eddie D were already out of school. Dean was a loverboy; he too was out of school. They were the men of the house. Big C was never home. For the longest time, I really thought she was a working woman, but not so; she didn't have to.

Jacob was the one everyone said could move something. Even when your eyes were looking directly at him, he couldn't be seen. He would steal sweetness out of gingerbread.

Poor Dog was the maid around the house. He was sweet like sugar. Buddy was a little whiner. His older sisters had him spoiled real good. He was a troublemaker and nothing but a coward—just like my brother Georgie Boy. They were two of a kind and the best of buddies.

Teddy, the baby, was the joy of all the Bakers' lives, and he knew it. Most all children know when they can get by with manipulation, but to his family Teddy was an angel. He could do no wrong in their sight—though he did. The family never saw what kind of "angel" he was.

I recall hearing Mrs. Phillips quote Scripture to describe Teddy. I didn't know at the time what she meant, but I was pretty observant. Even then, I had a strong, discerning spirit, and at that moment it was at work. He was a child up front—handsome, bright smile, a mama'a baby. Oh, but underneath it all was a hidden view no one could believe. Most people just said he was so handsome, he should have been a girl. His sisters and brothers loved him as much as their mother did, blinded as to what was right before their face. They refused to see what others on Rat Row saw.

Mallie and Pallie Lea were the twins. Mallie was on the quiet side. She never said very much, but she always smiled, and when she spoke, she mostly nodded her head. She was very pretty, with long hair and dimples in her cheek. Other than her twin, her cousin Paula was the only person she socialized with. They both were very private women. Mallie didn't take to people at all. She wasn't around very long; she got married and moved up somewhere round Mississippi.

Pallie Lea was what they called "a girl of interest," whatever that meant. She was a housekeeper, a good cook, and motherly. She was the spitting image of her mother, with a beauty that any woman would like to possess.

Belinda was the little supervisor. She and Buddy—the one who acted more of a baby than Teddy did—knew and did all the housework, the cooking, and the taking care of the smaller boys. Whenever time permitted, Belinda and I would play school. She was always the teacher.

My second year of school was the beginning of learning just how mean and uncaring an adult could be to children. I guess I had expected all the teachers to be as nice and loving as my first grade teacher, Mrs. Crowley, but I was really in for a rude awakening, I was placed in the last room on the other side of the building, all the way in the back, with old lady Funtain. She was as mean as she was hideous. Her skin approached black. She was the first person in my eight-year-old life (besides Ms. Onna Kingsley) whom I believed I actually could hate, without even knowing what hate was.

Because of who I was, the background of my life, she had already singled me out to pick on me. That lady didn't like me from the first day I walked through her door. I could feel the vibe from her, and it was not good at all. She hated me just as much as I wanted to love her. I was never able to satisfy her, regardless of how much I tried. My work was never good enough. She would beat the center of my palm for every mistake I made. Every word I spoke was wrong. If I didn't raise my hand before asking a question, she would beat me and then make me stand in the corner.

It was plain to me that she never treated anyone else in her classroom the way she treated me. I often wondered if she was beating me for who I was, or for who I was not. I could not tell. I only knew the growing pain that took root in my little heart aand required many years to heal.

Mrs. Funtain was a good teacher—in the days of my schooling, most teachers were excellent—but she was so mean that no one liked her, not even the grown-ups. I believe that was the worst year of my entire school life, and I couldn't wait for it to end.

The worst incident happened when I came home from school one day and Mama was waiting for me. She wanted me to sit with the children while she ran an errand. One of the kids tore the cover off of my schoolbook. I knew Mrs. Funtain would give me a good paddling when we got back to school. I was really scared.

But she didn't notice the next day that the book cover was not on the book. It took a couple of days before she noticed. I couldn't explain that my baby sister and little brother got hold of it and ripped it off. She didn't care. She said I was destroying school property and had to pay for it before I could get another one. I had no money to pay. She gave me till the next day to get the money or I was going to get a strapping.

Afer the weekend, I had the fifteen cents I needed, and she gave me another book cover—a used one she took off of another book, not new.

I escaped that time, but a few weeks later, Mama left the children down at Aunt Matilda's and again they got hold of my book and ripped the cover off. I was very afraid of what Mrs. Funtain might do to me.

Tonk came over to play and I was real quiet. He noticed I wasn't myself. I told him about the book cover. He had had the same problem with her that I was having. He made a plan with me.

On Sunday evening when church was over and no one was paying us any attention, we went up to the school. The old shutter that served as a door was just pulled shut. He went in and I stood watch. When he came out, he handed me a lot of book covers and told me he'd had to do it for himself.

When I returned to school, Mrs. Funtain noticed that the book cover was new and asked, "Where did you get that cover? It doesn't look like the one you left here with on Friday."

I froze in my mind, thinking she knew what we'd done. But I disputed her in every way I could and denied her accusation. She had no proof. She wanted to whip me, but I told her that I was going to tell Mr. Monroe. I knew she didn't want me to do that. She said, "You got one more chance. Do anything in my class and I'm gon tear your hide off."

I think this was when I picked up the sassy spirit. I snatched my head and popped my lips at her.

A new girl was placed in our classroom. She was my age, but she was taller than any of us in the class. She had just moved from New Orleans. Her name was Doletha Bradbusch, and she sat in the seat by me. It was a few day before she started to take to me. Skitter was my best friend. She and I played together exclusively until Doletha started to play with us.

At the end of the term, we had to turn in our schoolbooks. I was the first in line. She was so mean, she made me go to the back of the line before she would accept my book. I didn't comprehend why. I knew the woman didn't like me, but to do the things she was doing was just plain cruel.

I went and sat down at my desk. The line was long. I laid my head on the desk and started to snooze. I was awakened by pain: she was beating me across my back with a thick belt. I was crying hard.

In walked Mrs. Crowley. She said one of the parents wanted to see Mrs. Funtain. It seemed Mrs. Funtain had kept a student after school and beaten the girl. The mother came in and pointed a finger in Mrs. Funtain's face. "I will see you in hell for what you did to my child!"

Mrs. Funtain showed no remorse. They went outside. The next morning when she left to come to work, somebody set her house on fire. By the time she got out of school that evening, it had burned down to the ground.

I passed to the third grade by the grace of God. With the way she disliked me, I was sure she would not pass me, but she did. I had learned how to read extremely well; I was on a fourth- or fifth-grade level in my reading skills. My dumbest subject was math. It had been a long, hard school term for me, and I couldn't wait until it was over so I didn't ever have to be in Mrs. Funtain's classroom again.

Belinda Baker and I were after-school playmates, but I never had that friendly feeling toward her that I felt toward Skitter. Maybe even then I could detect the difference between real friendship and just plain playmates. Something about her my little spirit didn't agree with, and every time she and I would start to play, Buddy would come out and start something. If she and I played hopscotch, he would mess up the lines that we drew. If we were playing springboard jumping, he woud tear it down. I saw him being to her as I was to my brother Georgie Boy.

She and I stopped playing together when she started to play with Alma Benderson. Alma was the daughter of Duke Benderson, the eldest son of the Benderson clan whom nobody liked that had moved away to South Carolina. Mr. Duke and his family were different, like day and night. He was more like his daddy, Mr. Diggs—kind and loving. If folk didn't know otherwise, they never would have guessed that Mrs. "Bigmon" Benderson was his mother.

Belinda and Alma became playmates, and all our troubles began with the Bakers. They started to do all sorts of things. They threw rocks at us. If they caught us at the pump getting water, they beat us up. They was so big, we were no match for them.

It was cotton-picking time. I had always wanted to go pick cotton, but Mama said I was too small to go out into the fields. Still, I was anxious to go. I wanted to be a cotton picker like everyone else. They talked like it was something good to do. I never dreamed the nightmare from it.

It was hot one evening and we was out of school, bored with nothing to do but look after children. We were playing in the tire swing when a white pickup truck drove up in front of Mama's door. The driver blew the horn, but no adults were at home, so I trotted off to see who he was looking for. I went up to the truck and looked at the man sitting there. "Ain't nobody home, mister."

"It ain't?" he said. "Well, where's your ma an your pa?"

"You talkin bout my mama an my daddy?"

"Yeah, dat's right—your mama an your daddy. Do you know where dey is?"

"Naw, sir. I don't know where dey is."

"You think you might wanter pick some cotton tomorrow?"

"Naw, sir. We can't pick no cotton. We too little."

"Naw, you ain't. You just de right size to pick."

"My sister an my daddy could pick cause dey big."

"How you know dat you ain't big nough? You ain't never pick none before, is you? An I bet you ain't never had three dollar fore either."

As I was talking to the man, up drove another one in a brown pickup truck. Daddy was in that one. The first words that came out his mouth as he got out of the truck were, "Who business you tendin to now?" He lifted something from the back of the truck in a brown sack and carried it into the house. The white man who had been driving the brown pickup helped. I went in behind them.

They took a big jug from the sack and set it on the kitchen table. Daddy poured a big jarful out of the jug and topped it up with water. Then he turned the jar up to his mouth and drank down almost every drop. What was left he poured on the floor, then lit a match to it. It blew up like something was deadly in it.

I ran out the door and told Aunt Matilda that Daddy had set Mama's kitchen on fire. I came back with her, and Daddy knew I had told something. I just stared up at him and asked, "Is de kitchen burned bad, Daddy?"

Looking down at me suspiciously, he asked, "What you tell old lady Matilda?"

"I told her you set Mama's kitchen on fire."

"I know you went to tell a lie de minute you run your little ass out dat door. You bouter bigger liar dan Chicken Little. Now you take your little ass right back down dere wit old lady Matilda fore I beat you. Git!"

I didn't know that was how he checked the moonshine out—by the way it burned.

I took Aunt Matilda by her hand and led her back home as fast as I could. I watched from there as Daddy and the white man went over to the Baker house and talked to the oldest boys. I waited until they got back into the truck and drove off. Daddy said they were gathering up some cotton pickers. Nevertheless, that was the day I learned who the white man was that ran the moonshine still and supplied Daddy with the five-gallon jugs of whiskey that he sold. Clayton Wellow was that man's name.

Mama come in from work, looking fat and tired. She went into the bedroom. I heard her say, "Thank you, Jesus! He got it, all five gallons." She came out happy and talking to herself. "It's bout time. Who brought dis here jug in here?" she asked me.

"Daddy," I answered.

"Was anybody wit em?"

"Yeah, ma'am, he was wit a white man in a brown truck, and dey went dater way." I pointed in the direction of Flappy Boots's café.

Soon all the neighbors was flooding the house, buying up that moonshine. Daddy was seeking cotton pickers and they were all ready. Cotton-picking season was the biggest time of year. That's when all the blacks made their money, which meant school clothes and lots of moonshine sold.

It was getting dark out, and I had to beat it on home. Between the two houses, I heard voices—Aunt Matilda's and Daddy's and another one. They were teasing her about not having a man in her life. As I approached, I recognized Uncle Billy Roliver's voice. Daddy said how she and Uncle Billy would make a cool couple, and I mean she let him have it with both barrels. Her words were, "I been in dis old sinful world for way over eighty years, an I ain't had no man. I ain't neber had any man, an don't spect to needer. De good Lord is my man."

I didn't fully understand what she was saying, but whatever it meant, I believe it got Daddy's attention. Even I felt something, but what? She had that kind of effect on me. When she was sensitive about something, I could tell.

I read her the Twenty-Third Psalm out of the Bible before we retired for the evening. She really enjoyed every word; she got such a kick out of my reading to her. Even though she couldn't read, the good Lord placed me in her life to read to her. Reading was my favorite subject, and my favorite book was the Bible.

I was up like everybody else when I heard the rooster crowing. Voices came from all directions in the neighborhood. I pulled myself out of bed and looked out from the old shuttered window. I saw folk dressed in coveralls, blue jeans, and long shirts, their heads all tied up. I found a pair of coveralls that Aunt Matilda had packed in a box, and a dress twice my size. I also put on a long shirt and my brogans, and told Aunt Matilda that Daddy said I had to go pick cotton.

She didn't like the idea. She was furious that I was going to the field. She swore I was too small to be in a field picking cotton. She said, "He ought to be shamed of hisself makin you go out." She got me a straw hat down from the top of her shift row and told me to keep it on my head, because it was going to be real hot out there.

I took the hat and went on down to Mama's house. All the folk were sitting and standing around, full of excitement, waiting for the truck to come. When they saw me dressed the way I was, the smallest one in the bunch, they wanted to know where I was going. I was determined to pick some cotton, without the slightest idea what cotton picking was. I wanted to, just because.

Peadean was the first one to holler out, “Haley, where do you think you goin?” That was her way of getting everybody else started up about my going to the cotton field.

“I’mo pick me some cotton now. What y’all got to do wit it? Y’all always tendin to other people business too much.”

Gemmy BB was the next to ask, “Haley, where you think you goin?”

“Just like y’all; I’mo pick me some cotton.”

“Mr. Macky, you better come out here an see bout dis little nappy-headed gal talkin bout she gon pick cotton. Who she think gon look after er? Cause I sure ain’t,” she said angrily.

Mama came out to investigate. “Haley, where you think you goin, lookin like old lady Matilda?”

“I’mo pick me some cotton.”

“You can’t pick no cotton. All you gon do is git in somebody else’s way.”

Gemmy BB said, “I’mo git Mr. Macky wit your grown ass. I bet he’ll stop you.”

“Naw, you don’t, gurl, cause he ain’t know now.” I didn’t want them to go get Daddy. Besides, I had already lied to Aunt Matilda when I said he told me to go to the field.

Gemmy BB was determined to tell on me anything that she thought would get me into trouble. She was willing and ready. “Yeah, I’mo git em too. He don’t know you goin to de field. Let’s just see what he say bout it.”

Passy Kate was always my protecter. She told Gemmy BB, “Just wait an let’s take er. I bet when she git through and come back home tonight, she won’t want to go no more. Yeah! Dat’s what we do: take her little fast ass on out dere and work de s—— out of er.”

Gemmy BB was in agreement with this. “Come on over here an sat right here, cause we know if Mr. Macky come out here and see er, he ain’t gon let er go out dere in no field.”

The old man in the white truck, whom I had spoken to the day before, planned to come back and take them all with him. I had already hired him the cotton pickers, and nobody knew it. So I really hid. I went into the house and stood by a window, looking out as he arrived.

Everybody wondered what he was doing there. He noticed me standing by the window.

Daddy came out and watched as the old man counted how many people he thought he had: "Well, let me see how many heads I got here."

Daddy walked off the porch and asked him who he was looking for.

He answered, "I come by here yestiddy, an I talked to dat little gal over dere. She told me folk wanted to pick cotton and to come back, so here I is."

Daddy said, "You just made a trip for nothin. Anyhow, what little gurl you talked to?"

By the time he asked the question and the man pointed at me, I was no longer in sight. I had run on out the back door and was standing by the corner of the house, watching the fireworks from behind all the people.

Daddy looked back and saw no one. He told the man, "If you came out here on the word of a little gal, den you don't need no cotton pickers. All dese here people is already waitin on another man. But I spect if you go on down on de other end of dat corner down dere, you might be able to pick you up some. You might found a few dat will go wit you, but dese folk here is already been hired."

He started to walk away from the truck. Then he stopped to light a cigarette and turned back. He asked the man calmly, "How much you payin a hundred?"

"Well, I'm payin three dollars an fifty cent a hundred."

"Damn! If you payin three dollars an fifty cent a hundred, den your cotton must not be ready for pickin. Everybody else only payin three dollars a hundred an g'antee a hundred pound to a half row. If you payin dat much, you must have to scrap for a hundred pound of cotton, an dat'll take you damn near all day to git a hundred pound."

The old man spit a hunk of chewing tobacco on the ground and said, "Naw, it's good cotton. Well, I reckon you kin git bout a hundred to a row if you good workers."

Here came Clayton Wellow, turning the corner. Daddy said, "Dat's who dese people here is waitin for." The old man got into his truck and sped off, leaving Daddy wondering who he'd talked to. Daddy remembered the truck had been parked in front of the house when he arrived with Mr. Wellow the day before. He also remembered who had been standing at the truck, holding a conversation. "I bet it was fast-ass Haley."

Everybody was pushing toward Mr. Wellow's truck, running and shouting, before he could park. Daddy was distracted. Being the smallest out there, I crawled in between Gemmy BB and Passy Kate without Mama or Daddy seeing me. Before long, the back of that truck was jam-packed—as I heard somebody say, "Packed like sardines in a can."

Peter Junior replied, "We piled up in dis here truck like a pile of dirty clothes I seen in Ms. Jenny's Rue backyard."

My straw hat disguised me down among all those folks. For the the life of me, I don't know how Cousin Sattie Bell recognized me—and she had to open her mouth. "Who's little child dis is gon to pick cotton?" She turned everybody's attention on me, trying to see who I was.

Even Mr. Wellow came up and asked, "Whose little boy is dis?"

I took my hat off my head and replied, "I ain't no boy! I'm a gurl!" Everybody laughed.

Mama came up, shouting, "Git off of dat truck! Macky, dis here gal on de back of dis here truck talkin bout she gon pick cotton."

My little mouth stuck out like I was mad with the world. I did what I did best when I wanted my way—started boo-hoo crying. Mama was steadily shouting, "Git your little fast behind off of dere! You can't pick no cotton, gal. You just gon be in de way."

I shouted back, "Gemmy BB an Passy Kate said I kin go." I was crying real tears.

"But you don't know how to pick no cotton. Mr. Macky, come make this gal git off of dis here truck."

Daddy came around the side and for a moment just stared down at me squeezed in between all them folk. Then, with a slight grin, he asked, "Where do you think you goin?"

"I'mo pick me some cotton, cause Passy Kate an Gemmy BB said I kin."

Passy Kate said, "We gon show her how to pick. She need to learn how to do some else sides tell everythin she know. Watch! After today, she won't wanter come back no more. I g'antee you."

He agreed to their terms. "Yeah, take er little ass out dere and work de s—— out er."

Mama disgreed and said with concern, "Macky, don't let dat gal go out dere. Dat sun gon burn er up."

"Dat'll be good for er. Maybe she'll learn to not wanter go so damn much. Take er on," he said.

Mama sat on the porch with her thumb in her mouth, just shaking her head. She didn't want me to go to that field, but she went along with Daddy's decision.

As the truck drove off, for me it was like going on a minivacation or something. I was so tiny underneath everybody else, I couldn't even see which direction we went in. It was amazing listening to all those voices of people laughing and talking and joking loudly with each other. I was not able to see the laughter on their faces, but I could feel the laughter in their hearts flooding through my own.

I was all excited, thinking I was going to love picking cotton. Little did I know.

It was about a forty-five minute ride. The only thing I was able to do was hold on to somebody's pants leg and breathe as hard as I could to catch my breath. It was a miserable ride. I think they had just plain forgot about me, almost squeezed to death underneath them. I could feel the truck moving, but other than that I was in pure darkness.

I decided to get me some attention, and I pinched somebody's leg. I must have pinched five or six times before they acknowledged they were being pinched. Gemmy BB yelled, "Who in de hell dat is pinchin me on my leg? Lord, dat Haley down dere. I had forgot bout er just dat quick. Maybe de next time, she'll keep er grown tail home."

Some strong arm lifted me up through the crowd. The relief I felt was so comforting, like I was just opening my eyes into the world for the first time. I breathed in and out, absorbing that fresh morning air. I could see the laughter on some of those folks' faces and I joined in. The wind from the moving speed of the truck blew the sweat from my face. Someone said, "Poor little Haley. She so little, we almost forgot she was even down dere."

Another voice said, "But she sure do know how to git attention!"

The sun was starting to come out and we still hadn't reached the right cotton field. nevertheless there were cotton fields on both sides of the road, and I didn't need anyone to tell me it was cotton. I remembered the many bags they had brought to Aunt Matilda, and I had watched her make mattresses for Mama's beds. I was fascinated seeing it hang down out of what I later learned were called "cotton stalks."

Finally the truck started to rocking from one side to the other. The road had turned bumpy, like it was hitting big holes in an alley, which made me know we had come off the highway. The truck stopped under a big oak tree.

I was exuberant over the cotton—the height of it and how beautiful and white it was. And I was in the midst of it all!

Folk jumped off the truck and grabbed the long cotton sacks, which the cotton was put in as it was picked.

Someone lifted me off the ground until I was high above the rest. It was my cousin Chip; he stood about six and half feet tall. All of Cousin Big C's boys were six feet and over, and Chip was the tallest on the truck.

Once they had their sacks on, they raced to the field, claiming rows. All the grown-ups picked from two rows. Mr. Wellow called out to me. He had made me a little crooked sack with a strap cut out from around the top on one side. He put it across my shoulder and said, "Dis is a good fit for you. Now, little Ms. Macky, you kin go on out dere an pick you some cotton like de rest of de folk. I think dis will hold bout twenty pounds. Do you think you kin pick twenty pounds of cotton?"

Passy Kate was always the considerate one. She cautioned me to wait and showed me how to pick cotton without getting the sharp stickers from the buds in my hand. She encouraged me to pick from one side, not two.

As I stood at the end of the row, watching them all picking, it looked like a race. I thought, *Wow, picking cotton like this is fun*. But the sun hadn't yet started beaming down.

I did as Kate advised me to and picked on her row ahead of her, but I wanted to know why I couldn't have a row by myself.

Gemmy BB never missed a beat when it came to degrading me. "You know you can't pick no whole row of cotton by yourself. You just have to have your way bout everythin."

Kate stepped in and told me to stay on her row. She recognized how sloppy my picking was and guided me to the proper way, along with reminding me that it had been my decision to come and pick. She told me, "Pick from one bud at a time, an pick it clean."

Picking it clean was easy, but trying to pick fast was what tore my fingers up. The faster I tried to pick, the more I pricked my fingers. The sun was hot, and I started to actually feel it beating down on my head. Sweat dripped from my forehead, and then chunks of sweat, so thick that it was blinding me. The salt burned my eyes and ran down my back. I was feeling the real effect of picking cotton.

I looked across the field. Folk were hard at work, picking like they were pros at it. Scattered all over the field, they picked as fast as they could, like a prize was waiting for them at the other end. They were picking with all their strength.

Laughter echoed across the entire field. I never understood how they could turn so much heartache and pain into something exhilarating, but they did. Even after the day was over, when the field owner paid them that little amount of money they worked so hard for, they were laughing and talking all the way to Mama's house. They were thirsty for that damn moonshine.

I didn't get enough that day. I made myself forty-five cents of my own money, and I was anxious to go back for more.

That next day I returned to the field. I understood more in one hour that day than I had the whole first day. I picked enough cotton to feel the pressure of the sack pulling down on my shoulder. It got awful heavy, and I got more and more tired. I wanted to go home.

After just standing and watching all the other cotton pickers work for a while, a restless spirit captured my soul and sleep began creeping in. I could hardly hold my eyes open. I learned early how to protect myself from certain things, so I instinctively went to the middle of the row I was picking, where the stalks of cotton were very high and it would be hard for me to be seen by anyone.

I pulled that cotton sack off of my little shoulders and made it my pillow. I laid my body down underneath some of the tallest stalks to block the sun. Every now and then I felt a slight breeze sweep over my body. I slept until they caught up with me and insisted that I get up, since I was the one who wanted to come to the field so badly. They warned me that if I didn't get up, a snake was going to bite me.

That was all I needed—to hear a word about a snake. I jumped up in fear and saw the pickers going back toward the truck to empty their sacks. At first I didn't know what to think or what to do, until Passy Kate ordered me to come on. It was time to empty my sack and get some water. I was good and thirsty all right, ready for some water, but most of all I wanted to go home. I certainly didn't have much cotton; the weight from the morning dew was what made the sack heavy on my shoulders.

Once everyone had emptied their sacks, they lined up for a drink from a big old wooden keg that sat under the oak tree. Afterward we took about a five-minute rest under the tree, and then it was back to the field again.

I certainly did not want to go back out there among all the wet cotton stalks. I begged Passy Kate to let me stay under the tree. It was so hot that day, and I was miserable.

Passy Kate did have a little pity on me, but Gemmy BB had no compassion at all. "Dat's good for you. You want to always do somethin you ain't got no business doin. Maybe dis will teach you," she said coldly.

I followed them back into the field and did the same thing—ran up the row and put the sack under my head. But I was afraid to sleep because she had threatened me about snakes. The sun was beaming down, and it was getting hotter and hotter. With no shade anywhere in sight, even the big straw hat I was wearing didn't help any.

They caught up to me later that day, and I was for the first time compelled to do what I was told to do, without seeking help from anyone. Daddy wasn't around. Neither was Aunt Matilda. I was under the care of my evil sister. I thought, *Do as she say and everything will be all right*. I knew I hated picking cotton and would not be coming out there again. I picked along beside them in sorrow and fear.

I picked as slowly as I could. They were fast pickers. I'd never seen anything like it. They passed me and were a long way ahead of me. I tried to keep the buds from sticking my hands.

Gemmy BB grabbed my arm and yelled, "You wanted to come out here in dis field—now you gonna work! So you might as well git up dere, and you better not let me catch up wit you neither. Now git!"

I stumbled on down the row and began to pick as fast as I could. I went willingly, but my willingness turn into a total nightmare. The sun kept getting hotter and I didn't like being out there, period. I picked and I cried until I was plain tired of crying, soaking wet from sweat.

By the time Mr. Wellow brought us more cold water and the roadside store came for lunch, I was almost ready to pass out. That was the only time I felt at ease—not in waiting for the day to end so I could go home, but in coming to the conclusion I was not goming back out there ever.

The lunch hour rushed by. We ate, and everyone stretched out under the shade trees and slept until it was time to go back into the field. That was the shortest hour I had ever seen. Then they were calling, "It's time to go!" They all seemed to be having the time of their lives out there in that field.

I got up along with everyone else and grabbed my little sack and went back too. Halfway down the rows, it seemed like we were never going to reach the end. The rows was so long, and the stalks was so high, I couldn't even see where they started or stopped. The sun was burning down so hot, an egg would have fried.

I was miserable. I picked a few handfuls, and then I stopped and lay under the tallest stalks I could find. I rested until they caught up with me and forced me to get up. After a while, I had to use my charm on them. I would lie down until they was close to me, then jump up and pick as if I had been picking all the time.

Folk were nearing the end of the rows and the day was nearly done. I rushed to the end and sat down comfortably under one of the trees. I was dying from thirst. They were all shouting, "Where in de hell is dat damn cock-eyed Mr. Wellow? He s'pose to done been back here wit dat damn water!" Everybody was thirsty as hell, and the water in the old keg was hot.

Eventually a flame of dust rose through the air—it was Mr. Wellow speeding down the path. By the time he parked the truck, folk had surrounded it for the water. Men were men back then, and all the men stood back to allow the women and children to go first. The men drank what was left, and when they finished, the keg was empty.

Watching them empty their cotton sacks onto sheets and tie them up was fascinating to me. I whispered, "Oop, oop, dem dere people sure kin pick a heaper cotton."

As folk were drinking water, Mr. Wellow was weighing up the cotton, and he moved pretty fast. Some folk had picked over two hundred pounds of cotton. Passy Kate and Gemmy BB each picked nearly two hundred. Out of all that hard work, nobody made ten dollars.

I made forty-two cents. And I thought I had some money.

He paid everybody after weighing, by that time the day was over. Folk were tired, hungry, and ready to get home. We loaded up on the back of the truck and were home before we knew it. I knew Daddy was glad to see the truck when it turned the corner down by Pa Jack's café—but not as glad as I was.

It was just about dusk, past six o'clock in the evening. Aunt Matilda was sitting on the porch with Mama, waiting for me. Everybody got off in front of that house, and it was no secret what they got off for.

I hopped off that truck and ran to Aunt Matilda. She was all grins. I shouted, "You know what, Aunt Matilda? I ain't never goin back to no cotton field. Gemmy BB and Kate made me work too hard in dat hot sun. I was thirsty, an dat sun burned me up."

"You mean dey worked you in dat cotton field and didn't gib you no water? Dey need to be shame ob demselbes." She didn't stop till she went inside and told them a piece of her mind. She believed anything I told her, and if it was something she didn't like, she would blast them out.

As she was telling them off, Daddy came through the room. He asked, "What kind of lies you done filled old lady Matilda's head wit now?"

All I did was look up at him and roll my eyes, because I knew what was coming next.

My sisters tried reasoning with Aunt Matilda, but she was not buying a thing they were saying to her. I was as happy as a cat with a rat in his mouth. Gemmy BB said, "Ain't nobody made dat lyin gal go to no field!"

Daddy stood looking from me to Aunt Matilda. He knew me as well as I had gotten to know him, and he knew Aunt Matilda would protect me from anything I told her. He said, "Now you done took your little ass out dere in dat cotton field an got just what you deserve. Den you come back an fill old lady Matilda's head up wit a bunch of lies. When I git on your little ass, I mean I'm gon pay you for old an new. You bout a bigger liar dan Long Laura."

"Dat cotton field muster put er on er little ass. I bet she won't go back no more," Mama stated.

I grabbed Aunt Matilda by her apron, pulling her, hinting to just let's go. I knew if we stayed, Daddy was going to say, "Now cause you come back here wit a pack of lies, you goin back tomorrow." And I would rather have died than go back to that cotton field.

We left and went on to her house. She was as hot with them as that sun was in that field. She had supper ready and the kettle filled with hot water for my bath. She rubbed me down with liniment and told me that it was going to take the soreness out of my body.

That taught me never to do anything because somebody else does it. Learn about what you are doing before you do it—and about the consequences that come with it.

Each morning after that, when the cotton truck came, I didn't move. Not even to stand and watch the crowd load up.

***

The summer was ending. I lay in bed and heard the red birds out back, whistling and singing sweet melodies. I marched to the back door. Mama was walking back toward her house, whistling along with the birds. Things were pretty much going the way she liked it. Daddy's moonshine was selling, and there was money in the house. She was in a good mood.

Some of the neighborhood women were already gathered around to gossip. That was their everyday occupation—sitting in her backyard and gossiping about everything and everybody.

Second grade had been my last year at the old school. When we returned from summer break, we would be at our new school. Everyone was excited about it.

That morning, I got dressed and went to get my brother Georgie Boy. It was his first year of school. I came around the front of the house and heard voices coming out of Cousin Sattie Bell's house, yet her voice culd be heard coming out from Mama's backyard. I stood and listened, but I couldn't make out whose voice was coming out of her house.

Then my cousin Pallie Lea popped out the door. I could tell she didn't want to be seen, and she didn't see me because I was between the houses. She stepped off the porch and went around the other side. Shortly afterward, Daddy came out and walked toward Pa Jack's café.

I watched curiously until he turned the corner. Then I came around the house and saw that Pallie Lea had joined the other women in our backyard. At the time, I didn't know what I had witnessed or what was going on between the two of them, but I knew something wasn't right.

I entered the house to make sure Georgie Boy was ready, along with the Brimsley children and the Kingsley boys. We all walked to school together, and it was the longest walk I ever had to walk. It took us an hour and ten minutes to get to school. The street was full of children going off to our brand-new school. It was amazing.

Our first day was like heaven. My third grade teacher was named Mrs. Lizzie Miller. She was a tall, light-skinned, heavyset woman, and I liked her from the first day I was placed in her classroom. George was placed in Mrs. Cuties Johnston's room, along with Nookie Brimsley and David Kingsley.

It was the best time of my life, attending school. The books given to the class that day were "Little Red Riding Hood," another reading book called *On the Road to Hilltop Farm*, a spelling book, and a book of the three Rs: reading, writing, and 'rithmetic. I was so happy. I loved to read, but I was fearful of the arithmetic.

Once we got home that first evening, all the children gathered in our backyard. We went out back in the field behind the toilet, where we played catch ball, hopscotch, springboard, and hide-and-go-seek. Belinda and Bud came to join us. We played one game for a while, then played another one.

The last game we played was school. Belinda and I were the teachers. I was Mrs. Crowley and Belinda was Mrs. Funtain, because that's whose room Bud was in. I took it upon myself to get one of Gemmy BB's dresses and put it on, along with a pair of her high-heeled shoes. I took Teddy and Nookie and Belinda took Georgie Boy and Buddy. We began teaching them. Our chalkboard was the ground.

I was reading to the childrens when something happened. Out of nowhere, Buddy hit Georgie Boy in the nose. Some teacher I was—the moment I saw my brother's nose bleeding, I demanded, "Boy, you better hit dat boy back!"

But he wouldn't. He cried like a sissy, and that made me angry. He stood under the tree, blood pouring from his nose, and he wouldn't hit Buddy back. I went over to him and took the tail of Gemmy BB's dress and wiped the blood from his nose, scolding him at the same time: "You stand up dere an let dat boy hit you in your nose an you too scare to hit him back? You ain't nothin but a fool."

I began to plot that I was going to get Buddy the first time I saw him alone. I was going to pop him in his nose just like he did to my brother.

Buddy got scared. He must have known what was on my mind. He left, running as fast as he could. Then he told everybody that I made him and Georgie Boy fight—and he was believed.

I was trying to get out of the dress. The snap had got caught in my hair. Belinda and some others got back out there, and Mama was with them. I couldn't get out of the dress fast enough. She actually pulled a switch from the tree and whipped me, striking me with four or five whops across my back and sending me inside.

I ran straight to Aunt Matilda's house, screaming for her. Once she comforted me, I was even more eager to get Buddy. I could see him sitting in the alleyway, laughing at what he had done to me and my brother. I was angry at Mama for whipping me on the word of somebody else over mine. I kept saying, "Dat boy told a story on me an I got a whipping."

Buddy stayed with Belinda, his bodyguard, making it impossible to get to him. But I was not about to forget what he did.

***

Daddy looked at me angrily and told Snappy to go out and get him a switch. She brought it back and gave it to him. I just knew he was going to beat me for old and new. I yelled, "Daddy, please don't whip me! If you don't whip me, I won't never tell nobody you was in Cousin Sattie Bell's house wit Lea."

He hesitated for a second, then purely lost his nerve. He said, "I just be g—— d——. Git your g—— d—— ass on down dere to old lady Matilda an don't let me see you back down here no more dis week."

He didn't have to tell me twice. I jumped off the porch and ran. I was so relieved to hear him say that! Being with Aunt Matilda at all times was better than money.

Everywhere she went, I would go. I stayed as close to her as I could. To and from school, I went through the back to avoid him in every way I could. I did as he commanded me to do; the less I saw of him, the better off I was.

Mrs. George Ann had gotten real sick, and everybody gathered around in her backyard. Most of the folk in Rat Row were good about helping the sick, but at that point there wasn't much anybody could do. She was dying.

I sat in the backyard with Aunt Matilda with the other neighbors. They were saying she'd had a stroke and she was dying. Daddy came out the back door. He saw me and immediately called for me. My heart started pounding away. It had been a few weeks since I had been face-to-face with him, and I just knew I was going to get it.

For a second I sat still, close to Aunt Matilda and the others, pretending I hadn't heard him. On the second call, I got up slowly and started walking toward him. Once I was face-to-face with him, I dropped my head; I couldn't even stand to look at him. I could never tell what kind of mood he was in or what his next move would be.

"What ails you, gal? he asked.

"Nothin," I answered, still holding my head down.

"Well, damn it, hold your head up when I'm a-talkin to you."

"Yes, sir," I said, lifting my head up slowly. I could see he was drinking. He was up to no good; there was something he want me to do.

"Come on round here up on de porch. Hell, I ain't gon bite you." He spat on the ground.

I walked on round the porch and climbed up on it. I could feel my strength coming on, ready for whatever it was he was ready to dish out. He didn't look angry; neither did he have that intimidating look about him. He had a look of unconcern, yet purposefulness. "Old lady George Ann ain't dead yet, is she?" he asked, surprisingly.

"Naw, sir," I answered, shaking my head.

He got up from where he was sitting, paced from one end of the porch to the other, then stated, "Well, dat's too damn bad."

He stepped down to the ground and walked around the house, leaving me standing still and speechless. "Well, come on!" he said. "I didn't just call you to stand dere like a knot on a log."

When he got between the houses, he told me to go under our house and look behind the chimmey corner for a jug. Under that part of the house was where all the big rats bedded. It made me sick. But I got down on my stomach and crawled to the chimney and pulled out a five-gallon jug of moonshine, just as he told me to.

Rats of all sized started running from all directions. I was up and out from under there as fast as I could go. I came out trembling from fear but dared not show it. I hated that moonshine, especially the smell of it.

I thought he was finished with me, and I started to leave. He called me back, saying, "I didn't tell you to go nowhere. Come on over here and gimme dem dere bottles down dere." He had sack full of pint and half-pint bottles. I lined them up on the table, and he said, "Now it's bout time you learn how to fill up dis here bottle."

He taught me that evening how to pour pints and half-pints of moonshine without a spill. I had poured about five bottles without spilling a drop when a loud scream echoed across the room, fearfully loud: "Oh Lordy, she's gone! Lord have mercy, she's dead, y'all!"

I jumped and spilled some—not that much—and he went off. "Stop bein so damn nosy! Pay tention to what you doin and you won't waste my g—— d—— whiskey!" He turned his back, trying to hear himself. It was Ms. Mattie Willcot crying out that her sister was dead; Mrs. George Ann had passed away.

I hurried with the last bottle. He had me to stack them in a box behind the bed. He went back to the kitchen, and that was my chance to get the hell out of there as fast as I could.

Aunt Matilda was still sitting in the yard with the other ladies. I got close to her, remembering Letrolla's body and how cold it was. I didn't feel scared, but Mrs. George Ann's death did make me a little uncomfortable. It was either that or I was still in fear of the rats—all I knew was I was shivering like it was midwinter. We stayed until Funeral Bellow came and took her body. He placed it in the back of his old black hearse and drove away.

That night in bed, I was not able to get to sleep, twisting and turning. I hadn't been like that in a long time, but that night the nightmares started up again—the dead body of Letrolla and big rats running around the room, as well as Mrs. George Ann's death.

***

A whole year passed. I was in the fourth grade. Georgie Boy was placed in old Ms. Funtain's classroom, and I knew that since she hated me, she was going to hate him also. She was still as evil as a witch, and most of the students were afraid of her.

We hadn't been in school but a few days when she sent and got me out of my classroom. I had been placed in Mrs. Eddie Crainey's fourth grade class. She was teaching subtraction. I was really interested in arithmetic, and "taking from" was not easy for me. She called me up to her desk and told me to go to Mrs. Funtain's class. I couldn't imagine what she wanted with me; I sure didn't want to see her.

I went, and when I got there, I was astounded. She was standing outside her classroom with Georgie Boy, and he was crying. She looked at me and said, "You need to take your brother home. He done had an accident in his pants."

And he smelled terrible. I could see he had pooped on himself and it was running all down his legs. I believed he was sick or had diarrhea, and I had to take him on that long walk home.

I was going around the building with him and saw Passy Kate and a few other girls. They were at the side of the building, smoking. I called out to her and explained what Georgie had done. She sent me back to my classroom, saying they would take him home. They didn't know how glad I was to hear that.

Georgie Boy stayed home for a couple of days, but on the day of his return, the same thing happened. Passy Kate wasn't there; she had quit school. I ended up being pulled from my class again to walk him home.

On our way, I shouted, "Boy, you keep on doin it in your clothes, I hope Daddy beat your brains out!" I pushed him all the way home. He was nothing but a bag of water, crying about everything. I was his little protecter, but there was no one to protect me except Aunt Matilda.

When we got home, he was trembling from fear because he knew he was going to get killed. He didn't want to go inside the house; he wanted to go straight to the toilet. And heran right into Daddy coming around the house.

Daddy said, "Boy, you mean to tell me you done sh—— in your clothes again? You ain't got no diarrhea." Taking his belt from around his waist, Daddy beat him until the poop was spilling and splashing. He didn't have diarrhea; he had a serious nervous problem that no one had recognized. Living in that environment and having to encounter the dysfunctional family that we were, it was no wonder the poor boy was neverous.

Family homes should be about love and understanding, a safe place to express feelings and speak what is on one's mind. Not in our house. Georgie was the opposite of me. I spoke out every chance I got. I learned how to manipulate situations to my advantage. But if it hadn't been for Aunt Matilda, I probably would have been in the same situation as my brother. He was so far gone, his problem came out through his bowels, messing up his clothes.

Daddy kept Georgie Boy out of school for another week. When he returned, the same thing happened to him. There was no one to speak out on his behalf, only to criticize and scold him. I had to learn how to cope with him. I had to be strong enough for the both of us. I got up enough power to teach him to hold his hand up and ask his teacher to let him be excused to go use the restroom. At our house it was a toilet, at church it was a bathroom, and at school it was a restroom.

The last time Georgie Boy messed his clothes, I was most disgusted with him. He had gotten along well for way over a month. I was in my geography period when a student came to Mrs. Crainey and handed her a note. She looked directly at me, and I knew in my heart it was Georgie Boy again. Anger and shame rushed in and out of my body. I hated what he was putting me through.

When Mrs. Crainey beckoned for me to come to her desk, I got up slowly and walked up. She told me to go to Mrs. Funtain's room. By then, all the class knew about Georgie Boy and what he had been doing. Only a few in the class made fun and giggled about it.

When I got there, she had him standing outside the classroom by the door. She said harshly to me, "Take him away from here. He is not allowed back into my classroom until he is fully trained how to go to the restroom."

I couldn't help myself; I lit into him with all I had. "Boy, you mean you doo-doo'd in your clothes again? Now you know better den dis! You coulder told Mrs. Funtain to let you go to de restroom!"

He began crying as I was pushing him on down the hall and out the doorway. I knew Daddy was going to skin his ass when we got home, so I started to feel sorry for him. It penetrated my mind how to handle the situation. Maybe Daddy didn't have to know he had been kicked out of school again?

But the moment we turned the corner, Daddy was sitting on the porch. He knew what had happened for me to be bringing Georgie Boy home again.

We approached the porch. "Boy, you done s—— in your clothes again. Haley, go out back an bring me a switch. I'mo beat your g—— d—— ass."

Georgie Boy was crying with fear as I got a switch. His wails rose louder and louder before I ever got back. Daddy beat him till he begged him to stop. I stood helpless as Georgie was with no mercy. Daddy beat him until the switch was all broken up.

Wondering why Daddy had to beat him so long and so hard, I left, running across the highway and out to the field. It was the fall of the year. Rabbits were hopping wild and all the leaves were turning brown. I sat looking up to the sky. I asked God if he was up there, like everybody said he was, why he would allow Daddy to be so mean to us. Why couldn't we have a Daddy like Skitter's daddy, Mr. Monroe? In my mind, I could see Daddy continuing to strike Georgie's naked body. I felt Georgie's pain.

Georgie Boy was my oldest and favorite brother. He didn't seem to have anyone to look after him except me. I knew in my body that after that awful beating, he would stop messing up his clothes.

I didn't return to school that day. I stayed in the field all the rest of the afternoon, waiting for an answer from the Lord. But I didn't get one, and when I heard the other children coming home, I joined in like I too was returning home from school. As I was walking on home, something came to me: I would protect Georgie Boy in every way I could and never tell anything on him again. I didn't know if it was the answer I was hoping for or my imagination running away with me.

Georgie Boy was the first person I saw as I was going home. I called out to him, but he only looked at me and then turned his head in another direction. I knew he was good and mad at me. I said, "Come on, let's go play."

He was sucking on his thumb and spit was running down his hand. His eyes were cold when he looked at me and said, "I ain't gon never play wit you, and everythin I see you do, I'mo tell Daddy on you."

I didn't let it get me down. I said, "I don't care if you ain't gon never play wit me again, boy. You ought not to keep on doo-dooin in you clothes now."

I ran on down to Aunt Matilda's. She was quilting as she always did in her spare time. She made the most beautiful quilts anyone could ever lay their eyes on. The one she was making then was for Mama. She said, "Winter coming, an Jenny Rue need cober fur dem dere chilluns."

I watched her for while before she stopped stitching and asked, "What ails you, Haley?" She could always tell when something was bothering me. I guess it was the expression. I have never been able to get rid of a thousand frowns in my forehead; they always gave me away. I felt awful about George. I explained how he was having accidents in his clothes and how Daddy had whipped him bad. She looked at me and knew the right words to say.

This time he stayed out of school until after Halloween. I had grown so accustomed to being dragged out of my classroom because of him that I hated to go back to school myself. The day he returned, I walked him to his class and warned him he better not mess his clothes up again. "If Ms. Funtain come to git me out of my classroom one more time, I'm gon beat you upside de head wit my fist." I was hoping to instill fear in him so he wouldn't cause me any more embarrassment.

He stopped messing up his clothes, but he still sat in the classroom and cried, disrupting the class. Passy Kate and Gemmy BB had both dropped out of school. Tise now lived regularly with Aunt Lucy Sue. There was only me to deal with the problem. I was stuck, and every day it was something with him—just when I was getting comfortable in my classroom, someone would come a-calling for me to rescue him.

One day, Mrs. Funtain came herself. She called me out to the hallway and pointed her finger in my face. "I won't stand for this foolishness any longer. I have gone down to the principal's office and made a request that your brother be moved from my classroom. It's that or he goes home and does not return until he learns how to act. All he does is sit and cry. I've decided that he just don't want to be in school, and this is his way of acting out."

They eventually came up with a solution to the problem. Mrs. Funtain placed a student desk beside her desk. Students who were slow in their arithmetic would come to Georgie Boy, and he could help them. I learned he was a math wiz and was good in all the subjects.

Giving him a meaningful responsibility helped the situation tremendously. It worked out for all of us. I would go around to check on him doing recess, and he would be up to the board, writing out problems. He helped me to understand simple subtraction and multiplying.

I tried to find out what was bothering him so badly that he wouldn't tell anyone. I kept pressuring him, and learned he was furious with Daddy. He was so afraid of Daddy that it pushed him to become rebellious.

***

We came home from school one day and Mama's lips were busted up and her eyes were swollen and black. Daddy had beaten her face in. She was close to giving birth to another child, and he was beating her into bad health.

Her friends and associates tried to convince her to have him arrested, but she wouldn't. The reason he beat her up was, when he couldn't get to Pallie, he would take his frustration out on Mama. He had seen Pallie with another man, and he was mad as hell. Everybody knew the only thing Pallie wanted from Daddy was his money.

Mama said he was going with Pallie and her mama, Cousin Big C Lottie. I remembered the day I witnessed them both coming out of Cousin Sattie Bell's house. I hadn't understood it, but it was suspicious. Now it all begin to make sense. It felt like my brain shifted to another side of my head. I pitied Mama at the time, but I only saw her as other women did: as a big fool.

She was calm, but I could tell something else was troubling her, as if she knew something that no one else did. His behavior had gotten rotten. He was like a crazy man.

A few days later, we were all out of school on spring break. It was mid-March and the weather was good and windy. We were all getting along fine. Of course, just when we think life is good, something happens.

I was sitting underneath the house, feeling alone and playing doolie bug. I saw old Lund Cabb's Black Maria drive up. Right behind it was another black car, and two other men got out.

I came from under the house in time to see Cabb and that skinny Tommy Williamson go up the steps to Mama's house. She and Daddy were sitting on the porch. I thought something didn't match. I couldn't figure out why they were at our house, but something was spinning in my head that led me to believe there was more going on than I understood.

Everything that happened in the neighborhood drew crowds of people. Now they gathered on the porches across the road, where they sat and gossiped.

Then out came Lund Cabb and Tommy Williamson with all the jugs of moonshine. Everybody said they raided our house before Daddy had time to move his stash.

I witnessed a look on Daddy's face that day like I had never witnessed before; the sadness, the shame, the humiliation. Most all the neighborhood folk watched as he was led off to the back of the Black Maria. Somebody from Uncle Martel's porch said the men from the other car were revenuers.

Surprisingly, they didn't take Mama, due to her pregnancy and all the other children she had. The moment they drove off with Daddy, she took the children down to Aunt Matilda's house and trotted off to see what it would take to get Daddy out—only to return empty-handed. There was no bond. She was sure he was on his way back to the chain gang.

That was an unfamiliar word. I thought I had heard it before somewhere, but I couldn't remember where.

Word was out that somebody had turned Daddy in. Mama was so shook up by the news, she was crying. I couldn't undersand what on earth she was crying for. Knowing the treatment she received from him, she should have been glad.

For once in my life, I was. I was also inexperienced at life and not getting the wisdom I needed to think. I prayed for him not to return.

I heard from the gathering, gossiping neighbors one day that Mama had met Daddy on the chain gang. I was conceived on the chain gang. I did not get the full understanding of what that meant, and at the time I didn't care. Nevertheless, the thought invaded my mind and took residence.

Chapter 6: Experiencing What Prison Was Like for Inmates

Daddy had been in jail about two months. Mama was working every day to make ends meet for her and her children. I believed she was doing better without him there than she did with him. At least she didn't have all the drunks hanging around all the time.

One day, I watched her from Aunt Matilda's porch as she turned the corner, coming down Rat Row. She could hardly put one foot ahead of the other. It was noticeable she was in some kind of pain. The moment she arrived, she told me to go round to Aunt Frankie Reese and ask her to get the midwife—she had gone into labor and the baby was about to be born.

I ran all the way around Brake's quarter without stopping. Aunt Frankie sent Uncle to go get Mr. Alex Crow to get the midwife. Mama's house was full of caring neighbors. I could hear Mama groaning in pain. It wasn't long after when a lady came with a big black bag. They said every time she came, she brought a baby.

Some of the ladies were in the kitchen, cooking. Others were looking after the children. Some were just sitting around, doing nothing, waiting patiently, and showing much concern. Those were the days when all the neighbors gathered in unity when one was in need. All participated in whatever it took to meet that need.

Eventually it grew dark, and Aunt Matilda said, "Come on, Haley. It's pit dark out dere. We got to go git in de house now. Come along."

But early that next morning, I was down at Mama's. I could hear a baby crying as I came up at the back of the house. A few of the ladies were washing clothes: Ms. Estella, Cousin Sattie Bell, and Aunt Frankie.

I rushed into the house. The curtain was up that closed off the bedroom from the kitchen. I peeked around the curtain. Old Ms. Dani was standing by the bed, and Ms. Bonnie was in the kitchen, making breakfast. Mrs. Angie Rosa was in the bedroom, taking up room as Ms. Arketha stared.

I pushed my way on in and Mama said, "Come on up here an see your little sister." She was lying back with a red head rag tied around her head and the baby lying beside her. She had given birth to a six-pound baby girl and named her Willa Max after Daddy's deceased baby sister.

While I was standing there, Passy Kate and Gemmy BB came in along with Aunt Lucy Sue. We hadn't seen any of them in a few weeks. Passy Kate gave me a hug; I could feel her love whenever she touched me. But my oldest sister Gemmy BB made it known she didn't like me or anything about me.

I got up enough nerve to put my arm around her waist. My hand was on her stomach when I felt something moving around inside. It felt really funny, so I said, "Gemmy BB, you ate too much. Your somethin t'eat is movin round in your belly."

She pushed me away real hard and and yelled, "You too damn grown! Dat's why I can't stand y'all damn ass."

Folk looked at her, and she got no respect from the elderly ladies whatsoever. Aunt Frankie said Gemmy BB was more ashamed than anything; that was the only reason she said those mean words to me. But Aunt Frankie didn't know all the other mean things Gemmy BB had always said and done to me.

Aunt Frankie led me off to the kitchen with her. I wasn't sure what I had said wrong, but from Gemmy BB's tone, I knew I had done something that angered her. I was only repeating what I had heard others say when somebody's stomach would growl. Aunt Matilda would say that the large intestine was eating the small intestine. I concluded it was something else for me to bend down beside Aunt Matilda and pray about.

Three days later, Gemmy BB gave birth to a baby boy, right in the same room as Mama. She named him Bill. He was a real dark-skinned baby, but he was cute, and his skin was beautiful.

After the baby was three months old, Gemmy BB went out one day, leaving the baby with us. She didn't come back. She deserted her baby. Just when Mama was going through one of the roughest times of her life, with three toddlers of her own to support, Gemmy BB left a fourth one with her.

I fell in love with both babies. When Mama went off to work, she would bring all the children down to Aunt Matilda, and she and I would watch them. At an early age, I learned the real responsibility of taking care of younger sisters and brothers—that was how we looked at Bill, as a brother and not a nephew.

Daddy hadn't been sentenced to the chain gang yet. We had to take his supper up to the jail every evening because he was only fed breakfast and lunch. He was another mouth for Mama to feed.

I had to miss lots of days out of school to help watch the other children, and it was starting to affect my life. It was really hard on my mother. She worked hard in the white folk houses—cleaning, washing, ironing, and every other hard chore they could find to put on her for two dollars a day. Then she had to come home and cook for us, wash for her household, and tending to four small children, two of them babies. It started to show up in her drinking. She drank more each day. Everything was taking its toll on her. It made me tired just watching her, and that made me not want to have children. But as Scripture says in the book of Genesis, God always has a ram in the bush.

Old Ms. Dani Rhimes looked like a witch, but she was a true friend to Mama. She was there for us during the day when Mama was at work, and when Mama got home from work, she was there for her, always willing to give her a helping hand. Between doing Sister Greta's housework, Mrs. Angie Rosa's housework, and my mama's, it's a wonder Ms. Dani didn't collapse from exhaustion or have heatstroke. I thanked God for Ms. Dani, who enabled me to attend school. Because of the days I had missed, rumor was I was not going to pass from the fifth to the sixth grade.

It was late March. I recall the time because it was nearing Easter, and everyone was talking about the big Easter egg hunt that Old First Bethel Church was giving at the ballpark. Everyone was looking forward to it, and it was coming up soon.

Well, we were getting ready to take Daddy supper up at the jail that evening. We had to be there by five o'clock so Mr. Lund Cabb, the chief of police, could check it out before we sent it up. When we got there, we went the same way we always did. We called out to Daddy to let him know we were there, but he never answered. Georgie Boy started trembling with fear. He yelled, "Come on, Haley! Can't you see he ain't here? He done got out already."

"Naw, he ain't," I responded. "Boy, Mama didn't pay no money to git him out. She ain't got no money to git him out."

I could feel the fear coming from his body. The spit ran down his thumb from sucking on it. I commenced to get angry with him and demanded he wait by the window while I went around the back to ask somebody where Daddy was. Georgie Boy had that timid spirit about him just like Mama did, and he said again, "He ain't here, gurl. Don't you go round dere knockin on them dere white folk door."

He took off running and said he was going home. I told him, "You go on, den. I hope dem dere dogs git your ol' scary self."

I began to have the same kind of feeling in my stomach as I did the night Ms. George Ann passed away and Daddy sent me under the house to get the moonshine. I stood speechless for a moment, looking up at the window where Daddy usually answered from. Where was he?

Georgie Boy, he was scared of white folk, just like Mama was. I guess I must have gotten my braveness from Daddy, because he was not scared. Strengthening myself, I went around the corner and knocked on the back door.

Surprisingly, Sarah, one of Kate's best friends, came to the door. She was the sheriff's maid. She greeted me politely. "Haley, you come to see your daddy? You brought him supper?"

"Yes, ma'am. I call for him but he don't answer."

"Baby, ain't nobody told y'all? Dey come an took him down to de prison camp early dis mornin. Your daddy been put on de chain gang."

Those words "chain gang" again. I didn't know what it was nor what it meant, but I knew it wasn't anything good. I dropped my head as pain pierced my little heart.

Sarah said, "Your daddy got thirty-six months on de chain gang. Now you run on back home fore it git dark and tell your mama. Y'all don't have to come back down here to bring him no more supper. He's gone."

I left, walking slowly home. My heart was bleeding inside, and I didn't even know why. I suddenly took off running as fast as Georgie Boy had done, all the rest of the way home. I called out Mama's name before I got in the back door. She was nursing the babies on her breasts. I told her what Sarah told me to tell her. "Mama, Ms. Sarah said Daddy got thirty-six months on de chain gang. They put him on dere early dis mornin."

She didn't seem surprised at the news, but she didn't know he was gone. She stopped feeding the babies and laid them down on the bed. She stuck her thumb in her mouth and said calmly, "Well, I would rather see him dere dan in dat jail," looking at me with teary eyes.

Then she called out Ms. Dani Rhimes's name, and I knew what that was all about—they were going to "git a fifty-cent drink." Whiskey seemed to help her adjust to problems that she couldn't handle on her own. She needed that drink to do it for her; now she was dependant.

We were allowed to visit Daddy on Sunday only. I will never forget our first experience visiting him at the chain gang prison camp north of town. We were there on time at eleven o'clock. The chief prison guard was called Captain Showerhead. He was about six feet tall and weighed around three hundred pounds. He had this big potbelly on him that made anyone who came in contact with him afraid of him. He looked rough, and his voice sounded like a frog had landed in his throat.

But once we got to know him, we found that his looks were deceiving. He was always kind to us, and not just us—to any of the visitors.

We played down there just as we did at home. There were places set up for us in the back of the prison just like at home: a tire swing, a springboard, jump rope, and marbles for the boys to shoot. They even made a wooden wagon for us to pull each other in during our playtime.

I learned that playtime for the children was the time the married couples could get private time together. The only sad moment was when visiting hour was over; otherwise we had a better time playing at the camp than we did at home.

That first morning, we arrived at the camp. Once the guard opened the gate, he stood taking all the visitors' names and who they were there to visit. As each name was called, he checked it. The visitors came from various places, but no one was from Daddy's hometown.

The guard watched as all the visitors came through the gate. Another guard searched baby strollers and anything that was large or looked suspicious. Since we had never been in the place, we were a little on edge, especially when the gate slammed and we were locked in for the day.

Some of the prisoners who watched us as we played told us that when we came back inside, we were going to be in for a treat—whatever that meant. It was a day to be remembered.

Every Monday morning thereafter, the cook from the prison camp would come to the house with big boxes of groceries—foods that Mama couldn't afford. There were name-brand food of all kinds, celery, two or three different kinds of canned goods, cooking oil, salt pork bacon, bags of beans, salmon, sardines, eggs, butter, and grits, just to name some of it. I could truthfully say that as long as Daddy was doing time in that camp, we never lacked for food.

Mama was working for three different families. For Mr. Jack Henry, the assistant sheriff, she cleaned his house on Mondays and Thursdays. On Tuesdays and Saturdays, she worked for Terry Poole. And on Wednesdays and Fridays, it was her favorite lady, Ms. Connie Ray Poole. She was the sister to Terry. Mama only got paid two dollars and fifty cents a day, but not having to buy food except fish on Fridays, she got along fine.

Aunt Matilda said, "De good Lord sure is takin care of Mama an her chilluns." But what she didn't know was the terrible pain Mama was encountering from working all those jobs. Each house was different. When she got home, the first thing she did was take her shoes off, change out of her work dress into an old housedress, go straight to the woodstove, get the fire started, and begin to make dinner. Sometimes her feet were swollen and she was in pain, but she never would let it stop her.

One day I wanted to go and meet her. The children were down on the pallet, so I took off running. I was midway to meeting Mama when I saw her hand was waving to me. I didn't know if she meant "go back" or what she was trying to tell me. I happened to look back and saw my little sister running behind me.

I turned around to get her and, at the same time, yelled for her to go back. I grabbed her, and just as I did, the Brimsley's dog Lightning attacked me from behind. I hollered and screamed at the top of my voice, but by the time someone got to me, he had scratched and bitten me in several places on the backs of my legs.

I could hear Mrs. Angie Rosa shouting, "Boy, you need to be shame of your badass self, siccin dat dog on Jenny Rue chilluns. I'll come over dere an beat de red off of your bad ass. I'mo tell Jenny Rue you did it. You won't be able to lie you way out of dis one, cause I was satten right here on my back porch, watchin you untie dat dog and sic him on dem dere gurls."

Mama carried me on home and wiped the running blood from my legs. I wasn't hurt as much as I was scared. It seemed to feel so much better with her touching me. Mrs. Angie Rosa came bouncing in to fill Mama in on what had happened. "Jenny Rue, dat old red-cocked boy of Sara Lee's sicced dat dog on you young'uns. I was satten on my back porch, looking right at him, but fore I could holler to stop him, dat old big dog had already jumped on Haley's back and bit dat child. You ought to call Mr. Lund Cabb an have his damn ass locked up."

Mrs. Angie Rosa had a big bulldog herself. His name was Butch. She kept him tied up; he was a big, dangerous-looking dog. She was willing to let him loose on Lightning. She swore Butch would cut his throat. But Mama was against it completely. She said, "In the good Lord's own good time, he will fix it."

"Jenny Rue! I heard dey put Macky back down dere on dat chain gang. Honey, is it true?"

Reluctantly, Mama answered, "Yeah, Angie Rosa, they did."

"Well, how much time did he git dis time?"

"They first give em three years, but den dey cut it back to eighteen months."

Mrs. Angie Rosa's concern for Mama seemed genuine, but I along with Mama knew she had motive. She went on to tell Mama how sorry she was, and if there was anything she could do for us call on her. Frankly, after the pain she had caused Mama—because Mrs. Angie Rosa had once poisoned her—I was hoping Mama didn't need her. Telling on Tonk Brimsley was her way of getting to Mama. The information was appreciated, but her actions would always be remembered.

I knew she wanted to say something else, but something seemed to hold her back. She made her way home across the field. I was small, young, and very sensible. I thought with Mama alone with all these children, Mrs. Angie Rosa would come back and try to poison her again. Mama must have felt what I was thinking, and she said, "Now don't you go runnin down to dat prison camp, tellin your daddy Angie Rosa was over here. You hear me, gal?"

"Yeah, ma'am, I won't," I promised.

She must have used her ESP, because it started pouring down rain heavily that week. It rained from Wednesday on up to that Sunday. We were unable to go visit Daddy at the camp. Boredom occupied my time. I paced from the back door to the front, wishing the rain would stop. We learned the song:

> Rain, rain, go away,
> come again another day.

No, it didn't happen. I went from Mama's house to Aunt Matilda's in the rain. I got an old tin cup and stood at the back window to catch the water falling from the tin roof. I liked the sound of the rainwater dropping in the bottom of the cup, and I would drink it. Aunt Matilda said it was healthy to drink and wash your hair in rainwater.

The rain didn't stop the prison cook from bringing the groceries on Monday as usual. After he dropped them off, Mama prepared for work.

Before she left, she said, "We missed goin to see your daddy yestiddy, but if it's de good Lord's will, we'll go see em next Sunday."

I looked at her with my arms folded and said, "I hate rain. If it wasn't for dat old rain, we coulder went and saw Daddy."

"Gal, shut your mouth. You don't know what you sayin. It's de good Lord upper bove will dat it rain. While it was rainin, de good Lord was hard at work. He be workin all day, yesterday, all last night, all last month, an all last year. So you stop sayin things you ain't got no business in. When de Lord is workin, we be still. I had a feelin it was gon rain cause my knee was killin me."

I was curious as to what kind of work the Lord could be doing when it was raining. It was noticeable that when I asked her, she brushed me off. She pushed a baby into my arms, telling me Ms. Dani Rhimes would be coming soon.

Just as she said it, old Ms. Dani came through the door, eyes bloodshot, smelling like whiskey. For the first time, I took a real good look at her. She looked just like a witch that I had seen in some book, but she could have been a beautiful woman if she fixed herself up. She had long, thick, salt-and-pepper hair. All she needed to do was comb it out. She wore it packed down on her head, but every so often somebody would comb it out and make her two plaits.

She took the baby from my arm, and I trotted off to school.

No matter how Mama tried to conceal her true feelings, she was in a lot of pain—the kind that hurt deep within. Only the one feeling the pain can actually tell what it feels like, but I felt my mama's pains and they hurt me. I told her one evening, "Mama, I kin stay with you more nights if you scare to stay by youself. You want me to, Mama? You want me to stay wit you?"

I think I made her feel good. She grinned and put the baby in my arms and told me to hold her. She had to do something, because she was not responding to anything I said to her.

I suggested that she could allow Annie Dora to stay with Aunt Matilda and I could stay with her to help out with the other children. It was the first time since I had been residing with Aunt Matilda that I didn't want to leave Mama.

She stuck her thumb in her mouth, walked out on the porch, and told Aunt Matilda she was going to let Annie Dora spend the night with her. I cold tell by the look on Aunt Matilda's face that she didn't quite like the idea, but she went along with her. I only stayed that one night. The day after, Ms. Dani moved in with her to help out, so my little mind was clear for a while.

It was amazing to return to Aunt Matilda. She made our favorite dinner: fried chicken and mashed potatoes with hot tea cakes. Afterward, we sat on the porch, looking up at the beautiful full moon shining down to earth. and listening to the croaking of the bullfrogs sound over the neighborhood from the pond on the Kingsley property. We sat for hours.

Then one evening, old Ms. Dani left the house and didn't come back, leaving us to look after the children while Mama worked. I ran out to where Mama and some others were gathered in the backyard, washing clothes. I didn't stop to see who all was out there. When I was about to go up the back steps, someone yelled to me, "Hey! Come back here and help see bout dese here chilluns."

I turned and went back. Aunt Lucy Sue was there with her three children beside Georgie Boy, Snappy, baby Billy, and Willa Max, Mama got a quilt and made a pallet on the front porch. She laid the babies on it and I lay beside them. The other children played in my tire swing under the chinaberry tree, swinging with much laughter. I wanted to play, but I had to be the bigger one and look after the babies.

The Brimsley children and the Kingleys came to play too. As I watched on from the porch, I saw Georgie Boy pushing our cousin Tangy Ann in the swing. Then I recognized Tonk and thought he was playing with Georgie Boy, but he wasn't: he was fighting my little brother. Georgie Boy was nothing but a coward and wasn't even trying to fight back.

I hopped off the porch and ran to get Mama. She was putting sheets into the pot. "Mama!" I yelled. "You know what? Dem ol' bad Brimsley boys done come over here fightin Georgie Boy."

By the time we got back, Tonk was running across the field. Georgie Boy's nose was bleeding from where Tonk had punched him. The other

Brimsley children said he didn't even try to fight Tonk back. So I put one hand on my hip and pointed a finger into Georgie Boy's face. "Boy, you too scary! You just let dat old Tonk hit you an you won't hit em back."

He just stood crying—as my daddy would always say, "like a sissy." Blood was dropping from his nose, and that made me awful mad. I was determined to get hot. Mama wasn't saying a word, just wiping his nose as the other children watched in fear. Tonk had all the other children scared of him, but something in me did not fear him. He was only a bully. I noticed he fought those who wouldn't fight back, and he knew Georgie Boy was a coward.

I could see him watching from across the field, and I yelled, "You ain't gon git by wit hittin my brother in his nose! I'mo git you, Tonk!"

I know he would wait till later, as he always did, and think everything was forgiven. Then he would come back over to play. I plotted to get him back for sure.

I was right. Later in the evening, Aunt Lucy Sue had taken her children and left. All the others were gone home too. Mama got her children, and I went out to play in the tire swing. I saw Tonk and his brother Nookie standing midway through the field, watching me swing. So I beckoned with my finger for them to come and play with me.

At first they started over, but they stopped. Nookie took a few more steps and stopped again. Then I called out, and they came running.

I got up out of the swing and told Tonk to push Nookie first while I went to the kitchen and got some tea cakes. I looked around in the kitchen and found a stick about four inches long. I eased up behind Tonk as he pushed Nookie, and I struck him in the back of his head. I heard him cry out, and I ran back to Mama's house as if I hadn't done anything.

I went into her room and stood beside her bed. She knew me pretty well, and she knew I had done something I had no business doing. She took one look at me and said, "What you doin in here, Haley, looking sneaky? What you done did? I know you done did somethin."

Gemmy BB had stopped by and heard me tell Mama with a tremor in my voice, "I hit Tonk in de back of his head wit a stick cause he blooded up Georgie Boy's nose."

For the first time, my big sister had sympathy for me. She said, "Dat's good! You shoulda hit em. Maybe now dey will stay over dere where dey live."

We could hear Mrs. Angie Rosa and Mrs. Sara Lee's voices on Mama's porch. Mrs. Sara Lee was Tonk's mama. Our mama went out to see what they had to say. I peeped out and saw them telling Mama what I did. She yelled for me to come out, and as I did, they were all looking at me. Mrs. Angie Rosa asked loudly, "What you hit Tonk in his head for, gal? You coulda knocked his brains out."

I looked her directly in the eye and answered courageously, "Cause he blooded up my little brother's nose, dat's why."

She looked from me to Tonk and then to Mrs. Sara Lee, speechless for a few minutes. Then she said to Mama, smiling like they were best of friends, "Jenny Rue, dat damn gal of yours is a mess. She just like Mr. Macky, don't take no s—— off nobody. She done took up for her little brother. Tonk blooded up her brother's nose an she knocked Tonk in his damn head an I don't blame her. Maybe now he'll keep his black ass out from over him fighting on dese here chilluns."

Surprisingly to me, I felt comfortable with what she said.

She made herself right at home. Mama didn't want her there but was too kind-hearted to tell her otherwise. Mama welcomed her with a cold glass of water. The moment she drank it all down, she went into Mama's house. Gemmy BB was holding little Billy, the baby she had left on us, as if she were the perfect mother. Mrs. Angie Rosa played with the baby and laughed with Gemmy BB about how fat and healthy he was, complimenting her for being a good mother.

Mama went into to the kitchen. The moment her back was turned, Mrs. Angie Rosa came onto the porch and said to Mrs. Sara Lee in a typical loud, controlling tone, "Dat g—— d—— young'un look just like Macky. Dat ain't nobody's baby but Macky."

She was about to say more, but she saw me and we made eye contact. "Haley, git up an go play wit dem dere other chilluns an stop lookin in grown folk mouths," she ordered.

I gave her one of my dirty looks and moved toward Aunt Matilda's, with intentions to stand behind the corner of the house and listen to whatever else she was going to say. But I was interrupted. Mama called out for me to go get her a dime's worth of kerosene from the Shelmore store. I didn't want to go, but I didn't have a choice.

I took the can and started off to the store. After I got the kerosene, I spotted Tonk and Nookie. They were flying after me, trying to get me for what I'd done earlier. I broke into a wild run for home.

They overtook me just as I went to turn the corner by Pa Jack's. I yelled, "Boy, y'all better leave me lone!"

Tonk tried to yank the can from my hand, but I was holding on to it for dear life. But when I saw he was going to cause the kerosene to spill, I let go of it and fell back. Tonk gave me a few waps upside my head. Pa Jack came out, shouting, "Stop fightin on dat gurl, boy!"

The two boys took off running, but quickly turned and came back toward. I ran on, full of fear. Then I looked down and saw a nice-size stick in a ditch.

By the time they caught up to me, I was coming up out of the ditch and holding the stick. They both jumped down in the ditch. I took one hard swing with that stick, popping one of them against the skull. I swung again, and the other jumped back, running off across the field. It was Nookie running, leaving Tonk behind him, fearfully holding his head.

Tonk persisted in coming after me, reaching for the stick. I backed away, with no intent to hurt him again but incensed enough to defend myself against him. I let the stick fly—oops—upside the back of his head and anywhere else I could hit him. I said "Up! Up, boy, I'mo kill you now." Then I let the stick talk for me. I could hear the licks sound off on his head with each pop. I was faster than he was and able to keep him off of me.

Pa Jack shouted, "Stop dat! Gal, you gon kill dat boy!"

Angrily, I responded, "He ought not to come down here an be messin wit me."

Tonk tore out running as fast as he could, holding his head. People rushed out on their porches, but it was all over. Pa Jack walked home with me and told everyone how the Brimsley boys attacked me on my way home from the store. He assured them those boys wouldn't be bothering me again. His words were, as I would always remember: "Dey got just what dey was lookin fur. Now dey playin bad like dey old folks is ober wit, cause dat little Macky Keath-lookin gurl was on dey heads like beatin up on a drum. One thing fur sure, I don't think dey gon eber bother dat gurl ergin, cause dat stick talked."

The description Pa Jack gave of me protecting myself send a message to everyone else in Rat Row: size and age did not matter to me. I learned you have to bring it to get it. After that, I never had any more problems with the Brimsley boys—but I never turned my back to them either.

***

It was Sunday, a day we always looked forward to because we were going to visit Daddy down at the chain gang. I'd been staying with Mama for a while. She had adjusted pretty fair since he had been away. Though I was spending most of my time down at Mama's house, I was some content, but I still believed my place was with Aunt Matilda.

It was hot that Sunday. I got up early, as I always did when something exciting was going to happen. Aunt Matilda was angry because Snappy had peed her bed. That was the one thing Aunt Matilda did not tolerate. Even when she was angry, she was calm, never once raising her voice. But when she spoke, I knew she was serious. She said if I didn't come back, she would go get one of the Brimsley girls.

I was not about to let that happen. No one was going to take my place with her—no way.

Aunt Matilda saw how displeased I was, so she explained her reasoning. She just couldn't wash that big bed mattress, with the rheumatism in her arms.

I was old enough to understand grown folks' demeanors, especially hers. I told her after our visit with Daddy on Sunday, I was coming back home. She was so delighted, she kissed me on my left eye as always and smiled all the snuff out of her lips. She thanked God it was Snappy's last night.

She gave me and Snappy new dresses made from flour sacks to wear to see Daddy. Mama wore one of her Sunday-best dresses. As we walked to the prison camp, every so often I glimpsed Mama without her knowing, and I would catch that happy look on her face.

We approached the gate at the prison camp. Men were walking around the grounds as usual. The fence looked to be about twelve inches high, the building was newly painted white, and the men were all wearing white pants with blue stripes down the side. Two white men stood on each side of the gate, wearing big guns at their sides and holding rifles in their hands.

Daddy was standing in the yard, looking down that old, rocky highway at us. The gates slid open and we walked through. It was the first time I remember Daddy watching us enter through those gates. His face sparkled with joy like a little child, he was so glad to see us. Regardless of what I had heard folk say about him, I saw a side that was never revealed to them. He was tough, and some even saw him as no good and mean, but that day I saw pain and more pain. We brought him much happiness, and even though he didn't show it, I felt it.

Other prisoners took their wives in their arms and kissed them, lifted their children up and hugged them, but never once did Daddy kiss Mama. He took the baby from her arms, patted me and Georgie Boy on our heads, and led us all over into a little shack across from the building where they were locked up. This was the visiting room.

Walking up the steps, we could hear the most beautiful singing. It was the kind of singing that we only heard on the radio. I was amazed at the men's singing. It was like we were at a gospel concert, praising and worshiping God at the prison camp. I learned that God is everywhere at the same time. He is not only at the churches we attend; He is at the prison also. They sounded really good.

It was ambiguous to me at the time what it meant. But in no time I learned that this was how the men entertained their families, visitors, friends, and themselves. I will remember that song until the day I die, how beautifully it was being sung.

There were six men dressed in their white and blue-striped outfits, singing unto the Lord "See How They Done My Lord" and "Faith of

Our Fathers" and "Nearer My God to Thee." The clapping and the praising were touching. The Spirit was in that building like it was in the Old First Bethel Church.

The room was full of visiting families and friends from different cities. There was a drink machine in the corner, a piano in another corner, and in between was a snack machine and lots of benches around the floor. They were all filled.

The singing was breathtaking, leaving everyone speechless. When they took an intermission, two of the singers came directly over to where Daddy and we were sitting. They were his good friends. The leader of the group was Mr. Donnie Martin. He was very friendly and smiled all the time, and had a voice that sounded like Sam Cook's. He was as good-looking as he was friendly, but behind all those smiles, I saw much loneliness, sorrow, and pain. When I recall the look, the pain in it went much deeper than being in prison. I was too young to honestly know what prison involved, yet the more we visited, the more I perceived. I was watchful, and by then, living around Aunt Matilda, I had learned how to pray. When Mr. Donnie or any of the other men would pray, I could pray right along with them. It was like I knew exactly the words they were going to speak.

Mr. Danny Blocker was another one of Daddy's friends. He was huge; he weighed more than three hundred pounds and wore a black patch covering his left eye. He and Daddy had a lot in common. I was unaware of what it was then, but anyone in the room could see they were the best of buddies.

I also met Mr. James Blackmon. He was the prison head cook, along with keeping the books, doing the ironing, and providing many other services. Daddy called him the prison maid.

After a while, Mr. Donnie took me, Georgie Boy, and Snappy for a tour around the prison camp. We had more fun there that Sunday; it was almost a home away from home. I recall looking over the fields at big bulls grazing in the green grass out back of the camp.

There was a fishing pond, and on the other side of the pond we could see the white folk swimming in a white-folk-only recreation park.

Their laughter was echoing all over the camp. We could even see the signs that read "Whites only."

After a while, we were taken back to the entertainment center. I was most eager to know why Mr. Danny was wearing that patch over his eye. I noticed Daddy and Mama were not in the room, so I dashed right over to Mr. Danny. He was sitting off to himself, smoking a cigar.

Not knowing what to say to him, I kept looking at him. Then I asked him, with concern but mannerly, "Mr. Danny, where my mama an daddy? Did dey leave us?"

"No, darlin. Dey just gone for a walk like you did. Dey'll be back soon now. What else you want to know?"

Abruptly, I asked, "Why you wear dat thing over your eye like dat? You don't got no eye?"

He laughed at me with that long cigar hanging out of his mouth and said, "No, I don't got no eye."

"Den what happen to it?"

He stated slowly, "No, I don't got no eye cause a rattlesnake crawled up an bit it out."

I was surprised but more concerned than anything. "Did it hurt?"

"No!" he replied. "I didn't feel a thing. I think you done asked enough questions for one day; now allow me to ask you some. Will dat be all right?"

"Yeah, sir. You kin ask me a question if you want to."

"What's your name?"

"My name Haley."

"How old you is?"

"I'm ten years old."

"What grade you in?"

"I'm in de fifth grade."

"What your teacher name is?"

"Her name is Mrs. Ella Miller."

Just then, Mama and Daddy came through the front door. They were all grins. Daddy said, "I know she done just bout talked your head off an done asked fifty question to boot."

"We had a pretty decent conversation," Mr. Danny said. "She a little talkative. She ask what she want to know, just like you an me. I tell you, Macky, she gon be hard to handle one of dese days."

The guard called out, "Visiting hours is over in thirty minutes."

The men formed a line in the middle of the floor. The preacher, an older white man, came in and read the Twenty-Third Psalm. We recited the Lord's Prayer with him. Mr. Donnie Martin and a few other men sang "If Jesus Had to Pray, What About Me." We had church down at the prison camp.

The final song was led by another prisoner named Willie Bush, "I'm Coming Up, Lord." Once the singing was over, the guard announced that visiting hours were over and would begin again the next Sunday at eleven o'clock. People's faces flickered and sadness swept across the room as the light faded into darkness. Everyone commenced to walking out the door. I think everybody down at that camp that Sunday dreaded leaving.

Daddy said Mr. Danny and Mr. Donnie had no family to come visit them each weekend. They became our family to visit also. When time came for us to leave, they would walk out with us to the gate along with the other men walking out with their families. We all had to say good-bye, leaving the prisoners behind.

Once we were all outside the gate, it slammed shut. Everybody from inside and outside looked downcast through the holes in the gates. As we walked down the rocky highway, as far as we could see, they were watching. And then they were gone.

But we knew we would get to see them going through town on the bulldozers. They were working near our new school, and en route back to the camp each evening, they had to come through our neighborhood. We would stand on the side of the road by Pa Jack's café and wave to them until they were out of sight. Some evenings they would stop by and talk with us, and some evenings they would wave and keep on going. Mama said the days when they stopped were Captain Showerhead's good days, and the days they kept going were his bad days.

That became Georgie Boy and my regular routine after school. We gathered the wood, making sure there was enough for evening supper and breakfast. We checked that the lamps were all filled with kerosene, and there was plenty of water for cooking and bathing. Then off we ran down to the corner to get a look at our daddy and the other convicts headed back to the prison camp. Captain Showerhead would stand on the back, holding the rifle, as Daddy drove one side of an old yellow bulldozer and Mr. Donnie drove the other. Mama watched from the kitchen window.

We looked forward to doing this as we counted the weeks before Daddy got out of prison and came home to us. All we had were visits on Sunday and waving as they passed during the week. We experienced the pain on some evenings of getting our chores done hurriedly, running off to the highway, and waiting for the bulldozer that sometimes never came. I felt shame because of what folk were saying. We encountered a lot of harsh words. Once folk saw us, they would start singing the latest pop song: "That's the sound of the men working on the chain gang—that's Mr. Macky Keath."

I was firm enough to take the pain and pretend not to hear a word being said. I knew if they got close to me, I would beat the living daylight out of them. They knew it too. Georgie Boy was always the weakest link; therefore, I had to be strong for the both of us. I knew how to fight back in my own unique way. We were the most talked-about family on Rat Row, and I expected nothing less.

But I did learn something. No matter how we were disgraced, every visit I made to that prison camp was a learning experience for me. The day would come when I would have children of my own. I could tell the story to them, and hopefully they would learn from it and not end up in prison themselves. I promised myself, the last day I visited my father before he was released, that I would never go to prison or the chain gang or whatever they called it.

I was in between houses; I stayed at Mama's some and at Aunt Matilda's some. I was so hyper, I couldn't be still. The time finally came when Daddy had only three weeks left before he would be released from the chain gang, and our visiting hours at the camp would be over.

It was Annie Dora's (the sister we called Snappy) first year at school. She was assigned to Ms. Madison's classroom. Ms. Madison was the principal Mr. Monroe's sister. I was in the sixth grade and assigned to

Ms. Dorothy Brooch's classroom. Georgie Boy was in the fourth grade and assigned to Mr. Carnett's classroom, the meanest male teacher there.

The year started off well. We enjoyed getting to know our new teachers and getting acquainted with the new students. We were thinking the same thoughts on a positive note. I had even grown accustomed to coming home and helping with the children, facing life as it was. My own days as a child were over before I realized what childhood was all about. I didn't fret over the days I had to stay out of school and help with the children. I accepted what I didn't understand.

Gemmy BB got married and moved nearby, but Billy was still with us. Mama said she wouldn't allow him to go with Gemmy BB even if she wanted him to. He had become a part of us, our brother.

Kate was completely living with her grandmom, whom we called Aunt Pancy, while Tise was in between Aunt Lucy Sue's house and Mama's. But I was the one having to stay out of school and look after the younger children. It became a part of who I was. When I was alone, I pretended I was the mother and they were my children I was raising by myself.

One cold winter morning, unexpectedly, I had to stay home because Ms. Dani didn't show up. I was not allowed to go to school if she hadn't come by the time we were to leave. That day I babysat the two babies. They were now walking. Aunt Matilda hadn't yet come to check on us and take us back to her house, where we would stay until Mama come home from work. I was picking up around the room, wondering what life had for me other than babysitting all those young'uns. What was I going to be when I grew up? Would I even graduate from high school? Five years ahead of me seemed so far away. I couldn't begin to see a way for me, and I hadn't learned for myself what true faith was.

I heard someone coming in the back door. I first thought it was Aunt Matilda—but when Aunt Matilda came up, she called out my name before she came in. No one responded when I called out, "Who in dere?" Finally I went to see who it was. What a surprise—Daddy and Mr. Danny Blocker, his best friend, were coming into the kitchen. They had just been released from the chain gang.

They were like new men relocating in town. Daddy was dressed in dark gray trousers, a light gray shirt, and an imitation leather jacket. He had a gray derby hat and black shoes. He looked like brand-new money. Mr. Danny was dressed in brown in the same style. I stood for a moment, looking them both up and down. It was so astonishing to see the both of them standing in the kitchen. My facial expression said it.

Daddy looked back at me. He was never a talker until he was intoxicated off of that moonshine. Mr. Danny smiled with a long cigar hanging out of his mouth. He said, "You lookin like you is glad to see your daddy."

I was, but I didn't know how to tell him. I had no way of showing daughterly love except through a grin. Daddy never showed us any kind of affection; I don't think he even knew how. He never told us he loved us, not once in my entire life, but I knew he did—as much as an unaffectionate man could love anyone.

Aunt Matilda came to help carry the children to her house. She took one look at Daddy and grinned. "Mr. Macky, you done come back home."

"Old lady Matilda, I be damn. You git younger and younger. You done got married yet?" he joked. She grinned from ear to ear. They exchanged a few other words as I stood between them and the door, looking from her to him. He never said, "Thank you for helping look after my family during my absence." He didn't show love, and he didn't know how to say thank you. That concerned me.

Before long, our house was full again. It hadn't been that full since Daddy left over two and a half years ago. By noon, they all took off down to Flappy Boots's café, where Daddy stayed until Mama came home from work.

I had the babies pretty nearly under control. Once we got them to Aunt Matilda's house, fed, washed up, and dressed, I ran back down to Mama's house to finish cleaning before Mama got home from work. I was all stirred up that Daddy was finally at home. I was energized enough to go through the house in fifteen minutes. I was moving as fast as a freight train, with only the two beds to be made and some breakfast dishes to wash and I'd be done.

I was making Mama's bed when I looked up and there a man stood, grinning in the doorway, showing all his black gums. I went around the far side of the bed. His eyes looked cold, and the way he was staring at me made me feel unpleasant. An uneasy feeling rushed through my body, and my heartbeat began to speed up. I asked him with my voice in a shudder, "What you doin in here?"

He didn't answer, so I asked him again, louder, "Boy, what you want?"

"I want you." He spoke coldly as he made his way toward where I was standing. In one leap he was grabbing me. He wrapped his arms around my waist and wrestled me down to the bed.

I tried to push him away, fighting him off and yelling, "Naw, you don't neither!" Of course he was much stronger than I, and my little strength against his was nothing. I did let out one loud scream before he could stop me. I could smell a musky odor coming from under his arms, a smell like a polecat. He had a grip so tight I could barely breathe. I was so afraid.

When I let the scream out, he held me down with one arm. His right knee pressed down on one of my legs. He clamped a hand tightly across my mouth and said, "If you don't scream, I won't have to hurt you." I could feel the pressure of his hand as he tried to force my panties down.

Somehow his hand slipped from over my mouth, enough so I could open my teeth into the side of his hand. I bit down hard until he yelled. I couldn't speak because of the grip I had. I was afraid to let go.

Then I heard Uncle Billy Roliver's and Mrs. Sara Lee's voices coming around the house. I let go and let out a scream so loud, they came running through the back door. "Haley, what's de matter wit ye, baby?"

The man dashed like a scared rabbit out the front door. They were in time to see his backside.

Mrs. Sara Lee rushed over to where I stood with my panties down below my knees. She helped me pull them up and said, "Dat black-ass overgrown nigger was just fixin to mess wit dat little twelve-year-old girl. Go call de law. Put his damn ass in jail. We heard you scream an I told Billy, 'Dat sound like little Haley. We better go see bout er.' We know your mama was at work. If we didn't git in here, just think whater happen to you, dat black son of a bitch."

She held me as tightly as if I were her child. I was shivering with fear, but the comforting was warm. She took me to Aunt Matilda's and told her what had happened. Aunt Matilda said, "I had a strange feelin sumnutter bad was gon happen."

Uncle Billy said furiously, "If it was my daughter, he wouldn't live to try an hurt nobody else's child." He walked around the houses, looking if he could see the man anywhere, but he was clear out of sight.

Before long, the news that I had been physically attacked was all over town. Some said I brought it on myself. Some said I was willing, but just got caught. The nasty rumors were more than I could handle.

I relaxed the rest of the day on the front porch with the children until Mama and Daddy came home. I knew it was the grace of God that saved me from an ugly attack that day, but nothing was ever the same. It felt like war against me from all sides. There are some parents who never believe any wrong of their children nor appreciate anyone telling them of any wrong that the children may appear to have done, whether the appearance is true or false. I sadly experienced much fear that day, but wasn't sure of just what I was afraid of—was it the closeness of this attack, or when the next attack might be?

When Daddy heard about what had happened, he was calm. He kept his head down and never looked up as Uncle Billy and Mrs. Sara Lee explained to him what they witnessed. But I could tell anger was building up inside him by the way his temple was jumping. I learned from Aunt Frankie that that was the way to tell when Daddy was really mad and ready to attack.

He went into the house. By then, Snappy and Georgie Boy were out of school, and I had the opportunity to finish cleaning up Mama's house. It was dark. I had this awful feeling come over me. I pushed opened the shuttered window for some sunlight to shine through. I looked at the spot where I had been attacked, but I felt safe again. I picked up the chair that the man had knocked over running out the house.

Daddy asked me calmly, "Did dat nigger hurt you?"

"Naw, Daddy, he didn't hurt me. He is de one hurt because, I mean, I bit a big bite in his hand."

"I should not go nowhere. If I caught dat son of a bitch, I'd be right back on the g——d—— chain gang, dat's for damn sure," he stated bitterly.

With my mama and my daddy home, I felt safe from any and everyone that I had the slightest thought could do me harm. But from then on I decided to look at people differently, not knowing who could be trusted or who couldn't. I carried a knife as my own way of protection. If I had to get water from the pump alone, I had it with me. If I cut wood alone, I had it with me. I carried the knife everywhere, including school—when I was permitted to go.

Later in the evening, the sound of the bulldozer came. The other children went running to watch the convicts going back to the camp, just as we always had when Daddy was driving. I wouldn't go down there that evening; I couldn't bring myself to go. I stood by the window and watched as Mama usually did.

Georgie and Snappy went with Daddy and watched with him. The bulldozer stopped beside Daddy, and he talked to the prisoners driving it. I could tell Daddy was delighted he was not on that bulldozer. Mr. Donnie Martin was driving on the same side Daddy once drove, and another man was driving the side Mr. Donnie once drove. Captain Showerhead stood on the back, holding that rifle in his hand, guarding as usual.

Something was different that evening about the way it stopped. Mr. Danny and Pa Jack also went up to the side of the road. Joyfully, they learned it was the chain gang's last evening coming through the neighborhood. The highway was complete, and they were going to be moving to a new project, digging up trees off the India city road. That was the work they were doing, making all the dirt roads into paved ones.

Mr. Donnie congratulated Daddy and Mr. Danny for their freedom. He made them promise they wouldn't forget about him. All his family were in South Carolina, and he wanted the two of them to continue to visit him as often as they could.

Captain Showerhead told them, "Mack, you an Danny, y'all make sure y'all leave dat moonshine alone now. I don't wanter see either one of you back down at my camp, you hear? Good luck to you both."

They were off. We waved until they turned the corner and were out of sight. That was the last time we were able to greet the convicts from the highway. That evening seemed special to Daddy. I watched him when he and Mr. Danny got back.

Mrs. Sara Lee and Uncle Billy Roliver were conversing about the incident that happened to me. I wanted them to stop because I knew nothing good was going to come of it. Folk had already formed their opinions, and nothing more was coming out of it except more hurt.

Mama was real mad about it, but Daddy was still calm. He shocked folk who asked him what he was doing when he replied, "Nothin much." It was what he was thinking that worried everyone. I looked on with shame and pain. I didn't want to tell or hear concerning the attack. I didn't want any animosity among families. Daddy warned, "If he come back through our yard an looks at us wrong, I'm gon have him put in jail."

Mama cried later when they confronted the mother of that man concerning the matter. The woman cursed Mama out, not believing a word that was told to her. My mother said to her cousin, "Dem same young'uns one day gon make you wring your hands an cry." Lord knows I wanted to know what she meant by that statement. I concluded that something was going to happen to prove her right about them.

From then on, trouble was always lurking around us. Shortly after the attack on me, I was pumping water for Aunt Matilda. Usually she and I went to the pump together, but because it was light out, I didn't think that anything would happen. I was humming a song, and my cousins Jacob and Poor Dog sneaked up behind me. They snatched the bucket from my hand. I couldn't see which one of them did it, but whoever it was poured all the water out on the ground. They pushed me out the way and took over the pump, letting all the water just run over Mama's backyard for pure meanness.

They were pumping hard and wild. I stood back, watching. Suddenly the iron pump handle came flying up, knocking Poor Dog in his forehead. He fell backward, and blood was sheeting from his head down the side of his face. He was laid out for dead.

I took off running, shouting out Aunt Matilda's name. I met her as she was coming out the back to see what was taking me so long with her water. I told her what happened. She went to see if she could help in some way. When she arrived, Poor Dog was still stretched out on the ground, in the water that he had pumped all acoss the yard. She took her apron off and tied it around his head, trying to stop the bleeding.

Pallie Lea showed up and asked me, "What happened to him?"

I answered unfeelingly, "Dat's goodie for em now. He ought to leave people lone. He was pumpin de water out de pump in my mama's yard to keep us from gittin some, and de handle come off and hit em in his head."

"My God, he coulder killed hisself."

She watched on while her other brothers lifted Poor Dog up from the ground and carried him on over to their house. From there, they took him on to Miller County Hospital.

They were quiet for a long time before starting up again. They had Georgie Boy and I afraid to go out and play or go to the pump and get water. They were always lurking about us in some kind of way. Compared to us, they were grown men. We were afraid of them, and like always with Georgie Boy, it showed. I never let them know or see fear in me. If they said something to me, I said something back to them—even if I had to run after I said it.

Living around them became horrific. They started throwing big rocks at us. We were forever having to duck and dodge from them, and they were so slick, it was hard to catch them. When confronted, they always claimed the problem was us, little Georgie Boy and me, not knee-high to a duck as Cousin Sattie Bell said.

Though we tried in every way to avoid any contact with them, they got worse. I wondered what we ever did to make them so mean to us. We got rid of one mean family, the Bendersons, and then here came another.

I began to tell other folk of the things they were doing to my brother and me. When I told Aunt Matilda, she was very upset. She didn't allow us to pump water or go to the woodpile without her. We couldn't do anything except stay on the porch and play in the tire swing. In some ways, we were in prison. It was as if all of our freedom had been invaded. With Aunt Matilda keeping a tight leash on us, we barely moved.

Things seemed to settle down. We even believed they had left us alone. One day Mama came home, gave me three dollars, and sent us to the Shelmore store to buy her two number-two washtubs. On our way back, we were comfortable. Then suddenly we felt rocks being thrown at us. There was that long, tall Poor Dog, throwing rocks so fast that we dropped the tubs and ran home.

We told Mama and Daddy what Poor Dog was doing to us. She went back with us to get the tubs. Poor Dog and Jacob were standing on the corner by Pa Jack's café, looking like they hadn't done a thing. We got the tubs and returned home. They followed us and began singing the song "Chain Gang," added on verses. When I knew Mama wasn't looking, I tooted up and patted my rear end at them both.

That only made things worse. Rat row became a living nightmare. Lying on the porch with the children, feeling the breeze that every now and then swept across our bodies a torrid summer day, I said a prayer: "Dear Lord, please make Cousin Big C an her bad chilluns leave far away an leave us alone so me an my little sisters and brothers kin go outside an play ergin. Amen."

The cry of my brother Georgie Boy yanked my attention to him. I didn't see him anywhere. I called, "Georgie Boy, where you at, boy?" The sound had come from underneath the house, near where I stood. I jumped down from the porch and looked under in time to see Jacob grinning and crawling fast. He had gotten under the house without being seen. Georgie Boy had been sitting on the porch with his feet swinging off the side. Jacob dragged him under the house and beat him up.

I shouted out Aunt Matilda's name so loud, she heard me and rushed to the back door, thinking that was the direction my voice was coming from. She saw Jacob and Poor Dog running down the path toward where they lived. She didn't see me and came to the front, calling out, "Haley, where you at?"

I was pulling Georgie Boy from underneath the house and helping him back onto the porch. His nose was bleeding, shattered into pieces from many licks. Aunt Matilda took him on inside the house and cleaned him up. Then she went down to Cousin Big C's house and told them that if they came back to her house messing with us, she was going to call the policeman for sure.

Pallie Lea came to the back door, inquiring what she was talking about, and Aunt Matilda lit right into her. She told her the boys were demons from the pit bottom of hell. Pallie Lea tried to get a word in, but Aunt Matilda was talking so fast, she couldn't. Aunt Matilda pointed her finger and said, "Y'all better do sumnutter to dem young'uns fore somethin bad happen to em. These here chilluns don't bother em, an I won't stand fur dem to bother em no more. I'mo gwine down to Lund Cabb an have em locked up!"

She turned with her walking cane in hand and went back to her house as fast as she could, still mad as could be and talking to herself. "I mean, you better keep em home. If you don't, I'mo gwine up to Lund Cabb n habe them put in the big jail. They ought to be ershame of theyselbes."

Nothing she said made a difference. Those boys, like she said, were demon-possessed, and it was going to take a miracle from the Lord to put a stop to them. They stood in the pathway as we went into the house, grinning and mocking Aunt Matilda. They wouldn't stop. They didn't fear the threats she made against them. They didn't care; there was no godly fear instilled in them.

I don't know if they even knew of God. We attended church every first and second Sunday, but not a single one of Cousin Big C's family were ever in church. They were being used by the devil.

Once they were confronted, they sometimes paused for a second or two and we got a little peace. One Sunday after we came home from church, we were all in high spirits. Reverend Huffman had preached a mighty good sermon. It was one of those "take heed" sermons for warning. I was too young to understand much about sermons, not knowing the Bible. The only knowledge we received was what the preacher preached to us. But we sure knew when all the mothers and sisters got happy—hats were falling off heads, arms went up, and the ushers swung those fans. I knew something good had happened becauses of the unity and the smiles.

It was so good that when church was over, folk walking home were still thanking and praising the Lord. Even old lady Shelmore came out of her store, spectating. Ms. Geraldine Phillips said she believed Ms. Shelmore got some of the Spirit standing in the store doorway, which was unbelievable to everyone else. Ms. Phillips never moved in the church—as a matter of fact, she was about the only deaconess whom the Spirit didn't move. Folk said she had an evil blockage.

That joyful spirit was too good to be true. The moment we got home, Ms. Estella came to the back door and called Mama. She told her to come down to the hydrant when she got the time; there was something Ms. Estella wanted her to see. Mama changed out of her church clothes into a housedress, and we went down to the hydrant, not knowing what to expect.

Ms. Estella was standing beside Mama's tubs, her brand-new tubs she hadn't so long ago sent us to the store for. Several big nail holes had been driven into them. Mama bent over the tubs and looked at them—both were ruined. Tears fell down her face as she asked, "Who would do this evil thing? Who put all these here holes in my tubs like dis? Who?"

Ms. Estella said, "That boy of Big C's, Teddy, he done it. I was looking right at em when he did it. He used a big nail an this brick to drive the nail through um. I hollered at em, but I was too late. He ran screaming like somebody was out to do him harm. That was because he knew right from wrong. Having dat many darn boys, hell, I would stay gone too. They prob'ly will drive her stone crazy. Knowing her, she won't be back till late tomorrow evening."

Most of the neighbors were supportive of both Cousin Big C and Mama because they were family, and regardless of what happened, their lives weren't much different where motherhood was concerned. Just like all mothers, they were faced with some kind of dilemma. Little Teddy was the raw one, but he was as loved as he was devilish. All Mama wanted was for Cousin Big C to be held accountable for her child's actions, but we all knew who and what Little Teddy was to her—her baby, and she couldn't see beyond anything else. All the Rat Row neighbors came out and gathered around, supportive, knowing we were in the midst of neighborhood crisis where Teddy was concerned.

Cousin Big C Lottie didn't come through the quarters that Sunday. People were looking out for her, but she never came and was nowhere to be found. I didn't have a good feeling at all. I thought about the way she had carried on when Mama tried to tell her what had happened to me. She didn't believe anything about her boys. Everybody already knew what she was going to say whenever she did turn up. Some were even rehearsing her words and how she would say them. everyone knew she was going to deny that Teddy had anything to do with the incident.

Even though everyone knew she was not going to turn up, they all sat on their porches, fanning gnats along with the heat. Aunt Matilda and I retired for the evening.

Early in the morning, Aunt Matilda woke me up, groaning like she was in grave pain. At first I imagined she was having a terrible nightmare like I would. I got up and turned the lamp up. I tried to wake her, but she wouldn't wake. Her eyes were closed, but she was moaning terribly I didn't know what to do for her or what was wrong with her. I lay speechless, scared stiff.

The groaning worsened. I touched her face and she was hot. I thought she was hot from the summer heat. She always kept a kettle of water by the fireside, summer or winter. I got a rag wet and put it to her face, hoping that would cool her head off. I put the cloth against her head and called out her name. I knew something was dreadfully wrong when she didn't respond to me. I recalled she had never been a hard sleeper, and I had to get help.

I peeped out the window. It was still dark, but I did not let the darkness stop me. I ran out the door and down to Mama's house, banging repeatedly on her door.

Mama opened the door with look like a hundred frowns, asking, "What you doing out this time er morning, gal?"

"Mama, you got to come see bout Aunt Matilda. She real hot an she keep moanin an I can't wake her up."

Mama didn't hesitate. She grabbed her housecoat and didn't even put shoes on. Out we ran, barefoot.

Aunt Matilda was yet lying in the same spot. Mama placed a hand on her forehead, looking her over.

By then Cousin Sattie Bell and Uncle Martel were there. They said they would get Dr. Jenkins to come see about her. He was the house-call doctor for our race. Blacks were not allowed in the hospital; it was for whites only. He came and examined her and said she had stroke paralysis. It was serious. He left instructions on how to take care of her and gave her two types of medicine. We had to let her real kin know about her condition. She was to have an adult with her day and night.

I didn't mind taking care of her at all, because of the years she'd spent taking care of us. Everybody took turns taking care of her: Cousin Sattie Bell, Ms. Estella, Ms. Bonnie, and Mama. We were one, big, happy family, having enough concern for each other to live it, do it, and show it, just as the Bible instructs us. Jesus told his disciples he would know that they were his by the way they loved one another.

I watched folk come in and out of her house, the grown-ups and the church folk. I was old enough to know the friendly, caring ones from the just plain nosy ones. I learned that all church folk were not who they made out to be. There were churchgoers, and then there were the real Christian folk.

These two women came, saying they represented the church. I followed them around the rooms. They rummaged throughout her house and into her drawers, looking at her boxes of quilts and her dishes. They weren't there to see about Aunt Matilda; they were there to do just what they were doing. I heard them say, "No wonder Jenny Rue stick so close to er. She probably just waitin for the poor old soul to die so she kin git her hands on all her stuff. She dying now; she won't last the night out."

They sneaked around with nobody paying attention to them except me, and I listened to every idol word that came out of their false mouths. I knew they didn't have Aunt Matilda's health at heart—they wanted those quilts. They wanted the nice bedspread on her bed and the nice rockers in the room and the beautiful pictures that hung on the wall.

They strutted into the kitchen, saying, "I didn't know she had all dis nice stuff in er house. Jenny Rue let them dere pissy young'uns of hers piss all up these nice mattresses an quilts. Naw, she won't make the night out, an we kin git all them quilts outer dere fore she git her hands on em."

Listening to them, I got cold all over, and it was midsummer. Though I was not even thirteen years old, I had feelings of pure hatred. I knew it was against the value I had been taught by all the grown-ups never to disrespect my elders, but I couldn't hold my peace.

I stepped from behind the middle door that led from the bedroom to the kitchen, and I spoke out just like I was a grown woman. "Y'all need to be shame of y'all self. Aunt Matilda ain't gon die; she gon live cause God ain't gon let her die. He is gon make her better, an y'all ain't gon git none of her stuff either."

They both looked at me in fear. I believe God shut their mouths so that they were unable to respond. They turned and practically ran out the back door like they had seen a ghost. I followed, yelling at them, "She is gon git better now!" I couldn't help myself. I felt it was my duty to let them know I was there and had heard every word they said. There were sad, guilty looks on their faces. How could church folk come to visit the sick and never go to the bed where Aunt Matilda lay? I was so ashamed for them.

Something hit me in the pit gut of my stomach. It wasn't a pain, but a realization. I went outside and watched the two old ladies walking fast toward the highway, pointing and talking. They had said they were from Old First Bethel Church, but I didn't recall ever seeing them there—because they were not from there. They had just used the church to get into her house.

I felt an eagerness to pray for Aunt Matilda. Her words rang in my ears: "Always pray an tell de good Lord what you want. He will do it for you. Pray, pray."

I thought about the prayer I had prayed to the Lord to make Cousin Big C Lottie take her bad children and move far, far away. He hadn't done it.

But something in my mind wouldn't let me rest. I went to the other side of the house, to a room that was never used until somebody came to spend the night. I got in her rocker and placed my hands under my chin and said the Lord's Prayer. I added, "Please God, don't let Aunt Matilda die. If you let er die, I won't have nobody to take up for me an my little sisters an brothers, an I will have to stay back at my mama's house wit all dem drunk folk. So please, God, let er live an I won't have to go back an live wit my mama in her house wit all dem dere drunk folk. Amen."

I could hear Mama calling my name. I rushed in to see what she wanted. She was standing at the head of the bed where Aunt Matilda lay motionless. Mama had a towel and was wiping Aunt Matilda's forehead. I didn't know what good it was doing her.

The house was full of caring neighbors, so Mama wanted me to come home with her to check on the other children while Ms. Bonnie relieved her. We were on our way home when around the corner stepped Cousin Big C Lottie, coming home. She had heard Mama wanted to see her concerning Teddy putting the holes in the tubs. The moment she saw Mama, she lit into her like Mama was the villain. Mama told her to walk down to the hydrant with her to see the tubs for herself, and informed our cousin that a witness saw Teddy do it.

Cousin Big C walked with Mama down to the hydrant and looked. Then she told Mama, "Just cause somebody put holes in the damn tubs, it don't mean that Teddy was the one put them there."

Ms. Estella came out her back door and interrupted the conversation. She started waving her hands around, and a big dip of snuff was hanging out of her lip. "C Lottie, you kin take up for dat young'un of yours all you want to, but Teddy put dem holes in Jenny Rue's tubs. I was lookin right at em when he did it, an he know I saw him too." We all knew Ms. Estella had no reason to lie on that nine-year-old boy.

Teddy came running down to where everybody was hollering and screaming, knowing he was being told on. He denied every accusation that was made against him. "No, me didn't, Mother. No, me didn't. They tellin stories on me."

She lifted him up, his legs damn near touching the ground, and she laid his head on her shoulder, petting him like the baby she claimed him to be. He cried just like a baby too. He had her snowed. She believed him over anything or anybody. In her opinion, her children did no wrong.

Letting him down to the ground, she swirled around and in his defense stated, "He said he didn't do it, so he didn't do it. I don't give a damn what Estella or nobody else say, I believe my child."

Mama said angrily, "Big C Lottie, you my folk, we kinfolk. Why won't you believe an listen what people tellin you bout your chillun? Stop your accusin grown folk of lyin. Mark my word, one day dem boys gon make you wring your hand an cry."

Cousin Big C flew into a rage. She pushed Mrs. Estella down to the ground and struck Mama in her face. Mama struck her back just as hard, and a fight broke out between the two. Pa Jack, Uncle Martel, and Uncle Billy pulled them apart. Uncle Billy was still holding on to Mama when I saw Cousin C pick up a jar up over by the trash pile, draw her arm back, and released it, hitting Mama in her face.

Someone came out the door, yelling for Mama to come quickly—Aunt Matilda was dying. I looked on in despair, holding my hand over my mouth to keep from screaming. I was terrified. My mama's face was bleeding. I knew she was cut from the broken jar, but I didn't know how badly. I wanted to run to her and I wanted to run from her to go see about Aunt Matilda. I tried to move, but my feet felt glued to the ground. The pain I was feeling was so bad, I let out a scream.

Mama was brave, trying to get to Aunt Matilda and not worry about herself, but Uncle Billy was steady holding on to her. She tried to jerk away from him. He was drunk. He thought he was helping her, but if he hadn't been holding on to her in the first place, she probably wouldn't have been hit. But she was more hurt from Cousin Big C Lottie's words than the hitting.

Daddy came from the house and made Uncle Billy turn Mama loose. Nothing good ever came from violence; it never solved anything, and worse was on the way. It took all the strength both men had to get the women to calm down. Mama was crying, I was crying, and Daddy was saying no one won in that situation, families against families. He had a great deal of respect for our cousin. His words were always positive toward her. Often neighbors would see her coming home and say something negative. Daddy would say, "Hell, it take a hellable woman to raise dat many chilluns. She is a damn good one."

We went into Mama's house. Not long afterward, Cousin Big C Lottie came through the back door. The next thing, she and Mama were in each other's arms. Cousin Big C Lottie said, "All's forgiven. We are kin, two brothers' chilluns."

Ms. Estella washed the blood from Mama's face. I stood, quietly watching. I could see the wound was not deep, but it was kind of long. Ms. Geraldine Phillips said, "Keep butter on it, an when it heal, you won't be able to tell it was there."

Mama was being well taken care of, so I thought about someone yelling that Aunt Matilda was dying. I left to see what was going on with her. Was it true she was dying? Where was God? He couldn't let that happen. *Aunt Matilda can't die; she has me to help see bout.* I didn't know if that was being selfish or not, but I couldn't bear the thought of Aunt Matilda dying.

I went to the back door and looked out. Aunt Matilda's yard was full of people, even more folk than when we left. Cousin Big C Lottie was standing there and looking over at our house. For a minute I was lost in thought. Then, with my sights set directly on Aunt Matilda, I took off running to take care of my second mama.

I went into Aunt Matilda's room. Aunt Matilda Ann was standing next to her bed with a cool towel to her forehead, just as Mama had been doing. Folk were praying and singing. She lay still in the same position. I stood at the foot of her bed, not saying a word, looking down at her motionless body. I didn't know if she was dead or unconscious. I didn't see her breathing. I was so afraid, I yelled, "Is she dead? She dead, ain't she? Aunt Matilda Ann?"

She looked at me in disbelief. "Why you think she dead, Haley?"

I didn't tell her what we had heard. She assured me Aunt Matilda was not dead. She was getting better; she was only sleeping.

Aunt Matilda was sick for over a month. Then one day she recovered from her stroke and it didn't leave her impaired. She still had her speech. She was not paralyzed. She was up and able to take care of her house and her chicks It was like she was her old self again. I thought, *Look what the Lord has done! He touched her body. He healed her mind. He saved her life for me just in time.*

We praised the Lord the day we walked back into Old First Bethel Church. And in the back of the church sat the two women who had talked about my mama and planned to take Aunt Matilda's things. I looked at them with the evil eye so they would remember that day I heard every word they said. Aunt Matilda was very much alive.

Chapter 7: Hell on Earth but Miracles Do Happen

I missed more and more days from school that year. Reflecting back on my life, what stays in my mind was the cold, late winter. I had been promoted on to the seventh grade, and with all the days I missed, I don't see how I made it that far. I should have still been back in the sixth, but somebody was looking down on me. Daddy was back in his old habits—never home, gambling up every dime he got his hands on. Mama worked, taking care of the household. Daddy was still Macky Keath, fathering children but not half the father he could have been. Mama was having to be the mother and the father.

Georgie Boy was in the fifth grade and Snappy was in second. Some days old Ms. Dani Rhimes didn't show up, meaning I had to stay out of school and take care of little Billy and Willa Max. Nothing changed. We would go to Aunt Matilda's and stay until we saw Mama coming. Then we would go home.

I thanked the good Lord each and every day for Aunt Matilda. Only the good Lord knew we needed somebody. She was the second mama and the grandmama I didn't have.

I'd only seen my grandmama once. I was around five years old. We went up to Lee County, Alabama, on the other side of Columbus, and stayed with her for over a week while Mama was recovering from being poisoned by Mrs. Angie Rosa. The memories of that time were yet vivid in my mind—the cruel treatment Mama had encountered from Grandmom Mandy. She had a very strong dislike for Mama, like a mother should never have toward her daughter. But whatever the reason was, it was hush-hush. Grandmom Mandy never came to visit us.

Even though we didn't have her, God sent us Aunt Matilda. Wonderful miracles kept happening for me since she came into our lives.

One day, I was sitting on the porch with the children, playing. The weather was bleak, a little warm and windy. The sun wasn't shining much, but enough that we felt the cool of the breeze that sailed across every now and then. Aunt Matilda was taking seeds from some of last year's cotton folk had brought to her from the cotton fields.

Up drove a yellow taxicab from Aspen, Georgia. I had never seen a real taxicab before, and it was astonishing that one was stopping in front of Aunt Matilda's house. It drew the attention of all the other neighbors. They came out of their houses to look.

We wondered what a cab would be doing here when it was most unusual for a cab to be anywhere in that little town. Toby Kelly, whom everybody called Butternut, was the only person who drove as a taxi driver, but he drove his everyday car.

The cab driver stepped out car and looked toward the porch. "Is this where Matilda Rhimes live?"

Aunt Matilda was steadily picking seeds from the cotton, humming a hymn, not even looking up. I stood and said, "Yeah, sir, she do. Here she go right here." I pointed to where she was sitting.

He opened the back door of the cab. A beautiful, brown-skinned, sophisticated, rich-looking woman got out of the backseat. She was wearing a black-and-brown hat with a feather sticking out from the side of it, and a black-and-brown suit like she was dressed for church. She was smiling and her face was glowing. Gold shone from her mouth, bright and sparkling.

The cabdriver took about four suitcases from the car and placed them on the porch. That's what got Aunt Matilda's attention. The woman gave the cabdriver a twenty-dollar bill, said, "I'll see you in two weeks," and winked her eye. He got back into the cab and drove away. She stepped up to the porch slowly. "Is this where Matilda Rhimes lives? Is that her sitting over there?"

I looked from the woman to Aunt Matilda, wondering who the stranger was. It never occurred to me she could be somebody from Aunt Matilda's long-ago past.

Aunt Matilda watched as the woman walked toward where she was sitting. She was half smiling and half confused. The woman said, "Matilda, Matilda," smiling happily.

Aunt Matilda put the cotton bag down and stood up from the chair. She placed her hand across her brow as if she was blocking the sunlight from her eyes, trying to figure out who the woman was. "Who she want, Haley?"

"She want you, Aunt Matilda."

"What she want me fur?"

They stood still as mice, looking at each other. The lady placed her hands in Aunt Matilda's hair, saying, "Beautiful white hair. Much wisdom, much wisdom. It's been so, so long, my sister. So very long." A tear dropped.

She looked over at me, and I said, "If she can't see your mouth movin so she kin read your lips, she can't hear nothin you say to er."

She put her hands on each of Aunt Matilda's shoulders and looked at her straight on. "I know you don't know who I am, but remember your sister Montana? I'm your sister Montana from Chicago, Illinois."

Aunt Matilda looked as if she'd seen the dead raised from the grave. She backed away. "Who she say she is, Haley??

"She said she name Montana, Montana from Chicago," I repeated.

Aunt Matilda placed her hand across her mouth. She grinned and grinned and grinned before she shouted, "Lord have mercy, is this my sister Montana? Naw, you ain't!" She was in a state of shock. I guess she was expecting Montana to still be wearing slave folk clothes, not looking like a rich, dressed-up Northern woman.

"Tell her yes, I am. I am her sister Montana."

They both shed many tears on that spring evening, more tears than I ever saw Aunt Matilda shed. Finally, after huggng and kissing and crying, "Where you been? What made you come here?" they sat in the swing, talking over old times on the Sheffield plantation.

Montana was very proper-speaking. I was most fascinated by the way she talked, never splitting a verb. Her words were as complete as the English book taught us to be. I found myself staring her directly in her mouth. The gold sparkled shiny. I could see myself in it.

Montana caught my attention and asked, "Why are you staring me in my mouth so hard?"

I jumped. Fear swept across my body. I had never reflected I was staring. I knew better than to do that, but I was captivated by her beauty and her speech. I apologized to her several times.

She asked, "Did I frighten you, little girl? Come here and tell me what your name is."

"Haley. My name is Haley Keath."

"That's a pretty name. I heard you call my sister Aunt Matilda. Is she your aunt?"

"Yes, ma'am, she is."

"How'd she become your aunt? Are you my brother's daughter?"

"Naw, ma'am. She my aunt 'cause that's what I always call her—Aunt Matilda."

"So you are not related to her by blood but by name—is that right? Where do you live and whose babies are these?"

"I stay wit Aunt Matilda," I said with pride, "and these my little sisters and brothers. He my sister's baby. She left him wit us. Dat made him my brother. And she my mama's baby. She my real sister."

"I was trying to get your attention for a minute, but you were so busy admiring me or my gold, you didn't hear me." She was smiling as she spoke in that northern accent, and sparkle of the gold in her mouth covered her face. I twisted and turned, playing with my fingernails, not knowing what to say. The joy she had brought into Aunt Matilda's life could never be explained.

I felt a little shy of her. As much as I loved to talk, I was more in tune to listening. But the more she talked to me and the more I listened to her, it became easy to talk to her. She pulled me in by my arm and gave me a big hug. "So you stay with my sister. That's good." She looked at Aunt Matilda and said, "And you got yourself a little bodyguard."

Aunt Matilda was looking and smiling. She hadn't heard a word.

Montana said, "Yeah, that's a good thing. She is up in age. It's a good thing she has somebody smart staying with her. How old are you, Haley Keath?"

"I'm gon be thirteen years old next April."

"That's three weeks away! April is right around the corner, and you almost a teenager."

I was speechless. I didn't know that my birthday had come till Aunt Matilda took the ice cream charm out and sat one of her big chocolate cakes on the table and sang happy birthday to me. I didn't know how to answer her. She said, "Cat got your tongue now, you can't talk?"

"Naw, ma'am! Ain't no cat got my tongue."

"Prove it to me, then."

Mama was coming around the corner. That was my way of escape. "Here come my mama," I said, jumping down from the porch before she could ask me another question. I ran to tell Mama about Aunt Matilda's sister come all the way down from Chicago just to see her. It had been over forty years since they last saw each other.

Mama was shocked. She rushed up to Aunt Matilda's house to get the children. The sisters had taken them inside, and Mama went in to make herself known to them.

The sun was going down. It had a bright rainbow of color around it, something I had never witnessed before. I didn't know what to make of it. All I knew was that it was the most beautiful sun, moving slowly deep in the sky. It was so distant, but it looked like it was in reach. Something beautiful was going to happen.

Montana was the beauty that had happened to me, just showing up at the time she did. She greeted my mama as if she had always known her: "So you are this beautiful angel's mother. I'm Aunt Matilda's youngest sister, Montana. It's a pleasure to meet you."

Mama held her hand out to shake and responded, "My pleasure here." She didn't stay for long. She had to get to the kitchen. "Got to go git supper ready. I'll be back after the family is fed."

Montana looked at Mama as if reading her every thought. "Ms. Jenny Rue, is it? I want to get your name correctly. I can see where this angel of yours gets her consideration and gratitude from—she takes after her mother. I am grateful to you for allowing your soon-to-be teenage daughter to stay away from home and reside with my sister. I will forever be indebted to you."

Mama looked just as I felt—what did "indebted" mean?

Montana would never know how much joy we felt just by her coming to see Aunt Matilda after so many years.

I left with Mama to get the children home. I didn't give Mama time to put me to work; I rushed back to Aunt Matilda's. I didn't want to miss out on anything. Georgie Boy and Snappy were big enough to help out with whatever chores needed to be done.

When I got back to Aunt Matilda's house, she was in the kitchen, preparing supper. I peeped into Montana's room. She was changing into a beautiful purple robe and matching slippers. I thought she had to be rich, coming up here in a cab and wearing those kind of clothes. I'd never seen a black woman dress like that, not even Mrs. Crowley. I was fascinated by Montana; my whole body was drawn to her. I just wanted to sit and listen to her talk.

Before long, the porch was full of Rat Row neighbors nosying into who the mysterious woman was who'd come to see Aunt Matilda. She was excited, knowing that she was oh-so-surrounded by many caring people who really loved her. We were the family that she didn't come with but received once she arrived. It wasn't long before all the neighbors knew Aunt Matilda had a sister visiting her from Chicago.

Around seven o'clock, Aunt Matilda Ann and Uncle Emmet came to see the mother who had left Matilda Ann with Aunt Matilda so many years ago—yes, Montana was Matilda Ann's mother. They did not seem surprised to see each other. I could see there was a strong connection. It turned out that Aunt Matilda Ann had been constantly in contact with Montana; she just never told Aunt Matilda.

At the dinner table, Montana's eyes were all over me. I couldn't understand why she eyeballed me so hard. She was wearing that beautiful purple robe and I couldn't take my eyes off of her. She was like the kind of women we only saw in magazines. When the food was placed on the table, she ordered me to say grace. I knew it was a test to see if I knew grace or if we usually said grace before we ate. Well, she learned we never missed blessing our food before it was placed in our mouths. I said the grace loud and clearly, just as Lijah had taught me—with no shame, but with the anointing that was on my life: "God is great and God is good and we thank Him for this food, and Lord bless the cook. Amen."

She said, "My God, my God, what is this we have here? A wise little preacher. Somebody is teaching her the proper way in life."

I looked at her from the corner of my eye. She was well pleased with me and the help I was to her sister, but she didn't know the blessing her sister had been to me. There was no one like Aunt Matilda, and when the time came, she would know. I knew I had passed Montana's test with flying colors. There was no doubt in my mind.

She continued to look at me, smiling, her gold shining as bright as the lamplight that sat in the center of the table. I couldn't even eat my supper, I was so touched by her. We were two strangers sitting across the dinner table from each other, and the way she kept looking at me was like she was seeing the image of God in me.

That night, after Aunt Matilda and I had our baths, Montana watched our every mood. She came over and we talked. She asked me questions and I asked her questions—and she gave me the answer to every question I asked her. She became a role model in my life.

The next day, she went through my clothes and saw they were mostly handmade. She took me shopping and bought me a two pairs of shoes. I had always wanted a pair of Buster Brown shoes, but we couldn't afford them. The only kid on Rat Row who wore Buster Brown shoes was Sheila, Mrs. Angie Rosa's daughter. Montana told me to pick what I liked. Boy, was I glad I didn't know what to pick. Everything was so beautiful. She said to me softly, "Don't worry about the price. Get what you want."

The first two dresses, I chose. She picked out three for school and two for church. I never had any clothes more beautiful. Store-bought dresses were all new to me. Montana also bought me another pair of church shoes, bows for my hair, socks, and underpanties. I was treated as special by someone who had just come into my life.

Montana was home for over three weeks, and during her visit, she was no stranger. She was certainly a people person. She knew how to treat people. She never looked down on anyone. She even got to know all the drunks who hung around at Daddy's house. She treated them no differently than she did me or Aunt Matilda.

We made good use of the time she spent with us. The memory of her visit lives on inside me. We would sit on the porch at all hours of the night, watching the lightning bugs fly and the bright moonlight shine around us. I would count some of the stars in the sky, and we all would talk. I mostly listened to her and Aunt Matilda reminiscing about the many hardships they endured growing up on the plantation: the work they did without getting paid, the beatings their loved ones took from the evil taskmaster. Talk of their loved ones stirred up many memories that brought tears to their eyes.

Montana apologized to Aunt Matilda for leaving her with Matilda Ann and not returning. It was her son Tubby who was killed by the slave owner because the boy was accused of looking under a white girl's dress, which he didn't. White folk lynched him. He was hung in a tree and shot in his little head. I recalled how at Ms. Bertha's house, she had spoken of Tubby's death with Aunt Matilda. Montana said she was never able to come back to that kind of cruel treatment. But she tried to keep in touch with Sonny and Aunt Matilda Ann. She was sorry for leaving, but she had no regrets about getting out and making a life for herself. She said she had gotten married but had been a widow for twenty years. Her husband had worked on the railroad, and in his passing, he left her a wealthy woman.

The time came for her to return to Chicago. It was a time we all dreaded, but her leaving left me with a bolt of confidence that I could do anything in the world I wanted to do. Her last words to me before the cab arrived were, "Come here, Haley. Let Aunt Montana talk to you before I leave." She smiled as I sat on her knee. Her smiles were incredible.

She took my hand and said, "You are God sent. Has anybody ever told you that before? If not, I'm telling you. God is going to bless you one day for being so good to my sister. She is an old lady, and you are doing the work of the Lord now at your early age. I want you to keep going to school. One day you will graduate and be what you want to.

Stay in church. Continue to read our Bible. God is going to overtake you in blessings. When I get back home, I'm going to send you your school clothes and your church clothes, so you won't have to ever worry about clothes. Good?"

I nodded yes. She accepted that but warned me to speak whenever I was spoken to. "Now I'm going to say good-bye to your mother and thank her for everything she allowed you to do for my sister. I'll see you."

She walked out the door, and in walked Tonk, holding his slingshot in his hand. He and I went outside to play under the tire swing. We heard all the laughing and the loud talking coming down from Mama's house. Montana was saying her good-byes to all the Rat Row friends she had acquainted herself with during her stay. She was encouraging to everyone she came in contact with.

I was about to go see what was happening when Tonk shot me in the arm with his slingshot. Montana was walking up in time to witness it. She was furious at what he'd done. She didn't yell; she didn't show anger. She looked at him and said, "Young man, say you're sorry for shooting a little girl with your slingshot."

Tonk was astonished at Montana. He smiled most of the time, even when he was angry. He smiled now, and she smiled back at him.

From across the street came running his brother Nookie, holding their baby sister in his arms. Montana met him, but she was still looking at Tonk. He hadn't apologized. So she said again mildly, "Say you are sorry for shooting the little girl with your slingshot." She noticed his reaction toward the baby and added, "Is that your little sister?"

He said, "Yes, ma'am, she is."

She advised him about the importance of watching and taking care of your sister and protecting her from bullies. She insisted again that he apologize and do it right then.

In his eyes, I saw that he revived from an evil spirit that had been cast upon him. He was listening to what Montana was saying. He turned and said to me, "Haley, I'm sorry for shooting you wit my slingshot. I won't do it no more."

That seemed to please her. She gave him a handshake, then took the child from his arms and kissed her on her forehead. "That was satisfactory to me. I want you to remember this day for the rest of your life. Now, this little girl is about one or one and a half. When she gets to Haley's age, and you walk up on somebody round your age shooting her with a slingshot, don't you go knocking him upside his head. Remember this day and tell him to apologize to her with meaning." That day, Tonk and I became the best of friends.

Montana left that day too, and the mark she left can never be erased.

In church that Sunday, I wore one of my new dresses. All eyes was fastened on me during the service. The Brimsleys and the Robinson girls sat gazing with contempt and whispering among themselves. I knew it was about me. Every now and then, I looked out of the corner of my eye to see them staring at me and grinning. I grinned back. At one time I thought their grins were genuine.

I was proud of my new clothes like I'd never been proud of anything else. Very seldom could I step out in a new store-bought dress, and they wore new dresses when I couldn't. I had always said softly to myself, "One of these days, I'mo have me er new dress."

I recalled a Sunday when Arline and Della came in and they both had new dresses on. They sat beside me, gloating. I only looked at them and told them nicely, "Della and Arline, them pretty dresses." They each smiled and said thank you. I had been glad to see them in their dresses—why couldn't they be happy for me instead of being mad at me? I deserved to wear new clothes every once in a while.

I didn't know what the word *jealousy* was or how it affected a person. I was always complimenting. It was something I loved to do to make others feel good. Yet I was made to feel bad, so much that I hardly knew what it was to feel good.

That day I was really feeling good about myself. When church was out, I wanted so much to play with them. But the jealousy overpowered them. They stood at the side of the church, giggling and whispering just as they had done in church. I walked away and heard Arline say, "She ain't use to nothing. Look at er, like she ain't neber had no new clothes fore." She was always the aggressive one of Ms. Bonnie's girls, as Jonkey was of the boys. However, they still were our friends.

Della and Arline were the ones making it impossible for anyone to get along with them. They were nothing like the Kingsleys, Bendersons, or Bakers. In their own little, awful, mischievous ways, they could be tolerated. But that Sunday I was angry with them. They had no right, I thought, making fun at me when I had always been nothing but friendly to them.

I heard Montana's voice ringing in my ears, saying, "Stay focused on the good things in life. Stay in church. Read your Bible. Do good to others."

Those words convinced me not to pay those girls any attention, but it was so hard to do—just like it was hard to understand why I encountered so much pain. Pain was never far behind me. There was always something there to increase it. Pain pressed to overtake me.

Blue Monday was the day nobody went to work. They all gathered around Mama's house and juked like it was a Saturday night. Even Mama slacked off of her job on Monday. I didn't think it was too bad; at least I got to go to school.

I came home from a trying day at school, an unjust day of cruelty. Because of it, at lunchtime I had gone over to the other side of the playground and sat in the grass and watched all the other children play: swinging on the swings, climbing up and down the jungle gyms, and riding on the swirl wheel.

I was thinking of my cruel day when I spotted the porch full of drunks. I came through on the side of Pa Jack's café, and it was on the corner, so they hardly noticed me. I went through the backyard of Mama's house and on down to Aunt Matilda's, where I entered through the back door.

Once I let her know I was home, I changed my clothes and went into the room where Aunt Montana had slept while she was there. I sat in the corner, thinking out loud. I saw a sheet of paper on top of the pillow. I went over, picked it up, and began to read.

Dear Haley,

By the time you read this, I will already be back in Chicago. I was so glad to have gotten the opportunity to get to know you. You brought lots of joy into my life, just as you did for my sister the day she met you. I know you will, but I have the urge to say please continue to take care of my sister for me.

Next summer, I'm going to send for you and Aunt Matilda to come to Chicago and visit with me. Would you like that? I know you will. This is something you can look forward to: your first plane ride. I'm looking forward to it myself.

You and your family are the only family Aunt Matilda has, and I do appreciate it very much. Keep the good work up. And you will be rewarded. Next week I'm going to send you a big box of clothes, so any day after that, you may look out for them.

Give your mother my love, and tell my sister I love her very much. I love you very much. I will always carry a special feeling in my heart for you and your mama.

Good-bye,
Montana Missouri-Blackburn

I read that letter many times. Each time I read it, tears welled up in my eyes.

A few weeks later, I came home from school and there was a big box waiting for me. It was full of beautiful dresses, shoes, slips, training bras, skirts, and blouses. I had enough clothes to change my outfits and not be made fun of again. She included a nice winter coat with fur around the collar and cuffs.

As I unpacked the clothes, Aunt Matilda and I were so happy. I was glad to get those clothes. I looked at it as one of God's greatest blessings. He had somebody come all the way from Chicago, Illinois, to be a blessing to me. Nobody in school had clothes like mine. I couldn't stop laughing. I laughed like never before. I was one joyful little girl, and I was not about to let anybody take my joy away.

Two weeks went by, and another box came, mostly slacks and sweaters and all kinds of blouses. It was a miracle.

Montana wrote to me and Aunt Matilda every week. The last letter we received was all about our coming to visit her in the summer.

Then sadness struck hard, like it was too good to be true. Instead of the mailman leaving a letter, a red pickup truck pulled up in front of the door. The man Aunt Matilda always bought her chicks from got out of the truck, holding a yellow envelope in his hand. It was a telegram. I was on the tire swing, and he asked, "Is Matilda home, Haley?"

"Yes, sir," I answered. I went in the backyard and got her. She came around front, and he gave the envelope to her.

She gave it to me and said, "Open it and tell me what it say."

I slowly unfolded the paper. The message was a line and a half long. I read it to her as she looked solemnly into my mouth. The little chicken man stood at the end of the porch, watching resolutely.

I read out loud exactly the words that were printed on the paper: "I'm very sorry to inform you that your sister Montana Missouri-Blackburn passed two days ago in her home. She had a massive heart attack."

My heart speeded up till it was racing, and I couldn't stop it. I looked at poor Aunt Matilda. She didn't speak. A million thoughts spun around in my head. Montana's death came as such a shock, and the saddest thing of all was we couldn't go to her funeral and pay our final respects. It was more pain I had to encounter, bless God, and that was some pain to experience.

Aunt Matilda didn't say anything on the subject. She kept busy. She didn't seem to mourn. But suddenly she did a few days later. She cried day and night, calling out Montana's name and saying, "I'll be wit er one of these days soon."

She had been keeping that telegraph in her apron pocket. On the last day of her mourning, she took it out and placed it on her mantelpiece. That night, we were on our knees, praying. During all the years I'd known her, I had never heard what her words were in prayer. But that night, she said softly, "Lord, have mercy on my poor sister's soul. You answered my prayer after forty years when you brought er here to see me and to stay wit me for them three weeks. Lord, I do thank you for seein my sister one last time."

I never heard her mention her sister Montana again as long as I was with her. For her, it was over. But for me, the memory of Montana had just begun. I thought of her every day. When I put on an outfit she had sent me, it was like she was always with me.

Chapter 8: More Anguish Burns Inside

The month of November was cold in Georgia. It was the kind of cold that when it hit your body, it would cut. The wind would be so high, it would blow the tin tops off the houses.

This particular cold winter morning, I was up at seven. I went to Mama's house for Georgie and Snappy, to see if they were going to school or staying at home due to the weather. The wind was high, blowing so hard that it was almost impossible to walk to school without being blown away.

Inside Mama's house, the flames in the fire were swirling. Sparks flickered all around. I heard yelling coming from Mama's bedroom. She was telling Georgie Boy to go down to Aunt Matilda's house and get me to look after the young'uns while she got her wash started. I knew there was no school for me that day. The tears dropped down my cheeks.

I tried to stop them because I knew if Georgie Boy saw me crying, he'd poke fun at me. I could just hear him saying, "Gurl, you all the time crying cause you can't go to that old school." He didn't like school. If he'd had anything to say about it, he would never go. He had that attitude because there was no one to motivate him or encourage him. There was no father figure at all. Every chance I got, I told him what I learned from others and how much we needed to get an education.

But he was as stubborn as a mule. He wouldn't listen to anything about school. He took it as a joke because I was so adamant about going school. It was my major concern.

I went into the room where Mama was to let her know I was there. She was sorting out dirty clothes. I didn't have to say anything. She looked up, and for a second I thought she was going to tell me I could go on to school. Instead she yelled, "You may as well go on back an git outter dem dere clothes. You ain't goin no school today. You got to stay an help watch dese here chilluns. Do y'all spect me to do everything by myself?"

I so wanted to tell my mama that they were her children, not mine. But I knew if I did, I would get my face slapped.

I slowly walked out the back door in all that harsh, cold weather and went back down to Aunt Matilda's. She was watering baby chicks by the fire, keeping them warm. Otherwise they would have frozen to death in all that cold. She had quilts over the hens and roosters, and lanterns sitting around the coop so they could keep warm.

When she looked up and saw me, she knew I was not going to school. She was always able to tell when I was in pain by my eyes, and I could look into her and see the pain she was feeling for me. She put her arms around me and kissed me on my forehead.

I went into the next room and changed out of my school clothes into a pair of overalls and a plaid flannel shirt. I grabbed my old, faded car coat and marched on back to Mama's. She was feeding the children. I went into the bedroom to make the beds.

A feeling of hatred penetrated my heart—or what I thought was hatred for my mother for not allowing me to go to school. I asked myself the same questions over and over. Why was I the one who had to miss school all the time and watch the children? Why couldn't I go to school like other folks' children? I said out loud, "Them her chilluns. They ain't none of mine."

The moment I said it, baby Willa Max came crawling up to me. She reached for me to pick her up. She had just about worn my right hip out from carrying her around on it. Sometimes I would have her on one hip and Billy on the other, trying to give them the love that no real parents were around to give them. I tried to make myself understand that it had to be me because there was nobody else old enough to do it. I accepted I had to be the one to get the worst treatment of them all.

Mama came in the room and handed me a sheet. It was ripped in several places. She gave me a needle and thread and said, "Take this here sheet and sew it up and put it on Snappy, Georgie Boy, and Billy's bed." Then she rushed back out to the yard.

I sat for a minute on the side of the bed, and I cried painful tears. Finally I got up enough strength to thread the needle. I sewed that sheet up just as she would have. As I was putting it on the bed, she took Georgie Boy outside with her to tend the wood around the washpot.

I had made one bed and was making the other. I had placed Willa Max and Billy in the middle of the bed that was already made up. Snappy was sitting in front of the fire. When I turned my back, she got out of the chair and stepped up to the fire like a grown-up would, warming her back. I had warned her many times about getting too close to the fire, but she was the flip-mouthed one, as hard-headed as they come. She didn't want to listen to anything I had to say.

I had put the second quilt on the bed and was about to put the spread on when I noticed she was too close to that fire. I yelled, "Snappy, you better come over here and sit your fast self down in this chair. Quit fancing round that fire wit your bald-head self fore you fall in it."

Her words back to me were "I ain't studdin you. You don't tell me what to do, cause you ain't none of my mama now."

I put the spread down and walked over to where she was standing. Slap! I struck her across her head lightly and repeated, "Snappy, stop fancing by that fire wit yore hard-headed selb. you keep on, you gon git burned."

She started screaming like I had killed her. She had a voice on her that when she screamed out, it was like a death scream. Mama came running in the room, asking, "What is wrong wit dat gal? Haley, what you did to er?"

Before I could answer, Snappy cut the scream off instantly and lied, "Haley beat me in my head wit er fist."

Mama believed Snappy. I didn't get a chance to tell her of the danger Snappy was placing herself in, the risk she was taking. Mama jumped to her own conclusion and made me out to be the bad one. And I never tried to defend myself to her.

"What you beatin on dat gal for, Haley?" She slapped me upside my head as she spoke. "Now, you mad cause you had to stay home outer school, an you takin it out on dis here gurl. You better not put your hands on er no damn more, and I mean it. I'mo git me a limb and tie your ass up if I have to come back in here one more time." She turned and walked out the back door.

I didn't cry. I didn't even whimper. I went back to making up the bed. I didn't pay Snappy any attention. She crossed from one side of the fireplace to the other, back and forth, and I saw with my eyes and my heart. I could just feel that if she didn't stop, she was going to get burned or something else unpleasant was going to take place. It may have been a premonition I was having, but my vibes were not good where she was concerned. Finally I yelled again, "Snappy, why don't you quit fancing cross dat dere fireplace fore you fall in it?"

I was looking directly at her as she made a fast step closer to the fire. Suddenly, it happened: the tail of her dress caught fire. I was already in fear for her, and looking at her dress burning, my fear doubled. She took off running toward the back door. I started yelling, "Mama, Mama, Snappy on fire! Mama, Snappy on fire!"

Just as the blaze fanned into big flames across Snappy's back, Mama caught her. I watched in horror as Mama dragged her down with her bare hands, smothering the fire. She burned her hands so badly, I could see the skin hanging from them. Snappy was burned on her upper back and her left arm. I could see pink, and her skin was just hanging off too. What an awful sight for a twelve-year-old to have to encounter. I really grew up that day, and fast.

Though my mama's hands were burned almost as bad as Snappy's back and arm were, Mama had no concern for herself. It was all for her little six-year-old girl. She picked Snappy up from the floor.

I clung to the two smaller children, Willa Max and Billy, almost too frightened to move. They didn't know what was going on. I rested their faces on each of my shoulders to prevent them from seeing that painful vision.

Snappy was screaming to the top of her voice in severe pain. The burns that Mama sustained were bad, but nothing compared to what my little sister sustained. Mama had saved her child despite the pain. Her braveness showed me who she was that morning.

I watched as Mama laid Snappy on her stomach in the bed that I had just made up. She told me to take the children into the next room.

By then the house was filled with neighbors. It didn't take long for bad news to spread. Folk came all the way from Brake's quarter, and the majority of the neighbors were caring. Snappy's screams of pain were incomprehensible.

I put the little ones down and stood in the doorway, watching as all the neighbors gathered around the bedside, praying and showing their support. I commenced to relive the last words I had spoken to Snappy before she was burned: "Snappy, why don't you quit fancing cross dat dere fireplace fore you fall in it?" They rang in my ears as if I were psychic. I had just known it was bound to happen. I felt awfully bad for her and thought that I should have been more persistent or more demanding. Then maybe she wouldn't have been lying there with her skin peeling from her body like that.

Mama yelled, "Go quickly, Haley, to Angie Rosa and tell her to got git Mr. Tommy B. Hooker to come and talk the fire out of my baby." She was crying sorrowfully.

I grabbed my car coat from off the nail that hung beside the bed and put it on. I struck out running as fast as I could. I called out as I reached her yard, "Mrs. Angie Rosa! Mama said come! Hurry! Snappy got burn. Snappy got burn bad. She want you to git Mr. Tommy B. Hooker to come an talk the fire out ob er."

She pushed open the screen door. "What dat you say, Haley? Snappy got burn? Where bout she got burn at? Come on in here out dis cold, child. Poor Jenny Rue. She must be going crazy. She have such a hard time. If it ain't one thing, it's nother." Taking me by my hand, she pulled me on into Sheila's room, where she and Mr. Campbell sat calmly, watching a western. "Come on, baby, an warm your hands. Dey just like ice." She put her coat and hood on.

I looked around the big, nice room. It had a high ceiling, and the bed was high too. It looked like it had four or five mattresses on it; they needed a ladder to climb up in it.

"Come on, Sheila. Git your coat and boots. Let's go an see bout gittin some help for Jenny Rue's little gurl. She got burn. I got to go up to Korea and git Mr. Tommy B to come talk de fire out er, poor little thing. Lord help dat child." Mrs. Angie Rosa pushed some kind of funny-looking red bag into her bosom. Her house had some kind of odor that I had never smelled anywhere.

I was anxious to get back home. I knew my mama needed me.

We crawled into her shining black Chevrolet, and she pushed the button to get the car started. She said, "Lord, I sure hope we kin find him. It's a good thing it's through the week, cause if it was on Saturday, we'd never find his drunken ass. He'd be laid out somewhere in er ditch, drunk as a skunk."

Sheila and and I sat in the backseat. She had her doll. I couldn't help but envy her. It wasn't the kind of envy that I hated her or anything; it was the kind that I wished to be in her shoes. She had caring parents who loved her so much that they gave her any and everything she wanted. That's what made her so special.

She reached over and gave me a big hug and a kiss. She handed me her name-brand doll, saying, "Here, Haley, you kin play wit er if you want to." That was the closest I ever came to a doll such as that. She was a caring little girl, and she didn't mind sharing.

I wasn't focusing on the doll. My mind was only on my little sister. I held the doll for a few minutes and gave it back. Sheila sat quietly, sucking on her thumb and holding her doll close to her heart.

We arrived in the little Korea town outside the city. Mrs. Angie Rosa drove up in front of a small white house trimmed in black, with a black-and-white picket fence around it. She parked and told us to stay in the car. She got out, went up to the porch, and knocked on the door. A heavyset, light-skinned woman with curly white hair opened the door.

I recognized her as one of the ladies who came through the neighborhood some days through the week during the summer. With another woman who looked just like her, she sold greens, peas, okra, and other green vegetables. She was as fat as Mrs. Angie Rosa; they both weighed around three hundred pounds.

They greeted each other politely, and the woman invited Mrs. Angie Rosa to come inside out the cold. But Mrs. Angie Rosa declined and got directly to the point. "I come up here to git Mr. Tommy B to come an see bout Jenny Rue's little gurl. She got burn pretty bad and we need Tommy B to come an talk the fire out for er. Is he here, Ms. Fanny?"

"Naw, Angie Rosa, he ain't here, and I can't tell you when he'll be back. But when he do, I'll be sure an tell em."

They shook hands, and Mrs. Angie Rosa drove us back into town. The moment she pulled up in front of Mama's house, we could hear Snappy screaming at the top of her voice. Mrs. Angie Rosa went straight to Mama and informed her of what Ms. Fanny said.

She took one look at Snappy and begged Mama to let her take the child up to the hospital. But all Mama could think of was there was no money. Everyone in the house tried to convince her the child was burned too badly and needed medical treatment. Out of ignorance, Mama really believed that an old recipe was the solution to the problem, and no one was able to convince her otherwise.

Aunt Matilda and Ms. Geraldine were at the head of the bed with cold water, wiping away the burned skin from Snappy's body. Others were praying and calling on the Lord. Mrs. Angie Rosa stated, "I know the Lord is good and everything, but he put doctors here for such things as this, Jenny Rue. Dem dere white folk ain't gon turn you round wit your baby when dey see what kind of condition this gal is in. Stop being so hard-headed and let me take her to the hospital."

Mama wouldn't. She was set in her head that they wouldn't see about her child. It was at that day and hour I learned my mama didn't have faith in God. One of the ladies from the church said, "The Good Book says believe on the Lord Jesus Christ and thou shall be saved," but nothing anyone said convinced Mama. She still doubted while all of us suffered.

Sheila and I went into the other room where the children sat, frightened out of our minds, listening to the horrific screams that echoed across the room. Georgie Boy was holding Billy in his arms. Willa Max sat in the middle of the bed, looking scared as a mouse, not knowing what was going on around her. When she saw me, she was overwhelmed with joy. I picked her up and held her in my arms as if I were her mama. Sheila took her from me and played with her so gently, I was amazed. The love she showed the children and how right at home she felt allowed her to fit in with us like she was one of us. Sheila became our friend.

Voices were coming from all directions. Folk were outside, finishing up Mama's washing. Some were in the kitchen, cooking up batches of food. Folk were coming and going. Later that evening, folk had to go see about their own homes and prepare dinner for their families. I put the two little ones down for a nap and went into the room where Snappy lay crying. Aunt Matilda was kneeling beside the bed, praying over her burned body. Mama sat on the bed next to Snappy, crying. I didn't know if she was crying from guilt, from not taking her to get hospital treatment, or what, but she was crying like I'd never seen her cry before. Aunt Lucy Sue and Aunt Frankie came in and comforted Mama in every way they could.

Other neighbors gathered in a circle, holding hands and praying for Snappy's recovery. The harsh, cold wind whispered through every crack in that old house. Somebody put blue stuff on Snappy's burn wounds. I couldn't imagine what it was, but it had to be something that would help the burns. The wounds were deep. Word was, the ointment was to help restore her skin back to its normal color.

The house emptied except for the family and close neighbors. Cousin Sattie Bell talked to Mama, comforting her. She told Mama her little girl was going to be all right, because if it had been the good Lord's will for Snappy to die, he would have let her get burned up. But he hadn't. He had put little Haley in the room.

Mama said, "Lord, Sattie Bell, I done had one child git burned to death, and I'll die, I couldn't bear to have dis happen ergin."

Everybody in the house seemed to be crying. I wondered who the other child was that Mama had seen get burned to death. She said it was a child that had been born after Passy Kate and before Tise. Her name was Assie Mae. She was five years old when one day Mama was washing in the backyard. It had been a cold, windy day like today. Assie Mae found a candle, took it under the house, and lit it. Her dress tail caught fire, and before she could get to Mama to put her out, Assie Mae was burned beyond saving and died in Mama's arms.

There was one painful experience after another. Why did so many awful things just keep happening to our family? Aunt Matilda said it was because Daddy was so wicked and did so many bad things.

Daddy, Mr. Danny, and Uncle Cleo came in from a long day in the country. They all had been drinking, especially Uncle Cleo. It was never hard to tell if he had been drinking, because he giggled nonstop. Daddy talked a lot and started singing, and Mr. Danny just smiled. They didn't know Snappy had gotten burned. Once they learned of her condition, they all sobered up instantaneously.

Daddy bent over the bed where she lay. He didn't speak; he just stared down at her badly burned body. Once again I saw a caring man hurting over the pain of his little girl. After looking down at her for a long time, he walked over to where Mama was sitting and asked, "How did she git burned like that? Where were you?" I heard the blame.

Mama tried to explain, but her voice was in such a tremor and she was in so much pain herself, she could barely speak. He looked at Mama, as helpless as she was, and they were both too weak-minded to get their child medical help.

Mrs. Angie Rosa had left—nobody even remembered when—and returned with a jar of some kind of home remedy. She gave it to Mama and told her to give it to Snappy to drink. It would help ease some of the pain she was in. It would help her go to sleep for a while.

Mama accepted it without any hesitation. At that time, she would have tried just about anything to guarantee Snappy just a little relaxation—except get her to the hospital.

Uncle Cleo took me by my hand and led me into the other room. He said, "You don't need to be here wit all them grown folk. Come on ober here wit your uncle." He asked me if I knew what had happened to my sister. I told him every detail. The fire was burning nicely and it was warm in the house. Uncle Billy Roliver, along with Uncle Martel, steadily brought more wood for the fire.

I usually loved to talk to Uncle Cleo, but that day I didn't want to smell the whiskey scent on him. After I told him what happened to Snappy, he insisted on filling me in on the other sister Mama had lost to fire. He described her as the most beautiful child Mama had. He said she was so pretty, white folk would stop and compliment Mama on how beautiful she was. And he said she was as smart as she was pretty. Folk predicted she couldn't live on this earth because she was above what a normal human being was capable of being. He said she had thick, long, silky black hair that hung all the way down her back. She was the only black child who looked like her. She was loved by everybody she came in contact with, and when she smiled, her whole face lit up like a Christmas tree.

He said, "She had plenty sense, Haley, just like you. You even talk like she did. For some unknown reason, she couldn't stay on this earth. She was an angel sent from God to bring peace and happiness among mankind for a little while. Then God took her back in the year of nineteen hundred and forty-three, before you was born." He confirmed the details of her death that I had already heard.

Looking into the fire as the oak wood was burning, I could almost picture the death of my deceased sister. If it was anything as bad as what I encountered watching Snappy, what must it have been like for Mama? She'd had a child burn to death and now another one was lying burned near death. What must she be going through?

I asked Uncle Cleo, "Do you think Snappy gon die like Assie Mae?"

"Naw, I don't think Snappy gon die, cause the good Lord had you in the room wit er to save er life," he answered very convincingly. I thought I was hearing something from a storybook, but I acknowledged hurriedly that it was not a story; it was fact, the natural truth.

Aunt Lucy Sue called his name. I was kinda glad to get a break from him and the smell of that stinking moonshine. But when he got up, I felt cold chills run up and down my body. Sitting alone in the room suddenly made me feel uncomfortable. Maybe it was the stillness. Snappy had stopped screaming. The medicine Mrs. Angie Rosa had given to Mama for her must have helped, because I hadn't heard her scream in a while. But I couldn't shake that frightened feeling inside me.

Aunt Matilda came in and lit the lamp. As she set it on the mantelpiece, I could see that there was something different about the flame of the wick. It started to puff on and off, like it wanted to go out. Or like somebody was trying to put it out.

Aunt Matilda turned around and said, "Stop tryin to put de lamp out, Haley."

I said sincerely, "I ain't doin dat."

At that instant, the wick went out and she started. "See? I told you not to put dat lamp out. What you did it fur?"

Defensively I said, "I didn't do it."

"Don't lie to me. Who else done it?"

I tried to look into her eyes and watch her mouth move as she spoke to me, so I could tell what she was really feeling. She was about to light the lamp for the second time. She was not angry but a little disgusted.

Then the lamp gave two big blinks and went completely out again. At the same time, a door slammed shut without anyone touching it. Aunt Matilda said, "It just the wind that make the lamp keep going out," but there was no sound of wind coming through the room.

Suddenly there were strange sounds coming from the kitchen. Then they stopped. Aunt Matilda was unable to hear the sounds that I heard. The lamp went out for a third time. She lit it again and the light shone as bright as the flames from the fire. Everything was normal again.

My mind drifted to my deceased sister whom I never knew. I felt she was giving us a sign that Snappy was going to be fine. I did then and have always since believed it was her spirit.

Sometime later, I had the urge to get a drink from the water bucket in the kitchen. I went on over and tiptoed into the room. Snappy was lying naked in the bed, facedown and sound asleep.

Sitting in the chair across from Snappy's bed, Mrs. Angie Rosa was sound asleep, and Mama lay across the bed, sound asleep also.

My mind began to play tricks on me about the medicine Mrs. Angie Rosa had given to Mama for Snappy. I recalled the time she had come in with a large plate of potato salad, greens, and fried chicken and fed it to Mama shortly after she gave birth to Snappy. Mama had been poisoned. Negative thoughts sent my mind on a roller coaster spin, remembering all the horrible things I had seen done to my mama. I didn't think about the good deed Mrs. Angie Rosa had done by going up to Korea to try and find Mr. Tommy B. Hooker. That didn't faze me. I wanted some way to give Mrs. Angie Rosa a dose of her own medicine.

I didn't have but a little time to come up with a way to get back at Mrs. Angie Rosa, so I had to come up with something quick. She had been there when Mama needed her, but she had also tried to get rid of Mama through roots and voodoo. I thought that might be the reason why so much tragedy keep sweeping over Mama.

I couldn't distract the agony I felt. Mrs. Angie Rosa had her shoes off, her head tilted back, and her mouth wide open. She was snoring so loud, she could have waked the dead. I watched her sleep and snore, and I remembered the day Aunt Frankie, Daddy, and Uncle Willie came home with Mama from the treatment house.

Mrs. Angie Rosa came in the house, pretending to care so much about Mama and her well-being. Aunt Frankie got her shotgun and pointed it at Mrs. Angie Rosa and said, "If you don't git back in you damn car and git erway from here, lady, after what you done did, I'll blow you head slap off."

The words sang out in my ears. I wanted her to hurt as she'd hurt my mama. I looked at the fire burning fast and popping. The thought occurred to me put a hot coal on her feet and let her feel some pain too.

I got the small hanger and put it at the edge of the fire to get red hot. Then I crawled under the bed without being seen. I quickly put the hanger against her feet, then dropped it at the edge of the fire and scooted back under the bed. "Ohoooo, my foot!" she screamed.

Uncle Cleo was the first to get to her. A long burn spot was across her big foot. He asked her worriedly, "How in God's name you manage to burn your foot, Angie Rosa?"

"I must have put my foot too close to dat fire and hit dat hanger," she stated. Everyone raced to her rescue and helped doctor her foot, wrapping it up with gauze.

I didn't feel any remorse, even though she was helping Mama with my sister. Snappy still lay sleeping with second- and third-degree burns over her body. Who was to say Mrs. Angie Rosa didn't have an ulterior motive? No one could see me under the bed, but I could see everyone and everything.

"Angie Rosa, you gon be all right?" Mama asked. "What did you do, git your foot too close to the fire?"

"Yeah, I guess that's what I musta done. Damn, it hurt. I kin just magine what dat poor child must be feeling."

I lay still under the bed, wondering if the pain she was feeling was half as bad as the pain Mama must have felt for all those months. The burn was enough to show her what real pain felt like. Nothing ever seemed to happen to her or her family, always ours.

Out of the clear, I began to feel guilty. It didn't take long for me to regret what I'd done to her. But there was no way it could be traced back to me.

I wanted to come from under the bed, but the room was crowded and voices were echoing all around me. Uncle Cleo steadily put more wood on the fire every time it started to get low, making the room good and hot. It wasn't long before Snappy woke up, crying out. The pain was starting up again. Mrs. Angie Rosa told Mama to keep giving her the medicine she had got from up at Dr. Merrick's. It would keep her sleeping and help control her pain.

I lay still without being noticed. I started sweating from the fire heat, and that made me very uncomfortable and thirsty. The way still wasn't clear enough for me to come out. I put my thoughts together and came up with a solution: I would crawl out from under the bed on the right side, slowly and quietly, since everybody was focusing on Mrs. Angie Rosa.

Praying that I met nobody coming into the room, I crawled out from under the bed and made it out of the room in the length of time it took for Aunt Matilda to come calling me. It was time that we left for home; there was nothing else for us to do there. She promised Mama that she would be back early the next morning. She asked me, "Where you been, Haley?"

I didn't want her to talk loudly because I didn't know what she knew. I was extremely cautious of how to answer her. For a second, I refused to.

"You hear me talking to you, gal? I looked all ober in the other room an you wasn't dere. An I looked in here an you wasn't in here either."

I took her by her hand and pulled her on out. When I was out far enough not to be heard by the others, I just said, "Yes, I was in the room, watching Snappy sleeping."

Aunt Matilda looked me up and down. She knew I was trying to hide something, but I was not lying. Still, nobody else had seen me in the room; therefore I would have to explain where in the room I had been, unless I had become invisible. I gave her one of my tell-the-truth tales, but it didn't go well with her. She knew me. She said, not grinning, "Haley, you done somenother you ain't got no business."

I steadily shook my head, meaning nothing. I stretched my lids and rolled my eyes like I had something in them.

She said, "If you lying to me, the good Lord knows what you done, and he gon punish you if it's some bad."

That frightened me more than anything. If Aunt Matilda had ever done anything, she had certainly instilled fear of the Lord in me. It always seemed that she could see right through me, whether I was right or wrong, lied or told the truth. I would always get by with it until she mentioned God or the Lord.

I wouldn't get in bed that night. Normally I got in bed before her, but she didn't get in bed and neither did I. I sat beside her with a tight grip on her apron. If she'd tried to get loose, it would have came off in my hand. "What you holdin on to my apron fur? Now I know for sure you done done sumnutter you ain't had no business, and now you scare, ain't you?"

I was looking and stretching my eyes, knowing fully well she was correct.

"Go on to bed wit it on your conscience," she told me, "and just see don't God punish you fur it fore mornin." She made it so plain to me, I could feel God punishing me before it happened.

I shouted out in a panic, "I burn Mrs. Angie Rosa on er foot wit a hot hanger!"

I realized Aunt Matilda didn't completely understand what I had said, but I also knew she knew what I'd said wasn't anything nice. "Tell me what you say," she demanded.

I batted my eyes at her and took a deep breath and repeated what I'd said.

Her mouth flew open. She stared me down, speechless. Then she shook her head and said, "You better be glad you mama ain't in dis here room right now."

I was worried Aunt Matilda was going to tell Mama. She'd never told anything on me before, but then I'd never done anything so hideous before either.

"Go on to bed. You didn't mean to do it." She believed that I didn't—or she was just making excuses for me. I knew if Mama found out in any kind of way that I'd burned Mrs. Angie Rosa, my poor behind would be skinned. I begged Aunt Matilda not to tell Mama on me. I think I cried myself off to sleep, pleading with her not to tell, promising I would never do anything like that again.

Early the following morning, I woke to the smell of her fried meat and brewing hot coffee. My stomach was crying for some of those good tea cakes, hot biscuits, and grits to jump into it. Aunt Matilda was sort of quiet, making my plate and humming. Every now and then, I would get a glimpse of her talking softly to herself. I wondered what she was saying to the Lord. Was she speaking on my behalf? As soon as I ate, I dressed, and off I ran.

At Mama's house, folk had already gathered around Snappy's bedside. I wasn't sure what was happening, but something was. I moped around the other room with the rest of the children and heard the rest of the neighborhood children passing by, going off to school. I wasn't allowed to go. It saddened me. I desired to go to school and was torn between that and helping out with the children at home. I questioned myself about what was the right thing to do. I sat in front of the oak fire with my head down between my knees and wondered what it would be like to just take off and run away from all of the problems and the pain that surrounded me. I even said it to myself: "One of the days when I git bigger, I'm gon run erway from here and I ain't never coming back." I was speaking out of anger, but in my heart I meant every word of it.

Georgie Boy came into the room with his thumb in his mouth and spit running down the side of his hand, rejoicing that he was not going to school. I was in pain. I knew he didn't like school, and I knew he would never graduate, but I never knew why he hated school so badly.

It would be only a matter of time until the opportunity presented itself and he would drop out in a heartbeat. Not me. My entire future was based upon graduating from high school one day.

I could still hear Mrs. Crowley saying, "Stay in school and graduate, and one day you can be anything you want to be"

Now Georgie Boy was yelling, "Goody, goody, we ain't going no school! Mama said!"

I wanted to hit him hard. "I heard what Mama said, boy. I hope you be satisfied we ain;t going. You gon be dumb all your life."

"Yeah? I'm glad. I don't wanter go no school."

We argued back and forth until he told me I was going to be dumb too. It was as if something had been injected into my stomach. I went wild. I jumped up out of my chair and rapped him across his face, saying as harshly as I could, "Don't you never tell me I'm gon be dumb. You don't know what you talkin bout. I bet you I'm gon be smart just like Mrs. Crowley, an if you tell me dat again, I'll knock you over in dat fire."

I rushed outside in the cold and huddled beside the hot chimmey corner. I always found consolation there, watching the children trot up Rat Row to school. I wanted to go so badly.

When I thought all the children from our end had gone by, I squatted down in my old car coat, warming from the heat of the chimmey, with millions of things flashing across my mind. I saw Tonk and Nookie on their way to school—they were always late—and I tried to push closer in the corner so I wouldn't be seen. But they spotted me and came running over. They tried to persuade me to go to school. I told them my hair wasn't combed, covering my face from shame but not able to hide the pain. I was crying, and the tears were coming through my fingers.

Tonk put his arms around me and told me to come on and go. He said I looked fine. He was convincing; everything he said was so realistic and tempting.

I couldn't think about it long. I had to make a rash decision. I had on no socks, and my pants were high above my ankles because they were just play clothes. I guess that was a day of humiliation to match the pain: I let them talk me into going to school. I figured with all the attention focused on Snappy, I wouldn't be missed.

We took off running, going through Cousin Big C Lottie's backyard and down by the pond, taking back roads and shortcuts. We ran like a pack of wild rabbits until we were beyond the sawmill.

When we got to Tonk's cousins, Lorthy Kingsley's house, everybody there was fast asleep. I was shivering so hard, my teeth were knocking together. Her children were all snuggled up in the bed with rags stacked on top of them, trying to keep warm.

Tonk found a comb and began to comb my hair. It was nappy, and the comb broke. He took a shoestring and made me a nappy ponytail. He was familiar with the house, so he went in another room and came back with two pieces of cloth. He ripped them apart and told me to wrap my hands up in them so they could help keep me from freezing. He took his mismatched socks off his feet and gave them to me to put on. Then off we went running again. I ran so hard, I had to stop to catch my breath. The wind was blowing directly in our faces. Tonk cried, "Come on, Haley, you got to keep running! Ain't no time to stop now. We got to git to school before they lock up the doors."

He took me by one hand and Nookie by the other and we ran, arriving at school just in time. The janitor was about to lock up the doors. "Wait, Mrs. Bediford! Let us in, please," Tonk called out. She opened the door for us, even though it was against school policy.

I was glad to be inside that big, warm building. Once I got my breath, it hit me: I hadn't been to school in a while. My first thought was to thank God. I was shivering, but not from the cold. It was from nervousness.

Tonk and Nookie walked me down to my classroom. The students were already in and seated. Tonk was always brave, while Nookie was quiet and shy. Tonk said, "Go on in your room, Haley. What you scare of? You done come all dis way in all dis cold to git here, and then you git cold feet. Gurl, you crazy." He jerked my arm. "Git on in dere! I got to git to my class!"

I stood helpless, not knowing what to do. I seemed to have frozen with fear. I felt more shane than anything.

Tonk opened the door and gave me a slight push. I had no choice.

Devotion had just begun. The class was singing, "Jesus, Keep Me

Near the Cross." In those days, it was no problem to use the name of Jesus in schools. I went on into the classroom and all eyes turned on me. I went directly to the back of the room. I could hear some of the students whispering about the clothes I was wearing. Marie Lee told her cousin Doletha, "Haley Keath got on them high-water britches."

The class laughed out loud. One of the other students said, "Her mama sure need to comb er hair." I got an ear full I knew I was going to be the joke of the day. The teacher, Mrs. Caine, said, "Class, let's finish our devotion now. It's getting a little too noisy in here." It was hard for the class to concentrate with me being the center of their attention.

Skitter came over by me and placed her arm around my shoulder, smiling. She was the only one in the whole class who was glad to see me. When the Lord's Prayer was being recited, my voice rang out clearly along with the rest of the class, just like I'd been there every day.

The roll was called. When Mrs. Caine called out each name, the student said, "Present." She got to my name, and I couldn't stop shivering. She called it out and I was too ashamed to say anything. I stuck my finger up. She said, "Keath, you've only been to school six days out of the last three months. Why did you miss so many days out of school?"

I answered in a trembling voice, "Cause my mama got to go to work and I have to be home wit my little sisters and brothers. And my sister got burn."

Once she finished calling her roll, she called me up to her desk and said sympathetically, "That was your little sister who got burned down there on Rat Row?"

"Yeah, ma'am."

"How bad is she burned?"

I showed her my arm, demontrating where Snappy was burned. "It's a real bad burn. She could die."

She placed her hand on top of my head and said reassuringly, "She's not going to die. She's going to be all right, okay?" She accepted my situation and said, "It's good to see you in class today. You may return to your seat."

Marie Lee and Doletha continued to poke fun at me. I could see the expressions on their faces as I walked back to my desk. Skitter had pulled her desk close by mine, and she was already showing me where we were in the book. But I was so distracted by the other two, so fed up with them, that at one point I just shouted out, "Mrs. Caine, you better tell these here gurls to stop picking at me fore I git outer my seat and knock they heads off!"

Mrs. Caine heard me loud and clear, but she hesitated in speaking. She had a slight smile on her face. I think she was amused at how I said what I said, rather than what I said. With her chin resting in her hand, she beckoned for me to come back up to her desk. I can just imagine how I looked: high-water pants and a nappy head. I told myself, *Sticks and stones may break my bones but talk don't worry me.* That was the biggest lie ever told. Talk hurts, especially when it comes from folk who are much more fortunate than others.

I got out of my seat fast, stomping as I made my way back up to her desk. She said to me in a very low tone, "Keath, do you know you're not supposed to yell out in class like that?"

Speechless and hurting from humiliation, I refused to answer. She repeated her question and demanded an answer. "Yes, ma'am," I said angrily, crying and shivering. "But I wouldn't yell out if you stop them dere gurls from picking at me."

She promised me, "I'll take care of them. Now, don't you yell out in my class like that again. All right?"

She called Doletha and Marie Lee up to her desk. Marie Lee got up quietly, but Doletha jerked about as she went up to the desk. She gave me this ugly look. I saw the frazzled look Mrs. Caine gave Doletha. I couldn't help but feel envy of those girls: they both had long, thick, black hair, neatly combed. They were well groomed—in fact, Doletha was the best dressed, neatest student in the entire classroom, a poor little rich girl everyone looked up to.

Mrs. Caine asked her directly, "Why do you make fun of Haley's clothes, Doletha?"

She shouted, like everybody was supposed to be intimidated by her loud shouting, "I wasn't making fun of her old clothes! I ain't studied her!"

I saw she had disfavor toward me, and I couldn't begin to question why.

Mrs. Caine said calmly, "You don't have to raise your voice. I heard you, and I saw you also."

Doletha kept waging a war with her voice. "I don't care what old, pissy, smelly Haley Keath tell you! I know what I did an what I didn't!"

"Doletha, you may go to Haley and apologize to her, or you may stand in the front corner for the remainder of the day."

Then Mrs. Caine said to Marie Lee, "You may apologize to Haley, or you may go in the back corner and stand for the remainder of the day."

Marie Lee looked back at me and came directly to where I was sitting. She gave me a big hug and said, "Haley, I'm sorry for making fun of your clothes. Will you forgive me?"

Before the last word fell from her lips, I knew she hated it. The way she hugged me wasn't real. At least she admitted she was making fun of my clothes and she was sorry for doing it.

Doletha was still standing there, goggling her eyes. Once Marie Lee sat down, Mrs. Caine asked Dolettha, "What's it going to be?"

Doletha jerked away and started toward the front corner. Then she turned to look at me and said, "I'mo git dat old nappy-headed dog."

Then she stooped her way on over to the corner and stood with her mouth stuck out as long as her nose. She spent the entire day behind the door in the corner and did every little nasty thing she could do to antagonize me whenever she thought Mrs. Caine wasn't looking. Mrs. Caine pretended she was not watching, but every time Doletha licked her tongue out at me or even balled her fist up, Mrs. Caine saw her.

I was poorly dressed for school that day, but I was not a coward. I was waiting for the time when Doletha would tussle with me. I knew it was going to be a catastrophe, and God knows I longed for that day to come.

Skitter was an inspiration to me. Her encouragement lifted my spirit up to the place I needed to be in order to do the classwork that I was so far behind in. She gave me a ton of her papers to take home and study. It was not easy for me to study after working, but somehow I managed to do so with her help. Without it, I would have failed.

I focused on Marie Lee. She was a very beautiful, dark-skinned girl, and she was very polite to everyone, even me.

On the other hand, Doletha was as dominating as she was loud. She had a friend, Patrice Ball. They were good friends just as Skitter and I were. Patrice did all of Doletha's classwork for her. Doletha had a notebook full of As, but none that she earned. She copied from Patrice. Marie Lee made all As herself, and so did Patrice.

The joke was on Patrice, and she didn't even know it. The difference was that Marie Lee used her smartness to her own advantage, while Patrice was book smart only. Patrice could be manipulated to do anything, right or wrong, that Doletha wanted her to do. Patrice never used her intelligence, underestimating herself. She had no real smarts. She dressed very well and never missed any days from school, but for the wrong reasons.

All Doletha was was the class gang leader and dictator. I began to watch her like a hawk. I knew they all thought she was "it," but what was "it"? I didn't like any of those self-righteous heathens; I disliked them as much as they disliked me. Some of what was inside them rubbed off on me. I learned retaliation from them, and how to dislike. revenge raced through my heart and registered in my mind: "I'mo git them first."

Acceptance was all I wanted, but at an early age I learned acceptance came with a price. Fitting into their world was not who I was. I was the girl from Rat Row whom nobody wanted to be.

Half the day was over. I hadn't thought about what I was going do about lunch, but once again Tonk hadn't forgotten me. He came by and gave me a dime for cookies and milk. He only had twenty cents, enough for hot lunch, but he didn't eat hot lunch—he gave me a dime of his lunch money. I didn't go into the cafeteria. I sent Skitter inside because I didn't want to be picked at.

Doletha was allowed to go out for lunch. I had a sneaky suspicion that she was up to her same old tricks, so I told Tonk what had happened in the classroom earlier. He suggested I meet him over by the auditorium and I wouldn't have to be near them. He would be able to keep an eye on me.

Doletha was so determined to cause trouble for me, her gang came and found where I was. I wasn't hiding; I was only trying to stay out of trouble. They surrounded me, pretending that they wanted to play with me and be my friend.

I may have been a little weak, but stupid I was not. I tried to get past them. I looked around to see where Tonk was. Fat Patrice Ball pushed me into another student, who struck me in my face. Then they were hitting from all directions, calling me names like "nappy-headed" and "ugly."

I was the shortest student in the entire class. The others were taller and bigger, so I could only be seen by the ones who surrounded me. As they struck blows to my head and back, a teacher came out the door and asked what was going on. The leader of the disturbance was the first to answer: "Nothing. We just trying to git Haley Keath to play with us." She was lying through her teeth.

I didn't want any more trouble, so I backed her story up when I was asked. I don't know why I didn't tell the teacher exactly how they were beating up on me. I dropped my head and hid the tears that were welling up in my eyes. I hid them very well. I was not about to let any of them see me cry.

Tonk came busting through the crowd. One look at me, and he knew something had happened that I was not telling. I felt safe around him. He took up for me. He had been protective of me from the day Montana made him apologize to me. He never said a harsh word to or against me from then on.

I didn't want to go back to class that day; I just wanted to go home. But Tonk encouraged me to stay and show him who had attacked me. I hadn't seen who they were. I only felt the punches from their fists. He took off after them like a jet. He ran them down, and I took off behind him. He stood up to all of them, putting one hand on his hip. With a finger pointing directly into their faces, he spoke boldly. "I know who is behind all this funk. Skinny ass, big ass, it makes no difference what size. I dare you to mess wit Haley ergin. and I'll show you what picking on really is."

He had them scared stiff. Their bold, daring attitude was shut down.

He dared them to come down Rat Row. "Your country friends won't help you none. I guess you forgot they won't be wit you on weekends."

They didn't open their mouths. The leader rolled her eyes from him to me, not saying a word back to him. Her friends didn't say anything either. I think that was the first time it entered my mind that my little friend was sweet. He moved on his feet quick as lightning flashed. It was a good feeling to have somebody to come to my rescue, and I owed it all to Montana.

I recalled the time when it was Tonk picking on me and my brother. Now he and I were the best of friends. Montana was no longer around to see the difference she'd made in his life, but I did believe she was looking down from heaven, watching over the both of us.

An unexplainable feeling zipped through my body so fast, I began laughing. Braveness overpowered me. I took Tonk by his arm and pulled him away, saying, "They ain't talking they big talk now." What swept through my body changed me forever. I couldn't beat ten other girls; that was beyond my side. But I swore that cold winter day I was going to get all of them, no matter how long it took. One day I was going to pay them all back, though I didn't know how or when or where. That thought entered into my heart and dwelleth.

But it didn't help me. I kept watching their underhandedness. I read my Bible more often and vaguely remembered reading the Scripture like I was being warned: "Watch as well as pray." I learned to do precisely what the Good Book said. I watched them like hawks, and they were unaware.

School let out, and I reflected I had to go face another hard task. Turning the corner by Pa Jack's café, I saw smoke blazing from the chimney of Mama's house. I prepared myself for whatever awaited me, not fearing anything any longer. I was almost looking forward to whatever challenge was coming next; it couldn't be as bad as the other experiences I'd had that day.

I eased through the back door, looking to see who was in there. I heard voices coming from the bedroom. Snappy was lying in Mrs. Angie Rosa's arms. Ms. Geraldine, and Ms. Bonnie were gathered around the fire like always. I commenced to leave for Aunt Matilda's, and then I heard a baby cry. I stopped in my tracks with my ears attentive, trying to make sure that I'd heard a baby.

Whose baby was it? I peeped into the the next room and saw Aunt Matilda sitting on the side of the bed, holding a baby in her arms. Aunt Matilda Ann was sitting next to where Mama was sitting on the other side of the bed. Gemmy BB was lying in the bed. She'd given birth to another son, Collins.

I eased on into the room, knowing I was safe because I had both my bodyguards there to protect me. All eyes turned on me, just as they had that morning when I walked into the classroom. Gemmy BB was the first to yell out. "Gurl, where in the world you been wit dem dere short britches on and that nappy-ass head?"

I had no answer for her, but for the first time I felt the children had had good reason to make fun of me and the clothes I was wearing. I was a clown, so ugly that I was ashamed to act. I stood speechless.

Daddy came to the door and said, "Where you been all day? Could nobody find you."

Reluctantly I stared at him with my big brown eyes rolling up and down. All attention was on me. I said, frightened but brave, "I been to school."

"You did whut? I got to go now, but I'll git wit you when I git back."

In one voice, the women all busted out laughing with disbelief. "You mean you went to dat schoolhouse looking like dat?" Mama said. "You need your ass tore up. You know better den dat, gal!"

The voice of another baby cried out, and it was coming from where Mama was sitting. She too had given birth to another baby boy. His name was Alex.

I wasn't happy about either one of them having another baby. Everyone else seemed to be delighted about it, but not I. I asked Gemmy BB angrily, "Is you gon leabe that baby here?"

"None of your cotton-pickin business. Now git your grown tail outer here, bein grown. What's it to you?"

Aunt Matilda Ann stepped up and took me by my hand, pulling me as fast as she could out the door. "Stop your flip mouth now an come on here."

I was ready to tell her just what I thought: it was another baby for me to have to spend time out of school to help take care of, when I was already helping take care of Willa Max and Billy. I could hear everyone talking about my clothes and the way I looked, but the clothes were not what was on my mind. Anger and hatred were building up inside me all over again. No one could begin to know what was on my mind.

Aunt Matilda Ann led me over to the next room, where Snappy lay burned. Mama and Gemmy BB had given birth on the same day, and Mama couldn't even see about her burned child.

Chapter 9: Getting to Know Him and the Power of His Resurrection

My thoughts were interrupted by a loud noise. It was so loud, even Aunt Matilda heard it. The closer the noise got, the louder it became. Everyone rushed out the door at the same time to see what the commotion was. I trotted out, leaving behind Aunt Matilda Ann.

A long, black station wagon was coming slowly down the road. A big loudspeaker was on top of it. Music was playing from it. Suddenly the music stopped. By then, everyone in the neighborhood was out. From the loudspeaker came a man's voice: "Come out tonight at seven thirty and see how they done our Lord. In this film, I will be showing when Jesus was born in Bethlehem. We will see how he healed the lepers and raised the dead from the grave and took three little fishes and five loaves and fed five thousand of peoples. You see how Jesus went around and deaf ears were opened, blinded eyes could see, the dumb talked, and the lame walked. Come, come, see the miracle of our Lord! And that ain't all. You will see how his own disciple betrayed him with a kiss for thirty pieces of silver. And the most painful scene of all is how they crucified our Lord, how they beat him and nailed him to that old rugged cross. The greatest part of this film is when he died on the cross and they buried him. On that third day, he rose. Come see the resurrection of Jesus."

He circled around the neighborhood, inviting everyone to come out and be a witness that night. It was the best thing to ever happen to our town. We were so used to killing and hearing filthy words and bad news all the time.

I was as excited as everyone on Rat Row. I ran back into the house to get Aunt Matilda. I knew she didn't know what was going on. I had to translate to her what the noise was. I was calling out her name before I got to her: "Aunt Matilda! Aunt Matilda! Come on out here! Whoo-hoo, you got to come an see this man out dere!"

I explained what he'd said just as I had heard it. I led her to the front door so she could see all the folk outside, watching the black car as it drove slowly down our end of the road. She stood speechless but laughing with joy. I could always tell when she was happy about something. She would look down at me with all smiles, laughing—just as she was doing then.

Music was playing again from the loudspeaker, the hymn "See How They Done My Lord." That was the song Mr. Donnie Martin had sung at the prison. I could never explain the truth of what was happening to me, only that I was mesmerized by the joy that was overtaking me. I could feel what Aunt Matilda was feeling, and I knew she felt what I was feeling.

The music was heard all over the town, and it sounded good. All the neighbors' attention was on that man and the music.

The music stopped, and the man's voice echoed over the loudspeaker. He repeated his description of the real crucifixion of Jesus Christ and added, "Please don't forgit the film y'all also git to see about a boy killed his mother and ran all the way to the pit bottom of hell. And please don't forgit the most important film in all of history. I will show *The Crucifixion of Christ*."

The man drove right to where Aunt Matilda and I were standing. He stopped the car and got out, leaving the music playing. He walked around the car and stood directly in front of us. I never saw anyone who looked like that man. He was tall, about six feet, and weighed about one hundred and sixty pounds. His eyes were sparkling like a shining star on a Christmas night. His teeth were pearl white, and his beard hung down long on his chest. Out of all the people standing along the road and on their porches, he came up to where Aunt Matilda and I were. He took her by her hand, looking at the both of us and smiling.

I stood behind her, holding on to her apron and shaking, not knowing if it it was from the cold or his looks. He said in a hoarse but soft voice, "How are you doing, my sister?"

She looked like she had just seen a ghost or Jesus himself. As he was shaking her hand, she said "Fine."

"I know it's a cold, cold night out, but if you come out tonight, we'll forget all about the cold weather once we start to glorifying the Lord almighty. Don't you think so?"

She answered like she heard every word he said. "Yeah, sir."

Tonk came running from across the road. He stood beside me, shivering so hard that his teeth were clicking together. The man looked down at Tonk and me, then asked Aunt Matilda, "Do your children love the Lord?"

Before she could answer, I stepped from behind her and responded, "Yeah, sir, we do love the Lord. We go to church every Sunday, all day long."

He never stopped smiling. "Good," he replied, "cause he certainly love you too. Tell me, what may be your name?"

"My name is Haley, Haley Keath."

"Oh, guess what? I have one daughter, and her name is Haley also. She is all grown up and working for the Lord. And guess what else? She got beautful eyes just like you do."

I twisted and turned, my mind racing away. Something about that man and his voice sent a burning sensetion right through my heart, like only the Holy Ghost would send. He said, "If don't nobody else show up tonight, I know y'all three will." He made it clear to us to be at church, sitting in the front row seat.

Looking into that man's eyes was like looking into the eyes of an angel. I had never experienced anything so perfect.

Once he got back into that station wagon, he drove away slowly, waving, his voice resounding thoughout the the neighborhood. "See How They Done My Lord" was playing again. He turned the corner and was out of sight.

I lost all the ill feeling that had been antagonizing me. I had more important things to think about. It was no secret that the man only talked to Aunt Matilda. If Tonk hadn't came over, I don't think the man would have talked to him. I felt special.

I was still wearing the high-water pants with that car coat. I didn't care. I might have had on the shortest pants, and I might have had the nappiest hair, but I had been noticed. I had had the worst day in school. I had been humiliated and even beaten. But that evening, I got joy out of the visitation. I believed that through that man, God was making everything all right for me. I was the only child on Rat Row that the God-sent man had held a conversation with, and that made me extra, extra special. The humiliation I had encountered didn't matter anymore. In one moment, such kind treatment from a stranger made the difference in my life.

That evening, Aunt Matilda, Tonk, his brother Noonie, and I were the first to arrive at the church, other than the deacons who were making sure it was good and warm and the lights were on. The man was there, setting up his equipment. In came the Brimsley children and the Williamses, and before long the church was full. There were no vacant seats anywhere. Seeing even Uncle Martel and Cousin Sattie Bell there was a shock to all of us; the church folk were saying the world must be about to come to an end.

Skitter came and sat beside us. Doletha came in with her sister Barlena Jean and grandmother Mrs. Naddy G. I was so full of whatever feeling I was experiencing, I glanced at her and that was about all. Whenever I did look around, she was goggling her eyes at me, but I paid her no mind. She was so mean. There was a big different between her and her sister.

Once the devotion was over, the man who had sponsored the program came out, wearing a long black robe like he was Christ himself. All eyes were tuned in on him as he came walking down the aisle. Even Aunt Matilda said he could be Jesus. After brief remarks and welcome, the film started rolling. Across the big screen, big writing read, *The Crucifixion of Jesus Christ.*

I believe that film was the most touching film I had ever witnessed. I promised in my mind that night I would always live for the Lord. But making promises so young, I never had a clue that promises could get broken.

The film was two hours long. By the time it was over, there were no dry eyes in the church. I often wondered if Aunt Pancy and old Ms. Lila Bush were in a race or something. One would scream out, and the other one would scream louder.

During the short intermission before the next film, a collection was taken up. I was the first one to the table to put my nickel in the basket.

I was allowed to go to school the next day. I was overjoyed. I dressed beautifully in new shoes, new pants, a sweater, and my new coat with the fur around the collar and cuffs. There was no way the students could make fun of my clothes; I was ready for them.

The notes Skitter had provided helped get me caught up some, but I was still months behind. Mrs. Caine was proud of me for just trying. She said she was going to give me an A for effort.

Ms. Howard, Snappy's teacher, came to the classroom and told me to come to her class when school was out. She had something for Snappy, whom she called Annie Dora. When school was out, I went by her classroom. She had so many gifts for Snappy, she ended up taking me home—they were too much for me to carry.

Snappy was too sick to acknowledge she had been blessed. Ms. Howard had brought many gifts wrapped in Christmas paper. She had taken up a collection for Snappy, bringing money and all kinds of fruit like apples, oranges, bananas, and grapes—more than I had ever seen. Ms. Howard came inside to help me bring in the bags. It was the first time she had visited Annie Dora in that condition. She'd had no earthly idea my sister was burned that bad. Like everyone who saw Snappy, Ms. Howard had the same question: why wasn't she in the hospital? She sat helpless, looking at Snappy's burned body with tears in her eyes and much sympathy in her heart.

She wished us a merry Christmas as she was leaving, and asked where our Christmas tree was. I said, "We ain't never had no Christmas tree."

She smiled at me, rubbed her hand across my head, and was off.

Folk had been coming in frequently, but now they started to thin out some. We all understood they had their families to take care of, with Christmas only three days away and school out.

Mama was up on her feet day and night. Gemmy BB went back to her own house with her new baby, but they came to visit every weekend. I had to babysit. After Christmas, Mama went back to work. Even Daddy had a job with old man Benny. I had to stay home with the other children, watching Snappy every day, causing me to miss more days of school.

The days turned into weeks. A few of the ladies—Mrs. Bonnie, Ms. Tempt, and Mrs. Angie Rosa—were regulars. They didn't miss a day coming to help me. Snappy screamed day and night. She was in excruciating pain. Between her and the three babies, I thought I would lose my mind.

Then came the day everybody had something to do for themselves, and I was home alone with the three children. Even Aunt Matilda had to go uptown. I was totally on my own.

As the Bible tells us, God is a mysterious God, and he works in mysterious ways. This was really one of those days. If I'd had anywhere to go beside Aunt Matilda's, I would have run, changed my name, and disappeared without ever looking back. A million things were rolling around in my head, and Snappy was screaming nonstop.

A knock came upon the front door. Most people came in from the back. I opened the door, and there stood our mailman, Mr. Lester Doore. I thought he had one of those special-delivery letters he sometimes had me sign for when Mama was at work. He said, "Good evening, Haley. How you doing today?"

"Good evening, Mr. Doore. I'm all right," I replied.

"Haley, why do that child continue to holler all the time? Is something wrong wit her that make her scream like somebody is killing her?"

"Yes, sir. Cause she got burn, and she be hurtin real bad."

"She got burned? Where is she?"

I had nothing to fear from him, even though he was white; he was a very respectable mailman and well known. So I took him to the room where Snappy lay screaming. The tears were rolling down the corners of her eyes into her ears. Her complexion had lightened up until she was pale-looking.

He went up to the bed, took one look at her naked, burned body, and blurted, "Oh my God! What in the tornado happen to her? How did she git burned like that? I heard that one of Macky's and Jenny Rue's gurls got burned, but I never dreamed it was this bad!"

"She was fancing by the fire and her dress caught," I explained.

"I pass by here, and I keep hearin her screamin clean on the other side of Aunt Matilda's house, and I wondered what on earth kin make a child scream every day like that. I had no earthly idea. My God. Has she seen a doctor?"

"Naw, sir."

His face turned red. He turned away from the bed, then turned back. Looking at me with deep concern, he asked, "Do you look after her every day?"

With my eyes filled with tears, I said painfully, "Yes, sir."

Just then Mr. Danny came in the door. Mr. Doore glanced at him and said to me, "You and who else? You ain't but a baby yourself. Where your mama working at today? Is she at Mrs. Poole's?"

"Yes, sir. She at Ms. Connie Ray Poole's house."

"Then I'mo call her. Who round here got a phone?"

"Nobody but Mrs. Brittney got a telephone, down on the other end by Flappy Boots."

"Here's what I'mo do. Danny, you drive, don't you? Can you drive a stick shift?"

Mr. Danny answered, "Yes, sir. I kin drive anything wit er steerin wheel."

"I'mo go and make arrangements for this child to git some health care. Danny, here is my keys to my car. It's parked up at the post office. Go and git it. I'll call Jenny Rue and talk to the social worker about treatment for this gurl. Bring them up to the clinic. You know where it is, don't you? Once you take them up there, you kin park my car back at the post office." Looking down at me, Mr. Doore said with conviction, "Don't worry, little Haley. I'mo git help for your little sister."

Later, Mama came in, half out of her breath. I watched as they wrapped Snappy up in a sheet and took her off to the clinic. Deep within my heart, I knew this was the work of the Lord. It took that white man coming in and being compassionate enough to get help for a helpless, burned black child. It was proven to me that no matter how racist white folk may be, there is some kindness in some of them, and Mr. Lester Doore was one of them. Not all of them were like old evil Ms. Shelmore and Mr. Benny Lee Lang and old Lund Cabb. They were the meanest, most prejudiced white folk in all of the town.

Mama and Snappy were gone for what seemed like hours. I waited patiently with the other children for them to return. Late in the evening, they came home. Snappy seemed much better. Her arm was bandaged up. She wasn't doing all that screaming.

I was changing Alex's diaper when the car drove up in front of of the house. He was somewhat underweight, so much so that Uncle Martel nicknamed him Poor Pap. It was cold that day. The wind was whipping against the rotten wooden wall so hard, the house shook.

Daddy came in the back door around the same time the car drove up. Behind that car was another car. I peeked from the window and recognized Ms. Connie Ray Poole, the lady Mama worked for.

All of a sudden, there was shouting. I pressed my ear closer to the window and heard how that cracker was talking to my mama. The tone of her voice sent chills up and down my spine. The words were plain and very simple, with no misunderstanding about what was being said. Ms. Poole was demanding an explanation as to why Mama had left work unfinished.

Mama spoke in fear, trying to explain that she had to take her burned child to get treatment. She told her that it was only three shirts that she'd left unironed. But that inconsiderate, freckle-faced woman wouldn't even try to understand. I thought, *How kin she be that heartless?* She insisted that Mama give back the one dollar and fifty cent paycheck Ms. Poole had written her. Ms. Poole deducted fifty cents and gave Mama a one-dollar check.

I will always remember how Mama looked when she took the check from that woman's hand. Tears welled up in her eyes. She started to walk away from the car, thinking that the feud was over. But that woman felt she hadn't humiliated Mama enough. She ordered her to stop and shouted, "Don't walk away from me while I'm talking to you! You stand here and listen!"

It split my heart to watch my mama obey, looking from her master to her sick child, defenseless.

Mr. Danny took Snappy out of the car. Daddy went out and I came out behind him. That white woman saw the expression on our faces. If I didn't inherit anything else from my father, I inherited his boldness. I was not afraid of white folk.

Fear entered Ms. Poole's eyes the moment she eyed Daddy. He said, "Jenny Rue, what you just standing here in the cold looking foolish for?" She humbly told him she was listening to Ms. Poole. Daddy said indignantly, "Like she pose to be Mary, the mother of Jesus? Hell, I don't hear Connie Ray Poole sayin nothin."

Ms. Poole's entire demeanor changed. She looked at Daddy and me in fear and got into her car real quickly. As she drove off, I know she experienced our fangs clutching her, our eyes glued to her.

It was nice to finally get to hear what happened at the clinic with my little sister. We rushed in behind Mama, almost stepping on her heels. Mama was upset and I was the one she took her frustration out on. "Is you gon knock me down, little heifer?"

"Cuse me, Mama," I said sorrowfully.

Daddy said angrily, "Jenny Rue, you didn't holler at old lady Connie Ray Poole out dere, and stop hollering at dat damn gal. The white lady talking to you like a dog and you didn't say a g—— d—— word back to her; you just stood dere looking like a scared-ass child. Now your own child step on your heel, and you want to bite her head off. Now git up off of her right g—— d—— now."

Mama just stuck her right thumb in her mouth like it was something good to eat, ignoring every word Daddy said. Whenever she stuck that thumb in her mouth, that was her consolation. Nothing could humiliate her. But I was glad Daddy said those words to her. I hoped she would get some strength and stop letting that witch of a boss lady talk to her any kind of way.

We gathered around the fire. Snappy's arm was all bandaged up. She was sitting up in a chair and smiling and holding a conversation. She said, "Haley, de doctor saw bout me, dressed my burns, an said I'mo be like new again."

Nobody in that room knew the relief I felt and how thrilled I was that my sister didn't have to lie and scream from pain all day and night while I stood helpless. It was God Almighty who showed up through our mailman. Mr. Doore was the ram in the bush.

Daddy interrupted Mama's thumb-sucking and asked, "What doctor waited on er?"

She was so busy with her thumb, she didn't hear a word he said. He asked a second time and she jumped. "Dr. Hinson Merrick. She got to go back every Monday, Wednesday, an Friday, but I can't take er. Haley, you gon have to be de one to take er, an while you gon, I'll see if Danny kin come and stay with the other chilluns till you come back. You know Wednesdays and Fridays is my days I got to go to Ms. Dorothy."

Daddy said, "Jenny Rue, everybody know when it comes down to Ms. Poole, you break your damn neck."

"Aw, shut up, Mack. That's what help put food on the table when you was down dere on dat chain gang."

Mr. Danny called Daddy outside, and they both left, saying they had to git Mr. Lester Doore's car up to the post office. My first instinct was hurry up and find an excuse to get to Aunt Matilda's. Mama was entertaining herself, not thinking of anyone.

The first visitor through the door was Cousin Sattie Bell. Behind her was old Ms. drunken Jessie Luck, looking like a stone witch. All she worked for was a quarter drink. Give her a half pint of moonshine, and anybody could get a full day of physical labor from her. But she was there for Mama even when there was no moonshine to give her. Mama would give her a quarter, or sometimes fifty cents, and leave her with the children. I wouldn't have gotten to school some of the days I did go if it weren't for Ms. Jessie Luck being there to take my place. That's the way it was for a long, long time.

Again, I had to take Snappy to her weekly appointments every Monday, Wednesday, and Friday for the first six weeks. After that, she had to go twice a week for four weeks, and then once a week until she had taken all of her treatments. It wasn't bad. I rather enjoyed taking my sister up to the clinic. The nurses got to know us and treated us with the utmost respect. They gave us suckers every day, and on our last day, they gave us ice cream. They warned Snappy not to be so careless walking by the fire. "Now, Annie Dora, I don't want to see you back up here anymore unless it's for school shots, you hear?"

We got home one Wednesday, and something was happening. Daddy had lots of moonshine, and the house was full. Ms. Jessie Luck was sitting with the other children. That was my opportunity to go to Aunt Matilda's house before Mama got home from work. I knew Mama would work me from the time she got home until there was nothing left to do. So I left.

I was passing Cousin Sattie Bell's house and heard what sounded like Daddy's voice coming from the inside. I thought Daddy had gone out with Mr. Danny. As usual, my curious mind wanted to know. I put on my investigation ears and forced myself closer to the door so I could listen. I heard Pallie laugh out. That recalled the day I saw her come out of that house with Daddy, before he went off to the chain gang. What was she always doing around Daddy? If he was somewhere, she would soon show up.

A cab pulled up in front of Aunt Matilda's house, just as it had the day Montana came. Only this time it was Lijah getting out, wearing one of those nice, long army suits and a cap on his head. I waited until he paid the cab, and we went into the house together. I stood and watched as the two of them brought happiness into each other's life. I hadn't seen Aunt Matilda that happy since Montana stepped up on her porch. After six long years, the look Aunt Matilda had worn from the day I read the telegram that Montana had died vanished, replaced with a joyful look. Lijah made a great difference in her life, and that made me happy. He was trying to tell her something, but she was so happy, she didn't hear a thing he was saying.

"Come on over here, Haley," Lijah said. "Let me look at you. You don't look like yourself. You are all growed up now, but you were never too tall, although you did grow a few inches. Tell me what grade you in now. When I left, you was just entering your first grade. I know you ain't making nothing but As and Bs, smart as you is."

Oh, how I wished that were so. The expression on my face said differently. I looked up at him in shame.

He knew I was holding something back, but he didn't elaborate on it. He changed the subject and started to talk about his brother, Wesley. He asked Aunt Matilda when the last time was that she'd heard from him. She shook her head.

A knock came at the door. I was about to get it, but Lijah held up a hand. Apparently he was expecting who it was. He opened the door, and that short, dark-skinned, bald-headed woman came in, leading two little children and holding a baby in her arms. I remembered her from somewhere, but at the moment I couldn't think where.

She came over to the fireplace and stood in front of it, where Aunt Matilda usually sat. As soon as Aunt Matilda looked at her, the blissful expression on her face vanished. But when she looked at the two kids, she gave them a slight grin and some joy was restored to her.

Lijah got a chair and pulled it up. He set it before the bald-headed woman, saying, "Here, Essie Lee, sat down here in dis chair."

Then I remembered where I knew her from, her and that big dip of snuff in the corner of her lip. She was the woman Lijah married before he left for the army the first time. She was his wife and the mother of the McDaniels children: Joel, Becca Lee, and Hosea. She sat and shoved snuff from one corner of her lip to the other. Then she asked, "Do you remember me, little Haley?"

"Yes, ma'am, I remember you, but you look different from the last time I saw you."

"You ain't growed too much in seven years, have you?" she asked. "What bout me to you look different?"

I was not trying to be disrespectful toward her, but I said, "Your hair. It's white an gray like Aunt Matilda's."

She slightly smiled and said, "Gal, you still got dat babble mouth."

I didn't know if that was good or bad, but whichever—it didn't matter.

Lijah said, "Well, Essie Lee, you did ask her, so she answered de best she knew how."

Meanwhile, Aunt Matilda sat playing with the little children. Nobody had to say if they were Lijah's; they were both just like him. Aunt Matilda never liked Essie Lee, and she never accepted her as Lijah's wife, but she did accept her as the mother of his children,

He had thirty days of leave and then would be going overseas, not knowing when he would return. I watched Lijah sitting by the fire, warming and talking about the time he and Wesley came home. As he talked, I observed him closely. A sad, distant look appeared on his face, but I didn't know what to make of it. Was Essie Lee the reason? I wondered if it was because of their age difference. The word being spread down at Mama's house was that Essie Lee was a dominating, manipulative old woman who gave him children he loved more than life itself, and that was her weapon. In return, his life was sadness. Aunt Matilda had something Essie Lee didn't have, and it was that Aunt Matilda was a woman of truth. She was not a pretender; she was a true woman of God the Father of Abraham, of Isaiah, and of Jacob.

During Lijah's thirty-day leave, he and his family stayed up at Essie Lee's parents. Lijah spent most of the days with us until his time was up. He would be leaving his family behind while he was overseas.

The day before he left, he came early in the morning when he knew we were having breakfast. His advice to me was "Stay in school and study hard." Whatever grades I was making, he reminded me I could do better.

I watched Essie Lee and how she related to Aunt Matilda. I think she enjoyed boasting, and I believed she was flaunting her marriage at Aunt Matilda when his back was turned. When Essie Lee caught me looking, she would wink, and I surely didn't know what that meant. When Lijah left for Alabama to be shipped out, she didn't go. She stayed on, but she never brought the kids back to see Aunt Matilda, and neither did she visit. My conclusion, as usual, was that Aunt Matilda had been right about her all along.

After the long, hard, tiresome day of Lijah's departure. Aunt Matilda and I retired for the evening. We both were feeling chagrined, and once we were in bed, neither of us was able to go off to sleep. She tossed and turned for hours. I could hear her softly praying, and I knew she was telling God all about her situation. I could feel a breakthrough coming, and everything was going to be just fine.

Nothing is ever promised. We learn to take one day at a time and live the best day we can. Aunt Matilda was unhappy about Lijah, but she stayed in her place. She knew from looking at him that he was not happy in that marriage, no matter how many children he'd fathered.

Essie Lee left about six months later and joined him in Germany, where he was stationed. Every now and then he would write to let Aunt Matilda know he was doing fine. He always included some pictures of the kids, with another added to the family.

Chapter 10: The Bad Dreams Turn into Nightmares

Lijah had been gone a little over a year. There was no letter from him to me, but his encouraging words stayed with me. Each time I wanted to give up on everything, I would hear him say, "You kin do anything you want to."

It had been one of those awful days at school, and I was very mad. I was so mad, I could hardly breathe. I didn't eat much or say much. I was just mad and tired of those schoolchildren bothering me. I hadn't done anything to them, but they were making my life a living hell.

We retired to bed early, but unfortunately, I couldn't get to sleep. I just stared up at the ceiling, wishing and hoping. I began to feel congested. I wanted to fall asleep, but I couldn't. When I did go off to sleep, it seemed my eyelids wouldn't close tight. I could see the front door slowly opening. In came Ms. Onna. Beside her was Mr. Freddy Rudolph. They were moving toward the bed in slow motion. I tried to scream, but my mouth wouldn't open to get the scream out. As they got closer to the bed, I could see another person behind Ms. Onna who looked like Cousin Big C Lottie. She was coming toward me smiling, and then her facial expression began to change. Her nose commenced to grow bigger, and her eyes seemed like they were going back in her head. I tried to turn, but my body wouldn't move. I tried twisting my head, but it wouldn't move either. I just lay still, watching as those atrocious faces came directly at me. They circled around the bed.

Then another man came and stood at the foot of the bed. I tried to make out his face, but it was unclear. Suddenly the gold shining from his mouth and the long, curly, black hair familiarized his face, and I realized the man looked like Jesus Christ, the Son of God. He advanced, smiling, his hands stretched out. He moved slowly between Cousin Big C Lottie and Ms. Onna's face. They backed away, hurrying out the front door in fear. Then he just stood over the bed, looking down at me with that same smile. He whispered, "I am your Jesus. I'll never let no one hurt you, no matter where you are or what you are doing. Lo, I'll be with you always, even to the end of the earth."

My eyes blinked open. No one was there. I was a little frightened, but not to the point I felt inferior. I sat up in the bed. Sweat was pouring from my pores like a bucket of water had been poured over me. I told myself, "Oh, it was only a dream," but I was never convinced of that in my mind or in my heart. I knew it was more than a dream. Someone had been in that room, and I convinced myself it was Jesus. He ran the demons off, away from me.

In my head and in every picture I'd seen of Jesus, he was painted as a white man. Just as the thought occurred to me, a blare of sound came from the right-hand corner of the room: "My pictures are all painted white, but I am Jesus, your protector, and one day you will know."

I jerked the covers over my head so fast, it woke Aunt Matilda. She asked with concern, "Haley, what de matter wit ya? Is you sick?"

"No, ma'am. I was dreaming," I answered, worried. Something was happening to me, and I didn't know what it was. I couldn't tell that story to anybody because who would believe me? I didn't think even Aunt Matilda would believe me, as much as I trusted and loved her. I really thought she would think I was crazy, as most people would.

Anyhow, I never went back to sleep that night. I lay awake until I heard the roosters commencing to crow for day. It was almost like they were competing against each other. One would crow from Aunt Matilda's backyard, and then one would crow from Mrs. Angie Rosa's backyard, and then I would hear the two crowing from Mrs. Shaddy Mae Washington's yard. They would all crow in the same manner for what seemed like a solid hour. Unexpectedly, all the roosters in the neighborhood would crow together in one sound, and by the time they crowed that way several times, daylight appeared. It was overwhelming.

They crowed like that every morning, and when they stopped, it meant darkness had disappeared and light had broken through. A new day had been birthed out.

I hopped out of bed, thanking God a dozen times for letting me get up and to see another day. Aunt Matilda stared me up and down when she got up from praying, like she knew what was on my mind. I didn't know why I was not compelled to tell her of my dream, but every time I tried, something stopped me.

I imagined Mama coming through the door and me yelling, "Mama, I saw Jesus by my bed last night!"

She would have shouted back, her thumb fast in her mouth, "Gal, git you damn ass out of here, lying early this morning."

I visualized telling Daddy I had seen Jesus. He would have said, laughing, "Gal, you bout as bigg a liar as Chicken Little. He said de sky was fallin cause a piece fell on his tail."

I sat on the back step, thinking if Montana were living and I told her what I thought I saw, she would have told me to pray and ask God to let me see him again, because Jesus loves little children, especially little girls. The thought was so realistic, I set in mind to believe my thoughts and encouraged myself. It sounded far-fetched because she was deceased, but I prayed all the time: walking, lying down, playing, or whatever.

Meanwhile, I continued dreaming these dreams until I dreaded having to go to bed at night.

***

The sun was shining, and we had just finished having lunch. Passing by Cousin Sattie Bell's house, I saw Pallie Lea and Mr. Danny Blow. I had a discerning spirit so strong, I could see what was going on with a person by my first look at them. I wondered why they were coming out of Cousin Sattie Bell and Uncle Martel's house. I'd seen her coming out with my daddy, and rumor was she was going with him. I knew for sure Uncle Martel was now selling moonshine, and so was Daddy. I decided to wait by the side of the house, as I usually did. They walked past me, hugged up. Every now and then, he gave her a pat on her hip. One time he patted her on her rear end, and she said in such a baby voice, "Aw, s——, stop, Mr. Danny. That hurt."

As she completed her sentence, Daddy came around the other side of our house and ran right into them—his lover and his best friend. The expression on his face changed instantly. If his eyes had been a knife, Pallie Lea would have had a cut throat.

Something moved me. I was up on my feet before I knew what had happened. I ran and jumped into Daddy's arms like I was glad to see him. "Hey, Daddy's baby, where did you come from?" he said.

Casually, I answered, "I come from sittin down by the back door waitin for you."

"Waitin for me? What you waitin for me for?"

"Yes, sir. I was gon tell you to give me a dime."

He reached his hand in his pocket, pulled out a dime, and gave it to me. Then he turned to Mr. Danny and Pallie Lea. "I wanter see you later on, when you got time."

She asked, "Who you talkin to?"

"I ain't talkin to you, an dat's for damn sure," he retorted.

"Well! Cuse de hell outta me!" she said, pulling away from Mr. Danny.

Sly Mr. Danny answered sincerely, "All right, Macky. What time will you be home dis evening?"

Daddy spat on the ground and responded, "Round the same time as yesterday."

As we walked on back to the house, I looked into Daddy's eyes, and they were bloodshot red. I pictured him with horns standing out on his head. For a moment, I thought he was the redhead devil everybody talks about.

I was staring so hard at him, I tripped over a broken bottle and cut a deep wound in one of my knees. When I saw the blood, I panicked. It only took one scream and Daddy became the compassionate father I'd hoped he would be. He cleaned the wound and even asked me if I thought I needed to go to the doctor. I had never been to a doctor, and the word infuriated me. I hurriedly answered, "Naw, sir."

It wasn't long before Cousin Pallie Lea came down from Pa Jack's café. She was intoxicated; I could tell by the way she was staggering. The only three women who staggered when they were intoxicated were Ms. Dani, Odessa, and Pallie Lea.

She got to our back door and called Daddy outside. He went out to meet with her. I was not about to let any little thing slip by me. I hopped out the front door and ran around the side in time to see him slap her face as hard as I'd ever seen him punch Mama in hers.

She saw me and cried, "Mr. Macky Keath, what you do that for? You gon make folk start talking." She knew folk were already talking of how his best chain gang buddy had beat his time with Pallie Lea.

I assumed we were going to have a miserable weekend. Whenever folk saw Daddy and Mr. Danny pass together, they sang, "The Chain Gang." For the longest time, I thought they were singing because that's where Daddy met Mr. Danny. But the more I heard talk around the backyard and in our kitchen, the more I understood what was going on. Daddy had started drinking heavily. He was in and out and back and forth like a restless spirit. We knew it didn't take much of anything to set him off, but I was yet in darkness concerning a lot of things.

Each night I had those awful dreams of the same faces, the same people. The man that I thought looked like Jesus would rescue me from whatever they were trying to do. The man was my protector, and they were never able to get to me.

On this night, I had a totally different dream. It was about Mama. Daddy came in. He had found Cousin Pallie Lea and Mr. Danny over in the ballpark, and he came home and took his frustration out on us. He started beating me with his belt, and I was screaming for help. The man came into the room and stopped him.

Daddy cursed like he was demon-possessed, Mama had been drinking, and I could smell the scent on her breath. When she was intoxicated, she wouldn't hush. Daddy hit her in her mouth, and the blood sprayed from it. He hit her a hard slap, sending her flying across the water bucket. I was jumping up and down, shouting for him to stop. In walked Uncle Billy Roliver and grabbed Daddy, pulling him off of Mama and saying, "Macky, what is wrong with you, beating up your wife in front of your chilluns like this? What's the matter wit you, Macky?"

I was determined to help Mama up from the floor. Her face was swollen, blood poured from her mouth, and she was crying. I was crying along with her. Some other women came and helped me to get her stabilized.

I twisted and turned, trying to come from under the dream, but what woke me was Mama coming into Aunt Matilda's house with the baby in her arms. The dream was reality: Daddy had beaten Mama up badly. But it hadn't been me who tried to rescue her; it was Cousin Sattie Bell. She brought Mama down to Aunt Matilda's for a cooling-off period. I was so disgusted with him. I sat up in bed as Mama was placing the baby beside me, and I saw her face. I began to hate the man I called my father. Aunt Matilda was humming the hymn "Somebody Prayed for Me."

Mama tried to make excuses to go back, but Aunt Matilda and Cousin Sattie Bell were more convincing then she was. Aunt Matilda got a pan of water and washed her swollen face and bloody mouth. She said, "That old man gon burn in hell one of these days."

Daddy didn't come home that night. He came back the next morning with five gallons of moonshine and set it down on the table. He called me into the house and gave me another lesson in how to bottle up moonshine into gallons, quarts, pints half pints, fifty cent shots, and quarter cent shots. The more I poured, the more I hated him. There was nothing positive about my father. What kind of man teaches his own flesh and blood to be bootleggers? I did not spill a drop—I dared not.

Shortly afterward, Daddy and Mr. Danny went into partnership selling wood. They tore our play area back behind the toilet, where Papa relaxed in his spot, watched us play, drank his shine, and ate his cheese, sardines, and saltine crackers all day. They made our playground into a woodpile, a moneymaker.

They bought a long, rusty, faded-out truck and a woodcutting saw from old man Benny Lee. They worked long and hard, cleaning up and repairing the saw and the truck. In no time at all they had everything running. Mr. Danny's wife—Big Lillie was what she was called—moved in town, and they lived in Brake's quarter. He and Daddy worked closely together. No one would have thought they were not brothers.

We no longer had to go gather wood. All we had to do was bring it inside the house. I learned how to cut wood on the saw. It was fun doing it until I was forced to. They would go down to Tylerville, gather the wood from the woods, bring it back to the yard, and cut it up. Folk were ordering and everyone was profiting from it.

Mr. Danny didn't go with Daddy to get the wood one day. Daddy took Georgie Boy and I with him to get the load. We were all excited because we had never been outside the town limits. We thought we were really going someplace. It was certainly a pleasure for me because we didn't have to cut and we got the opportunity to ride in the big truck. It popped all the way there and back. The muffler was so loud, we could be heard coming miles before we arrived.

We made two trips that day, and after the second trip, we were surprised to arrive home and see a big truck parked in front of Cousin Big C Lottie's house, loading up the furniture. They were moving away to another town. How glad that made me feel! I thought Pallie Lea was moving with them, except that didn't happen. But the others were moving to a better life.

Once they were all loaded up, Mr. Danny came over. I was smiling. He wanted to know what I was so happy about. "Cause dey movin from by us. Cause dey beat us too much an dey bad."

Daddy stepped from behind the door and asked, "Who in de hell kin you call bad, Ms. Angel? Why you call dem bad?"

I explained as well as I could. "Cause Cousin Big C raise her boys like her want dem to be raised, and her big old boys fight me an George, an one of dem hit me in my head wit a big rock an made my head bleed. Dat's why!"

That day was the happiest day for me since Mr. Lester Doore set up Snappy's appointment at the clinic. But watching the Bakers move off of Rat Row was a sad day for many. The entire neighborhood gathered in Mama's backyard, watching Daddy and Mr. Danny cut wood and the Bakers moving out. One thing I learned about nosy neighbors: the ones who threw the rock and hide their hands were the ones came the earliest and stayed the longest. They gossiped about everything and everybody until all Cousin Big C's children were loaded up in two separate cars. Pallie Lea's children, Lester and Nadine, got into one car. They drove off, waving, knowing they were going to be missed. And they were—just not by me. I wondered who the next neighbor was going to be.

Cousin Sattie Bell, Mrs. Estella, Mrs. Angie Rosa, and Aunt Pancy Suller continued to hang around. They moved back around the woodpile, making it impossible for me to hear what they were saying. Daddy was cranking up the saw, and when he got finished winding it up, the motor would damn near bust your eardrums. It was fun to watch Daddy cut the wood; men would help just for the fun of it. It was the most exciting work going on in the town. They did it like they were real professionals.

Things were working out for everybody, no fussing and no fighting. The business was a success, with everyone cooking on woodstoves. They procured summer and winter wood. The pile stood as tall as the old toilet. They were really making good money, and people started to say we were rich. All was good while it lasted.

Pallie Lea moved into the apartment next door to Cousin Sattie Bell and Uncle Martel. I would always see Mr. Danny coming and going while the children were still out of town. Iit was known he was the man.

This was around the year 1958. I was in school every day. We were living the best life had to offer us, but something was dreadfully wrong. Mama was drinking constantly. It seemed she stayed intoxicated all the time. Daddy was gambling up every dime he made from selling moonshine and wood.

One day I came in from school and heard Mama and Daddy arguing and cursing at the top of their voices. It was all about Pallie Lea. Mama screamed, "Just wait till Danny find out you is still messing wit er! We gon see how long you gon be big shot in round here! We gon see how long you gon be partners then, you cripple bastard!"

She was holding a bottle in her hand. "Hit me so I kin break this bottle cross you bald-ass head!" she demanded.

For some reason, Daddy wasn't saying anything. He'd stopped

arguing with her. It was all her, cursing and arguing by herself. He held his head down, soaking in every cruel word she was passing out to him. What I heard suggested he had lost a large amount of money that was needed in the house.

She continued with the "m——f——" and "SOB" language until I guess he'd had enough. He jumped up from the chair and yelled, "Jenny Rue, I'm tired of your g——d—— mouth. If I throw erway a thousand damn dollars, it's mine, g——d—— it! I'm sick of your mouth!"

I knew I had to do something fast before the physical abuse began. I got between the two of them, pushing Mama on out to the other room. She would not shut up. I begged her, "Mama, be quiet!"

Folk were now all out on their porches, listening. Daddy rushed in after us and grabbed Mama's collar, shouting, "You keep running your g——d—— mouth or I'll break your g——d—— neck!"

I got strength and shoved him back as hard as I possibly could. He told me, "You better git your tantalizing ass on somewhere and sit down."

I had to do something to stop her from running her mouth before we all suffered the consequences. I got her seated on the bed. Dear Lord, that was one of those times I wished she would put her thumb in her mouth and stop it up. She certainly was not understanding what was happening, but she did put her thumb in her mouth.

That entire week was a disaster. Nothing was right. Everybody was doing their own thing, and it was a revealing time. The whole neighborhood was nothing but drunken cheaters and liars. I woke up nightly in fear of tragedies happening or about to take place. It led me to despair.

A major tragedy took place between Uncle Emmet and Aunt Matilda Ann, whom I had put a lot of my confidence in. They were spending the weekend at Aunt Matilda's. They had been down at Mama's house, drinking all day. Aunt Matilda Ann was like Mama in so many ways. When she drank, she was uncontrollable. Their mouths ran like speeding freight trains.

Before when they stayed, Uncle Emmit would be out cold and Aunt Matilda Ann would slip out the door. I only suspected she went back to Mama's house with the other women, but the truth was totally different. That night when they came in, Uncle Emmet was not as drunk as he pretended to be or as she believed him to be. She got him down across the bed, and he was snoring like he was asleep. She waited a few moments, peeked in the next room to see what Aunt Matilda and I were doing, and then tiptoed out the back door.

Uncle Emmet jumped up and followed her down to old man Willie Pricehart's house. He had moved into one side of the house that Cousin Big C Lottie had moved out of. I followed Uncle Emmet out of the house. I was afraid to go farther, because in my spirit I knew something was going to take place that was not pleasant.

A few minutes later, I heard loud voices. I ran inside. Uncle Emmet dragged Aunt Matilda into the house. He held her by the top of her head and slammed her down on the bed. He strangled her by the stomach, and she screamed. I'd never thought anything would get her down or shake her. She was as brave as they came, and he seemed like the henpecked one. Now his licks were sounding from her head. Anyone would have thought he was killing her.

It had been proven she was no different from the rest of the sneaky-ass women in Rat Row. Uncle Emmet had caught her and old man Willie Pricehart in the act. It seemed Willie was hitting up quite a few Baptist mothers and sisters of the church, and Aunt Matilda Ann was one of them. Uncle Emmet beat her down, and when it was over, he went out back, got old Bessie the mule, hitched her up, and left for the country.

Once he was gone, she came out of the room with a look of hatred in her eyes. I didn't know if it was because Uncle Emmet had caught her in the act, or because she had just gotten the ass-whipping of the year. She always looked mean, but if looks could kill, that one would have. She grabbed her shoes and left.

I followed her. She went directly back to old Willie Pricehart, and no, he hadn't wasted any time. He had old, drunken Ms. Dani with her legs way up in the air, and he was on top, working her. Aunt Matilda Ann stood in the kitchen and watched for a few minutes. I was at the side of the house, listening through a door.

She turned away, and I thought she went around the house to the front. She came around the front all right, and went right on around to the side. She caught me standing with my ear glued to the door, listening to what was being said and the noises being made. "Haley," she said angrily, "what in the hell do you think you is doing?" She took me by my arm, squeezing it. "I'm gon tell your folks what you round here doing. How long you been round here snooping on grown folk business? I'mo make Mr. Macky whip your ass."

"No, ma'am, Aunt Matilda Ann. Don't tell. I promise I won't do it ergin." I still didn't know what "promise" meant, but I found myself saying it a lot. The promise I made to her that day, I never broke. But I picked up many other habits to take its place.

She led me back down the path from Willie Pricehart's house back to Mama's. She wanted to stop in there. I wanted to continue on to Aunt Matilda's, but she didn't trust me and insisted on my going into Mama's house with her.

***

Papa was moving in with Mama. Aunt Lucy Sue's family was steadily increasing, and there was no room for him up at her house. She was almost ready to give birth to her sixth baby, and they lived in three rooms. At least Mama had an extra bed in the boys' room. Papa's health was failing him rapidly, and moving in to where all the whiskey was certainly was no help where his health was concerned. Since he was directly in the middle of the moonshine, it was available for him whenever he wanted it, and that was daily.

The only benefits of the move to me were that the fighting stopped, and we got to play with our cousins more often. Up on the corner of Brake's quarter, where they lived, there wasn't much room to play. With Flappy Boots's café being so close to where they lived, we weren't allowed to be there much. But whenever Papa felt like walking up there, Georgie Boy and I got a chance to go along with him. Mostly we were looking after him.

We walked up there with Papa one Sunday evening, and I got my first opportunity to experience the surroundings where Aunt Lucy Sue lived. I remembered the many times we'd spent with them up at the Sawmill quarter, and the fun we'd had playing on the sawmill piles. They were like sliding boards. We missed that. I sat listening to the music playing from the jukebox in Flappy Boots's café. I thought it was a little strange that the juke joint was so close to the church. I assumed it was natural.

I saw Passy Kate and her friend Antoinette Slaughter walking across the road, popping their fingers and dancing as they walked. People went to and fro between Butternut's café and Flappy Boots's. I thought to be like Passy Kate and her friends was cool.

I called out to Passy Kate just to wave and say hey, nothing specific. She turned and came over to where I was. She and Antoinette were smiling like they had something planned. They took me by my arms and carried me into Flappy Boots's café. The music was playing and it was filled with wall-to-wall people. They sat me down in one of the booths, and I started to feel good, being in there with all the grown folk. I popped my fingers and shook my shoulders. Before I knew how it happened, they had me out on the dance floor, teaching me how to dance.

I was not a slow learner, after being in Mrs. Crowley's dancing class. I had rhythm. I followed their steps and watched their movements, and in no time I was dancing like they were, shaking my hips. People surrounded me, clapping and yelling, cheering me on. I was liking every step.

I looked up, and Daddy was standing there, looking disappointed. I knew he didn't like me being in there, not at all. But before he could express his feelings, Passy Kate and Antoinette took full responsibility for my being in there. He said mildly, "Don't you think you better git home?" I knew that was not the last of it, but he didn't shake the blissful feeling I had experienced. I didn't know that was the hook of a demonic spirit deposited into my body. Once the deposit was made, I began to draw on it.

It was past three o'clock in the afternoon when I arrived back at Mama's house with Papa. He was spinning from the moonshine he had drunk. The moment I treaded upon the grounds, I didn't feel quite right. I had a tormented feeling I couldn't define.

I was taking Papa through the back when I saw old Lund Cabb's Black Maria come speeding up and park in front of Cousin Sattie Bell's house. Her back door was open, and angry voices could be heard. Some of the noise was coming from Pallie Lea's apartment, and it was loud.

I took Papa on inside the house and made my way to the front porch, where a lot of other folk were watching what we called "the picture show." We watched in sorrow, anger, fear, and mostly pity. It was the most unthinkable thing we witnessed that year.

Uncle Martel came stumbling outside like he was being pushed. He was bleeding profusely. I witnessed old Lund Cabb right behind him. He struck Uncle Martel hard upside his head with his blackjack, in practically the same spot where the blood was already pouring from his head. The blow knocked him off the porch to the ground. Blood covered his face.

As Uncle Martel lay helpless on the ground, Lund Cabb took kicked him in the stomach. I will always remember the hot-tempered feeling that went through me. All those Negroes stood around and wouldn't lift a finger to help. They were as scared of that cracker as I was of a snake or rat.

Then out came old, skinny, long-necked Tommy Williamson, holding on to Cousin Sattie Bell. Her clothes were torn from her shoulder down to her waist.

Uncle Martel was trying to get up from the ground. Old, nasty Lund Cabb stood over him and constantly hit him across the forehead, opening the wounds wider. Aunt Matilda went up to him and said sadly, "Mr. Lund, don't hit em no more. Please. You gon kill em."

He looked at Aunt Matilda and stuck his blackjack in the black holster he was wearing on the side of his belt, next to his gun. He snatched Uncle Martel up and threw him in the back of the Black Maria like he was nothing or nobody. Old man Tommy tossed Cousin Sattie Bell in behind him like some kind of dead dog. Tommy slammed the door, and the two white men got in the front seat and drove off.

The second they drove off, voices sounded all over the porch. The only ones who didn't seem scared were Uncle Billy and Mrs. Sara Lee. They called all of those niggers the cowards they were. Apparently those two had come up at the end and had seen the Black Maria driving away. They locked up the house and went immediately to see what could be done.

When they came back around seven thirty that night, they had Uncle Martel and Cousin Sattie Bell with them. Uncle Martel was bandaged all around his head. His face was swollen, and both his eyes were closed. He had to be led up his porch and into the house. Sympathy was in my heart. He had to be in so much pain. Everyone watched on, helpless and very sad. We had all witnessed it, and not a single one had been strong enough to help.

A nasty, prejudiced cracker had beaten a helpless man down to the ground. I don't know what would have happened to Uncle Martel that evening if Aunt Matilda, a woman over ninety years old, hadn't pleaded in his defense. I wondered if Lund Cabb would have just beat him to his death. There wasn't a weekend that he didn't come circling the neighborhood and beat some drunk man into bad health.

Tommy Williamson, when he was around Lund Cabb, was totally different from the way he was when he came through the quarters alone. I learned that it was because Daddy was supplying him with all the moonshine he could drink. Alone, he was about as scary as old Barney Fife on *The Andy Griffith Show.* He looked just like Barney, but always played the big bad wolf. He was really no more than a sheep in wolf's clothing.

Once all the commotion had vanished, I realized I hadn't seen Mama outside. I knew Daddy was down in the bottom, and I noticed the house was mighty still. I heard the baby cry out, and followed the cry over to the bed. Mama was stretched out, dead drunk and asleep. I lifted the baby. Little Pappie was soaking wet. The whiskey scent was strong; I had to hold my nose to keep from getting drunk from the smell. I got Pappie out of there as quickly as I could and carried him on down to Aunt Matilda's. I handed him over to her without any explanation. My mind seemed to have gone on remote control; I couldn't think.

I hurried back to Mama's house so fast, I don't know which door I went through. There were drunks asleep all over the house. I called out for Papa but got no answer. I began to seek for the other children. I called out their names, and Georgie Boy answered. I followed his voice out to the woodpile. Papa had cleaned off another sitting place under the trees. He had all the children playing outside with him. "What you want?" he asked in a grouchy voice.

"I just wanted to know where y'all was at, that's all."

Papa was drinking, but he was sober enough to make sure the children were fine. Now that I knew they were safe, I went directly to the water faucet. Then I went around the room and poured water on the drunks' faces, waking every sleepyhead I saw. As I poured, anxiety came over me, but I shook my head and continue right on. Some got up cursing. Some got up lost, not knowing where they were. Some got up wanting more to drink. It didn't matter to me. All I wanted was them up and out of that house.

At first I showed no compassion. But looking at those sorry people, I had to show humanity to them. I did everything possible to compose them.

After I got the last one up, it wasn't ten minutes before old Lund Cabb drove smack in front of Mama's door. He jumped out of the Black Maria and up on the porch like he was trying to catch someone. I met him at the door. He brushed past me like I was not even there and went through to the kitchen.

A chill rushed through my body. I was afraid he was going to get Mama. I held my breath, praying under my tongue that she didn't wake up.

He made a fast tour through the entire house and quickly came back out with his nose turned up. Between the whiskey smell and the piss smell, it was a wonder he could breathe. When he got to the end of the porch, he stopped and looked down at me. In a ferocious tone with a look that could kill, he asked, "Where your daddy at, little gal?"

"Dunno where he at," I answered coldly.

I saw the fear in everyone when Lund Cabb came around, and how he intimidated the blacks, but I was never in fear of him. He did make me a little nervous, the way he treated and beat up on blacks. But there was something in my body that allowed me to respect him without fear. I feared no man, black or white, and if there was any man in that town to fear, Lund Cabb was the one.

Aunt Matilda came around the corner, holding the baby in her arms. Lund Cabb spoke kindly to her. "How you doing, old lady Matilda?"

She looked at him. I remembered how she pleaded with him to stop beating up on poor Uncle Martel. She pretended she didn't hear Mr. Lund, so he got close up to her and asked loudly, "Who's baby you got holding there? Don't tell me you done waited till you got damn near er hunderd to go an have er baby!"

I saw she didn't find what he was saying amusing in the least, but she answered him. "Oh, naw, sir! Ain't got no baby. Ain't nothing so precious as a little baby, but the good Lord didn't see fit to gib me none. Sometime I'm kinder glad he didn't."

He slyly smiled at her, got into his Black Maria, and drove slowly off. Folk were looking on and were too scared to move from their spots. I believe Lund Cabb got his biggest kick out of coming down through Rat Row, terrorizing the Negroes. I got a lot of my strength from watching them. It motivated me to be determined I was never going to allow myself to be intimidated by a man such as that.

As he was driving away, Aunt Matilda looked at me teary-eyed and asked, "What did he want?"

I shook my head, meaning I didn't know, but told her he'd asked where Daddy was. She and I went into the house. The sun was starting to go down. We got Papa and the other children inside, safe. She was concerned about me getting home and ready for school. I knew it was a school night, but I didn't know from one day to another if I was going. It had started to not even matter to me.

I insisted on taking the baby to Mama's house with us to stay the night. She asked why, and I said angrily, "Because Mama in de house drunk an she can't see bout em." Aunt Matilda stared at me with pity. She was astounded to hear me speak so maturely. She closed her mouth tightly and went into Mama's bedroom. She touched Mama lightly on her shoulder.

Mama sat straight up in the bed, looking around the room like she didn't know where she was or who she was. Aunt Matilda said only, "Jenny Rue, you need to git up an see bout dese here young'uns now. It's gittin dark outside."

There's one thing I've always remembered about my mother: regardless how Aunt Matilda spoke or what she said, Mama listened. She got up in pure shame. I watched on from the side door as she crawled out of the bed, looking wild and lost. She started closing up the house and lighting the lamps. She told Aunt Matilda she was all right and had everything under control. I didn't want to, but I believed her. I couldn't help but see the the nightmare I was in, and I couldn't awaken from it.

We had got the other children in bed and Papa was in his bed too before I heard Daddy's voice singing, along with many others. I knew he was bringing more drunks home with him. I got Aunt Matilda and started out of there. But I was too late; he came in, calling out my name. I answered as brutally as I could, "What, Daddy?" I also sent Aunt Matilda on her way. I didn't want her to be caught up among drunks. I told her I was coming on behind her.

"Don't you 'what' me. Git me three half pints and bring em here right quick," he demanded.

These men I had never seen before. I just wanted to get as far away as I could. I obeyed him, trotting off sorrowfully and bringing the whiskey back to him. I thought that was all he wanted me to do. As I commenced to walk out the door, he called out, "Wait er minute. I didn't tell you to go nowhere." My knees got weak and my heart pounded away. I goggled at him and stood silently as he pointed me out to all of his drunken customers. "This here is my oldest daughter," he said.

They looked lustfully on me. One of them could barely keep one eye open. "Mr. Macky, you got a g—— d—— sure pretty daughter, now. I wouldn't lie to you."

Daddy looked either like he was pretending to be stupid or I was stupid. I recognized he was on top of the lust. He said loudly and very sincerely, "I will cut a son of a bitch's g—— d—— throat bout any of my chilluns if anybody f—— wit em."

One was a tall man with feet as long as his arm. He was about as tall as Gemmy BB's husband, John James. He was too drunk to speak. He couldn't even stand, but he was steady in his drinking. There was something about the way he looked at me. When I looked into his eyes, I saw nothing except pain and more pain. It pierced my heart. Something was rooted down so deep inside him that only he could feel it. Nobody else gave a damn about him or noticed he existed. I kinda pretended I was paying him no mind, but I was almost in a trance watching him. Who was he? Where did Daddy find him? Did he have a family?

The other one was somewhat hostile. He had a nasty personality, a filthy mouth, and a dirty look about him that couldn't be trusted. It was a terrifying look that said, "I am a rapist, and I don't care who knows it."

In no uncertain terms, I asked Daddy my question. Pointing my finger directly at the pain man, I said, "Daddy, what's his name?"

Daddy said jokingly, "Dat old son of a bitch, dat's old Willie Shangle. He bout as ugly son of a bitch if you ever saw one."

Gosh, I really deplored him. He was in no shape to speak, much less answer any questions I may have had. He looked up with his painful eyes and laughed. I knew in that instant—it was nothing but the Holy Spirit revealing it to me—that he was a loner and had no family in this old world. And he didn't know Jesus Christ.

Daddy called out the tall man's name: Dor-Roa. Dor-Roa was watching me, and I was watching Mr. Willie Shangle. Willie Shangle distracted Dor-Roa's attention by blurting, "Nigger, what you doing, watching Mr. Macky's daughter like you doing?"

Drunk out of his senses, Dor-Roa said, "Aw, hell, she don't look like no little gurl to me wit all dem dere tits sitting up dere looking at me."

Whatever else he had in mind to say, he never got the chance. Before he knew what hit him, Daddy had collared him from behind, dragged him to the back door, and slung him out. He landed on his head hard. Daddy jumped down over him, holding a hawk-bill knife. He shouted, "Nigger, I'll cut your g—— d—— throat!" When he got angry, he was famous for making that threat. This time, he was about to do it. He put the knife to

Dor-Roa's throat. I think Dor-Roa sobered up right fast, begging for his life: "I didn' mean nothing by it, Mr. Macky. Don't kill me."

Mr. Willie Shangle begged and pleaded with Daddy not to cut him. Finally Willie got Daddy's hand from around Dor-Roa's throat. Dor-Roa lay there, lost for words, fear screaming from his face. I stood behind the door, watching. It was a frightening experience but also a happy one, to see my father stand up for me against a disrespectful drunk. Daddy was so angry, he was actually foaming from both corners of his mouth. He placed his knife back into his pocket and said to Dor-Roa, "Bitch, you better not neber let me found out you said any g—— d—— thing to my daughter. I'll kill you dead as you got to die."

When Dor-Roa got up from the ground, that nasty, lustful look was no more. He backed away in a rush, holding his neck. I could just imagine what was going on in that dirty mind of his after coming so close to losing his life.

Uncle Billy Roliver was never far away when something troublesome was happening. He convinced Daddy to go on back inside the house before somebody called for old Lund Cabb to come back in the quarters. He pointed out a few important factors to Daddy, especially the role Daddy played in the proposition. He told Daddy it was all his fault; he had no business allowing me to sell moonshine to his drunk customers. I was a young lady, and not all the men were men. Dor-Roa was proved to be no man. He was a stranger from God knew where. Uncle Billy told my father the confrontation could land him back on the chain gang.

Uncle Billy was the only man that my father would listen to besides my uncle Cleo. Daddy sat listening to what Uncle Billy was telling him. I don't know if it went in one ear and out the other, but the expression on his face said, "You're right." Daddy was not the kind of father who told us he loved us. Half the time he didn't show love, either—only when something terrible was taking place. But he listened to the positive advice for once without saying anything negative.

I was old enough to trust my own judgment and never allow myself to be caught alone where Dor-Roa was concerned. Going through difficulties was part of growing up, and the life I was trapped in was not the life I wanted at all.

Chapter 11: The More They Came, the Worse They Got

Brake's quarter became a nightmare. Judge Brake was the owner of those houses. The regular families were having to move out due to him renting houses to a puck wood owner named Rosco Henry out of Bullfrog Town. It was a sad situation, old families moving out for new families to move in. Across the street from us, Antoinette's mother, Ms. Suzie Mae, and her fifteen children were out. The house became a whorehouse.

Things changed for a lot of people once all those strangers came into our neighborhood. Daddy had made me into a woodcutter, a bootlegger, and a live-in babysitter. There was no light in my life anymore. I traveled through pure darkness, feeling my way. Life had become lifeless. At the age fourteen, my self-esteem was as low as the ground. I didn't want to go to school. I saw no future.

I thought Daddy had banned Dor-Roa from the house, but at some point all was forgiven and he came back. Daddy sent for me, and when I got to the house, Dor-Roa was standing in the kitchen with his head dropped. Daddy demanded I tell Dor-Roa what Dor-Roa had said to me, stirring up those old ill feelings again.

I didn't want any part of it. I wanted the whole matter to be quenched. But Daddy insisted. Dor-Roa had come pleading for forgiveness, pretending he didn't have any recollection as to what had taken place.

I did. I recalled the words he'd said, and I repeated them. He apologized—to Daddy. "Mr. Macky, I'm so sorry. I swear fore God and three er four more Jesuses. Forgive me. I won't disrespect you or your little gurl ergin."

My stomach commenced to boil. It got jittery and was never the same. I don't think I listened to another word that came out of his mouth.

Dor-Roa was not sorry. That was who he was—a damn pervert. The way he pleaded for a second chance did not go down smooth with me. I didn't trust him then, and I never would again. I didn't know who my father was, allowing that man back into our lives. He was only asking for trouble. They both made me sick.

I walked out. A thousand different thoughts flashed in my mind. I could hear all the children heading off to school. It was a day I also had the chance to go. I walked slowly down the lonely highway, trying to efface the awful thoughts that were clouding my judgment. The words from Dor-Roa's lying mouth played over and over in my head. The sound wouldn't leave me alone; it became real bitter to my taste.

Up ahead of me, Ruthella and Glory Ann looked back and yelled for me to catch up. "You better hurry up, Haley Keath! You gon be late if you don't hurry!"

They waited for me. I didn't understand why my life was so messed up and their lives seemed to be so together. They didn't appear to have a care in the world. They never missed days out of school and they dressed very well.

But behind what I saw, there were not-so-perfect stories. Glory Ann was Passy Kate's cousin through her father's brother. Ruthella was O'Bera Walters' oldest daughter and Cousin Sattie Bell's niece. She had an older brother, Henry, and a sister, Sandette. Word was her mama O'Bera was expecting another baby at any moment.

I answered, "I'm coming. I'll be there by the time y'all git there."

Ruthella was always flip-mouthed, though easily terrorized. "Not walking like that."

I ran and caught up to them, and we all three walked on to school together. That's the way it was. They were a grade behind me, but that day we became friends.

***

Mrs. Crowley came around to the higher grades. She was choosing girls to be in her dance class. She made sure to choose mostly the town girls, because the country girls couldn't stay after school for practice. They had no way home except the regular school bus, and some of them lived far out in the country. The old saying was "they live plum Nellie"—"plum" meaning way out of town and "Nellie" being slang for "nearly beyond the woods." I was delighted to be chosen for the dance class. That was one of the fun things I looked forward to. I felt I was doing something positive in my life there. Dancing took away the emptiness that I was unable to dismiss.

I also looked forward to spending my recess time with Skitter. Sometimes Glory Ann and some of her schoolmates would come around, and we all had a wonderful day. It made the time pass by quickly.

I was placed in Mrs. Dell Brimsley's eighth grade class. The entire class suffered from animosity that built due to a change of student seats. I had been up front beside Skitter, and was switched to a place between Doletha and Marie Lee. I didn't like it there at all. Whenever I started to feel confident in myself, it got cut from under me. All the good feelings I started with vanished a little each day. Doletha and Marie Lee exchanged notes while whispering and looking at me. Hurt pierced my heart. Contempt built up inside me, ready to explode. But this was one of those times I learned to ignore them and keep my composure.

The last bell rang for the day. It was dance rehearsal time. I rushed out without saying good-bye to Skitter. She caught up with me and encouraged me not to pay Doletha and Marie Lee any attention. She had seen them from the back, where she was now sitting.

Before we reached Mrs. Crowley's dance class, Doletha's gang had surrounded Skitter and I. I tried to move past them. One of them gave me a hard push in my back. I turned to see who did it, but I couldn't getting anywhere. They were going to lie, looking all innocent.

I made a serious threat. I warned them that whoever it was, I was going to knock that girl's head off. I had all intentions of making good on my threat, regardless of the consequences.

That wasn't enough. I made a quick turn to walk away, and someone deliberately stepped on the heel of my shoe, causing it to come off of my foot. I whirled around again with a hard swing, hitting Marie Lee smack in her nose. I grabbed her hair and tried to pull out every strand I could. That was hard to do, since she had so much—it was long thick hair.

A couple teachers pulled me away from her. Her nose was bleeding. I felt in no way sorry for her. She swore she hadn't done it but refused to say who did, and she got what was due for someone else. Everyone knew it was Doletha, and they covered for her.

I was led off down the hall, blamed for the fight. I looked back in a rage and yelled out, "I'll break all y'all m—— f—— up from messing wit me!"

The teacher took me to Mrs. Crowley's class. Everyone was there, waiting on me to arrive. Mrs. Crowley got her dance class started and took Marie Lee and I back into her classroom. She asked why I fought with Marie Lee. I was angry and crying about having to explain my role in the fight. I was so emotional, my words weren't coming out right. Mrs. Crowley gave me a second to compose myself and had Marie Lee tell her side. Marie Lee told the truth; she admitted she was the one who stepped on my heel, causing my shoe to come off.

Mrs. Crowley asked why she did it, and who else was involved. Marie Lee paused for a minute and began to cry. "Doletha pushed me up to do it. She said if I didn't, the other gangs wouldn't play with me and she would tell everybody in the gang to beat me. I'm so sorry."

It was already known to Mrs. Crowley who the instigator was. She warned Marie Lee about allowing herself to be bribed or influenced by others. "Let that bloody nose along with your hair being pulled out be a lesson to you." She was a sharp teacher. Nothing got by her where Doletha was concerned. It was known that Mrs. Crowley thought Doletha was getting by with her manipulation. Doletha wasn't aware that she was being observed.

Mrs. Crowley took Marie Lee and I back to our homeroom. The moment we got there, Doletha's was the first name Mrs. Brimsley called out, along with Patrice Ball and Patty Topkins. She had been watching the four of them all that day, and she knew Doletha Bradbusch was behind the entire problem. She excused me back to dance practice, promising she was going to take care of Miss Gang Leader and her followers. I knew they were going to get what was coming to each of them.

Skitter was standing at the door, waiting for me. We took a shortcut back to Mrs. Crowley's dance class. She had the girls lined up, selecting partners. Gloria Ann selected Barlena Jean to be her partner. Doletha usually stood so no one else could get to Barlena, always keeping Barlena to herself.

For the first time, I had the chance to observe Barlena Jean's mannerisms without Doletha around. It amazed me, the difference between the two sisters. Barlena was prettier, friendlier than most, and had exquisite intelligence. She had pretty, pearl-white teeth, and she always smiled. She was well loved by everyone she came in contact with. Lord knows she was nonviolent. She had all the qualities any young lady should have, and many of us could have taken a page from her book. She carried the most beautiful spirit, like no other. I believe everybody in the dance class wanted to be like her. I sure did.

Barlena didn't hang around too many girls. She mostly stayed to herself. I learned that was because of the jealousy she encountered from others. Glory Ann tried to condescend to her because Glory Ann thought she was the queen of the town. But Glory Ann couldn't hold a candle to Barlena. She was a light-skinned, Indian-looking girl with a shape like a European model.

Ruthella was paired off with Hanna Brookwike, and Skitter and I were the last to be paired. It was one of the last times we danced together. Not long after, Skitter started taking piano lessons that were at the same time as dance pratices, so she had to give up dance. But she and I remained friends. I was given another partner, Jessie Bell McDaniels.

***

It was coming up on our yearly school dance contest. It was going to be held in Wormwood. We were practicing often. Mrs. Crowley informed us that if we won at Wormwood, we would get to go to Aspen College for a tour. We worked really hard. Things were going well. I hadn't missed any days out of school, and that was in my favor. With Papa and Tise back home, I got to go to school much more than I would have if they hadn't been there. When the time came, our dance class didn't make first place, but we did come in third.

Tise and I took turns staying home with the children. The weekends were rough on me. Tise had started going out on dates, and now Gemmy BB had four children. She would bring them and her husband and stay the whole weekend. She would leave home—beautifully dressed, sober, and well-mannered—and then return drunk. That's when all hell would break out like a bad rash.

Tise and I were up the weekend of Mama's birthday. I was exhausted. Tise had tests that week in school, and so did I. There was a conflict over who was going to stay home and babysit. Tise had the upper hand, so I fibbed and told her Mama said for her to stay. She and I argued.

Then Daddy took it up, and he and Tise got into a real heated confrontation that led to a big fight. Tise plainly beat the hell out of Daddy. He was a man, but she was swift as she was tall, and he couldn't do anything with her. He managed to get her on the bed, holding her down, but she bit him. He got a chair and threw it at her. It didn't hit her, but she lay for dead. Mama came in, misinterpreted what had happened, and yelled, "Call the law! He done almost killed my child!"

Papa came running in, pulling out his big switchblade. Daddy panicked; he thought the chair had hit her, though it hadn't. While everyone was raving over Tise, Daddy walked out. He crossed the field that led to Mrs. Angie Rosa's yard and on across the wooded area behind old Funeral Bellow's funeral parlor, walking as fast as he could.

There wasn't anything wrong with Tise, but when it came down to her, Papa didn't care. Truth or no truth, he was involved. She sat on the side of the bed, pretending to be hurt. They was asking where the chair had hit her. I walked up in front of her, and she dropped her head. She knew I was not going to stand by and watch her lie on my father, no matter who or what he was.

The police came. I stood around the side of the house, listening to every exaggerated word she was telling Mama and the police. I recognized that when a person carried hatred in their heart, they would do any kind of hurtful thing and not spare another's feelings.

Tise was not completely truthful, and my father was going to be arrested based upon what she told them. He did hit her first, but that was all. She did the fighting. But she told Mama Daddy tried to choke her. They were both fed up with him and wanted him punished.

Old Lund Cabb asked, "Did you see which way your daddy went, Haley?"

I lied as fast as they did. "Naw, sir, I didn't see which way he went."

"If he is anywhere round here, we gon find him." Lund Cabb got into the Black Maria and slowly drove away.

The next day, Papa was still holding Tise in his arms, babying her, and she was eating it up. I knew I was going to get blamed for everything, so I got out of there as fast as I could, with the intention of going to school.

I heard somebody calling out my name down by Aunt Matilda's. I dashed around the house and answered softly, hoping no one from Mama's house would hear me. It was Glory Ann and Ruthella, asking if I was going to school. They said they would wait for me on Pa Jack's corner.

They walked on, and I noticed they were about thirty minutes early. I had time to put my clothes on. Then, as fast as my legs could run, I trotted on after them.

As we were walking past the Shelmore store, Ruthella went in and Glory Ann asked me abruptly, "Haley, did Mr. Macky beat Tise with a chair?"

"Naw!" I answered, angry. "Who said dat?"

"Well, dat's what dey said yes'day on my mama's porch." The news had gone through Brake's quarter all twisted and backward, and now was spreading like a wildfire all over town.

I happened to look up, and there was Daddy, standing on the corner by the funeral home. I quickly turned and pretended I had left something at home. Glory Ann and Ruthella walked on slowly. I had to be careful that I didn't draw any attention to myself as I ran to where he was. Ruthella called out, "Come on, Haley! What you waiting on?"

I had learned to be a perfect little liar. "I'm waiting on Tonk. Y'all go head and I'll catch up."

The moment they turned away, I ran over to Daddy. He looked rather apprehensive. I didn't think they had seen him. He asked me point-blank, "What did Lund Cabb say?"

I responded, "If you round here, he gone git you. Is you got lunch money?"

Running his hand in his pocket, he gave me a quarter. Boy, was I glad to get that quarter. He said, "Git on to school."

I saw something in his eyes. I couldn't make out what that look was, but it was painful, acknowledging he hurt too. He stayed away for a few days before he returned. I don't know what came of it, but I knew old man Benny Lee had a lot to do with no arrest being made and no charges being filed. Daddy came back home and did not go to jail.

I went on to school. My lunch most of the time contained tea cakes and cold meat. Every now and then I got a peanut butter and jelly sandwich and a dime for cold milk. I knew I was going to be picked on today because I had lunch money, but it didn't matter to me anymore. I had already accepted that I was not good enough to be counted as one of Doletha's gang. I felt that I was not good enough to be classified in their league. The other girls were more her type. they wore the finest clothes ans had money for hot lunch daily, as well as afternoon snacks. Most of them were smart academically, though not Doletha—she was graded by other students' brains. There were a few girls in the same category as I was, but they bought her friendship. She was the queen of Sheba, but not I.

Mrs. Brimsley was writing arithmetic problems on the board. Doletha's gang started in the moment I held my hand up for hot lunch. My day was ruined instantly, but I waited to see what was coming up next. Sure as I thought, Patrice Ball passed me a note that read, "Doletha want you to be our friend. Sit at our table and eat lunch with us ." As I was reading, I could see all their heads together. I had a strong suspicion they thought they were making a fool out of me, except I outsmarted the fox. That time the joke was on them.

I told Patrice yeah, knowing full well I had no intention of sitting with them. The moment class dismissed for lunch, she was the first one to put her arm around my shoulder in the lunch line. But Skitter had a spot for me. I stood behind her, and once we were served, we went over to another table by ourselves. I never looked back at the gang. That day, I learned to laugh in front and scheme in the back. I was learning from the best.

One thing about Doletha and her gang: they never gave in. If they were blocked one way, Doletha was so conniving, she stopped at nothing. She came back with something new.

Once lunch was over, Skitter and I had all intentions of just going back to the classroom and catching up on some overdue homework. But the second we emptied our trash, the gang was waiting. I thought it was suspicious when Doletha had little Linda Smith to do her dirty work. Linda never spoke, never commented on anything ever. She was included only when she brought something to Doletha. She was like a little frightened rabbit. Skitter and I knew right from the beginning she was being used. She was doing only what she was ordered to do.

"Hey, Haley Keath," Doletha said. "You an Skitter come round in front of the school an play with us."

Skitter flat-out refused, but I was determined to see just what scheme Doletha had plotted for us. If we didn't go along that day, I knew she wouldn't stop. My suspicion was she was really up to no good. No one ever played in front of the school. But Skitter had informed me her father, the principal, had assigned a teacher to sit in the teacher's lounge and watch from the window. Most of the teachers met in there after lunch anyway.

All sorts of excuses flashed through my mind, but nothing settled. So I went along, and we joined them.

Doletha had her plan all mapped out. "Let's play ring around the roses," she stated. It seemed a fairly harmless game to play. We formed the line and began. Doletha was the first to get put out. Then she changed the game. "Let's play fighting, y'all," she said. "We ain't gon fight for real; we just gon play fight." Not too many wanted to take part in that. But she was persuasive, and they were all afraid of her, so they agreed.

Skitter was the only one to step forward and say, "No, I don't want no part of fighting because my father don't allow it. And beside, it is not a good game."

I wondered in my heart what Doletha was really up to. She knew Skitter and I were friends before we came to the new school, and our friendship remained. But Doletha insisted on Skitter and I fighting each other. We both said no at the same time. Somebody pushed Skitter into me real hard. Before the gang could gather around us, Ms. Howard saw from the teacher's lounge window and called out.

I had turned to swing on whoever did the pushing, but I accidentally hit Skitter in the lip. Ms. Howard witnessed what I did. Someone else pushed Elanda Burke up on me. She and I started fighting, and it was not play. Mella Kempton struck me as hard as she could, hitting me across my back with a stick. Teachers witnessed everything.

The gang took off running. Skitter ran off to get her father. I was still on the ground where I fell after the blow from the stick. When the teachers came outside, Mella threw the stick down and Ms. Howard insisted she pick it up. The principal, Mr. Monroe, along with a few other teachers, lifted me up. "You!" he called out to Mella Kempton. "Go to my office immediately."

The whole gang shouted out in one voice, "It wasn't none of me!"

"All of you go to my office and wait for me there," he demanded angrily.

Ms. Howard gave him the full details of what she saw. She told Mr. Monroe it was all Doletha's instigating. "She was the one who had those girls attack Haley Keath, and the one who was pretending to break up the fight was hitting Haley from the back also." I guessed they had been hitting me so fast and hard, I didn't recognize there had been more than one.

"Keath, go to my office. Skitter, go to Mrs. Brimsley's classroom and tell her to come to my office. Have her ask one of her mature students to watch the class. This won't take long at all. Doletha won't get by this time, I promise," Mr. Monroe said.

Once everyone was in his office, Mella Kempton, Patrice Ball, and Elanda Burke each got ten hard strips in each of their hands with his belt. It felt good to watch, but Doletha escaped again. The gang lied for her. She was the leader, she encouraged the whole thing, and she walked away scot-free.

My face was burning terribly. Skitter, Elanda, and I went into the bathroom. I washed my face and looked in the mirror to discover one of them had scratched my face awfully bad, like a cat had clawed me. I was furious at the only person I could blame—Doletha.

That day brought Skitter, Elanda, and me closer. We played together and had lunch together. The gang didn't like that very much, but they had to lie low. The only time we were separated was when I was not in school and in dance practice.

That day ended in much regret. I had to return home and face Mama and Tise about the morning's issues. I wondered if that was the day for fighting.

I left through the side door. A good-looking, dark-skinned guy came up to me and called out my name. He introduced himself as Ernie J. Major, Tise's boyfriend. He handed me an envelope and said, "Please, will you give her this letter?"

The first thought that came to my mind was he had heard what happened to Tise and my daddy. I never looked up at him; I didn't want him to see those deep scratches in my face. I took the letter and said, "Yes, I'll give it to her."

He said, "I got to git to my bus. Thank you, Haley," and he was gone.

But when I got home, Tise had moved out to Rooks Iron quarter.

***

Two weeks later, we were all set to go on stage for our third dance contest. I had put all of my effort and time into it. Right at the time to go, I was told I was not allowed; I had to stay home and take care of the children.

The neighborhood was swarming with new neighbors. Families were steadily moving into our town.

Our grandmom, Mama's mother, hadn't been to see us in a long time. I barely remembered what she looked like, but I could remember Mama leaving Daddy and taking me to live with Grandmom for a while. The cruel treatment we received from her during our stay was rooted deep in the core of my soul.

We arrived at Grandmom's house on a Sunday evening. It was far down in the middle of a large field, surrounded by cotton and peanuts. She worked out in the fields for the whole two weeks we were there. I wore one pair of pink corduroy coveralls the whole two weeks too.

I recall the long walk we had to take and how hot it was when the bus driver stopped and we had to get off. he said we had to walk about ten miles; that was as close as the bus went to where we were going. We walked for so long, and then we sat on the side of the road under a tree and ate hot plums that had fallen to the ground. A preacher man came by in an old Model T black truck and gave us a ride. That took a long time too. He said that on foot, we wouldn't have made it there until three or four o'clock in the morning. The name Morrow Junction, Georgia, would always stay with me, and so would the name of my grandmom, May Lee.

I was curious as to why our grandmom never came around us, why we didn't ever see her or go visit her, and why her name was never mentioned in our house. I wanted to find out, but I had to wait until time permitted it.

An old white man named Rosco Henry was the owner of the puck wood that all the new families worked for. He practically owned them. He had rented all of Brake quarter, and that was the beginning of a terrible nightmare for the married women. The bootleggers' houses became nothing more than whorehouses. It was an ugly sight to see the women and men who were slipping around with each other, they were so bold and open. I thought it was all right for a woman to have an affair with another woman's husband, or a husband to have an affair with another man's wife. It was so visible, there weren't too many who weren't.

Mama had begun to drink more and more. It was like watching her drown, and there was nothing I could do about it. She knew all the drinking women who had moved into the quarter. Roxie Longfellow was a beautician. She practically put Ms. Bracy and Ms. Trudy out of business. They were good, but she was better, and she became their enemy. I didn't understand it. There were enough folk, and they all made a decent living.

It was the year nineteen hundred and fifty-nine. The date stays with me because of a big field day at the school. We all thought it was the most popular one ever.

Mrs. Crowley knew my potential in dance. She didn't hold it against me because I couldn't make the last contest. She never cut me out. She made sure I came to practice. If I missed school because I had to watch the children, she would come and get me for practice after school. She was so good to me. She kept my faith built up and encouraged me to always believe in God first and myself.

Mama came to the school with me for the next dancing contest. We walked home under a beautiful full moon and a sky that surrounded us with stars. Mama had a blissful look on her face that shone like the stars. She was proud of me. She was never good at speaking her feelings, but it always showed in her facial expression.

Tthe moment we turned the corner, we heard the music from old Fred Solomon's guitar, and the porch was full of drunks like always. Mama's expression faded instantly. She said, "You keep right on to Aunt Matilda's. If he try to stop you, keep going."

I was hoping Daddy wouldn't be on the porch, but it just so happened he was. I pretended I didn't see him. He called out my name, and just like Mama, all my ecstasy vanished. I goggled at him as I walked up to the porch to see what he wanted.

He was drinking, and he was preposterous. The profanity he used made me flagrant toward him. At the same time, I was very uncertain. No matter where we went or what fun we had, he always found a way to spoil it.

When I got up to where Daddy was sitting, he was talking to one of the new men in town. Daddy called him Charston Sneed. They ignored that I was standing there in the middle of all those drunks. I busted in on their conversation and asked, "Daddy, what you want?"

Daddy turned and eyed me with a cold, cold look, as if I was under some kind of punishment. Then he went back to talking to Charston Sneed.

Mama looked at him and walked on inside the house. In one of his ferocious tones, Daddy murmured, "You was just gon pass on by and weren't gon tell me or let me know how this here dance thing you was in went?"

I didn't speak, just nodded my head. Suddenly his entire demeanor changed. He seemed like the most concerned, warm-spirited person in the world—like the father we wished he was and knew he could be. "Tell Daddy all bout de dance thing. Did you make old lady Crowley glad? Well, she damn sure work y'all hard enough. Did y'all git any money?"

I shook my head and rubbed my eyes like I was sleepy. He demanded, "Tell me, how did my daughter do? When you tell me dat, you kin go on down dere wit old lady Matilda an git to bed."

He made my night then. My response was, "Mrs. Crowley said we did real good. We came in second place, an we worked really hard."

Just like that, he lost interest. "Damn de dance. Go in dere an git me a half a pint of whiskey."

I followed his order to the letter. He was so busy talking that, when I pushed the jar into his hand, he never stopped. He opened the whiskey, drank half of it down, and passed the bottle to Mr. Charston Sneed, who finished it.

Before Daddy could give me another assignment, I was gone—through the house and on out the back door.

Passing Pallie Lea's apartment, I heard loud shouting and crying. I stopped to be nosy. It was Mr. Danny Blow and Pallie. Sounding viciously angry, he said, "I'll kill you! You don't know who you f—— wit! How do you think I feel? You round here f—— my best friend, good as I is to you!"

"Naw, Mr. Danny, you got it wrong."

"Naw, *you* got it all wrong! How long this g—— d—— s—— been going on?"

Pallie was crying horrendously, like the sound of Benny Lee's braying donkey. For a few minutes, no one said anything.

Then Mr. Danny's voice could be heard, sounding chagrined. "Macky and me is friends. We did time on the freckin chain gang together. We is in partnership together. How that look, me and my friend screwin the same woman?"

She said, "Mr. Danny, that was fore he went to the chain gang. You wrong! I use to go wit him, but since I been wit you, I ain't had no dealing wit him. Whoever told you dat done told you a damn lie. I don't do dat no more."

I stood frozen in my tracks, visualizing the evening Mrs. Lara fell from the back door of Cousin Sattie Bell's kitchen. Daddy stepped over her without lifting a hand to help her up. He went in between the houses and embraced Pallie Lea. That hadn't been so long ago. She was lying. Mr. Danny had found out the truth, and she was trying to lie her way out of it. Listening to that horrible confession was so hurtful. I never looked at my mama's cousin the same way again.

***

I was awakened in the later part of the night by another dream about the man with the long beard. He said, "Revival is starting, and I want you to join Old First Bethel Church. It is time for you to accept Jesus as your personal Lord and Savior." On the other side of the bed stood Sister Greta Garland, and there was the sound of drums beating and tambourines playing. Awake, I could not get those dreams out of my head. I wondered what they meant. I didn't know, but I felt something good was going to come out of those dreams.

***

Nookie, Carl, and Georgie Boy were playing behind the woodpile. School was out, and there was nothing to do. I was bored as well as angry. I was sick of watching children and washing diapers. I couldn't pick blackberries; they were not ripe. The cucumbers were just getting started up at the cucumber house, where most of the town children had summer jobs. I was stuck on the porch, watching the children.

I spotted Mrs. Phillips's ducks plucking away at the grass from her backyard to ours. For some reason, they irritated me, and I targeted them to take my frustration out on. Or it could have that the dreams were going around in my head and I was hoping something pleasant would happen, but my mind was overpowered by evil thoughts.

I heard somebody call out my name and rushed to see who was calling. It was Tonk and Nookie. They said vacation Bible school was starting on Monday. That was something positive I had to look forward to. If I could attend, it would give me some kind of consolation, but I didn't see how I could, because of the children.

It worked itself out. Aunt Matilda agreed to watch Billy, and Willa Max was old enough to come with us. But I still wasn't satisfied with having to take Willa Max with me. An evil spirit was taking over my body, and I was powerless to stop it.

***

Daddy came in and said he had to run to Tylerville. He didn't have to say for what; I knew it was more beer and moonshine. I had to watch the house while he was gone.

When I got inside, I heard moaning and groaning coming from Papa's room. He was lying faceup on his back in the bed, like he was in terrible pain of some kind.

I put my hands on his forehead and he felt warm. I couldn't tell if it was from the summer heat or if he had a fever. There wasn't any air stirring inside or anywhere else. Aunt Matilda's words rang in my ears: "Hell is ten time hotter than this."

The groaning increased. The way he sounded was frightening. I knew for sure something terrible was wrong. Not knowing what to do except get help, I called out for Tonk to fetch Mrs. Angie Rosa.

She came quickly. As always, before long the house was running over with caring neighbors, including Mr. Funeral Bellow. Mrs. Angie Rosa shouted, "Git de hell back outer here! Git outer Jenny Rue's house, Funeral Bellow. Ain't nobody dead."

He replied, "I got a call to come down here to Jenny Rue's house. Said er daddy was dead. Hell, I'm de undertaker. Dat's what I do—pick up de dead."

"Ain't nobody told you a damn thing. You tellin a lie. You ain't had a body since my brother Nathan. Now you desperate and circlin round like a buzzard, waiting for sumnutter to die."

We all waited patiently until Dr. Morrison came and examined Papa. He diagnosed Papa as having a stroke. It was serious but not fatal.

I was tired of sickness and fighting drunks. I ran out to the woodpile, looking over the land that we lived on, the air we breathed, and the sun that was burning through our skins. All sorts of imaginings swept through my mind. I felt like I had to do something spontaneous, mischievous, cruel, or destructive,

I looked, and there was all three of Mrs. Geraldine Phillips's ducks, quacking and shaking their tails all around Aunt Matilda's chicken coop. It felt like I watched them for hours, quacking and quacking. The quacking began to disturb me something awful.

One of the male ducks chased after a female duck. He ran her down and was on top of her, pecking away at her body. Another duck quacked, and he chase after it also. I picked up some rocks and threw them after him. He ran at me, and I ran from him in fear. I ran right into Nookie and Georgie Boy around the side of the house. I ran up on the porch to sat down to catch my breath. Anger rushed into my head.

I called out to Georgie Boy and Nookie to come. They came, and I told them to catch the big male duck and bring him to the back. I waited for them beside Aunt Matilda's chicken coop. The boys had a timid look upon them. I began to get a little impatient.

Mr. Danny came around the corner. He said he wanted me to do something for him. I lied and said I was doing a chore for Aunt Matilda. He looked at me suspiciously and walked on. I rushed in through the back door to see if he was gone, and spotted the ax standing at the side of the stove. I picked it up and walked back outside.

Nookie and Georgie Boy were still watching the duck, reluctant to catch him. I ordered them again to do so. The duck was quacking as they reached for him, and I realized he was smarter than any of us. Hell started to build up inside me; I was getting madder by the second. The way the boys were running around like two cowards made me even madder. Anguish pumped though my body and destruction ran around in my head nonstop.

The sun was hot. Sweat was pouring from the boys' bodies. In a flash, they stopped running after the duck and ran back toward me. The duck was chasing after them.

Something came over me that was beyond my control. I shouted angrily, "Go back and git em!" They tried to explain they couldn't catch him, and I refused to hear anything they had to say. I accused them of not trying hard enough.

I went over to the fence, grabbed a dog finder from the bush there, and hid it behind my back. I called the boys over to me calmly. Neither of them was wearing a shirt. Without saying another word, I slapped each of them across their naked, sweaty backs with all the strength I had. They both yelled out, but there was no one in sight to help them.

I didn't care how they hurt. All I wanted was for them to catch the duck.

They didn't want me to hit them again, so they took off after him and got him jammed up in a corner. They grabbed him from behind and brought him to me. I made them put his head on the bottom step and hold him down. I pulled the ax out. Tonk came running up; this was right down his alley. The three of them held the duck, and I chopped his head off.

Instantly, blood splattered all over us. I dropped the ax in a panic. I was shaking and couldn't stop. The duck lay kicking, and blood poured everywhere. I started screaming.

The boys were in fear and took off running, leaving me standing. I had to regroup. I covered my face. Reality had set in. That was a horrible thing I had felt compelled to do. What on earth provoked me to do such a vicious thing?

I knew I had to come up with something fast and not let anyone look into my eyes. One thing I had learned from Daddy was he could always tell when I was lying by looking in my eyes.

Daddy was just pulling up in front of the house. I could hear Mrs. Angie Rosa's voice. The boys had told her what I made them do. I knew I was going to get killed. She came rushing across the field, and I ran into the house,

By the time she approached Daddy and told him what I'd done, I had already changed out of my bloody clothes into clean ones. The duck lay dead on the ground; that was proof I couldn't lie my way out of. The boys were not going to jeopardize themselves for me. The only thing left for me to do was lie on them.

I started shouting before Daddy got to me. "Oooh, Daddy, Georgie Boy and Nookie done cut Mrs. Geraldine Phillips duck head off!" Knowing fully well I had done that horrible thing.

"What was you doing while they cut the duck head off?" Daddy demanded.

I hadn't thought of that complication. I was a little awed and instantly sorrowful. Remorse was all over me like an ugly stick.

"You can't even think of a good lie. I'm gon beat you g——d——ass!"

Out came Aunt Matilda, waking up from her afternoon nap. She had no knowledge of anything that has taken place. I lied to her before she could ask. "Them boys done cut Mrs. Phillips duck head off and they puttin all on me and Daddy gon whip me."

I got the surprise of my little lying life. She looked into my eyes and knew I was lying through my teeth. "Haley, Haley," she said, "stop you lyin. You gon go to hell wit all them lies. What done happen to you? All you do here lately is lie."

I was embarrassed. I couldn't deny the lie. I had committed the most hideous sins I ever committed and then tried to lie my way out of them all.

The boys came and faced me with the accusations I'd made against them. They faced me like two champs. Daddy asked me angrily, "Who cut that duck head off? And you betta not stand in front of my face and tell me no lie."

Nookie and Georgie Boy shouted out loud and truthfully, "Haley made us do it. She hit us on our back with that dog finder. We was scare, so we caught the duck. Us hold his head down, and she cut the duck head off and now trying to put it on us."

Daddy looked at me in so much anger. He knew I was lying, just as Aunt Matilda did. I kept my head down and didn't allow him to look into my eyes. I watched Aunt Matilda. For the first time since I got to know her, she didn't come to my defense. She couldn't allow me to go unpunished.

I was spared for the moment because Daddy's moonshine was delivered just then, and that got his attention. I knew he wouldn't forget it, but I tried to find a way to make him forget. As everybody scattered, I climbed up the chinaberry tree.

Everybody who came by that day was cold to me. I withdrew into my own world and shut everyone out except the two people I loved the most: my mama and Aunt Matilda.

Later that day, Daddy came to me and turned my world upside down. He said it was time I moved back home and learned from my mistakes. That was worse than any whipping I could have gotten.

Chapter 12: My Cotton-Picking Days

Daddy ordered me to go to the cotton fields and pick one hundred and twenty-five pounds of cotton every day. I would rather have gotten the whipping than go out in those hot fields each day and work like a slave. Working in the cotton fields also meant more days out of school come the fall.

I lay in the chinaberry tree and watched Mama sadly apologize to Mrs. Phillips. Mama offered to pay for the duck, but Mrs. Phillips refused the offer. She said she was sick of the ducks anyway and wished something would happen to the other two. The only reason they were there was because of her uncle Bentley; they belonged to him. Her last words to Mama were, "Forgit the duck."

But Daddy was determined to punish me for the killing of the duck. He promised Mama that I wouldn't be around to get into any more trouble. And I knew he had more up his sleeve.

I may never know the real reason I took my frustration out on the duck. It was a terrible thing to do, but I couldn't seem to stop myself. My life was starting to become hell on earth. The devil was slowly railing me in. I began doing treacherous things, and I could out-lie any child in the quarters.

Nothing was the same around Rat Row. I stayed angry all the time. I was never satisfied. I was furious at my mama and daddy, and I never had any remorse at what I did. I began to think how easy it would be for me to chop Daddy's head off the same way I did the duck.

Some days I cared about school, and then other days I didn't care if

I put my foot on school soil ever again. I had no one to share my deepest secrets with. My innermost thoughts became my darkest.

I worked in the fields that whole summer, along with Georgie Boy. Every penny we made, we gave to Mama.

The new school year was half gone before I was able to return to class. I was the laughingstock. My motivation was zero, and I had zero tolerance where anyone was concerned. By early January, I had been to school for only two days since September. Mrs. Crowley was the only person who did everything in her power to keep me encouraged. She never dropped me from the dance program. She was sure I only needed a few practices and I would be right up with the big shots. Some felt she should drop me, but she heard them not.

The day came for the first field day of the term. I was all dressed to perform—and then I was told I was not going to school. Ms. Jessie Luck was sick and nowhere to be found. I would have moved heaven and earth to get to school that day. The field day was the biggest event of the year. I thought Daddy was too stupid to know what was important. Or he was just as I always thought, evil as hell. I felt myself birthing out some of his evil spirit.

That morning, the sun was shining. It was a cold but beautiful day. Around ten thirty in the morning, I was inside the house with the new baby Mama had given birth to, James. A knock came to the door. I open it to see Mrs. Crwley standing in front of her 1956 blue-and-white Chevrolet Impala. She was wearing a look of disgust. "Haley, why aren't you in school? We go on stage in an hour."

I wanted to just bust out in tears. I tried hard to hold them back, but the impact of her words was too forceful. My voice trembled and I broke down crying. She took me in her arms and asked, "Where is your father?" I pointed inside.

She rushed inside with her hand stretched out, introducing herself to him politely. "Mr. Keath," she said, "I'm Mrs. Crowley, Ruth Crowley, Haley's dance instructor."

He never looked up.

She went on, "We are having our field day at school, and Haley is in the dance group. She tells me you won't let her participate in the dance."

I finally stopped crying long enough to hear what his excuse was. He sat quiet in that chair. Finally he cleared his throat and said, "Naw, she ain't gon no school. She under punishment, and beside, she got to stay here and see bout dese here chilluns."

I felt so uncomfortable and ashamed to have an evil daddy like him. She pleaded with him and detailed the importance of my being on the program, but he refused to let me go. "Mr. Macky, can't you please make this one exception? Just this once, let her go be in the play, and once it is over, I will bring her back home."

He wouldn't compromise at all. In a ferocious voice, he said, "Naw! Did you hear me de first time? I said naw and dat's what I mean."

She wiped the tears from my eyes, and her own eyes were full. She said, "It's going to be fine, Haley. Don't you worry. I have to run downtown and get some ribbon. I am so very sorry you can't come, but you take care."

I was not about to let that day end and I not be a part of it. I knew something had to be done, and I was the only one who could make it happen. Just because Daddy was ignorant, that didn't mean I had to be ignorant too. He didn't care anything about education, and he cared less if we got any. He was down to nothing, and it would suit him great if we ended up bootleggers like he was. But I would rather die.

I moped around the room, watching him until he fell asleep. Then I eased out of the house and on down to Aunt Matilda's, looking for my dance clothes. I found the jeans and shoes; unfortunately, I couldn't find my white shirt.

I knew Mrs. Crowley would be coming back through to get to school—at least, that was what I was hoping. I put on the first dress I could get my hands on, grabbed the pants and shoes, and ran out the back door without being seen.

I went around the woodpile and on to the corner by Pa Jack's café, close by the stop sign. I saw Mrs. Crowley approaching. When she came to a complete stop, I ran up to the car and hopped in so fast I frightened her. "Haley, my God! Where on earth did you come from?"

I was breathing so hard, I had to wait a second before I could speak.

Half choked from fear, I said, "Drive fast, Mrs. Crowley, so I kin be in the dance. I ain't got my blouse. I couldn't found it."

"That's fine. Getting a blouse is no problem," she said.

She drove downtown and bought me a white blouse, and we got back to school thirty minutes before the performance. The school was running over with folk from other schools. We went directly to her classroom. We were both so excited, neither of us realized I didn't have on any socks until I sat down for her to comb my hair. She made me a ponytail up on the top of my head and tied the red ribbon around it. Then she noticed my bare feet. "Haley, you don't have on any socks, baby. Never mind. I'll take care of that too. Maybe someone in here has feet your size." She was more determined than I was for me to be in that play.

"But all these children is too little. They is just in the first grade," I said.

She placed her hand to my face and said, "Honey, the grade doesn't matter. They come in all sizes. Don't you worry your pretty little head none. I am going to find you a pair of socks."

A student came in who was taller than I was. Her feet were larger, and she was wearing white socks. She said loudly, "Mrs. Crowley, that boy out dere keep on messing with somebody."

"Come over here, Johnson. Now, what have I been telling you about 'somebody'? Who is somebody?"

"Me I'm talking bout. He messin wit me."

Mrs. Crowley looked at her watch. "Oh no!" she said, panicky. "We're going on in fifteen minutes. I'm sorry, Lulu, sweetheart. I'll deal with whoever you're talking about later. But right this minute, I have to get my girls in place." She looked down at the girl's feet. "By the way, what size shoe do you wear?"

"I wear size eight."

"I need to borrow your socks for about an hour, please. I will make sure you get them back. This little girl need them to be in a program, if you will be so kind? I will make it worth your time."

The girl looked at me, smiling, and I could tell she was overjoyed to do it. It was like an angel came down from heaven to be my helper.

The socks were too big for my little feet, but I tucked them under my toes and in five minutes we were in the back of the stage. The speaker of the program said, "To the principal, faculty, students, families, friends, and visitors, we will now present a dance program by our own finest jamboree dance group, orchestrated by none other than Mrs. Ruth Crowley."

We lined up and walked out on that stage, and we came in first place. The audience's clapping and yelling made Mrs. Crowley really proud of us. The other girls had their families there to support them. The only person I had was my sister Tise. When the curtain opened and we took our final bow, I saw her smiling, sitting beside her boyfriend and her friend Millie Mae.

My day had been rewarding; now I had to face the consequences of my actions. I dreaded going home, but I had something inside me not even my father could take away. It would have been worth the whipping, but he was nowhere to be found.

The spirit was flowing and voices were coming from Mama's kitchen. Mrs. Alice and Roxie were there, two of the new women who had moved into Brake's quarter. They were discussing my sister Passy Kate and her friends Lila and Antoinette.

This was one of those eavedropping days. I wanted to know what they were talking about, but I couldn't relate to what they were saying. I decided to get closer by moving to the front side of the room.

Papa was groaning so loud, I forgot all about the conversation. He looked really sick. His eyes were dim and had no color. He looked up when I called out his name. He could barely hold his head up. His chin trembled. I asked softly, "Papa, how you feeling?"

He managed to blink and said, "I'm doin pretty good, I guess." He didn't seem to recognize who I was. Instantly he was down again, his his eyes looking directly up at the ceiling. I watched him for a few seconds, then quietly left the room.

The women was leaving the kitchen like they had accomplished something. Their facial expressions weren't looking too pleased. I was pretty uncomfortable with the way Mama was sitting at the table, almost in tears.

Mrs. Angie Rosa and Passy Kate's grandmama, whom everyone called Aunt Pancy, came up about the same time the other women were leaving. They came to see how Papa was doing. I knew when they came around, I would learn all the gossip in town. Mrs. Angie Rosa was the garbage can, and Aunt Pancy was the dumpster. So I decided to hang around a little while longer.

As always, Mama welcomed them in, inviting them to make themselves at home. And believe me, they did.

It was no secret that Aunt Pancy hated Mrs. Angie Rosa, and the feeling was mutual. Mama told me, "Go on outside and don't be listening to grown folk conversation." (She must be turning over in her grave as I write this. She never knew the many conversations I sneaked around and listened to. If she had, I probably wouldn't be writing these stories.) I left the room as she insisted, but I didn't go outside. I went behind the icebox, put my ear to the wall, and heard every ugly word they said.

Aunt Pancy had a mouth on her. She went from neighborhood to neighborhood, gossiping about everything and everybody. Whenever Pancy Suller came around, we all knew it was nothing but trouble brewing. Everyone in Rat Row hated to see her come. Once she got the hurricane roaring, she would stay away for weeks. When she thought everything was forgotten, she would come slithering back like the snake people said she was, ready to bite somebody else.

***

The school year was ending. I could imagine what the summer was going to be like. I kinda looked forward to going to the cotton field. I passed my grade, God knows how. Georgie Boy and I both went to the cotton fields, working hard for our school clothes.

All the families on Rat Row worked on the same farm for Sheriff Fonda. He was the brother of that low-down dirty Lund Cabb, the police chief. There was a big difference between the two of them. Lund was unfeeling and hated blacks. To him, we were just filthy niggers. On the other hand, Fonda was caring, compassionate, and very sympathetic to blacks. He called us "colored folk." But we all still knew he was a white man.

White folk went up and down the roads, seeking cotton pickers from all parts of the county. Daddy chose to work for Fonda Cabb. Word was he paid more than the rest of the croppers, and besides, the sheriff was in Daddy's hip pocket.

Sheriff Fonda was never around in the field. He had a right-hand man named Bon Alp Lopaze who looked after the crops, picked up the hands, and drove us to and from work each day. He was an old coon hunter and as poor as we were.

He had a daughter named Marlene Lopaze. She was around seventeen years old when we started and had already dropped out of high school. She kept the books and recorded how many pounds of cotton each hand picked. She did the weighing and totaled the wages and paid us off every evening.

His oldest son, Bon Alp Junior, worked in the field right alongside us. Nobody could tell him he was not black.

The beginning of the day was hell. The cotton stalks were wringing wet. It wasn't the piece of cake I thought it would be; I had forgotten how wet we got, picking down those long rows until the sun came out. Those were not easy times for us. But other than our parents working in white folks' houses as maids and handymen, the cotton fields were the only means of making any money. I wanted to buy more clothes. I hadn't had any new since Montana bought them. I had worn those until I grew out of them. They were good while they lasted.

The rows were long. The cotton stalks sagged from one side of the row to the other. The cotton was wet and cold, making it hard to pick. When the sun came out and dried the dew up, we all worked faster. We got through the days with laughter, joke-telling, and blues-singing.

Every now and then, one of the sisters would break out in a hymn that echoed all across the field. Afterward, one of the the brothers would send up a touching, delivering prayer that everyone in the field could relate to. They would say the good Lord had heard the prayer when a cool breeze swept across everyone's faces. Voices were constantly heard all across the fields, and that helped the day go by quickly. Those days became a lifetime of memory.

Picking cotton was hard physical labor. Some folk seemed really enjoy it. If there wasn't cotton picking, there was hoeing peanuts, pulling corn, or digging roots. What a way of life, and the little money that the white man paid was inhuman.

No matter how I tried, I could not get used to that hot, hot sun beaming down on my body every day. I wore a large straw hat on my head, yet it was not enough. I never understood how older people made it through the day, why they didn't die out there from heatstroke. Later, I thought of it as the goodness and mercy of God.

Many times, Cousin Lula Purkinson stood up in the field, tall like Aunt Lucy Sue. You could tell her from anyone else in the field. She would pour a big dip of snuff into her bottom lip, take that big, wide, Mexican hat off of her head, and fan with it for a minute or two. She used her apron to wipe the sweat that was blinding her vision. Then she would shout out, and her voice echoed all over the field: "Hey, Lord, he ain't sleep. He see what we going through, and he'll send us a cool breeze after while." Lo and behold, soon after the coolest wind would sweep across the field, and that would drive us to go a little bit farther.

There were times I thought I was going to collapse from the heat, and pulling that old, long sack on my shoulder was unbearable. I had to get used to being out there five days a week and sometimes half of Saturday. I hated being worked like a slave. But that was the only thing I had to look forward to every summer. I had no choice but to make the best of a bad situation, learning how to get better at what I was doing to make as much money as I could.

But to work all week and have an evil, mean man such as my daddy take my money became too much to swallow. Nothing was ever right at home. Daddy was a daddy in name only. You would think he would learn from other fathers in the quarters how a father should treat his family.

It wasn't just folk from Rat Row out in the fields. Every now and then we looked across to the other side of the field and saw the white folk picking. No matter how poor they were and how ragged they looked, they were still white and thought they were superior to us.

***

Old John Sap was the raccoon catcher. Lord knows he gave us many of them. When Mama cooked them, she boiled them half done and then surrounded them with sweet potatoes and finished baking them in the oven. Raccoons made the best meals, and at times they saved a lot of hungry stomachs.

Sunday was our day of rejoicing. It was the most enjoyable time of the week. I depended on church to help me get throught the rough times. I often tried to be like the rest of the workers picking cotton. To them, Sunday meant sitting down to the kitchen table after church on a beautiful evening and eating a good dinner.

Aunt Lucy Sue lived out in Rooks Iron quarter. She gave us some pleasure when we went out to visit on weekends. We were dog tired, but something about being up at my auntie's house was different. The atmosphere was different; the breeze felt different.

That summer was unforgettable. We worked hard but never saw a dime of our money. I didn't mind Mama having it, but to learn Daddy was taking what we earned so other women could enjoy it was more than I could stomach. The more Georgie Boy and I picked, the more Daddy expected us to pick. By the end of the summer, we were each picking over a hundred pounds of cotton a day.

Daddy went on one of his drunken sprees. He didn't go to the field with us but put Mrs. Mattie Willop to be our overseer. What a nightmare that was. She had no compassion for us at all. She was mean, one-eyed, and controlling.

She worked Georgie Boy and I like we were her own personal slaves. She made it perfectly clear that she was not Macky Keath, but we better act like she was. She would take the two rows between us, making it impossible for us to talk to each other. She always reminded us that she didn't want to hear any talking; all she wanted was to see the cotton stalks moving. She had us too afraid to even look across at each other. I grew to hate her, so badly that it became painful.

At the start of the day, she would choose the rows for us. Mine always had cotton running over out of the Freddys. Then she'd get between us and say, "I don't want to hear a mumble or a wimple out of none one ob ya. I mean y'all better take them rows down to the other end, and you better not let me catch up wit ya neither." Snuff would pop from her lips as she spoke. She had some kind of vindictiveness toward us for whatever reason.

Once she picked a few stalks, she would look along the row and find the biggest, tallest stalks. Pulling up two, she would skin all the leaves off of them and plait them together. Then she would go back to picking. If she caught up with us, she would beat the skin from our bodies with those stalks. She was one who loved to pick cotton and had enough experience that she could pick four or five rows to our one. Still, we tried our hardest because I didn't want her beating on us like we were animals. I worked and cried. She would almost be upon us, and the good Lord would give us more strength to pick a little faster.

One time, Mrs. Angie Rosa told a joke about the rabbit and a man. Everyone laughed except Georgie Boy and me. Tonk called, "Hey, Haley Keath, what go all way round a house and don't make a track?"

I wanted desperately to answer, but before I could say a word, Mrs. Mattie Willop shouted, "You ain't got time to talk. You better be working, and don't let me catch up to you neither."

I guessed she was about thirty steps away from us, and I was determined she was not going to catch me. I started putting stems, leaves, rocks, and all into the sack, filling it fast. The sack commenced to get uncomfortably heavy, dragging so hard on my shoulder that I could hardly pull it.

When they called across the field, "Empty time!" I was relieved. My prayer had been answered. Without a shadow of a doubt, the Lord was my shepherd.

It was no secret how desperately Mrs. Willop wanted to whip me. After we had weighed in the cotton, she said, "You better be glad you didn't let me catch up wit you, cause I want to whip your ass so bad till my own ass itch."

I was convinced she wanted to skin me alive because she had that lusting kind of hidden vendetta against my father. I watched her reactions whenever she was in his presence. All of the town knew Daddy was a womanizer, but she was not one of his women. She lived on Rat Row too, but had a good, respectable reputation, and we were as nobodies to her. She thought her children were better than any other children in the neighborhood. I'd be damned if I was going to allow her to beat me or my brother again.

I noticed that her boys picked cotton, but her girls Marjorette and Annabeth didn't. Marjorette was a very quiet young lady with long hair down to her back. She acted as if something was terribly wrong with her, and I learned she had several ailments. These caused her to be unfriendly and deprived her of socializing. She seemed to be very shy. On the other hand, Annabeth was overweight and light-skinned. She was so light, she looked white. She was the friendliest one in their household. The only time they were seen was in church on Sunday, walking to or from the store, or sitting on the front porch.

My determination was to find out as much about the Willops as I possibly could. I detested old Mrs. Willop as much as she did me. I learned an eye for an eye and a tooth for a tooth. As long as she couldn't catch up with me, then she couldn't whip me. Something had happen to her, and it was hidden, but not for long.

We were out of work for a couple of weeks due to rainy weather. I had the opportunity to go to school. When the rain was over, I had to return to the fields and work while her girls attended school. Our first day back in that damn field was pure hell. The cotton was really wet. That was a good thing in the beginning, until old Bon Alp started to deduct pounds from our sacks. We only picked half sacks because the wetness made the cotton so heavy and the sacks impossible to pull. Our clothes were soaked from the stalks. When the sun came out, that was a blessing.

But that last sack of cotton before the sun came bearing down was too heavy for me. I called out Mrs. Willop's name several times. I knew she heard me calling, but she refused to answer. I pulled the sack off my shoulder and started walking toward her, still calling. She stood up between the rows with her hat in her hand. Sweat rolled down her face, covering her good eye. Her other eye was bad and prevented her from seeing me clearly.

Her hearing, though, was not dull. I was about five steps from her face when I said, "Ms. Mattie, I can't pull dat sack of cotton on my shoulder no more cause it's too heavy. It got my back and shoulder hurtin real bad. Kin I go empty now?" I was shivering, mostly from fear of the evil eye she was giving me.

That woman looked me up and down with her one good eye and in a cold, flippant tone said, "You ain't got no back. You got a grisser. An if you let me catch up wit you, which I'm bout to do, your little ass gon hurt."

I knew there was no reasoning with that woman. I hated Mrs. Mattie Willop with every part of my body. As I stood there, speechless, soaked, and shivering in front of her, I urinated on myself.

She never knew I did it, because God stepped in; other hands called out "Empty time!" Tonk came over and took up my sack for me. While I had been standing before her, he had been picking from my row, giving me a lead. She was made to look bad. If it hadn't been for Tonk that day, I wonder if she would have caught me, given the condition my back and shoulder were in.

When we returned from weighing, the cotton was beginning to dry up. I picked as fast and hard as I possibly could. I was two sacks of cotton ahead of Mrs. Willop, making her wonder how I got so far. She was not going to be outsmarted. She stood over me and asked, cold and nasty, "Who helped you pick this row up here? I know you didn't do it by yourself."

"Who help me? Nobody help me."

She spit out a big hunk of snuff. "If I found out you lying to me, I'mo put this cotton stalk on your black ass. Now git on up dere on dat row, and dis time I want it all the way to the end wit no slowing eround neither. I wanter beat your ass so bad, I could just taste you."

Looking to the author and the finsher of my faith, I thought, *Lord, help me to know why this old, ugly-ass, cockeyed woman want to beat my ass so bad.* No one else in that whole damn field got as cruel treatment from anyone as I did from her.

I had to be obedient in those days. Not a mumbling word were we allowed to speak back to an adult, whether they were right or wrong. I fought back tears and swallowed my pain until I was at the end of the row. I wanted to do bodily injury to her so badly, I could hardly move.

By the end of the season, I was picking over one hundred and twenty-five pounds of cotton per day. But at least we didn't have to be under her supervision for the last two weeks. Daddy came and worked with us. I knew any time he came out to the fields, the whiskey was out and he had to get money to replenish it.

School had reopened, and Georgie Boy and I were sure we were starting along with the other children. School was my major priority; I wanted so much to finish high school. I had positioned myself to believe we would at least go two or three days out of the week, but I was wrong again. We went for one week, and were out again for the three months before Christmas. By then I dreaded to return for the little time we had before the holidays, but I accepted what I could get, even being as far behind the entire class as I was.

My homeroom teacher, Mrs. Brittney, knew all about our life, that we were the products of our environment. She lived on Peer Street in a beautiful pink-and-white house surrounded with sunflowers, roses of all colors, and honeysuckle that we could smell all the way from her end of the street to the end where we lived—but our end was Rat Row. She always had her nose stuck up in the air as if she were smelling her own lips. That's who she was, but she was an excellent English teacher.

I returned to school feeling ashamed and sad because I knew she was going to ask in front of the whole class why I hadn't been to school, though she knew full well what I had been doing. She was one of those old-fashioned, educated teachers who didn't care about humiliating anyone, especially me, because we didn't live up to her level.

She called the roll. For each student name who been absent, she asked, "Why haven't you been in school?"

Everyone had the same answer: "We were out picking cotton."

I felt easy that I was not the only student who had not been coming to school. The entire class had been absent except Doletha and her gang. And when Mrs. Brittney called out my name and I said present, she only said, "Keath, it's good to have you back this morning."

Doletha, Marie Lee, Patrice Ball, Mella Kempton—their eyes fell on me. It was all starting again. They whispered, and I knew they were whispering about me.

But Elanda Burke and my good friend Skitter pulled their seats up close to mine and clung to me with all the love they could muscle up. Doletha and her henchmen did everything they could to discredit me to Skitter and Elanda, but they didn't fall into her net.

Later that week, they somehow managed to get to Skitter in the lunchroom. During recess time after lunch, I saw the gang approaching the jungle gym, where I was standing. I sensed trouble but didn't know they had lied to Skitter. She was coming behind them. I started to make my way toward her. She had an unpleasant look on her face. The gang formed a circle around us, and before I knew what was happening, someone pushed me into her hard.

That was the start of an awful fight between us. Then the gang saw the teachers coming and took off running like the cowards they were. Elanda and a girl from another classroom stopped Skitter and I. We were separated and taken to Mrs. Brittney's classroom.

We both were crying, so ashamed of ourselves. Mrs. Brittney was sitting at her desk, ashamed for us too. She didn't even have to ask us what happened because she had witnessed the whole sordid ordeal from the foyer. What she didn't know was why the incident happened. She asked angrily, "What on earth were you all fighting about? You all are supposed to be friends."

I answered as truthfully as I possibly could. Skitter said, "I don't know why we were fighting. She told Doletha a story on me, but I wasn't going to fight with her about it. I just wanted to know why she told that story on me." Neither of us knew the real reason we were fighting: Doletha had told Skitter a vicious lie.

Skitter and I hugged and made up. Doletha wasn't so lucky. Mrs.

Brittney knew she was behind it all, and did not let Doletha get away with it.

She made her way to the door and quickly opened it. In fell Doletha with her ear practicaily glued to the door. She had to make it seem like someone had pushed her in. But we all knew she was an eavesdropper; she couldn't lie her way out of that one. "Get in here, Bradbusch," Mrs. Brittney said harshly. "What you got to say about yourself?"

Immediately, Doletha's mouth flew wide open. "Ball, why you pushed me up against that door?"

As usual, Patrice Ball took the bait. "I didn't mean to! I was trying to git into class fore the bell rang."

Mrs. Brittney was calm. She knew Doletha like the back of her hand. She said, "I was about to go out and look for you, Doletha, but look—faith just blew you in." She was furious. I had never seen her that angry since the day the Benderson girls stuck her nose-down in the outdoor toilet. She made Patrice and Marie Lee go outside and said she wanted to speak to Doletha alone.

They went out the door, mumbling something no one could hear. That made her even angrier. "Girls," she said, "don't talk under your lips. If y'all have anything to say, say it when I finish with Bradbusch. You will get your chance."

Doletha sat between Skitter and I, all huffed and puffed like she was about to blow us up. Mrs. Brittney closed the door, turned around, and stood directly before Doletha. "Doletha, I'm surprised at you. I am tired of you continually disturbing my class. Well, guess what? It is over. I've got only one question for you: why did you go to Skitter and lie about Keath so they would fight?"

Doletha began to shout, as she always did when she was caught in a deception. "I ain't caused nobody to fight!"

"Look at you, getting all hysterical. Why you got to shout? Can't you discuss this in a calm manner?"

Shame struck Doletha silent. Mrs. Brittney grilled her with one question after another until she gave the truth—that I never told her anything about Skitter. Mrs. Brittney heard her, but she was not pleased, so she made her repeat it. Then Mrs. Brittney cautioned her that there would be severe consequences if Doletha did anything like that again.

Mrs. Brittney got her strap and made Doletha stand up and hold her hand out. She gave her five hard licks in each hand. Doletha didn't take it too well. She goggled her eyes and shed not a single tear. Afterward, she ran out the door, slamming it as hard as she'd been hit, making sure she got all our attention.

Once she was gone, Mrs. Brittney allowed Skitter and I to apologize to each other. We hugged, and our friendship continued even stronger.

***

That year started off pretty rough for Daddy, and what affected him affected the whole family. Mr. Danny and Pallie Lea moved in together. He pulled away from Daddy in the wood business and went solo. Before long, he had taken the majority of the customers, ending their friendship. Everything was now out about that affair, and they continued to have it right under Daddy's nose. It was obvious Mama was too weak to do anything about Daddy and Pallie Lea, but Mr. Danny was not.

From then on, nothing seemed to work for Daddy. His wood business was practically shut down. Whiskey was scarce, leaving him penniless. The only money coming in was the ten dollars Mama earned from the maid work she was doing at Connie Ray's and Jack Henry's houses. She had a heart of gold. What she had, she made stretch farther than even she could imagine. She made barely enough to pay the rent and buy food for us.

Her friend Odessa was there for every meal. She made sure Mama's house was clean on her work days, and she helped Mama around the house, taking some of the load off of me. She and Aunt Matilda were true friends to my mother. I wondered what she would have done without them. God always has a ram in the bush. If it had not been them, it would have been someone else.

Going to school became more and more abominable. There was just no escaping the pain. Doletha and her gang never missed an opportunity to take advantage of my mishaps. But no matter what happened, Skitter was always there to help me.

Can-cans and poodle skirts were popular. I wanted to look decent, like the other students. We were allowed to keep all the money we made on Saturdays. I worked really hard to earn more than six dollars. The can-cans were only one dollar, and the dress was two dollars. I got myself a beautiful black dress with yellow stars and moons on it. I had enough money left to get a pair of black loafers.

All excited about my new clothes, I couldn't wait until Monday. I stopped by Mama's after shopping to show her my new outfits and to look in on Papa. Daddy was in the kitchen with the rent man, Mr. Leman. They were drunk asleep. I could tell Daddy's shipment of moonshine had come in.

As I was about to pass through the kitchen into Papa's room, a ten-dollar bill lying under a chair caught my eye. I was in a daze looking at the money. I made sure they were not pretending to be asleep. I didn't know what to do.

One part of my mind said, "Get the money! Losers weepers, finders keepers." I rushed over, picked the money up from the floor, and didn't stop running until I reached Aunt Matilda's. It was my lucky day. I didn't feel nervous or afraid. I felt brave for taking a chance with pride. I could eat hot lunch for ten weeks at a dollar a week. The good Lord, I was always told, worked in mysterious ways.

Monday was chapter day at school. I wore my new dress. I had to admit to myself I wasn't feeling hideous, as I normally did. I felt beautiful. Skitter met me at the side door. She and I walked on together. She gave me compliments and I felt more beautiful.

We arrived in the auditorium, and all eyes fell on us. I could literally see the envy and jealousy on Doletha's face. She started whispering, and I knew trouble was going to follow. I was well prepared, I thought.

After the chapter service was over, it was recess time. Skitter and I made a beeline for the door out to the playground and lay back in the lovely sunshine.

All hell broke loose. The gang lay down on the grass a few feet from where we were, so Skitter and I moved. Everywhere we moved, the gang would move. I was about to get up yet again, and that long-legged Paulette Loomis, Patrice's cousin, stepped on my dress. She ripped my can-can off me.

The gang broke and ran when they saw Mr. Garnett coming out of his room. He warned all of us that if any fighting broke out, we were going to get it. He hadn't seen Paulette standing on my dress, so the warning was for all of us.

I was so damn angry, I rushed up to Paulette. She stood about five feet five inches, the same height as Doletha and much taller than me. I hit her hard in the face. She had long arms. I backed away, and when she swung at me, I went under her. I managed to get my hands in her ponytail and I dragged her to the ground. I got my shoe off and beat her in the head till someone pulled me from her. I was like a hungry lion, even after I was separated from her.

I never hated anyone as much as I hated those girls on that day. I hated them more than I hated my father. From then on, hatred commenced to consume me. I believe if I'd had any weapon besides my shoe, I would have used it on them all.

I was taken to Mrs. Brittney's classroom, and she and my sister Tise came in. Tise told me I was nothing but an embarrassment to her. She believed I was the one initiating the fights. She didn't know I was defending myself in every way possible. I explained how the gang attacked me and ripped my can-can to pieces. They were shocked to see my can-can dragging and torn to pieces. All the gang were yelling and lying, but Mrs. Brittney knew better. She warned me not to be near them, but what she was not getting was that I was never near them. They made it their business to come find Skitter and me.

Because I fought Paulette and beat her in the head, I ended up getting fifteen stripes in my hand. I wasn't hurt so badly over the striping. My pride was hurt more because of the lies the gang told.

Skitter had tried to explain that I was taking up for her, thinking that would help me. Tise's friend Millie Mae said in a loud voice, "Honey! You can't just be fighting for nobody else. You got to fight for yourself and let Skitter Monroe fight for herself."

I looked at her angrily and said, "I took up for her then, and I'll take up for her ergin if need be."

Millie Mae took that as I was sassy, and told Tise to leave me alone because that was the Macky Keath in me. I took it as an insult, but she meant it as a compliment. As I was walking home after school, they caught up to me and tried to give me the best advice they could, since they were older and wiser than I. I took it as caring until I felt they were taking up for the others and not me. Millie Mae said, "You keep on taking up for Skitter Monroe and see if Mr. Monroe gon gib you an A for it."

I got mad and yelled at her. "It ain't none of your bald-headed business. And leave me erlone!" I didn't know those words would haunt me for many years to come.

She refused to allow me to get the last word in. "Well, you need to cut out all this fighting and making your sister shamed!"

Tise said nothing. I wondered why Tise let her talk to me that way. Finally she told Tise to leave me alone, that nobody could tell me anything. I felt as though Tise took Millie Mae's side against me. Millie Mae had somewhat of a controlling spirit, and Tise was very humble and soft-spoken. I took off running away from both of them, more angry and confused than ever.

Later that evening, I was sitting all alone out by the woodpile, drawing on the ground. Tise came out and tried to give me a sisterly pep talk without knowing all the facts. "I wouldn't taking up for nobody, Haley. It just that every day, somebody is coming to me telling me, 'Tise, your sister fightin.' How do you think that make me feel? Havin to hear that all you come to school to do is fight?"

I explained, "I fight cause Doletha an her gang picks on me and Skitter all the time, in the class an out the class. What are we suppose to do, nothing?"

She listened to what I had to say and promised that from then on, she would be looking out for us. Wherever Skitter and I played, Tise and her boyfriend Ernie J were always close by until school ended for the summer.

Chapter 13: Everything Has an Ending; Nothing Lasts Forever

Being out of school that summer seemed like a whole new beginning to me. I was no longer that nappy-headed little pigtail-wearing girl from Rat Row. I was growing into a beautiful young lady. I looked at life in a brand-new aspect, thanks to Glory Ann and Ruthella. They persuaded Daddy to let me get out and go to the picture show with them. It took some doing, but they did it. They both were very convincing. He gave in to them and allowed me to go if I did all of my chores.

All that week, I prepared to go to the picture show. It was a brand-new outing for me, and I was certainly looking forward to it. This was also the last week of revival at Greater New Salem Baptist Church. During the next week, the revival would move to Old First Bethel Church, and the preacher would be from Montgomery, Alabama. Everyone looked forward to the revival.

I liked Greater New Salem, where Mama was a member. The members there were friendlier than Old First Bethel's congregation, where all the high-class folk with the beautiful homes, nice cars, decent jobs, and education attended. The Jones-Williamses and the Harrises went there, just to name a few. They mostly looked down on poverty-level families such as ours. But that never mattered to me, because there were some at Greater New Salem who were the same way.

Each church held services on its own Sunday once a month, so everybody went to the same church, rotating from one to the next. But folk were members of or "attended" a specific church. Skitter attended

Old First Bethel, and that was where I wanted to attend, though I knew that would never happen.

Monday night of the revival week, we arrived at church early. We were one of the first families there besides Skitter's. Colleen and Theresa were preparing to usher, passing out fans and leading us down the middle aisle to be seated, Aunt Matilda sat on the front row alongside the other mothers, where she always sat. Skitter and I sat on the third row. I spotted Doletha sitting with Della and Alicia and some more of her relatives. The moment they saw us, the whispering began, just like they did in school. We knew they were saying things about us. Skitter always said, "Pay them no never mind, Haley," but I was not as intelligent as she was. I couldn't hold my peace. I goggled my eyes and licked my tongue at them until they no longer looked our way. People steadily came in, and before long there was standing room only.

Deacon Phillips and Deacon Williams began the service with the opening song "Won't It Be Grand." Then old Mr. Phillips broke out with Hymn 96, "A Charge."

Prayer was led by Deacon Martin Cainey. He prayed like no other. Once the prayer was prayed, Mrs. Rachel broke out singing. Then the preacher came forth.

Rev. Sandles was a middle-aged preacher, around fifty-five years old, with salt-and-pepper hair. He wasn't long-winded at all, but his sermon was meaningful. Folk shouted, fainted, and hollered as they usual did on Sunday, and it was always the same ones.

Old lady Lila Bush popped her jaws before she began hollering, "Yes, Jesus, preach his words." She shook all over before jumping to her feet and slinging her arms every which way, hitting and practically knocking over everybody who tried to hold her down. It took three or four deacons to carry her out.

This time it seemed every woman in the church was shouting. The sermon was about forty-five minutes long, and then Rev. Sandles walked out, saying the doors of the church were open. He broke out in a song, and the ushers came down. They placed two chairs before the pulpit. The entire church joined in, singing "Come to Jesus" and then the hymn "Must Jesus Bear the Cross Alone."

The reverend held both of his hands out, asking, "Will there be one tonight? Will you come to Jesus?" No one came. The congregation sang, and he walked up and down the aisles, waving his hands, asking, "Won't you come tonight?" Some of the sisters were still shouting and thanking the Lord for his many blessings.

The pastor called the deacons up for the collection. They knew the right words to say to get every cent of the people's money. They drilled into the minds of the people that Rev. Sandles had preached a very spiritual sermon, and now it was time to show him just how much they really loved the Lord. I sat wondering how come the preacher got paid so much money when he was supposed to be doing it for God. Later I learned that the Scripture said Jesus warned the disciples to "freely give as they had freely received" the Good Word.

The two deacons pulled the table out to the center of the floor for the collection. Folk began to form the lines. Mr. Eddie Kirkland walked up to the table, pulling his billfold from his back pocket and repeating what the deacon had said: "The Lord said give all you can, and before you get home, he will provide." He was so eager, he pulled out a ten-dollar bill and laid it on the offering table, saying, "This here's my last ten, so I'mo try God." By the time everyone had gone by, the table was full of money. The talk on the church grounds and all the way home was about Mr. Eddie Kirland giving his last ten. The most faithful Christians were the main ones talking about how foolish he was.

On Wednesday night after revival, when Aunt Matilda and I got home, something continued to nag me from inside. My mind was focused on the man in the dreams I continued to have. I could hear Rev. Sandles's voice ringing in my ears, saying, "Will there be one tonight? Come as you are."

After going to bed and entering into a sound sleep. I saw the dream man's face. This time, he was dressed all in black, and he looked angry. He came toward me in slow motion. At one point I thought my blood had stopped circulating. I started to take in slow breaths. The slower he moved, the farther away he seemed. He pointed his hands toward me. I was trying to wake up, but I couldn't.

Then he was up to the bed. He bent over me. I tried to speak, but my lips were sealed. He said in a gentle whisper, "Tomorrow night is your night. When Rev. Sandles comes around waving his hand, you will get up and give him yours."

I kept my eyes as tight shut as I could. I didn't want to open them. With all that black on, I couldn't tell what he looked like. He bent even closer to to me, as if he was about to kiss my lips. "Promise me! You will join Old First Bethel Church tomorrow night."

In that dream, without any hesitation, I made a solemn promise that I would join. I said it over and over again: "Yes, I will join Old First Bethel Church. Just leave me alone. I promise. I promise."

He backed away silently. "I will be beside you, with you, to protect you all the way." And he was gone.

I sat straight up in the bed, shaking like a leaf on a tree. I opened my eyes and looked all around the room, but no one was there. Aunt Matilda was sound asleep. I wanted desperately to tell somebody about that dream, but there was no one to tell.

Early that morning, Mama come a-calling. She was getting all of her chores done. Out of all nights, she had decided to go to church on that one.

I thought, *Joining Old First Bethel Church was only a dream*. I knew with her being at the revival, joining was out of the question. But like I said, it was only a dream. I had nothing to fear.

When we arrived, it was like the whole town was there. I got the most uncomfortable feeling I had ever felt. We were at Old First Bethel Church, where all the members were nose up. I sat down with the voice of that man ringing in my ears. I was in fear but I was also coherent. I thought that joining that church was not for me, but something was happening to me that I couldn't explain. If I couldn't understand it, I knew nobody else would understand either.

Mama and Mrs. Essie Mae Tilman sat right behind where I was sitting. The church was soon standing room only. The singers in the choir stood, all geared up and ready for the preacher to bring the Word. I looked around in fear, so obvious that Mama tapped my shoulder and scolded, "Stop that turning round looking at people like you ain't got good sense, gal."

I jumped in my seat and started to cry. But once the deacons began the service, I felt a calmness come over me. As the church was singing, I looked to the back of the choir and saw the face of the man who had been visiting my dreams. I was not asleep, and I was not dreaming. I saw him: the face, the beard, the complexion, the height, and the smile. He looked directly into my eyes and said, "Cheer up, my child. I am with you." Then he was gone.

I quickly blinked my eyes twice as if something was in them. I couldn't believe what was happening to me. I was not hallucinating. What I experienced was real.

A deacon was imploring prayers for everybody. A sensation moved down my shoulder to the soles of my feet and sent waves of shock all over my body. I was no longer frightened. I felt proud. I knew it was the power of God. I felt the Holy Ghost for the very first time in my life.

People were shouting in every aisle. Mrs. Angie Rosa, Ms. Lila Bush, and Aunt Pancy were leading it. The Holy Spirit was certainly moving there that night. I often wondered if it was the Holy Ghost on them or just their emotions.

The reverend came on with his sermon. We knew he wouldn't be up long. He preached on the five wise and five foolish virgins, then took us to the cross. The church quieted a little, but he jumped up and down and got them all started again. Everybody was clapping their hands. Ms. Lila Bush shouted, "Amen! Preach it," and Mrs. Angie Rosa shouted too.

The ushers set the two chairs out in front of the pulpit, and everyone sang. The reverend walked up and down the aisles with both hands out, pleading for someone to come give their life to the Lord. "Will there be one tonight? Will you come give Jesus your life? Jesus can save you. Won't there be one tonight?"

The dream man's voice began to speak to me. His voice sounding far off, as did the preacher's. I was in amazement when the preacher stopped directly in front of me. "Brothers and sisters, we need Jesus in our lives. When we get Jesus in our lives, everything else comes natural. Can I get an amen?"

And all the congregation shouted out in one voice, "Amen!"

The preacher continued to ask, "Do we have one tonight?"

Skitter got up and placed her hands in his hands. Then Christine Stronglove got up and gave her hands to the preacher. The ushers placed two more chairs beside them.

The congregation sang, "Come to Jesus." Rev. Sandles was yet asking, "Will there be another man, woman, boy, or girl tonight? This might be your last chance. Will you come?" And he did something that sent chills up and down my body. He quoted the Scripture passage in which the Lord said, "Suffer little children to come unto me, and forbid them not: for of such is the kingdom of God" (Luke 18:16 KJV).

Two of the Brimsley girls walked up and seated themselves in the added chairs. For the first time, I experienced myself floating in the air, as if I had lost consciousness of what was happening around me. The dream man's voice steadily rang in my ears: "I'll protect you all the way."

Before I knew it, I was walking slowly up to the reverend. I could feel all eyes on me as I sat down in a chair. Aunt Matilda was smiling and crying happy tears. She shouted and clapped her hands, praising the Lord and thanking him for me. "Thank you, Master! Thank you, Jesus! Thank you!"

Mama had the most terrified look on her face. There was no excitement in her eyes, no smile. It was the opposite of Aunt Matilda's reaction.

I quickly dropped my head. I even felt like going back to my seat, but I was too ashamed. I didn't know what to do, or what I was doing for that matter. All I knew at that moment was that I was obeying a man I had only seen in my dreams.

The singing suddenly stopped. There was nothing but silence. I had everything sorted in my mind about what I was going to say when the preacher asked me to stand. I wanted to say, "I feel like the Lord has forgiven me for all of my sin, and I came to join this church and be baptized."

But when he stood before me and asked me to stand, my legs were shaking from fear. I quickly looked out of the corner of my eye and saw that same awful look on Mama's face. I was lost for words, swallowing fear like water.

"Do you want to join this church?" the preacher asked.

My eyes were glued on Mama's eyes. She was shaking her head, telling me no. I could never explain the many thoughts that went rushing through my mind at that moment, but they did not feel good. It no longer mattered what she said.

I said boldly, "Yes, sir, I do."

He took hold of my hand. "What's your name, little girl?"

"Haley. Haley Keath."

"Is your parents here tonight?"

"Yes, sir, my mama is." I spoke so only he could hear me.

"Will you tell us, in your own sweet words, why you want to join this church?"

I tried to get the words out, but my mind went blank. I felt everyone staring at me. My knees were knocking against my seat.

He looked into my eyes and said, "Don't be afraid. Say whatever you want to say, whatever the good Lord lays upon your heart. Just say it."

I said with my voice in a tremor, "I don't know what to say."

The congregation whispered. Some even laughed out loud. Doletha's voice was the first I recognized. I felt ashamed and humiliated, so much so that I began to cry.

The preacher took me in his arms and patted me gently, speaking softly. "Don't do this to yourself. The devil is trying to hinder this anointing that God has on your life, but we won't let him tonight. Jesus love you."

Then he stood and walked directly to where Doletha and Della were sitting. "You know, it's not good to laugh at the Lord's work, girls, and this is the Lord's work. This little girl has come to give her life to Jesus tonight, and I know she didn't do it alone. The Holy Spirit is guiding her. The Bible says when one soul is saved, the angels in heaven rejoice at that one saint. If I were you, I would stop and think about what it is you are laughing about. Because if you are not careful, God will put a curse upon you that you won't ever laugh—not only at this wonderful child, but at nobody ever again."

The church was as still as a mouse. You could hear a pin fall.

He turned and walked back to me, took my hand, and said, "Do you feel any better? Do you think you can go on now?"

Bravely I stated, “Yes, sir, I is.”

“Go on. Tell the church why you want to join this church. Tell em,” he encouraged me.

I said, loud and bold, “I feel like the good Lord has forgiven me of my sins, and I want to be baptized.”

Everyone started yelling amen. The motion was seconded by the deacons. I was officially set for baptism on Sunday morning.

I ran out of church as soon as service was dismissed, and stood beside the building, waiting for Mama to pass. She never saw me, but the expression on her face revealed that my ass was grass. Her good friend, Ms. Essie Mae, came out behind her, trying to get her attention, but Mama was not hearing her. She was not saying anything that Mama wanted to hear.

Mama said, “You just wait till I git her grown ass home. I’m gon beat her brains out.”

“Now, Jenny Rue, I know you ain’t gon beat that child bout joinin no church.”

“Essie Mae, you my friend, but you ain’t got nothin to do wit me an my young’un, so don’t you go tryin to tell me what to do.”

I walked slowly behind them most of the way home. When I got past the Shelmore store, I waited until they passed Pa Jack’s corner and then dashed on down the back so I wouldn’t have to go by Daddy. I knew if I made it on down to Aunt Matilda’s house, I was in safe haven. I was feeling uncomfortable because I knew Mama would tell Daddy what I’d done, and I didn’t have either of their approval.

But in time, I had to face them. “Come here, Haley!” Daddy called. “I hear you join Old Bethel Church tonight.”

“Yes, sir, I did.”

“Who told you you kin join de church?”

I almost said, “That man who comes to my bed at night,” but instead I said, “Nobody,” sadly.

Mama said loudly, “You see dere, Macky? See dere? Dat’s what I’mo talkin bout. I told you dat gal done got too darn grown.”

He shouted, “Jenny Rue, g—— d—— it, shut your damn mouth an let me talk!”

"Hell, Macky, you just talkin stead of pulling your belt off an beatin er damn ass. She done got to where she do what de hell she want to do."

"Aw, go on home to old lady Matilda," he said. "I'll talk to you tomorrow."

Mama slapped that thumb in her mouth as I was walking off the porch. She was really upset with me for joining that church without her consent. She promised she was going to git me, and I knew she would the first chance she got, but I didn't care. I did not honestly know whether it was me or something else she was angry about.

I hurried off to Aunt Matilda's, where I was safe from anyone and everyone. I stayed inside the house to prevent having to face Mama. I knew I couldn't hide forever. I would walk to the front porch and watch her go in and out of her house. I had antagonized her in some way by joining the church. I had thought it was a good thing. I didn't expect it to bring so much attention.

She got me when I least expected her to. I was playing under the house, and she had Nookie catch me. She had a shoe and she got me good, beating me across my head and my back until she was satisfied.

Rev. Huffman saw me. I was kicking and screaming, not so much from the licks but from my natural heart hurting. He came up to the fence and called, "Haley, get up. Get up from the ground. It gonna be all right."

I got up slowly, filled with anger. But once he promised me everything was going to be fine, I believed him.

He never asked me what was wrong, as if he already knew. Snot was running from both my nostrils and tears poured from my eyes like rain. He pulled a handkerchief from his back pocket and handed it to me. "Wipe your face, child," he said.

Suddenly a calm, serene feeling came over me. I stared at him across the fence. He gave me a quarter and said, "Go buy yourself a candy bar and a cold drink." It was as if he knew something I didn't, or he felt something I couldn't feel. He walked up on the porch and I went inside the house. The whipping was over, but the pain I felt never left me.

On Saturday, everyone was to meet at the church at three o'clock in the afternoon. I was all set to go. Glory Ann and Ruthella came up, inviting me to go to the picture show with them. I was amazed at the invitation. I trusted no one. If someone did me a kindness or invited me to something, I wondered what their motive was. I said, "I can't go. I have to go to the church for orientation." They laughed like it was so funny, and made a joke about me joining Old First Bethel and trying to be like Skitter. Neither of them considered that maybe this was from my heart.

Glory Ann got a little defensive and said angrily, "Okay, then, go on to church. I won't ask you to go nowhere else now, an I ain't gon come at you no more."

"No care if y'all don't come an git me. I didn't ask y'all to come in the first place."

I could tell when they left me they was not pleased. I just went back inside the house to fetch Aunt Matilda. We were on our way when Georgie Boy came running. "Haley, Daddy want you."

I knew it was trouble. "What he want wit me now?"

"Dunno what he want? But you better come see."

"Georgie Boy, tell him we already in church and the doors is already shut up and locked an you can't git in. Tell em, boy."

He was a coward and flat-out refused. It wasn't that he couldn't lie; he was too afraid where Daddy was concerned.

So I translated to Aunt Matilda was was going on. She didn't want me to get into any trouble with Daddy. We turned back.

Daddy's eyes were as red as blood. He stood in the front doorway and asked, "Where do you think you goin?"

I answered, unafraid, "We goin to church."

He was drunk, beyond impaired. He looked from me to Aunt Matilda. "What y'all going to church now for? Y'all didn't git ernough church on Sunday, you got to go on Saturday? An since when dey start having church on Saturday?"

I said, "The preacher gon tell everybody bout the baptizin tomorrow."

"Who told you you was gon be baptized tomorrow?"

I knew the devil was busy. I answered sarcastically, "Aunt Matilda."

He demanded I march my little grown ass right down to old lady Matilda's, get my things, and them back to Mama's house. I was forced to move back into that rat hole with all those drunks, and there was nothing I could do about it.

Aunt Matilda knew something was wrong by the flicker of my facial expression. She asked several times, "What he say?"

I was so angry, I could have spit blisters on a brick. I couldn't even answer her. My eyes filled with tears. I just ran off as fast as I could. I didn't want to tell her what Daddy had demanded. I was hoping he didn't mean it, but I knew he did.

Aunt Mailda came up behind me. "What did he say to upset you?"

I blurted out painfully, "He's making me move back down there." I couldn't make myself even say the word *home*, for I didn't feel like that was my home at all.

She looked at me and I at her. "Oh Lord, mercy!" she cried, and her eyes welled up with tears also. She quickly took the end of her apron and wiped them dry, trying to be brave for me. She said, "The good Lord will fix it. Just you watch an mark my word. Did he say when for you to come back?"

"Now."

"You mean right now."

"Yes, ma'am."

She didn't speak another word. She moved slowly up the steps, lips moving silently. I knew she was telling the Lord all about our problems. I couldn't keep the tears from falling down my face. I ran in behind her, imploring, "Please talk to Daddy and make him let me stay on. I don't want to go back to that house around all them old nasty, stinkin, drunk folk. Please, Aunt Matilda. He'll listen to you."

She hesitated for a moment, then agreed. "I'll do what I kin but don't know what good it'll do."

It made me feel better just hearing her say she would talk to him. After all, she did have a way with him like nobody else in all of Rat Row.

I stood at the end of the top step, watching folk move from one bootlegger's house to another. I kept looking for Daddy but didn't see him. I assumed he had fallen asleep, and when he awoke, he would have forgotten all about his silly demand for me to move back to that house.

Soon all the church folk started passing by from the orientation.

Deacon Flucken drove up in front of the Phillipses' house. Mr. and Mrs. Phillips got out of the backseat, and then the Rev. Huffman. They stood by the car, talking a second. Rev. Huffman started walking toward the end of the steps where I was standing. I was all puff-eyed from crying and tried to hide by covering my face with my arm. He stepped up to the porch and said, "Hello, my little girl. How are you doing this fine evening?"

Wiping tears, I said, "Fine." I waved my hand as if I were fine, but I was not fine. I wanted to die. But I pretended I was fine all the same.

"Is your grandmama inside?"

"Yes, sir. She in the kitchen. You kin come on in. She don't mind none."

Aunt Matilda came out the kitchen as we were coming through the house. Wiping her hands on her apron, she greeted the reverend with a handshake.

"How you doing, my sister?" He asked with a serious look about him.

She was smiling and responded, "Doing good, Reb. Doing good."

"Well! I stopped in to see what happen to you and Little Haley Keath here when we didn't see y'all in the orientation class this evenin. Hope all is well."

I knew she wasn't hearing what he was saying, so I translated. She answered, "Well, Reb. Only the good Lord knows upper bove."

"Will Haley be participatin in the baptism tomorrow?"

She looked at him in despair, knowing it wasn't going to happen. "It's up to her daddy. You got to go ask him. I can't tell you."

"I see it's a right smart of folk down there right now. I don't think it's a good time to go down there, do you think?"

"I don't know," she said sadly.

"Well, do you think it'll help any if I go down there and talk to Mr. Keath?"

I blurted out, "Naw, sir. He drunk. Don't ask him."

"That's all right. I've talked to drunk people before."

I knew I had to do something to keep him from going down there to talk to Daddy. I was sure he had spoken to many drunk folk, but I didn't believe he had talked to anybody like Macky Keath. I said, "But he's sleep."

Just then Daddy came walking through the door, all red-eyed. Rev. Huffman looked at him with a slight smile and said, "Mr. Keath, I was just asking your little girl and her grandma about you."

I was hoping Daddy didn't say anything. He had no respect for anybody, preacher or deacon. I stood speechless, waiting for him to bite Rev. Huffman's head off. He surprised me by asking calmly, "What you want to know bout me for?"

"I was wonderin if you'll let Haley take part in the baptizin tomorrow."

"Naw. Haley ain't gon be no baptized at no Bethel Church. If she do it, it'll be over my dead body." He turned around and walked back out the door.

It must have been the good Lord who stopped Rev. Huffman from carrying on the conversation any further. We watched Daddy limp down the steps. It was painful, but I held back the tears, looking as if I didn't care.

Rev. Huffman said, "Well! I had to try. I couldn't stand by and not ask. Well! I got my answer, but I do feel he is makin a terrible mistake. The Bible say to suffer little children. Maybe he don't think what he is doin is wrong. After all, she is his child, and I have to respect his decision. But I don't have to like it."

He shook my hand and Aunt Matilda's hand and said to me, "Don't worry, my dear. Everything is going to be all right." He left a few minutes later.

Ms. Essie Mae, Mama's best friend, came rushing past the house and went down to Mama's house. She looked like she was about to burst with anger. She leaped up to the porch, calling out, "Jenny Rue! Ohhh, Jenny Rue!"

I sped on down to Mama's house as fast as I could go. I got to the back door just in time to hear Mama say, "Hey, my friend, come on in." She really believed it was one of their friendly visits, but by the tone in Ms. Essie Mae's voice, it was not a friendly visit at all. I had wisdom enough to see that, but Mama was drinking. "This is my good friend Essie Mae!"

Angrily, Ms. Essie Mae asked, "Jenny Rue, is it true that you and Macky wouldn't let Haley be baptized Sunday? Is it true?"

The expression on Mama's face flickered. I believe she even sobered up. She said, "Now, Essie Mae, you ain't got nothin to do wit what Macky and me do wit our chilluns."

Essie Mae pointed her finger in Mama's face and said, "You mean to tell me it's true? You kin keep your own child from givin her life to the Lord? If you do, you and me ain't got no more friendship."

I discovered that day what friendship was about. Though she was standing up for my defense, I didn't like the fact that Ms. Essie Mae was pointing her finger in Mama's face the way she did. I witnessed hurt in Mama's expression. Humiliation overwhelmed her, and she seemed lost for words for a little while.

Then she said brazenly without a flinch, "You kin do what the hell you want to. If you don't want to be my friend cause we won't let Haley go be baptized with y'all so-call high an mighty folk, that's you business." And she walked into the kitchen, leaving Essie Mae standing.

For once I was proud of Mama standing up, even if Essie Mae had been standing up for me. I knew I inherited that part of Mama's personality: we only allowed ourselves to be pushed so far before we pushed back.

Ms. Essie Mae didn't find Mama's words remarkable. A slight smile crossed her face and faded into tears. "Jenny Rue, it's your child, true. She is yours an Macky's, but you an Macky neither one is gon ever have any good luck for denyin this child from givin her life to the Lord. If either of you had any kind of heart, you all would rethink this decision. She is old enough to know where she want to fellowship. I kin see Macky, but you on the other hand is total different. What do you think this is doin to her? All of her schoolmates, neighbors, and friends gon be baptized, and she is the only one that will not be able to participate. I took you to be better than that. If you kin do this to your own child, then I kin do this to you."

She turned and left, crying real tears, never to be my mother's friend again. My mother lost a very dear friend in Ms. Essie Mae that day, and I became the devil's chaser.

Folk were in and out, too drunk to recognize what was going on—except Cousin Sattie Bell. She winked at Mama as Essie Mae was leaving for the last time.

Daddy ended up making me come back home to stay, and Annie Dora went to live with Aunt Matilda. I was allowed to be down there during the day. But it was never the same.

My attitude changed. My behavior was unbearable. A don't-care spirit entered my body. I would go out in back of the old toilet and look up at the sky, to what I called heaven. I would pray to God with all of my heart for him to let me move back to Aunt Matilda's and let Mama and Ms. Essie Mae be friends again. It didn't happen.

***

I rose early the next morning. It was pastoral day up at Old First Bethel Church. I dreaded the fact that I was not going to be in the midst of the others. The birds were singing outside the window, and the smell of honeysuckle covered my nose. I couldn't even be happy for the new members. I tried, but something inside me forbade me from sharing in their happiness.

Old man Fred Solomon was already beating on that guitar and singing his church songs, though he wouldn't go to anybody's church. I could always tell when he was full of moonshine at seven in the morning, because he started church right on Uncle Martel and Cousin Sattie Bell's front porch. It was a little breezy, causing the chinaberry tree to shake. I looked at old Fred Solomon with all sorts of ideas racing across my mind.

I hurried back into the kitchen, where Aunt Matilda was starting to prepare our breakfast. Who could eat after being faced with such awful pain? I didn't want food. I wanted to just disappear and hope never to be seen again.

I went over to the kitchen window and pushed it open in time to see Rev. Huffman and the Phillipses sitting outside, drinking coffee and puffing on their pipes. They didn't see me. I watched until they went inside. Not long after, Rev. Huffman came out and walked down the road toward church. It surprised me when he came up on our porch. Nosiness filled my mind. I jumped close in time to hear Rev. Huffman plead with Daddy for the last time to reconsider and let me participate in the church baptism.

Daddy was cold and so damn disrespectful. He cursed and said, "I told you one time an ain't gon tell you ergin. She ain't gon be no baptised at Old Bethel Church, and dat's all it is to it."

The reverend's last word to Daddy was sincere. "I heard you before, Mr. Keath, but I just thought you might have had a change of heart. I see you haven't. I want to leave you with this: for Haley to join the church, she must be ready to accept Christ as her Lord and Savior with her sins now on her. It is no longer on you or your wife. It is very brave of her to want to give her life to God. I have to accept your decision, except I will never understand it. That was a wise choice Haley made. You may not know the braveness of her action at her age. Nevertheless, it's you who will be held responsible for denying her at this time. May God bless and keep you."

He walked down the steps. Then he stopped and turned back. He asked Daddy, "May I ask you one other question?"

Daddy said, "Yeah, I don't give a damn what you ask me. You kin ask me anything."

Rev. Huffman smiled. "What church are you a member of?"

Instantaneously, I saw anger rise inside Daddy. He answered in a terrible tone, "For your information, ain't no member of no g—— d—— church, and ain't got no intention of joinin none neither. If I did, it damn sure won't be no Bethel church."

Rev. Huffman didn't actually speak the words, but his eyes said, "My God, he do need the Lord seriously." He reached out to shake Daddy's hand, but Daddy was too evil to do even that. I could see hostility ripping through his body. The devil had a grip so tight on him, he would never get away. I knew we were all in for pain and sorrow the rest of the day.

Rev. Huffman walked away with his face tilted up toward heaven and shook his head. That morning after baptism, he resigned as pastor from Old First Bethel Church and never came to that church again.

Daddy stood helpless. He was so bounded by Satan, he didn't see good in anybody. Sin was his best friend, and it was being passed down from one generation to another.

I was determined I was not going to become what I saw in my father. I ran back to Aunt Matilda's house and buried my face in her lap. I cried. All she did was rub her hands through my hair and allow me to empty out all of my pains.

The question I often asked myself was who Macky Keath really was. To me, he was none other than the devil in a man's body. What other kind of man would deprive his child of being baptized?

Aunt Matilda Ann and Uncle Emmet had walked over thirty miles to see me get baptized, and it didn't happen. Daddy had the whole town mad at him. Everyone could see exactly who he was. Aunt Matilda Ann was as shocked as I was ashamed. She had made me a beautiful white dress with ruffle trimming around the sleeves and the hem. It was the prettiest dress since the one she had made me for Easter.

I decided not to give up. I could still hear Rev. Huffman's last words to me on that Sunday. He came up to the fence where I sat quietly under the chinaberry tree and said, "Even though you weren't baptized today, God is all in you an every plan. Maybe this is not his time, but you will be baptized one day. Can you remember this?" He looked down at me with what I called his Holy Ghost smile and patting me on my head.

I reluctantly said, "Yes, sir." That was the last time I saw him.

I went into Mama's house through the back door and heard loud voices. Aunt Matilda Ann was blessing Mama out. Mama was always blamed for my father's actions. I turned around and went down to the corner of the house, where I listened to her tell Mama, "Jenny Rue, I never woulder thought you would do this. God gon whip you with many stripes fore you lebe this here world, for keeping that child from bein baptized. you just mark my word."

Mama wept. Not only did she have something to feel bad about, she had lost a lot of respect from folk that liked her, not only her very best friend, Ms. Essie Mae. I didn't like what she was being put through because of what Daddy did.

I tiptoed round the house and went back to Aunt Matilda's. I was about to tell Aunt Matilda all about my morning when in walked my sister Tise. I hadn't seen her in a month or so, and she looked strange to me. I rushed into the other room because, for some unknown reason, I didn't want to see her. She asked Aunt Matilda for me. Aunt Matilda looked around and said, "Well, Lord-a Lord, she was here a minute ago but now she gon. She muster went outside to play."

Tise turned to leave, and I saw her stomach was big. I thought, *Gosh, Tise really done gained a lot of weight in her stomach.* I didn't realize then that she was expecting a baby. She went down to the bottom with her friend Eldora.

I didn't go inside the rest of that evening. I was too ashamed and humiliated to show my face. I went to the chinaberry tree and sat out there. Along came Eddie Kirkland. The sun was setting as he was coming from between the two houses. He went out behind the toilet and stood looking up to the sky, speaking to himself. I do believe he was crying but I wasn't sure.

Old man Fred Solomon was playing his guitar. The sound flowed all through the neighborhood, along with the filthy language from some folk's mouths. It was hard for me to hear what Mr. Eddie Kirkland was saying.

I ran up to the side of the toilet in time to hear, "Now Lord, I'm begging you to give me all of my money, cause they told me if I gave my money that you will double it back to me. I did that, and that was my last ten dollars I had to my name, and Lord, it's late. The sun is going down and I still don't have my money. I don't mind if I got to wait on the double, but I need you to give me my ten now."

A bird flew over and dropped a drop in his hand. He shouted out angrily, "Lord, I don't want no g—— d—— s——! I want my money!"

I rushed away around the house. Ssomething convicted me of laughing at him, but I couldn't help but wonder why he cursed God.

Aunt Matilda called out my name and I went to see what she wanted. Out the back door came Daddy, drunk as old Fred Solomon, but not too drunk to yell, "I thought I told you I wanted you to come back home!" I stared at him, hatred spinning around inside me like I was on a merry-go-round. "Do you hear me talking to you, gal?"

I looked down on the ground and answered, "Yes, sir."

Inside, I prayed that Aunt Matilda would talk some sense into his head, but that was one time she kept silence. He insisted that if she just had to have somebody to stay with her, it would be Snappy or Willa Max.

Chapter 14: Moving Back to Hell

Aunt Matilda heard Daddy shouting. She never spoke; she just turned around and slowly walked away from him, straight to her house, and commenced to gathering up my clothes.

I refused to take them. For the later part of the evening, I stayed as close to her as I could, like it would be my last time in her company. She convinced me that my leaving would not be for long, like she knew something was going to happen. "Don't worry yourself none. You won't be gone forever." She began smiling.

Just at pitch-dark, she took me by the hand and walked me to my mama's house. A few people were still sitting around, but not like they usually were. She didn't come in with me, but she watched from the end of the porch as I moved on inside the house, leaving her. My heart ached. I waved to her, looking into her teary eyes. She waved back and left.

Aunt Matilda was accepting the move too calmly. I couldn't imagine what she had up her sleeve. Whatever it was, the good Lord was in the plan.

Around nine o'clock that evening, Mama finally woke up from her drunk. Georgie Boy and I were listening to Papa tell us about some of his unpleasant times raising his children after he and Grandma split. I was at the age when I understood more of the discomfort he'd felt. Papa was in his last days. He was sick, but he got pleasure telling us his story as a father and grandfather.

Mama was in her own shameful mood not knowing what was going on. Surprised to see me there, she asked with concern, "How come you ain't with Aunt Matilda?" She rubbed her hands over her face for consolation.

I blurted out loudly, because I was mad, "You know why! Cause y'all just mean, makin me come back down here to stay! When I git bigger, I'm gon to run away from here, and when I do, I will never come back here. Never!"

She drew her hand back to strike me. Papa scolded in his weak voice, lifting his head from his pillow, "If you hit her, I'll break your sorry neck."

She looked up in fear and rushed out of the room. Sick as he was, he could hardly hold his head up to speak. But he had the strength he needed to say what he did to her.

Papa was always good at putting the best on the outside, but the time had come when he could not hide his sickness. I asked him if he was all right. He looked at me as if he didn't know who I was. I realized his mind would go and come. He was in and out.

Georgie Boy insisted that I come to the kitchen with him to get some water. I knew immediately he wanted me to come because he was afraid to go by himself. I refused, and he implored me to go. So I gave in to his demands and got the lamp.

As we entered the kitchen, three big rats jumped from the table, ran behind the stove, and disappeared through a crack in the floor. I jumped in fear. The movement shook the globe from the lamp. I was unable to catch it before it fell to the floor and shattered to pieces.

That got Mama's attention. She came running to see what had happened, only to be concerned about the lamp globe and not her children. She scolded me and said I hadn't been back in the house one good night and was already disturbing it. I tried to explain I was frightened, and she literally slapped me across my face, shouting, "You ain't scared of no rats!" That was a time I wanted to hit her back. I do believe if she had not been my mother, I would have.

I ran back into the room where Papa was and sat in the corner, crying inside silently. All sorts of terrible ideas raced around in my head. I wished I had never been born.

I took my mind off of myself and looked over at Papa. He slept with his mouth wide open. He looked as if he might be dead. As I was getting up to check him, in walked my sister Tise. Without giving me time to say anything, she asked crossly, "What you doin down here, Haley? Why you not at Aunt Matilda's house?"

Being nothing but a bag of water, as Mama always said, I felt my eyes well up with tears. I was not strong enough to withhold them.

She saw them falling and took me by my hand. She said, "That low-down dirty Mr. Macky is behind whatever it is, I know."

I detailed what had happened, and that it all initiated because I joined the church. She used her thumb to gently wipe the tears from under my eyes. She said really sincerely, "I hate that man. He need to be shame of his low-down self."

"I do too, Tise. I hate em too."

She changed her skirt, and for the second time I saw her stomach was big and round like a watermelon. Her navel was sticking out. I said, "Oh, oh, Tise, your stomach is big like Bessy Royce. Is you gon have a baby like she is?"

Whirling around, Tise looked at me in disbelief and answered, "Yeah, Haley, I is. I'm gon have a baby in early October. Anyhow, how do you know Bessy Royce is gon have a baby?"

"Now, Tise, you know dese niggers round here can't hold water. Everybody know bout Bessy Royce. Mrs. Angie Rosa said dat ain't de first one, it's just de first one she havin."

"Pay no mind to everythin you hear. Everythin you hear might not be de truth."

Tise jumped in bed. I took my clothes off and jumped in beside her. It was like old times, being at home with her.

Late that night, we were awakened by Papa pulling down clothes and yelling, "Git dem damn cows outer here! Hurry! De world is on fire! Git dem cows outer here quick!"

Mama and Daddy came running into the room like this was something they encountered often. In a few minutes they had him calmed down and he was back in bed. They restrained him so he couldn't get out, and before long he was sleeping.

I didn't know what to think, so I asked Tise what was wrong with

Papa. She explained that his mind came and went, and when he was out of his mind, he hallucinated. She tried to convince me that no matter what state of mind he was in, he would never hurt any of us. I was not so sure. I was frightened out of my mind. I wanted desperately to go back home to Aunt Matilda's house. That was my home.

I got back into bed, but I could not sleep. I must have prayed till daylight.

After about a week, things were not working out with Snappy staying the nights with Aunt Matilda. Snappy's asthma was getting the best of her, and Aunt Matilda's rheumatism was taking its toll on her. Neither of them was able or healthy enough to accompany the other.

Aunt Matilda made arrangements with Mrs. Bonnie for Della to stay at night. I knew Mrs. Bonnie had been wanting that for a long time. I was not about to let it happen. I had to find a way to prevent it from happening but could not think of a thing.

I was astounded to learn that Aunt Matilda had tried to get out of bed in the middle of the night to see about Snappy, and had fallen. She had deep cuts over her eye, and she had bruised her hip and leg, causing her to limp when she walked. My heart cried out for her. We were her only family. No matter who she brought in to spend the night, they were not going to make her feel as comfortable as I did. I had sense enough to know Della was not going to spend the night out of concern. She was only spending the night so she could gloat and get what she could out of Aunt Matilda.

I went to Aunt Matilda's house early one morning, before any of the others had gotten out of bed. She was already up. I looked directly into her eyes and saw the pain as I spoke to her. My heart hurt real bad all that day. I didn't eat; I just sat around moping.

I do believe that was the first day I learn how to scheme. I didn't think it was very bad, but I did know it was not a nice thing to do. I took a verse from Scripture: "And from the days of John the Baptist until now the kingdom of heaven suffereth violence, and the violent take it by force" (Matt. 11:12 KJV). I interpreted it as I wanted so it would fit my purpose.

I didn't care what I had to do to get Della and her family out of my way. Controversy was beginning, and I had my own plan about how I was going to prevent anything or anyone from getting in my way. I wandered from room to room, back and forth, thinking about how to get back to my rightful place.

I realized it was getting late. I looked into Aunt Matilda's beautiful gray eyes and said, "*Wait*! I'll be back direckly. Just you wait. I'm comin back and stay wit you."

She smiled, showing her snuff-colored teeth, and that sad look on her face vanished. She asked, "What you gon do, child?"

I gripped her hand just enough for her to feel my real concern. "I'mo come back, don't you worry. I'mo come back when dark come. I swear I will."

As I went out her back door, she was grinning hard and tears were running down her face. I knew they were happy tears.

I ran on down to Mama's house, crossing Cousin Sattie Bell's backyard. I heard voices, and they were having themselves a good time. I rushed on into the house. Folk were gathered around for the evening. Snappy was sitting on the couch, wheezing as if every breath would be her last. No one helped her or did anything for her. Papa was lying at the foot of his bed with his eyes rolled back. Mama was sitting out on the front porch with Aunt Pancy and a few other nosy, gossiping biddies, discussing everybody's business. They were all intoxicated, talking loud and making jokes.

I went over to Snappy and put my hands on her forehead for comfort. It was like I was being guided. I turned the covers back on the bed and told her to get in. I made her as comfortable as I could, encouraging her to get her some rest despite the racket around us. I gave her the asthma pump and let her use it, then watched as she drifted off to sleep.

Millie Mae and Tise came in through the back door, on their way to the cafés. While Tise was dressing, I went out on the porch and saw Della and her mama coming to Aunt Matilda's. I ran as fast as my legs could go to reach her front door just as they did. I told them there was no need for Della to stay the night, because I was back. I even told them Aunt Matilda was not there; she was down at Ms. Estella's house. They looked disbelieving, but didn't see her, so they turned and left.

I watched until they were back to their house. Then I went into the kitchen, where Aunt Matilda was. I told her I had to tidy up Mama's house and make sure the other children were in bed, and I would be back.

The streetlights had come on, and I knew my time was limited. I rushed back to Mama's. Daddy had not came home from the bottom. Mama and Odessa were plotting how to find Daddy's whiskey. I cleaned up the house and made sure the children had their baths and were safe in bed.

Snappy was in the spot where I normally slept. Nothing was left but to make sure Odessa got out of there and Mama got in bed. That didn't take any doing at all. Odessa starting saying, "Jenny Rue I gotto go now, but I'll see you the first thing inner morning, if the good Lord willin." Whatever her conversation was, the Lord was in it. Odessa ended every sentence with "if the good Lord's willin." And the way Mama jumped into her bed, she had been waiting for Odessa to leave.

I hurried to close the doors and the old shuttered windows. Then I was back in Aunt Matilda's house almost before she knew I was gone. She smiled when she saw me, believing I had Daddy's permission to come back and stay. I didn't see a reason to bother her with the truth about my manipulation. The happiness on her face gave me all the pleasure in the world.

That night, we both slept like newborn babies. I was home at last, like I'd known I would be.

I was awakened by the crowing of the roosters the next morning. The sounds came from all directions. I lay awake until I knew everybody was getting up. Then I rushed back to Mama's house and got in bed, as if I had stayed the night.

Before long, Daddy was calling out for me to bring him two half pints of whiskey. I jumped out of bed, stretching like I was just waking up. I made my way to the back so I could be seen rubbing my eyes. I got the bottles and brought them to Daddy, who was standing by the table with Watch Marshall and Willie Shangle. They were shaking like leaves falling from a tree. Daddy gave them each a bottle. They turned the bottles up, and when they took them down from their mouths, the bottles were empty. I wondered what that whiskey tasted like to them. I had never seen them eat a home-cooked breakfast. Their breakfast was drinking, in the morning and all day.

Watch Marshall pulled a quarter from his pocket and offered it to me, but the one thing I was not allowed to do was accept money from any man. Mama always said that if you took money from them, they felt like they could ask you for something in return. Whatever that meant. So I declined his quarter.

I made my way back to Aunt Matilda's. She was making breakfast, and the smell was all throughout the neighborhood. I ate and thanked God I was home again.

After a couple weeks of maneuvering, Daddy gave in and said I could move back to old lady Matilda's house. I was thrilled that I no longer had to slip out every evening and pretend. He never found out what I'd been doing. Whatever was going on with Daddy at that time put him in a good mood. I could practically get my way with anything.

One Sunday afternoon, Passy Kate and her friends Lila and Antoinette were at Mama's. We seldom saw much of Passy Kate; she was busy running with her friends. I was hearing all sorts of things that were going on with her.

I was happy to see my sister. She was hugging Georgie Boy when I came through the door. She said, "There you is! I was just asking your little brother bout you. I should have known where you was. Look at you! You done put on a little weight and growing you some tits, I see."

She pulled on one, and that did not feel good. "Ow!" I said. "Passy Kate, that hurt!"

She laughed. "You done been round Aunt Matilda so dag blame long, till you startin to look just like er."

Lila said, "Passy Kate! That hurt her. Don't pull on her little tits like that. She just growing up." She put her arm around my shoulder, showing some compassion for me.

Passy Kate sure didn't have any. She replied, "That don't hurt that old Macky-Keath-lookin gal." Those were always her words when she did something mean to me.

Smiling, pretending I was joking, I said, "Just like you look like Aunt Pancy."

In walked that sneaky, dirty-looking Dor-Roa, a man I did not like or trust. I hated the way he looked at me. I hated when he came to our house. Many times I said, "Why don't he go buy all his whiskey down at Millie Lee's house? And he won't have no reason to come here a'tall."

He grabbed Antoinette. He was keeping it all in the family; I knew he was with her mama, Ms. Jonnie Mae and he ended up married to her older sister, Loueva. It didn't seem to faze either of them.

He saw the look I gave him and said sarcastically, "Macky, your daughter just don't like me. Must be cause she still member me from what happen when I first moved down here."

Daddy turned and said meaningfully, "Yeah, you g—— d—— right. She just like her old man. She don't forgit nothin been done to her, and I damn sure don't either."

Dor-Roa tried making what Daddy said into a joke, and Daddy didn't smile at all. They were both half-drunk, and I knew before long they'd be good and drunk.

While Passy Kate was there, I made sure she helped me get the kids into bed. Dor-Roa waited around until we were about to clear the room. Then he responded, "Yeah, mother f——, I don't either."

Passy Kate and her friends walked me down to Aunt Matilda's house, making sure I was safe. They stayed a while. When they left, a cold, shivering feeling came over me like something was going to happen. But nothing did that night.

***

With Tise waiting to deliver any day, I was feeling good about having a little niece or nephew. It was a joy having her back at home and having me back where I belonged. Things were calm.

Early on a Saturday morning, I went to Mama's house. Everyone was up. Tise had the house all fresh-smelling and clean. Daddy came in to shave Papa. When he had finished, he and the other gamblers headed off across the field to Mrs. Angie Rosa's, leaving Tise and I sitting in the room.

Tise was straightening her hair, and I was watching. She started to tell me about her baby's father and of her plans once the baby came. She was going to move back out to Rooks Iron quarter.

Suddenly I heard a funny noise coming from Papa's direction. He was lying at the foot of the bed, looking up at the ceiling. His mouth was open and he was making those weird sounds. I asked, panicky, "Tise, what's dat noise?"

"What's what?" she inquired.

"Be quiet and listen for a minute."

We both got real quiet, and another sound came from Papa. Tise knew what it was and started crying. "Oh my God, Papa dyin!" She jumped up and ran for the front door.

Mama was crossing over to the back road by Mrs. Angie Rosa's house, headed to Lessie Lee's house. Lessie Lee had given birth. Tise screamed, "Mama! Come back! Papa's dyin!"

The whole neighborhood heard, and they all came running. Papa had expired.

It wasn't long before the house was crawling with caring people. I followed Tise back into the room. Cousin Sattie Bell took baby Pappie over to her house. I stood back in the doorway, watching from a distance. Mama was down on her knees beside the bed, crying painfully. "Lord, have mercy. Jesus, my poor daddy. He's gone." Everyone in the room was crying.

Arms came around her shoulders and lifted her up from beside the corpse. "Get up, Jenny Rue. Ain't nothing else you kin do. He's in God's hand now."

Minutes later Dr. Henley came in and asked everyone to clear the room. He pulled the covers back and took Papa's pulse. He used a stethoscope and tried to listen for a heartbeat. He shook his head when he didn't find one and pronounced Papa dead.

He left, and in came Aunt Lucy Sue. She was screaming loud and hard; she cried more than anyone in the room. News traveled fast. Not much later, Uncle Head Henry and Aunt Rita came in. They had been on their way to visit Papa, but was a little too late. They arrived in time to see the body before Funeral Bellow came and took it away.

Uncle Martel put a towel under Papa's chin, pulled his mouth closed, and tied the ends behind his head. Funeral Bellow talked to all the family members and took the body away. That was my first experience of a body being taken away from our house, the body of a close member of our family.

We lost a wonderful grandfather. His death that day will always stay in my mind. I was a little frightened and didn't know fully what I was frightened about. I couldn't say if it was the death of Papa or his dying in the room where we all slept. I was more than glad to know I didn't have to sleep in that room anymore—not for a long, long time, anyway.

Everyone helped to strip the bed down and wash up all the bedclothes. Mama didn't have to lift a finger. In no time the clothes were hanging on the line to dry. Some folk were in the room, scrubbing the floor. Others were in the kitchen, cooking. That was the kind treatment you got from your neighbor back in those days.

Passy Kate, Antoinette, and Lila were in the kitchen. I heard the names Lussie Mae and Alice mentioned. It was nothing for me to walk out of one room and into another and hear everything I shouldn't have heard. By the way they were talking, trouble was on the rise and Passy Kate was in the midst of it.

Antoinette stated, "It's that so-call friend Lussie Mae you need to watch out for. She is the one grinning in your face and running back to tell Alice all about you. All Lila is telling you is to be careful, cause words out dem damn puck-wood-ass women. Dey all totes straight razors and will steal you."

Passy Kate didn't have a fearful bone in her body, nor an ounce of common sense. My mind raced back to a day some months ago, to a conversation Roxie had with Mama. Rumor was Passy Kate was about to take Lussie Mae's husband. Now it was more vivid for me as to what that confusion was all about. I started to have some concerns about Kate, because she did a lot of drinking, and a drunk person weakens. She commented like she was the most powerful queen since Jezebel:

"They kin tote dey mammies for all I care, I ain't worry bout em f——wit me."

Aunt Matilda Ann called out my name. Realizing that I was there, they changed the conversation and started talking about Papa. It took my mind off of what was being said about my sister, but I had heard enough to know that trouble was brewing fast.

"Come here, Haley!" Aunt Matilda Ann called. "I want you to go to the store an git me a box of snuff." She gave me a quarter, and I hurried out the back door to the Shelmore store.

Old Benny Lee never missed a beat when somebody black came into the store. I had got the snuff and was paying for it when he said, "Well, another one of the niggers done kicked the bucket down dere in Rat Row." I was impressed he didn't get any feedback, not even from that nasty Ms. Shelmore. She gave me the fifteen cents back and I shot out the door, running as fast as I could.

Passy Kate and her friends were gone, but other folk were still discussing Papa and the family man he had been. It appeared that Papa had raised all his children by himself. He learned that Grandmom May Lee had another relationship and kicked her out of the house. He wouldn't allow her to take either of his children with her—Mama and Aunt Lucy. Uncle Head Henry and his two other children were from a previous marriage to Aunt Ceily. After he put Grandmom out, he had moved out on the farm and worked sunup to sundown. He didn't allow Grandmom near the children. Papa guarded those children with his life.

I pondered all that night. Grandmom May Lee was so distant from us: she was never in our lives, and she never got to know any of Mama's children. She was a stranger.

Papa was funeralized that next Friday. I recall Grandmom coming to the funeral. After it was over, she and her daughter went up to Aunt Lucy Sue's house. Grandmom always blamed Mama for her troubles and her wrong decisions, and that is putting it mildly.

I was a grown woman at the age of fifteen. I knew more about the lives of my family than I had brains. It was no secret that when a family member passed, that was the time to learn things that were important. I regretted having heard those things about my mama, but they helped me to understand her more and the things she did, like why she drank so much. It all started to become clear to me. She was a victim of a violent abuser, and instead of her mother defending her, her mother rejected and blamed her.

***

I was on my way to Sunday school, and I stopped by Mama's house. It was no different than any other Sunday: the house was full of customers. I walked through the house, and in Papa's old bed lay Passy Kate. She was bandaged up around her head and her arm, and folk were gathered around her bed. Somebody was holding a cigarette to her mouth. I stood speechless, wondering what was wrong with her and why she was bandaged up.

To keep from being seen, I crawled under the bed to listen. The name Lussie Mae came up again. They were discussing what had taken place, but I didn't get all the details.

I eased out from under the bed just in time for Sunday school. My mind wandered the entire time I was in there. Ms. Pughsley asked me a question, and I was unable to answer because I'd heard nothing she said. I was glad when it was over, and I believe that was the day my mind became the devil's workshop.

I rushed home when church was out, directly to Passy Kate's bedside. She was in a lot of pain. Tears rolled down the sides of her face into her ears. I asked, "Passy Kate, what happen to you? who did dis to you?"

Her tears fell harder, and she said, "I got cut last night."

"Who did it?"

"A woman I was fightin wit."

"What er name?"

"Lussie Mae."

"Is dat one of dem old puck-wood women?"

"What you know bout dem puck-wood women?"

Mrs. Shonnie Mae, another neighbor on Rat Row, came through the door to Kate's bed. She seemed very concerned about Kate. She took her hand, rubbing it, and said, teary-eyed, "Kate, baby, just look at you.

Dis is all because of your hardheadness. You could have lost your life." I couldn't tell if she was pretending to care or really did.

Lila and Antoinette were whispering to each other. Lila was saying she and Walter Leech were on the dance floor when someone came in the café, saying Passy Kate had got cut. Passy Kate had about beaten Lussie Mae's unborn baby clean out of her. Passy Kate could go to jail for making her lose her baby. Antoinette said, "Lussie Mae need to git up out dat hospital and take herself back to wherever she come from."

The story was starting to come together. But I was being summoned, so I had to leave. As I passed by Cousin Sattie Bell's house, somebody was saying, "Dat woman done caught Passy Kate wit her damn husband and done f—— her wanter-be-bad ass up. Dat's just all is to it."

Cousin Sattie Bell said, "She sure muster caught er wit her drawers down."

Everybody was speaking and forming their opinions. Some were for Kate and some were against her. I tried to hear everything I could about what had happened to my sister.

It wasn't long before Mrs. Shonnie Mae came wobbling through Cousin Sattie Bell's back door, and the moment she came in, her demeanor changed. She was not the caring friend she had portrayed herself to be at Mama's house. She declared, "Whether she caught her with her back turned or not, going with women's husbands and tryin to be bad about it don't git you nowhere but a early grave."

She spoke loudly enough that Lila and Antoinette overheard the remarks she made. Lila commented, "See that big bitch? I told Walter she ain't no friend of Kate's."

After that, Antoinette gave full details of how it all went down. She was with Passy Kate up until the fight took place. At that point, she was in another car, but she could see all that happened. She never tried to lie for Kate or dress anything up. It was a mess.

Kate and James, Lussie Mae's husband, were getting ready to leave for Baker County. Kate told James to go back in the café and get her a pack of cigarettes. He parked the car and went back to honor her request. While Kate was waiting, the puck-wood woman came up and tapped on the window. Kate rolled the window down, and Lussie Mae asked her to get out of the car. Antoinette couldn't hear what Passy Kate answered, but she heard Lussie Mae say, "Wait here till I git back."

Antoinette believed Lussie Mae went home, got a knife, and came back. That's when the attack happened. James got back to the car and pulled Passy Kate away from Lussie Mae. Howard Lomax held on to Kate, and Antoinette heard her tell him to let her go; she had been cut. Then so many people had surrounded them, Antoinette could no longer see until someone came out, carrying Passy Kate in his arms, and said he had to get her to the hospital before she bled to death.

Lila said, "I need to get er drink." From where I was eavesdropping, I could most likely be seen, so I moved on. Shonnie Mae and Lila passed one another where I could see them, and I witnessed the contemptuous look Lila gave her. Her friends were all standing up for Kate, no matter how wrong she was. That was because all of them were sleeping with some other woman's husband. It was a popular thing. I believe there were not enough men to go around, so they had to share.

I had no one to talk to about what I had heard except Aunt Matilda, and she couldn't hear me. I concluded that Antoinette was telling exactly what had happened. It was the talk of the town for a long time. If I ever believed that our family was cursed, I believed it then.

***

Music from the jukeboxes was blasting in the distance as we sat on the porch. Aunt Matilda stared up at the beautiful stars shining down to earth, speaking silently to herself. I watched, wondering what was she saying. My mind wandered in thoughts about the fun I thought everyone was having.

I could hear Millie Mae's and Bessy Royce's voices, and the more I listened, the more I wanted to become part of that good-time life. I pictured the boyfriend I would have in the near future. I commenced to believe that nightlife was more than going to church. The only thing church seemed to have brought me was pain. Maybe I could drink myself happy like the rest of them, like nothing else mattered. Drinking, dancing, running from one juke joint to another, cursing, fighting—all those seemed to matter.

The devil had creeped in unaware. I based my vision of the future on the folk I lived around. Between negative and positive, I really didn't know the difference. The fantasy was no more than a sin birthed out in my mind, an iniquity seeping through my pores. I was drunk in my sin, sick in mind. I lived it. I smelled it. I sold it. There was nothing left for me to do except taste it. Never for one moment did I consider Paul's words: "Touch not; taste not; handle not" (Col. 2:21 KJV).

I had no willpower and no one except Aunt Matilda to be an example for me. She was getting up in age. I started to wonder if I might come home one night and find that she was deceased. The thought turn around in my head like a freight train coming down a wet track on a winter night.

Suddenly gunshots rang out from right side of the road, near Butternut's café. I heard screams, and voices getting loud. I recognized some of them. It was hard not to know Candis Wilkes's big mouth. There was no other voice like her's. Standing up and looking down, I saw folk running and cars speeding off in different directions. I do believe Aunt Matilda heard the gunshots, but she thought they were firecrackers. Nonetheless, she hurried us into the house.

I got nervous. Something terrible was going on down in the bottom. Aunt Matilda and I at the same time uttered, "Oh Lordy, have mercy." I wondered if any of my sisters were down there fighting again. Kate had not so long ago recovered from her injuries. The screams were so loud, it was like they were coming from just a few feet away.

I opened the window, and the road was filled with people. The cafés were closing down, and folk were going to every bootlegger's house. Mama's house was the first one they came running to.

"Haley! Git back inside and close dat window. Dem damn fools down dere shootin like dey in the Wild West some darn where."

I hurried to close the window. Tire wheels squealed. Folk kept screaming. I didn't try to go to sleep; I sat up. Aunt Matilda knelt down and prayed, so I jumped down beside her.

I concentrated hard and the words outside came clearer. They were saying something about Marcus J being hurt real bad. I identified Arketha's voice yelling out his name. Others were saying, "Them damn puck-wood men." Apparently the town men had been fighting, and then the Baker County men jumped in and it was a battleground down in the bottom. I distinctly heard Antoinette say, "Lloyd is hurt bad."

Then the sound of Old Lund Cabb's Black Maria came speeding through. I peeked out to see folk running through Mrs. Angie Rosa's cornfield and in between the houses, because they knew what he was all about—handcuffs and the blackjack.

Everything went quiet and still. The Black Maria circled the roads for a while. Then I didn't hear it anymore. The voices started up again.

By then, everybody in the neighborhood was awake. The lights were out down in the bottom at Ms. Hilley's café. Everyone knew something awful had to have happened for her to close her café early. Her customers brought all their troubles down in the quarters to Rat Row. Nobody got any sleep.

Daylight came, and the first opportunity I got, I went down to Mama's house to find out what had happened. It was the topic of the morning: in the kitchen, on the front porch, and in the backyard. It appeared Lloyd and James had had some words concerning Passy Kate. They got into a terrible fight. Marcus J tried to break up the fight, but others jumped in and the fight escalated. Several Baker County men got cut, and most of the puck-wood men were cut. Nothing was life-threatening, or so they were saying.

As people began to spread out, the view became clearer of what had happened. Quite of few people had been hurt pretty bad, and somebody shot Lloyd in his side. The fight was against some Alabama men. The Baker County men got involved later; the puck-wood men were the initiators. Lloyd was the only one who was laid up in the hospital for three days. Marcus J was treated and released. Rumor was a couple puck-wood men were in critical condition.

Later in the week, Lloyd got out of the hospital and came to our house with Passy Kate. He drove up in a black Chevrolet convertible, and Kate was sitting right up under him. He was bandaged from his head down, having been cut around his neck, his nose, and his arms.

The way folk gathered around him, it was like he was a movie star. He was the black king of Rat Row. I was right in the midst. They all helped him into the house. I could tell he was still physically weak, but he was strong-minded. The first question he asked was, "Have anybody heard how Marcus J is doin?"

Arketha answered, "I just come from down to Aunt Millie Bee's house, and they were sayin he is doin pretty good. He sure is one lucky fellow, cause if they had cut him a little deeper, they woulder cut his juggler vein and he woulder bleed to death. But he all right now. He'll live."

Lloyd responded, "I owe that cat my life. If he hadn't came up when he did, them cats would have did me in for good and I wouldn't be here now. I owe Marcus J my life."

Old Fred Solomon came through the back door, playing that old guitar. He always knew how to cheer up a dying man. Daddy sold some moonshine, and we all benefited from it. Lloyd, even though he was cut, was in a great mood.

Before long, he and Passy Kate were head over heels in love. Everything else was sane, and folk were back to their normal selves. Judge Brake evicted the puck-wood men and their families. Some men ended up staying on in town with some of the single women there. The neighborhood folk were back to their old, joyous selves. Peace was among them once again.

***

One hot summer evening, folk did what they normally did after supper—they gathered on Mama's front porch to chat. They were all sitting around when up drove Lloyd. Kate was with him. He announced he was leaving for Allbright, Tennessee, and he was taking Kate with him. Mama did not like the fact that her daughter was leaving town with Lloyd. According to her, there was much more to Lloyd than good looks, much that Kate didn't know.

But it was what they both wanted, and there wasn't anything Mama could do about them leaving. In two days, they were off. Two weeks later, Mama got her first letter from Kate and they were in Allbright. Kate sounded like she was in heaven.

For the next two months, Mama received a letter every week. Then suddenly, no more letters came. She would come home every day, asking, "Did a letter come from Kate today?" Having to tell her every day for weeks and weeks that no mail had come? It was heartbreaking. Mama would sit sometimes with her head hanging down. She would stick her thumb in her mouth and cry. I wondered if the thumb-sucking made her feel better or took her mind off of her problems. The way she sucked it, she had to find some kind of satisfaction in it.

Then one day I came home from school and she called me to read a letter. It was from Kate. Mama was so happy, she was teary-eyed. I opened the letter, and the first thing I noticed was the new address. This one was from Buckerton, Tennessee. The letter was about a third of a page long.

My dear Mama,

I'm so sorry I haven't wrote to you before now, but I have been so busy moving, I just have not had the time. I wanted you to know I left Lloyd and I live in Buckerton now. He don't know where I am, so if you hear from him, you don't know where I am either. I'm working, and when I get myself settled like I want to, I'll send you some money. Don't worry about me. Tell Haley I said I want her to make sure she go on and finish school. If she don't do it for herself, please do it for me. I'll write again soon. Give everybody my love. I love you.

Much love, Kate

I thought of nothing else except her encouraging words. She didn't know how badly I wanted to finish school. That was all I lived for.

But things were happening to me that I couldn't explain. I wanted to make something out of myself. I didn't want to end up like my parents, that was for sure. Tise was the only sister I had left who I knew cared anything about me. I could go to her about anything when I couldn't even go to my mother. She and I got closer, and when she gave birth to her first son, it changed my life.

But Mama's drinking had increased tremendously. It was so bad that Tise couldn't stand living in the house. Daddy didn't help at all; he was as mean and nasty to her as he could be. So Tise finally moved back with Aunt Lucy Sue, leaving me practically alone. Though I was living with Aunt Matilda, I had to take on all the responsibilities Tise had had, and it took take its toll. Anger entered and wouldn't exit. It seemed to control me in every way. Being the oldest of Daddy's children, I was needed at home more than Aunt Matilda needed me.

I was torn between my sisters and brothers and the woman who had been a better mother to me than the woman who gave birth to me. I didn't have the role model I should have had, and I resented the one I had.

***

Aunt Matilda was in the kitchen, cooking for Thanksgiving dinner. I had got all the children down in their warm beds, and I was sitting in front of the fire, thinking of the many ways I could get out of that place. I was suffocating from the horrible scent of moonshine, working from morning to evening, and hardly getting any rest. My life was spinning out of control.

I wasn't strong enough to get my Bible and find a passage that was fitting for my condition. The noise from old Fred's Solomon guitar sounded all over Rat Row. He was in the other room. I took a look, and the room was full of drunks. Long Laura was sitting, pissy as she was drunk, snuff running down both corners of her mouth. Odessa and Jean Otis were on the floor, dancing to the beat of Fred's music. Mama was lying at the foot of the bed, dead drunk to the world. My head filled with rage.

I think anger broke my spirit completely. Willa Max, my baby sister, was old enough to stay with Aunt Matilda. All Aunt Matilda wanted was someone to be in the house with her at night. Willa Max could stay with her, and I could be home with the other children. Snappy was big and sickly, and all those drunks were hanging around. I would be there for her and the others. They did need me, more than I had realized.

I got Willa Max up and took her to Aunt Matilda's to stay. Aunt Matilda was glad to have her. She laughed and hummed her usual gay tune.

Chapter 15: My First Love and My First Heartbreak

I got Willa Max settled in with Aunt Matilda and ran back to Mama's like I was going to put out a fire. It just was not the kind of fire you put out with water. Everyone was in their same positions. I didn't see Daddy anywhere. I paused for a second, and then all hell broke loose inside me. I shouted, "Git up and git out of here! Go home! My mama is sleep and my daddy ain't here. Now all y'all git outer here and go home where y'all stay!" I opened the door and shouted again, "Git out! Git out! Git out of here now!"

I had no sympathy for them. They could go to Uncle Martel's house; it didn't matter to me where they went as long as they got out of there.

Odessa was the first one to respond to my demands. She was drunk, but she was not too drunk to fight back. "Now, little Haley, you done got too damn fast. I'mo tell Mr. Macky on you. He gon whip your little grown black ass, and you know it too."

"Git out, Ms. Odessa, an don't worry bout my ass whippin. One thing bout it: a whippin don't last no longer dan you git it in. I done had plenty of em. Now git your drunk, ugly-lookin ass out of our house an go home to Mrs. Angie Rosa."

She was shocked. The look she gave me showed her surprise. But I was not that nice little girl anymore. I was a very angry teenager with an uncontrollable attitude.

I continued to yell for them to get out until they all left. I walked behind them until the last one was gone.

The house was a filthy mess. I started cleaning up, many thoughts running loose in my head. I wanted desperately to run away. I thought of many places I could run to, but again my little sisters and brothers were my first piroity.

I made sure the back door was closed, and I placed the slab across it. I went to the front door, and there stood old man Willie Shangle and Dor-Roa, pushing their way in. I didn't push back. For the first time, I got the perfect image of them both. Mr. Willie Shangle had the mind-set of a child. I saw a lonely spirit on him. He was a drifter in the land of nowhere to go. Dor-Roa as usual had a nasty look on his face. His eyes were cold and fearsome. I was a little scared, but I was not about to let him know it. I looked them both in the eye and told them Daddy was not at home. I was getting ready for bed, and they had to leave.

At that moment, I heard Daddy at the back door. That gave me great relief. I had to go let him in, while they made their way inside. When he came in, Daddy went to pull out whiskey as if he knew they were there.

I looked at them with real hatred. Anger hit me all over again. I went into the other room where the children were sleeping, to guard them.

A noise in the kitchen sounded like a rat. It sent Daddy to investigate. He looked over in the bedroom and spotted me. The first thing that came from his mouth was, "Come here and git me two half of pints of whiskey."

I didn't say anything. I did as he ordered me to do. I felt Dor-Roa's eyes on me. I looked back out the corner of my eye and saw that awful expression on his face, as if he wanted to attack me. I put my guard up where he was concerned.

I got the whiskey and brought it back to Daddy. Then came another knock at the door. I couldn't imagine who it was. I had worked so hard to get the other drunks away, and now here came another set.

I opened the door, and there stood Tar Baby, so drunk he could barely stand up. I said "Daddy, dis Tar Baby."

Daddy said, "Come on in, man, if you comin."

It was cold outside, one of the coldest nights we had the whole winter. Tar Baby came in cursing and ordered a half pint of shine. I knew I had to get it, so I did—just in time to see Tar Baby slap Dor-Roa hard.

Fire rose in Dor-Roa's face. They were about to tie up fighting. Daddy and Willie Shangle reached out to separate them. Mr. Willie Shangle was so drunk, he couldn't do anything, so Daddy got between them. Dor-Roa's anger flew up beyond control and Daddy was not able to constrain him, so he demanded Dor-Roa get out of the house immediately.

Before Dor-Roa left, the hidden, demonic spirit in him boiled up. He said, looking directly at Tar Baby, "You black mother f——, I will see you again. Dis ain't near bout over."

Daddy pushed him out the door and slammed it closed. Dor-Roa shouted vindictively, "I'll be back!" Nobody took him seriously, not even Daddy.

I was terrified of what Dor-Roa might do. His capabilities were far more than anyone could predict. At that moment, I was the only one who seemed to really think about his treacherous behavior. Something in my heart told me it was not over.

I walked over to the bed where my two baby brothers were lying fast asleep and began rubbing their heads. I turned to look at Mama, lying fast asleep.

The door was kicked open. Daddy jumped from his chair and started toward the door. In came Dor-Roa with a double-barrel shotgun in his hand. He yelled out, "Don't nobody move!" Then he blasted a shot into Tar Baby's right leg, I believe at that moment everybody in the house was too frightened to move a muscle and too astounded to comprehend what was happening right in front of us.

Dor-Roa quickly turned and ran back out the door. Blood was pouring from Tar Baby's leg profusely. If he hadn't been sitting in the exact chair where he was hit, that bullet would have hit my baby brother James C directly in the middle of his head. In fact, neither of the boys woke up.

Mama did. She woke up astounded. I don't think she realized what was going on, but it didn't take long for reality to set in. She started crying, frightened that her baby could have been killed. She seemed stone sober and alert, shouting, "Git de law! Git de law! Lord have mercy, dat crazy damn man coulder killed my baby! He coulder blowed his brains clean outer his head!"

My parents not only lived dangerous lives, they placed our lives in danger also. They were so dysfunctional that they didn't realize what they were putting their own children through. They may not have had any education, but they should have had common sense. I often wondered what was on their minds. Looking back, I see how God kept us throughout all those years. "If my people, which are called by my name, shall humble themselves, and pray, and seek my face, and turn from their wicked ways; then will I hear from heaven, and will forgive their sin, and will heal their land" (2 Chron. 7:14 KJV).

Once old man Lund Cabb came up in that Black Maria, I knew everybody was going to be talking about it. Shame took over my body. After that, I stopped smiling. Frowns grew on my face. When folk look at me, they automatically think I am mean—that is the presumption about me to this day.

Lund Cabb questioned Daddy, who gave him all the details. Tar Baby was taken to the hospital, and a hunt went out for Mr. Dor-Roa. Lund Cabb arrested him that night. He was home, snuggled in bed like he hadn't done a thing. He was sentenced to five years down on the chain gang.

For the first time, I saw my father shake from fear. But what he was afraid of, I couldn't tell, because there was so much he had to be fearful of. Was it fear of dying and going to hell? Fear of what had taken place among his children? Fear of the next time? What exactly was he in fear of? Fear certainly was not one of his philosophies. Many times, remembering that night, he said, "There's only one bad luck, and that's to miss heaven and go to hell." Only he didn't fear that either, in light of the way he lived.

Neither Daddy nor Mama knew anything about prayer. In all of my born days, I never saw or heard my father pray. Daddy had never been inside a church, and Mama had completely stopped going. The children were growing up in devastating surroundings.

I lived on at the house because of what happened that night. I knew if anyone ever needed security, it was my siblings. Willa Max stayed nights with Aunt Matilda regularly, and we all spent every possible minute with her. She was never alone.

There wasn't a day went by that I didn't miss staying with her myself. What I missed the most was the calm, serene feeling of going to bed at night and not having to fear what we would wake to. For a long time, all I'd had to look forward to were sweet dreams, and now they were all gone. Being back at home meant awakening each morning to a terrible nightmare. Mama's drinking got worse each day, and Daddy was uncontrollable. Folk were saying he was chasing his outside woman like he was a teenage boy with his first crush.

Mama kept going to work. Some days I got to go to school. The majority of the time, Daddy had us in fields—pulling corn, pulling roots, or any other kind of work he could get for us once cotton season was over.

The first time Georgie Boy and I had to stay out of school to pull corn, Daddy made us believe it was only for a week. But every time he needed money for moonshine, women, or gambling, I knew we had to be the ones to miss school and work hard. Nevertheless, Georgie Boy and I worked extremely hard that week. We even thought that, just maybe, he would have a heart and give us something for ourselves.

On Friday, Daddy collected the money. We never learned how much we got paid, but I do know we filled up two trailers of corn that week. All I asked for was a pair of Slim Jim pants—they were the latest fashion—and a pair of loafer shoes. The two items ran about two dollars and twenty-five cents. He promised I could have them. But when the time came for me to go downtown, he couldn't be found anywhere with all our hard-earned money. I didn't get one dime from him.

The good news was my mother came up with the money. Not only did I get the Slim Jims and the loafers, but I got an evening at the movies.

***

Later that week, Glory Ann and Ruthella came by, certain I would be able to go to the teen center with them. Daddy came storming in from only God knew where and absolutely forbid me to go. We begged him, but it was no use.

Mrs. Brittney had bought the place from Mrs. Ola Mae and turned it into a social center. That Saturday was opening night, from five to nine o'clock. Everyone was going except me. Glory Ann and Ruthella were even more disappointed than I was.

After they left, I went to Daddy in the most respectful manner and reminded him about his promise to give me the money for pants and shoes. He said he had no damn money. I just accepted the no.

The room was the same as always—a drunk here and a drunk there. Pretty soon Daddy was stretched out across the bed, dead asleep, with a twenty-dollar bill hanging from his pocket.

I did not hesitate. I took that twenty from his pocket and caught up to Glory Ann and Ruthella. I told them I would meet them at the teen center. I had made up my mind that I was going to do what I wanted to do if it killed me.

I went downtown with the twenty dollars and bought myself another pair of Slim Jims, a sweater to match, and another pair of loafers. I made myself happy, and I had five dollars left over to go to the center and have myself some fun. I knew there would be consequences, but I really didn't care.

I took the clothes home and changed. As I made my way to the center, an unfamiliar voice called out, "Hey, Haley Keath, where you goin?"

I looked back to see who it was. Surprisingly, it was good-looking Andy Malone, son to Sister Greta. I didn't know what to think. I was shy and had such low self-esteem, I hardly knew how to answer him.

Without meeting his eyes, I pointed toward the center. A few other teenagers were scattered about the grounds, and they seemed shocked to see me. Andy approached and, out of the clear, asked if I was going inside. I said yes. The music was playing, and it sounded good. He asked if he could walk in with me. I was astounded. He opened the door, and we walked in together.

The dance floor was filled with the girls and boys dancing. They were in a circle, doing the pony. Andy asked if I wanted to join in, but I wanted to watch so I could get the hang of it. I looked around to see who was sitting where, and then took a seat.

That was the most enjoyable evening I'd had in my whole fifteen years. I danced my first dance with Andy to "Cry Baby." The pressure of his body against mine made me fall in love with him at that very moment. He looked into my eyes. He was never a talker, but his eyes spoke what his mouth didn't say. Yes, his eyes said everything I wanted to hear. He was the most good-looking guy any young lady could want for her companion.

As he danced close, he whispered in my ear, "Can I be your boyfriend?" I was in hog heaven, but he knew I was also nervous. He added gently, "You don't have to answer me now. You kin give me your answer when I walk you home." All eyes were on us, as if we were a show or something. My heart was flowing with excitement.

When the song was over, I hurried to a booth and sat down. Andy stood off on the side and watched me. I was nervous, but I felt special for a change. I even allowed myself to believe he really cared about me. I had felt so abandoned and shut in for so long, and now a free spirit of belonging was all over me. It was the first time a young, handsome, respectable guy like Andy had shown interest in a girl like me.

He asked again if he could walk me home. That sent chills up and down my body. The good time I was having vanished. If Daddy caught me walking with a boy, he would half kill me. I told Andy no, and he wanted to know the reason why. I was not a good liar. I explained my fear of what my father would do. Andy didn't let that stop him. He got Glory Ann, Ruthella, and Jonkey to come with us, and they all walked me home.

The house seemed real quiet. When I got inside, Mama was awake but Daddy was fast asleep in a chair. I wanted desperately to tell Mama about my evening and what a wonderful time I'd had, but I just didn't know how to approach her. She was not the kind of mother I could just talk to about anything.

I watched from the doorway as she was getting the boys down for the night. I was not about to let her or anyone else spoil the wonderful feeling I had.

***

Things brightened up for me. Each weekend, I was allowed to go to the center—as long as I was obedient during the week.

For a long time, Andy and I were together at the teen center. He would walk me home from school whenever I went. One Saturday evening, I met him at the center. We danced for a while. At one point, he was standing off to himself with his arms folded. He was looking at me in a very different way. It didn't make me feel comfortable. Something was on his mind. The first chance I got when he was not watching, I eased out the door and ran home, practically running away from those looks I couldn't understand.

For the next two weeks, I was under punishment for stupid things like spilling a few drops of whiskey. When the two weeks were up, I knew Daddy would find another way to keep me from going to the center. I was prepared for whatever evil plan he conjured up. I was on my best behavior, because I knew the least little thing I did would be a strike against me.

Lo and behold, I was so right about him. Daddy came in on Friday night and the house was filled with people as usual. He was in a vicious mood. He started in on Mama. She had no control over him at all. She was washing the children, awake and sober for once, and her only weapon was her mouth. She bluffed him off with every dirty word that she could use. I do believe the good Lord was in there watching over us, because Gemmy BB and Charlie John came in with their little army, distracting everyone.

As long as I was being the little slave sitter for all the kids, I was in good standing with Daddy. It wasn't long before Charlie had him and they were gone. I knew when they came back, nobody in the house would get any rest until Sunday evening.

Charlie John and Gemmy BB fought all the time. He was either catching her out of place, or she was too drunk. She was a very disturbed woman. She was in a marriage she was miserable in. At age twenty-five, she had more children than Mama had, and was steadily having them.

On Sunday evening, they packed up their long station wagon and left for home early. I was glad to see them go. I got dressed and left for the teen center before Daddy came home. I wanted to surprise Andy, but mostly I wanted to capture that first look on his face when I walked in.

I arrived at the center with a few other teenagers. There was a circle going around on the dance floor, doing the pony. The moment Andy spotted me, he got out of the line, came over, took my hand, and pulled me into the line beside him. I felt so special. Going out with children my own age and doing what normal teenagers did was now in my bloodstream. All eyes were on Andy and I. We danced to every record that played, slow and fast.

The last song of my night was "There Goes My Baby." Andy held me close to his heart as we moved slowly to the beat. When it was over, he kept holding me.

I looked up at the clock, knowing I had to leave. My curfew was up. I was the only one who had to leave, but if I wanted to come out on weekends, I had to be obedient.

We were about to leave. Andy had his arm around my waist. Out of nowhere, Doletha came up to me with the fake smirk she wore when she was up to her ungodly tricks. "Hey, Haley Keath, you leavin, gurl? It's early! Everybody stayin out till ten. Why you got to go so early?"

"Yeah, Doletha, I got to go. Some got it and some don't. You got it."

"Well, at least Mr. Macky let you stop sellin moonshine whiskey long ernough to come habe er little fun."

Everybody heard her embarrassing remarks. I wanted to slap her, but instead I said, "Yeah."

Andy, his arm steady around my waist, pressed against my back and moved me on out the door. We never mentioned Doletha as he slowly walked me to my house.

We were standing out front when I heard the door opening. My first instinct was that it was Daddy. Me with a boy was the last thing I wanted him to see. I might not be allowed back to the center for a year. I took Andy's arm and pulled him around to the side of the house.

It was a beautiful Saturday night. There was a full moon, and the light shone down right over us. It was a perfect night, and I was in the arms of someone I had fallen deeply in love with. I could feel he had fallen in love with me also. We looked into each other's eyes, and his eyes were the same color as mine. He took me passionately into his arms and softly kissed my lips. It was my very first kiss.

Suddenly the old toilet door opened, and out stepped Daddy. He walked right up to us and struck a match to light a cigarette. He pointed the match in our faces, asking, "Who is this boy you got with you?" I was speechless. He went on, "This here Greta Garland boy, ain't it?"

Andy answered very intelligently, "Yes, sir. I'm Andy."

"Yeah, I thought so. Well, Haley, don't you think you better be gittin on inside outter dis dark?"

The only darkness out there that night was him. "Yes, sir," I said. I knew I was going to get it. Daddy was calm in front of Andy, but I knew. I was nervous, but more angry than anything.

Andy and I walked on behind Daddy. When he went inside, Andy kissed me gently on my lips and said, "I'll see you tomorrow."

I went inside, knowing I was in big trouble. There was no way I could explain what we were doing at nine o'clock at night in the backyard. It was innocent, yet Daddy would never understand. I took my clothes off and jumped into bed as fast as I could.

The next Sunday, I got ready to go to the teen center. Daddy had been gone all day, but as soon as I was ready, he popped up out of the thin air, intoxicated, smelly, and sweaty. He looked as if he was ready to skin a bull.

I showed no fear of him, just stood before him like a prisoner. He told me I was not going to "no damn teen center." He ordered me to go only to work. I was not allow to attend school or any school function. No picture shows, no nothing.

I hated him with every bone in my body. I wished he would die or just disappear. I had no choice but to obey his demands. The heathen had taken my life away from me. Living in that house was living in pure hell with fire.

I worked from six in the morning until six at night, no school, no church. There was only working in the fields through the week and selling moonshine, beer, and home brew on weekends.

I still had Aunt Matilda in my life to encourage me in my painful moments. She was always up when we left for work, and waiting when the truck put us out in the evening. Georgie Boy and I were the only children working during school season.

I spent a lot of time awake, lying in bed and looking up at the ceiling. I thought about what my life would be like away from there with no education. My one desire was to finish school.

My hatred of Daddy was so strong, I began to think of ways I could get rid of him myself. One night, I came in from a hard, depressing day. After eating dinner and taking my bath and cleaning the kitchen, I was putting away the dishes in the cabinet. A big rat hopped out and ran down through a hole in the floor. I got the bottle of rat poison, put some on food scraps, and put the scraps down in the hole. I began to fantasize about putting some in Daddy's food to kill him.

The thought became a vision in my mind. All my thoughts focused on how to get rid of him. He was no father; he was an evildoer with no compassion toward anybody.

As always, something happened. I went to Aunt Matilda's house, and she had made her favorite meal: tea cakes, fried chicken, white rice, and gravy. As we were eating, out of nowhere a light shone from the ceiling down onto the table. I couldn't imagine where it came from. The day was cold and dreary, and there were no light fixtures in the ceiling.

Then Aunt Matilda laughed out loud and began to clap, giving praise to the almighty God. Though I didn't know what she was giving praise for, I began to give praise also. We praised for about five minutes, and suddenly a strong belief of provision swept over me. Georgie Boy and I wouldn't have to go back out to that stupid cornfield.

That night, I went back to Mama's house and lay awake practically all night. In the early morning, I got up, went to the kitchen, drank down all the water my stomach could hold, and got back into bed without being heard.

Around five o'clock, Daddy's usual time for getting up and starting the fire burning, I ran my fingers down my throat and commenced to throw up all that water. I rolled over, moaning and groaning as if I were dying from stomach pains. Mama rushed into the room, full of concern. "Haley, gal, what's the matter wit you?"

I faked the worst illness anyone could ever fake. She rubbed her hand over my forehead and swore I had a high fever. She felt the bed and it was soaking wet from my throwing up. She called out to Daddy, and he came in. He was unconcerned that I was sick but concerned I was not able to go work in the field. Mama stated, "She can't go no field in dis kind of condition, Macky. She just gotter stay home."

For once in his sorry life, he agreed to something other than having his way. Once they left the room, I covered up my head and let out a soft laugh until I cried. I had successfully faked an illness so I could go to school.

I waited patiently as they left for the field. Then I crawled out of bed and told Mama I was feeling better. Could I go to school?

It didn't take me long to get dressed in my Slim Jims and loafers, ready for my first day in school after missing over three months. I knew it was my plan, and God had nothing to do with my faking, but he allowed me to pull it off.

That is, until I stepped into the kitchen, dressed for school, and Mama saw directly through my deception. She looked me up and down and said, "You got well might fast. You wait till I tell your daddy what you did. He gon beat your damn ass."

I shouted, "I git tired of workin in the field all the time! I want to go to school, an if dis is de only way for me to go, den I'mo go, even if it just for one day."

I didn't give her time to say another word. I ran out the door, all the way past Shelmore store and the funeral home before stopping. I was almost up to the old Sawmill quarter when Andy caught up with me. He and I walked on to school together. When we arrived, he walked me to my room and kissed me right at the door. I walked in, and all eyes fell directly on me. It didn't make any difference to me. That morning, I was willing to risk getting my ass whipped. I wanted to go to school, and that was my only opportunity.

Skitter was so pleased, she called out joyfully, "Haley Keath!" She ran right into my arms, showing much love and concern. She was as glad to see me as I was to be in class.

I got settled, and when I turned around, there was my favorite troublemaker, Doletha. It was no secret why I hadn't been to school, but she couldn't wait to try and embarrass me by asking, "Why you ain't been to school, Haley Keath?"

I responded, "I had to work, Doletha. Do dat answer your question?"

"I'm glad my mama don't make me stay outer school and work in no field. If she did, I think I would run erway."

"I prob'ly would feel de same way if my daddy was dead an I was gittin er check from him like you do."

Not giving her time to say another insulting word, I sat in my usual seat next to Skitter. I was amazed—Skitter had a notebook full of extra copies she had made for me to help me catch up. She said encouragingly, "Don't let them git next to you. Sit down and put your name on these papers so you kin turn them in, an you won't flunk all the lessons."

She never knew how blessed I felt to have a friend like her. She never knew how much she helped me that day. Mrs. Brittney thought that I had been keeping up with the work when I had not done schoolwork for three months. Skitter had prepared at least three papers a week for all the classes, and they were accepted unquestioned.

Doletha was still very popular, and she wore the best dress in our entire classroom. I could not understand why she antagonized me the way she did. Her harassment began to annoy me. As I was walking back from the teacher's desk, she rolled her eyes at me as if I was her worst enemy. Skitter wrote me a note: "*You see, Haley Keath? Before you can get back in school, good Doletha is already picking, but don't pay her no mind.*"

I wrote back: "*Yeah, before school is out in June, I am going to beat the hell out of her. You watch and see what I tell you.*"

I knew that was not what Skitter wanted to read, because nonviolent was who she was. I was surprised when she wrote back, "*I hope I be around so I can get me a lick in (smile).*"

I managed to ignore Doletha and her gang that morning. During lunchtime, the picking and instigating continued. At one point I almost reached for her, but Mrs. Pughsley touched me on my shoulder and told me, "Keath, girls don't fight each other. Only cats and dogs fight." I heard the words and they soaked into my spirit, but Doletha was yet on my mind.

I was walking home from school and didn't know Andy was walking behind me with his two little brothers, Poppie and Norman. Norman ran up behind me and in a cute little voice said, "Hey, Haley Keath, Andy told me to give you dis."

It was a letter. I stopped so Andy could catch up to me.

"Who you waitin for?" he asked.

"Waitin for you."

"That's why you walkin so far behind the other children?"

"I didn't realize you was behind me until my new mailman delivered me my mail special delivery. So I decided to wait for you. I just didn't feel much like no crowd."

We walked on home. I didn't care if Daddy knew I was yet seeing Andy. There wasn't much else Daddy could do to me. I had made up my own mind I was not going to stop seeing my first love.

***

I believed I would not be going back to school until mid-December. I must have prayed a dozen times, asking God to let me go back to school. And he answered. It was a cold, rainy, windy autumn, and we were unable to work. Therefore, we had to go to school. It was not refreshing for Georgie Boy, but it was a fresh beginning for me.

Every morning, Andy and I walked to school together, and every evening we walked home together. I didn't know it at that moment, but he and I were going steady. Things were looking up again. I was allowed to go to the teen center and the picture show.

We had a wonderful time over one weekend. I had been to church with him and his mother, Sister Greta. She was doing everything in her power to help me receive the baptism of the Holy Ghost. Monday was a normal school day. I walked home with Andy and his two brothers.

As we passed Pa Jack's café, I saw it was blue Monday at our house. The porch was full of drunks. I decided not to enter from the front. I went through the back of the café grounds and on down to our yard, hoping to come in through the kitchen. But it was full. My mama was sitting at the table, crying, and she was surrounded by our neighbors. I went in to see what was wrong, and I heard her say, "Poor Big C. Her baby is gone."

I was puzzled. It had been a long time since Cousin Big C moved away.

The news was some members of the family got into a disagreement, and it escalated into violence. Gunshots were fired, but with no intention for anyone to get hurt. The family had gotten everyone calmed down, and they thought everybody was safe, when Little Teddy came around the corner, holding his stomach. He said a wasp had stung him. Everyone believed that until he collapsed. When they got to him, his eyes had rolled back in his head. He was rushed to the hospital and pronounced dead on arrival from a gunshot wound to the abdomen.

It was a sad occasion. Little Teddy was gone; God had taken him and made him an angel to watch over the rest of us. All I heard from the kitchen that evening was, "Oh my God, Teddy is gone to be with the Lord."

They brought Little Teddy's body home and funeralized him at Greater New Salem Baptist Church. It was a funeral that will never leave my memory, the saddest of the sad. The pain among the family could not be hidden.

For the first time in my life, I witnessed Cousin Big C's weakness. She had lost her baby boy, the light of her life. She loved all her children, but Teddy had been special. They had had a special bond between them, and it could have been for many reasons. But though he was gone on to the far place beyond, he had been a loving child.

He had had everybody in the neighborhood wrapped around his little finger, and now the whole town was in pain from his death. Folk said the reason for his early death was that he was too pretty. God couldn't allow him to stay here.

The family sobbed on that warm Sunday afternoon. I knew everybody in the sanctuary felt what I felt and remembered what I remembered. But we could only feel the pain that swept across the hearts of the people who loved Little Teddy.

Late that Sunday night, a terrible thunderstorm came up. Lightning flashed and the thunder rolled throughout the entire night. The storm lasted for days. Word was that when the Lord called one to death, after the funeral rain came and washed the footprints away.

I never liked thunder and lightning, but I was not minding it now because I knew I could go to school every day. My belief was the bad weather was the work of the almighty God, showing his power.

The last thing I remembered about that week was old man Wilkerson had a major stroke, and he never recovered.

***

I always knew that somehow and some way, I was going to make a liar out of Macky. I knew my field days were coming to an end. But the problem was I had missed so many days of school, my desires no longer existed. I was so far behind in my schoolwork, there was no way I could catch up, even with Skitter's help. It would take a miracle for me to pass my grade, and it didn't matter to me anymore. The only thing I was concerned about was Skitter moving up and leaving me behind. The thought saddened me, but other than not sharing classes, we would still remain friends.

The weather was calm, and folk were back to their old routines. Tise came by, surprisingly. I hadn't seen or spent any time with her in what seem like months. She didn't stay long, but long enough for me to see her stomach was pushed out again. She didn't look happy to me; she seemed distant.

Shortly afterward, her visits became regular. I was old enough to relate to some of her pain. It must have been an uneasy feeling for her, knowing that the father of her child had married someone else. That made me take a real good look at my life. I didn't want to end up like my sister. With a mother like ours, who was not really a mother figure, Tise and I had built up a relationship that allowed us to confide in and depend on each other. I had gotten to know her remarkably well. As soon as she entered the door, the look on her face would tell me if she was unhappy or worried. I wanted to be depended upon, and she could depend on me.

One day, she came in with a new man in her life—a tall, light-skinned fellow with pearl-white teeth. He was the quarterback for the high school he attended, and we thought that was real cool. She introduced him as Buster, saying he was very popular and from a good family.

The moment I took a good look at him, I knew in the pit bottom of my gut he was not the grinning, happy-go-lucky man he pretended to be. I never saw a man who grinned as much as he did. Maybe it was because he had white teeth and wanted to show them off.

My first instincts instructed me he was not to be trusted. He had a hidden personality that none of us could imagine. Tise was not as happy as a young woman should have been when dating the quarterback of the football team. I knew in my heart that no matter who Buster was, he was no J. R. Hayward. And he would never be the love of Tise's life. I was also concerned about the father of the baby she was carrying.

Not long after, she and Buster became engaged to be married. I didn't want her to marry him. She knew just what I was thinking. She put her hand on top of my head, smiling, and said, "Don't worry, Haley. Your sister knows exactly what she is doing."

I had to trust her judgment, but I was set against her decision for many reasons. He was graduating and already had a four-year scholarship to attend college away from home, yet he would rather marry than take advantage of such a great opportunity? A college degree meant a better job and more money to take care of a family and live a decent life. Who wouldn't want that? Something was there that had not yet been discovered.

The only thing left for me to do was wait for the film to start rolling. I didn't like him because I felt he was taking Tise away from me. But I felt if my suspicions were right about him, Tise would see it also and maybe think twice before marrying him.

When they left that evening, Tise took little glance at me, trying to be strong. I saw the pain in her eyes that said she didn't want to marry him. It was her stomach saying she should.

She said she would be back on Monday, but she didn't come until that Wednesday. I was hoping she had come to her senses and would not go through with the marriage. I even hoped for something to intervene.

But Buster was smarter than any of us imagined. They got married the same week he graduated from high school, and they moved to Whiskey, Georgia. Tise wasn't completely alone there. Uncle Head Henry was there and his family—Aunt Rita; her mother, Aunt Mattie; the twins, cousins Rosette and Posette; Dolly; and and the baby girl, Milford, who everyone said was Uncle Head Henry's heart. Tise was one of his favorite nieces. That gave me a great consolation, knowing he would be there as much as possible for her. Cousin Louise and her daughters Della, Pauline, and Eartha were also living in Whiskey. So I didn't worry too much about Tise.

***

It seemed like everything hit me at once that year. I flunked my grade and had to be retained. In a way, I was released from having to put up with my classmates. It put me back with Glory Ann and Ruthella, so that worked out for the best. I wondered why Doletha didn't fail, but then realized it didn't take a genius to figure that one out. All her friends did her work for her. She was going to come out, as Mrs. Brittney would say, empty as a barrel with no bottom.

We were all out of school and waiting for cotton season. Normally everybody jumped on the first truck that came along. One Sunday evening, I was sitting on the porch, hoping somebody would come and rescue me from that hell hole. A blue-and-white Ford drove up and a voice called out, "Hey, gurl." I recognized it was Buster's voice.

Immediately I asked, "Where's Tise?"

"She's at the house. She sent me to see if you would come and stay wit er till the baby come next week, if Mr. Macky and your mama would let you come. We thought she was gon habe it this mornin, but it was a false erlarm. Since I have to work and she home wit only Glance by herself, she gon need somebody dere wit er so she sent me to git you." "Glance" was what we called Tise's first child.

Boy, as much as I disliked Buster, I forgot my feeling. I was overjoyed at the chance to get away from that enviroment. Whiskey was only thirty-seven miles away, but to me it was like going to New Orleans. "You bet I'll go," I replied.

Daddy was entertaining in the back. Buster went in to where he sat with his customers and drunken buddies. When Daddy was in that kind of mood, you could get him to do anything you wanted him to do. They were singing their usual gospel songs, and old Fred Solomon beating away on his guitar. The song was "See How They Done My Lord." That bunch wouldn't go to anybody's church, but every Sunday they got juiced up and you couldn't tell them they were not a quartet.

I waited patiently on the porch and prayed that Daddy would let me go. Buster was gone a long time. When he finally came back, I gathered by the look on his face that Daddy had said no. But Buster said, "It took some doin, but I finally convinced him to let you come back. You better hurry an git you some clothes fore he changes his mind."

I hurried to the bedroom, grabbed a brown paper bag, and threw some clothes in it. I jumped into the car before Daddy could get to the door. Buster drove off at high speed. I didn't say good-bye to anybody, not even Aunt Matilda.

Tise was standing in the door with Glance when Buster drove up. She looked sad. Maybe, I thought, it was because she was ready for her new baby to come. The first three days of the visit were pleasant. Tise tried to be cheerful, but I could see she was very unhappy. When we finally had a conversation alone, she confirmed everything I suspected, including about her unborn child. She was having a difficult pregnancy, and that certainly didn't help her situation.

I took Glance for long walks in the cool of the evening, and he enjoyed them. I watched him around Buster. Buster was not the loving father that he pretended to be.

He worked eight hours a day, and that was when Tise and I got our girl talk in. She gave me great advice. She thought I was sexually active until I convinced her otherwise. Somebody had told her I was sexually involved with Andy Malone, and that was a lie.

When she and I weren't talking, she was sleeping. I mean, she slept a lot.

I had been there for a week when the girls next door came over. Janice and Rita were their names. They reminded me of Doletha and Patrice. They had a friend named Haley also. What a coincidence! They were very friendly girls. I was invited to Rita's sixteenth birthday party on Saturday night. I felt special being invited to their party when they didn't know anything about me. I was happy for the moment.

That Saturday, the local Haley came to get me for the party. Everything was well. I made sure Glance had his bath and was in bed before I left. I had never been to a house party before. I was shy as well as a little edgy under the circumstances, not knowing anyone at the party except the girls who were hosting it.

I stayed close to Haley, Rita, and Janice. They were having the time of their lives. The backyard was full, and guests were steadily coming in. There was a young guy who kept looking at me. I was looking at him too, but only because he looked so much like Andy. Only his complexion was different.

Janice was a very pretty, tall, light-skinned girl with a nice shape, and was a great dancer. Her sister Rita was silent but very observant. Janice and I talked. She gave me the news of their lives. They worked pulling roots during the day; that was why they hadn't come over sooner to meet me. She told me if I wanted to go work with them, I could, but I didn't feel comfortable leaving my sister.

The crowd did the pony and then the hully gully. They danced the same as we did back home Rita finally called over the guy who had been eyeballing me. His name was Andy Ross; I couldn't believe I had met someone who resembled my Andy *and* had the same name. I saw a big fall-off in Haley's attitude toward me, and it didn't take any time for me to put it together. Neverthless, Andy and I danced to the record "Two Lovers." I could tell he was ha slick charmer.

When the party was over, he insisted on walking me next door. I suggested that he stay and have the last dance with Haley, but he declared there was nothing between them. The last dance was "Pride and Joy," and as we were all dancing, I eased off the dance floor and went home. I knew the tension between Andy and Haley was because of me, and that was the last thing I wanted. I questioned why I caused problems for others unknowingly.

Tise was waiting up for me. She had been watching the party from her kitchen window and had witnessed everything that took place. The first question she asked me was, "Who was the boy you kept dancing with?"

"Would you believe his name was Andy Ross?"

We laughed. She understood how much Andy Malone had become a major focus in my life.

I was glad I was there for her. Telling me her innermost secrets seemed to help her a lot. She couldn't hold back the pain. I witnessed more pain in her face that night than I had carried around in my heart my entire life. I wanted to know why we had so much pain. My pain alone could have killed ten elephants, but her pain and mine together could have killed a whole jungle. I was not old enough it do anything about Tise's situation, only to be there for her. There was much I understood, yet much I didn't. Somewhere in the back of my mind were words I wanted to say, words that might make her feel better, but I could never articulate them.

We said our good nights and went off to bed, but I could hear her crying. Buster was not home, so I went into her room to see if there was anything I could do for her. She said she just wanted the baby to come so she could do something with her life. I was in no hurry, because I knew as long as she was pregnant, I didn't have to go back home. The moment she gave birth, I would have to return.

I was too restless to sleep. I lay awake for a long time, feeling bad for the other Haley. I was proud of my refusal to let Andy walk me home. I knew he was a player, and I had denied him the opporituity to score on the new girl in town. Janice and Rita were still friendly toward me afterward, but I never saw Haley again.

Tise had the baby, an eight-pound girl, two days later. She named her Shannon Huntington. I was allowed to stay on another two weeks with her.

I left on a Sunday. Buster bought me a Trailways bus ticket for my first ride on a bus alone. Janice and Rita came over to say good-bye, and that meant a lot. They were the first new people I had ever met. They walked me to where the bus stopped, so Buster could stay with Tise. I never saw them again.

I hated to leave Tise that Sunday. She cried, and so did I, because I knew what I was going to have to face when I got home.

The bus was right on schedule. Once I boarded, sadness hit me from all directions. I arrived around five o'clock and walked home, entered through the back door. I could hear Daddy cursing. He was in one of his devilish drunken states. From the door, I didn't see Mama, but Gemmy BB and Charlie were holding on to Daddy like the man had gone mad. Drunks were scattered around the room, loud and filthy.

Suddenly I heard a whisper from behind me. I turned, and it was my mama. Her hand was wrapped in a towel, and it was soaked in blood. I pulled her into the bedroom and unwrapped the towel to see why she was bleeding so badly. Her hand was cut in several places, and her thumb was the worst. "What happen to your hand, Mama?" I asked. She cried and shook her head and shushed me. "He did this to you," I said. "What did he do?"

It turned out he had tried to cut her with his hawkbill knife. She had grabbed the knife, and that's how her hand got cut. It was bad. She needed stitches, but I couldn't convince her to go to the hospital or put his black ass in jail.

I pulled her out the back door, down to Aunt Matilda's house, like I was leading a little child. I wondered, *How can she be that gullible? How much more is she willing to adjust?* Daddy's behavior was so contaminated. The children saw it, I lived it, and Mama wore it.

They were all fearful, but I was no longer afraid of him. I was so filled with rage, I couldn't even speak.

Aunt Matilda heated up some water and placed Mama's hand in the pan to soak a little. Then she poured a small bottle of Mercurochrome into the wounds, and I wrapped the hand in gauze. We insisted on

Mama going to bed there, and in a matter of seconds she was asleep. I watched as she slept and saw the tiredness in her face.

I thought about the children at the house, so I left Mama with Aunt Matilda and went back. I was ready to take Daddy on with rat poison, a butcher's knife, or whatever means were necessary. But when I arrived, most of the customers were leaving. Odessa was sitting on the couch, and the younger children were sitting beside her. Georgie Boy was in the other room, sober, his thumb in his mouth, scared out of his wits.

When Ms. Odessa saw me, she was pleased. "I don't know where your mama is, but I'll be right here wit dese chilluns till she comes back, little Haley."

I looked out the door. Daddy was strolling down the road just past the Williamses' house, headed toward the bottom. Something hit the pit of my stomach, as if my body was getting prepared for disaster. Word was that Daddy and Pallie Lea were all over each again since Mr. Danny had had a stroke. I hoped he would stay down there and not come back home that night.

Voices came from the back of the house. It was sundown, and Gemmy BB and Charlie John were returning. My God, if Daddy wasn't raising hell, they were. They brought their problems directly to our house every weekend. Gemmy BB was as far gone as the rest of them. How could anyone win for losing?

Ms. Odessa and I cleaned the house and got the children down for the evening. I wondered if Mama had woken up and went to Aunt Matilda's house to check. Mama was awake and sitting on the side of the bed. I told her she could come on back home if she wanted to, and she did. We got her home and settled in her own bed. She was much calmer but still sad. Aunt Matilda came later with peroxide and some other solutions for the cuts on Mama's hand. She made Mama as comfortable as she possibly could. I could see she was feeling a lot of pain. But with Daddy and the drunks gone, the house was quiet and clean, and we all felt some peace.

I walked out to the backyard just to look up toward heaven and say a prayer. *Dear Lord, please help us to git out of dis awful mess dat we are in. Git my daddy away from us so he won't hurt my mama again, and please God, don't let him come back to dis house. I know we ain't suppose to hate nobody, but I have to tell you, I don't hate nobody else in the world like I hate him. I do hate him. If you don't want me to hate him, move the hatred from my heart. I don't want to hate him, but de things he do to us make me hate him. Amen.*

I turned to go back inside, and Andy was coming around the side of the house. I was so glad to see him. We locked into each other's arms, and he kissed me gently. He held me so close. I needed that hug desperately. He asked, "When did you come back?"

"Around five o'clock this evenin. How did you know I was back?"

"I didn't. I come down here every evenin this time to see if you had come back. I really missed you."

My heart beat up against his, and it was like one heartbeat. I knew he loved me as much as I loved him.

Then that uneasy feeling I had felt before came over me again. Something terrible was about to happen or had already happened. Andy felt my body tense up. He took my hand and said, "Let's take a walk over to the ballpark."

We did, and sat on the bleachers, watching the sun finish going down. He knew how my father was, so after about an hour, he told me he didn't want me to get into trouble and walked me home, making sure I was safe inside the house after we kissed good night. That uneasy feeling was still with me. I couldn't shake it, but I was strong because of the love Andy felt for me and the difference he made in my life.

I checked on Mama and the children. Snappy was sleeping. Georgie Boy was sitting up. Gemmy BB and her boys were gone. Everything seemed normal again. I couldn't remember the last time our house had been that still. I said to myself, "God must be working out my prayer for us."

Just then Jonkey's older brother, Tighteye, came running up on the porch, screaming out my name. "Haley! Haley, you need to come quick. Your daddy done got hurt."

My heart must have skipped a beat or two; I couldn't believe what my ears had heard. Tighteye was out of breath. He had run all the way from the bottom. "Mr. Charston Sneed done hit em in his head wit a two-by-four," he panted.

I didn't even know what a two-by-four was. It didn't sound too serious. "Dat's good for em."

I hadn't noticed Mama was standing behind us. "Watch your mouth, Haley. Don't you let me hear you talk like dat bout your daddy. What you say, Tighteye? Did I hear you say Macky got hurt?"

"Yes'm. Mr. Charston Sneed done hit em in his head wit a two-by-four."

She just looked sorrowful. She would always show compassion toward that evildoer. I was not sorry for what I said; I was only sorry for her hearing what I said.

Before long the porch was full of people coming with the news of my father being hurt. Charlie John drove up and came running to say Daddy was in the backseat of the car. Daddy was hurt pretty badly, but he wouldn't let Charlie John take him to the hospital. "Mama, he needs to go."

She stepped down off the porch and walked over to the car. I was right behind her. Daddy was lying in the backseat, and his forehead was split wide open. It was the most frightening wound I had ever witnessed. I lost control of myself. I knew then I didn't hate him. I screamed, "Oh Lord, don't let him be dead!" For the first time in all my years, I saw my father helpless. He was groaning as if he was dying. The big, bad Macky Keath had got a taste of his own medicine.

I was in a new frame of mind, broken between love and hate. The love I had for him was deep, far beyond the hatred. I only pitied him. I couldn't feel anything else. Once I got my composure, I could see things in a different light, and I had questions.

Mama was still holding a towel around her hand. She told me to get back. We stood looking on as she got into the car with Charlie John and they drove off. I looked at everyone standing around, watching the show. There was always some action at our house, never any real peace.

The porch was filled with caring people. Not all of them were there just to gossip. Tighteye was still there, and I asked him why Mr. Charston Sneed hit Daddy. Everyone knew Mr. Charston Sneed had been Cousin Sattie Bell's male friend since she left Uncle Martel. He never bothered anybody—just anybody's woman. I couldn't remember him doing anything except drinking and chasing women. Why would he bust Daddy's forehead open when they were supposed to be friends?

We went to the backyard so we wouldn't be overheard. Tighteye said, "I was comin from de picture show when I passed by your cousin Sattie Bell's house, an I saw your daddy down on top of Pallie, beatin her. So I hung around and watched two other men pulled em up off of her. A few minutes later, Mr. Charston Sneed come out and hopped off de porch. Dat's when your daddy got at em, and Mr. Charston started runnin. Your daddy was chasin behind em wit a long, shiny object, what look liked a switchblade knife in his hand.

"Mr. Charston ran until he got up to the woodpile, over across from Ms. Pallie's and Mr. Danny's house. He reached down an picked up a two-by-four. Just as Mr. Macky swung at him wit de knife, he jump backward and swung de board at Mr. Macky head. He struck him in de middle of his forehead, knockin em completely out cold, and blood started skeetin from his head. Dat when I took off runnin down here to git y'all. Dat's what I saw, but I won't tell nobody else if you don't want me to."

I knew there was no need; others saw what happened, therefore it was already told and strowed. I knew Tighteye was being truthful, and he had no reason to lie to me.

I heard voices by the back door. Odessa came out, and she had the cow by its tail. "Ms. Jenny Rue work so hard to take care of er poor little children, an now dis Mr. Macky caught Pallie an Charston Sneed in Sattie Bell's house makin out, and he done beat her g—— d—— ass an broke both her legs. Dey had to take er up to de hospital. An Charston Sneed done hit Mr. Macky in his head, so now both of dem up in de hospital in bad shape. De good Lord sure don't love ugly. I bet you anything Ms. Jenny Rue gon have to see bout both of em."

I was sick to my stomach, devastated, speechless. I went into the house and sat watching as the children slept. Glory Ann and Ruthella came in. I knew they had heard some version of what happened, and they couldn't wait to tell it. I asked if they actually saw what happened.

They both said, "No, de only thing we witness was Mr. Macky lyin in a pool of blood."

Ruthella said, "It was a good thing Mr. Danny was nowhere to hear dat."

"Where is Mr. Danny?" I asked.

"Oh! Haley, you been gone so you don't know. Mr. Danny had another stroke last Wednesday. He is up in de hospital too, paralyzed from his waist down to his feet."

After a while, Charlie John came back with Gemmy BB and said Mama was staying up at the hospital and wouldn't be home till next morning. I had to face the fact that her loyalty was with Daddy, regardless of how he treated her or any other circumstance. No matter what he did to her, she was always by his side. And he didn't seem to give a hoot about her—or us, for that matter.

It was past midnight when Gemmy BB and Charlie John left for home. Odessa stayed at the house with us. I was the oldest of the children left behind, and I knew my school days were over for a while. There was nothing for me to do but look after my little sisters and brothers.

Early on Monday morning, before we were awake, Mama came home only to wash up, change her clothes, and return to the hospital. I was young, not mature in many things, but for the love of this life, I couldn't understand why she put that man first. I swore I would never allow anything or anyone to come before my children, if I ever had any.

The next day, she came back again. I saw in her face that she was tired. Dark circles were under her eyes. Maybe that was why I took her to Aunt Matilda's house. The two or three hours of sleep she got there were better than any she had had the whole night.

Flip-mouthed and very outspoken I was, but I was never sassy to Mama. The one thing I would do was let her know what was on my mind. She was in the bedroom, preparing to take her bath. I waited until she was finished and was coming out the door, pushing more clothes in a brown paper sack to rush back to that hospital. I asked, calm but a little angry, "Mama, when you coming back home?"

She was teary-eyed. "I don't know. Your daddy is unconscious. He got forty-eight stitches in his forehead. De doctor say his skull is cracked up like an eggshell. But I got to stay up dere an see bout em. He ain't got nobody else. I know he been nasty to us, but dat don't mean I got to be nasty to em. I won't do it. I won't turn my back on em, not now. De good Lord will fix it, but he won't bless us if I turn my back on your daddy. You stay and see bout de young'uns. Ms. Odessa gon help you. I'll be back as quick as I kin."

As she was walking out the door, I yelled, "But look at dis picture, Mama! You is leavin your real obligation on me an your friend! You did try to do what was right, an you always tried to keep peace, an now you say you wanter do de right thing even though he got his head busted open over another woman."

She was speechless for a second. She looked like I had pushed a knife through her heart. "You know bout what happen to Lea."

"Yeah! Who don't know bout it, Mama? It's de talk of de whole town!"

She didn't get angry. She paused a second and then said, "You look, gal. You heard what dey say, but some dey ain't said dat. De good Lord is done already fixed it. Whateber dey done to me, both of em layin in dat ward, him wit his head busted open an her wit both her legs up. She turn one way, an he turn the same way. Neither one of em kin do er thing for the other one, an the good Lord got me waitin on both of em. De Good Book say, 'He will make your enemy your footstool.'"

I didn't know what she meant by that statement. It was clear she was pretty sure something positive was coming from what she was doing. I asked, "Mama, how kin you wait on dem like daey done done you? People sayin you ain't nothing but a fool. Just as soon as dey git up, dey gon do it again."

Bam! She slapped my jaw hard and said, "Don't you let me hear you say nothin like dat ever again de longest day you live."

I could tell when she walked away from me that she was hurting, the kind of pain that only she was able to feel. And she used her pain for good. I couldn't imagine that life, bearing that kind of pain for anyone.

Three days later, Daddy regained consciousness. Mama was standing directly over his bed when his eyes opened.

When Mama came home at noon for a fresh bath and clothes, I was in the kitchen, bottling up moonshine the way I had been taught. Bootlegging was at that time our only source of living until cotton season. She went directly into the bedroom and took a bath. I could smell her Avon catalog scent.

She couldn't spend one hour after that with her children; she had to get back before he woke up again. I called out as she was heading for the back door, "Mama, I wanter see Daddy. Now is er good time for you to lay down and git you er few hours of sleep while I go up to de hospital."

She looked back at me in disbelief. "You can't come up to no hospital, gal. You got to stay and tend to dese here chilluns. Now he done woke up, he'll be comin home in a few more days." And Mama practically ran out the door.

I made up my mind that I was going to the hospital regardless. A car drove up, and I heard Buster's voice. It was him and Tise. I asked how long they were going to stay. They said they had got the news about Daddy and Pallie Lea, and had come to help out at the house.

They settled in, and I said to Ms. Odessa, "I got to go to de store. I won't be long. Will you look after de chilluns till I come back?"

"Why sure, little Haley. Go on. Take your little time. I'll be right here when you come back," she said convincingly.

I knew she wanted a drink, so I poured out a fifty-cent shot and gave it to her. I hid the rest of the moonshine where she couldn't find it. Then I made my excuses, not telling anyone the real story about where I was in such a hurry to get off to.

I took off running. I knew I still had the opportunity to get to the hospital ahead of Mama, tired as she was. I ran every step of the way without stopping, and when I arrived, I was half out of my breath. I made my way to the colored ward and paused to compose myself. Many awful things rushed through my mind that I wanted to say. But when I got my first look at them, the words that had tossed around in my head vanished.

Daddy had bandages all around his head, and his face was swollen hugely. Both of his eyes were bloodshot, and he could barely see out of them. Pallie Lea was lying across the room from him, both of her legs in casts from her ankles up to her knees. She recognized me and, in a low whisper, called my name. It appeared that she was in a great deal of pain.

I walked slowly over to her bedside and stood, lost for words. I believe when she looked at me, my facial expression spoke for me. Lea had the kind of voice that on its own could charm any man, married or single. She asked sadly, “Will you give me a cup of water?” I did as she asked: poured a cup of water, put a straw in the cup, and gave it to her to drink. Once she drank it, she took a deep breath, groaned painfully, and said, “I ain’t doin so good. I’m hurtin all over.”

I placed a finger over her mouth, meaning *don’t talk*. I couldn’t help but wonder how much of that pain she was feeling was guilt or shame—shame that she got caught, or shame of what she’d done to her husband and my mother.

The nurse came in to check on them. Mama came in directly behind her. As the nurse was taking Daddy’s temperature, Mama sat watching me. For some reason, I believed she was proud of me. But I just could not feel the same pride in her. I did feel a great deal of sympathy for them all, but I was disturbed over everything.

I left the hospital and walked slowly down the dusty, hot road, more disturbed than ever. I wanted to understand what I had witnessed. Was Mama being good, or was she being the biggest fool in the town? Did Pallie Lea or Daddy know the suffering they had inflicted upon us? What was going to happen once they were released from the hospital? Were they going to continue their sordid affair, or would they have the decency to end it and stop the pain? I was more confused and angry when I left than I was when I got there.

The only way to free myself from so much pain was to throw myself into the chores that waited for me when I arrived home. After supper, when the children were all in bed, I sat in the the old wooden rocking chair and stared up at the ceiling, hoping that God would send me an answer. After a long while, I got into bed. But I couldn’t sleep, so I stared some more at the ceiling.

Sometime during the night, I fell asleep, but not for long. I woke up from what I first thought was a bad dream that someone was in the room, watching me. I lay still with cold chills running up and down my body. I recall tilting my head toward the middle door that led to the kitchen. Without a shadow of a doubt, I saw Dor-Roa peeping around the doorframe at me.

I rubbed my hand across my face, took a couple of deep breaths, and turned my back, praying that it was a dream. I always slept on my stomach, but that night I lay on my side with my face turned to the window. A little moonlight trickled in. I thought, *Dear Lord please protect me and my sister and brothers and don't let nothing happen to us.*

Suddenly the lamp in the kitchen went out. Someone was in that room. They came directly over to where I was lying and put their hand across my mouth. Somehow I got strength enough to wiggle out from under and let out a scream for help. Ms. Odessa came running from the other room, and whoever it was jumped out the window. Ms. Odessa lit the lamp and called, "Haley, is you all right? What's de matter?"

I was so shaken up from fear, I could barely speak. When I could get the words out, I said, "Mr. Dor-Roa was in dis room, Ms. Odessa. I saw em. It was him. I know it was. He put his hand over my mouth, but I managed to wiggle out an scream. Dat's when he ran."

"Haley, what's de matter wit you? I don't think nobody was in dis house. You mighter been dreamin, child."

Georgie Boy said, "Yeah, it was too. It was er man. I saw em too."

"Who it was, den?"

He answered, sucking on his thumb, "Dunno who it was, but it was er man an he jump out de window when Haley scream out. It was er man."

"Yeah, it was! It was Dor-Roa! He put his hand over my mouth!" I said.

Ms. Odessa went to the window and made sure it was closed and wired up tightly. She insisted on all of us going back to bed. I got in the bed between my two brothers, but I didn't sleep. I was much too afraid.

"I'm scared," Snappy said after a while. "Kin I git in de bed wit you too, Haley?"

All five of us bundled up together. I watched over them for the rest of the night, having to be strong for my little sister and brothers, making sure they were safe.

Around nine o'clock, Mama came home, and we all commenced to tell her what had happened. She said, "It probly was some of dem old drunks lookin for Mr. Macky."

I almost called her a liar. Why would whoever it was be looking for Daddy by putting his hand over my mouth? She had no other comment, just told us Daddy was finally coming home from the hospital the next day.

I was not interested in Daddy coming home. I wanted her to acknowledge what had happened. She had not been there to protect her children; she was more concerned about a man who did nothing except beat her and cheat on her.

When I informed her that I believed it was Dor-Roa I had seen, she doubted me. "It couldn'ta been em, cause nobody seen em since he shot Tar Baby in his knee."

I thought, *Just because nobody in town seen em, dat don't not make em be out lurkin.*

But if Daddy was being released from the hospital, our house wouldn't be broken into, at least. I could feel a little safe from outside intruders. Again, the thought of him coming back into our lives made me just sick to the pit-bottom of my stomach.

Around four o'clock that evening, Daddy came home. Mama was glad—why, I would never know. I was in much distress, hating myself for feeling the way I did toward Daddy. I just couldn't find a place in my heart for him. Often I sat and recalled the many prayers Aunt Matilda had prayed and the encouraging words she had said to me.

He was settled in the bedroom. Folk were in and out to see him. I kept in mind the exact Scripture passage Aunt Matilda quoted from the Ten Commandments: "Honour thy father and thy mother: that thy days may be long upon the land which the Lord thy God giveth thee" (Exod. 20:12 KJV). I didn't want to be rude or show any disrespect toward him. I just kept my distance. But I wanted to know about the mother and father honoring their children. I asked the Lord to help me understand what I didn't understand.

It wasn't easy getting to sleep at night, even though Daddy was back in the house. And with good reason. In the wee hours of one morning, I drifted off to sleep and was awakened by a sharp object—it felt like a knife—pressing against my throat. A hand was over my mouth again. Then came a hoarse whisper in my ear: "If you make a sound, I'll cut your throat."

Trembling from fear, I didn't move. My sister Snappy was in the bed with me, and she was sound asleep.

The hand moved from my mouth. He pressed the knife harder against my throat and attempted to remove my undergarment from my bottom. He almost succeeded.

I wiggled my knee hard, striking Snappy. I prayed she would wake up. She didn't.

It had to have been the good Lord stepping in once again and saving me. I don't know what made my brother Georgie Boy wake up, but he sat straight up in the bed. The light coming from the kitchen lamp shone in the room just enough for him to see that someone else was there. He scrambled bravely out of his bed and leaped for my bed.

The man jumped off of me. As Georgie Boy reached for him, he swung at Georgie Boy with the knife. I let out a scream. He climbed out of the window and ran out through the backyard.

But it wasn't light enough for either Georgie Boy or me to recognize who it was.

Mama came running into the room. "What de matter wit you, gal?"

I sat up, shivering. "Oh Lord, have mercy!" I don't know how I survived two attacks in two days. This time, Georgie Boy and I both could have lost our lives.

Mama was mad as hell. "Could y'all see who it was?" We told her we couldn't.

She ran out of the room. Quickly she was back, fully dressed. She told us to shut the door tight and she would back. I was afraid for her, wondering if the attacker was hiding out back someplace and might attack her.

She wasn't gone long. She came back with old man Tommy Williamson and Lund Cabb. They did a complete search all over the grounds for footsteps that might give them a lead as to which direction the attacker went.They managed to follow a set of footprints from our window on down the path that went by Pa Jack's café. Then they couldn't pick the prints up any farther because they crossed the highway. They took the matter very seriously and began watching the house more closely.

***

People were in and out all day long, visiting Daddy. Some cared; some were nosy. I watched him the entire day. He was awfully quiet. He didn't have a lot to talk about. That was how and who he was when he didn't have any whiskey in his system. He barely spoke a word sober, but when he was full of whiskey, nobody could tell him he wasn't the best gospel singer ever heard, or the best lawyer who ever won a case. I knew it wouldn't be long before he got started. I watched him, and I didn't stop watching him. I was watching him when he didn't know I was watching him.

I concluded that Daddy did love us in his own way—as much as a man of his caliber could love his family. It was just that he didn't know the meaning of love, and therefore he couldn't show what he didn't have in him. There was something deep within him that prevented him from showing love, and we all suffered severely.

At first, he appeared to be very restless. I didn't know if it was because he learned of the break-ins or because he was too ashamed to sleep because of what he'd done. I even thought that he might leave—move back to where he came from, and we could have our lives.

Around ten o'clock the next night, we were still up in our room. Folk had thinned out, leaving Daddy to rest. He came into our room and looked around the window, checking it out.

He sat down in a chair. In a totally different demeanor, one I had never witnessed, he asked, "Was you able to tell anythin bout de son of a bitch dat broke in here?"

I shook my head no.

"You couldn't tell whether he was tall or short? Or nothin bout his voice?"

"Naw, sir. He didn't talk loud; he was whisperin."

"Did you tell what he smelled like?"

"Yeah, sir, I did. Like whiskey."

"So you couldn't tell nothin else bout em."

"Naw, sir, I couldn't."

He lifted himself up from the chair, saying "I'll found out who de damn nigger was an dat's for damn sure." He said it with strong concern and conviction: he meant it.

I got a kitchen knife and slept with it under the pillow for several weeks. No more break-ins happened I began to feel normal and had no difficulty sleeping. I even positioned in my mind that the break-ins were over. Whoever it was was not coming back again.

On a harsh, cold, rainy Monday night, I was in the bath, scrubbing my weary body. I longed for somebody to confide in. If only Tise had been there, I could have told her my deepest, darkest secrets. All I needed was a listening ear.

I began to feel that I was being watched. I hastened to my feet and got out of the tub, shaking. I dried myself off. I got dressed and planted myself in bed, with my head buried deep in the pillow. I had a dream that night, and when I woke up the next morning, I was unable to remember any of it. But a poem was in my head that I never forgot.

My Last Dream

My last dream, I wonder what will it be
My last dream, I know it is especially for me
My last dream is soon to come true
My last dream—Dear Lord, I know my plans
And my future all depend on you

My last dream is fascinating to me
There are frowns, smiles and anger
With pain that I face each and every day

But thinking on the goodness of the Lord
I know love overshadows in every way

My last dream, a nightmare to fear
Each night I close my eyes to sleep
But when I open them each morning
My last dream stares at me until I weep

My dream is like my shadow, following me
And endures me forever more. If it wasn't
For my Jesus, whither shall I go?
In my dream, I always see Jesus
He stands beside me day by day
That is one of the reasons that I dream
And I know he'll never lead me astray

A few months passed without any disturbance. Daddy was fully recovered and back to himself—drinking, bootlegging, gambling, and entertaning drunks from morning till evening. Every word that came from his mouth was a curse.

Violence made our house its headquarters. When we got up in the morning, we had to clean up somebody's bloodstains from the floor. People were always getting cut or busted in the head. It had become our daily routine.

On a Friday evening that haunts me to this day, I was home after working hard in the field. All I wanted was a hot bath and bed, knowing completely well that that was damn near impossible. When the truck drove up in front of our house, the yard was already full of drunk niggers. I got instantly sick to my stomach.

Would it have been a damn crime for us to have a normal childhood? Or were our lives predestined for pain and shame? We were poor, but we still could have had a decent life. We definitely were not the only poor family in Rat Row, but we were the only poor family that lived this life of horror.

I jumped from the truck and hurried into the house before Daddy could see me. I went into the bedroom and looked out the window at the people in front of the house. I saw our lives as not a story, but real, true facts. The memory of them are so rooted inside my heart, they can never be erased.

I closed the window and prepared my bath. By eight thirty, I was in bed.

Around ten o'clock, we were awakened by Snappy. She had one of her asthma attacks. The coughing and wheezing made it impossible for me to sleep. I finally pulled myself out of the bed and went over to Mama's. "Can Snappy sleep in your bed?" I asked. "Or wit de boys? I just coan't take er anymore."

Mama surprised me and said, "Yes."

I got Snappy up and took her to Mama. Then I hurried back to bed.

It must have been around three o'clock in the moring when I was awakened a second time. The nightmare had started again. Someone had wrapped a strong cloth around my neck, strangling me. I couldn't scream. The strangler crawled on top of me and tried his damnedest to get my undergarments off. I knew I was about to be raped.

The butcher knife was still under my pillow. I pushed my hand under the pillow and felt for it. His body was on top of me, and because of that, he couldn't get my underwear down. He moved the hand that was tightening the cloth around my neck and whispered, "If you scream, I'll kill you."

I let out a fearful scream anyway. I had my hand on the knife, but I couldn't get it out. I screamed so loudly, Daddy and Mama came running. The strangler slapped me across my head and jumped from the window. Daddy made it to the window behind him and fired off a shot.

Mama had the lamp and said, "That looked just like Thomas Cravis. I'll stake my life on it." Odessa was standing behind her and agreed that it looked like Thomas Cravis. I couldn't see who it was, but his general shape sure did fit the description of Thomas Cravis.

I couldn't believe this had happened to me again. I cried and cried. I was ashamed to face anyone.

Next morning, Doletha came by. She wanted gossip to take back to school. I played along. I had started to think as she thought and pretend as she pretended. Let the game begin.

Her first question was, "Haley Keath, who keep breakin in on you?"

"I don't know who it is breakin in our house, but de police have a pretty good idea."

She said, "Well, I for one will be glad when dey catch whoever it is."

For a minute, I could almost believe she was sincere. Knowing her, it was words. Although I wanted to give her the benefit of the doubt, my instincts were not to believe or trust her at all. I knew it wouldn't be long before she would prove me right.

"Can you come to de café dis evenin?" she asked.

"I think so. I got to help round de house, an den I'll see."

"I'll come back for you after we come back from downtown."

She did come back, and I was ready to go. When we arrived at the café, she eased away from me to a few of her country friends. I stood on the sidelines, the target of more of her underhanded scheming. She acted as if she was ashamed to be seen with me.

That day it was her, O'Bera, and Jettey B sitting at the counter. Their eyes seemed to be fixed upon me. As I looked around, it seemed everyone was looking at me. I didn't know what the looks were for, but I felt extremely uncomfortable. Something was going on that I didn't know about. All I had to do was play it cool and wait; whatever it was, Doletha was sure to spill it.

I went and sat directly beside her. The record "Rome Wasn't Built in a Day" started to play, thank God. My hero Andy came over and took my hand to dance. In the beginning, I was hesitant, being a little nervous. He pulled me gently, and we danced to that song and many more, taking my mind completely off my problems. As we danced, he held me close but very respectfully.

He put his arm around my shoulder and walked me back to my seat. "Mama want to see you. She told me to tell you to come by de house," he said.

"See me?" I replied, curious. "What do she want to see me for?"

He smiled. "Go see."

I couldn't began to think what Sister Greta wanted to see me about, but that was my signal to leave. I didn't hesitate. I told Doletha I was going to see what Sister Greta wanted. She gave me a nosy look, but before she could say anything, I was out the door.

Andy was right behind me. He wanted to come with me, and I didn't want him to. For whatever reason, Sister Greta wanted to see me for me. I had no idea what in God's name such a well-respected woman could possibly want to see me about. She was a holy woman of God at Pentecostal.

The first thought that came to mind was, "I'm not good enough for her son Andy." I had grown accustomed to thinking the worst of myself, especially with all the break-ins—those had made me the talk of the town. I convinced myself that was exactly what she intended to say. Despite the negative attitude, I was calm when I arrived.

Andy's sister Nena came to the door. "Hey, Haley," she said in a friendly way. "Come on in. Mama back in de kitchen." She led me through the house to the kitchen.

Sister Greta had her hands in flour, making biscuits. She looked up at me, smiling. "Oh, hey, Haley. I see Andy told you what I said." Her tone was happy and very kind. "Let me wash my hands an I'll be right wit you. Have a seat if you kin find one."

"Here, Haley, you kin set ober here in dis chair," Nena said softly, moving clothes from the seat next to her and pulling it from underneath the table.

I sat down, watching as Sister Greta washed her hands. I didn't know what to think or say. She had welcomed me so kindly, I forgot all my negative thoughts.

I looked around the house. They were not living any better than we were. Theirs was a much better house than ours, but the upkeep was nothing to equal our house on Rat Row.

She washed her hands, pulled another chair from the table, and sat down beside me. She got directly to the point. "I guess you wonderin why I wanted you to come round here and see me, huh?"

"Yes, ma'am, I was."

"Well, don't you worry. It ain't nothin bad. It's good—at least, I hope it is for you and for me. I wanted to invite you to come to our church wit us on Sunday."

I was astounded at her invitation. I didn't wonder about it; I was glad and accepted gracefully, without any hesitation. I was elated one of the most respectable women of all saw fit to take up time with me. My instinct revealed that she saw something good in me that the good Lord could use. I was overjoyed. "Yes, ma'am, thank you. I've always wanted to come to y'all church, but I thought only sanctified folk went."

"Now you don't have to wonder no more. We'll git you round nine o'clock. Is dat too early for you? I figure we kin go to Sunday school and on into de eleven o'clock service. Den we'll have dinner at de church, and four o'clock service. You know we stay in church all day?"

"That's okay. I'll stay too. Thank you, Sister Greta, thank you!"

She hugged me as she got up and said, "Oh, I almost forgot. My boss lady gave me lots of clothes. Nena can't wear em, so if you like, look through em an take what you want."

I had never felt so welcome and cared for since Aunt Matilda's sister came from Chicago and took me shopping. Sister Greta had a plastic bag full of skirts and blouses and nice, pretty dresses the white folk had given her. She gave them to me, and I couldn't thank her enough. I left there exhilarated. She never said anything about me and Andy, though I knew she knew about us. I fell in love with her that day. She became my spiritual mother, my friend, and a woman I thought of as my future mother-in-law. I couldn't begin to express what it was like for me to be invited by a holy, sanctified woman to come to her church, the Mount Pentecostal Church of God.

Sister Greta had Gary, Andy's brother, help me carry the clothes home. I still had time to go back to the café and hang out before my curfew was up.

I went to the teen center first. There weren't many teens there, so I made my way on down to Butternut's café. That was the most happening spot. All the gangs were there on the dance floor, ponying away to "Pony Time." They looked good, and everyone was in step.

I stood back, watching. I didn't see Doletha, and I wondered where she could be.

Andy spotted me when the dance was over and came directly to me. By then, I didn't have long before my curfew was over, so he walked me home. I had such a good feeling about myself, just the way he made me feel.

When we arrived at the house, a few people were there yet, so we walked on down by Pa Jack's café. The place was dark; they were no longer open as much as they used to be. The back of the place had been turned into a gambling house. Andy and I sat on the swing under the pecan tree, near the streetlight. The stars were shining down upon us, and I was definitely in love. He kissed me gently.

Suddenly a strange vibe shook me. He stopped kissing me and began to stare into my eyes. I could feel the magic steaming from both our bodies. Point-blank he said, "Haley, I want you to let me make love to you."

I thought he had lost his mind. My mouth flew wide open and I was unable to close it. That beautiful night had turned into a nightmare. I was serious as a heart attack when I said, "What did you ask me, Andy Malone?"

Again he pulled me close, and that was the first time I felt a hard penis rub up against me. I was being pressured into doing something I had no desire to do. Angrily I said, "I'm only fifteen years old, an you are seventeen. No, you cannot."

His expression changed to anger. That did not rattle me in the least. He looked very disappointed, and he was silent. I pushed away from him like he was out of his damn mind. I could see he didn't want to take no for an answer.

He said furiously, "You is my gurl, ain't you or not?"

I responded, "Yeah, but we ain't gon have no sex, I kin tell you dis right now."

"Well, come on. I'll walk you home. Think bout what you want. It seem like other guys don't have to beg you."

I couldn't begin to think what he meant. What had happened during the time I left him to go to his mother's house? My heart was pumping faster and faster. "Oh my God, what is you talkin bout?"

"Just forgit it."

Nothing about him was the same. I smelled whiskey on his breath. He had been drinking.

That was all it took for me. My world crumbled before my face that night, under a sky filled with beautiful stars and bright lights.

He walked me home and left me. I went on inside. For the entire night, I thought of nothing else except how I had felt when I met him, and what I was feeling now that he had left me. Rumor was the majority of young girls were sexually involved. I didn't know who was, but I knew it wasn't me.

Sister Greta did come and get me as she promised. I went to church with her. Andy came to the backyard after I got home, and we talked. He asked me if I had changed my mind, and I told him no. His words to me were, "I do love you, Haley, but I got needs. If you can't supply my needs, let's just call it quits."

At that moment, I thought I would die. I didn't understand how something at one moment was so perfect and in the next moment was so screwed up. I learned the difference between having a crush and being in love.

I looked up into his eyes and said, "Okay, Andy. If dat's de way you want it, den dat is exactly how it will be."

I sped off in pain, leaving him standing in the moonlight without looking back. It was over. When I got into bed, I cried until I was dehydrated and no more tears would come. I thought about everyone staring at me in the café that evening I went with Doletha. Something terrible must have gone on, but what could it be? I was determined to seek out whatever was being said secretly and reveal it openly.

***

One thing about a town as small as ours: it didn't take much to learn what was in and and what was out. Andy had become friends with Alford Malone, his cousin. Alford was dating Say Lou, and she had a friend named Emma Joe. She was a pretty, real dark-skinned girl. She looked like Midnight the Cat from the TV show *Andy's Gang*. She had pretty white teeth and was more Andy's type. Word was she was dating Andy—they were a couple, but he loved me. I hurt for a long time.

I was going to church with his mother every Sunday, and I was experiencing what holiness was all about. The Pentacostal church was different from the Baptist churches I had attended. I was starting to feel what it was like to be transformed. My feelings toward Andy commenced to fade. I would see him and Emma Joe, and yet I didn't see them. I had gotten good at ignoring people.

Chapter 16: Unforgiveness, Deceit, and Lies

In school, Doletha pretended to be my closest friend. I didn't care if she was pretending or not. I was able to discern truth from fiction, though she couldn't. She didn't know I was studying her like a book. It was not hard to read. She was a dressed-up dummy with an empty brain, and all the teachers knew it. In school with her country friends, she would talk about me and make fun of my clothes. But on the weekends, when her country friends were nowhere around, Doletha made me out to be her best friend. I knew better, but really she was all I had.

I was able to turn the other cheek because I had comprehended her weakness, but she could not comprehend mine. She didn't know I had a heart of gold. She didn't know I loved her like she was my very own sister. I wanted desperately for her to like me half as much as I loved her, but it was not in her to love anyone but herself. To this day, I don't think she knew me at all. I didn't have the expensive clothes that she had. I didn't live in the kind of house that she lived in. I didn't have money to spend like she did. But I had something she never knew: I had a heart filled with love, and it was genuine. I loved her regardless.

We were in Mrs. Daisy Grady's classroom. Every student in there who was not under Doletha's spell knew Mrs. Grady was completely fed up with her. Doletha could keep up confusion that would go on for weeks nonstop.

One time, she had many students fighting each other for no reason. I came to school that day, and there was so much confusion going on that Mrs. Grady strapped Doletha good. Doletha ran out of the classroom and got her grandmother, Aunt Nanner. Aunt Nanner and Mrs. Grady got into a heated confrontation. Threats were made. Mrs. Grady put them both out of her classroom and told Mr. Monroe, "If I have to teach Doletha another day in my classroom, I will resign this job. These lies are unforgiving lies, and they will get somebody killed."

Everyone sympathized with her. Many of the smart students from the country stopped having anything to do with Doletha: the well-respected country girls like Lindsay Wales, Elizabeth Donalson, and Louise Crowday. Doletha was placed in another classroom, separated from the students she had control over except Patrice Ball. But Doletha was still popular in the school overall, and she was highly esteemed by her gang. If the school had had a contest for the Miss Popularity, there's no doubt in my mind Doletha would have won.

Nevertheless, there was something terribly wrong with her life. Her insecurities prevented her from developing a beautiful personality that corresponded with her looks. Behind her back, students called her who she was, but in front of her face, they laughed and said what she wanted to hear. I could see they didn't like her. But in spite of all the things she was doing to me on the weekends, I was there for her. She needed me far more than I needed her.

Still, I hadn't forgotten that night at the café that ended with Andy and I breaking up. I knew she had something to do with it, and I was determined to find out what it was. I was in her good graces, but this time she had gone too far. I no longer fell for her tricks. I wanted to know what Andy meant when he said, "Other guys don't have to beg you." Doletha was going to tell me. To get her to do that, it was up to me to use my head for more than a hat rack.

I decided I was not going to go to the center that Saturday. I was not ready to face Andy or watch him with Emma Joe and Say Lou, both of them with their lips filled with snuff. I knew what Andy was up to, and it was fine.

In came Ms. Odessa. I heard her ask Mama where I was. I stepped out of the room and made myself available to her. "Hey, little Haley," she said, turning up a jar to her mouth and gulping down that fifty-cent drink as fast as she could. When she was done, she wiped her mouth and said, "Little Haley, Sister Greta said come round there if you kin."

Sister Greta must have learned that Andy and I were over, I thought. *I might as well go on and git it over with.* I asked Ms. Odessa if Andy was home, since Ms. Odessa would have just come from cleaning Sister Greta's house.

"No. He done got so grown, he stay out all night."

I felt cowardly all the way there, but I never turned back. I met Joel, Andy's oldest brother, coming out the front door. "Come on in, Haley. Did Ms. Odessa tell you Mama want to see you?"

"Yeah, she did."

Nipsey and Paul came out the front door, speaking and smiling like they were thrilled to see me. Sister Greta was dressed for church. She was such a beautiful lady. Her first words were, "You going to church wit us, ain't you?"

"Yes, ma'am, I is."

That was the day Joel and I got real acquainted. There was a difference between him and Andy. Joel was like his mother. He was her chauffeur; he drove her everywhere she went. He was as into the church as she was. They often included me. When they went to another church out of town, they took me with them. Andy and I were no longer together, but his family became like my second family. I went to Mama's church on the first Sunday, but on the other Sundays, I was with Sister Greta. I really felt modest, not knowing what to say as part of such a beautiful family. The ecstasy that moved through my body was indescribable. Those felicitous feelings stayed with me for a long time. The more I went to church with them, the more I felt at home.

The Pentacostal service was nothing like other church services. The preaching, the people speaking in tongues, the tambourines and drums—they even shouted differently. I will never forget the first time I shouted. My feet got light, and something hit me from the top of my head and centered down to my stomach. My body felt like it was on fire, and my feet started moving. I couldn't stop them. It was like I was in a whole new body. Sister Greta swore I had the Holy Ghost for sure. I didn't want to go to any other church but theirs. I felt a sense of belonging. Something inside me woke up that had been asleep for a long time.

Before long, a year had gone by. It was the best year since I left Aunt Matilda's house. I was gaining respect and wasn't being talked about, so I was comfortable with myself. I loved attending school. Joel was my best friend. He was so encouraging, he had me believing I was good enough to go to college. I was thinking positively for a change and feeling good.

One day after church, we were walking down a dirt road. I had on a pretty tangerine dress and tangerine shoes to match. Joel told me I had grown up to be a beautiful young lady. I began to set goals for myself, with the help of one of my classroom teachers, Mr. Jacob Harrison, and his excellent teaching. I thought he was the best. I noticed the difference between street men and church men—how amenable the church men were, and how they treated their families.

Mr. Harrison had a beautiful wife. She was brown-skinned and he was light-skinned. I remembered how he used to meet my sister Gemmy BB out behind the chimney corner. I followed them out there one night and fell and cut my butt. I knew every time he looked at me, he remembered me also, and now he was my history teacher. He was good at his work. He extolled all of his students as much as he could. He was a churchgoing man who sang in the male choir at his church. I couldn't help but wonder why I didn't have a daddy like him.

We were at midterm and all hell began to break loose, at home as well as at school. Daddy was back to his old dirty tricks again. Joel came by the house after church. He invited me to walk down to the center for an ice cream. I thought it was a good idea to get out. My feelings for Joel's brother had not changed, but I was adjusting to Andy's new life.

Unsurprisingly, the moment we arrived at the center, the main people I didn't want to see were the first ones we ran into. Alford, Andy, Say Lou, and Emma Joe were coming out the door as Joel and I were about to enter.

Andy dropped his head. I gave him a look and a slight smile before going inside. That was the beginning of a doomed night.

Doletha was on the dance floor. I was surprised to see Marie Lee too. She was expecting a baby, it seemed, so no wonder she hadn't been to school. Joel was mingling, and I sat in one of the booths.

Up came this thin, handsome guy, and he asked me to dance. I danced with him, and he introduced himself as Neal Ruskin. I had heard the name before, but I couldn't remember where. The moment Doletha saw me dancing, she didn't hesitate to inform me he was the young man who had been in Marie's life before she left school. It was shocking. As smart as Marie Lee was—an honor roll student with perfect attendance—she was now about to be a mother, and her friend Doletha didn't mind letting it be known.

Joel and I got ice cream cones and headed home. I saw a crowd forming down by Mama's house, and I knew something was wrong. It turned out Daddy had been beating up on Mama again. He had fought her like a man. Her face was swollen, her lip was busted, and both of her eyes were bloodshot. Mama said Daddy had drawn a gun on her and fired a shot in the house.

I was angry. I was not about to let him get by with it. I was ready to stop him by any means necessary. The Phillipses had called the police, and Lund Cabb was looking for Daddy.

The police stopped by the house a little while later, asking if Daddy had come back. He hadn't. Nobody seemed to know where he was. Old man Tommy Williamson said they would find him and bring him in, and warned us to call them if he came back to the house.

When Daddy came in around eight o'clock, I ran all the way to the police station as fast as my legs could go. Old man Tommy was in the office. "Come quick!" I cried. "Come, Mr. Tommy! My daddy is back beatin up my mama."

He told me to get in his car. When we arrived at the house, though, Daddy was gone.

This time Mr. Tommy told Mama to go up to Jack Henry and swear out a warrant for Daddy. She didn't want to do it. Many people wanted to see Macky Keath pay for how he had beat her, and they persuaded her. But she didn't want to ride in the police car; she wanted to walk. I walked with her.

The warrant was written, and we took it to the police station. Up drove Mr. William with Daddy in the backseat and old Benny Lee behind him. The moment we saw him, I smelled a rat somewhere. We all knew Daddy was supplying Tommy Williamson with moonshine, and in return received certain favors. I knew some lies were about to be told.

In walked the chief of police, Lund Cabb, the meanest cracker in the whole town. He was not going to hear a word Daddy had to say. Lund said Mama's face was living proof of what had happened. But old Benny Lee called Lund outside and convinced him to arrest Mama also. She had told them about Daddy firing the gun. It was in the warrant. They asked Daddy if he had a gun, and he said no. Benny Lee called that perjury. So Daddy and Mama both were arrested and sent to city hall.

I wanted to scream. I looked at my mama's swollen, bloody face. Daddy didn't have a scratch on him anywhere. I could have killed him myself. Tears were pouring down her face and mine.

While they were processing through, I ran all the way to the city hall. By the time they arrived, I was already there. I watched as they took my mother out of the car and placed her in a cell and locked the door. I promised her I was going to get her out of there, no matter what I had to do.

I turned for home, but an idea hit me. I went back into the police station. I didn't even knock; I just pushed the door opened and walked in. Lund was sitting, reared back in the seat, his legs resting across the desk. I walked in like I was a grown woman and stood directly in front of him. I looked right into his eyes, eyeball to eyeball.

He asked tough, "What kin I do for you, gal?"

"Why you locked my mama up in de city hall?"

"Cause she lied on Mack. Said he shot at her and he didn't have no gun. That mean she gave false information on a warrant."

"No, she didn't lie. He is de one lied."

"How do you know he lied? Did you see the gun?"

I dropped my head. I knew I had to be strong for my mother, and I concluded this was lying time. "To every thing there is a season, and a time to every purpose under the heaven" (Eccles. 3:1). That was a time I had to help my mama, no matter what.

I answered in a very careful, dignified manner, "Yeah, sir, I did see em. My mama don't tell lies, and her taught us not to tell lies neither."

He stared at me from my head to my feet and then said in a snippy tone, "Well, you bring me twelve dollars and fifty cents, and I'll let Jenny Rue out. The only way she kin git out is the money."

I was not accepting that. God gave me wisdom that night, along with two of the nastiest white nigger-haters in all of that town. Bravely, I said, "I don't got no twelve dollars and fifty cent. But mister, if I kin found dat gun and bring it back here, won't dat be proof dat she didn't lie? And you kin let her out of dat place so she kin come home to her chilluns."

He was so astounded at my statement, he looked at me in disbelief. He hesitated like his jaws had locked up on him. When he could speak, he said coldly, "Well, you sure is a smart little old gal, ain't ya? If you kin bring me that gun that she said Macky had, then I'll let Jenny Rue out."

I didn't give him time to utter another word. I was out that door and running straight home. I had no idea how or where I was going to find that gun, but I was determined to find it. Mama's freedom depended on it.

I got home, and the house was empty. The kids were all down at Aunt Matilda's house. I went into Mama's house, searching everywhere I could think to look, but no luck. I knew in my heart I was close to finding it. I looked underneath the house, behind the old toilet, and every place outside.

At one point I was beginning to feel that it was a hopeless case. But I recalled Aunt Matilda's voice saying, "De Good Book say ask an he'll gib it to you. Look for em, and he'll be dere fur you."

I went into the house again and started cleaning. I cleaned the bedrooms first and commenced sweeping the floor in the kitchen. I didn't even think about rats. It appeared Mama had been clearing the table when he attacked her. I finished up, hoping that something would trigger my mind and lead me to where that gun could be. I knew Mama was not lying.

I kneeled down in front of the dining room table, and I prayed with all belief for God to lead me to that gun. "Dear God, I know I haven't done all the things right like you want me to, but I'm doin de best dat I kin. If you please, show me where dat gun is in dis house so I kin take it back up to de police station. Den dey will let my mama out of dat city hall an she kin come home to us, her chilluns. Dear Lord, if you do dis one thing for me, I will git holy like Sister Greta an live right for you as long as I kin. I promise. Amen."

The moment I got up, I was terrified of being in the house alone. Something spoke to me and said, "Look." I looked around the room and no one was in it except me. I was shaking from fear and about to run.

The voice spoke to me again and said, "Look over by the kitchen cabinet."

A knock came upon the door. I rushed to open it and found Buster and Tise standing there. I don't think I have ever been so glad to see anyone. I immediately began to tell them what had happened. Buster took off for city hall while Tise and I continued to search for the gun. We searched all over again, and in practically the same places. Buster returned and said that he had seen Mama. He assured her I had everything under control at the house, and the children were fine. The children were her main concern.

I tried occupying my time by playing with my little niece Shannon and nephew Glance. They were adorable, and the joy they brought to our lives was just what we needed. Glance had grown and was handsome just like his father. Shannon was bigger too. But even they couldn't take my mind off of my mama.

I fell asleep on the couch. In the middle of the night, I sat up quickly and remained balled up on the cushions until the roosters started crowing. I jumped to my feet. I had altogether forgot about the voice speaking to me before the knock came upon the door.

I ran into the dining room and pulled the icebox out to look behind it. Nothing. As I was pushing the icebox back into place, the voice spoke to me again and said, "Look over at the kitchen cabinet."

I looked over and saw a shining white cabinet. I walked slowly to it and commenced to pulling it back. Two big rats jumped from behind it, frightening me half out of my mind. It didn't stop me. There had been times when, if a rat jumped out before me, I would never have gone near that cabinet again. This was not one of those times.

I took hold of myself and took a deep breath. I noticed the part of the cabinet where the rats jumped from was where the flour was kept. I opened it. A white towel was stuck down inside. I touched it and felt something was wrapped up in it. I took it out of the cabinet and unwrapped the towel. God bless, there was the gun–black plated, with a white pearl handle. I yelled so loud, I could have woken up the neighborhood. "Tise! I found the gun!"

I was so excited, I went into the bedroom and pushed open the window—in time to see Daddy come walking across Mr. Benny Lee's yard. I ran out the front door with the gun in my hand all the way to the police station. I knew Daddy was coming to get the gun, and we would never have found it then. It would always have looked as if my mother was guilty or lied. I ran without stopping to catch my breath.

Lund was sure surprised to see me come walking through the door. He said sarcastically, "Oh, it's you again."

I didn't speak. I just laid the towel on the table in front of him and unwapped it, the gun lying before his face. Then I said gloatingly, "Dis is what you wanted. Here it is, Mr. Lund. Mama said Daddy drawed on her. Yes, sir, here it is."

He took the gun from the desk and opened it up, checking the bullets. He said, "It look like this gun been fired."

I didn't have any doubt. I had proved to that nasty, prejudiced cracker what he told me to prove. I had called his bluff. I outsmarted a white man, and the chief of police at that.

I looked at him and he at me, like he was lost for words. I said, "My mama said Daddy shot at her. But everybody believed Daddy dat he didn't. Now here is de proof. You need to free my mama."

He looked over at old man Tommy, laid the gun back down on his desk, and said, "Tommy, go round there to the city hall. Let Jenny Rue out, and take her and her daughter home."

I dashed out of that door so fast, by the time Tommy drove around, I was already at city hall, telling her, "Mama, I found de gun! Mama, Mr. Tommy is on his way to let you out. You git to go home."

The reunion began when he opened those double doors. Mama's face was unrecognizable. Both of her eyes were shut, and her face was swollen. She couldn't stop crying. Yet she didn't want to ride—we walked home, the two of us.

I couldn't imagine what kind of monster would beat his wife in her face as Daddy did my mother. I begged her to get rid of him. She had just nursed him back to health from having his head busted open about another woman. That should have been enough for her to kick that son of a bitch clean out of her life.

That day, I learned that there was another man who was in love with my mother—a churchgoing, hard-working, loving, respectable man. And she wouldn't give him the time of day. Daddy knew all about it. I concluded that was his sick motive for beating on her.

This churchgoing man—Fat Frazer was his name—stopped through the quarters later. Mama was in the house, and he didn't hesitate to go in and ask her when she was going to have enough. What was it going to take for her to wake up? I saw him put something in her hand, and he left. I never questioned her about what it was or what her feeling was for him. I waited to see for myself how long she would allow Macky to destroy what was left of her life.

Fat Frazer confronted Daddy down in the bottom that evening. Word was he said if Daddy beat my mother like that again, Fat Frazer would kill Daddy himself.

Mama thought I had paid those crackers twelve dollars and fifty cents to get her out of that city hall, until I explained how I had looked that entire house over and the Lord spoke to me. She just laughed and said, smiling with her swollen face, "You sure is smart," and she thanked me.

Tise washed Mama's face in something she said would help take the swelling down. I didn't want to go to school the next day and leave Mama with that evil maniac. Every time I looked at him, I could feel myself turning into the monstrous villain that he was. I hated him, and I knew it was hatred. But with Buster and Tise there, I was comfortable.

The jerk had the nerve to ask me what I did with his gun. I goggled my eyes at him from head to foot, just as Lund Cabb had done to me when I made that deal with him. I said as harshly as I possibly could, "I gave it to Mr. Lund Cabb to git my mama out of dat city hall."

"You gave it to Lund Cabb," he repeated.

"Yes, sir, I did," I said, bravely speaking as I felt.

"Who do you think you talkin to?" he asked coldly.

"You asked me a question and I answered. I gave de gun to Mr. Lund, de one you told dem you didn't have, so she could git out of dat city hall where she didn't have no business bein in de first place."

He slapped me across my face. I didn't resist. My face was burning, but I couldn't cry. I just looked him in his face and said, "I hate you. I wish you had died when Mr. Charston busted you in your head with dat two-by-four."

He took his belt off and beat me all across my head, back, and anywhere else he could.

The Black Maria turned the corner by Pa Jack's, and Daddy stopped beating me. He went out the back door, practically running from the law, though he would abuse us like we were animals. I took that beating, and when it was over, I showed him a brand-new side to me. I no longer was afraid of him. Whatever the odds were against me, I would be candid with him. I positioned in my mind that I wasn't going back to the damned field and work like a slave. Nor would he take my hard-won earnings and spend them on other women or gamble them away at some skin game.

All of my innocence vanished. I reversed the situation to my own advantage, but with that man, there was no way of escape except by force. My personality changed in every way except my going to church and believing in God.

Tise and Buster lived on with us for about a month, and then they moved into the house next to Pa Jack's café. They weren't there long before they moved up in the Moses Cainey quarter, which they were pleased about. I would stop in some evenings after school to play with the kids before going home. It became a meaningful routine.

Glance's fourth birthday was that October. I had all intentions of going home and coming back later. There was bad weather, and it started to rain hard. A severe thunderstorm swept through the town. By the time I got home, I was soaked, so I got changed.

I went into the kitchen. Mama had cooked black-eyed peas, fried chicken, white rice, corn bread, and iced tea. Daddy was sitting at the table, eating. That was his favorite meal. I got sick, wishing in my heart he would choke to death. I had so much animosity stored up inside me, it was clouding my judgment.

Mama had given me her permission to visit with Glance on his birthday. Daddy heard her give it. Out of pure meanness, he insisted on me going into the kitchen and making him some eggs, though it hadn't been five minutes since he ate enough food for two hogs. He smelled like liquor and was still staggering drunk. I shouted, "I ain't cookin nothin!" He pulled his belt off, and I picked up the iron bar from beside the fireplace. I was not about to be intimidated by him anymore.

Old man Fred came through the door and said loudly, "Macky, why don't you sat you drunk ass down an leave dat gurl alone? What de hell de matter wit you?"

For a moment, I believed Fred had shamed him. I left and went up to Tise's house. Once I informed them of Daddy's latest stunt, they suggested that I move in with them. I agreed it would be for the best, because I would kill him before I allow him to beat me again. I thought that at least I would be safe with them. The contempt I felt for that atrocious man was beyond my comprehension.

We were having a wonderful time, sitting around the table and watching the kids, who were our greatest enjoyment. A knock came at the door. When Buster answered, he was shocked to find old man Tommy Williamson standing there with Daddy. None of us had the faintest idea what they were doing there. All I knew was Tommy would do anything Daddy wanted him to do for a half pint of moonshine.

"Buster," Tommy said, "is Macky's daughter Haley in here? And don't lie for her, less I'll take you and your wife down to the city hall."

His demand was so strong, Buster was astounded. Tise looked at me and I at her. We both stood up at the same time. We went into the living room. From the look on his face, I could tell Daddy was up to no good. I really didn't want Tise or Buster to get into trouble because of me. I looked directly into Daddy's drunken eyes; they were red as fire.

Tommy said, "Come outside, Haley."

I walked out.

Daddy said, "You call yourself runnin away. If you wanter go somewhere, I'll send you to de reformatory school. Take er an lock er up, Tommy."

I said to myself, "Dis ain't true."

"Come on, gal. Git in de car."

I got into the backseat of the police car. Daddy got into the front with Tommy. Of all the cruel things I had encountered in my life, that was the pits. Tommy drove us up to city hall and took me out of the car. It wasn't until he actually opened the cell door and said "Git in" that understood I was really being locked up—and for what? Daddy watched as Tommy Williamson put me in a cell in back of city hall. I felt there was nothing any worse that could have happened to me. I believe I lost my mind that night.

The cell contained a toilet and sink that were so filthy, I began to throw up. I thought I would throw up all of my insides. The bunk was covered with a green army blanket filled with holes that was beyond repair.

Tommy slammed the door and locked it. I was left in pitch darkness. All I could think of was the night Mama was locked up in there and what she must have felt like. I cried some. The tears stopped when I heard someone at the door. I was not able to see who it was. The door only had five bars midway. A voice called out my name. It was my mama, and she was crying. She said, "Dat low-down, dirty son of whoever gon pay for dis. I promise, Mama gon git you out. Don't you worry none."

Around midnight, I heard what sounded like keys rattling. I couldn't see anything. My first instinct was that someone else was being brought in to another cell, but as the rattling drew closer, I knew they were coming to my cell. It was that old Tommy. He unlocked the cell door and said, "Come out, Haley. I come to let you out."

I was too glad to be out of that place. As I was walking out, he said,

"Now you go on back home and mind your daddy, and you won't git locked up no more."

I was glad to put my feet on the ground, but my heart was about to burst from hatred. I was not only filled with it, I was sick with it—so much that I could have died from it.

When we got into the car, Daddy was sitting his red-eyeball ass in the front seat. I could smell the moonshine on both of them. I realized it was true what folk had been saying—Daddy was supplying old Tommy with all the moonshine his belly could hold, to get him to do whatever Daddy wanted. He was Daddy's white flunky.

I had to listen to Daddy lecture me on obeying him. "I don't want to have to kill your damn ass, but if you think you done got so grown where you can't mind me, I'll put you somewhere you will mind." I was as silent as a mouse. I had learned how to be humble. "Do you hear me talkin to you?" he demanded. "I locked your black ass up tonight so you'll learn a lesson, to let you know I kin show you betta dan I kin tell you."

I heard him and I didn't hear him. What he said went in one ear and straight out the other. If he thought for one second I was going to let that stop me, he had another thought coming. I was more determined than ever to find a way to get the hell out of Rat Row. I didn't know how or when or where, but I knew one day for sure I would. My only regret was having to leave my mama there with him.

I noticed a lot of attention surrounded me after that. Folks' attitudes toward me changed immensely. I didn't give it a second thought, mostly because I really didn't know why they were frowning at me. At one time I thought it was because Emma Joe had gotten pregnant, and word was it was from Andy. It didn't put a pleasant taste in my mouth, but I kept my head up.

***

It rained continuously throughout an entire week. Some mornings we got rides to school, and other times we had to walk in the rain. The intimidation between Doletha's gang and Skitter and myself escalated.

I didn't want to do any fighting with anybody, but the way things were going was forcing me to fight.

Skitter came to school on Friday, upset in one sense and happy in another. Her parents had arranged for her to leave school and return to her father's hometown. They couldn't tolerate the intimidation from the gang any longer. They had Skitter's best interest at heart: her future was at stake, and her education was very important to them. I could understand that. At first I thought her parents were sending her away because she and I were so close, and I was not the kind of girl they wanted their daughter to socialize with. But that wasn't so. Her parents were not prejudiced against me, because they were wonderful Christian folk who loved everybody.

Skitter was not thrilled to leave school, but she was more than ready to leave those cruel children. When she announced it was her last week, they started in on her. She was never violent; neither was she a fighter. She was just beautiful, inside and out. She and I always went out of our way to avoid any kind of confrontation with Doletha and her gang.

On one particular day, however, they followed us everywhere we went. During our fourth period class, I learned from Skitter that something was written on the wall in the bathroom: *Haley Keath went to jail cause her mama caught her and her daddy in the bed together.* That blew my world apart. I wanted to die. Who on earth would write such an ugly, lying, scandalizing rumor? Who could hate me so badly that my name would be tarnished forever?

I went into the bathroom to see for myself. I examined the handwriting exceedingly carefully, and the more I scrutinized it, the more I credited it to Patrice or Doletha. But there was something about the letters that made me think it was not just one person who wrote it—it was the gang. They all took turns writing letters, making it hard to determine who actually was the source of the gossip. I knew in my broken heart Doletha didn't write all the words, but she instigated the thing.

I was hot to confront Doletha, but Skitter showed she was truly a dear friend in every way possible. She convinced me not to get even with Doletha, to let it go. Skitter and I prayed. Her last words to me, before we said our good-byes and she left school, were "Hey, Ha-ley Keath, let—let it—it go! Like my parents told me: let people talk. Talk don't hurt nobody. One day de good Lord will pay every man accordin to his work."

I heard her, and I appreciated every act of kindness and friendship she showed me. The kind words will always stay with me, but she didn't know how deeply wrong she was when she said talk don't hurt. My heart was melting. It wasn't just talk; it was slander, and for what? Doletha was the one who had the good life. Why was I so picked on? She pretended to like me on weekends and hated me throughout the week.

I walked along the railroad track. I looked up at the sky with tears rolling down my face. I made a promise to the Lord. I swore on my grave, and I was not even in it. I said if God continued to let me live, I would find a way to make Doletha pay. I hadn't learned that vengeance was the Lord's. Every premeditated word I spoke from my mouth, I meant.

From then on, I waited on my time. I didn't think on any one level; I was thinking every evil thought I could. I was going to one day make her pay. One pain would make up for all the pains she'd caused me for five long, miserable years.

After Skitter left town, I always heard her voice in my ears. I listened to her and the advice she left me with. It was just not enough to make me me to let it go.

That rumor was thick everywhere. Any door I tried to get through was slammed in my face. I was being talked about on every corner, down every road. I couldn't hold my head up. I read my Bible, and that didn't seem to help. I prayed, and my prayers were—I thought—unheard. I went to church more and tried to be more active. Nothing seemed to matter to me anymore. I wanted to die. I thought I would be better off dead but didn't have the nerve to take my own life. I begged God to take it for me. I had to learn be careful what I asked God for.

A week went by. On a hot summer Saturday evening, Glory Ann—bless her, she never changed toward me—insisted on my coming to the center. I had permission to go, so I gave it a try. After all, I was sick of being around drunks day and night.

The moment I walked in, I was surprised that everyone was so nice to me. I didn't know how to take them. I noticed Rudy Salkman stayed near me, and I mostly danced with him. He showed me kindness, and I could feel it was real.

We walked down to the bottom. I was standing outside Flappy Boots's café, having a relaxing conversation with Glory Ann. Ruthella came up, and then up walked Neal Ruskin. He looked at me as he passed, then turned around and came back to me. He asked, "Haley, kin I speak to you a second?"

I guess I looked puzzled. Glory Ann said, "Go on, Haley. You come out to have a good time. See what he want."

I could tell he had something on his mind, and I was curious as to what it was. As I was about to go with him, up walked that drunken, whorish, menacing O'Bera, looking like she had just finished turning a trick. Her eyes were red as fire, and she was staggering. She called to Ruthella, "G—— d—— it, what I done told you bout dat Haley Keath?" She slapped Ruthella all across her head in front of everybody.

The pain resurfaced, rushing back like heat waves on a beach. O'Bera had no mercy on her daughter. She was determined that Ruthella have nothing to do with me. Whatever Neal wanted to say to me vanished from his mind, as it did from mine. O'Bera put on a show, and everyone came out to watch.

Neal took me by my hand and walked me over to his car. He had just purchased a gray-and-black Ford, and it was shining. I could tell the lie had hit his ears. The way O'Bera was carrying on didn't make matters any better. After a while, Neal point-blank asked me, "Is it true? Did your mama catch you an your daddy in bed together?"

For a minute I was speechless. It occurred to me to wonder what this must be doing to my poor mother. No one had given her feelings a second thought. I answered Neal just the way the enemy intended for me to, and I didn't care who heard me. I had been around enough filthy cursing all my life to know how to put it back out. Unfeeling and disrespectful, I blurted out, "Hell, naw, dat ain't true! That's a g—— d—— lie, and I am just bout sick of sons of bitches spreadin damn lies on me!"

Fear hit Neal hard. He threw up his hands and said, "Whoa! Good golly, Miss Molly! Calm down. You don't have to be so darin. I just asked you a question. Calm down, Haley."

He didn't know I had that bad side in me. Neither did I. It took him to bring it out of me. I demanded he tell me where he got that gossip from. He was embarrassed; I could see it all over him. "Sit down in de car," he said. "Let's talk about dis calmly."

His persuasion helped me to snap back into reality. I knew the language I'd used was not me. "I'll calm down when you tell me where you git dat damn lie from."

He said, "From Candis."

I was candid with him. I wanted him to know my sordid life. I started off by telling him the kind of father I had. I knew Neal was from a Christian background. His grandfather was a great pastor up in Webber, Georgia. It seemed everyone had decent, respectable parents except me. I was in an awful place. I wanted to fit in. I wanted to belong. But it was just not there for me.

I told Neal what my life had been like for the last five years. I didn't owe him an explanation, but I wanted him to know what we had to live through with Daddy. Neal's informant hadn't told the sad, just the nasty. I told him the pain I was feeling at that moment. I explained what had happened the night I was arrested. Neal was in total shock.

Candis Wilkes was one of Passy Kate's running partners. She was good friends to Lila and cousin to Doletha. It all led back to Doletha. From the writing on the bathroom wall right down to that moment with Neal, everything was on Doletha.

I so wanted my life to be better. I wanted the gossip to stop. But no one cared except Sister Greta. I continued to go to church with her, and the service at the Pentacostal church helped take my mind away from all the talk. With Skitter being gone, Sister Greta was the only one left who I knew cared about me. I rededicated my life to the Pentecostal church; I knew I belonged there. I felt at home, for I knew I was with folk who loved me and were really holy. I knew as long as I lived on the earth, I would never get another friend like Skitter.

Chapter 17: First Down Payment

As usual, Doletha, Patrice and the rest of the gang were sending notes across the classroom to each other and whispering among themselves. I knew they were saying things about me, but I ignored them with everything I had. Our teacher had placed me in a seat right behind Doletha. Why? I don't know. I didn't want to sit there, but the teacher was the boss.

I sat quietly, studying for the English test we were about to take. Suddenly Doletha swirled around in her seat and looked me up and down. I was dressed nicely, but I could see from the corner of my eye that Doletha disdained me. I was good and ready for her when she asked, "Haley Keath, you done got sanctified now, huh?"

I just looked up at her and goggled my eyes without dignifying her with an answer. I hoped that was enough to let her know that I was not interested in anything she had to say.

She really allowed the devil to fool her. When I didn't answer, she took it upon herself to slap my face. I instantly elevated myself from my seat and was all over her head like a flock of wasps defending their nest. I beat her all around that classroom. She got one slap in, and that was all. I got my fingers into her hair so I can bend her neck and beat her head against the wall, just like I wanted to. It was my day to shine.

Astonishingly, the teacher just stood back and watched along with the students. She didn't allow anyone to stop us; she just let me do what she wanted to do—beat the hell out of Doletha. When considered it enough, the teacher allowed two of the guys to break us up. Winston grabbed me, and Jimmy took Doletha.

Doletha was enraged and yelling harsh words at me like she wanted more, but everybody knew she didn't have a chance. The joke was on her. I won and was proud of it. My only regret was that Skitter was not there to witness it.

After the fight was over, the teacher sent us to our homeroom teacher, Mr. Josh. He heard both sides. As usual, Doletha told so many conflicting stories, it was pathetic. I didn't lie about any details, but because of the fight, I had to be chastized also. I received ten hard strokes in my hand, but Doletha got double in hers for fibbing. She left the school running to get her grandmother, as she always did.

That weekend, the Pentacostal congregation was invited to Clayton County, and I was included. It was the most inspiring service I had yet attended. When I got home, the house was still. I was surprised when Joel came back after dropping his mother off. He invited me to walk down to the center. Daddy wasn't at home, so I took the chance.

We stopped in the center, but the crowd had vacated, so we took off down to the bottom. Butternut's café was our first stop, and the first faces I saw were Candis and her friends. I could hear them whispering about me. Joel was very encouraging. He said, "Don't even give them a second thought. You don't see them." But it was hard.

I decided the only person who could deal with her was my daddy. I knew every one of the name brands who were slipping around with my father, and he was the one who could put them in their places.

I went over to the gambling hole and walked directly in the door. When Daddy looked up and saw me, he got up instantly. I said, "Daddy, I want you to do somethin for me."

"What is it you want?"

"I want you to go stop dat old, yellow, bald-headed Candis Wilkes from spreadin lies bout me. What she spreadin round bout me is what she is doin."

I didn't have to say what. He didn't hesitate. He started walking fast, and I was right behind him. He stopped at Butternut's café, but they had left. He went on to Flappy Boots's café, and there he found Candis. This was the first time I witnessed him defending me.

When he walked in the café, they were all on the dance floor. He went directly up to Candis and grabbed her by her collar. "Look, bitch!" he said angrily, without any concern for anyone else. "I done laid you, Lila, O'Bera, an half de g—— d—— sluts in dis town. Dat rumor y'all got goin? Can it right g—— d—— now! If I hear one more word bout it, bitch, I'll turn your ass as black as me!"

She turned dark in the face. The few strands of hair she did have on her head stood straight up. She and her friends were in shock. It did me all the good in the world to watch Daddy put them to shame. I knew he was not lying about having them. I had caught him with them on different occasions. They were tricking with him and all the other men in town.

Daddy was holding that big hawkbill knife in his hand. He had her so scared, she didn't move. They all were in fear; even the jukebox was so afraid, it stopped playing. O'Bera started to open her mouth, and he turned a look on her and said, "I don't want to hear a g—— d—— thing you got to say cause it ain't nothin but a damn lie. I kin and have f—— you bitches for fifty cent any night or day I want to. I don't have to have my daughter."

Candis finally opened her mouth and said, "I didn't spread de lie. It came from her friend Doletha. She de one been tellin everybody dat bout her so-call friend."

Daddy looking from one to the other. "An you, red bitch, caught de cow by its tail an hauled ass wit em." He pushed her big ass down to the floor.

Daddy didn't realize I was there, listening to all those horrible words and his confession to adultery. I didn't want to hear any more. I eased outside and waited for him.

As I was waiting, who came up from behind and placed his arms around my shoulders but Andy? We stood speechless, staring into each other's eyes. I knew he loved me. I was his first love. I still loved him too, but I was not going to spoil my goods with him.

A few tears rolled down my cheeks. He used his thumb to wipe them away. He looked like he had something heavy on his mind. But before I learned what it was, Daddy came out of the café. I knew the sermon that Reverend Scott had preached up in Clayton County was for me: "The battle is not yours; it's the Lord's."

A question rose up in my mind: "How do I overcome hurt when I was born to be hurt?"

I received it then and forever. I knew Daddy was never interested in gossip. But the gossip was hitting me, and he did put a stop to it. I didn't want Daddy to get in trouble. I just wanted the gossip to stop. With the rage he was in, I was so sure he was going to jump on me for allowing Andy to put his arms around me.

But Daddy surprised me. He gave Andy a look and told me to stay as long as I wanted to. If any of those women came near me or said anything about me, I was to let him know. Then he reached in his pocket and gave me a five-dollar bill. To Andy, he said, "Take care of her."

I was thinking, *What do Andy want from me? I don't want him takin care of me de way he takin care of de others.*

Daddy left. Candis came out, crying and smelling like the drunk she was. She didn't deny the role she played in scandalizing. I was only interested in one thing from her—to repeat what she'd said inside and confirm my suspicions about Doletha.

And Candis did. At first, she tried to cover up for Doletha by lying. She said she'd heard some of the girls at school talking about me. I told her to get out of my face or I would get my daddy. Then she admitted Doletha was the one who had spread the gossip.

Doletha had lit the match without being seen, and the fire had spread. I swore, "My right hand to God, all of you will be sorry."

I don't know why, but I took Andy by his hand and we walked toward Butternut's café. Andy begged me to take him back, to give him another chance. He promised he would never hurt me again. I couldn't trust that, though my feelings were yet strong for him. I could only appreciate his standing by me.

***

During the spring, Greater New Salem had a big Easter program.

Mrs. Brittney had given me a part in the Passion play. When I accepted the role, I had good intentions to go through with my commitment. But the night before Easter, Mrs. Dani came around to the house and informed me that Sister Greta wanted me to be ready to leave at nine o'clock. We were going to Alabama. There was no way I was going to miss an opportunity to get out of the state of Georgia.

Tise had bought me a beautiful beige dress, and Mama bought me shoes of the same color. Surprisingly, Doletha showed up to the house, once again pretending to be my friend. She really just wanted to see my Easter dress. She had told two other girls, Delta and Allie, that if my dress looked better then hers, she was definitely going to get another. How pathetic.

Mount Pentecostal Church of God was a big church with a medium-size congregation. We were like one big, happy family. Dear Lord, did we have some church up there!

Sister Greta put me up to sing. It was the first time I had sung outside of Mama's church, and at first I couldn't think of a solo. The only song I was used to singing was "See How They Done My Lord." But it was fitting for Easter Sunday. I really sang it, and it felt so good. They had me to sing another, "On Calvary." I felt that I was worth something. I got so many compliments. I made Sister Greta really proud of me.

Folk began to look at me as if I was somebody, but my enemy wouldn't let me be.

It was not until we were on our way home that I realized I had stood Mrs. Brittney up. When I saw her at school, she told me she would never put me on another program again. I told her how sorry I was, but she was Mrs. Brittney. No one did that to her. And there was nothing I could do to undo what was already done.

Nonetheless, even in school I was asked to sing a solo in a different teacher's program. Doletha couldn't stand it. She began to pull her old tricks again. Doletha thought she had found a weak spot in Idella Lompkins, who pretended to be interested in Joel and started questioning me about Sister Greta's family. I had no idea what Idella was actually up, to and I didn't care. Idella was always quiet and very sneaky.

It was a Saturday evening. We had been up at the church, where the choir was practicing. The moment I arrived home, I heard Daddy's voice. He had been drinking. He knew when I came in because the door made a *squee* noise when it opened. "Come here, Haley," he called out.

I went on into the other room to see what he wanted. There was a tall, handsome, light-skinned young man standing in the room with him. He looked up at me, and our eyes made contact. He had eyes that would make any girl or woman melt. They were grayish-green. I was looking so hard, I didn't hear Daddy tell me to get him a half pint of shine. He shouted, "Is you deaf? I told you to git me a half pint of whiskey. What done happen? Old lady Greta done had you singin so you lost you hearin?"

I turned and did as he asked. As I went to the other room, I heard him say, "Matt, how did y'all crop turn out last year? You think dis one be better year?"

"Yeah, Mr. Macky, it was a pretty good year. It more likely be bout de same if we git enough rain."

I stood quietly at the end of the kitchen, listening. Matt—what a handsome name.

As I gave the whiskey to Daddy, I was still looking at the guy and he was looking at me. Matt asked, "Is dat your daughter, Mr. Macky?" He was looking me up and down. I had a nice figure and pretty well-shaped legs.

Daddy took the bottle from my hand and said, "Yeah, dat's my daughter."

"She sure is a pretty little thing," Matt said. He winked his eye at me. A warm spirit pierced my heart. Daddy liked him, and when Daddy liked someone, he would talk to them about me in an intelligent manner.

I left, wondering what I was going to wear to church on Sunday. Ms. Dorothy had given me a lot of dresses, and some needed a little altering. I rummaged through them and found a beautiful orange dress. I hoped it would bring me some good luck.

From that week on, on Saturday evenings, Matt came down to our house. Each time he came, it was as if I had never seen him before. I wondered about him—who was he, and where did he come from?

***

"What is it you want, Doletha?"

Doletha was grinning, not a serious bone in her body. But I was very serious about getting her. She claimed she wanted me to forgive her for all the trouble she had caused me. I was astounded, and willing to forgive her to the extent that she was sincere "Haley Keath, forgive me, please. I want to make up for de way I been treatin you. I do want us to be friends."

Reluctantly, I said, "Sure, Doletha. I don't see no reason why we can't be friends. Old things have passed away, and behold, all things come new. We need to put away childish ways an act our age."

"Where did you hear dat? I ain't never heard dat before."

"From de Bible. After all, we both all grown up now. Why not let bygones be bygones?"

It was about two weeks away from school ending for the summer. I figured one of her reason for wanting to hang around me was because she had nobody else to hang out with during the summer.

I had been up late, selling moonshine for Daddy. I was so sleepy, I made up a story that I had a headache so I could stay in, put my head on my desk, and sleep through my lunch hour.

Doletha had been under my nose, matchmaking between Andy and Idella. She came into the classroom and said, "Haley Keath, git up an come outside. You need to see dis, gurl. Idella an Andy round de schoolhouse kissing."

I was hip to what was going on because Tonk had already told me, and so had Glory Ann. I pretended to care and followed Doletha to where they were. It was true; they were kissing. When Andy saw me, he refrained quickly. His head dropped in shame, and he walked away, leaving Idella looking odd. She seemed scared and started smiling at me if she was saying, "Oops." She apparently didn't know I was no longer with Andy and had not been his girl for a good six months. Doletha and Idella were waiting for me to act the fool, but I didn't give any of them the pleasure. I smiled and backed away. Andy had become a real gigolo, it seemed. Other girls came running to me at other times and told me gloatingly that Andy and Idella were kissing again, and I never responded.

I learned that a girl named Rolene Slater was Matt's sister. She came to the door of Mama's house and said, "I been looking for you all day. Matt told me to give you this." She handed me a letter. It was an invitation out to meet with him.

I met Matt at a café, but not because I wanted him. I wanted to let Andy know I was wanted. Andy was watching as Matt came over to my table and sat beside me. Matt wasn't much of a talker, but he could certainly stare. His eyes had a charming glow.

Glory Ann came and sat down at our booth. "Haley, ain't you gon innerduce your friend to your friends?"

"Yeah, Glory Ann. Dis is Matt. Matt, dis is my friend Glory Ann."

He smiled and said, "My pleasure."

We all got up to pony. I showed off my nice-fitting, tight blue skirt with a deep kick pleat. My white blouse emphasized my breasts, and the white saddle shoes wrapped around my nice legs spoke for themselves. A twenty-two waist, thirty-four bust, and twenty-seven hips was not a bad figure. Andy watched me in despair.

Finally, he couldn't take me any longer and left. I believe that was the night he became a natural stalker. Everywhere I went, he was there. Ee started going to church. But he knew he had lost me. I couldn't care less what he felt. He started drinking heavily and losing himself.

But, back to my meeting with Matt. He, Glory Ann, Ruthella, and I made plans to go to a picture show the next Saturday. Matt left for the evening, and Glory Ann cried, "Gosh, Haley, who is dat good-looking guy? I never seen em around here before."

"Matt Slater. He's Rolene brother."

"Where did you meet em at?"

"Would you believe I met em at my house through my daddy?"

"Mr. Macky!" she said, shocked. "Gurl, I know de world is comin to an end now for sho'."

Over the summer, I spent more time with Matt. Knowing him increased my courage to believe in myself. He told me how beautiful I was when I believed I was so unattractive. His demeanor was formal, different from any other man I knew. He convinced me I was the kind of woman he wanted to marry. He never addressed me with any disrespect. I set a goal in my life: finish high school and go to college.

There were times when I was around Matt that I could feel there was something pressing on him mind, like he was in some kind of trouble. His advice to me was, "Haley, I want you to finish school and git the hell out of this town as fast as you kin. You kin make it, but not in this honky-tonk town."

He was the second person to give me that kind of advice. And I was really taking it in. He made it sound profound.

I was really surprised to learn that one of my mother's best friends and drinking partners, Mrs. Ella Sue, was Matt's mother. She was at our house every weekend, and she was a bigger alcoholic than my mother. But she had seventeen children and worked on a cracker's farm from sunup to sundown—what was left for her to do but get drunk on Saturday? He filled me in on all of his family. He was the eighth out of seventeen siblings. I knew several of his sisters.

After that conversation, he left the café where we were talking. I didn't have any reason to stay on, so I was thinking go home so I could be up early. I looked over by the jukebox, and my good old friend Doletha was watching me real hard. I knew she was asking herself what Haley Keath doing with that good-looking fellow, but she didn't have the nerve to ask me directly. I got up and left.

The moment I got outside, the most uneasy feeling came over me. Andy was over by Mrs. Brittney's house, standing under the light pole. I started walking fast. He came walking behind me and placed his arm around my shoulder as if we were girlfriend and boyfriend. My response to that pressure let me know I was not completely over him. He said, "Come walk over here wit me, please. I just wanter talk to ya, an when you hear what I have to say, then if you don't wanter have anythin to do wit me, I won't bother you again. I promise."

He and I walked along the back road and the open field in between the Willops and Mrs. Angie Rosa's house. We stopped under a tree, and he kissed me. It felt so good and so right. He was an excellent kisser.

But then he was kissing so hard, it was not even good. He was rough with it, and I stopped. He got very aggressive, until I had to push him away. He took a tight, remorseless grip on my arm. His eyes were sparkling with desperation. "Is dat guy you been with at de center your boyfriend now?" he asked boldly.

I didn't feel it was any of his business. I snapped back in the same tone, "Is Idella Lompkins your new girlfriend?"

Suddenly his bold look turned into a frightening one. I used smarts and not sarcasm, because by then I was a little fearful of him. I didn't know what he was going through with a baby on the way and no job. I immediately said, "No, dat guy ain't my boyfriend. We're only friends."

I was steadily trying to get my arm loose from the grip he had on me, but the more I tried, the harder he pulled. "Ow! Andy, you hurtin my arm! Let me go!"

I felt choked, not brave enough to say what he wanted me to say. Before I knew it, he had me down on the ground. I pushed him away, telling him to stop. "Andy, this is not the way! If you do this, I will put you in jail, and I mean it. I will have you arrested!"

With his face rubbing against mine, he said, "Haley, please. I need you and I want only you. If I hurt you, I'm sorry for it."

I knew he atill felt for me what I had once felt for him, but having sex was the farthest thing from my mind. My mind was on finishing school. I could tell he was furious with somebody, but I didn't think it was with me. I was his escape. I stopped trying to fight him off, but I repeated, "If you force me into doing something I have never did and I don't want to do, you are going to jail."

He begged, "Please, Haley. I need you and I want you bad."

"I don't want you if I got to have sex with you!" I shouted. "Go back to where you been having sex!"

He instantly got up and left without another word. I pulled myself up from the ground, brushed myself off, and stood under the oak tree until I got my composure back. I couldn't even cry. I didn't feel hurt; I was damn mad/ I knew he had lost himself. His life was headed downward. I didn't know where mine was headed, but it was not with him. Idella and anyone else who wanted him was welcome to him.

As I was walking home, I heard a voice say, "The battle don't belong to you. It is the Lord's. Let it go."

I pretended I didn't hear it. It got louder. I wanted the voice to stop, but the more I tried to ignore it, the more it sounded off in my head. I really believe I lost some of the good mind that I did have. Hatred penetrated my heart, for Daddy and for all men. I never looked at men the same again. To me, they were all alike. I swore I would get them before they get me.

I was coming out of the path by Mrs. Angie Rosa's house and met O'Bera. I knew she had been out there spying. She wasn't going to allow me to walk by without her saying something sarcastic. "You out mighty late, ain't you, Haley?"

I was dying to say, "It ain't none of your g—— d—— business," but I sped up, not giving her the satisfaction.

I was home long before my curfew was up. I sat on the swing on the front porch. I heard voices coming from Mama's room. I asked, "God, if you git revenge on people, like Aunt Matilda say you do, help dose people dat dey stop bein so mean to me."

Something turned over inside me, spinning round and round. I believe I could have murdered someone that night. All I could think about was getting even. I wanted the people who had caused me pain to suffer severely. Like Scarlett O'Hara in the movie *Gone with the Wind*, I promised, "I'll never be hungry again." That was my solemn vow to myself. "I promise I'll git every damn body ever did me harm. One day they will feel de effect of the girl from Rat Row."

If those were God's words speaking to me, letting me know the battle was not mine, then why did my every thought come out negative?

I couldn't get old O'Bera Walters's face out of my mind. She was holding many dark secrets in her heart. Her look made my hair stand up on my head. In that sick mind, she was thinking wrong. I was wrong, yes, but not in the way she was speculating. I sat in that swing for hours, trying to put together what it was about me that she detested so harshly. Passing judgment on me was one of her hobbies. She was so busy spying on me, she was overlooking what her own daughter, Ruthella, was doing.

I didn't want to cause Sister Greta any type of problem. She had been good to me. Out of all my evil thinking, Sister was my major concern.

I was starting to have mixed feelings about myself and my life. Once I got into bed, I began to pray. I asked God to please deliver me from all sin and evil. The faces of Candis and O'Bera vanished from my mind. God gave me a vision of their deaths. It frightened me for a second. I wanted to think it was only my imagination.

***

Time was not long before Doletha started coming round me regularly. By then I was in a place where I didn't trust anybody. I was struggling with a low self-esteem and had no destiny in mind. A two-letter word was dictating my every move: "if." If she was my friend, why did she treat me the way she did? If my mother was like her grandmother ... If folk liked me the way they liked her ... My daddy's words came to mind: "If a frog had a tail, he wouldn't bomb his ass every time he hop."

Doletha and I had been to the picture show; everybody went to the picture show on Sundays. As we passed by Mr. Norris's fish market, someone called out, "Hey, little lady."

It was Matt. He was sitting in his car with a guy named Homer. It seemed they were good friends. Matters of fact, Homer was Matt's only friend.

I smiled. "Oh, hey, Matt."

"So you were gon walk right by me an not speak?"

I was glad to see him, but not in the way I used to be. My entire personality had changed. I was good at keeping it hidden. I didn't know if I was having some kind of breakdown or what. I didn't know what was happening to me, but I knew it was something different.

I was starting to lie when Doletha interrupted. "Haley, dis dat guy you been wit? Introduce me."

"Doletha, dis is Matt. Matt, dis is Doletha."

"Oh, Haley, he's good-looking. Gurl, you struck it lucky."

Glory Ann came up at that point and took my hand. "Come on, Haley. Why you even fool wit dat fool anyway? You know she don't like you. All she doin is pretendin and tendin to somebody else's business. She should be tendin to Barlena Jean an de mother she bout to become. I bet she ain't mentioned dat, is she?"

Shocked to death, I said, "Naw, she sure didn't mention not a word."

"How come she done got so friendly wit you an always tellin folk she can't stand your guts now?"

"Yeah, I know more about her dan she think I know. But ask me why I forgive her all de time."

I didn't let Glory Ann in on my secret. My time was God's time, and he would get my just reward. My daddy often warned me about women friends, saying some women were treacherous and back-stabbing. If anyone knew, he did. He said if a man stabbed you, it was for money or a job, but a woman would stab you for any reason at all.

That night, Doletha and I and some of my other friends were out on the dance floor. Doletha was a terrific dancer, but Barlena Jean was better. It seemed to me she had everything most girls could hope for.

I stepped outside to breathe the nice cool air. I felt good. I was not about to allow anything or anyone to trouble me. Then up walked Matt.

I didn't see him come up. He was just there, standing beside me with his arms folded, looking up at a beautiful red-orange sunset. He said, "I wish I was dat big, beautiful sun, shinin down on de earth witout a care in de world." That was a kinda odd statement. Something major was pressing on his mind. I looked at him and saw a halo around his head. It was an anointing too strong to miss.

He said, "Walk with me. I have something to tell you." He took my hand, and we walked over by Greater New Salem Baptist Church. As we stood under a big oak tree, he informed me of a girl he'd been dating. Her name was Joann, and she was from Hawkins County.

I laughed slightly, but I couldn't blame him. I didn't feel comfortable under the tree. It reminded me of the night Andy attacked me. I told Matt I was ready to go back inside. He said he was waiting for Homer to come out and drop him off home; Matt had to be out in the field at five o'clock in the morning. We said our good-nights, and I left him standing there.

***

Doletha said, "Haley, how come when you git wit Glory Ann, you try to act so funny?"

I thought that was funny, so I laughed at her. "Is that what I'm doin, actin funny?" She didn't mean that; it was just her sly way of getting up on me. I got up on her instead. "Doletha, where's your boyfriend?"

"My boyfriend? Why you ask me bout my boyfriend?"

"Just curious. No real special reason," I said, being mischievous. I thought I would irritate her a little, since she was always getting her kicks from antagonizing others.

Sarcastically, she answered, "I really don't have one cause all of dem is just alike. Dey all out for one thing."

The next week, Barlena Jean and Javlin got married. This was a very embarrassing time for Doletha. After all the trouble she had inflicted upon others, it had come back.

For the time being, the commotion was off me and on Barlena. When a crowd gathered around like buzzards circling over something dead, it didn't take a rocket scientist to know what the topic of their conversation was. They talked about Barlena as if she had committed some hideous crime. If anyone could understand what that was like, God knows I did.

I happened to walk up on a particular circle—Ruthella, Glory Ann, Sheila, and Harriet. They were talking about Barlena and her pregnancy, and no one had anything kind to say except Harriet. "She ain't no faster dan any of us is. Many of us would be pregnant but is not because we ain't been doin what it take to git pregnant."

In one voice, Glory Ann and I said, "Not me. I'm still a virgin."

Up popped O'Bera, drunk as she could be. "Did I hear you say you is a virgin, Haley?"

"Yes, ma'am, you did."

"Do you even know what a virgin is?"

Anger stalked my tongue, and I shouted angrily, "Ask your daughter do she know?"

"Well, a virgin is a woman dat ain't never had a man's dick. An if I had as many jives in my eyes dat you done had dicks in your ass, I would be blind as de blind man dat passed de fish market an said, 'Good morning to all you ladies.'" O'Bera grinned. Everyone looked at her, and on to me, and then to Ruthella.

The humiliation I experienced at that moment was enough to last me a lifetime. My heart pounded. I started to hyperventilate. Trying to catch my breath, I turned and walked off.

Joel called out, "Haley, wait a second." He was coming around the corner by Butternut's café. He took my hand. I felt so embarrassed.

I heard Glory Ann's mother yell out, "O'Bera, you need to leave dem dere teenagers lone fore you git yourself in some more trouble. You know what Mr. Macky Keath done told you an Candis bout Haley. Now you damn sure wrong, O'Bera."

Joel had proven to be a dear friend. When I needed him the most, he was there to comfort me. "Haley, don't pay dat drunken woman no mind. She don't know what she talkin bout. Forgit er."

That was easy for him to say. He didn't feel the pain that pierced my heart when O'Bera said those terrible words about me. I couldn't have detested her any more than I did that day. I saw that Joel was trying to make me feel better, but there was no way I could forget that. Not ever.

He walked me home, holding my hand like he was my big brother, the kind I longed for. I cried hysterically, asking over and over, "Why do dat woman hate me so badly? Why do she keep on embarrassin me?"

He stopped on the side of the road and said comfortingly, "Haley, she talkin bout er own daughter. She ain't got no room to try an embarrass you, an nobody else for dat matter. Just between me and you—and you know me, I don't talk bout no gurls or women, but—she sayin to you what er daughter is. She know what she is cause she just like er."

"Oh, oh, Joel, you lyin!" I said, shocked. "Dat's sad."

"No, I ain't neither. An just between me an you, I know for sure she ain't no virgin cause I done been dere. So is two or three more of de guys I know done been dere."

As a man, he knew things that I didn't, and I learned from him.

"Bro," he said, "Haley ain't droppin no draws. Now if my brother ain't never got none, I know ain't no other nigger got none."

He made me laugh, but most of all he made me feel good about myself. I knew what I had to do: hold my head up and keep it moving. I really trusted him. He was the only friend I could trust and confide in at that moment.

Joel Malone became the kind of friend any male or female could want. I trusted him with my life. He was well respected in the community. He checked on me daily.

One day in the middle of the week, I was home, cleaning up the rooms and thinking of everything that had gone wrong in my life. From the doorway, a voice called out, "Whatever it is you thinkin bout so hard, it ain't gon do you no good to dwell on it, so forgit it an move on."

Laughing and wiping tears from my face, I said, "Joel! How long you been standin dere?"

"Just long enough to know dat you were thinkin bout somethin dat made you unhappy. Come on, walk to de store wit me. Git out of de house."

Walking past the Bolitter house, he said, "I got somethin I want to tell you. After I left from walkin you home last Sunday, I decided to walk back around by de cafés, just to see what was goin on. At Flappy Boots's café, I heard noises comin from de side. Somebody was cryin out, but it was like dey was tryin to keep from bein heard. So I followed de sounds, an apparently a certain somebody dat been singin your name caught her daughter over by de church, makin out in the backseat of Benjamin Donley's car."

I didn't take pleasure in somebody else's pain, but that information made my day. Maybe O'Bera the witch would leave me alone.

In fact, O'Bera never looked at me straight in the face again. I witnessed firsthand, "Be not deceived; God is not mocked: for whatsoever a man soweth, that shall he also reap" (Gal. 6:7). God sure don't like ugly, and he don't care too much about pretty either.

***

Through the summertime, we worked in the fields. I looked forward to buying new school clothes. I was full of joy. Everything seemed to be going right for me for a change.

But I was only allowed to go to school the first day, to register and learn whose classroom I was in. I was in homeroom with Glory Ann. She got to go to school, but I had to continue working.

I was not going to turn over all the money I made that summer to Daddy, for him to go gamble up or spend on other women. I made around forty-eight dollars for the summer. Daddy took all of Georgie Boy's money, and I knew he was headed for mine. But my mind was made up. He was not getting one red penny.

When we got home from work that last week, Daddy was waiting with both hands out. I mean, he was avaricious when it came to our money. I thought of telling him I lost the money, but I knew that was not going to fly. I asked Mama how we were going to get our school clothes, and she said, "Ask your daddy." Daddy eventually gave Mama enough money to get us one outfit each, including Anna Dora, Willa Max, and Billy.

Meantime, I did decide to tell him I lost my money. I had to make it look real good, so I started patting my pockets and pulling them inside out, searching, right on the back of the truck. Everyone helped me look, and they were all convinced I had lost my earnings. The moment we got home, I ran into the house, yelling about my lost money.

For the first time, my brother Georgie Boy supported me in a lie. He ran ahead of me, babbling, "Haley lost her money!"

Daddy came into the room. He was a little intoxicated, but not dangerously. It was my time to perform like never before. I started crying, so hard I couldn't get a clear word out of my mouth. Daddy shouted, "Haley, what de hell you doin all of dat boo-hooing for like a damn fool?"

I knew he was more concerned about the money than he was about me, but I had him going my way. Georgie Boy answered for me. He was sucking his thumb, saliva running down his hand. "Cause she lost her money."

By then, I was sniffing more than I was crying, so I used my hands to cover my face. I peeped through my fingers.

Daddy said more moderately, "You mean to tell me dat's why you doin all dat doggone howlin like somebody done damn near killed you? Gal, if you don't shut up dat fuss and wipe your face, I'll kill you my damn self."

I hurried and cleared my face. Not another whimper came from me. I stood wiping snot from my nose. Daddy even patted the top of my head, uttering kindly, "Ain't nobody gon kill you cause you lose de money. Stop your cryin."

"Yes, sir," I declared, feeling proud of my accomplishment. I beat that daddy of mine at his own game.

He was headed out the door, and suddenly he stopped and slowly turned around. He asked, "How much money did you make this week anyhow?"

Batting my eyelids fast, like they were filled with trash, I said, "Twenty-six dollars."

"Well, just so you know, dat was your school clothes money."

He turned back around and walked out the door. I started grinning from ear to ear. I had learned to lie better than a grown-up, and it felt good.

Bond Alp showed up to the house not long after. He blew the truck horn, and I raced to the front door. He stepped out of the truck, holding money in his hand. "Haley, I understand you lost your money," he said.

I was so nervous, I didn't know what to say. He smiled. I remembered hearing somewhere that if you tell one lie, then you got to tell another lie to cover it up. Before you know it, you've become a liar.

I knew it was wrong, but I didn't care. I stuck to my lie.

"Yes, sir, Mr. Bond Alp, I did."

"Well, dis is your lucky night. I founded it, and Marjorie Ann told me it was yours. I know y'all work hard for your money. I told her to let me git back down here to you cause I know y'all need it. So here it is."

What it boiled down to, though I didn't realize it, was I had lost my money for real. Old Bond Alp had found it and brought it to me when he could have kept it. I took that as a warning not to lie, no matter what.

***

Another weekend, another week in school, and another problem with my dear friend Doletha. My mental state and my personality were changing, and nothing seemed the same with me. I had Joel as my friend, but he wasn't enough. I didn't know what was happening to me. It was like I was losing all control, lying and plotting. Anger stirred inside me. But I didn't stop going to church. I loved church, and I knew that was what was keeping me going.

Joel drove Sister Greta and her friend, Ms. Broddie Trodman, up to Johnsburg to a pastors' convention. I didn't go; I couldn't bring myself to go with them. I didn't know if I was being controlled by the enemy or was just being stupid.

Early the next morning, word was out that they had been on their way home and Joel got into a terrible accident. Ms. Broddie's neck was broken, and Sister Garland was unconscious.

I went under the house and sat close up to the chimney. I prayed, crying out to God not to take them. I needed Sister Greta, and Ms. Broddie's children needed their mother. I overheard Arketha saying, "Dem holy women, see? Dey are livin witness what God kin do."

The patients were in the hospital for about four or five days. Then they were released, made whole again.

From then on, trouble seemed to lurk about the women of God. Sister Broddie lost her youngest son. He was getting off the truck one evening after picking cotton. Some children in the truck bed were throwing cotton buds at the ones getting off. Little Koop ducked a hit and jumped down directly in front of a car. He was hit and killed instantly. At his funeral, I heard Sister Broddie cry out, "Please, Lord, help me to bear my burden!"

Not long after, Sister Greta lost her husband to another woman. It shocked the town.

Being godly, these women bore up under their trials. God helped them to be examples for others who didn't know God for themselves.

***

Harriet took Ruthella's place as Glory Ann's friend. I was learning to abide in Daddy's word about nasty women: if I was going to have a friend, he was going to be male. And I did have that in Joel. Sitting in the center of our social circle was Doletha.

We were at a café one night, and in walked two guys we didn't know. They went up to the counter and watched our booth from there. Both of them goggled at me. I couldn't tell if they were serious or just playing games. I didn't flirt around with anyone. I had Joel as a friend, and I didn't need anyone else.

The song "Summertime" came up. The new guys came over to our table and asked Doletha and me to dance. They were both as handsome as all outdoors. The one with the process asked Doletha to dance with him, and the other asked me. I agreed. He introduced himself to me as Rosco Graham. He was absolutely fine: tall and light-skinned.

When the music stopped, Doletha and I decided to walk on down to the bottom. Rosco said, "You gittin ready to leave? Can my friend and I come with you?"

"What's your friend name?"

"Haley, this is Ezekiel. Ezekiel, this is Haley Keath," Doletha said.

I said, "This is Rosco. Rosco, this is Doletha."

We walked on to Flappy Boots's café, and it was packed like sardines in a can. There was no sitting room and barely any dancing room. We walked on to Butternut's café. His girlfriend Sooner was working behind the counter. It wasn't as congested as Flappy Boots's, but it was full. At least there was some dancing room. It didn't take me long to learn Rosco was only a slow-drag dancer, but he was good at that.

Popularity went to my head. I was starting to feel like I was the soul mate of every available guy who came through the door. I was having what I thought was the best time of my life.

As I danced with Rosco, in walked German Lompkins, Idella's handsome brother. He was the talk of the high school, and about the most egotistical and arrogant male there. He had all the girls chasing after him.

Our group was sitting in a booth. Another song came on, and German came over and asked me to dance. I was all for it. I didn't know Rosco. He was sitting with me, but he was nothing to me.

Doletha and Ezekiel had walked outside. I believe that was the night her life became meaningful for her; it was love at first sight.

Once I completed my dance with the great German, I knew it was time to go home. I made my way outside to let Doletha know I was leaving. Rosco asked if he could take me home in his car. I told him right away I was not allowed to get into anyone's car unless Daddy gave me permission. Doletha and Ezekiel volunteered to walk with Rosco and me. We all agreed, and they walked me home.

In front of my door, Doletha and Ezekiel said good night, leaving Rosco to say good night privately. He asked me if he could see me again. I told him the next time he came to town, I'd let him know. He said he would be back the following Sunday evening. Before he departed, he kissed me, and it was a kiss of death. I was afraid of him. For some reason, my spirit didn't agree with him, and I didn't know why that was.

I went inside and thought I heard Matt's voice coming from the other room. I went to look and he was sitting with my father. They were drinking. I didn't know why Matt was with my father. The last I'd seen of him, he'd slid down in the backseat with one of the Rant girls.

I went into the bedroom, but I couldn't go to sleep. I think I brought every malicious spirit home with me from the cafés. Evil thoughts ran through my mind. I was in a silent rage, considering revenge on everyone who had caused me pain. I wanted to get even. The night couldn't end fast enough for me.

I set my mind on flirtations. I thought it would help me to be popular. I was not ugly. I had a nice shape. I became contrary. My demeanor became intractable, giving my teachers a hard time. I didn't listen to anything they had to say.

I anatomized anyone who tried to help me. The only time I wasn't taking people apart in my thoughts or in my words was when I was asleep. We never got much sleep at home because of the traffic in and out at all times of the day and night. The moment daylight entered the window, we were ordered to get up. Therefore, my desk at school became my bed.

Rosco visited as he said he would and made a date to take me to a game. It was a few days before the Fourth of July. The game was Dothan against Jacob County. All the girls had been up there except me. I had never built up enough nerve to go. Rosco said that he could come and get me, but Doletha was going up with Ezekiel, and she invited me to come along. Both of these plans fell through: Ezekiel had family come in from up north, so he couldn't go to the game, and Rosco had a car accident on his way to get me. But we still had a great time that weekend. Folk were home from everywhere.

***

Matt was a perfect gentleman, a great friend, and a man with a strong calling on his life, a calling that he was fighting hard. We became good friends. One evening, he shared his plans with me, which helped me to realize he trusted me and wanted only the best for me.

My attraction to Rosco was strong. I kept the feeling hidden, even from him. I could feel myself drifting back into the same low self-esteem I'd felt so often in the past, a feeling of not being good enough for anyone. I thought that it was only his looks I was attracted to. I positioned my mind to believe that all boys were only out for one thing.

Doletha and I were hanging out more, and I was starting to like her more than I thought I could. She was changing. I concluded that she had finally met somebody who really lit her fire: Ezekiel. When she wasn't with me, she was with him.

One Sunday, he didn't show up. Doletha and I paraded from one café to another, having what we thought was the time of our lives. As we crossed over from Butternut's café to Flappy Boots's, German Lompkins came out of nowhere. It appeared he had an angry spirit. "Why did you lie to me?" he asked.

I retorted, "What did I lie to you bout?"

"You promised me a dance at de school dance, but you didn't, an every time I tried to come near you, you avoided me."

"Dat's cause you was wit Frances, Endora, Ellen, an should I go on? You was wit who you wanted to be wit."

"Well, what bout tonight? Kin I git a dance?"

Yes, I was a great dancer, so he became my escort for the evening. When the evening was over, he walked me home. I don't know what happened to Doletha. She disappeared.

The high school was having another dance the following Friday. Each homeroom teacher was responsible for one dance each month as a fundraiser. That Friday, who walked in but German, and Frances with him. I was not mad—I didn't even care, for that matter. The dance was swing, and everyone was having fun.

I saw Joel going out the side door. I ran to catch up to him. "Where you goin?"

"Down in de bottom. Too many of my gurls is in de same room. I got to go."

That was my way to get out of there also. He and I walked to the bottom together. The first car I saw was Neal's car. I could recognize that Ford anywhere. Ezekiel was getting out of it, and Doletha was with him. She told me Rosco was looking for me and had gone up to the school dance. I was not anxious to see him, so I left for home without telling anyone, not even Joel.

I was halfway home when German ran up behind me. "Haley Keath! Didn't you hear me callin out to you?"

I felt cowardly but tried to be courageous. I remembered the night Andy came up behind me like that, and I ended up almost being raped. I couldn't see into German's eyes, but his voice made me feel uncomfortable. I had never liked him. He was a prime example of male chauvinism. I could smell the scent of alcohol all over him. I thought, *Why de hell do all de damn young men drink?* They all seemed to.

A car was coming, and it got my attention as a way to get out of my situation. As it passed, I recognized it was Neal's car, but he was not driving. It was Ezekiel and Doletha, and they seemed involved in conversation.

I didn't focus on driver or passenger. I had to stay alert because I had to cope with German. My spirit revealed to me to be cautious.

"Did you hear what I asked you, Haley? I asked you a question!"

Filled with anger, I yelled, "What did you ask me? Now turn my hand loose! I didn't want to answer you. What you doin, followin behind me? Where is Frances?"

He didn't seem pleased at the mention of her name. Either she'd dumped him for another guy or for his drinking.

German was known to be dating Endora, and we had to pass her house. I made use of the opportunity. "Don't you think you need to turn around? What if Endora see you when we pass? What are you going to tell her?"

I must have hit a nerve. Before I knew what had happened, he pulled a long switchblade out. I don't know what got him so mad, but he said angrily, "I'm German, better known as German, and don't you never tell me what to do."

I had to talk fast, and I did. I talked him into putting the knife away. He did, smiling like he was God's gift to women. Not to me. I was not interested in him at all.

I was frightened of what might happen next. He wouldn't turn around. When we were a few feet from my house, he said, "I hear your old man is mean. I don't think I should walk you all de way home. But Haley …" In a different tone of voice, he added gently, "I will be back to town next Saturday. Kin I see you?"

Just to get him away from me, not meaning a word, I lied, "Yes, German, you kin." But I never wanted to see him again. I despised him from then on. At school, I dodged him in every way possible.

***

I was basking in the sun, lying in the grass out by the basketball court. Doletha came to join me. She looked restless.

My grades had fallen. I wanted to be something. I wanted to be noticeable, but not the way I had been over the years. I wanted to do something daring or dangerous. Hell, I thought my name was already mud, so what more could happen? I was torn between living for the Lord and living for the devil. After all, the Bible says that God forgives us everything. So I would live according to my feelings. My life was in turmoil.

Doletha and I sat and watched other students playing. I happened to glance over at her, and she looked like she was in deep thought. I tried to gloat. I hoped it was something that made her as miserable as I was. But I saw she was extremely worried, and her problem seemed more devastating than mine. Her eyes welled up with tears, and I asked, "Gurl, what's de matter wit you?"

She seemed agitated at my question. She turned and looked up at the sky.

"What happened to you and Ezekiel last Saturday night?" I asked. "Y'all disappeared awful fast."

She answered harshly, "What you mean, what happen to us? I had to go home."

She didn't know I'd seen her in Neal's car with Ezekiel, and the car had not been going in the direction of her house.

Doletha stood up and walked away. When she returned, she had Idella with her, and once again, they were laughing at me. I had no idea why. I asked what was so funny, but Idella just laughed even harder, showing all that gap between her teeth. "Haley Keath, ha-ha, my brother told me what happen last night."

"Oh, he did, huh? What did he tell you? Tell me, so I kin laugh too."

As if it were the funniest thing to her, Idella repeated every detail of what had taken place the previous Friday night. I wondered how on earth she could find something so humiliating and painful so amusing. Her brother pulled a knife, and she was laughing?

I made it perfectly clear that I didn't think it was funny, and he better be glad I didn't report him. "How funny would it be if he was arrested?"

Doletha said, "I didn't know you was seein German. I thought you was seein dat Rosco fellow."

"I'm not seein no German. I only danced with him a couple of times, and now I'm goin to die for it. He got many gurlfriends. Idella, your brother is crazy. I don't never want to see em or hear his name called."

She grinned. "Yeah, he told me he started to cut you."

"And for what?"

"He didn't say why. He just told me you made em mad."

I turned to say something to Doletha, and she was spaced out. She hadn't heard a word we said.

The bell rang for our last class period of the day. I had old Mr. John Ticks, and I knew he didn't like me. He was the only teacher I had that year that I detested, and the feeling was mutual. I hated to go to his classroom. I had come to the conclusion that he took out on me the way my father lived. I was his punching bag. The things he said to me, I could never live down.

Once the roll was called, he taught us songs. That day it was "Danny Boy." Some students were acting out in the back, and he blamed me. I had absolutely nothing to do with it. I was not in the mood to be put down by him, so I stood up. My punishment was to stand behind the door with my face to the wall until the period ended.

Dropping out of school was the only thing on my mind. I was feeling the pressure from all his criticisms. He told me regularily that I was dumb and would always be dumb, and I had begun to believe it. I believed I could not learn like other students. He even told me that it would be better for everyone if I just quit school and saved the teacher the trouble and the ink to flunk me.

I stopped studying. I discontinued working on my assignments. I slept all the time I was in his classroom. One time I was asleep on my desk, and he shook me awake before the entire class, yelling, "Wake up, Keath! You need to listen to everything I have to say with your dumb self!"

I woke up half out of my mind, not really knowing where I was until I looked in his face. I yelled back, "Mr. Ticks, I don't care what you say, and I don't want to hear nothing you got to say!"

"Yeah, but one day you will."

I really wanted to tell him where to go, but I held my peace and just rolled my eyes at him.

As he walked away from my desk, he said, "I don't have to worry about you taking up space for too much longer."

I hated him. I got to the point where I would cut his class and spend my time in the bathroom, and that made him even angrier with me. He reported me to Mr. Jacob Harrison.

Mr. Harrison sent for me to come to his room on that Friday afternoon. I wanted to make up some excuse. Beside Mrs. Pughsley, Mr. Harrison was the nicest teacher I had.

When the bell rang, I went to Mr. Harrison to receive what was waiting for me. The minute I walked through the door, Mr. Harrison greeted me and got right to the point. "Keath, I've been getting some rather disturbing reports about you. Now don't get me wrong—I'm not saying it's all true. I'd like you to tell me your version, and then maybe we can compromise. Have you been skipping Mr. Ticks's class?"

"Yes, sir, I have," I answered.

"Can you tell me why?"

"Cause he talks bout me in front of de class an make me shame. He call me dumb all de time. It look like he git his kicks out of pickin on me."

"Can you explain that a little more?"

"Everythin somebody tell him I said or did, instead of em tryin to find out if it's true or not, he call me dumb. He tell me I won't be round here much longer, takin up space. It gotten to de point I hate school, special his class."

"Keath, believe me, I understand your feelings. I am not taking sides here. But let me give you a piece of advice—not as your teacher, but as your friend. Education is important, especially where us blacks are concerned. You might not see it now, but I promise you: without an education, you and anyone else will be lost. There will be many days you will wish that you didn't let these great opportunities slip through your fingers. Please don't let what Mr. Ticks says keep you from getting all the education you can. You only have three years left, and if you had worked a little harder, you wouldn't have but two. Do you hear what I'm saying? Please. Someday, when you get married and have a family—and I don't mean to put you down—can you honestly tell me you want to live the way you do today?"

I busted into tears, saying "Oh no, God, no, I don't want that!"

"Then promise me you'll try to do better." He handed me his handkerchief. "Wipe your face and stop crying. Believe me, I'm right, and one day you'll look back over this day and thank me for this little talk."

I left the room with my eyes filled with tears. I knew Mr. Harrison was right and had my best interests at heart, which was more than I could say about Mr. Ticks. I don't know what Mr. Harrison said to Mr. Ticks, but I knew from the way Mr. Ticks changed his attitude toward me that Mr. Harrison had got to him also.

I felt better in many ways at his kind words and good advice. Yet there was such a void inside me that it couldn't be filled. The words that kept nagging in my mind were "I don't care." The one thing I wanted Mr. Harrison to tell me was that Mr. Ticks was wrong, but he never did. Ticks had his education and couldn't care less if I got mine, and that stayed in my heart.

After my meeting with Mr. Harrison, I got outside and Glory Ann was waiting for me. She thought I had got a strapping about something, because I was crying. I assured her he didn't strap me—I was whipped, all right, but not with a strap. Once she saw I was fine, she said, "I have somethin to tell you bout your friend Doletha."

"What bout Doletha? What she done did now?"

"You mean you ain't heard what she done to Ezekiel? Go ask her."

I went directly to Doletha's house. I wanted to hear it from her own lying lips. I blurted, "Doletha, I heard you were assaulted."

"Who told you?"

"Never mind who told me. Is it true?"

She said in a low tone, "Yeah, he did."

"Doletha, you lyin on dat boy. You know he ain't assaulted you."

"He did!"

"Where is he now?"

"He's in jail."

"Now, dat is pitiful."

"Well, it ain't like he in a prison."

"But he goin if he's found guilty."

"He ain't gon go no prison cause his parents come up here last night and dey gon pay us five hunder dollars if we take up de warrant."

"So what you gon do? Is you gon take de money and take up de warrant? Or he goin to de chain gang?"

"Yeah, why not?"

"Yeah, what?"

"Yeah, take de money."

Glory Ann and I went up to the jail to see Ezekiel. Even in jail, he was in good spirits. He told me what happened, and I knew he was not lying. I knew Doletha so well—her words, her promises, her lies. He told us everything was going to be over with within a week. But he also told me he didn't want his parents to give her a damned dime. He wanted to take his chances in court. I knew Doletha was not going to be outdone in anything. He got out, and I knew she had gotten paid five hundred dollars.

***

It was mid-August. Glory Ann came down early on a Saturday evening and me at the café. Flappy Boots and Ms. Hilley had added another room to the café where we could sit and eat. It was nice and cool. Glory Ann and I were dressed alike, only in different colors. She was wearing a red-and-white pedal-pusher set, and I was wearing a pretty lime green. Each of us had on white sandals.

In came German, and he called me to come outside. He claimed he wanted to apologize to me. I hesitated, but he was persistent and I gave in. Like a fool, I went outside with him, thinking, *What harm can he do?* Maybe he would apologize and go on about his business. I told Glory Ann I would be right back.

I walked into the parking lot and stood by a car with him. I asked, "What you want?

At first, he was so apologetic that even I believed he was serious. He showed me a gentle side I had never seen. I didn't have any reason to fear him. For a second, I let myself believe he was interested in me.

He took me gently into his arms and passionately kissed me. It was so good that I could have really gotten used to it. I was too naive to know what he was planning and too stupid to understand why.

German persuaded me to sit in the car with him, just to talk. We hadn't been in the car for long when he started thrilling me all over. His kisses got sweeter and sweeter. I liked what I was feeling.

Then Glory Ann tapped on the window. She had been watching, God bless her. She could see in him what I couldn't. Her tapping broke up his little romance and snapped me back into reality.

German was furious, and out came that knife. I was speechless.

Glory Ann called, "Haley, come on back inside! Your food done got cold."

German was pressing the knife into my side hard. I murmured, "My hot dog done got cold."

He whispered, "Don't worry bout dat hot dog. I got one for you."

Worry entered my whole body. I was thinking, *All dese gurls he got chasin after him, why he doin dis to me?*

Glory Ann was unable to see the knife, but my facial expression let her know something was not right. I said to German, "Let me let de window down," and he did. I rolled the window down enough for me to speak to her.

She said, "Haley, git out de car. What you doin out here wit German? Rosco lookin for you. Git out de car, gurl."

It was no secret that there was no love lost between Glory Ann and German. She was more bright when it came to guys than I was.

German pressed the knife into my side even harder. I believed it went into my skin. I cried out, "Let me out! Dis what you did to me de other night."

He said, "Tell your friend to go back inside, and I'll remove de knife. I promise."

I did as he said; I convinced Glory Ann to go on back inside. The look on her face told me she didn't want to. She looked at me strangely and said softly, "I'm goin and find Mr. Macky."

She left hurriedly. The moment she left, he put on his charm again. telling me he was not going to hurt me. But he kept on holding me with one hand and the knife with the other. He never put it away.

All I could think about was getting out of that car. I told him to open the door because it was hot. He let the window halfway down, enough to feel a little breeze come through. He had the nerve to pretend that he was sorry for what he was doing. He was a bigger liar than Chicken Little. He said, "I'm sorry bout de other night an Frances. She was after me, not me after her. She don't mean nothin to me. It's you I want."

I wanted to literally puke. I despised him for the lying demon he was. I didn't know what to do. I decided to try for the door as fast as I could. I got it opened and leaped out, but he grabbed me and moved his knife to my neck. I was terrified. He demanded, "Close de door an don't try dat no more. I don't want to hurt you, but don't make me. All I want to do is talk."

I thought, *If I git outter here, dis red Negro is goin to jail.* I shouted, "I don't want you! I don't want to be out here wit you! You will be sorry for dis!"

Glory Ann was back, saying, "Haley, what he doin to you? I thought you was comin behind me. Git out de car, gurl. You ain't got to be scared. I know what I'mo do. I'm gon git Mr. Macky."

"No, Glory Ann. He got a knife!"

"He just bluffin, Haley Keath. He ain't gon cut you. I'm gon found Mr. Macky on dat low-down yellow punk."

German said boldly, "I don't know why you actin like dis. Other guys done got some. Why can't I?" Then he pressed me down with his body and took me with no remorse, like I was nothing.

When he was done, I busted out in tears. I couldn't stop myself, and he had the nerve to mock me. He said, "What you cryin so for, Haley? It ain't like it's your first."

I didn't try to explain to him the extent of what he had done to me. Even if I'd had ten other guys, he had no right to touch me. He thought any woman was a freebie. I lost my virginity to somebody like that, and there was not a damn thing I could do about it. My life was ruined, and for what?

I jumped out of the car running, and I didn't stop until I got home. I washed my body as hard as I could. I tried to wash the pain off of me along with his scent. I was in a daze, trying to pretend it didn't happen. I thought about having him arrested. I thought about telling everybody I could tell. But nothing made any sense to me. The worst part was, I couldn't even tell my own mother.

From that day on, I felt dead inside. I stumbled as I walked. I constantly cried—during school hours, walking to and from school. I stayed home for weeks, not socializing with anyone.

One Saturday night, I was sitting on the front porch, watching the stars shining and listening to the music sounding from the cafés. Nothing mattered to me. I didn't care if I lived or died.

Daddy and Matt came walking from Mrs. Angie Rosa's direction. Matt sat down beside me, and I almost jumped out of my skin. He could see I was in great distress and insisted on me telling him what was bugging me. He held my hand and discovered I was shaking. He asked me over and over again to tell him what was wrong, but I couldn't bring myself to share my raw experience with anyone.

We both were staring up at the stars, and I glimped that sad, lonely look about him I had witnessed before. He revealed that he was getting ready to leave town. He shared the calling that God had on his life. It was leading him away from that town.

I lay in my bed that night, crying my eyes out silently. I just couldn't understand, for the love of God, why the Lord allowed something so evil to happen to me.

When I fell asleep, I dreamed that I was at the Pentecostal church, and I was shouting all over the place. I shouted away all my heartache and pain.

I hadn't actually been to church in over two months. I rose up early on Sunday morning as if nothing was wrong, and went back to church. Just as it was in my dream, the service was filled with the Holy Ghost. I shouted until I couldn't shout anymore. Sister Greta was glad to shout right alongside me. I shouted because I wanted to shout away the pain and dirtiness I was feeling.

But it was not that Sunday the Holy Ghost came upon me. God was preparing me for a major victory that was about to take place. I could feel it all down in my body. I was a changed individual, but from what into what?

I thought I must have disappointed God for him to let what happened to me occur, as if rape were his way of punishing me. Not so. He was purifying me in his own way. He was God Almighty. He knew what I needed to go through, because he allowed it to happen when he could have prevented it.

A feeling came over me that electrified my body and my mind. My feet moved and they wouldn't stop. My tears turned into happy tears. I felt as if I were floating in the air and the wind was beneath my wings. I couldn't explain it. The service was magnificent.

After it was over, Joel came to the house. He was determined to know why I was not coming to the café. I wanted to tell him of the horror I had encountered, but I couldn't. It was like it was locked inside me, and there was no key to unlock it. I could only feel the effect from it.

I don't know why, but he confided in me and told me all the girls he dated. The new girl in town, working for Mr. Hill, was his main girl, but he was in love with the pastor's daughter. I didn't lose respect for him, but I saw him in a different light. He was a guy out for what he could get. It changed my whole attitude toward men. He was a kind, loving man with strong desires. No one woman could fulfill those desires.

Who those women were is what gave me chills. One of them was the best choir singer in the whole town, not just at Old First Bethel Church. Joel was what any girl wanted.

The subject of sex made me ill, but he was educating me in an area I wouldn't have learned about in home economics class, and it took my mind off of my own problems. I never had a friend as dear as Joel. No matter what was said or what I was faced with, Joel never forgot about me, the girl from Rat Row.

***

It was late October when I learned I was with child—sixteen years old and expecting a baby.

Matt had left town that Monday. He stopped by the house on Saturday to tell me he was leaving, and we said our good-byes. I never told him the deep feeling I had for him. Although I didn't want him to leave, I knew he had to fulfill his calling. He had a duty to the almighty God, and it could not wait. I wished him well, knowing I would never see him again. But I would always have his memory.

His last words to me were, "Promise me you gon finish school and git all de education you kin, now. Don't let nothin or nobody stop you. You promise?" Whenever I got depressed, I would recall his words: "Finish school, Haley. You kin be anythin you wanter be." Dear God, I had to fight back tears like never before.

I acknowledged again just how important school was to me. I wanted to finish, but in the condition I was in, there was no way I could.

Nobody knew about the pregnancy except me, but it wouldn't be long before my belly showed and the whole town would know. That was pressing terribly on my mind. I thought about doing something to end the pregnancy. I had heard many stories of girls getting rid of babies, but I didn't know what to do or anyone trustworthy to ask. All I knew was I was an expectant mother with nowhere to turn.

Coming from school one afternoon, I saw Joel walking Candis home. Afterward, he ran and caught up to me just as I passed the funeral home. He said, "Okay, let's have it. What's the matter wit you? I know somethin is weighin heavy on your mind, so out wit it. You kin tell me. I won't tell nobody."

I knew I could trust him, and I couldn't keep that big secret any longer. It was ripping me apart inside. I shared my most hideous secret: what was growing inside me was life, but was life worth living? I was almost convinced dying had to be better. At least if I were dead, I couldn't feel all that hurt.

I felt comfortable talking to Joel about it, but there was nothing he could do. The damage had already been done.

But Joel insisted on confronting German Lompkins.

That Sunday evening, Joel came and got me after church, and we walked down in the bottom. I told him I didn't want to go inside the cafés; I wanted to stand out in the parking lot and watch.

We watched the crowd go in and out of Butternut's café for a few minutes. Joel said he was going to get us a cold drink. I didn't want it. I wanted to go home.

I waited for him to come back. It was taking a while, so I walked over to see what was happening. I found Joel in time to stop him from confronting my attacker. I didn't want Joel to get hurt or get himself in trouble over me, but it made me feel better knowing that I had someone on my side.

When we were outside, Joel said, "Haley, you should have let me bust dat punk in his face. You ain't de first gurl he done took advantage of, and if he is not stopped, dere will be more. But don't you worry. It won't be but two licks and he gon hit the doggone floor."

***

I was having morning sickness and sleeping all the time. I could be walking and I would have to fight sleep. One morning I was in a program at school. We had to demonstrate some behaviors in the lunchroom. I was asked to sing "We Are Climbing Jacob's Ladder."

No one knew how sick I was. I could feel the baby moving inside me. But somehow I got through it. I sang that song with all my strength. It was the first time I had been on stage in a long time. Just for a moment, it helped my ego. I received many compliments, including one from old Mr. Ticks. "Keath," he said, "you surely have a lovely voice. If you keep using it, it might get you someplace one day. You was really great. I never knew you had it in you."

The morning sickness got worse, and I knew my time was limited.

It wouldn't be long before I would have to drop out of school. I had to come to terms with it: I was going to be a mother. I had no idea how. My life seemed ruined. The only thing I had to look forward to was a baby who didn't ask to be born.

***

Endora Blue came out of her classroom, and she spoke to me as if we were the best of friends. I was shocked. It seemed nobody else would have anything to do with her anymore—not even the love of her life, Calvin A. It was noticeable that her stomach was much larger than mine. I didn't question her, but it was obvious she was at least four or five months gone.

One day she ended up in the bathroom when I was in a stall, having just finished vomiting. I stood on top of the toilet and watched her vomit in the next stall, her head hanging over the commode. I asked if there was anything I could do for her. She said sadly, "Naw, Haley, it ain't nothin you kin do. I done had too much done to me already. I never thought I would end up like this. I know now what it feel like when you ain't got nobody to care bout you. Now I'm pregnant, I ain't got no friend. Dey all turned dey backs on me. Will you be my friend?"

From then on, she stayed around me. Her secret was out, though I pretended I didn't know it. Mine was yet a secret. I was not telling.

***

Mama received a letter from Passy Kate. Kate was coming home for Christmas. It had been about three years since she left town. Lloyd had been killed in prison. I wanted to see her, but I didn't want her to find me in the condition I was in. In the letter, she said, "Tell Haley I'm looking forward to her graduating. When I come home I'll bring her lots of pretty clothes."

Christmas was only a couple of weeks away. Not only would Passy Kate have to be dealt with, but I had yet to deal with Mama and Daddy. I wondered what I was going to say. No words could make a difference.

If I told them about the assault, I knew they wouldn't believe me. I could tell Mama was already suspicious.

That afternoon, Endora and I walked down to the ballpark and sat on the bleachers. She started crying and admitted that she was expecting. Her family was forcing the father of her baby to marry her. She was sick about it because he didn't want to marry her by force. He was one of the town's finest basketball players, and he was still very popular, just as she used to be. The teachers had high hopes for him, and he had major plans for himself. Neither she nor her family were included in those plans.

She told me that it was all settled and they were going to the courthouse to get married. That was what happened in those days when a boy impregnated a girl—he had to marry her. There were a lot of shotgun weddings going on. Endora was so in love with Calvin, it made her no never mind. She would do anything to keep him.

Eleven girls dropped out of school that year. The majority of them got married and relocated to other cities. Marie Lee and I were the only two who were stuck in our situation. She quit school just before Thanksgiving. I sympathized with her because I knew I was going to be next.

On the last day of school before the Christmas holiday, a big fight broke out on the ball court. Students gathered around two boys, but I couldn't see who they were from where I was sitting. Some older boys broke it up. One of the fighters remained on the court while the other one was taken away. After everyone thinned out, the remaining boy played ball like nothing had happened.

Then the fighter who had been carried away returned, and he had a bat in his hand. He drew the bat back and hit the first boy on the arm, as hard as he could swing. It was Brock who got hit, and the one who did the hitting was Matt's nephew, Wilbert. Wilbert busted Brock's arm, and Brock was screaming death as they carried him away. He shouted, "I'm gon git you, bitch, if it's de last thing I ever do! I'm gon git you for dis!"

Both of them were vindictive and both were violent. But no one really believed Brock's shouts. They thought he was blowing smoke.

But in my heart, I could feel he had something evil on his mind. It was not cheap talk.

That evening, Endora came down to the house. She was very upset. Calvin A had married her, and she said he had left. She didn't know where he was. After listening to her cry and share her most intimate feelings with me, I thought I could ease her pain by sharing the news of my pregnancy with her. "Endora, don't feel rained on. I won't be returnin back to school after de holidays either."

"Why, Haley?"

"Cause I am too."

"I don't believe you, gurl. You just sayin dat. You ain't."

"Yes, I is, an in June you will see I ain't tellin you no story."

When I told her my secret, I trusted her not to tell anyone else. I begged her not to say a word, and she promised me on a stack of Bibles she wouldn't.

But she did. She couldn't wait.

A week before Christmas, I was sitting around the house, minding my own business. I looked up and there was Arketha, watching me. She came right up and said, "Haley, you pregnant, ain't you? Don't be scared. You kin tell me. You ain't the only one got pregnant; Endora pregnant too. Tell me. You don't have to keep this kind of secret. Tell me."

She convinced me, and I confided in her. I had to admit it was like a heavy burden lifted off of my shoulders. But Arketha didn't stop until she got to my mama and told her.

It was out in the open. I don't know why I told Arketha; I had never liked her. She was no more than the neighborhood news carrier. But her persuasion was more than I could hold out against. It never occurred to me that all she wanted was for me to confirm that I was in the same condition as Endora was. Arketha had no intention of helping me. She wanted to expose me, and that is what she did.

Before the sun went down, Mama called me, yelling. I knew that was an attack yell. And as I was going into the room, who was leaving but that Arketha? Not only had she broken my trust to Mama, the news was already spread all over the quarters. The look on Mama's face when

I walked into her room said everything. Each frown line said, "You is in for it dis time, an it ain't pretty."

Mama did all the scolding she could do in one evening, and nothing she said made any difference. When I left the room, I could still hear her calling me all sort of names, and as usual I just cried.

Passy Kate arrived a few days later. It took the attention away from me for a while. Then Gemmy BB came with her little army. I dodged Passy Kate as much as I could. I heard her asking for me, but I was in my secret hiding place and I was not about to come out. I was not ready to face her.

She left the house, and when she came back, I was asleep. Her voice woke me up. She was discussing my condition with Mama. Speculation was circulating all over. I listened to every word they said, reliving in my mind the horror of that awful night when my unborn child was conceived. I knew I had to face my sister sooner or later, and I was finally prepared to get it over with.

Mama fussed steadily, saying I was bringing another mouth into her house to feed. I was not about to allow my baby to encounter any of the environment I had lived in. No way.

I amazed them when I walked into the room. They were gathered around the big oak fire and gave me the third degree about my life. Neither of them knew the anxiety I'd had to bear alone, trying to measure up to everybody's expectations. Nothing I did was ever good enough. Now I figured it was time I stood up to them.

Passy Kate shouted, "You Macky-looking heifer! You knew your black ass was stiff big when I sent my money to you."

"Aw, hell. Ten dollars out of three years an you call dat money?" I retorted.

I looked her up and down. I really didn't have anything to say to her. She didn't have to take care of me or my baby.

Their conversation was all about me, and I was tired of it. I had no intention of debating anything with them. "Lord," I said, "I kin tell dis is gon be one heck of a day."

Passy Kate kept on. "Now you done let some little old boy fool you up, and look what it done costed you."

I shouted, "I ain't let nobody fool me to do nothin!"

She busted out laughing. "You little liar. Who you think gon take care of your baby?"

"You sure ain't. I kin take care my own baby."

"How, gurl? Tell me how you gon take care of er little baby?"

"De same way as now! I work an they take my money! I kin work and keep my own money and take care of my baby wit it now."

When I said what had happened to me, it was like some kind of joke to them—a story made up out of some book. They talked among themselves, and I eased out.

But Passy Kate followed me to my hiding place. She grilled me for what seemed like hours. She believed in her heart that I had deceived her. Apparently, because she came home with four cheap outfits and a pair of boots for me, I owed her my life. She yelled at me and I shouted back. "Yes, I'm pregnant, and I'm glad I is! Dat make me grown just like you, an I don't have to listen to none you and nobody else gotter say."

Jeff came into the room and demanded she let up. She had no sympathy for me, but he certainly did. "Don't scold her like dat, Kate, for cryin out loud. She is in family way. She don't need everybody scoldin at er like she done committed a crime. Just leave de gurl erlone."

"Jeff, she *lied* to me! She had me thinkin she gon finish school, an I come home, an she big as er damn bear!"

"Still, you ain't got no right to scold er. You didn't finish school. And you is doin what it take to be pregnant, so maybe you just can't. Leave de gurl erlone and let's go. I'm ready to go back up to Baker Town."

I explained to Jeff I was not lying to her. I had intended to tell her myself, but my sister Gemmy BB had already got to her. To be honest, I didn't give a damn what any of them thought anymore. I stopped crying over it. I accepted it. I prepared for what was coming next: the birth of my baby.

Jeff pulled Passy Kate on out the door and they left. They returned around seven o'clock that evening, dressed to go down in the bottom. They left after drinking two pints of whiskey down like water.

Something happened down at the bottom that night. Passy Kate was never the same. I noticed she was in the bed the next morning, and she stayed in bed all day. Word was she accidentally took more pills than she should have.

Her friends Lila and Candis came down late Sunday evening, concerned about her. I made it my business to hear what they were saying. It reminded me of the time I overheard them warning her about the puck-wood lady before Passy Kate got attacked and cut. They told her how the pills got mixed up.

Christmas was in two days, and folk were in town from everywhere. The house was joyful. Everyone was in good spirits. The Christmas spirit was flowing. The weather was cold but was sunny. I stood on the front porch, watching folk drive by and walk to and fro. A blue station wagon drove up in front of our house. A white man was driving, and a white woman was sitting on the passenger side, holding a baby in her arms. She rolled the window down and asked me if Passy Kate was there.

I told her yes and went into the house to tell Kate. She didn't ask who it was. She jumped up from her chair and went to the door. I heard happy shouts. It was a beautiful sight: the white lady and Passy Kate were locked up in each other's arms, smiling and hugging like they were sisters.

Passy Kate was saying, "Mrs. Massay! Mrs. Massay!"

And the white woman was saying, "Passy Kate! When did you git back home, gurl? We've missed you so bad!"

It was obviously Passy Kate had been working for Mrs. Massay before she left town, and Mrs. Massay was trying to get Passy Kate to come back. She told them she couldn't. I had never seen any white folk seem so glad to see a Negro, other than the time we were downtown and Aunt Matilda met with Ms. Bertha Wiggler. It was real. No matter what, all whites are not bad, nor are all blacks.

I watched Mrs. Massay beg Passy Kate to come back and take care of her eight-month-old baby, Kateleen. She said, "You see, Passy Kate? I gave her part of your name." Her husband stood back, rejoicing over the love the two of them showed each other.

But Passy Kate still refused, saying she was not home to stay.

I called Passy Kate to the side and asked her to introduce me to Mrs. Massay. I thought I could work for her, since I was not going back to school after the holidays, and I needed a job. Kate was so damn mean, she wouldn't hear of it. I implored her to do it. I even told her if she would do that one thing for me, I would never ask anything else of her as long as I lived.

She finally did it, with regret. I didn't care how many regrets she had. Mrs. Massay hired me and told me to be up at her house at seven o'clock that Monday morning. She warned me not to be late, because Boyd Bellford, her husband, left home at seven to open up at work, and her job shift started at seven; she left home at six thirty.

My new job was heaven sent. I thought it must be nice to have such outstanding jobs as the Bellfords had. She was a high-paid registered nurse at the hospital, and he was the highest-paid employee in the post office, a postmaster general. They paid me only twelve dollars a week, but compared to what some folk made working in the white folks' houses, that was my blessing. I thanked God for that job. Now I could be responsible for my actions and could take care of my baby. God had fixed it for me again. I woke up early Christmas morning, all excited about my new job.

The job started the day after Christmas. I walked up to the Bellfords' house, and I was amazed. It was big and beautiful, and the central heating was like nothing I had ever felt. They had three children besides the baby Kateleen: the oldest was Beth Fran; the second oldest was Frazer, the only boy; and the knee-high baby was Sandra Lyn. She was the most beautiful child of them all.

During the middle of the week, Passy Kate and Jeff left for Tennessee. On Friday, I received my twelve dollars and thought I was rich. It was the most money I'd ever for one weekof work. I gave my mother half to help out around the house, and I kept half, realizing the baby was my own responsibility and I had to live up to it.

***

I found a small New Testament Bible, and I read it daily. I started in the gospel of Matthew, with the genealogy and birth of Jesus. That Bible became my life. I had no recognition that the enemy knew more about me than I knew about myself and the calling God had on my life. The devil had bigger plans.

One Sunday morning, the weather was cold and dreary, like there was something in the air that spelled trouble. I got up to the smell of coffee and Mama's biscuits coming from the kitchen. I washed up, then put on a pair of black slacks and a black-and-yellow blouse with a design of moons and stars. I heard voices coming through from Mama's room. They got louder and louder. At first I thought somebody was laughing, but the more I listened, the more I realized the sounds were painful screams.

I went into the kitchen and met Rosetta. She was the one screaming. Her face was covered in tears. "Haley," she cried, "dey killed em, cold-blooded killed em!"

She wasn't making any sense to me. "Who killed who? Who is you talkin bout?" I asked.

"Oh Haley! Dey killed Wilbert! Brock an his daddy caused Wilbert's death last night! Oh my God, Brock an Pluto did it."

I squeezed her tight and whispered, "I'm so deeply sorry. I'm sorry."

I remembered the words Brock yelled the day Wilbert broke his arm with that bat: "I'm gon git you, bitch, if it's de last thing I ever do! I'm gon git you for dis!"

I thought I was going into premature labor. I took a seat beside Rosetta, still trying to calm her down. "Tell me what happen, Rosetta. Why did dey do it?"

In came Mrs. Loudella, Matt's mama, calling out Rosetta's name. She told me what appeared to have happened. Wilbert was dating one of the Moncellar girls. Brock was interested in her, but she was not interested in him. She made it known that she loved Wilbert, and they had an eight-week-old son together.

Wilbert was up at the house, visiting with them, when Pluto and his son Brock showed up. Predictably, an argument started between Brock and Wilbert, and then a fight broke out. One man cut Wilbert and the other man shot him in the head. The coroner's report stated that when Wilbert was shot, he was already dead. Brock had made good on his threats.

Wilbert went down with a fight, kicking ass until he couldn't kick anymore. The town was saddened by the loss. Wilbert's family had the support of all races; they were well loved.

Mama's house was filling with customers. I held Rosetta for what seemed like hours. By the time Mama came out, she and Mrs. Loudella were both feeling the moonshine along with the hurt.

Wilbert's funeral was the following Saturday. Matt came home for it. Word was a pregnant woman should not go to a funeral; if she did, the baby would be born blind. I didn't know if it was true, but I didn't take a chance. I watched from Pa Jack's corner as they drove to the graveyard. I didn't see Matt. He did come to the house, but I was too ashamed to let him see me. By the next time he came to town, he was married, had three kids, and was preaching the Word of God. He'd answered his call to preach.

***

Working for Mrs. Massay Bellford and taking care of her baby, I learned what a mother's love was all about. She was not like my mama. The love that baby received was the kind of love I wanted for my baby. That was what I mostly focused on—being the best mother I could be. I knew my job was my only security, and each day I thanked God for it.

I started preparing for the arrival of my baby girl. I wanted a boy, but in my heart I knew I was going to have a girl. I had a long way to go, and with the help of God, I would get there. I learned the special needs of a baby from Mrs. Massay's baby girl. Even with the experience I had with my mother's and sister's babies, my experience with Kateleen was important.

Mrs. Massay and my relationship expanded. She liked me—not as much as she liked my sister, but she liked me. When something was bothering me, she knew it. I learned to confide in her. There were also times I was evasive with her, and she could tell that also. Whatever state I was in, she was supportive of me in ways she never knew.

I learned about her, just as she did about me. I recall watching her mouth as she talked. Her lips were different from black folk's lips. White folk had no lips. Daddy always said to pay close attention to white folk's mouths. They had mouths like snakes. Black folk always had to be careful of them, because when we least expected it, they would bite. They were deadly poison, just like a snake.

I was in my sixth month of pregnancy. Morning sickness still troubled me. I was so sick, I began to get slack on my work. I never stopped taking good care of that baby, though—at least, I didn't think I did. My slackness caused friction between Mrs. Massay and me. My attitude started to get out of control. I wanted my baby out of me.

Ms. Massay's oldest daughter, Beth Fran, was twelve years old, and she was unpredictable. She was the only one who had a prejudiced streak in her. Mr. Bellford didn't seem to be prejudiced, and Mrs. Massay certainly was not prejudice. Neither were Bellford Junior or Sandra Lyn. For me, it didn't take a lot of nothing to love them, regardless of their race.

Sandra Lyn was the kind of child who made you feel better just by looking at her. She was the prettiest child and had a great sense of humor. Her room was always kept nice and neat. She never allowed the fact that I was their housekeeper interfere with her sense of responsibility, and that went a long way with me. Mostly what attracted me and attached me to her was how very sympathetic she was toward everyone she came in contact with, no matter what race they were. It made me know that she would follow in her mother's footsteps, taking care of people. There were times I was so sick, and Sandra Lyn knew it. She would take me into her room and tell me to lie on her bed for a while, saying, "This is our little secret."

***

It was a beautiful spring day around the beginning of April. Birdsong echoed through the window. It was Mrs. Massay's day off from the hospital. She rose early, ate her breakfast, then relaxed at the table, drinking her morning coffee. She said, "Come over here, Haley. I want to talk to you."

I pulled a chair out and sat down beside her. She had a mysterious look in her eye. I couldn't tell if it was good or bad. She eyed me up and down. My stomach was sticking out. She said, "Today we're going to do some spring cleaning. Do you think you is up for it? Sandra Lyn tells me you be sick a lot."

"Yes, Mrs. Massay. I'm up for whatever you want me to do. I do be sick, but it don't stop me from doin my work."

She laughed and asked, "How many months along are you? Six or seven? You shouldn't be still having morning sickness."

I didn't know if I should or not. All I knew was that I was so ready for the sickness to stop and the baby to come. Meantime, I would get that spring cleaning done with and go home.

She said, "I kin make room by giving away a lot of things. I hope your baby be a little girl. A lot of Sandie's baby clothes, she has outgrown. I want to give them to you so you won't have to buy them. I know your baby could use them." Mrs. Massay was a pretty woman, but her inner beauty showed in her speech.

I watched her drink down several cups of coffee. She was looking at me with that mysterious look again, and I could tell something was heavy on her mind. She asked, "What do you want the baby to be, a girl or a boy?"

"It really don't matter. I just want it to come here alive an healthy. Whether it's a boy or a gurl, I want it to come outta me."

She laughed. "That's good judgment." Out came the big question. "Where is the baby's daddy? Will he help with the responsibility of this child?"

"No, ma'am. He left town and moved, an I don't know where."

She turned red in her face. "Haley, you telling me that son of a bitch left you here to deal with this responsibility all alone, and you just a child yourself?"

Tears welled up in my eyes. I didn't have to speak; she had her answer.

The advice she gave me stayed with me for many years. It ate away inside me every single day. "Haley," she said, "you know he done ruined your life at sixteen years old. Do you know he kin be made to marry you and live up to his responsibility? I kin call Jack Henry right now and have him to come out here. He will make a call and have his deputy pick that man's sorry ass up. Do you have an address on his parents?"

She was deeply concerned about the welfare of me and my baby. But I didn't want any of that. I wanted to take care of my baby myself. I knew it was going to be hard, but as long as I had her, I didn't have anything to worry about.

I told Mrs. Massay no, I had no address, and I didn't have any way of getting one. I didn't want anything from him because he'd done enough to me already, but the good Lord had provided for me and my baby through the Bellfords. I knew without a shadow of a doubt that one day German Lompkins would weep for what he did to me. And my baby would never have to worry about anything as long as I lived.

I prayed under my breath, "Dear heavenly Father, please let me live to raise my baby myself and see her grown."

Mrs. Massay said that I was only confused about what I wanted due to the shock of being pregnant. Once the baby was born and the shock wore off, she said I would be more alert about what I wanted.

I looked at her and thought, *Dat's what white folk do.* I excused myself from the table before she could ask me any more questions about my business.

When I came out from cleaning the bedrooms, she had cleaned the kitchen and was in the garage, cleaning out the storage chest. She told me to come and see what I could use for my baby.

I had never seen so many pretty baby clothes in my life. She had gowns, bibs, diapers, diaper shirts, dresses, pants, suits, blankets, shoes, sweaters—they were all beautiful and they all could be mine for my unborn child. When I went home that evening, I had everything I needed. Some things were used, and some were still new.

As I carried that baby to full term, I learned that there was always more than meets the eye. I never told Mrs. Massay about the rape, but still I learned to trust her with my life. And she trusted me. She shared things with me that I will take to my grave, and I shared some of my horrible stories with her. She was the first white friend I ever had, and not only my first but my best.

***

Wednesday was Moa India Halloway's day to go up to the clinic and get treatment. I had heard a lot about her. She would sit under the pear tree in her front yard and smoke a pipe. That was an unusual thing for a female to do. She wasn't long returned home from a lengthy stay in the hospital.

When I got off from work that evening, I stopped by to see how she was feeling. She was basking in the sunshine and smoking her pipe. She was wearing a brown paper bag on her head. She said, "I know you mad wit Endora."

The old saying back then was that when more than one woman was expecting, and one had her baby, the others would get mad.

I heard her and asked, "Why would I be mad wit Endora?"

"She had er eight-pound baby gurl dis morning. You next."

I got curious as to why she was wearing that paper bag on her head. She didn't get defensive when I asked. She took the bag from her head, and she took the pipe from her mouth. And in the holy name of our Lord and Savior, Jesus Christ, in a few seconds tiny bugs commenced to come from her nose and the corner of her eyes and her ears. I couldn't believe what I was seeing. And her head was as clean as the palm of my hand.

Shocked, I asked, "Good God, Mao India! What happen to all your hair?"

A sad look came over her face. "I was cursed wit er voodoo an witchcraft curse. It was put on me by a woman."

"What she do dat for?"

"Cause she wanted my husband, Uncle Billy Bob. Now she dead, an I can't git it off me."

"What's voodoo an witchcraft?"

"It's a spell dat mean people kin cast upon a person if it's some you got and dey want it. Or dey hate you bad ernough, dey kin do evil things to you like what Lizzie Ruth Johnson done did to me. Take it from me for what it's worth: be careful who you trust and who you eat from."

It was a good warning I didn't take heed of. The advice I received, I didn't do much justice to. To know how dirty and cruel people could be was overwhelming. Lizzie Ruth Johnson was known for calling loud on the Lord. Who would ever believe that she would do something so evil to a woman as sweet and respectable as Moa India?

I began to understand more about church folk. If anyone was suspected of doing evil, they screamed the loudest. They were at the church the moment the doors opened.

It was Easter of 1963 when Moa India expired. I didn't go to her funeral, but I watched the many cars line up and drive slowly to the graveyard for her burial. I said my final good-bye to Moa India Halloway. To be absent from the body is to be present with the Lord.

After her death, the cracklings were never the same. Nobody could cook them like she did. Not even the pears from her tree were as good as they had been when she was living.

Later that summer, we were all awakened by the loudest, saddest cry from Mrs. Angie Rosa's house. I was big in my stomach, so I could not move as fast as the others, but I watched from the front porch. Old Lund Cabb's Black Maria came around the corner, driving slowly, and behind it was old man Funeral Bellow's black hearse. It was carrying Mr. Campbell's body to the funeral home. The cries turned into screams, and I heard clearly, "She stabbed my daddy cause he went to sleep and de hog feet burned up! She blamed him!"

Folk were talking all around town. "Mrs. Angie Rosa was arrested for the death of Mr. Campbell Connelly over some pig feet."

Nobody was able to sleep. The death of our neighbor was shocking, painful, and unbelievable. Not even Lund was ready for that one.

Before her bail was set, no one would go visit her. She sent for my mother, and I was surprised when Mama said she would not go.

But before the day was over, Mama went. She braided Mrs. Angie Rosa's hair so it could be fresh for her when she went to court. When Mama came back, she said Sheriff Fonda Cabb searched her. They never did that. He wanted to make sure Mama was not going to give Mrs. Angie Rosa a weapon or anything. When he unlocked the door to the cell, he said, "Now, Angie Rosa, don't teach Jenny Rue how to kill Macky like you did Campbell."

I asked Mama why she went up there, knowing what Mrs. Angie Rosa did to Mr. Campbell.

She stated, "Mrs. Angie Rosa is still er human bein. De devil used er to do his dirty work. God still love er, no matter what." As she always did, she reminded me what the Good Book says: "Jesus said to de unrighteous, 'When I was hungry, you didn't give me bread; when I was naked, you didn't clothe me; an when I was in prison, you didn't come visit me.' Now who would I be if I didn't go visit Angie Rosa when she in trouble, no matter what she did?"

Mrs. Angie Rosa made bail and got out of jail. When her trial came, she was found not guilty on the grounds of self-defense.

Everyone knew Mr. Campbell. He loved his family and would never hurt them, no matter what. Whites and blacks were upset over her being found not guilty. Her little girl's testimony was believed to have freed her. An innocent, hardworking, respectable, loving man was taken, and no one will ever know the real story of what happened in that house.

Chapter 18: The Stranger Entered

The first Sunday was always a big Sunday, and a first Sunday that was also Easter Sunday was the biggest. I bought myself a beautiful, dark blue maternity suit for the occasion. My sister Tise was also expecting her third kid. Everyone relocated to the bottom after church, pregnant women included. I sat outside, talking with Glory Ann. Ruthella was in town with her friend. It was strange that O'Bera was not around, and neither was Candis. I expected to see those two, since they had become my favorite friends. I felt like gloating that Sunday, but they were nowhere to be found.

Up drove a blue-and-white Ford and parked beside where I was standing. A tall, dark-skinned image of a man, like a model you would only see in a magazine, got out of the car. Something strange whirled around inside me. My baby started to kick like crazy. I almost fainted.

The man looked me up and down. He took me by my arm and asked with concern, "Are you all right? You not goin into labor, are you?"

"Yeah, I'm all right." Big drops of sweat popped out of my face and all over my body. I was practically unable to breathe.

"No, you are not. You look just like you is bout to pass out. Come sit down in my car."

He walked me slowly to his car and seated me in the passenger's seat. He hurried around to the driver's side, started the car, and put on the air conditioning. Within a few seconds, I was feeling my old self again. "You sure you all right?" he asked.

"Yeah," I answered. "I never had anythin like dis to happen to me. I don't know what happen."

He smiled sarcastically. "Dat Little Freddy charm got you."

I didn't know what he meant by that statement. I laughed when he said it. He looked at me, and from that moment on, I was hooked. I started to get out of his car, and he jumped out and ran around to open my door like a perfect gentlemen. He asked for a third time, "Are you sure you all right?"

"Yes," I answered.

"Den prove it to me. When you git ready to go home, let me take you. I don't want you to start walkin an pass out."

I did promise, but only to get away from him.

Glory Ann was looking on, and Barlena Jean was also standing there, holding her bundle of joy. I was mostly ashamed. I didn't know what had happened to me. All I could do was thank the young man.

I asked Glory Ann who he was, and she smiled. "Haley Keath, you know dat's Little Freddy Justin. Everybody know his good-lookin self. He want to take you home, let em. I'll go wit you if you scared, but ain't nothin gon happen to you. He'll take you home just like he promise."

I trusted her. I stayed around the the bottom until it was starting to get dark. Buster came for Tise, but Glory Ann persuaded me to stay on a little while longer, reminding me that I had a ride. When we were ready to go, she ran and came back with Little Freddy. We got into the car, and she said, "Don't take us home, Little Freddy. Ride us."

He drove us out into the country gladly. I found he was hilarious, as funny as any comic. He played the radio and we listened to all the oldie-goodie music. He told a joke about a sixteen-year-old girl who was in her seventh month of pregnancy and had been deserted by the father. She was desperately in need of real love for her and her baby. I didn't quite understand the joke until he said, "Never fear, Little Freddy is right here. I kin love you an your baby if you let me." He touched my stomach and felt my baby kick. I laughed it off, not giving him or his remarks a second thought.

Around five o'clock, he drove us back to the center of town. He and Glory Ann tried to encourage me to stay out with them, but I just didn't want to. I was enjoying his company too much, pretending that he was my man and I was expecting his baby. All sorts of nonsense was racing around in my head.

Glory Ann went into the store to get us something to drink. Little Freddy and I were having a pleasant conversation—he was a great conversationalist and kept me laughing. I hadn't laughed like that since I could remember.

Up came the Three Musketeers: Lila, Candis, and O'Bera. I really didn't want them to see me. I tilted my head sideways, hoping they wouldn't recognize me. As they got closer, I got more uneasy. I didn't want any more humiliation from those people.

Little Freddy noticed. He said sincerely, "You don't have to be shy an you don't have to hold your head down. You wit me, an you don't have to worry bout anythin or anybody as long as you is wit me."

I sat straight up in that nice new Ford as Lila came tapping on the driver's side window. He rolled it down and said, "Hey, Lila, what's it like?"

"Oh, nothin but bout a half a pint of moon."

She beckoned with her hand for the others to come over. "Who dis you got in de car wit you, Little Freddy? Oh, dis little Keath."

He placed his hands on my stomach and murmured, "Don't let dem or nobody else spoil your Easter when you carryin your first Easter bunny."

From then on, every Sunday until the baby was born, Little Freddy took me and Glory Ann for a ride. One Sunday, I was about to get out of the car, and he looked into my eyes and said, "You know, you got de prettiest big eyes of anybody in dis town."

I was flattered for a few seconds. His words left me speechless. I really didn't know what to think about this older man paying me all this attention. I couldn't let myself think of anything but my unborn child.

I began to open up to him more and let him in on some of my issues. Everybody knew I was that Keath gal from Rat Row. Who could get serious about her? I felt sorry for myself, convinced nobody wanted me. I didn't fit in, no matter how I tried.

Little Freddy didn't stop. He would come by the house through the week and bring me fruit. He knew I loved pears, peaches, and watermelon. I knew he had to have someone special in his life, but I didn't care. I was being treated well, and I didn't want it to end.

At the end of my eighth month of pregnancy, I was big, swollen, and afraid. The closer I got to my due date, the more afraid I became. I was too sick to fulfill my obligation to Mrs. Massay Bellford. She suggested she find someone to fill in for me until after my baby came. She ended up getting a girl named Delta to work for her. I disliked the fact that she was working in my place. Everywhere I turned, Delta's sister Mary Ann was bragging that Delta had taken my job. I knew Mary Ann believed that, but in my heart I knew Delta hadn't, because that was my job given to me by God.

***

On a beaming hot summer day, Daddy was working somewhere. Glory Ann had come down and braided my hair for me. I was due to deliver any day.

I looked down the street and saw Daddy coming home. I don't know what came over me. That hatred flared up inside me. I knew he was going to be hot and thirsty. I waited until he was halfway to the house, then ran to the icebox and got the cold water. I poured it out the window.

When he came in, he went directly to the icebox, as I knew he would. He yelled out, "Haley, you mean you been here on your sorry ass all day and didn't put no water in de box?"

I ignored him, to my satisfaction. He was so angry with me, I believe if I hadn't been so pregnant, he would have struck me dead. He started to chip ice to make himself some cold water.

I saw Theola and Millie Mae walk up to Mary Ann's door. I heard my name mentioned and couldn't begin to think why.

Millie Ann called out to me. When I walked up to see what she wanted, it was Theola who said, "Haley! What is all dat you told Massay bout me?"

I had no knowledge what in the hell she was talking about. "What is you talkin bout? I don't know nothin to tell Mrs. Massay. I don't know *you*."

"Well, my boss lady is wife to Mrs. Massay's brother, Dr. Reynolds. She de owner of de Freelance store, and Mrs. Massay told er a lot of things er maid told er bout me."

It didn't take a minute to figure out who that maid was, since I was no longer working. Theola was a pretty, dark-skinned lady with front teeth full of cavities. I told her I hadn't told Mrs. Massay anything; she should check with Delta. She apologized for accusing me, and they left.

I had never liked Millie Mae, and when they left, I knew there was more to it than them confronting me about some "you say, I say" nonsense.

Later that week, Little Freddy stopped by on his work truck and asked me what happened. I told him. He immediately said, "Dat ain't what dat was all bout. I think de reason why Theola come down here is cause I used to go wit her, but I don't no more."

I'd known he had somebody. Now I knew who. I didn't want to know, but since I did, I didn't care. We weren't doing anything wrong, and I saw no reason for him to stop seeing me. He was my company in pregnancy and sickness. Besides, he was one of the best-looking, best-dressed, and most intelligent men in town. Who wouldn't want to be with him?

On Friday evening, he stopped by again and brought me a whole bag of Elberta peaches. They were the best peaches I had ever eaten, and I ate many. On Saturday, around three thirty in the morning, I was awakened by sharp pains in the lower part of my belly. I thought it was from all those peaches. I couldn't lie down and I couldn't be still, so I walked the floor until daylight.

I walked out on the porch and sat in one of the chairs, questioning what any man would want with me, a girl who was sixteen and with child, from the poorest neighborhood in town. I couldn't begin to imagine what Little Freddy was hanging around me for.

The pains got increasingly hard. I went inside and called out to my mama. She got up and got Daddy up. He left the house. I still did not know I was in labor.

I was in so much pain I couldn't even think. The pains seemed to speed up. I recalled a Scripture verse that instructed us to pray in season and out of season. I couldn't pray enough. I thought I had to use the toilet, but I couldn't. That was when I figured out I was in labor. I wanted that baby to make its entrance fast.

I was walking back to the house from the toilet when a pain hit me so hard, it knocked me to my knees. Arketha was standing in the back door, watching. She helped me up. A few seconds after, I was comfortabaly in bed.

The house as usual filled with caring and nosy neighbors. I was in labor all that day. I got tired of bearing every pain that hit me. I started to get angry.

The midwife then was Mrs. Lottie. She was the sister of Candis's mother. She arrived around three o'clock. Odessa and the women of my family were the only ones allowed to remain in the room after that. I was drenched with sweat from the torrid heat. No air circulated. I begged them for something for the pain, but there was nothing they could give me. They all said I had to bear that pain alone.

Glory Ann came in, and that made me feel somewhat more comfortable, like the pain was easier to deal with. I thought it was ironic that Glory Ann had been there the night the baby was conceived, and here she was again as I was trying to deliver. Mrs. Lottie encouraged me to take a walk around the house, to walk some of the pain off, and Glory Ann and I walked for about thirty minutes. She never knew the comfort she brought to me that Sunday.

Back inside, Mrs. Lottie had made me a pallet on the floor. A chair was turned upside down to support my body. I lay there for hours. Mrs. Angie Rosa came in with a big plate of food, and I wouldn't eat a bite of it. She begged me to put some food in my stomach, but I refused.

Mrs. Lottie looked me over, her glasses hanging on the tip of her nose, and stated, "It is now ten o'clock. I want to get her up in the bed. She is dilated enough that this baby will be coming in about another hour."

The moment I got in bed, I dozed off. When I woke up, pain was all over my body. I had to bare myself to everyone. All I could hear from every direction was, "Push! Push! Push!" I pushed so many times, I had no strength left. The pains didn't stop. They were hitting me every five seconds, or so it seemd, and harder than I remembered. I thought I was dying. At one point, I even tried to give up. The voices kept saying, "Hold your breath an push. Can't nobody have dis baby for you. Not your mama, not your sister, not your friend. Haley, it's time you bring your baby on into dis world."

I thrust with all the strength I had left, and it was only enough to bring her on. I felt one more unyielding pain, and I did just as I was told—I held my breath, gritted my teeth, and pushed hard.

I felt my baby when she came out of my stomach. I looked down, and Mrs. Lottie was cutting something—what I heard somebody say was the umbilical cord. The baby let out a loud scream. She had strong lungs.

I had given birth to a nine pound, three ounce, beautiful baby girl. I was so sleepy, I wanted to just doze off, but I was not allowed to. The women kept me awake until they had washed me and the baby.

They placed the baby in my arms. She had a head full of beautiful, black, silky hair. Her cheeks was like a pomegranate. Her skin was soft like cotton, and the smell stayed with me. She belonged to me. I experienced a mother's love for her child. She was the precious gift that God had so richly blessed me with. That was the most beautiful feeling I have ever encountered. I was a mother. I had a baby girl whom I loved dearly. Nothing else mattered. She became my pride and joy from that moment on. I named her Rejetta.

I prayed, *Dear Lord, I never asked for dis baby. I never even thought of havin a baby out of wedlock. But dis is what you have gave me. Now, God, since she is here, I want you to know I am gonna be de best mother to dis baby dat I kin be. All I ask is for you to let me live to raise er and be a good mother to my little gurl. She won't never have to be under de footstool of nobody else. I love er so much, and dear Lord, I love you. Amen.*

I acknowledged I had it all to do alone, and I was willing. I had to double-love Rejetta, be the mother and father for her.

My first step was to get her out of that house, away from all those drunks. Getting my strength back had to come first.

***

Rejetta was in her second month of life, and I hadn't heard anything about returning to my job with the Bellfords. I was in need of that job. I feared that Mrs. Massay was going to keep Delta on and not rehire me.

But I was wrong. As I was planning to meet with another family about working for them, a shiny blue station wagon drove up in front of the house. It was Mrs. Massay. She had Sandra Lyn and little Kateleen with her. They got out of the car and came up on the porch to me. "Haley," Mrs. Massay said, "you had the baby! Let me see her. Can you come back to work?"

They came into the house. I had Rejetta beautiful and clean, dressed in one of the outfits Mrs. Massay had given me. That white family held my little black baby without any prejudice, and I was rehired by Mrs. Massay on the day Rejetta turned two months old. Oh, I was so glad to see them.

But my going back to work meant Delta was out of a job. I made an enemy out of her. I went to work the following Monday, and it was a shock to everyone who had been so sure Delta had my job.

Leaving my baby was the hardest thing. I breastfed her when I was home, and she took the bottle while I was gone. My breasts paid the price. By the time the day was over, they were full of milk. Not only did my breasts ache, my whole body ached.

As I approached home, I would hear my baby crying. I rushed directly to her and picked her up. She looked up when she heard my voice, and stopped crying instantaneously. She was small, but I believe she was as happy to have me as I was to have her. She knew who I was. I nursed her, and she enjoyed the milk, sucking like she'd never had a meal since she was born. I enjoyed watching and feeling her mouth sucking on my breast, deflating it like a slow leak in a tire.

One day, Daddy came home drunk after tying on one of his blue Mondays. Just hearing his voice made me ill. He didn't know I was home until he walked in the room and saw me nursing my baby. He demanded I go in the kitchen and cook him something to eat. I had not seen what he was up to all day, but I knew he was not hungry. He thought I would stop nursing my sucking baby to serve him? He had to be sick in his mind.

I clutched my baby closer, ignoring his cursing. I was not going to be intimidated. My baby came first, and nobody was going to get in the way of that. But he was persistant. "Don't you see me nursing my baby?" I shouted.

He shouted back, "Who you talkin to? You can't do what I ask, you take your baby an git de hell out."

I thought he was a damn fool. "Who you think I'm talkin to?"

He slapped me. "Don't you damn holler at me!"

My first instinct was to hit the bastard back, but I had my baby in my arms. I didn't let him get the last word, though. "If you think I'm gon stop takin care of my baby for you, if you think I'm gon cook for you, you got another thing comin."

Without giving him a chance to respond, I walked straight out the back door to the path that led from our backyard to the highway. I walked down to my sister Tise's house; she hadn't so long moved round to Brake's quarter. I asked her if I could stay with Buster and her until I found my own place. She talked it over with Buster, and he agreed to let me stay with them for as long as I needed to.

Tise was thrilled to have me move in with her. "Gitting you and your baby away from round there is the best thing you could have done," she said.

I believe always, in God's own good time, he will fix everything the way he wants it to be. A special healing took place instantly. I declared the time and hour. I had waited for the day to come for me to walk away from that house on Rat Row. Daddy didn't realize the favor he had just extended to me. I got my three-month-old baby out from that environment. For the first time, I saw a future for me and my baby. My intention was to raise my baby in a uninterrupted, placid atmosphere. My life was already half normal. But my determination to give my child a decent, normal life was just the beginning.

I left my baby with Tise while I went back to Mama's house to get my clothes. The moment I arrived, I could hear my mama screaming.

Daddy was beating her. He was straddling her and beating her face like a raging maniac.

I jumped right in on him. I lost all sense of what my place was. I was audacious. I raged, grabbing him around his neck, "Git off my mama, bitch!" I spotted a whiskey bottle on the floor and smashed it on the back of his bald head.

Daddy jumped up and started toward me, but Uncle Martel, Mr. Danny, and Uncle Cleo grabbed hold of him. That gave Mama time to get out, and I ran behind her to help her get somewhere safe. Daddy was like a bull charging once he sees red. Of all the times I witnessed him in action, that was one of the worst. He was totally out of control.

Mama and I went around to Tise's place, knowing Daddy wouldn't go there. I hated that man. Oh God, how I hated him. How on earth could Mama love someone as heartless and cruel as he was? Who was Macky Keath? What kind of human being was he?

With all the persuasion I could muster up, at every opportunity I got, I encouraged Mama to leave him. I may not have known how she could love him, but I did know one thing: she was all alone in that house with no one to help her. Annie Dora was sickly, Willa Max was with Aunt Matilda, and the boys were just boys. I had to find a way to get her away from him.

Chapter 19: On My Own, Looking for Love in All the Wrong Places

One of Mama's cousins passed, and they brought her body to lie in her house that Saturday night. During those days, it was common that the family of the deceased would bring the corpse back to the residence the night before the funeral. Everybody in the neighborhood mourned together.

Afterward, the family cleaned the house and moved everything out, and it became available for rent. That was the first house I rented for my baby and me. The rent was only two dollars a week. I was making twelve, and in those days, such a small amount was still good living if it was used properly.

I didn't have any furniture. Aunt Lucy Sue gave me an old, rusty iron bed, and Mrs. Massay's mother-in-law gave me a nice new set of mattresses. Cousin Lula gave me a dresser and a chest, and I bought myself a decent couch from the furniture store. I decorated the house with little whatnots Mrs. Massay gave me, and it became our home.

Early one morning, Mama came beating on the door. Daddy had launched another nasty attack on her. I was astounded to learn she had beaten the hell out of him. She fought back and won. I wanted to put her up in my place, but she wanted to go back because I only had one bed. There was no room for the boys and Snappy.

The good Lord looked down from heaven upon us again. There was a house with more rooms over on Keed Street. It was not where either of us wanted to live, but for the moment it was all we could get. I had to beg and plead with Mama to take that house together. I was determined that Daddy had made his last attack on my mother. I was willing to do just about anything to keep her from going back to him.

With Tise and I begging together, we finally convinced Mama to leave Daddy and move to Keed Street. We already knew who the neighbors were, and we felt we could probably get along with everyone. Mama schooled me that we could live anywhere as long as we minded our own business and let others do the same.

The rent was sixteen dollars a month, but between the two of us, we could do it. The house was also wired up. We no longer had to use lamps; we had electric lights for the first time. The house was much the same as those on Rat Row, but the lighting made everything better.

However, we had to come up with forty dollars to turn the electricity on. I went to the Bellfords. They didn't change words with me—they just gave me the money.

Move-in day was the beginning of much happiness. But no matter where we went or lived, we were the black sheep and the most talked-about family. Most of the neighbors were no different than we were, but they all thought they were better. I wonder who they thought gave them the right to be judgmental?

Across the street lived the Gardens and the Carltons. Mrs. Louise Carlton was the mother and Mr. Carlton Senior the father. The oldest child was Pearly Mae, followed by Ollie Lee, Lorene, Lonnie, Frankie, and Jean. The three oldest had the same father and carried his name of Garden. They was good neighbors, quiet and very family-oriented. Like everybody else, they were working folk. And, like everybody else, they were human.

To the left of us was a hell-raiser, Ozeda Seagall, and her husband John Seagall. Living with them was an adopted friend named Louise, and she had a daughter named Addie, a real pretty girl. Every time I saw Addie, she was working. All Mrs. Seagall did was sit and give orders, when she wasn't dipping in everybody else's business. Louise and Addie were nothing but slaves in exchange for a place to live.

Below them were Marcus Mac J and his wife. She was still having babies, and each time she gave birth, her cousin Emmaline came and took the baby home with her. She said she wanted them raised right in the house of the Lord, and their mama didn't go to church, not even for a funeral. Cousin Emmaline was a quiet, well-respected woman. Once I began to see what was going on, their lives became a part of our lives.

On the right side of us were the Tills. Mrs. Cindy Tills was the only gambling female in town. Her mama, Moa Rosalin, lived with Mrs. Cindy, Mrs. Cindy's daughter Mrs. Dorothy, and Mrs. Dorothy's daughter Kaynanna. Mrs. Dorothy was the only honest worker in the house. Mrs. Cindy hustled more than any man. She eventually had a baby at a late age and named her Farmer.

We were getting ready to pay our second month's rent. Pearly Mae and I were becoming pretty close. Rejetta was going into her ninth month, and she was as big and beautiful as she could be. We were comfortably settled in with the boys, Snappy, and Mama.

Then I came home from work one day and Daddy was there. I don't think anything in the world could have made me madder than that. I was so mad, I could have spit blisters on a brick. I knew right away he was moving in, but I made it perfectly clear he better not put a hand on Mama. I promised him on my baby's life that if he did, I would not be responsible for what I did to him.

He gave me a look, but he promised he would not harm my mother, and he did keep it.

***

I went out on the back porch and sat down. Little Freddy had taken the day off for pleasure, but when I sat, he disappeared. I got up because I thought Rejetta had awakened from her nap. As I was coming through the door, there was Little Freddy, walking into the kitchen with the baby in his arms. He held her as if she were his. I knew it was not my imagination.

The first time Little Freddy saw Rejetta, she was around two weeks old. She was lying in the center of my bed down on Rat Row. He had gone to the icehouse for Daddy. I put the ice in the icebox, and Little Freddy bent over the bed, looking at Rejetta like the precious gift she was. She was smiling happily, just like a baby does when she sees her mother's face.

He watched me love on my baby: the big hugs she received and the sweet kisses I placed on her thick cheeks. His said passionately, "I kin sure use some of dose."

"Some of dose what?" I asked. I knew full well.

"Some hugs and kisses you plantin on her cheeks."

"Oh my goodness, Little Freddy, dis is my baby."

He said sincerely and convincingly, "I'll be your baby if you let me. I sure want you to be mine."

"Den what bout dem other gurlfriends?" I asked smartly.

"What gurlfriends are you talkin bout?"

"Lurie an Penny Lee an who knows who else."

After that, Little Freddy and I started to date. We got really serious. My feelings for him grew into love, and he loved me and my baby. I saw all the good qualities in him. I got to know only what I wanted to know. Nothing else mattered.

Folk were talking about it. For that moment, I was "the" woman, and I backed down to no one. Little Freddy was my lover and my friend. He told me how a woman should carry herself. He taught me not to be so flip at the mouth, to think before I spoke. I was head over heels in love with Little Freddy, and he was all I knew.

I and the other neighborhood ladies were sitting around on Ozeda Seagall's porch one day, talking about soap opera stories. *Love of Life* and *Search for Tomorrow* were the two hottest soaps then. Up drove Theola's mama, Mrs. Nadine. She jumped out of the car with a terrible attitude. Pointing her finger at me, she demanded, "Haley, is you f—— Little Freddy?"

I was so shocked, I didn't have time to think. I just blurted out, "What business is it of your?"

"It is my business when he is stayin wit my daughter."

"Livin wit your daughter? Who gives a damn? What business is it of your to run up on me, askin me bout who I'm spendin my time wit? Hell, if I didn't know any better, you're actin like you was sleepin wit em yourself."

With one word leading to another, it got heated. She told me to leave Little Freddy alone or I would be sorry. I guess she had something planned that I was unaware of, but it didn't take me long to learn she was a strong believer in voodoo and roots. Once she was gone, the revelations started.

I expected to see Little Freddy later, and I couldn't wait to hear what he had to say about his not-even-mother-in-law confronting me.

***

Before I knew what hit me, I was pregnant with another baby, unmarried, and in love. Buster and Tise moved up in the project, and their house in Brake's quarter became available. I rented it the same week Sister Greta moved to Ohio. She gave me most of her furniture. I really thought that was the life.

I had backslid out of God's hand right into the devil's. That was the beginning of longsuffering. I had read that it was one of the fruits of the Spirit, but in turning away from God mine became the fruit of evil.

Pearly Mae learned of my pregnancy. She knew things I didn't know, and she encouraged me not to have the baby. She suggested that I do a self-abortion. I didn't feel comfortable having such a gross conversation, but I inquired for more information from her. She said she could get the pills I needed, called quinine capsules. I was to take them and go to bed, and when I woke the next morning, everything would be over. I could go on with my life without any complications.

It all sounded so simple. I went along with her to get the pills, and I shared that information in a phone conversation with a friend of mine named Darcus Lee.

Unexpectedly, Little Freddy came by, and I could tell something was weighing on his mind. We went for a drive, and he told me all about my conversation with Darcus Lee. Neither one of us had known we were being eavesdropped on. Ethel Highland had been listening to every word on the party line. She told Little Freddy all about it. He begged, "Don't git rid of de baby, Haley. It's my baby. I'll take care of it. We'll do dis together."

I denied it all. "Dat bitch was so wrong. She had no right. She never heard me one time say positively dat I was gon do dat. She heard us discussin de possibility. I was told what to do an how to do it, but I never said I was." I was very convincing.

When Little Freddy dropped me off, Pearly Mae was up waiting for me. She gave me the pills. It was a terrible, freezing-cold night out. Everyone in the house was smuggled up in bed. The fire was nice and hot. I sat in front of it with whiskey in my hand and pills in my pocket. I stared into the flames, the different colors sparking in front of me. I was so mixed-up inside, I didn't know what to do. Pearly Mae's voice played over and over in my head like a broken record, but I was also hearing another voice in my heart saying that this was murder.

I took the pills from my pocket. Each time I brought them up to my mouth, something would happen. I just couldn't take them. I was confused, considering what was the best way out of an awful situation. A small, still voice spoke again to me and said, "Have that baby. Don't take the pills. If you do, you will be taking a baby's life. You are too far gone, and you could take your own life."

I dropped the pills in the jar of moonshine I was holding.

A knock came upon the door. I jumped from fear and dashed the jar's contents into the fire. When the moonshine hit, the flames spread up as if I'd thrown kerosene on them.

The knock came again. I went to the door and opened it. Little Freddy was standing there. Surprisingly, he didn't show any anger or suspicion. He said he was on his way home and just wanted to say good night.

But before he left, he admitted, "I didn't come to say good night. I come to tell you somethin about dese so-called friends." He warned me about talking on the phone. Most of the lines were party lines, and I would never know who was listening.

All the advice he gave me, I should have listened to—except I didn't. He knew things I didn't. Many times I thought about the conversation I had with him that night, and I knew he had been warning me about Pearly Mae as well as others.

The very next day, Pearly Mae called me. I ignored Little Freddy's advice and talked with her. She asked me if I took the pills. I told her I did. Within a week, it was all over town that I had got rid of the baby.

The news got back to Little Freddy, and this time he was mad as hell. With all the talk, he started drifting away from me. I was pregnant, and my life was a shambles. It appeared that he was living with Theola. She did not matter; she was one of many. But her dear old mama didn't think so.

This was one of the trying times of my life.

***

I had been to work. That evening, Mr. Boyd Bellford had gone bird hunting, and I had to walk home. It gave me time to think. My stomach was showing, but I hid it real well for as long as I could.

I passed by Moa India Halloway's house, and I remembered her. I was filled with despair and lost in thought, not knowing how I was going to cope with a second child.

It was Christmas time. Everybody was in the Christmas spirit. The joy of Christmas rang out all over the town. Everything was decorated. And I was as low in spirit as I was pregnant.

When I got around the last corner before my house, I saw a strange car parked there with a Florida tag on it. I thought it belonged to a neighbor's family, come home for the holidays.

When I got on the porch and looked in, I saw my little daughter's father. Seeing him blew me away. German Lompkins looked back with no remorse. Before he could speak, my little brother James C came out, holding Rejetta in his arms. She was laughing blissfully. Her daddy took her and looked at her in shock.

I don't know if it meant anything to him or not, but German said, "I'm sorry, Haley."

He asked if she could spend the day with the Lompkins. Because of Idella, I allowed him to take my baby. I didn't even know why I did. Daddy called me every kind of damn fool, and I felt like one. But it wasn't his call. In my heart, I wanted German to be a part of Rejetta's life, but I was not going to force the issue.

Pearly Mae and I went downtown to the barber shop and got our hair trimmed. As we were coming out, we met Delta going in. She spoke and we spoke, all very friendly. Then we took the bus to Dothan and got our Christmas outfits. Pearly Mae wore a red suit and black shoes, and I got a black suit with red shoes.

I hadn't heard from Little Freddy.

Christmas morning was a cloudy, no-sunshine day. It wasn't misty or anything, but it was weird. I felt just about like the weather. That night I was sitting in a car, talking to a guy named Ned, getting more acquainted with him. All of a sudden, a knock came on the window. Ned rolled the window down, and there was Little Freddy. He asked, "Haley, kin I see you a minute?"

I couldn't believe him.

I made my excuses to Ned and stepped out of the car. Little Freddy asked me if I was involved with Ned. I told him no. I asked him if Theola Knight was living with him. He didn't lie to me; he said yes. But he also said that after that night, she was not going to be anymore. He was bringing her back to her mama's house.

He kept his word. A few weeks later, Theola moved down from the café by the slaughter pen. He promised me that night that it was only going to be him and me, and he did just what he promised. It was good while it lasted.

***

Right after Easter, I was at work. I lay down on the couch to take a five-minute snooze. I had a frightening dream.

Then Mrs. Massay came in and woke me, furious. She'd heard I was pregnant again, and she wanted to hear it from me. I couldn't deny it even if I'd wanted to. My stomach was looking directly at her.

She fired me that week. She told me she needed somebody dependable to work for her, not someone who was going to have a baby every year. "Tell me, when is this baby due?" she demanded angrily. I told her September, and she ended the conversation.

Later, after the Fourth of July, she told me she had hired somebody else. She was still good and mad with me, and I didn't try to convince her otherwise. She hired Mrs. Louisa.

Thank God it was cotton season. I worked in the fields and took in ironing to support my baby and me. It was one of the hottest summers I could remember. Each day, I didn't know if I was going to faint or have the baby in the middle of Pete Case's cotton field. I prayed over and over again for God to help me make it through. I worked all the way through my ninth month.

One evening, I got off the truck at Tise's apartment to pick up Rejetta. Tise looked after her during the day. I was so tired, I could barely put one foot ahead of the other. Tise was always pleasant to be around, always knew the right words to say. She saw how exhausted I was and suggested that I spend the night with her. She even made my favorite dinner: fried fish and grits with hot biscuits.

With her husband around, I felt uncomfortable, and in the beginning I turned her down. But she made me a proposition I couldn't refuse: a hot bath that I could just lie back in and soak my tired, dirty body for as long as I liked.

I got in that tub, and I soaked. I dreamed of the day I would have my own tub that I could soak in any time I felt like it. Once I had the bath, we sat down and ate hot fish right out the frying pan, with good, creamy grits. I made it to the sofa and fell asleep.

I was awakened by sharp stomach cramps. I thought they were due to me pulling that heavy, six-foot cotton sack on my shoulder. I fell back to sleep, but was awakened again around four o'clock. I thought I was soaked in urine. *My God!* I thought. *What have I done?* Thankfully, it was a leather sofa.

I was urinating steadily and couldn't stop. I got up and made it to the bathroom with streams of pee running down both my legs. I panicked and screamed out for Tise. She came running. "Haley! What de matter wit you?"

"Tise, I can't stop peein," I cried. "And my stomach won't stop crampin."

"Is it time for you to have dis baby?"

"Naw, not now. It's not due till de end of de month."

"It *is* de end of de month. It's only two more days before it'll be September, gurl! You done gone into labor."

We both laughed. I was afraid, but I was ready.

She sent me into another room, and she went into her bedroom to change. I heard Buster telling her he didn't want me having a baby in his apartment, and it led to an awful argument. My pains were severe, and so was my heartache.

Buster left for work, and Tise left to get Mama for me. During her absence, Mrs. Willona Willis, a retired midwife, came over.

I was thinking about the day I went into labor with Rejetta. That had been so tiresome. I was praying that this labor was not nearly as tedious. I was sure this baby was coming, and there was no way I was going to make it to the hospital in time.

Mrs. Willona was a miracle worker. She placed me into position. She told me to put my hands on my knees and said, "I kin see the head. Push as hard as you kin!" I gave that one push and she popped out: another baby girl.

Mrs. Willona rushed to the door and called out for somebody to get the doctor up to the apartment. Then she came back and had me put my hands together and blow into them like I was blowing a whistle. She said, "You got to bring out dat afterbirth now, cause ain't no tellin when de doctor will git here."

I did just as she commanded. I blew as hard as I could, and out popped something. She took a deep breath. I learned from her that Theola Knight's sister Rebecca had died because some of her afterbirth was left in her. It mortified her whole system, and she died two weeks after giving birth to a fine, healthy baby boy.

I wondered if that would happen to me. I prayed, *Lord please don't take me away from my two babies. I promise I won't have another baby out of wedlock. Please, Lord. I don't want to die like Rebecca did, leavin her two-week-old baby behind. I will be a good mother to em. I promise in the name of Jesus. Amen.*

But it stuck in the back of my mind as I lay helpless on the bed, waiting for my mama, Tise, and the doctor.

When Dr. Henley finally came through the door, he shone a light in my eyes, pushed around in my stomach with his fingers, cut the umbilical cord, pushed my stomach again, and said, "I see the afterbirth is already out"—as if that were impossible for me to do.

I said, "Yes, sir. I coughed real hard, and it just came out. I thought it was another baby."

"That's real good," he said, looking over at Mrs. Willona. He knew she did for me what he should have done, yet he charged me twenty-five dollars and told me to get to the clinic as soon as possible.

The next weekend, I went back home with my new baby girl. I named her Vermont Andreka Keath.

When he went out the door, I saw my little Rejetta looking through the doorway, sad and apprehensive. I wanted to pick her up, but I couldn't. I was unable to move.

Mama and Tise cleaned the new baby up and dressed her in a beautiful rainbow-colored gown. They put booties on her feet and laid her in my arms. She was dark and had a head full of jet black hair. My mind stayed on poor Rebecca and how she brought life into the world and it ended hers.

I knew there was something wrong with my baby. I didn't say anything. I wanted to see if anyone else would notice. I was drenched with sweat and in pain, but was holding my own. I named my baby Vermont Andreka.

I tried to pay Mrs. Willona for the service she had rendered me. She looked at me and said, "I would be less dan a woman. You got one little gurl an just had another, an God blessed me wit de gift I have. Ain't no way I will charge you for it. Be a good mother to your little gurls and dat's my pay. Jenny Rue, I'm goin on back to de house. If you need, you know where to find me."

Bessy Troyce was the first visitor I had from the bottom, and she was the first to notice something wrong with my baby's eyes. She warned me that her babies had been like that. She delivered at home and then called the doctor because of the discharge. She encouraged me to call the doctor and tell him my baby couldn't open her eyes, and they were bloodshot. Pus and blood seemed to be coming from them.

I called the doctor as she suggested. Dr. Morrison came out

immediately and examined Vermont. He called in a prescription for eyedrops, and I put them into her eyes right away. In a few days, they cleared up.

Bessy Royce was also nosy about Little Freddy's whereabouts. She got absolutely nothing from me about that. But she became the news carrier about my baby.

Vermont was three weeks old when Little Freddy first saw her. He had been locked up in jail the day she was born. I placed her gently in his arms. He looked her over and kissed her forehead. He said, "Thank you for givin me a beautiful daughter. You kin always tell a Justin by de head. What did you name her?"

"Vermont Andreka."

"I promise you won't have to worry bout er bein taken care of. Neither one of dese gurls. As long as I'm alive, you don't need to worry. I'll be dere when you need me to be."

***

One Sunday night, Pearly Mae and I were going around to the cafés, having a little fun. Then I went over to her house. As I was coming out to go home and nurse my baby, I met Delta. She spoke to me and Pearly Mae as she passed, just as nice and intelligent as any human being could speak. Then she walked on down in the direction of Marcus Mac J and the Blandi's house.

Pearly Mae and I went on our way. Suddenly Delta came running back up to us. With a very nasty attitude, she asked me, "Why couldn't you pay Buky for my haircut? And why you and Pearly Mae couldn't git y'all hair cut when I was in de barber shop?" Lila and Candis were right behind her. It didn't take a scientist to know what was happening—those two witches were behind her problem. And I was in the right mood to solve it for her.

I looked her up and down, I looked at Delta like the ignorant human she was and didn't even dignify her with an answer. I was about to walk away from her. I heard Lila tell her to get me. When she grabbed my shoulder, I bashed her with a left hook right in her temple, knocking her backward. She hit the ground.

There was some history there. On a hot Friday night years ago, Delta and her sister Lula Mae had jumped my sister Tise. I was only thirteen years old, but I promised revenge that night. On this night, I made good. I beat the living daylights out of her. I beat her fast, and every blow was payback for the marks she'd left on my sister's face.

Marcus Mac J. came and pulled me off, begging me to stop. I was not even tired.

I started to walk inside the house. Somebody cried out, "She got a ice pick!" I reached down in the yard and picked up a rock. Delta was coming up on me. I waited until she got within arm's length. Then I drew the rock back and slammed her right in her forehead. I tried to bust her brains out. She had to be taken to the emergency room.

I was out of control. Daddy picked up the ice pick. I could hear Lila lying about Pearly Mae and I double-teaming Delta. She was smoking a cigarette, and Marcus Mac J slapped her so hard, the sparks smeared across her face and she fell backward. He made sure everyone knew Lila and Candis pushed Delta on me.

My blouse was ripped, but it was just my blouse—not my face. I went in, changed my clothes, and came out again, because I was determined not to let Delta ruin my night.

A little later, I was at Butternut's café, and in came Delta's three sisters: Lazy Mae, Eliza Lee, and Mary Ann. I watched them from every angle. I knew they wanted to jump me, and I was dying for them to do so. I wanted them to get within five feet of me, and it was going to be on.

I overheard gossip that Delta had sixteen stitches in her forehead, and she was vowing to get me. I also heard talk that I didn't do it; my daddy cut Delta. That lie didn't last long.

I was coming from work the following Monday and I met Cousin Emmaline. She was standing on the corner by the slaughter pen, down the road from her house. I smelled trouble. She said, "Haley, do you have anythin on you?"

"Anythin like what?"

"Somethin to protect yourself from Delta and her sister Mary Ann.

Dey was waitin on you down by de church, an I went down dere after hearin everybody gossipin. Dey decided dey gonna git you. I think I may have got through to em, but I don't know. Dey coulder just moved on somewhere else so you can't see em. Be careful."

I thanked her and clamped my teeth tight to keep from uttering what was really on my tongue. I was ready to kill those dirty, fighting whores. I picked up a good, strong limb that had fallen from an oak tree, and I took out the knife I carried in my bosom. I was ready for anything they were ready to dish out.

My brothers Pap and James C met me in between Flappy Boots's café and the church. I was walking down the middle of the road. I didn't see Delta or her sisters, but Lila and Candis were sitting on Butternut's front porch. I knew they were behind all the stupid stuff that was going on. I did as Cousin Emmaline told me: "Go home and don't start no trouble." When I walked by those two, they were so quiet, a mouse could have been heard.

I had been friends with these girls once. I knew for sure that Little Freddy was behind all that confusion. He was the reason Lila disliked me so much. Candis was just her road dog. Living in a town so small, your business was out the moment it happened. There were no secrets. Word was Little Freddy and I were over, and that was Lila's opportunity to go for him. So be it. I had learned to hide my real feelings very well.

***

I wished Joel Malone was still around. He was my friend, and I could talk to him about anything. He was certainly a good listener. The thought of having to raise two kids out of wedlock was terrifying. But he had moved to another town and started a new life with his family. I missed him like crazy for the first time since he moved away.

I also couldn't put out of my mind the words that came from Buster's mouth when I was in labor. All the distasteful things I had been thinking concerning him were starting to come true.

As for Little Freddy, we talked. I told him I was going on with my life without him. He agreed to take care of the baby and allow me to do whatever was necessary without any interference. It was over for us, I thought.

During my recovery from having Vermont, I had been out of touch with what was really going on. He was dating Lila. She had moved in two houses down from me. Her being that close to me, and Little Freddy practically living with her, the situation was almost unbearable. But I never saw them. She always seemed to be with Candis.

Then word came that somebody had poisoned Candis Wilkes up in Baxter County. She died instantly at thirty-four years of age. Lila was torn up.

Just before Candis died, I started seeing Duke hanging around in our neighborhood. Duke was the husband of my cousin Bracey. When he saw me in the yard, he would stop and speak, but he never got out of his car. I didn't pay much attention to him.

One evening he stopped in front of Lila's house. She, Gwendene, and Nitta Blackmon got in the car, and they were all drinking. I went on about my business and thought no more about it until after Candis's funeral. That evening they were all partying again in front of Lila's house, and I had a suspicion that one of them was messing around with Duke. The indications all led directly toward Lila.

On another evening, I was coming back from buying kerosene for my lamps, and Duke stopped as I was passing the corner by Pa Jack's old café. He gave me a ride to my house and offered me a cold beer. I didn't see anything wrong with taking the beer. When he put me out of the car, I watched as he went on down to Lila's house. She and her friends got in the car with him and left.

The next morning, Little Freddy came knocking on my door just before I left for work. He asked if he could leave his clothes in my house for the day. Not aware of the whole truth behind his request, I allowed it.

I learned later that Lila had married Butternut and was moving in with him. Butternut was in love with her—she had his old nose wide open, as the word was. Then I learned from my friend Vonnie that Lila had married Butternut to get rid of Little Freddy. She didn't really want Butternut; it was Duke she wanted, but she was using Butternut to get him.

I recall thinking about what Scripture says: what we bind on earth will be bound in heaven, and what we loose on the earth will be loosed in heaven. Candis was dead. Little Freddy was rejected. Lila was married to the wrong man. I knew that was the beginning of sorrow for all who had come against me. Even in my sin, I was hearing from the Lord.

Halloween was a really spooky night that year. I got my baby and I inside early. It was just cold enough for a nice fire. My little girl Rejetta had just plain moved in with my parents. James C and Pappie brought her to my house, and when the boys left, she took off with them. "Bye, Haley," she would say. "See you later, alligator."

I was off from work the rest of the week, and I was expecting to stay home and enjoy my baby. But a knock came upon my door. It was Delta. I knew she had something big to tell me—one thing for sure, she didn't want any part of me in a social way. And I didn't mind giving her another ass-whipping if I needed to.

She was civil. "Gurl, you know you got it lookin good in here, an dis damn fire feel so good! You heard bout dat O'Bera? She up dere in de county hospital, and de doctor done gave her up."

"Naw, Delta, you de first one I heard it from. Are you real or you just jokin?"

"Naw, I ain't neither. She is. Dey say she dyin. Her whole body is mortified inside. Dat mean her whole system is toxic."

I tried to feel sympathy for O'Bera, but I couldn't. My heartbeat increased as I tried to feel something, but there was no remorse, nothing. Candis had not been two months buried, and now her instigating buddy O'Bera was about to join her. I very clearly the night she humiliated me in front of all my schoolmates: "Well, a virgin is a woman dat ain't never had a man's dick. An if I had as many jives in my eyes dat you done had dicks in your ass, I would be blind as de blind man dat passed de fish market an said, 'Good morning to all you ladies.'"

Those words would never leave my memory, and neither would she. I read somewhere that you can't cut a man up and not draw blood, but Candis, Lila, and O'Bera cut me many times. God knows they cut me into pieces. Only my blood spilled inside, leaving barely enough to keep my heart pumping. I believe I was glad she was dying. It might sound wrong or even cruel, feeling the way I did, but it was not unknown to God.

During that entire weekend, the weather was cloudy, chilly, cold, and bleak. It rained nonstop. I could feel in my spirit there was something happening. No one else seemed to know about it except me. It was like the world was coming to an end.

Mama said she was going up to the hospital to see Mrs. O'Bera. I had an urge to go too. I wanted to see for myself what everybody was saying: that she was dying, that she looked like a skeleton, that she lay in a fetal position, that her eyes was rolled back in her head, that she was chewing like she was eating food.

When we arrived at the hospital, we met Cousin Sattie Bell and her sister Hassy coming out of O'Bera's room. They were both teary-eyed. Cousin Sattie Bell said, "Little Haley, always right wit your ma. You go on in. O'Bera gone. Ain't no more nobody kin do for er."

We walked up to O'Bera's bed. I never witnessed anyone so pitiful. She didn't look like the O'Bera who had harassed me on every corner. She was dried up to skin on top of bones. Her jaw was sunken, and the bones were revealed. What on earth had happened to this woman?

My mother looked down with tears on her face. I wondered if she knew the terrible things O'Bera had said about me and to me. I never said an unkind word about O'Bera to my mama, because they were distant cousins, and my mother was nothing but love.

As for me, I stood over O'Bera's bed and wished for her to die. I prayed that God would take her out of that misery.

Suddenly, words came from O'Bera's mouth: "Git dem babies out of my mouth." I was not quite sure what she was saying. Some, including Mama, translated every word. Mama commented softly, "Lord, she eaten every one of dem dere babies she done done erway wit."

We left the hospital, and a rainstorm appeared out of nowhere. Hard rain fell, and big chunks of hail. It was frightening, like nothing I had witnessed. It lasted for over an hour. We had to wait out the bad weather. The news was being discussed by the time we arrived at

Mama's house. "Mrs. O'Bera Walters," as Daddy put it, "done kicked de bucket."

I went on to my house and was surprised to find Little Freddy there. He had moved in with me. I didn't know how to handle him; he was much more advanced than I was.

***

Mr. Lester Doore, the mailman, came up to my door and reminded me of the day he knocked on our door down on Rat Row, saving my little sister's life. I didn't expect the kind of blessing he was delivering on that day. He said Dorothy Kingsley had sent him. He was seeking someone to look after his mother, who was coming home from the hospital. She'd had major surgery up in Thomasville, Georgia.

At that time, soon after Vermont's birth, I had no regular job. I accepted the position to look after Mrs. Doore, and I began work that same evening. I had to be at her house when the ambulance arrived with her.

Due to my working, I was not able to attend O'Bera's funeral, much as I wanted to. The good Lord didn't see fit for me to attend. Everyone who went said it was a sad day for her family, especially O'Bera's baby girl. She was only eight years old. Cousin Sattie Bell took in her sister's children and raised them as her own. She loved them as if she had given birth to them.

The awful storm that came up so suddenly on the day of O'Bera's passing was nothing compared to the day of her funeral. It seemed like a tornado came up out of nowhere. Sharp lightning and loud thunder were all over town, like I had never heard before. The mourners were not able to leave the church until the weather ceased. Mama said it was like a fireball from hell. We always recognized the work of God whenever it rained or stormed. Nothing was allowed to move in our house. We learned to fear the almighty God.

Candis Wilkes died and O'Bera Walters died, but my pain never died. I feel it every day. But I do believe in my heart that one day it too shall pass.

***

Blessings were coming from all directions, and so was the devil.

My new job was an answer to my prayers. I was paid twenty-one dollars a week, and that was good money back then. It brought me more and more enemies.

Mrs. Doore was a short, chunky white woman with beautiful white hair. Mr. Lester told me that many people had encouraged him not to pay me but two dollars and fifty cents a day. He was a humble, kind, and Christian man. I worked seven day a week and was never late. I cooked three full meals every day for Mrs. Doore. I cleaned her house and washed her clothes. She and I were friends. Mr. Lester was her only child, and she loved him as much as he loved her. It was easy to see where Mr. Lester inherited his kind demeanor from.

One day, my baby had come down with a bad cold, and I was about thirty minutes late for work. Mrs. Doore's strength had increased, and with it, her attitude had hardened. When I arrived, she treated me as coldly as her worst enemy. I explained to her my reason for being late, but she wouldn't understand.

I made her breakfast just as she liked it. I made sure everything was in order. While she was eating, I went into the bathroom and said a silent prayer. When she finished, I asked her to tell me why she was so different toward me. She didn't hesitate to say she'd had a phone call from someone who told her I was a thief. I was nothing but a drunk, and I was overcharging Mr. Lester for working for her.

Jealousy is just what the Word says it is—as cruel as the grave.

I asked her if she had ever missed anything in her house. Had she seen me come to work drunk? And if she didn't want me to be paid the salary I was being paid, then she should cut my hours and my days.

She looked at me and said, "That wouldn't be right. Who will take care of me if we did that?"

"I don't know. What I do know is dat I'm gittin paid for de long hours I work. Whoever called up here is somebody dat hate me and is jealous of de money dat I make. But I earn every dime."

She looked me up and down and then told me to give her a big hug.

She had tears in her eyes. She asked me to open the closet door in the living room and pull out a big box. She went through it and gave me a soft feather mattress, bedspreads, sheets, and pillowcases. They were beautifully handmade. She apologized and pleaded with me not to leave. She also set out to find who the witch was that made that phone call to a sick seventy-nine-year-old lady.

She didn't stop until she found proof. It was Delta and Mary Ann. Even I was surprised. And Mrs. Doore did not let them off the hook—she had them arrested on the word of an old lady that she was being harassed.

She continued to make tremendous progress. Her operation had been for colon cancer. The doctors got as much of the cancer as they could, and estimated that she had eight to ten months to live. She took each day as it came. I stayed on for another three weeks after the time of our original agreement was up. Then the Doores were going on a three-week vacation, so they let me go.

On my last day of work, Mr. Lester gave me a ride home and said he had already gotten me another job. I had an interview with Mrs. Webster, Judge Brake's daughter. I had had a dream about working for her, and in fact she gave me the job. I started work for them the next day. God kept proving himself to me. Even then, everything the enemy meant for evil, God turned to my good.

I worked five days from eight until two, and was paid fifteen dollars a week. The new schedule meant my children and I were able to get back in church.

And when we went to church, we were really dressed for church. We looked *good*. I changed my membership from the Mount Pentecostal Church of God to Greater New Salem Baptist Church, and I attended faithfully. I didn't serve because I feared the Lord. I was fornicating. I didn't know how to even get myself out of all the sin I had gotten myself into.

I wanted so much to do right and live right, but sin was ever-present. Little Freddy was becoming a headache. He was living with me and doing anything he was big enough to do. I was so blinded with love, I couldn't do anything about it. My drinking got worse. One drink and I was drunk. My life was spinning out of control right before my face.

***

I had been working for the Websters for maybe three or four months, and Mrs. Webster was very pleased with my work. She never knew the pressure I was under. I had established a good working relationship with her.

One day, I came home and found a note in my door. I hadn't yet picked my babies up from my mother's house. I opened the note and read it. "*Haley, I want to see you. Will you please call me as soon as you get this note? Mrs. Massay.*"

I went over to Nanna B. Brittney's house and phoned Mrs. Massay. She didn't hesitate to tell me what she wanted: "Haley, I need you to come up here if you will and do some ironin for me. My clothes is all piled up, and you know for some reason you bout the only person that kin satisfy me when it comes to your ironin. Will you come up here? I kin come and pick you up if you want me too. Please—I've got a lot I need to talk to you bout."

I could hear she was serious. I wondering where Mrs. Louisa was, but I didn't have time to think about her. All I knew was I could go up and do Mrs. Massay's ironing, which meant more money for me and my babies.

I told her yes, to come and get me, and in ten minutes she was there. Those jealous-hearted niggers Delta and Millie Mae were standing out nosying. They watched as I got in Mrs. Massay's station wagon. Her daughter Sandra Lyn was with her. She was delighted to see me.

I ironed from three o'clock to seven, and she gave me six dollars. When I finished, she and I sat down for a drink. I had a Coke and she had her coffee. She asked why I hadn't called her. She said she had been by many times, looking for me, and had left several messages with a heavyset, short girl down the street. I told her no one had given me any message from her.

She made herself plain. "Haley, I want you to come back and work for me. The kids miss you. I just got to be honest with you: I was wrong, but we all learned from our mistakes. I fired that woman Louisa, and I really need you to come back."

I didn't hold any ill feeling toward her for looking after her family during my pregnancy. I got along just fine. But I couldn't work for both her and the Websters, and I turned her down. "You know I work for Mrs. Webster now."

"Yeah, I do know, but you just gonna have to quit. I got to know something, though—is you planning on having more young'uns?"

"No, I do not."

"I'm glad to hear that. You don't need to keep having young'uns with no husband."

That was one thing we both agreed to 100 percent. I didn't want more children. I hadn't wanted the ones I had, but now that I had them, I loved them more than anything in the world.

I was torn between the two white women. I didn't know what to do. I wanted to say to Mrs. Massay, "No, I can't," but something wouldn't allow me to.

I thought of my sister Tise and suggested, "Now, Mrs. Massay, I can't quit workin for de lady and come back to you just like dat. I know my sister need a job. I'll tell her to come up dere and work for you."

"Naw, Haley I want you. You know the house and how I like everything to be. The children know and like you as much as I do. Come back and work for me, and let Tise go work for Mrs. Webster."

I tried everything I could to convince her to let Tise work for her, at least for two weeks while I gave Mrs. Webster my notice. But she would not hear of it. We came to the agreement that I would come back to her and Tise would go work for Mrs. Webster. To be honest, I thought that was a good idea.

At the time, I enjoyed the situation. I was a black gal from Rat Row, and here I had this white woman begging me to come back and work for her. I really loved Mrs. Massay and her children. I knew white folk had feelings, and that she loved me too. But my feelings were also ripped between two people who needed me. That was not a easy decision to make. Both women had my children's welfare at heart—but Mrs. Webster didn't have any children herself, and that made the difference.

I called Tise. She was willing to go work for Mrs. Webster. Then I phoned Mrs. Webster.

The phone rang twice and she answered. "Hello, this is the Websters' residence. Virginia Webster speaking."

"Mrs. Webster, this is Haley. I'm sorry to be calling you so late, but I have a little problem that couldn't wait until morning."

"That's all right, Haley. I told you, anytime you need me, just call. Is the kids all right?"

"Yeah, ma'am, they fine. I wanted to let you know Mrs. Massay wants me to come back and work for her, and I decided to go back. But I have you a good housekeeper that kin come and work for you. She will work just as good and hard as I did."

Mrs. Webster was not pleased. Silence struck for a moment. Then her voice changed, and she said, "You mean you gon quit workin for me and go back to Massay? Why, Haley? Haven't I been good to you? Don't I pay you enough money?"

"Mrs. Webster, you been real good to me, but I feel that I owe Mrs. Massay. Both of y'all been good to me, but she got chilluns that need me too. But my sister is just as good as I is, and if you give her a chance, y'all see."

"This is very disturbin to me. I never expected this. When do you plan on makin this transition?"

I didn't know what the word *transition* was, so I placed my hand over the mouthpiece and asked Mrs. Massay. She said, "It means to change over from one place to another one, like you bout to do."

I said to Mrs. Webster calmly but not cheerfully, given what I was doing, "Well, tomorrow, Mrs. Webster. Mrs. Massay wants me to start tomorrow. I already talked to my sister. She said she kin be up dere to your house at seven thirty fore you leave. I'll tell her all bout what you like an how you like it done. Mrs. Webster, I promise she'll do just like I would."

"Haley, I don't like this short notice. Well, you kin tell your sister

I really do need somebody, so I'll give her a chance—but I won't forgit this." And she hung up.

White folk did not like to lose to a Negro. If she had fired me, it would have been fine, but I made the decision. She didn't like that. She was disappointed, but there was nothing she could do about it. The two white women had words over me, but I ended up going back to Mrs. Massay.

Tise started to work for Mrs. Webster the following day. I was glad to be back in Mrs. Massay's house. It was like my own, and I was a part of her family.

I was vacuuming the den when Mr. Boyd Bellford came home for lunch. He had an unusual look about him. I didn't know what it meant, but it made me very uncomfortable. I ran over the carpet right fast and went off to the living room. I vacuumed the carpet there, then bent over to unplug the vaccum. My butt was up toward the hallway. When I stood and turned, there he was in the doorway. He was smiling, with his wallet in his hand. I was astounded. I said, "Oh! Mr. Boyd, do you want me to do something?"

"Yes, I do, matter of fact," he answered. He stood square in the doorway, making it impossible for me to get by without touching him. I said, "Excuse me, Mr. Boyd." Then he pressed past me, his elbow brushing against my breast.

I didn't pay it much attention because he was a white man. I put the vacuum in the closet, shut the door, and returned to the kitchen, preparing to do the lunch dishes. He followed me and stood up behind me at the sink. I could feel his eyes all over me.

I turned the water off and said, kind of panicky, "Mr. Boyd, if you don't need me to do nothing, I'll just go outside and hang out the clothes that's in the washer." And before he could answer, I dashed for the back door.

The phone was ringing, and he said, "All right, Haley, go right ahead. I got a few more minutes." He was still smiling as he reached for the phone.

I had hung up most of the clothes when he called me to the phone. Mrs. Massay wanted to speak to me. Kateleen was waking up, so he handed me the receiver and went to get her. Once I hung the phone up, Mr. Boyd told me he wanted me to do something for him—but he would tell me about it later.

***

I had been working for the Bellfords for over six months, feeling right at home. My job, life, and children were good, and I was in church every Sunday. I even stopped drinking. It appeared that my life was on the right track.

On Mrs. Massay's off days, she would go out of town to shop, and she always included my two girls. They already got all of Kateleen's outgrown clothes. They were not lacking for anything.

But my love life was a trigger point. Everything had come out about Lila and her so-called marriage to Butternut. She and Duke had moved in together and opened up a place they called the Art Juke Joint across from where Butternut lived.

Worse was yet to come. The Fourth of July wasn't far away, and people were coming home from all different directions. My feelings for Little Freddy were changing daily. Something was happening, and the signs all pointed to Theola. I didn't care about what he did or who he saw, but I did care about his well-being. She hated Little Freddy, and even then I could see her mojo working.

At work, Kateleen was my priority. At Mrs. Webster's house, I had been able to sleep for a couple of hours every day, yet get my work done before she and Mr. Webster came home for lunch. At Mrs. Massay's, I couldn't sleep. I had to make sure Kateleen was taken care of every minute.

On the Friday before the Fourth of July, after the cafés were closed up in town, everybody headed out to a place in the country we just called "the shack." Sheila Ann and I got a ride with the butt boys—guys who just wanted somebody to ride with them. They didn't have sense enough to try propositioning a woman.

We arrived at the shack around eight, and it was jumping. Sheila Ann was dating RB and they had drinks in his car. His friend Nicholas

Anthony had accompanied RB, so I joined them. In the mood he was in, I could pull anything out of Nicholas Anthony that I wanted to know. RB reminded me that I would only be causing trouble if I messed around with Nicholas Anthony, because that's who Millie Mae was going around with. Regardless, I stuck with Nicholas Anthony.

I learned someone had convinced my cousin Bracy that I was dating her husband Duke, while all the time it was Lila. Most of the town folk had migrated to Lila and Duke's café, leaving Butternut in a frail state. He hated the way Lila had used him to get rid of Little Freddy and make room for Duke. But meantime, I had been made the scapegoat. I had too much respect for Cousin Bracy to do anything like what people said.

Lila claimed she wanted to make up to me for all the pain she, her deceased friends, and her sister had inflicted on me. She befriended me, and I didn't have the sense of a gopher to know it was a setup. She would persuade me to sit with her, play tonk, and drink. My drinking became astonishing. There were times I would go in there and have only one drink, but nonetheless come staggerring out like a man who had drunk a gallon of whiskey.

One day I had a drink with Lila, and as soon as I drank it down, it came speeding back up. It would not stay in my stomach. I made it to Mama's house and sat on the back porch.

My daddy came out and lit directly into me without hesitation. "I thought you did have a little sense. Every time I look around, you got your nose stuck up Lila's damn ass. She don't like you, never have and never will. When a bitch don't like you, dey won't never like you. Right now, if I was to take your brains out of your head and put em in dat bird's head, I bet you dat damn bird would fly backward."

I was so drunk and sick, I didn't care what my father thought of me right then. When I got stable-minded, Daddy and Little Freddy schooled me on the type of women I was up against. They were older, more experienced, and as evil as a rattlesnake curled up to strike.

But I was too blind to understand. I wanted to be needed or accepted. I was naive or just outright stupid.

Apparently my father and Little Freddy had other conversations on the subject, because Little Freddy came into town on Riff Groves's chemical truck one day and demanded I stay away from Lila and Millie Mae. He insisted they were my enemies. I asked, "Why would dey hate me? I never did anythin to em."

"I kin give you three reasons. Cause of me, number one. Cause you got my baby, number two. And cause you look better dan both of dem ugly bitches, number three. Is dat enough reason for you? I thought you had a little sense, but I see now you ain't got a damn bit. Do I need to go on? Or do I got to watch your every move? Haley, babe, *dey don't like you*. Can you git dat through your thick head? You shouldn't trust not a one of dem bald-headed witches, and old Delta neither. Dey all is settin you up. Long as you wit me, I got you covered, but what bout de times I'm not around? Haley, listen to me, babe. Stay way from dem dirty whores."

I think that day Little Freddy became my protecter. He was so sincere.

***

I was over at my mother's house, watching the drunks go in and out. Daddy had turned the house into a gambling house, just like our old house on Rat Row. Having to leave my babies there every day was my main concern. I was not about to let my children grow up in that environment. Marcus Mac J had taken over as the biggest moonshine seller on the block. But Marcus only sold; he didn't let the drunks hang around his house. So they would come and wallow in their drunkenness at our house.

On this day, a guy came in. He and Daddy seemed to know each other. Daddy asked him, "When did you come home?"

He said, "We got in last night."

"You still livin in New Jersey?"

"Yeah, we still livin there. Who dis pretty young lady?"

"Dat's my oldest daughter, Haley."

"I know Tise, Passy Kate, and Gemmy BB, but I don't know Haley."

"She was a little old thing when you left town. Muster been round ten or eleven."

"Hey, Haley, I'm Rocky. You kin call me Rock. I got to go up to Neck Town, but I'll be back around six. I'd like to take you and Sheila out on the town and show y'all a good time."

Rocky came back just as he promised he would. He gave Sheila and I a great time. I also discovered he had a strong antipathy for Little Freddy. The two of them hated each other; there was no love lost.

***

My life was spiraling out of control again. I worked every weekday, and I partied on the weekends like each one would be my last.

I was cleaning on a cold winter day, only a few days before Christmas, when Mr. Boyd came home early from work. I noticed that mysterious look about him I'd seen before. This time I was more brave and bold; I wasn't uneasy.

He put more wood on the fire, and when he finished, he passed me. I smelled alcohol. He had been drinking. He went into his bedroom and quickly came out again. I went into Sandra Lyn's room to finish cleaning, and I came out, he was standing at the end of the hall. His wallet was in his hand.

I froze in my tracks. He whispered, "Don't be frightened, Haley. Come here. I don't bite." He held his wallet out, and it was packed with money.

I was broke. I didn't know what to think or what he was up to. All sorts of ideas starting clamoring in my head.

It's a setup.

Git the money.

Don't touch it.

That's a white man.

Oh Lord, what in the world was happening to my life? I looked at him and at the money in the wallet, calling out for me to take it.

"Take what you want out of it," Mr. Boyd said. "And I can get what I want."

I felt possessed by some type of evil spirit. Why was he challenging me?

Something inside of me blanked. Then I was pulling out twenty-dollar bills. I took five. He asked, "Is that all you want?"

I quickly backed away and said, my head hanging down, "What you want from me? It don't feel right, me takin money from you."

I needed that money. At that moment, I believed it was a gift from God.

Mr. Boyd placed his wallet in his back pocket. Taking hold of my chin, he lifted my head and said, "It's all right. You haven't done nothin wrong. You don't have to do anythin for the money. I know we don't pay you for all the work you do. I just want you to have what you need for you and your babies."

He was smiling like he had just gotten off on me taking money from his wallet. Before he walked away, he said sincerely, "You know, just between you and I, black folk have far more fun than white do."

That was the day we became friends. We both had a secret.

I was still thanking him for the money when Mrs. Massay called and said she was coming home early. She had something urgent she wanted to discuss with me. When she arrived, I went to the kitchen table and sat with her. She said, "Oh, Haley, everything looks real good—all nice and clean. Now, listen to me for a minute. I have this marvelous idea."

I gave her my undivided attention. She was more excited than for Christmas.

She said, "There is this new protection out now for women to prevent them from gettin pregnant. It's called the Loop, and I already set up an appointment with Dr. Carlton for you. He is going to insert it in you. It cost thirty-five dollars, but I'm gonna pay for it so you don't need to concern yourself none bout the money. I got it. Go on up there. It will only take bout ten minutes, and then just take the rest of the day off."

I was not pleased about her setting up an appointment for me to have a procedure done without discussing it with me. But it didn't take me long to adjust to the idea that she was only doing what was best for me. I realized that I was a single, unwed mother with no skills in life. I didn't want to sound ungrateful, though I also didn't want to jump into something I might regret later. Even so, I was unlearned, and she was a registered nurse.

I went to the appointment. Dr. Carlton demonstrated the insertion beforehand and assured me everything would be all right. Everything he said would happen did happen, and in thirty minutes it was over. Still, for some reason I knew deep down in my heart that I would never be the same again. Leaving his office, all that was on my mind was to get to my two babies as fast as I could.

I picked them up from Mama's house and brought them home with me. Little Freddy was at our house. He demanded to know where I had been. I explained to him the procedure I'd had done. He was astonished, even speechless. He really didn't believe it. I showed him the booklet with all the instructions in it as proof. It was satisfactory to him.

But it wasn't to me. Two weeks later, I began to have severe cramps in the lower part of my stomach. My cycle came, flowing heavily. I could tell it was different from normal, and it lasted for weeks. I was losing my strength, and my eyes started to get blurry.

When Mr. Boyd came for me one day, he noticed that something was wrong with me. I was staggering like a drunk person. "What's wrong with you, Haley? You have such a scowlin look about you. Is you in pain?"

"Yes, sir." I hardly could talk.

He suggested I stay at home, and he would take Kateleen to his mother.

I went back to the doctor, and he removed the Loop. It left me with a terrible infection.

Chapter 20: Lost Soul

Buster and Tise had set a moving date. He was to leave for New Hampshire in three days to find a job and somewhere to live. Then he would send back for Tise and the children.

Tise and Lora Lake had become best of friends, so they got together and planned a surprise going-away party for Buster. It was held at Chloe Spikes's apartment. I was not in the mood for a party, nor did I have any intention of attending. Buster was not one of my favorite people, and with the Loop complications, I was going through a terrible time.

I had let Sheila move in with me. She was having problems with her mother, Mrs. Angie Rosa. Sheila had had a baby young, and it really put a damper on their relationship. I was letting her live with me for a few weeks until she made other arrangements. Around seven o'clock, I was already lying down, not feeling my best. Sheila came home from taking her daughter Terleda to Mrs. Angie Rosa and was getting dressed for the party. She insisted on me getting up and coming with her.

I didn't want to go. I was not led to go. And when I look back on that night, I know it was the Holy Spirit urging me not to go. But I hadn't yet learned that obedience was better than sacrifices. So Sheila convinced me to go, reminding me it was for my sister, not Buster.

I got up and dressed in a beautiful pantsuit Mrs. Massay had given me. When I looked in the mirror, I had to admit I was looking real good. I was sure to make some others jealous. But I couldn't get the thought completely out of my mind that something unpleasant was going to happen.

We arrived at the party around nine thirty. It was rocking. The dance floor was full. I stood back and watched, and then made my way to the kitchen. They were serving all kinds of good food and booze. Everybody was having a good time. Folk had come from everywhere. Some I knew and some were strangers, but I knew who liked me and who didn't. I believe it was that night I acknowledged that I was not a likable person. Even so, I didn't understand why some who didn't like me were the ones who grinned in my face the most. I didn't like phoniness.

Lora Lake was one of them, always the comedian. She never resisted the opportunity to pluck my nerves. She eyeballed me from head to toe because I was a size five and she was a size twenty-five. She was a friend to my sister but an enemy of mine. I was cool. I kept a very low profile until she gave me a sneaky grin and asked, "Haley, what you gon do bout Little Freddy? Is you gon help git him out of jail?"

I was too astonished to react. I didn't know that he was in jail until that moment. "Is Little Freddy for real in jail, Lora Lake?"

"Yeah! You mean you didn't know?"

"Naw, I didn't know. How you know?"

"Cause my brother Oscar come by de house dis mornin an said he got locked up Thursday night for beatin up Tiff Ruffin. Said he beat him so bad, his daddy had to pull em up off of em."

Gossip was her second name, with no division between fiction and nonfiction. I kept my real feelings inside me without giving her a clue. I left her, saying contemptuously, "Oh well, dat's good. Now all dey got to do is throw away de key."

I wanted to get to the bathroom and get a deep breath. I glanced back and saw them making eyes among themselves. I rushed directly to the nearest whiskey bottle and poured a shot down my throat as fast as I could, hoping it would smooth my feelings for the rest of the night. One drink led to another, but something wouldn't let me have a third. If I had, I would have been beyond impaired.

I was coming out of the bathroom when I heard voices from Chloe Spikes's bedroom. One of them sounded like my brother-in-law, Buster. The other was Sheila Ann. I heard Buster say, "I'll be round dere bout one thirty." I didn't know what to make of it or who was concerned, so I forgot that I even heard anything.

People started to leave. I got a ride with Lora's brother, Oscar. When I got inside my house, I undressed and went to bed. I was awakened around two o'clock. Hell had come alive in my skull. I remember throwing up. I was lying on my back, and someone was in my bed. I was unable to lift my head. The room was spinning. I could hear voices and somebody groaning.

I called out Sheila's name, but she didn't answer. I must have called her several times. Eventually I passed out.

Around four o'clock, I woke again and the bed was shaking. I called, "Sheila, who over dere wit you?"

I still didn't get a response. I managed to sit up. There was wetness, and it smelled like whiskey.

She must have known what I was doing, because she finally answered. "Haley, what you doin?"

"Fixin to light de lamp. I can't see."

She had to let me know that she was not in the bed alone. A guy named Larry Junior was with her. He was getting up.

I was angry. I could smell trouble. I remembered hearing a door shut in the night. Somebody had gone out earlier—or had it been Larry Junior coming in? That didn't make any sense. I recalled somebody in bed with me earlier. What was going on in my house?

I sat on the side of the bed, hungover but no longer impaired. "Larry Junior, you git up and git out of here fore somebody see you coming out of my house and start a damn lie sayin you was in here wit me."

They laughed, and that angered me more. "What the hell so g—— d—— funny?" I asked harshly. "And who went out my g—— d—— door in de middle of de night?"

I didn't get an answer, so I threatened to put Sheila out along with Larry Junior. Then she said, sly and innocent, "Haley, it was Buster."

"Buster who, Sheila?"

"Buster."

"What! What the hell Buster doing in my house dat time of the damn morning? And how did he git in?"

Then I remembered: I had heard him and Sheila making plans to meet. "Sheila, what was Buster doing here?" I demanded.

I got up, made my way to the lamp, and lit it. She was covered up in the bed. I ordered her to get up. She was silent. I turned around and stepped on a piece of glass. It caused a deep gash in my left foot. I was so devastated by what was happening, I didn't really feel the hurt. But I could feel the blood pouring from the open wound.

A lamp globe had been broken. I sat back down on the side of the bed and pulled the glass from my foot. My head felt like someone had struck me a blow that knocked all the sense out.

Sheila was now sitting up in her bed, and the look on her face frightened me. I demanded again, "What was Buster doin in my house?"

When she answered, I knew she was lying. "He came here to see if you had any whiskey. Me and Larry Junior had just laid down when he came. I let him in an he came in and stood by the dresser. He said that he didn't want to go home cause he wasn't through partying. Everwhere he been, nobody had anything to drink, so he decided to come by here. I dozed off to sleep an I don' know what happen after then."

I turned to Larry Junior and calmly asked him, "What happen after Sheila Ann went to sleep?"

He fumbled with his words. "I-I-I d-dozed off m-m-myself."

Day was breaking. Larry Junior left, and I had to get dressed for work. Mr. Boyd would be coming within an hour. I hoped the day would be over rapidly.

I brooded over the situation at work, sitting alone while the kids were playing. The pieces just didn't add up. I could feel in my heart that something was terribly wrong, and we all were the ones who were going to be hurt the most from it.

I felt as if I were the lowest slut that I had ever been called. I felt like I was the dirtiest person on earth. And for what reason? I still didn't know. I dreaded having to pass through the neighborhood with everyone staring and whispering about me behind my back.

I was in luck in that respect, at least. Mr. Boyd offered to take me home. The kids wanted to ride too/ Sandra Lyn was always so cheerful, and she always had the right words to say to me. But that day, nothing she could say made me feel better.

I found Tise sitting on my porch, waiting for me. Tears steadily flowed down her face. I said to myself, "Oh no!" I knew she was hurt, but from what?

I started to unlock the door, and she said softly, "Haley, you are my sister. Tell me it's not true. Tell me you didn't do what I heard. I just have to know."

My mouth flew wide open. I tried to speak, but I didn't have any words for her. I was that ashamed, and I didn't know why.

As I turned the key to unlock the door, I moticed everyone in the neighborhood was out. I saw Millie Mae's big, pregnant belly before I saw the rest of her.

Trembling, I managed to get inside. The unmade bed stared me in the face. I looked down to see the broken glass and my blood on the floor. It all started coming back to me. I commenced to moving around the room, explaining to Tise my version of what happened.

In walked Sheila. The moment I spotted her, all the dirt came flushing out of my mind. It was not hard to put the missing puzzle pieces together. I said in humiliation and grief, "It was you! It was you! Buster came round here to meet you in *my house*! I heard him say he would be somewhere around one thirty. I didn't know what he meant then, but I do now! He got here, and Larry Junior had beat him to it. Bitch, you knew all along that's what happened. You was going to trick with Buster! I give you a roof over your head and this is how you repay me? You did this. *You did this*!"

"Wait a minute now!" she cried. "I didn't tell Buster to come up here, and I didn't tell him to git in your bed while you was drunk. But nothing happen! You woke up!"

"Is that pose to make it all right? Look at my sister, Sheila! Just look at her! I want you to git you clothes and git the hell out of my g—— d—— house right now!"

She tried to explain with more lies, but it was a little too late for her. Thanks be to God, the story had been revealed right in front of my sister, and she knew it was the honest truth. She also knew me, and that

I would never do anything so sluttish. We had a good conversation. We knew we could get through the rumor together, and we did.

When she left, she was satisfied. And she made me a promise: the moment Buster sent back for her and the children, I could come too and make a life for me and my kids.

***

I had something positive to look forward to. I went to Mama's for my children, head held high.

Surprisingly, Little Freddy was there. He had just been released from jail. I knew the moment I looked at him that the rumor had reached his ears. He wasn't angry. He was very honest with me as we talked about the story, and he believed me. He knew that I would never do anything so contrary to my sister, and he knew the ones who spread that gossip were my haters. He described how he put Millie Mae and Delta in their places and told them both off, leaving them empty.

Little Freddy certainly was not one to deliberately hurt someone else's feelings. Undoubtedly he had his flaws, but he also had intellect and wisdom. The talk he gave me was more educational than the high school diploma that I never received, and he was on my side 100 percent. I was encouraged by him. He was good for my self-esteem, which had dropped to damn near zero. Especially when he put his hand across my face and rubbed it like I would do for my babies. He promised me things were going to be different.

Our favorite song to dance to was "You Really Got a Hold on Me," and we danced to it that night. If those women didn't hate me before, I knew they did then when they saw Little Freddy singing softly in my ear.

I felt comfortable with him after that. I was very content. That night he moved back in with me, and it was him and me against the whole town.

***

Little Freddy was good friends with the sisters Canora and Aroanna.

They were beautiful women, both older than I was. They had grown up with him. I became good friends with them through him. Canora was very much a people person, but Aroanna was more like I was—she didn't give a damn. She had just separated from her husband, Bonky Blackmond.

Tise left for New Hampshire on a sunny fall Saturday afternoon. In some ways, I was delighted for her to go, but in many ways I was sorry. Tise was my mentor, someone I looked up to, and now she was gone. Little Freddy and I shared a lot of love, and I was getting good treatment from him, but I knew it was not going to last. I enjoyed the ride for as long as it lasted, but I could feel something was missing, and it didn't take a genius to know what that was.

Gradually, things changed. We argued about stupid stuff, things I had no knowledge of. And other things were happening around me.

Canora knew more about Lila and her friend Gwendene. It appeared that Lila was the cause of Gwen and her husband Wallace breaking up. Wallace was brother to Rocky, and there was no love lost between them. Canora warned me that if Little Freddy and I had some back and forth, Lila was probably behind it. And now Butternut didn't like Little Freddy because of the women they had shared. All hell was knocking at my door, and Little Freddy was in and out of jail.

I was coming home one day, walking by Lila and Duke's place. Lila stopped me, and I ended up drinking and playing cards with her. Before long, I was stone drunk.

Lila supplied me with all the booze I could drink and was killing me at the same time. Unknown to me, I was in grave danger. The roots were working in the enemy's favor. Lila knew how to butter me up with kindness.

Little Freddy had been in jail for over a month. Lila told me people were laughing at me; I was the joke of the town. She poured me drinks, and I didn't know what I was drinking. Drinking with the enemy was my weakness. I had become dependent on Lila, and she was becoming more and more of an alcoholic.

I was drinking with Lila on a Friday evening with her friend Gale. They laughed and called me Miss Little Freddy. I didn't have sense enough to know they were making fun of me. I looked up, and there stood Little Freddy. He demanded I get up and come home with him. He strongly disapproved of what I was doing, and his facial expression said so.

He and I got into a heated argument, and it was not nice. I wouldn't stop running off at the mouth, making all sorts of accusations that had no meaning. Whiskey won't let you keep quiet—it makes you lie and cry. We broke up that night.

Weeks later, word was he was dating Lora Hornet. Maybe I drove him to her, or maybe he was already doing her and it was just time for it all to come out. I was as foolish as Mr. Vinegar in the folk tale. He started off with gold and traded the it for a cow, traded that for a bagpipe, and traded that for a stupid stick. When he realized he only had a stick to take home to his wife, he sat under a tree, wondering what he was going to say. A little bird was up in the tree and called him foolish. Mr. Vinegar threw the stick at the bird, and had to go home with nothing. That was how I was feeling: a fool with nothing.

During this time, I was alone, with no one to share my life with or tell my troubles to. But I remembered that I had the Lord, no matter what. I could always turn to God, and I did.

***

One Monday, I was at work and the phone rang. I answered, and it was Millie Mae. The moment I heard her voice, I knew it was nothing good. "Yeah, Millie Mae, what you want?"

"I call to ask you, did you know where Little Freddy is?"

"Naw, Millie Mae, I don't know where Little Freddy is. But I know you is dyin to tell me."

"I figured you didn't, cause de law got him shortly after your boss man came and picked you up for work."

"Okay, Millie Mae, thanks for tellin me."

"Lila told me to tell you to stop by on your way home," she added.

I hung the phone up, feeling insulted. I thought I could handle the devil, but I had forgotten what the Good Book says: "Wisdom is the principal thing; therefore get wisdom: and with all thy getting get understanding" (Prov. 4:7). I had gotten so rooted in sin, I didn't think there was any hope left for me. I certainly didn't have any. It was the devil's time with me.

Chapter 21: It's Time to Leave

When I give my life to the Lord, good things always happen.

I hadn't been to church in a while, so I took my girls and we returned to God's house at Greater New Salem. It felt so good. I felt so much peace within myself. It didn't take me long to realize this prescription would renew my strength. After being out of church for so long, I had started to believe that God wanted nothing to do with me.

I will always remember the sermon that Rev. Conley preached from John 14:1–7: "Let not your heart be troubled." He preached it like he was preaching directly to me. I rededicated myself to the Lord with all intentions of never turning my back on God again.

When the preacher shook my hand, he said, "God bless you, my daughter. You made a wise decision. Stay with God, and he will stay with you." No one in that church knew how grieved my heart was that Sunday, but I do believe the man of God did. When his hand touched mine, the grip was different from any other hand I shook that day.

I attended every Sunday for months without missing, until the weekend when everyone was saddened. News spread that J. R. Hayward, who fathered one of Tise's daughters, had been killed somewhere up north.

I sat down to write to Tise about that and the death of another man we both knew, Bud Cleaver. I had no intention of seeking anything from her, only informing her. But as I was writing, I felt an emptiness in my body. I knew I was missing her. Tise had been all I had, and now I felt so alone.

I asked her in the letter if she would send me a ticket to come up to New Hampshire. I promised I would pay her every cent the minute I found myself a job. In each letter I had received from her, she had always reminded me that if I wanted to come up there, she would send for me. That night, I called her on her offer.

A week later, she wrote me back, telling me when to expect the ticket. That made all the difference in my life. There was hope for me at last. I didn't say anything to anyone. I waited for that ticket, and on the day she said it was coming, it arrived just as she said. I make a quality decision to leave that town with everything and everyone in it. That place was evil. The stench of contamination was far more than I needed. Anybody who wanted Little Freddy could have him.

My imagination turned optimistic for the first time since I had become a mother. I had a vision, and it was a positive vision. I knew it would be constructive and beneficial to me and my kids.

I was holding the letter in my hand, and a loud knock came on the door. I knew it was Little Freddy. I knew his knocks. I sat without moving, but the knocking didn't stop. He called out, "Haley, I know you in dere."

I could tell by the sound of his voice that he was intoxicated. When he was like that, all that was on his mind was fornication. I refused to be dominated by him anymore. At one point I thought he was going to break the door in, but I continued to sit silently, still as a mouse. I was not afraid, just tired as any human being could ever be of anyone.

Then came one extra hard knock, and the latch fell to the floor. Little Freddy came in and stood in the center of the floor like he was God's gift to women. He did not like to lose; he had to be the one to call all the shots. He didn't know I had a trick up my sleeve, my one-way ticket out of that hellhole.

"Didn't you hear me knockin?" he demanded. "What de hell you doin, ignorin me or something?"

"Little Freddy, what you want?"

He grabbed me and held me in his arms, squeezing me tightly. I was not amused. I knew he was up to something. I pretended I wanted him as much as he wanted me, knowing that fulfilling those needs was never enough for him. His heart was beating hard, as if he had done something strenuous or guilty.

I was right. The next day, I found out he'd beaten the hell out of Ruthella. I was strong and courageous. I said nothing about what he had done. I was counting the days until I got on that train and out of that town, away from him.

***

It was a cold winter night, the coldest I could remember. The year was 1965, and my baby Vermont was two years old.

Little Freddy was spinning out of control. He came and picked me up from work, and I knew when I saw him he was up to something. I left the kids at my mother's for the night and went home. I made myself a nice fire and heated up the house. I had me a drink or two, bu I was sober enough to see Little Freddy for who he was. I was also drunk enough to play him.

He was not over the humiliation of the way Lila had dumped him. More recently, Theola Knight had met him at Rothy's house. She got in his car with him willingly, but it was a setup. The next day, she had him arrested on a kidnapping charge.

Now I saw another side to Little Freddy I had never noticed before. Nothing could satisfy him. He was a little boy trapped in a man's body. He had what it took to get any woman he wanted, but he was like Peter Pumpkin-Eater, who had a wife and could not keep her. He could not keep his women, and when they walked away from him, he did not take it well. Given that I was planning to leave too, I had to plan carefully.

I don't believe even he knew how messed up he was inside—and so was everyone else who was involved with him. We all were uneducated, unlearned folk, getting by in life on a wing and somebody else's prayers.

I made up my mind that if he put his hands on me again, I was going to do like all the rest of his women seemed to do—put him in jail.

***

My question was, do the sins of the parents fall back on the children if sin is never dealt with? If it is not defeated, sin is passed on to the children. Children are always the ones to get caught in the middle. Husbands disrespect their wives and wives disrespect their husbands, opening the door for adultery, whoremongering, and lying. Before long, all God's commandments have been broken.

I studied the lives of Little Freddy's parents. I remember the day he took me to meet his mother. I didn't know where he was taking me. I had met his dad many times, but never his mother.

We drove up in front of a big white house. Little Freddy came around and opened my door, saying, "Come on. Git out."

A woman opened the door of the house. I asked, "Little Freddy, who live here?"

"You'll see," he said, smiling.

"Y'all come on in and have a seat," the woman said.

We sat down in a beautifully decorated living room, and he introduced me. "Mama, this is Haley, your soon-to-be daughter-in-law." He was clearly jiving.

Mrs. Justin smiled and took my hand. "So you are Haley Keath. Little Freddy told me bout you. I'm glad to meet you."

I wondered what on earth he could have told her. Whatever it was, she showed no dislike or lack of welcome. "Same here," I said, feeling very uncomfortable.

After a great visit, I told him I was ready to get back. I had to get my babies. Mrs. Justin asked me, "How many babies you have?"

I answered, "I have two."

"A girl an a boy?"

"No, ma'am. I have two gurls."

Little Freddy said, "One is your grandbaby."

Fearful, I looked at Mrs. Justin. She was still smiling. "When am I goin to see my grandbaby? Bring her by. If you need me to keep her, I'll do that too."

"Yes, ma'am."

Many times after that, one or the other of his parents came to my house for him, but they never came inside.

Still, there was no reason to believe he was raised the way he turned out. That was not his parents' doing. He was too intelligent and respectable. But sin entered when he least expected it, as it did with many of us.

***

Just before my last weekend in that town, there was a tragedy. As the Bible says, the wages of sin is death. This one occurred in a gambling room. An argument occurred. A man pointed a gun in a woman's face. There was a tussle, and the gun discharged, striking Nicholas Anthony between his eyes—a fatal shot at the age of twenty-four. Half the town seemed to have witnessed the shooting. Folk walked away saying, "It could have been me."

I had my time set to get to the train station in Cairo, Georgia. I was ready to say my good-byes to all in that wicked town. I hinted around at work that I was leaving, and one day Mrs. Massay caught on. She asked, "Haley, are you goin somewhere and you ain't told me?"

"Why you ask me dat?"

"Because of the things you been sayin lately."

"Naw, ma'am. It's all just some things I need to git solved in my life."

That Friday night, the cops showed up, looking for Little Freddy. I opened the door to a loud knock. Fonda Junior, the son of the sheriff, was standing there. "Where is he? Do you know where I kin found him?"

"He's sleeping."

"Damn! Little Freddy got all the women. I'd like to know what he do to y'all, that y'all keep lettin him beat the hell out of one and then run to the other one. He beat that gal Ruthella, busted her mouth, and blackened both of her eyes, but here he is, sleepin in your bed."

I stayed out of the way as Fonda Junior went to the bed and gave Little Freddy a hard shake. "Justin, git up! You're under arrest! Git up!"

Little Freddy rose in a daze, not understanding what was happening.

Fonda Junior said, "I got a warrant for your arrest for beating up on Ruthella."

As he was being taking away I never let Little Freddy see me. He was arrested for Ruthella, and also for all the charges Theola had against him. He seemed doomed, but I didn't worry too much. If there was a way to get out of those charges, his parents and bossman would find it.

I had a dream that night like the ones I had in early years of my life. A man came to me and bent over my bed, whispering, "Take your children, get out of this town, and never come back." He quoted Scripture to me, from the gospel of Matthew. It was the story of the angel of the Lord who came to Joseph in a dream in the middle of the night. The angel told him to take Mary and baby Jesus and get out of that town. They had to flee into Egypt because the evil king, Herod, was out to kill him. I knew this was the same man I had seen before in my dreams: the same voice, the same black robe, with a halo over his shoulder.

I woke up in fear, not knowing what the dream portended. It nagged at me over and over. It had a lot to do with me getting out of that town.

It was a good thing I hadn't revealed to Mrs. Massay that I was leaving. I stayed another week to work and get traveling money. I couldn't see what the good Lord was doing for me then, not the way I do now, but he has been favorable to me for many years.

That was a nervous week. I was sure Little Freddy wasn't getting out of jail, but until I was on that train, I worried. I was all hyped up like I was on some strange high. Halfway through the week, I started packing. I wondered how I was going to break my news to Mrs. Massay. She had been so good to me and my kids—I didn't want to disappoint her, but I had no choice. Truthfully speaking, I had come to really love her. She was the only white person that I actually loved. Her daughters Kateleen and Sandra Lyn were favorites with me. I had even won over the oldest, Beth Fran. Oh, how I was going to miss them—but I just couldn't bring myself to tell them I was leaving town for good. Instead, I wrote a letter that Friday afternoon and placed it in Mrs. Massay's top dresser drawer without her knowing.

I went to Butternut and explained my situation to him. I asked how much he would charge to take me to the train station, which was nearly fifty miles away. He was so elated that I was getting away from Little Freddy, he said he would charge me nothing.

My mother was my last stop. All the way to her house, I was in so much pain. But when I got there, the house was running over with gamblers.

Old man Bussey Bell William had lost all his money and was trying to win some of it back before going home. Rolling the dice, he stated, "If dat damn seven fall, I'mo have a damn heart attack."

"Death and life are in the power of the tongue" (Prov. 18:21 KJV). It didn't happen then. But eventually, the seven did fall, and when it did, Bussey Bell fell over dead from a massive heart attack in Marcus Mac J's kitchen. He spoke it, and it came to pass.

Once Mama's house cleared, I took Mama to her room, all the more determined to get my children away from these unfit surroundings. She and I sat down on the side of her bed, and I said to her sadly, "Mama, Tise sent me a train ticket to come to New Hampshire, and tomorrow de kids and I will be leavin on de train."

"You what? You takin de kids? Naw, Haley! You go, but don't take de gurls. Let dem stay here till you git yourself settled in your own place, den come back and git em. Don't take em now." Her words were full of pain, but there was nothing she could have said to make me leave my babies with her. I would have had to have been out of my mind.

I hated having to bring that type of news to her. She loved the girls with every fiber in her body. I did my best to explain my reasons. She understood, but she still hated the idea of me taking my kids.

Finally, in just a few hours, I would be departing. I had all our clothes folded on the bed, and I thought, *I don't even own a suitcase.* The word "luggage" was not in our vocabulary. So I packed our clothes in boxes.

I couldn't just leave and not saying anything to Mrs. Massay, so I phoned her house, hoping one of the girls would answer. Sandra Lyn answered, "Hello?"

"Hello, Sandra Lyn, this Haley. Is Mrs. Massay around?"

"She's taking a shower."

"Okay. Look in your mom's top dresser drawer. I left a letter in it for Mrs. Massay. Please, will you git it out an make sure she gits it?"

"Sure. Haley, why you ain't coming in today?"

"I got to be somewhere. I got to go now, Sandra Lyn. Good-bye."

I hung up the phone hurriedly before I began to cry. I really did love them all.

Chapter 22: Leaving at Last

I was awakened by loud voices coming from the kitchen. Daddy's voice was the first one I recognized. It was cold and raining that Saturday morning. The raindrops pounded the tin roof of that old wooden house. I will always remember that sound. I went to the front door and stood, watching the rain. *What a awful day for travelin. But it is my day*, I thought.

The wind blew vehemently, and the trees were shaking like they were coming up from the roots. Later, I learned a tornado had touched down near town, and we were feeling the impact from it.

Mama came to the door. She and I watched the rain together silently. I didn't want to say anything because I knew she was hurting.

It was getting along time that we got ready. I knew Butternut was coming, and I didn't want to keep him waiting—not a minute. Mama delivered a last speech about how important it was that I leave the kids. I didn't answer her because I didn't want to hurt her feelings any more. But under my tongue I was saying, *No way. I'll leave my kids in dat bootleggin hole when hell freezes over.*

Butternut arrived at ten o'clock, just as he said he would. "Haley Keath, gal, let's go! Got to git you to de train."

I was so happy. Finally I was leaving, intending that it would be for good. Before I closed the car door, Mama said, "Uncle Head Henry will be at de train station, waitin for y'all." I waved to her as Butternut was driving off. I waved until we were out of sight.

When we arrived at the station, my uncle was there. The train was on time. At first the conductor said I wouldn't be able to take the boxes on the train. I told him to let me get my kids a change of clothes and diapers. He looked at me and said, "Wait, ma'am. I think I kin put em somewhere for you. Good luck to you." I knew that was nobody but the Lord. When the conductor said, "All aboard!" I was ready to go.

That inward voice said, *Don't go. Send the ticket back.* But there was no way in hell I was going to give up an opportunity such as this. At eleven thirty, I was rolling down the track on my first train ride, bound for a new life.

It took us three days to get to New Hampshire, due to the awful weather. A terrible and unforecasted snowstorm hit our route, and we had to travel in a whole different direction and lay over for nearly twenty-four hours.

I awoke early in the morning after we lay over. The train was about to leave, and my children were gone. I panicked immediately. "Oh my God, my babies! Where is my babies?"

People gathered around me in concern. After a few minutes, a fellow I had met the night before appeared with my girls. He had taken them to the bathroom, changed their clothes, fed them breakfast, and packed us bags of food. Lord, I don't know how he knew that my money was low. It wasn't enough to last for another day. I was so grateful. He even made sure we were comfortably seated in the correct seats on our train The good Lord always has an angel guarding us.

We were some hours late arriving, but Buster was at the train station waiting when we got there.

Tise introduced me to her neighbor, Mae Lyn Forester. She was a beautiful woman, a factory worker by day and a nightclub singer by night. Dionne Warwick didn't have anything on her voicewise. She was the mother of six children and a very single parent.

Mae Lyn helped me get hired on at Lloyd Products, working as an inspector. My first formal job paid one dollar and fifty-five cents an hour. That beat fifteen dollars a week. It was by far the most money I had ever made. The environment was perfect and the coworkers were excellent. For the first time in my life, I saw a future that shone bright.

The flip side of the story was that living was expensive, and each pay period, it showed more and more. I had to pay for living with my sister plus babysitting for my kids, and she was home every day. I had never charged any of my sisters for watching my nieces and nephews. That was the pits.

Watching the snow fall to the earth became my daily occupation. Even that was better than the South.

Buster was drifting into his old habits, and I was watching him with everything I had. I still was haunted by the memories of the night he got into my bed, knowing I was intoxicated. I slept with a knife under my pillow every night. I didn't trust that bastard farther than I could throw him.

I made some friends in New Hampshire. Buster had a cousin name Leslie Mae, and we hit it off great. She was the mother of two handsome boys. When I was promoted to another department, I met Juanita, who also happened to live across the street. I was mesmerized by her. She did something for my self-esteem.

Heeding Juanita's caution, I noticed there was a big difference between the whites back in the South than those in the North. Down South, we knew what they were. But up in New Hampshire, they were as sneaky as a person can come.

One evening, Leslie Mae invited me to come out with her. We ended up going to the Club Haddad, where our neighbor Mae Lyn performed. She was a great singer. I hadn't been out in so long, I had almost forgotten what it was like to have some clean fun.

There was a big difference in the nightlife between North and South. Folk went out late in the North. Back home, the cafés opened early and closed early, and folk went home at a time when folk up North were just coming out. By midnight, I was ready to go home. I could tell Leslie Mae was not. She was having the time of her life. She rarely went out, because of the two kids.

We were sitting back in a dark booth when in come these two guys, good-looking and well-dressed. That was the night I met the love of my life, Robbie, and I didn't see it coming. We had our first dance to "When Something Is Wrong with My Baby." He asked me for my name. I hesitated, but as we danced close, I whispered, "My name is Haley."

He caressed me and I didn't ever want him to let me go. His manner was overwhelming. When the dance was over, he joined me in our booth. I knew in my heart he was mine. I made him my earthly heaven, not knowing who he was. Not having billy-goat sense, I was lost in my own attraction. I think I was more aggressive than Robbie was, moving a little too fast to realize what I was moving into.

I made Robbie a part of my life and my kids' lives, along with his friend Will. They were living in a hotel near downtown. I didn't know if that was good or bad. Their visits became more frequent, and that caused a big stir with Buster.

Buster was seeking the least little thing to nag me about, and then he would take his frustration out on my sister. He had a hidden jealousy—he didn't want Tise around other men. She was then in her sixth month of pregnancy with her fifth child. I would lie awake all hours of the night, listening to her having to fight him off of her while she was expecting.

I tried to stay out of their affairs, but it was hard to watch the cruelty she was taking from him and not say anything. I couldn't understand why she continued to have babies with a man she said she despised. He was a woman beater and very abusive. I was looking for an apartment that I could afford on my own.

My life was different. I felt different, and I was living differently, but my life was really no different—the devil was in control of my going out and my coming in. The enemy was working on me through my brother-in-law. Buster treated me like a child, monitoring my actions and causing great disturbance in the household. I was mouthy and didn't care what I said when I got angry or was pushed. Hatred stirred up inside of me for more reasons than I cared to remember.

There was habits and ways in Buster that I had never known were in him back home. And I would always go back to that night when he was in my bed. He was just a two-legged dog. He reminded me so much of my father.

I began to study men. I was fascinated by what took place during slavery. Why were our men so damn weak and frail as to allow white men to control them? Black men did nothing except take their frustration out on their wives. This was what was happening to my sister Tise. I had witnessed it with my mother, my older sister Gemmy BB, poor Cousin Sattie Bell with Uncle Martel, and the list went on.

I could feel the nasty attitude from Buster when he came home in the evening. He had lost all consciousness of what a man was. When Robbie and Will came around, the respect they showed Tise and I was more than Buster could handle.

One evening I had got off from work and was in my room with the kids, enjoying them, when Buster came in and asked me when was I going to move out. "Just as soon as I kin found myself a place dat I kin afford, an I hope it's soon," I answered sarcastically.

"De reason I asked is cause my brother Amos done got released from prison. He want to come up here an live, an I just want to give em de same opportunity as we gave to you."

"When do you expect Amos to come up here?"

"Oh, I really don't know yet. He ain't worked everything out with his probation officer. I was just letting you know what to expect."

I looked at him with both eyes and said, "By de time de day come, I will be out of here."

It wasn't long before I learned that it wasn't Amos who was anxious to leave; it was Buster trying to get Amos to come up there. Bessy Royce wrote to me that Amos's wife, Cora, was having a relationship with someone else, and she was so into that relationship, she was not planning for the family to leave town anytime soon.

***

A coworker named Molly invited me to go out with her, and I saw nothing wrong with that. I was riding with her to work and starting to trust her. I thought she and I would go out like Leslie Mae and I had done. I was looking forward to going, and I didn't feel like explaning to Robbie my whereabouts. So I didn't tell him.

Molly picked me up at eight o'clock, as prompt as when she picked me up each morning for work. I wore a beautiful dress and black heels, my hair well-groomed. When we arrived at our destination, I saw nothing like a club or restaurant—it was a beautiful apartment building in a breathtaking neighborhood. She said, "We're here," and parked the car. I felt I was in for a real treat, not yet hip to this new way of life.

She rang the doorbell, and a voice responded through the intercom, saying, "Come on up." Before that moment, I didn't know what an intercom was.

The door opened and Molly said, "Come on, Haley; let's go up. We're bout to have some real fun, girl." I was all ready for some real fun.

To my surprise, when we got upstairs, a white man who looked like a movie star reached out to Molly and embraced her. I really didn't know what to think. She introduced us: "Mike, this is Haley, my new friend from down South I was talking bout. Haley, this my good friend Mike."

He seemed charming, friendly, and most respectable. "Haley, it's my pleasure to meet you. I have heard so much about you from Molly, and now we finally meet. Come in!" He took my hand and kissed it. "You ladies look splendid." I really thought I was somewhere special.

We stepped into a large room circled by a bar with black and gold stools. Tables and chairs were centered before a wall with a picture of the president hanging on it. At the side of the picture, Mike touched a button, and out of the wall came all the booze you could name. The floor was covered with oriental rugs. I really thought I was going to faint. This was unbelievable. But I also wondered who this man was to her.

Molly had a shape like you see on television. She had more ass than I had tits—and I had tits. She was shaped well but was not a dresser. The old-timey dress she had on, I would never have worn, and when I looked down at the shoes she was wearing, I knew I had to teach her to dress.

Mike took us up to the bar and seated us. Another guy was coming down the hall to the left of where we were sitting. I could have sworn he looked like the King of Rock 'n' Roll. I immediately recalled a movie I'd seen at the picture show back home—*Jailhouse Rock*. Elvis and this guy could have gone for twins. He walked up to me, and Mike introduced him. "Lance, Haley. Haley, this is my roommate Lance."

Lance kept looking at me as if he had a case of déjà vu. I was astonished and fascinated by where I was and who I was with. I was in another world.

They were all laughing as if this was a well-planned evening. Surrounded by all those brands of liquor, I had to maintain myself and not get out of control. Lance asked what I would have to drink. I wasn't used to anything except moonshine and bourbon. I spotted Canadian Club and recognized that, so I asked for it. He made my drink and the same for himself.

Lance told me he was from Italy. I could see he was rich, and he said he was a college student. He and Mike lived right around the corner from a medical college, where he was in med school. I was so ashamed. I was only a high school dropout with two illegitimate children. I had no sense of direction except having to work to take care of my babies. I had no idea what some of the words he used meant.

Then he asked, "What do you do? What's your career?"

For a second, I thought I could go right through the floor and never return. I had no answer.

My head filled up with many lies I could have told him. I felt sorry for myself. I don't know what made me be truthful, but my honest answer came out in a humble way: "My career is my two kids. My one dollar and sixty-five cent an hour job is my livelihood, along with a high school dropout is who I am." Then I swallowed down a nice, stiff drink.

He took my hand in his and looked me directly in the eyes. "Where do you work, Haley?"

"For a factory named Lloyd Products, as a drop-out inspector."

"Why do you say 'drop-out inspector' like that? You don't like the job?"

"No, I don't, but it's all I have for now."

"So in other words, you have to settle because you have two kids. Is that correct?"

"Yes."

"How old are your kids? They can't be too old because you are not that old yourself, right?"

"My oldest girl is three and my baby is two."

"Haley, may I ask you what you are planning to do with yourself?

You don't have to settle. There are so many other thing you can do, like go back to school. Do you plan to do so?"

"Yes, I do! That's all I think bout is goin back to school. But it's too late for me. I got two kids, an I can't go back."

"No, it isn't. It's never too late, only if you let it be too late. Before you leave tonight, there are some addresses I'm going to give you and some phone numbers you can call to help you get started. They have day care and rides and much to offer for young unwed mothers. There is nothing to it except to do it. It's all up to you. I can tell you want more—then go for it!"

All I had ever known were white folk and crackers, and here was this Italian college student giving me perfect advice. We danced and played darts, and we enjoyed a nice, clean party unlike any I had been to.

At the end of the night, Molly had disappeared. Lance asked if he could drop me home. I was nervous. It was my first time out with this total stranger, in a new city. But I didn't know how else to get back to where I lived.

All sorts of thoughts rushed through my mind. Lance was a killer. I was all alone with him. Then I remembered I had God. God knew I was innocent and wanted to go home to my young'uns.

Lance took me home, walked me up to the door, and kissed my cheek like a perfect Italian gentlemen. His final words to me were, "Go back to school, and take care of you and the kids." I never heard from him again, but he left me with the thought that it was all up to me if I wanted to do better. That thought always stayed with me. I hadn't received that kind of encouragement since Aunt Matilda's sister Montana passed.

***

I was sitting in a lounge where Mae Lyn was singing. I was with Leslie Mae and a woman named Ruby, who was an acquaintance of Leslie's. For some reason, Ruby confided in me. She had learned her husband was having an affair, so she had moved out and left him. Something didn't fly with her story. A friend was involved who seemed nosy and suspicious to me. I was led to encourage her to go back home. She listened, and we fitted like a glove. She gave me a ride home.

The next morning, Buster took it upon himself to go down the street to a rooming house. No one but men, and those men wineheads, lived there. But Buster took a room there and put me and my children out. I had no choice but to accept the room. I knew God was with me.

I moved on a Sunday, and Tise came down to help. She laid out her plan to get Buster out of her life. I'd never seen her cry so hard. She promised once she had this baby, she was going to do something about her marriage. I didn't know what to tell her. I was her only ear.

It hurt her deeply to see me and the kids residing in that rooming house. I told her I was not going to work that Monday; I was going to take the day and find an apartment. We promised each other that we would always be close and could tell each other anything.

I didn't feel anything for Buster. He had been revealed to me the first time I laid eyes on him back home, when he was all grins. Daddy said. "You catch a nigger always grinning, they will cut your throat. always watch that sucker." Even then, there was something about Buster I didn't like.

When Tise left that evening, I closed the door to my room. The children were asleep, and I prayed. I knew the Lord heard my prayers because when I had finished, a bright light came across the ceiling. It rested there until I fell asleep.

Later, I was awakened by a knock on the door. My first instinct was that one of those wineheads was trying to get in on me, but when I asked who was there, he said, "Robbie."

What a surprise! I had totally forgotten that I had promised I would go out with him that night. He was my bright, shining armor while I was stuck in that room.

The next morning, I dropped the girls off with Tise and I was on my way to look for a place. It was my lucky day. I met Ruby when she spotted me walking. She stopped her car and rolled the window down, saying, "Girl, I was just coming to look for you. I took your advice and I moved back home yesterday. You kin take my apartment. The rent is paid for the month and I can't git the money back. And you kin have most of the things in there. Git in. I'll take you to see the place."

That was my miracle day. The apartment on Jackson Avenue became my apartment. I bought food, and then I only had enough money for bus fare to get to work. I thought I would let the kids stay a couple of days with Tise until I got paid.

It was too much of an assumption. On Friday, I went to get the girls, and I met Satan in the flesh. I was accused of everything. That was my first time seeing that side of Tise. I gave her my new address and left that house.

I had to return to work, but I had no one to keep my kids. Another miracle took shape. I had a coworker named Lillian whose girls were home. They took care of my kids along with their infirm Uncle Blankey.

***

I had been on a break at work. When I got back to my station, I noticed one of the white line workers was already back at hers. Her name was Mimi. She was always the first one back, but I noticed she was in an area that she shouldn't have been in. The look on her face spelled trouble for somebody. We all knew she was as prejudiced as a rattlesnake was poisonous, but I didn't say anything. I just started up my machine.

Before the day was over, a big argument broke out between Mimi and and my friend Juanita. Mimi called Juanita a nigger, and that didn't go well with Juanita. She slapped Mimi so hard, the woman went flying across the paint area. Mimi didn't retaliate physically, and I wondered why.

The supervisors came and heard both versions of what happened. Because Juanita hit Mimi, she was terminated. Because Mimi did not hit Juanita, she kept her job. Mimi knew what she was doing all along.

We were all on Juanita's side. Lillian proved it by resigning her position. I just watched; I couldn't afford to lose my job for anyone.

The fight broke out because Mimi had put broken vases in Juanita's boxes, so they didn't pass inspection. I realized that's why I'd seen Mimi in the wrong area earlier—she was sabotaging Juanita's work. But the supervisors were white, Mimi was white, and it was all pushed under the rug. As always, the whites didn't have to step back, and the blacks had to stay back.

Living was not easy in those days, with all the prejudice. Blacks had to deal with racism among whites but not ever forget that whites were not all the same, just as blacks were not—though whites looked upon us as if we were. Something that rattles in my mind to this day is this: we blacks know where we came from, which is Africa. But where do the white folk come from? I have been told they came from Europe, but their skin color doesn't match the complexion of Europeans.

In any case, the supervisors' excuses never left my mind. No matter how good white folk are, they cannot be trusted. They are the same in many ways, wherever we go.

***

Lillian and I grew closer. She came to get her last paycheck during one of my breaks. She warned me to be careful of Mae Lyn, because she was the company's snitch. I recalled hearing something similar before, but I just couldn't believe that about her.

I soon found out it was the truth. Mae Lyn snitched on me and said I was sleeping on my station. Well, she didn't lie about it—I was. Not long afterward, two supervisors, Holly and Leann, came to me with the accusation. They were not rough about it; they only cautioned me that if the bosses came through and saw me, I could lose my job and so could they.

I explained, and they knew, that I was sleeping on my own time, not on company time. I was staying at my station during breaks and lunch when I didn't have the money to buy food. I found them fair and understanding. Still, it was true we could all get in trouble if the bosses saw me doing it.

As they were walking back to their offices, they stopped. Leann spoke to Holly. Then they came back to me. Holly said, "Haley, I need you to corroborate Juanita's version of what happened between her and Mimi. She said you were a witness."

"Sure. What you want to know?"

"Did you see Mimi during that time in Juanita's section?"

"Yeah. She was unpackin bottles out of de boxes. I thought it was odd for er to be doin it, but I didn't know if she was followin orders or what, so I overlooked it."

"What else do you know about the feud between Juanita and Mimi?"

"Mimi been harassin Juanita ever since she come here to work. She was always sayin somethin negative about her, but I never knew why. I discovered that she set Juanita up, and it was proved when she confronted Juanita about the breakages. That was when she called Juanita a black nigger and Juanita slapped her."

"Thank you, Haley. You have been most helpful."

As they were walking off, I overheard Holly say, "That's pretty much the same story Juanita told. Get Mimi in the office."

Once Mimi had been called in, I was also summoned. When Mimi looked up and saw me, her face turned red. I had to repeat the same information I had told the supervisors earlier, and Mimi was terminated.

She was as hot as a oven set at the highest temperature. She got back to her station to turn the machine off, and she yelled out, "All these damn nigger all just a bunch of damn liars!" Then she ran out the door and was never heard from again.

I kept silent because I needed my job more than I needed to get even with her.

***

I was settled in my apartment with my kids, and my relationship with Robbie was untouchable. It wasn't long before I was head over heels in love with him. But he didn't know what came with the love—I was a stone alcoholic with no signs.

Robbie made me and my kids very happy. I really didn't know what happiness was until he came into my life. I learned the difference between needing love and true love, the kind that I knew was a many-splendored thing. It came with laughter, sharing, trusting, and believing. Nothing would ever take the place of what we found in each other.

Will saw that love, and I witnessed a tremendous change in him. That was the beginning of trouble.

Both Robbie and Will loved to party. Their lives were based on partying. We partied every night, and I thought that was cool. My past was right on my heels.

***

Tise and I made up our differences. She had the baby, a little girl, and named her Teresa. I gave her the nickname Mama Moochie. She was the spitting image of Mama, and she became my favorite niece. Buster and Tise moved to Coleman Avenue. The weather was still nice, but winter was setting in. It hadn't yet started to snow, but snow was in the making.

Cora showed up early one Saturday morning, surpising me. She and Amos had moved North after all, and they'd had a terrible fight. It appeared that Buster had been inquiring about the relationship she had been carrying on back home, before they relocated. Buster revealed it all to Amos.

I didn't turn Cora away, but I didn't have room enough for her, me, and my kids. So I talked her into going back and making the best of her situation. She was not working and had two kids. It wasn't easy to make it with kids alone—I knew from firsthand experience.

I had promised the landlord I would be out of the apartment in six months, and those months were coming to an end. My focus was on getting a larger place. I found one, and the girls and I moved.

Will and Robbie also moved out of the hotel into a rooming house that was owned by a real live prostitute. I learned that bootlegging was not just in the South. It was in the North also, and the white man was behind it all. This prostitute was driving Will's car, and Willie was walking half the time, with Robbie supporting his bus fare.

I kept my eyes on Will. He got involved with a girl who lived across the hall from me, Lucy. He was grinning with Amos and sticking it to Cora every chance he got. I had an acquaintance named Dossey Webber. She was related to Ruthella back home and worked with me at Lloyd Products. Willie was involved with her too. I saw myself getting entangled with the game he was playing, and I didn't know what to do about it.

Lucy invited me to come outside and sit with her and few friends. They all welcomed me to "the hood." I didn't know what they meant. It turned out that was their name for the apartments. We all got along like family, and I didn't even know them. I was not alone in having a drinking problem. None of us were rational enough to recognized the others' problems. It was the blind leading the blind.

I was in love, but I was still desperately in need of belonging. Getting to know my new neighbors became my focus, and I couldn't see the inevitable. There was not a single person in the entire building complex who did not call themselves friends and were not backstabbing each other. I was able to see the negativity that surrounded me, yet I was blind to what it was doing to me. The drinking, gossiping, and underhanded tricks were just another reminder of my life back home.

One of my new neighbors, Jerri, gave me the rundown on Will's and Robbie's love lives before I came into the picture. It seemed Robbie was still seeing someone else—Jerri's sister Loretta. I didn't know if it was a secret from everyone or just me, but that was the first I'd heard of it.

One night I went to a lounge. Lorretta and Robbie were on the dance floor. His back was turned toward me when I walked in. She was facing me. The moment she saw me, her arms tightened around his neck, and they grinded like they were about to get one on.

I left. Robbie didn't know I was there at the time, but Will told him later. Robbie immediately came to me to explain. He knew from the way I was acting that Jerri had been in my ears, but I never let on that I knew about him and fat Loretta.

Will shed some light on who Jerri really was. He'd been seeing her too, but he claimed he only used her for money and head. Dumb as I was, I didn't know what he was talking about. I thought "head" meant her brain—that she was smart. He warned me she was a extremely untrustworthy and a peace-breaker. He also denied that Robbie was seeing Loretta.

I realized later that he would lie for Robbie in a heartbeat. They were both nothing but men.

***

I had gone over to visit Robbie, and I fell asleep. He and the kids were in the pool room, shooting pool. They didn't wake me—I learned later that his landlady, Rose, said I needed the rest.

I came out of Robbie's room into the kitchen. There was a very tall, dark-skinned, nice-looking woman there, and I knew from Robbie's descriptions that this must be Rose. Her hair was up on top of her head in a pompadour style. She said, "Come in, Haley, and have some coffee. Little Brother is teaching the girls how to shoot pool. I'm Rose."

Coffee was the furthest thing from my mind. "Pleased to meet you, Rose."

"Little Brother talks bout you and the girls. You are as pretty as he described you. That boy loves himself some Haley Keath. Come and sit in the dining room. I got to be leaving for work in bout an hour."

"Where do you work?" I asked, just making conversation.

"I work on Pinecrest Avenue in the prostitute house. It's the biggest prostitute house on this side of town, and I'm one of the head prostitutes that work there."

Lord forgive me, I didn't even know the meaning of the word "prostitute." I guess the look on my face told her I was ignorant. "Why you look so puzzled?" she said. "Is there anything you want to ask me?"

I knew it something about the word was not respectful, but I didn't know what it meant. "What is a prostitute?"

"Little Brother said you was from down South. I don't speck they have prostitutes out in the open down there. A prostitute is a woman like me who tricks for a living. She sells her body for money."

I was really puzzled. I had heard the word "trick" many times, but I didn't know it had the same meaning as "prostitute." I said, "You mean you do tricks like a clown at a circus?"

She busted out laughing. "Haley, let Rose school you bout life, cause I see you don't know nothing. A prostitute is who I am. Selling my body is what I do. That is my occupation."

My mouth flew open, and I was lost for words.

She further stated that it was no different than a woman lying with a man for free. "If I was going to lay, I may as well git paid for it." Rose told me she was a first-class prostitute and got paid well.

My mind was racing. My question was how did she know Robbie, but I dared not ask.

Everything I did ask, she revealed. There were so many ways to have sex, I was lost. She stated, "When you deal with white men, you learn all kind of ways to have sex. Black men don't know but one way to make love, and that is git on top, stick his dick in, make babies, and git down."

My ears had heard enough for one evening. Her conversations, then and later, were always fascinating, and I learned from her, but I would never be like her.

Women never really know who they are married to and what men's capabilities are. It's hard for a religious man to live decently, so what does that tell us about a non-Christian? It takes God to keep the flesh under subjection. Sex has a strong hold on a man. Oral sex is a deadly sin, and who is able to withstand it? I had never heard of oral sex or beating someone with a wet towel or walking on somebody's back. God made man and woman. These other madnesses are of human invention, and many people suffer as a result of it—child pornography, child molestation, baby killing, kidnapping, and selling our children into slavery.

I was encouraged to be a good mother to my children. My biggest concern was to protect them from predators, pimps, and drug dealers.

I never got to close to Rose. I was not judgmental against her, but I was somewhat cautious. From time to time I would run into her downtown at Kress Drugstore, and she and I would talk. She always told me how much Robbie loved me.

One particular day, I ran into her and she was in a stinky mood. She wanted Will out of her house. He had lost his job, and he wasn't paying his rent. She said he was using Little Brother like a stepchild. I promised I would talk to Robbie, but I had no intention of doing so. Robbie knew Will. He had known Will long before Rose or I did. I wanted Robbie to see for himself.

***

Lillian picked me up for an outing. As we were riding along in her car, a Jeep passed us, just flying by. A man and a woman were inside. Lillian said the man was Walter, her husband. She U-turned and tried to follow them, but by that he had lost her. She was hurt, seeing her husband with another woman, but she was the kind of woman who put the best on the outside.

We had lost all track of time and had to get back home so she could let her kids in the house. She dropped me off home. I was unsatisfied with the hurt I knew she was feeling, so I got my girls and we walked around to Lillian's house, which wasn't that far.

I rang her doorbell, and an elderly man with a pipe in his mouth opened the door, smiling. "Hello," he said, "are you looking for me?"

"No, I'm looking for Lillian. Do she live here?"

"Yes, she do. Who shall I tell her is calling?"

"Tell her Haley, and you must be Uncle Blankey."

"Yeah, how did you know? Lillian must have told you. Come in. I'll git her for you."

Lillian heard my voice and came running down the stairs. "Haley! You almost beat me here! Come on, have a seat. I guess you read my mind that I'm bout to lose it. Come in, girl."

I could see nothing but sadness all over her face. She was a beautiful woman, but she had deep, dark circles around her eyes from crying. I wondered why black men hurt the women who love them so deeply. Lillian loved Wallace so much, and they had four children together. Yet he treated her like she was the other woman.

I hurt for her. I hurt for people regardless of who they were. I guess that was why my hurt never showed. I never had time to really think of mine; I was learning to put the best on the outside and keep on moving. It was never easy, but I think God was carrying me in the direction to see that my pain was no different from anyone else's. Scripture was always a reminder that we must bear one another's burdens. Though my problems were far from subsiding, that attitude gave me more to focus on than myself.

I spent the rest of the evening with her. I shared some of the pain I had experienced back home with the man I thought I was in love with. I discovered Lillian was a highly religious woman. Her faith in God was superior.

I hadn't gone into a Northern church building, but I carried the Lord with me each and every day. Still, I was sinking deeper into sin. I hadn't yet learned that I was the church and our bodies should be temples of the Holy Ghost. But God does not dwell in unclean places.

We all talk about God as if he is a faucet that can be turned on and off as we need him—only on Sundays, or when we have gotten ourselves in trouble. We turn the faucet on until he brings us out of whatever we've gotten our ungodly selves into, and then we repeat the same old cycle.

Lillian lived the faith, and that's where I wanted to be. But there was nobody in my whole apartment complex who went to church. I was in the midst of nothing but sinners. My past was lurking right behind me.

We talked about the children and her uncle Blankey. He was standing in the kitchen, pretending to look on with a lustful eye. He was so cute with that pipe in his mouth. I would smile at him, and he would wink, and Lillian would ask with a straight face, "Haley, did Uncle Blankey make a pass at you?" And we would all laugh.

We sat talking for hours. She needed to get a release from all that pressure she was under. I was getting ready to call it a evening when her husband drove up in that Jeep. He came strolling inside as if he were innocent. She introduced us, and showed me kindness. He didn't display any of the symptoms that she had described to me earlier.

"Honey," she said, "I'm about to run Haley and her kids home. I'll be back soon."

"Sure, hon. Take your time and drive careful. Jackson Avenue is wild."

I protested that I could walk home, but Lillian said, "No, you will not do any such thing. I'm driving you, and that's just all there is to it." She winked, indicating that I should not say another word, just follow her lead.

Driving us home, she asked, "How did he seem to you? What do you think? I know you are a good judge of character."

I was honest. "He seemed to be the perfect, lovin husband. Polite. Intelligent. Like a man in love wit his wife."

"Well, the old Wallace is who you just described. I don't know who this one is. Believe me, girl, he is a nasty son of a bitch. He puts on the biggest front in front of my friends, but behind closed doors, he is the devil."

I advised her to trust in God, pray, and let God fix it. One of the Ten Commandments is "Thou shalt not commit adultery."

Lillian stayed at my place for dinner. The more she talked, the more I saw how deeply in love with her husband she was. Lillian was the kind of friend anyone would be proud of. She was respectful, loving, understanding, and very encouraging. She didn't drink and she didn't smoke. She was a good wife and mother who worked every day and loved her family as well as she loved the Lord.

***

My neighbors, on the other hand, were more on my level. We were all were alcoholics and liars. Gloria was the superintendent's wife and was a bigger alcoholic than the rest of us put together. I had to learn why she was such an alcoholic. I gained her trust, and she confided in me. I learned from her that my neighbor Louisa had a husband who was being a man, just like the average man. So Louisa was doing the same, and one of the men she was screwing around with was our superintendent, Gloria's husband. Gloria was too weak to do anything about it except turn to alcohol.

Louisa was a tall, skinny, and light-skinned. She had gorgeous black hair and kept it well-groomed. When she smiled, she showed a deep dimple in the middle of her cheek. She was a sharp dresser and had a very sarcastic, arrogant mouth. She was married to Joseph. He was different from the other guys in the complex. All he did when he came home from work was sit at the window and watch us. He had Louisa timed. Before she would leave and go back upstairs, he was gone. When Joseph did come down the stairs and mingle, his eyes were all over me, and and it was noticeable.

Another couple were Campbell and Sally Jean. She was dumb but beautiful, inside and out. She was also as humble as a lamb. Campbell didn't want her, for whatever reason. They had two kids, and not long after I moved in, he left her and moved back to Georgia. She ended up having an affair with the owner of the building.

Caroline and Lucy were mother and daughter, and they became my dearest friends.

Then there was Louisa's brother, Davey, the most good-looking man God ever made. He was shacking up with a woman and her two sons, but that wasn't enough for him. Like Joseph, Davey eyeballed me every chance he got. I wondered which of them was eyeballing me the most. But Davey was very laid back.

Larry and Clary were identical twins. Larry was Lucy's man, and Gloria was making it with Clary. Caroline and Lucy were the bootleggers in the complex and were the biggest root workers anyone ever wanted to be around.

God forbid, the Jackson Avenue apartments were nothing but *As the World Turns*, *Love of Life*, *The Guiding Light*, and *Search for Tomorrow*, all in one. Joseph and Louisa were the only married couple in the entire building after Campbell left Sally Jean. The rest were living together. And it seemed like all of them were stepping out on one another.

I was so reminded of back home. It was all so familiar. The memories were more than I cared to acknowledge. I was ready to get the hell out of there.

***

Buster and Amos stopped by with good news. There was an apartment coming available near them. The landlord was doing repairs, and it wouldn't be ready for a couple of months. I considered it, but I was still looking on my own.

After Buster and Amos left, I had to go to the store. I left the kids in the apartment with Lucy. I wasn't gone long, and upon my return, I heard Rejetta screaming. It was a life-threatening scream, like somebody was dying. I ran on up and found Lucy's daughter Sheneice had accidentally closed the door on Rejetta's finger. It was cut down to the bone.

Davey volunteered to take me over to the hospital. While the doctors were working on Rejetta's hand, Davey kept me company in the waiting room, and he and I got better acquainted. He was so handsome. Just like Louisa, he had dimples in his cheek. The sideburns down his face would sober up a drunk dog.

Rejetta was fine. They gave me a prescription for her pain.

Davey drove us home, and that evening I could not forget the time I'd spent with him. I was not able to shake it.

Will was waiting at my apartment. He said he needed to talk to me. Once I cooked dinner and got the children fed and down, he begged me to let him bunk on my couch. Rose had kicked him out. I had only enough room for me and my kids, but as usual I was eager to do anything I could for anyone. I didn't want him to stay, but the kids slept with me, and what would a few days hurt? He had nowhere to live.

***

Things were steaming around the complex. Joseph got busted. Some major stealing was going on, and he ended up in jail. The paper said he was a big heroin peddler. The superintendent moved out, leaving Gloria. Louisa didn't hesitate; she moved in with him without a moment's remorse.

I moved into a four-room apartment that the welfare office gave me. I had been fired from Lloyd Products, and I ended up on welfare. I hated every minute of it. I was job hunting every day. The apartment wasn't what I wanted, but it was close to my sister. I was happy with that little.

Cora and Amos had found their own apartment too, and Will

ended up living with them. I had put him out some time before, and the next place he stayed put him out too. Will was just a monster in the guise of a human being.

I went to Rose to get some light shed on his behavior. She swore that Will had been lying since the day he moved into her house. Little Brother had been feeding him and paying his room rent. I knew Robbie meant well—they had both come from the same hometown, and Robbie just couldn't turn his back on Will.

Rose had no patience with that. She cared absolutely nothing about Willie. And she did not exaggerate the situation: he was who he was, a user and a loser.

The picture that stayed in my mind about Will was from the day he left my Jackson Avenue apartment. I had gone riding with Lillian, and when I got back, the living room looked like a hurricane had been through it. There were about twelve beer cans scattered around, the chair covers were all messed up, and the kitchen table was filthy.

I didn't say a word. I just started to clean. Cora stopped by unexpectedly and joined in. She mopped the kitchen floor—I believe he had urinated on it. I couldn't believe it. I was reliving my growing-up days back home. Anger pierced my stomach and caused me to tremble.

But thank God Will was no longer my concern. For me, he was just a memory, but Cora was just beginning to learn who he was. After a few weeks, she too came home from work and found her place demolished.

Months passed. Robbie had never mentioned Will. Then one day, out of the clear, he began to talk. That was unusual; Robbie was not a talker. He asked if had I seen Will. I told him no. Robbie said Will had just left him after trying to borrow money. I could see the frustration on Robbie's face. He was fed up with Will at last, and I was glad.

We discussed Will's behavior. He couldn't keep a job. When he did get paid, he would disappear. When he reappeared, he was broke and hungry. He always wore long-sleeved shirts, summer and winter. What could the reason be except heroin?

Robbie decided he was cutting all ties with Will. He knew Will refused to change—not that he was incapable of changing, but he had a problem and wouldn't try. Frankly, I didn't think Will wanted to change.

***

While I was still on welfare, I babysat for Cora's kids, Eartha and Ron, for a little extra income. The apartment was not the way I wanted it to be. I had to get myself a job to furnish it the way I wanted to.

Caroline had told me that whenever I needed a job, she and Louisa worked at Enterprise Company and they would get me in there. I called her that evening, and in two days I had an interview. We went up to the Mercury Lounge to celebrate.

My interview was that Monday. I was hired to commence work in two days. Everything was going according to my plans. I could see my future looking brighter—a job, a man, and my own apartment. I was just as proud of those welfare iron beds and the wringer washing machine. It didn't matter about the old furniture. I was safe in my own place, and my kids had their own room. I was happy my kids and I could snuggle in comfortably at home. The neighborhood wasn't the best, but neither was it the worst. It certainly beat Rat Row.

I had acknowledged I was an alcoholic, but I was doing a pretty good job of hiding it from everyone I knew. Robbie had this saying, "One little drink won't git you drunk if you just don't keep on drinking." Sometimes when we were having a social drink, he would say those words and I would feel so guilty. I told myself that he must know, but there was no way he could have.

It was down in the twenties, cold as hell was hot, on my first day of work at Enterprise. The moment I walked in, hell hit me smack in my face. A woman named Benny worked there, and she was the sister-in-law of Loretta, Robbie's ex. I smelled trouble a mile away, but I didn't entice it. I concluded I would stay as far away from her as I possibly could.

I needed to talk to someone, and I called Lillian. She met me for lunch. I gave her the history of my drinking problem that I felt was getting out of hand. I didn't know how to control it.

As always, she was supportive. She knew the right things to say that encouraged me to cope with the problem. She asked, "Haley, what do you *want* to do bout it?"

The question caught me off guard. Teary-eyed, I said, "I want to stop drinkin."

Her cure for me was to go to church. "Only God can fix what ails you. I can't, you can't, and nobody else can. Only God. Come to my church with me. I'll pick you and the girls up on Sunday morning at ten thirty."

She did, not a minute late, and I was too hungover to go.

But Lillian didn't give up on me. She came again the next Sunday, and the girls and I were ready. Being in church again was a blessing. I hadn't been to church in over a year and a half. I just had turned my back on God. But he never turned his back on me.

Every Sunday for months, Lillian came and got us. I was almost my old self again, like the days at home with Sister Greta. I loved going to church.

Lillian wanted me to formally join, but I wasn't ready. I was being cautious, one step at a time.

Meanwhile, Lillian, Uncle Blankey, and Wallace prayed with me and for me. I could feel their prayers working, but my weakness was more than the prayers, or so I thought.

All the time Lillian was helping me, Wallace was divorcing her for another woman. She was so strong, she didn't let it get her down. She drank a little wine, but always in moderation.

One Sunday she was bringing me home, and I caught that sad look in her eyes. I said, "Lillian, you been so wrapped up with me and my problem, tell me how is everything going with you."

She busted out crying and said, sadly yet joyfully, "Wallace wants a divorce, and I am ready to give it to him, Haley. I don't want Wallace anymore. He gave me something, and that I will not forgive him for. He wanted to make amends, but I don't want him. He kin have the woman he have mistreated me for all these years. I'm done."

Two months later, she left Wallace and moved back to her hometown in Virginia. We stayed in touch until I moved later, when we lost all contact.

***

When a three-bedroom apartment up over Tise's became available, I moved there. It was a better neighborhood and a better building, so I thought I was settled.

Once Lillian left, there was no more church for me. My excuse was that I had no way to get there. Other churches were closer to me, but somehow with Lillian gone, I lost my desire. That was one thing I had not yet faced. I had to learn how to be my own woman. I had to make the right decisions for myself and stop depending on someone else to be my crutch.

The last letter I received from Lillian said she was in church and was involved with a new guy there. She sounded happy, although her uncle Blankey had expired. The children were off to college, and everything was working out according to God's plan.

She wrote, *Be honest with Robbie. Tell him your problem.* But I didn't. I couldn't. I had decided he didn't have to know, because whenever I was drinking, we were all drinking. He had to be an alcoholic himself.

My nightmares had become terrifying. In my dreams, I heard old Mr. Willie Shangle: "Looker, looker, looker hear, Mr. Macky. Just let me have one quarter drink. I'll pay you tomorrow."

I hated my father. Even more, I faulted him for my problem. He was the cause for why I was like I was. I didn't see any way out of it. The devil had taken control of my life. Demons were residing in my mortal body, rent-free.

Chapter 23: Sinking Deeper and Deeper in Sin—More Trouble for Me

My job was my life. I enjoyed each day the good Lord allowed me to get up and wade through that snow to get there. I had gotten to know most of my coworkers. Everybody was nice except that Benny woman. Verla Benny had a hangup about me from the minute she learned who I was. I worked in the same row she did, but farther down. The work was not hard, but it was steady. There was no time to play around as the carts kept coming down.

One cold December morning, everyone was in the Christmas spirit, making plans to attend parties. Christmas carols echoed around the building and made me think of home.

I got paid that Thursday and back to my apartment in the spirit to cook and spend a quiet evening at home with the girls. I knew we wouldn't be there alone. Robbie would show up with his friends and we would all sit around and chill. Robbie's friends were nice young men, very respectable, and their demeanor did justice to their upbringing.

Another day, a week before Christmas, I was up practically half the night entertaining Robbie and his company. Rose was moving out of her house, and Robbie was planning on moving in with me and the kids. He wanted me to put up a friend of his temporarily too. My sister Passy Kate had relocated and was already residing with me, causing my apartment to be overcrowded. I felt smothered—there was no privacy, Christmas was around the corner, and I had *no money.*

The reason I had no money was because I had been fired from Enterprise. Verla Benny had pushed me one step too far, and I had assaulted her, just as my friend Juanita had assaulted Mimi all those months ago. Caroline and even Louisa spoke up for me, but the supervisor, Bill, had zero tolerance. I didn't blame him; he was only doing his job.

The dreams about the man started again. One night he warned me that many heartaches and disappointments awaited me. The loss of this job was not the last of my sorrows. I had been hexed. He said three women were responsible: Delta, Theola, and O'Bera. "O'Bera blamed you for her daughter turning out so early. She was not able to face the fact her daughter was identical to her. In her heart, she knew you were not the way she painted you. It was her own reflection in Ruthella. She had to take all the focus off of her and shift the slander onto you."

The hex that had been worked on me was taking a strong effect. I would always be like a faucet, constantly running. I would move from job to job, and I would spend the biggest part of my life in lack, which will play a major role in the ungodly decisions that I would make.

I blocked that dream out of my mind for many years. From time to time when I drank, flashes of it would reappear, and I would dismiss them.

I looked for work for months. Nothing came my way. The good Lord did look down, and I took on some babysitting—three children for thirty dollars a week. Cora had gotten a job at Enterprise, and I babysat her little boy Ron. It wasn't all bad. I thought making an honest living was all that mattered.

***

Passy Kate was still living with us. I was learning that I didn't know her. She had left home at an early age. What I was getting to know, I hated. She was an alcoholic.

Willie left New Hampshire for good, moving to Connecticut. Amos and Cora separated briefly, but got back together. I was so tuned in on my sister Passy Kate, I wasn't noticing very much going on around me. My problem—and Passy Kate's—were much deeper than I could ever have anticipated. I began to question my sanity. Who was I? Why did

I get myself entangled in such awful situations? What was it going to take for me to get out of them?

I fell down on my kitchen floor, flat on my face, crying out to God sorrowfully with a repentant heart. I asked sincerely, *Dear Lord, how come I have to continue be in so much mess? Why can't I found me a good job and move in a nice neighoborhood and raise my children? Why do I have to drink every day just to cope with this raggedy life I have? Why don't you just take me away from here?*

I wanted out from the people who surrounded me. I wanted out of the neighborhood I was living in. I wanted to stop partying and drinking and get back into church. But the more I examined my circumstances, the more it seemed there was no way of escape for me.

***

An apartment became available up over Tise and Buster: three bedrooms, living room, and kitchen, with one bath. I took it and gave one of the rooms to Kate. The girls had their own. I had a conversation with Kate, and she went out and got herself a job. She was starting to do better, and peace eased into our lives. I could breathe again.

Robbie and I had a loving relationship. The kids were happy. I was considering going back to school. Things were finally starting to reach a turning point in my life.

Cora stopped by my old place as I was moving out. A few minutes later, a guy named John came by. I wondered why he was visiting me. Was Cora secretly meeting him?

Then Buster stopped by to pick up some boxes. I didn't want any problem, so I had John hide to keep Buster from seeing him. I could tell by the expression on Buster's face that he was up to no good. He was snooping around, and when he snooped, nothing good was coming out of it. He didn't stay, and once he left, I got John out of the apartment as fast as I could.

I asked Cora not to give John my new address. She did. Robbie got curious and asked me if Cora and John were meeting at my apartment secretly. That was a problem. The way it was happening, it appeared that I was in on it.

Not long after the move, we all went out to the Mercury. I needed an evening out after cleaning, cooking, washing, watching children, and listening to other people's problem. Cora came along; Amos did not.

We were having a wonderful time. The evening was beautiful. John was a great singer, and he and his friends had cut a record titled "Don't Neglect Your Baby." They played it. I was drinking my favorite wine and feeling the effects of it.

Cora asked me to come upstairs with her. I followed her up the stairs. She was meeting John. Amos came in downstairs, and we were trapped up there. When intermission was over, John slipped away. Amos found Cora and I up there, and I was blamed for the situation.

I came down the stairs, and Robbie walked away from me. Amos had Cora cornered. She said I had torn my dress, and she was helping me fix it. Everybody was giving me the cold shoulder. Robbie said, "You need to take that cloaking s— back to Georgia."

I never was good at taking orders.

***

My cousins Lenny and Ross Junior—Aunt Frankie Reese's boys—came in from the country. I remember the first time I was introduced to the two brothers. They were really, really close, like jam and jelly. They stopped by frequently and were no strangers. I didn't know them as well as Tise did, but I was determined to learn more of them.

Lenny and his wife Rhudene came to see us and took my baby Vermont Andreka back to country for two weeks. Now that Tise had given birth, they came around regularly. We all drank together, as families and friends do, but I learned to be careful what you wish for.

Ross was hilarious, but Lenny was the comic star. He was so funny, he could make King Kong laugh. He was the kind of fellow anyone would like to be around.

Some weekends when they drank, they would spend the night at Tise and Buster's apartment, not wanting to drive. On one such weekend, they had stayed over but I didn't know it. I was going shopping and needed to leave the girls with Tise for a couple of hours.

I stopped by Tise's apartment and something was wrong. I could sense the vibe in the room. I felt unwelcome, like I was intruding. I didn't stay, and I didn't bring the girls down there.

I had also noticed that Tise had started grumbling if I left the kids down there. She would ask me if I'd brought food for them too. My God, she threw away more than my two little girls ate.

Tise was my favorite sister and she was my mentor, but I knew her in ways that left a bitter taste in my mouth. Something was going on. I knew Cora and Amos had something to do with it, but I couldn't put my finger on it. No doubt Buster was in the midst of it. Her dependency on him handicapped her.

***

I was still looking for a job as time permitted. Kate was working at one of the big hospitals. She had started hanging out with a friend named Lesley, and that was not working out for either of us. It didn't take a genius to see what kind of user Lesley was. She was short and round like a polar bear's ass. She had two little boys that her mother took care of. Lesley herself apparently lived in the streets. I saw failure, and she was eventually going to take Passy Kate right down with her.

Kate had begun to stay out on the weekends when she got paid. She would come home unrecognizable. I realized something terrible had happened to her during the years she was away from us, whether during the time she was with Lloyd or after they parted. Whatever it was would affect her for the rest of her life if she didn't get help.

I didn't mention Kate's situation to Tise; I just kept my eyes on her and Lesley. Each weekend, Kate's demeanor degraded further, like she was losing control of her faculties.

Passy Kate came home drunk one night and was upstairs, sleeping it off. The usual crowd was downstairs in Tise and Buster's apartment. It was party time. Only Lenny was missing.

I went upstairs for a change of clothes for my baby. I heard a slight noise coming from Kate's room. I pushed the door open to check out the noise, and saw Lenny on top of Kate. She was stone cold drunk. I was astonished.

I pulled the door shut, intending to get Tise, but I was so angry I couldn't think straight. I couldn't believe my eyes. I lost all respect for Lenny. What was done to her had been done to me, and I would never forget the pain I felt. I didn't want anybody to know how low-down he was, so I kept that secret.

Not long after, Lenny got real sick. He was diagnosed with leukemia and died a year later. I said to myself as I prepared for his funeral, "The wages of sin is death." What I witnessed him doing to my sister was a secret that died with him. I never revealed it to anyone. Yet I often wondered how many others there were.

***

I knew it was time I got myself a job. As long as Tise was getting paid, she would keep the kids smiling. I got up early one morning and walked over to another factory that had hiring signs posted all around. I didn't realize you got hired by passing a test. I had never been good at testing. Matter of fact, I was downright terrified of tests. Never did I think factory work would rely on testing. The jobs that I knew called for high school diplomas, I stayed clear of.

I filled out the application, and the interviewer said I needed to take a test. She led me into a room where about twenty other women were testing. She gave me the test and said I had twenty minutes.

I wanted to faint. I wanted to take wing and fly away. I sat in the chair and opened the test booklet. It contained English and math questions. Adding, subtracting, and multiplying—they were nothing. But when I got to the dividing, I panicked. My mind seemed to have gone blank.

I looked around and everyone else was testing away like there was nothing to it. It made me see just how dumb I was. Common denominator? Mixed fraction? Improper fraction? I had no idea how to work them.

Time was passing. I went on to the English questions. I did have some knowledge of the four kinds of sentences and that each sentence began with a capital letter. I also knew the eight parts of speech. I really thought I was home-free until I got to the subject and predicate questions. There was so much I didn't know or remember.

The room was almost empty, just a few other women left. I gave up. I stopped working and left. In my heart, I believe I flunked the test out of pure dumbness.

The interviewer came into the waiting room, calling my name. I answered and went into an office with her. She said, "We don't have any openings that would fit your skills at the moment, but we keep applications on file for one year. If anything comes up, we will give you a call."

I said, "Yes, ma'am" in a trembling voice. My eyes filled with tears, and I glued my lips together to keep from busting out crying. I walked out of her office feeling like I had been kicked by a horse.

All I could think of was my father. It was his fault I was in the condition that I was in. I couldn't even pass a simple test. Hatred induced the idea that I needed to go back to school. I cried all the way home with my mind only on that one idea.

Arriving at Tise's apartment, I didn't enter right away. I had to pull myself together. I dared not let my girls see me so broken in spirit.

There had been a James Brown song that was briefly popular when I was young: "Don't Be a Drop-Out." The line I remembered was "Without an education, you might as well be dead." Word was the record had to be pulled from the market because so many uneducated dropouts were attempting to commit suicide. I was in that frame of mind. But my two little girls kept me focused.

I looked up, and Cora was coming down the street. She was so busy with her own problems, she never paid any attention to me. I went inside. Tise could see I had been crying, but she was as sharp as Buster was nasty. I just wanted to go somewhere and hide. As I was gathering up my kids, Tise kept winking at me to stay, but I couldn't.

For the first time since I was forced to drop out of school four years before, regret overshadowed me, leaving me with a void that only I could fill. I couldn't share that hurt with anyone, not even Tise. I left my sister's apartment broken into many pieces. I wanted to die, but instead I turned to alcohol for my comfort.

I drank every day, but I took care of my children. I kept them close and had them under good control. If I drank too much and took a nap, they would not open the door for anyone. They would come in my room and wake me up. Poor kids, they didn't know I was drinking. They thought Mama was tired.

One morning I was making breakfast for the kids. They were playing in the living room, innocent of everything that surrounded me. I recalled the utility bill was due and I had no money. The rent was due and I had no money. I was so depressed, I squalled. I felt a little hand touch my shoulder. I looked around, and it was my little Rejetta. Tears were rolling down her face. I lifted her into my arms and quickly wiped the tears from my face. I asked her why was she crying, and she said, "Cause you cryin, Mammy." I held her close and comforted her. She said, "It's gonna be all right, Mammy."

I had to get a grip on my life for the sake of my babies. Nothing mattered to me except them.

I knew I had to get a job. I tried getting into schools and taking up trades, but my test scores were too low. After I flunked yet another test, a secretary told me about a GED class that might help. I could get the equivalent of a high school diploma. The class was only offered in the evening, and that created another obstacle. I had no one to take care of my kids at night. I made up every excuse I could to keep from attending that class. It was fear and fear only.

I remembered that old teacher Mr. Ticks's voice: "Keath, you need to pay attention to what I'm teaching. One day, you're going to need all the education you can get, and now is the time."

I heard my science teacher, Mr. Willow, yell out, "Keath! Turn around in your seat and sit up like a young lady! Pay attention!"

And back to Ticks: "You won't be here long. I know your kind. I see how you live. Your kind don't make it. You will be like so many other statistics and end up with a house full of children, who will end up like you."

They scolded me so much, I believed them. But I would always hear Mr. Jacob Harrison's encouraging words echoing in my head: "Keath, stop following the crowd and pay attention. You will need an education one day. You can be anything you want to be, but you have to apply yourself. You need to try and do better."

Mr. Harrison was the only one who advised me without scolding. He could have criticized, but he didn't. He always spoke with real concern for me.

I made up my mind that I was nothing—nothing but a mother. I decided that at least I was going to be the best mother I could be to my children. I bought them books to read, books with animals and geography and math. I drilled into them the importance of education. I didn't ever want my children to face life as I had to.

We lived off welfare with no means of advancing except the two-percent raise each year. Every month, a old social worker came around, snooping in our business. That was life for me. I had no hope, no goals set, nothing except my kids. I had even stopped praying to God. When I put my kids into their beds, I would say the "lay me down" prayer with them, but I never would ask God for anything for myself.

I was standing at my window, looking out, feeling sorry for myself. Suddenly I cried out to God like I used to at church. I asked God who I was and what my purpose was on this earth. I didn't get an answer from God, but I felt something inside me that was unexplainable.

From then on, it was like I was being pulled in two different directions.

***

It was our second Christmas in New Hampshire. I made sure my children had everything I wanted them to have. We were happy. My mind was content with who I was at that moment, but I knew in my heart that something better was waiting for me.

I had moved to another apartment because the old landlord kicked me out after I refused to sleep with him. No one knew I was carrying around that burden. I had to laugh to myself. Nobody but the Lord allowed me to get an apartment after being told to get out in thirty days on no money with two babies. God fixed it for me. I had to recognize that only God could do the impossible.

Down at the Baker Street settlement, they were giving away Christmas toys. I was getting ready to take my children down there, and the doorbell rang. I ran downstairs and opened the door. Surprise! It was my sister Tise. I hadn't seen her in a while.

She was crying. That low-down husband had jumped her again, and as always, it showed. When I saw her like that, I couldn't help but remember all the many times Daddy fought Mama. That was just the way Buster would beat my sister. With five children, she felt she couldn't leave him.

Instead of me taking the kids to the settlement, she encouraged me to go home with her and let her oldest child, Glance, and Shannon and their friends take mine to pick up their toys. Tise had just gotten her first phone installed, and we were going to call our mama over at Mrs. Brittney's house back home. I was all for it. Just to hear my mother's voice would be a blessing.

I really didn't like the idea of the children going out alone, but under the circumstances, I agreed. We spoke to Mama, and I felt so good, hearing that she was fine. It made my day. Of course, she would say she was fine if she was dying, but I could hear the truth in her voice. She really was fine.

We were sitting around Tise's kitchen table when the children came through the door, shouting, "The little girl been hit by a car!"

I saw all the children except my Rejetta. I took one gal, Pinky, by her hand and asked, "What little girl got hit by the car?"

She pointed at me, crying profusely. "Your little girl. It was Rejetta."

I lost it. I ran every step of the way to Baker Street. Rejetta was already in the ambulance, being prepared to be taken to the hospital. I said, "That's my baby in there!" The medical attendant helped me into the ambulance.

Rejetta lay with an IV hooked up to her arm. She was very calm and had a melancholy look to her. She said, "Mammy, the car hit me."

"You okay, right?"

"My arm hurt."

"But it's going to be fine. Mammy promise you, everything gon be fine."

We arrived at the hospital, and she taken directly to the emergency room. She was checked out thoroughly. X-rays were taken of her body. Nothing was broken. There was no fracture to her skull. All seemed well except the bruises to her knees and elbows.

Throughout the treatment, she was in great spirits. We spent the evening at the hospital, and the driver of the car was there the entire time. Pastor Lee was his name; he introduced himself to me. When I was getting into the ambulance, he was giving his statement to the police. He came directly to the hospital the moment he completed his statement.

He was very sorry for the accident. I was convinced it was nothing more than an accident, and thanks be to God she was not hurt. I told him it could have been worse, but both of us knew it was God who kept my child from being hurt.

As we waited for the doctor's final diagnosis, Pastor Lee explained the full details of what happened. The light had changed, and he was waiting for all the childrens to cross over. When the light changed again, out of nowhere a little girl ran out in front of the car. He saw her and hit his brakes instantly. If he hadn't, I couldn't began to think about what could have happened. I was so grateful to the good Lord up above for saving my child.

The children later told me that Rejetta had dropped one of her bags. She reached down to get it, which was why the pastor didn't see her. Just when the light changed again, she ran out.

As we continued to wait, the police came. They had not finished up their investigation. They asked for my name, and I gave it.

"Are you the little girl's mother?"

"Yes, I am."

"I'm Officer McCarthy, and this is Officer Leary. We are appointed to take your statement. I have just a few questions for you, and we can wrap up the investigation. I know you are anxious to get her home."

"Yes, I am."

"This won't take long. Is her name Rejetta Keath?"

"We all call her Jetta, but yes, her name is Rejetta Keath."

"How old is she?"

"She is four years old."

"Where does she live?"

"She live with me at Seventy Coleman Street."

"I understand she had been to see Santa Claus. Tell me, Ms. Keath, who was she down at the center with?"

"She was with her cousins, Glance and Shannon."

"How old are Glance and Shannon?"

"Glance is twelve years old and Shannon is five."

"That wraps up our questions. I see the doctor has released her. You all have a merry Christmas, and thank you for your cooperation."

They were cops with jobs to do, and they were very professional in their questions. They shook Rejetta's hand and wished her a merry Christmas too, and they were off.

So were we. Pastor Lee insisted on bringing us home and gave me the information of his insurance company. Dear Lord, I was so dumbfounded, I didn't know the importance of the information until a couple of days later. An insurance man came out to my apartment and offered me five hundred dollars.

I accepted on the spot like a damn fool. New Hampshire law was they had to pay all the medical bills. I didn't know that her pain and mental state deserved additional compensation beyond the five hundred dollars. That was another factor of being unlearned. Faced with an educated insurance agent who knew just what to say and how to dangle the right bait in my face, I bit. I took the five hundred and signed the paper. I was later told I gave away over twenty-five thousand dollars. In the 1960s, having that amount of money was being rich.

When everybody learned what I had done, I was called just what I had called myself, a damned fool. Everybody except for Telvin. He was the brother of Robbie's friend Will, but very different from Will.

I was sitting at my kitchen table with my head resting in my hands. He came in and insisted I sit up and hold my head up. "Pay no tention to them runnin off at the mouth. If you gave it away, what the hell they got to do wit it?"

Telvin helped me to understand how I made a mistake. He helped me to see myself in a different light. I began to see him in a different light also. He was a good friend carrying around a heavy burden. I saw loneliness, heartache, and much pain in his eyes. But he was so caring, he never focused on his problems. He was always reaching out to help out someone else. What a big difference between him and his brother.

At that time, all I knew was that he was Robbie's friend and Will's brother. We accepted him based on them. He could have been a serial killer for all we knew. I had let him into our lives, my children's lives, but I was a good judge of character. He was harmless, lonely, and at that moment, helpless. I knew what it was like to be down on your luck with no one to turn to in a strange city. Will had abandoned him and moved to Connecticut. He had a choice: to stay and try and make it there, or go back to Tennessee.

The more I talked to Telvin, the more I got to know him. He was a kind, decent person, very caring and considerate. I took Telvin as the big brother I didn't have but had always dreamed of having. I made him welcome to what I had: food, a couch to sleep on every now and then. I could tell him anything. But he started dating my sister Passy Kate, and that was not promising.

Chapter 24: Hell-Bent with Fury, Don't Seem Like No Way Out

Kate and I had started off with a good relationship, but we were slipping apart. I had thought it would be good for her to reside with me. We could be a help to each other. She would be an aunt that my girls could look up to and be proud of. Residing with us would help her right herself.

But from the moment she'd moved in, her entire demeanor had changed. That friend Lesley had found her. It appeared they were old acquaintances. My spirit had been vexed ever since my eyes met Lesley's. Something like acute appendicitis weakened my whole body. I wondered if it was just my imagination, seeking someone else to blame for Passy Kate's problems. I questioned my own motives as to why I wanted Passy Kate living with me.

Passy Kate had a job, and I didn't. She didn't have any children to hold her back, and I did. She was earning a paycheck every two weeks, and I was on welfare each month, waiting on handouts. She was free-spirited and I was tied down.

Lesley could do and go wherever she pleased without any concern, because her mother lived with her and took care of Lesley's two boys. I wasn't sure if I was being unfair to her. I had a million questions rolling around in my head, and not a single answer to any of them. It was taking its toll on me. I knew I had an acute discerning spirit; I was only too weak to relate to it.

When Passy Kate didn't come home, I worried. I worried more about her than I did my own kids. She had become like more like a kid than a big sister. Her drinking was distasteful. The girls loved her, but I didn't want my children around her, period. She often was so intoxicated, she couldn't stand up straight.

Lesley stood tall, as short as she was, and the more she came around, the more I resented her. I tried to put Passy Kate at fault, but there was something in the back of my mind that kept focusing on Lesley. Suspicion took root in my heart. I despised her. I didn't believe she was that genuine friend she portrayed herself to be. Unfortunately, I had no proof of any of my suspicions.

Passy Kate was giving me twenty-five dollars a week, fifty every two weeks, and it had gotten t the point where she was not dependable at all. I supported her cigarette habit as well as her liquor habit, not to mention she had to eat and sleep. Since she was working, we both could have had it good together, but her habits and sick mind overpowered her.

I had accepted the fact that we were all sick people. I didn't get physical help; I got spiritual help and guidance from God. I never had a psychological evaluation. I knew by reading that the life I lived was not normal, and I did a self-examination. It didn't take a genius to know we were a dysfunctional family. We were sick from our parents down to the children.

I could see there was a terrible sickness on my sister, and I didn't know how to help her. She was Lesley's dupe, and it pushed us into one dissension after another. I was unable to be objective, believing and seeing the worst but helpless. No one in our family ever got any kind of treatment for our mental problems. Therefore each of us grew up with sick minds that never got fixed. I had to think of a sincere way of approaching this problem.

Something inside of me remembered the man who use to visit me in dreams when I was faced with uncertain issues. I was no psychologist, but I knew how to pray and seek God for the right guidance. We were sick people with no way to turn but to God for help. My goal was to prevent my girls from having to face these kinds of life issues. The curse was going to be broken, no matter what I had to do or how long it took.

I prayed to God day and night for the right guidance. I accepted that there was mental damage that all of us possessed, and the Keath family had severe problems. My first approach was reading the Bible. The curse began with Adam and Eve in the garden. God demanded they not eat the fruit of the tree, but they did. Their disobedience brought about many curses, and there is nothing new under the sun.

A Scripture passage came to my mind. I had never heard it preached on, but I had heard the words being used: "And if the blind lead the blind, both shall fall into the ditch" (Matt. 15:14 KJV). It caused me to face a lot of concerns I hadn't before, which forced me into copeing with them. How do you cope with situations when you're ignorant as to what can be done? As with everything else, turn to God. That is the only way.

***

One evening, there came a loud banging on my door. I rushed to open it because I didn't want my children to wake. It was Passy Kate and her friends: three hideous wineheads, all as drunk as a skunk was stink. Memories from my childhood flooded back, and all the shame, pain, and humiliation I had felt came with them. Passy Kate looked up at me, and her eyes were red as fire. I don't believe she knew who I was. The smell of them was despicable.

One of the men reminded me so much of old Mr. Willie Shangle—the face, the voice, the problem, all staring at me. Sometimes I thought that I had magnified the vision of Willie Shangle so much that every drunk I came in contact with reminded me of him.

I tried to feel contempt, but I only felt pity. I demanded that her friends go back downstairs; it was too late for visiting. They didn't say a word. They just turned and left. Passy Kate tried to start cursing, but no words came.

I called out, "Passy Kate, what is wrong with you?"

She had a sad look in her eyes. There was so much hurt and pain inside of her, a little girl trapped in a grown woman's body, crying to come out. She needed rescuing. A light came on inside of me: there was yet a ray of hope for us. My healing came from recognizing her illness and helping. I was still sane enough to reach out to my older sister and help save her. I may have been a little dim, but I was not blind. God gave me the strength I needed to reach out to her.

My first thought was to go to Tise and fill her in on what I had learned. But I couldn't wait until the next morning to have a heart-to-heart talk with Passy Kate. She was not in a comprehensible mood. That next morning, I got up and waited until she came out of her bedroom to start the conversation again.

Passy Kate was an eighth-grade dropout. She didn't seem to remember the mental and physical abuse she had encountered from my father. She hadn't known her own father. She didn't have any children of her own, and she didn't seem to know the value of being a mother. She didn't have motherly instinct.

She never looked at me as I was talking to her. She looked out the window and had this evil, nasty expression. I warned her if she didn't do better, she would have to find somewhere else to live. That didn't seem to faze her at all. I explained she was an alcoholic with many issues, more than I could cope with. Nothing I said to her made any difference. She was so far out in left field, there was no right field in sight.

I went downstairs to fill Tise in about who, what, and how. Buster opened the door with a thousand frown lines on his face. It didn't take a rocket scientist to tell me what his problem was. He said, "Y'all muster had a party up dere last night, or shall I say dis mornin." I knew he was angry.

I was too, but there was nothing to be done about what had already happened. My concern was what was going to be done about Passy Kate to prevent this kind of problem from recurring. Regardless as to who caused the noise over his head, the blame was on me, so far as he was concerned.

I answered him calmly, "Naw, we didn't have a party." Pushing past him, I asked, "Where is Tise?"

"She's in de bedroom, probly tryin to make up for dat sleep she lost last night."

I had learned to overlook a lot of things that came out of my brother-in-law's mouth. "And good morning to you. Tise!"

She was up. She came out to the living room, smiling. She knew what was on my mind—I could tell by the way she spoke "Yeah, baby?" she said sincerely.

"I didn't have no party, but your sister would've if I'd allowed her to. She brought her hideous drinkin partners up after one o'clock in the mornin, an I met em at de door."

"Haley, what is wrong wit her?"

"She is sick in the damn head, an she needs help. I want to know how kin we help her?"

Tise didn't know any more than I did. But she was willing to try to talk to Passy Kate and get a better understanding of what we were dealing with. She hadn't experienced the awful side of Passy Kate that I had; it was not a pleasant sight to see.

I stayed downstairs with Tise's kids while she went upstairs to try and talk some sense into Passy Kate. I could hear the moment she entered my apartment. Before she could get out what she wanted to say, Passy Kate lit into her with every angry spirit housed in her body. The word "respect" stood out when Tise said, "Haley got two little girls she is tryin to raise. She was good enough to bring you into her apartment an give you somewhere to live. The least you kin do is respect her an her kids."

"Respect, bitch? I pay my m—— f—— way, I kin bring any g—— d—— body I want to here."

From those words alone, I was convinced the woman was even sicker than I understood.

"You git outta my face wit dat bulls—— fore I throw your poor ass down dem dere stairs. Respect dat, bitch."

Tise came running down the stairs. I met her on the porch. She said, "Haley, my God, dat's pathetic. Who is dat up dem stairs? What done happen to Passy Kate?"

"Now you see what I'm talkin bout. Our sister is in big trouble, an if she don't git some help, I'm afraid she is gon self-destruct."

I never completed our conversation about Kate. Tise's phone rang. She went inside to answer it. I sat outside on the porch, thinking out loud, asking over and over, "What is gon happen to her if we don't do somethin?" My insides rushed up and down.

I heard a voice say, "Demon possessed." I wanted to ignore those words. I had not gotten to the point, or I was not faithful enough, to understand the meaning of good and evil spirits.

At the moment something was about to trigger inside me, Tise came to the door with the phone. "My goodness, dis is a surprise, Haley. You is really gon be surprised who dis is. Here, she want to talk to you."

I couldn't imagine who it was at that hour of the morning. Taking the receiver from Tise's hand, I placed it to my ear. "Hello?" I said as politely as I could.

"Hey, Haley, dis Millie Mae. How you doin?"

My entire demeanor faltered the moment I heard her voice. The feeling that touched me was all too familiar. God knew I didn't want to be rude or show any kind of animosity, but that was the last voice I wanted to hear that morning. Her voice took my mind completely away from what I had been focusing on. "Millie Mae, what a surprise."

"Yeah, girl, I was talkin to Tise, and she told me you lived upstairs an y'all was on de front porch talkin, so I told her to let me say hey to you."

The reason for her phone call was a man named Roland. She had been seeing him, but now he was living in New Hampshire. The same day, I got a letter from Bessy Royce comfirming my suspicion: Millie Mae was planning to come to New Hampshire too.

But Millie Mae had nowhere to stay. The next week, she phoned back, wanting to know if she could live with me until she got a place for herself and her kids.

Despite the heartaches she had brought me, anytime anyone wanted to get out of my hometown, it was my pleasure to help them. After talking everything over with Tise, I concluded I would give Millie Mae another chance. What a mistake.

She phoned back the third week and I extended a warm welcome to come and reside with me. On the day she was scheduled to leave, she called to say her trip was delayed for about a month. When she finally arrived, I took her in and treated her as if she were my own flesh and blood.

It appeared that she had already been in contact with Roland. One evening, we were getting ready to have dinner, and he showed up out of thin air—unexpected by me, anyway. From then on, my apartment became his.

Within weeks, Millie Mae was out of control, Roland was the head demon, and Millie Mae's little children were caught in between. There was no peace, no communication, no appreciation. Everything became cold. My apartment was like a refrigerator. I would have been better off putting a rattlesnake in my apartment. I realized that once a person doesn't like you, they will never like you. What was it in me that allowed me to go against my better judgment?

I had made my decision based on who I was and not on who she was, believing that she would change and I could help her do so. I was only wishful thinking, hoping for the impossible. I could let go, forgive, and forget. I had to learn that all people were not like I was.

***

Robbie and I entertained everyone, and their problems became ours. His friend Stephen was close and always around. So were Dexter and Leland, who were brothers. Robbie made sure Stephen got me and the kids wherever we needed to go, such as the grocery store or the doctor. We could always depend on Stephen. Leland and Dexter had nothing to offer except their friendship, and they were Robbie's good friends in more ways than one. They was nice, intelligent young men—and as sneaky as a dog love bones. That's just who they were.

It was twenty-two days before my birthday. Robbie told me I could do whatever or go wherever I wanted to. I chose to go out to the Mercury Lounge and just dance and have a good time. I bought myself a beautiful outfit.

Leland and Dexter came over. Robbie went out to the pool room with them for a few games. As they was preparing to leave, I was in the bedroom, relaxing across the bed. They were carrying on a strange conversation concerning Leland and Dexter's sister. Once they left, I fell asleep.

The slam of the door woke me. I got up and came out to the living room. The children were playing in their bedroom. Millie Mae came into the kitchen as I was standing at the kitchen sink, getting myself a drink of fresh water. She had a nasty look on her face, like she'd smelled a foul smell. I sensed immediately that she had been downstairs, instigating, but I brushed that off. I told myself I was not going to allow her conniving, hateful ways to destroy anything I had worked so hard to put together.

Tise came to the top of the stairs, calling for me to come down. As I went to see what Tise wanted, Robbie was coming upstairs.

Tise was grinning from ear to ear when I walked in, but I could tell right away the smiles were not real. "Haley," she said, "Shannon told me you were upstairs cryin an said you were gon have a baby."

I was shocked at what her five-year-old lying daughter told her. Why was Tise bringing me something so petty? Everyone knew the liar that Shannon was. The lies she told were funny to them.

They weren't funny to me. I knew she needed to be stopped. I believe that children should always stay in children's places and keep out of grown-up affairs.

So, not trying to hurt her, I took her by her arm and pulled her toward me. "Shannon," I said, "when did you hear me say I was gon have a baby?"

She answered, "Millie Mae told Mama you gon have a baby."

Tise called out, "Buster, Haley tryin to whip your daughter!"

I don't know if she meant it jokingly, but Buster didn't take it that way. He came out of the bedroom and grabbed my hand prying it away from Shannon as if I was trying to kill her. He said harshly, "Don't you be hittin on her!"

"I didn't hit her, but somebody need to hit her little lyin self! Dat's what wrong with dat gal. Now you take up for her in everythin she do. She is a little lyin demon from the pit bottom of hell."

Shannon faked up a cry. She was never in any kind of danger, but he'd made an issue out of me holding on to her hand.

Why had Tise even called me down there for that lie? And what made her call Buster? Anger penetrated my mind, leaving me confused.

I took my frustration out on Robbie. I blamed him for the fight, accusing him of not doing anything about Buster attacking me. Maybe I wanted to blame him for the terrible mistake I had made by letting Millie Mae back in my life. I knew she was behind all the stink that had been stirred up.

Some weeks later, Tise and Buster moved. Roland and Millie Mae moved also. They never told me they was moving out; Millie Mae just got up at five o'clock one morning and took everything downstairs. By the time I got up, their things were all out.

***

I was out one night with Robbie and his friends when Davey, the good-looking brother of my former neighbor, Louisa, sat down beside me. "Mind if I sit here?"

His eyes locked with mine, and neither one of us was able to unlock them for a while. "What are you drinkin?" he asked. He ordered a round: Scotch for him and Canadian Club and Coke for me. Davey's eyes were charming. I remembered how he'd stayed with me the night my daughter went to the hospital when she got her finger slammed. He had dimples in his cheeks that made me melt, and his eyes said what his mouth didn't. Yes, Davey was a great charmer.

I was compelled with destructiveness. Davey turned on something that had been off inside me. It came on like a flash of lightning.

Robbie, meanwhile, was sitting with his buddies and another woman. I thought she had to be Leland and Dexter's sister, who had just arrived in New Hampshire. Robbie had captured her mind already, based on the conversation I'd overheard. Her name was Mildred Pearl.

I decided to take full advantage of Davey. I thought about Robbie, *If I don't do it to him, he gon do it to me, and where is that gon leave me and my girls?*

I started to seeing Davey on a regular basis. Every weekend, Robbie went out with his friends, leaving me home and stranded with the kids. He went his way and I went mine: I would go out with Davey and be back before Robbie was.

I was beginning to think about taking the kids back to my mama, with all intentions of returning to New Hampshire myself and finding a job and a decent place to live.

On a holiday weekend, Robbie got Stephen and Stephen's girlfriend Sadie, and we all spent the day out at SkyBreeze. It was a day I will never forget.

Robbie said to Stephen, "We got to git Haley on the Bunny Jerk." It was a popular ride I had never been on before.

We stood in front of it, waiting for the girls to finish their ride. I said, "No way am I gon git on that dangerous thing."

Robbie said, "I know you ain't scare of that Bunny Jerk, bad as you is."

I was not about to let either of them think I was chicken. Their persuasiveness was more than my fear, and I was more sentimental than I gave myself credit for. It was a fun ride that one could take over and over again, forgetting all troubles.

Robbie was such a perfect gentlemen that day. He won me all kinds of goodies for my kitchen and living room that I could not afford to buy on a county check. I dreaded the end of the day, knowing once we got home, he was going to leave us for the evening. Who knew what he and Stephen would get up to? As always, my mind ran away with ideas.

Early the next morning, Tise came over. I hadn't seen her since they moved. She was devastated and apologetic. She had found out about Millie Mae.

Tise told me how Millie Mae had gotten together with Amos's wife, Cora, and they'd had a field day about me. Tise knew now that it was Millie Mae who had stirred up all the mess. I wondered what it took so long for Tise to figure that out. I had forgiven Millie Mae and was moving on with my life.

My sister and I had a wonderful talk that morning. I told her of my plans to take the kids back home. We resumed our relationship, as we had always done in the past. But for some reason I could not shake the thought of Millie Mae.

***

I was home alone, feeling down and abandoned. Robbie came home late, and flipped the light on. I was not asleep, but I was so heavily intoxicated, I could barely hold my head up. When he cut the lights off, I buried my head in the pillow.

Suddenly I felt his hand on my head. The bed seemed to go around and around in circles. I mustered up the strength to lift it. Robbie held me like I was a baby, his touch affectionate.

I felt myself losing him, and he felt himself losing me. I wasn't deliberately trying to hurt him. I was safeguarding myself from more hurt, but going about it the wrong way. I wanted to make the pain go away for both of us, but how could I?

He caressed me as if I were the only woman in his life, though I knew I was not. No one loved me as he did, and I loved no one as I loved him. But even I knew that love was not enough. What he needed, I did not have. The spirit that I carried was agitating to me, and I couldn't be the woman that he wanted me to be.

I woke up at the breaking of daylight. I pulled myself out of bed and made my way to the window, watching the sunlight shine down on the earth. I knew I had to escape. I had to leave the best thing that had ever happened to me. I hurt Robbie, and it was done deliberately. My only way out was to go back home and let him get together with someone who was more capable. My first instinct was to take my children and run like hell.

Robbie went off to work. I was waiting on the delivery of my first washing machine. I was all excited, and it wasn't even a new one.

The children were in their room, playing, when a knock came upon the door. Elated, I opened it—and there was Millie Mae. I was astounded. The nerve of her, showing up at my door after all she had done to me!

The men came up with the washing machine at nearly the same time, so she had to come inside out of their way. She had a night scarf tied around her head. She was telling me something or other about Cora; it was all lies. I could hear the guilt and fright in her voice. I opened the door wide again and said without raising my voice, "Git the hell out of my apartment and don't you ever come back."

She knew me, and she got out as fast as she could. My violent streak was not gone, and someone like her brought out the worst in me.

Chapter 25: Bitten by the Viper

I start to lose all control again. Drinking was all I desired and depended on. Intoxication was the only thing I trusted. I had nothing to hold me up—no friend, no one I could confide in. I was losing Robbie, yet I continued to ignore the signs.

Robbie always got up early on Saturday, and by eleven o'clock some of his friends would come around. They called it their hang-out day. They would go to the barber shop and end up at the pool hall. When he got back, it was time for him to go to the Mercury Lounge.

I don't know if I was being selfish or was outright tired of him putting his friends before me and my kids, but I started to make a joke out of his staying out on Saturdays. Then I got myself a babysitter one night and showed up to the Mercury without him knowing I was there. I sat and watched him from the bar as he danced to one song after another.

Just before the band took its intermission, I made my way up to John, who was in the band, and asked him to sing their hit song, "Don't Neglect Your Baby." I told him when they sang, they should add in how the man neglects his baby by spending all day at the pool room with his friends.

As John sang the song, watching me from the stage, he was smiling.

Revenge consumed me. Davey and his sister Louisa took me out to the Green Dollar Club. We had a marvelous evening. The next few weeks was unimaginable.

Then I faced the mistake I had made. There was nothing left for me to do but go home to Mama.

***

Once again, I met a wonderful man at the train station. He shook my hand and said, "Micah, Micah is my name."

He was drawn to my kids. Immediately, he picked up my baby girl and asked if he could get us anything. When the time came for our departure, he carried my baby and my footlocker on to the train, and made sure we were seated correctly in coach. Oh, how blissful it was to meet someone so charming! I threw my arms around him and hugged him in a genuine thank-you.

The conductor made the call. I was about to thank Micah again, and he interrupted me. "You don't have to thank me. It was my pleasure to have met and helped you and these beautiful little girls. Maybe our paths will cross again one day, who knows?"

He never knew my tremendous gratitude. I actually felt his generosity live on within me. He was not Tonk, my childhood protector, but he was a gentleman.

We arrived in Georgia on schedule. For once in my life, I was glad to be back home. The taxi drove up in front of the old wooden house. Mama and Odessa were sitting on the porch swing. Half the paint had peeled off of it. They were using a towel to fan away the gnats and flies.

When the driver stopped, they both looked up, their expressions uncertain. My girls crawled out of the backseat and Mama jumped to her feet with great joy. We gave her something to celebrate.

Odessa shouted, "Now, Jenny Rue, go git us a nice, stiff drink!"

Mama cried loudly, "Lord my chilluns done come back home! I knowed you was gon send my young'uns back home to me." Her face lit up with warmth. For the first time in my life, my mother and I embraced each other, and it felt oh so good. She whispered, "You ain't gon take my chilluns way from here again, is you?"

Before I could answer her, my eyes met those of Little Freddy. He was coming in the door with Daddy. "Haley, babe, you made it back home! I just finished tellin Mr. Macky if y'all didn't come home, I was gon take me a trip."

We laughed it off. After a while, he and I took a stroll around the old neighborhood. We met some old neighbors. He told me to speak and keep on walking. But at Millie Mae's mama's house, she recognized who I was and insisted on us coming in and having a cold beer.

The moment we stepped into her living room, I saw a photo. I had had the photographer from the Mercury come to my apartment and take my girls' pictures. Millie Mae put her little girl in there with mine. I paid to get the pictures made, and Millie Mae sent one home—then cut my girls off.

I was blowed, but I kept my cool. I shared the story with Little Freddy after, and as always he had nothing but good advice for me.

We walked in between Benny Lee Lang's place and old Pa Jacks's café. I looked across the ballpark and had a vision of my two girls and Millie Mae's playing in the field. All of a sudden, Millie Mae's girl disappeared, and my girls just kept turning flips and laughing.

I shook away the vision. I knew it was meaningful, but what did it mean?

Little Freddy told me with confidence and pride, "One day, Haley babe, you an our little girls gon climb Jacob's ladder, and each time you go higher, you'll look back on all of dem wit love, joy, an happiness, an you will smile."

The best times in my relationship with Little Freddy were when he was schooling me about something I needed. Those words were inspiring to me at that moment.

That night after Little Freddy left me, I was awakened in the wee hours of the morning. I heard the voice of Jesus say, "Fret not thyself because of evildoers, for they shall soon be cut down and wither like the grass."

Lord knows I didn't understand a word of what I heard, but I felt something strong hit my spirit I shook my head and went back to sleep.

The first thing I remembered the next morning were those words. As I was cleaning the house, I came across a little Bible. It opened to Psalm 37: "Fret not thyself because of evildoers." I read the entire psalm and knew that was a strong message for me from the almighty God. It set my mind at ease for the first time in a long, long while. I felt a peace in my heart and mind.

***

Millie Mae was lying near death from a gunshot wound. Her man Roland had shot her. I prayed hard for her recovery. Coming home that evening, I met Casey, Roland's brother. I asked him where Roland was. "Locked up in de big jail, but he won't be dere long," he stated.

"Why did Roland shot her?"

"For tryin to be slick!"

"Casey, you act like what Roland did was right."

"Naw, dat ain't what I said. But dat's what bein slick git you. You ought to be de last person to take up for her like she done been round here, talkin bout and low-ratin your name. What if Little Freddy shot you over some of de lies she been tellin on you?"

"Well, if a man feed you stones, the Good Book say feed him bread. The good Lord up above knows all about me, and he is my shepherd. Little Freddy knows me too. I ain't worried."

No matter how my mind said I hated Millie Mae, my heart said to love her. The Bible said to judge ye not that ye may not be judged. She was lying in the hospital, fighting for her life. She only had two things working for her: God and time.

I was yet standing, preparing to return to New Hampshire to try and get the man I loved back and raise my two girls in the way they should be raised. Casey was in love with me, and everyone round there knew it. Word was I was going with him, but God knew the truth—it never happened.

The journey I was traveling was not a good example, but no matter how many blocks were placed before me, no matter how many ditches had been dug for me, those who placed the obstacles would one day get caught in their own traps. "The Lord will fight for you; you need only to be still" (Exod. 14:14 NIV). I was taught that, I lived it, and I knew it to be truth.

I was so confident in myself that on Sunday morning, I paid Millie Mae's mother a visit. She welcomed me in, and I told her she had my sympathy. I said I was wishing Millie Maw a speedy recovery, especially for the sake of her children. Her eyes were swollen from crying. She told me word was I had said "I wish Millie Mae had died."

I had been treated awfully cruelly by Millie Mae, but never in a thousand years would I wish death on her. Sister Greta's was to pray for your enemies, and I did. I never held any animosity in my heart because that was too much energy to burn unnecessarily.

Millie Mae's mother said Lila was inside. I went into the room, and there Lila was, all wracked in pain. I asked her how Millie Mae was doing. "She is in intensive care. Dey had to remove one of er kidneys. Dey wasn't able to git one of de bullets out of er. She listed in critical condition. Gurl, you just don't know how good it made me feel to see you an Little Freddy up dere visitin."

"I'm very sorry, Lila. She is in my prayers."

"Thank you. I heard you said you wished she died. Ollie Burns convinced me dat was a lie, cause you and her been together since you an Little Freddy was at de hospital dis mornin. Somebody told a damn lie on you."

Ollie Burns and Lila had been friends for a long time. Ollie knew I never said anything so evil. What I did say that day out of anger was, "One day somebody gon kill that lyin Delta." It was in Delta's nature to lie and keep hell going. That story had been twisted and told by her, for sure.

I was sick and tired of lies and deceitfulness around me. I always seemed to be in the midst of some kind of confusion. There was no need for defense, though. I was getting ready to hightail it away from that town for good.

I saw the same symptoms in Delta as I did in Millie Mae. They were two of the most miserable human beings I had ever known.

I had a phone call from Tise over at Mrs. Brittney's house. News had reached New Hampshire that Millie Mae was dead. I assured Tise that she was not dead, but she was in critical condition. Tise said my return ticket was on the way. I decided to get out on Monday

I was reluctant to utter a word to Little Freddy, but I did. I told him I planned to leave on Friday. He made it known to me that he wasn't pleased. I knew he loved me as much as he was capable of. And I had made sure all of his spare time was spent with me. I led him to believe that I was still romantically in love with him.

On Thursday night, he implored me to wait until Monday. I let him persuade me a little before pretending I had given in. He had played right into my hands. He made the entire weekend a very social and enjoyable one for us, and drove me to the bus station on Monday morning.

I hadn't known how hard it would be to leave my kids until the time came for me to do so. At the last minute, I wanted to back out. But my mama was happy, and they were in the best of care. As Little Freddy drove off, the girls sat waving at me from Mama's lap. I couldn't fight back my tears, no matter how hard I tried.

When we arrived at the bus station, he implored me to take a later bus, which wasn't leaving until five o'clock. He wanted us to spend the rest of the day alone. That was the furthest idea from my mind. I refused. But my scheduled bus was about an hour late, and that gave us a chance to talk.

He reassured me that he would be checking on the kids as often as he could. I knew he had loved Rejetta from the day he laid his eyes on her, and I could depend on him looking after her as well as Vermont Andreka. He couldn't stop telling me how pretty I was to him, like I was the only woman he ever said those words to. In a way, I didn't doubt him, but it was a little too late.

The bus finally came. I couldn't wait to board it. He walked me inside. I took a seat midway down the aisle, by the window. Our final good-bye was harder than when I left the children. Tears dropped from his eyes, and that brought tears to mine.

"I love you, Haley babe," he said sincerely. He waited for a response from me, but I could not give it. His tears came faster and faster, and he made sure I saw them.

I did love him in the way we should love, but I was no longer in love with him the way he wanted me to be. That love was gone. The only person I wanted to tell that I loved him was many miles away, and I couldn't wait.

Chapter 26: In Spite of It All, Life Goes On

I arrived at the New Hampshire bus station at five minutes after ten on Tuesday night. I called Tise. "Tise, baby, I'm back."

"You are? Where you at now?"

"At the bus station."

Buster arrived fifteen minutes after my call, and drove me directly to their house. Tise was waiting for me with open arms. I had never been so glad to be in New Hampshire as I was at that moment.

She filled me in on everything that had been happening there during my absence. I noticed she didn't mention Robbie nor Passy Kate. I had a feeling she was waiting on me to mention them. I hinted that it was late and I had to get home. Tise smiled as if I was kidding about going to my apartment. "Do Robbie know you back?"

"No, he don't, unless you told him?"

Did I expect to return and find him the same as when I left? Despite everything that had happened, I didn't consider that he might have replaced me during my absence or might not be there at all. I had to get there fast and straighten everything out. I acknowledged the danger into which I had placed our relationship. I didn't know if the damage was repairable.

I told Tise I had to leave.

"You mean you goin on over there?"

"Yes, I got to."

I walked up on the porch. The house still looked the same, but it was dark. I thought maybe no one was at home, or they all could be asleep. "Tise, will you come up with me?" I asked, frightened.

"Sure."

I had a feeling she was holding something back, something she was dying to tell me.

She led the way upstairs and knocked twice on the door. My stomach was overflowing with butterflies. No one answered. She knocked twice, a little harder.

This time Passy Kate answered. "Who is it?"

"It's Tise, Passy Kate."

Passy Kate opened the door. Tise and Buster walked in, and I behind them.

When Passy Kate saw me, her eyes lit up like a Christmas tree. I put my finger to my lips to signal her to keep quiet. We embraced with great joy. She was happy that I was back, but not half as happy as I was.

I pulled her aside and quietly asked, "Is Robbie in dere alone?"

She said, "Yes, why?" And looked directly at Tise.

That really made me believe that there was something going on.

"Well, I guess we better be goin, Buster," Tise said.

"No, you don't, either, wit your sneaky-ass self," Passy Kate said.

It was time for me to go into that bedroom and find out just how things stood between Robbie and myself,

I took a deep breath. Instead of knocking, I walked boldly into the room. Moonlight shone through the window onto the bed. Robbie was sleeping soundly. I walked quietly up to the bed and just looked at him. He'd cut his hair. My thoughts became dreams of what our lives should have been.

Then he turned over and saw me standing over his bed. "When did you git back?" he murmured.

"Tonight. Buster picked me up at de bus station."

I looked around and saw Passy Kate and Tise peeking through the doorway and giggling with happiness. I was unsure how to handle the situation.

Robbie got up and put his robe on, and we all sat in the living room. I discovered Passy Kate had put in a new sectional. It was lovely. I tried to avoid the subject of my trip for as long as I could. Robbie was dying to know how the kids were, but I knew if I said anything about home, it would only lead to more questions. I wanted to deal with them later. Everything was going so well, I didn't want to spoil it.

Passy Kate undoubtedly hadn't considered any of that. She was the first to mention Georgia. She wanted to know how Millie Mae was doing. "When I left, I heard she had been taken out of intensive care," I answered reluctantly.

"How bad was it?" Robbie asked.

"It was bad. One of de bullets damaged a kidney, which had to be removed."

"How many times did Roland shoot her?"

"Three times. De one in er stomach did de most damage."

"Isn't that something," Tise said.

"Why did Roland shoot her?" Buster asked.

"I really don't know. Rumor was dere was some new men in town, an she was slippin round wit one of dem. Whatever it was took place out behind Mrs. Hilley's café. De real reason, I don't think nobody know except Millie Mae and Roland. You know how them lyin-ass niggers is down South. They git the cow by his ass an run away with em."

"Yeah, Haley, you right about dat."

I got up and made my excuses. "Y'all wait, Tise. I just got to take me a bath. Dem two days travelin on dose buses have really got me tired an misty."

Tise got my grip and said, "Naw, Haley, we won't wait. It's gittin late, and Buster have to git up early in the mornin. I know Robbie and Passy Kate do too."

"Naw, I'm off tomorrow," Passy Kate stated.

I went into the bathroom and took a good hot bubble bath. Lying in the tub with hot water soothing my body was one thing I had missed since I left for Georgia. I thanked God as many time as my tongue could move.

Passy Kate knocked on the door. "Come on in," I invited her. She came in holding a beautiful red negligee in her arms. I had never seen anything so beautiful in my life.

"I bought dis for you," she said.

"Oh, Passy Kate, it's beautiful!"

"Thank you. I thought you would like it. After I gave Tise de money for your ticket an bought that livin room suite, I went shoppin for myself. I seen dat negligee and it looked just like you, so I got it for you."

"Thank you again. If you don't mind my askin, where you git all of dat money?"

"I knew dat would be your next question. You know I ain't been stayin here regularly, an de week you left, I got in an accident. Before you git all excited, I wasn't hurt as bad as it seem, but bad enough to git three thousand dollars."

"My God, girl, you been in an accident an I didn't know!"

"Like I said, I wasn't hurt bad. I end up with a knot on my head an painful whiplash, an my nerves was shot, but no broken bones. Other dan dat, I'm doin good."

"Den I'll say good night an see you in de mornin."

***

The next morning, the light from the sunrise shone through our bedroom window. I stared at it bleakly. It was nearing Robbie's time to set off to work. I felt like a new person, but I couldn't escape a guilty feeling.

After he left for work, Passy Kate and I sat down for a hot cup of coffee. My body felt heavy from the guilt I was feeling. I wanted to talk over everything that had happened. I didn't think Passy Kate was the right one to talk to, though. I tried to hold back.

Somehow Passy Kate seemed different. I admired her integrity. Her intemperate manner somehow compelled great admiration. I wanted to know if she had broken her alcohol problem. But I dared not ask her, because I knew how defensive she got when anybody stuck their noses into her personal affairs. Our relationship was commencing well, and I wanted to keep it that way.

Tise came over, anxious to reveal what she had withheld from me the night before. We went out to shop. As soon as Passy Kate was out of earshot, Tise blurted, "Robbie is seeing another woman. Her name is Mildred Pearl. She's Leland an Dexter's sister."

It didn't amaze me that Robbie was involved with another woman, but who that woman was surely did. It put a damper on the hilarious mood I had been in, leaving me feeling frigid and withdrawn. "Tise, I think I want to go back home. I need to be alone. Tell Passy Kate."

"Tell er what, Haley?"

"I don't know. Anything you want to. I got to go back home."

"Haley! Passy Kate warned me not to tell you bout dat. If she found out, she'll kill me."

"Then just tell er I forgot somethin an went back to git it!"

I left, running. Anguish swept through me. I ran all the way back home, almost hysterical. As I walked up the stairs to the apartment, I recollected a conversation I had overheard between Robbie, Leland, Dexter, and Stephen months before I left New Hampshire. I had heard Leland mention something about his sister, who hadn't so long before come to the city.

I was unsure of what to do. I knew I loved Robbie, and regardless of who he was seeing, the hurt and the questions did not justify me accusing him without proof. I remembered Davey and Little Freddy and thought, *Who am I to say anything?* If I had been the woman that I set out to be, maybe this would not have happened. I tried to convince myself that I was to blame for something that I was not even sure of. I did try to keep an open mind, seeking answers that were not there.

Cora stopped in for a visit. She looked as if she had lost her best friend. "I been stoppin by your apartment after job huntin, tryin to catch up wit y'all."

"You lookin for a job? What happen to your job at Enterprise?"

"Haley, child, after Amos left me for dat little ugly woman, he and I had a big fight at work an we both got fired."

We exchanged our problems with each other, mostly laughing our hearts out at her hilarious jokes. We were in the same boat: upstream with no paddle. I didn't have the kids, so I wasn't eligible for public assistance. We were both desperately hurting for money and having no luck finding a job.

Robbie came home in a cheerful mood, greeting me with one of his passionate kisses. Nothing could take away his joy. He sprung some news on me: Leland, Dexter, and Stephen were coming by. I kinda felt rejected. I had hoped for a quiet evening.

Acting was never one of my favorite activities, but since I hadn't seen them in so long, I dared not allow what I was really feeling to show. They arrived on schedule and showed the same charming, attractive manners they had always done. Leland was still as tall, deep-eyed, and handsome as ever. Dexter was slow-talking and equally handsome, toting his guitar. Stephen brought laughter wherever he appeared. It was really great having them all around again. They were Robbie's best friends.

Neither Leland nor Dexter smoked or drank. Robbie, Stephen, and I did. I observed Leland and Dexter. They were certainly well-mannered boys. It was visible that a solid foundation had been laid for them. I didn't feel anything except happiness for Robbie, having such friends. They were the kind of family he needed. He fit right in with them with no hesitation.

I made them feel welcome and showed just how gracious I could be. The evening started off casual, with a warm, pleasant atmosphere. They had always loved my cooking.

After dinner, I left them in the living room and went into my bedroom. I sat alone, looking out the window and drinking down as much Canadian Club as my stomach could hold. I puffed cigarettes one behind the other, listening to their voices.

I suddenly got annoyed. They were having a laughable good time, and I wasn't. I went out to the living room and asked courteously, "Guys, did you all have enough to eat?"

"Yes," they all answered simultaneously. Leland added, "The food was really good, as always."

All eyes were on me, like I was the coming attraction. It was noticeable that I'd been drinking. Intelligent guys that they were, they overlooked it. Leland asked encouragingly, "Haley, how was back home?"

I really don't think he meant anything by asking, but my alcohol told me he was meddling. Before I could answer, Dexter complimented me on how beautiful my skin was, adding, "Pretty as a big Georgia peach!"

I was flattered by his charming compliment. Along with a thank-you, I asked him to play us a tune on his guitar. He was a little modest, but he had a benevolent sense of humor. He played a novelty tune about a bear. I got carried away, not realizing the CC had taken more effect than I anticipated.

While everyone was listening to Dexter play and bantering their smart remarks, hell flew up inside me. I looked Leland in the eye until I got his undivided attention. Then I said, "Leland, you a good-lookin man. Does you sister Mildred look anythin like you?"

Dexter stop playing his tune. Robbie's glass dropped from his hand. Stephen began to light up another cigarette with one already in his mouth. Leland's eyes flashed from me to Robbie, and I knew he was ransacking his brain for the right words to say.

Reluctantly, he said, "Yeah, everybody say me and her do look somewhat alike."

Dexter stated suspiciously, "Haley, you know our sister?"

I answered, "I know of her." I was filled with anxiety, not sure what I hoped to accomplish.

"Well, Haley, we enjoyed this evening," Dexter said bravely. "You keep your face looking like that Georgia peach!" They knew I was on to them. They left and never returned.

***

I woke up early the next morning, filled with excitement. I went to Passy Kate's room and discovered she hadn't been home again. I got dressed and waited for Cora. She was going with me as moral support while I applied for a job at the hospital.

We reached the hospital at nine o'clock. I asked the receptionist for an application. Cora said she was going around to the emergency side to see a friend of hers. I completed the application and gave it back to the receptionist. She told me to have a seat and someone would see me shortly. I sat down in the waiting room, lit a cigarette, and crossed my legs.

Not long after, a middle-aged, tall, gray-headed lady came out, holding my application in her hand. "Miss Keath," she called gently.

I put out my cigarette and stood up. "Yes?"

"Will you come with me, please?"

I followed her into her office. It was tidy. She told me to have a seat. "I am Ms. Stockade. I will be interviewing you today."

I sat across from her desk very properly, her eyes on me at all times. She looked over the application and said, "Your last employment was at Enterprise Company."

"Yes, ma'am," I answered nervously.

"Why did you leave?" she asked.

It was so unexpected, I almost choked. I didn't want to lie because I was smart enough to know she would check out what I told her. The only thing I could think of was to be honest. I took a deep breath and explained the fight.

From the way she looked at me, I knew I had blown any chance of getting hired. She asked me a few other questions, then said, "Well, Miss Keath, at this time our housekeeping and dietary departments are all filled, but I will keep your application on file. If anything comes up, I will give you a call."

I had heard those words before. I dropped my head with deep regret and said, "Thank you."

I rushed out the door, then immediately discovered I had left my purse behind. I opened the door and saw Ms. Stockade putting my application in her trash basket.

"Excuse me, Ms. Stockade, I almost left my purse in your office," I said pointedly.

She never looked embarrassed or sorry.

I picked up my purse and stormed out the door as fast as I could. I ran to the elevator. My heart fluttered with hurt. I felt humiliated and desperate. I just cried.

I took the elevator down to the emergency room to find Cora, wiping my eyes so she wouldn't see that I had been crying. I searched all around the emergency room, but she was nowhere to be found.

I left for the bus stop and discovered I had missed the bus by about two minutes. I had to wait thirty minutes for another one. As I sat, I was thinking every negative thought. I watched the students go in and out of the medical school. It all seemed so easy for them. I wished so badly for an opportunity to return to school, but no matter how hard I wished, I concluded it was too late for me. I had convinced myself I was nothing but a no-good loser, and that's what I would always be.

Finally the bus came. I hopped on and trotted all the way to the back. I didn't know how cold I had gotten until I sat down. My face felt like a chunk of ice, even with a scarf covering my ears.

I arrived at the apartment. Without my kids, it was so empty. There was so many voids in my life, and I couldn't begin to fill any of them.

Suddenly that old dream flashed through my mind. Three women had hexed me: Delta, Theola, and O'Bera, and O'Bera was dead. It was all making sense. I was having a hard time and couldn't prosper. I couldn't even find a job though the advertisements were plentiful.

I started to accept I was doomed to failure. The only thing I had to live for was my kids, and I couldn't help but wonder if they would be better off without me. At least if I were dead, they would get a social security check every month.

I wanted a drink, but there was no whiskey and no money to buy any.

***

Robbie got paid and gave me the money to take care of expenses. I headed downtown to pay our gas and electric bill, but my route went past the liquor store. I fought with all my strength to keep on without stopping. It was like gravity drew me into the store. I thought maybe I could borrow from the bill money and delay paying until the following week, not knowing another bill was due. I spent our bill money on whiskey.

My drinking got worse. My nagging at Robbie became unbearable. I was totally untrustworthy. I hated myself.

One day I got drunk and passed out. I must have been out for hours. When I woke up, the house was freezing cold. I looked out the window, and it was snowing. I looked up at the clock, and the hands were at 1:10. My head was spinning so much, I couldn't figure out whether that was a.m. or p.m. I hit the light switch, and the lights didn't come on.

Then I realized I hadn't paid the bills, and everything had been shut off.

Robbie came in to find a dark and cold apartment. He was furious. Out of anger, things were said that I took personally. I contracted unforgiveness in my heart. I didn't fight back or exchange insults. I took all of the accusations exactly as he put them to me. There was no way I could rectify what I had done, because I had no job and no money. I had already decided what I was going to do.

He left the apartment, looking devastated. The only thing I could do was finish drinking the rest of the booze and crawl into bed to stay warm.

Robbie came back later that evening with a bag of hot food. I was too ashamed to eat any. The next day, he took off from work and went downtown to try to get the service back on. But he was unable. The bills were already three months past due, which totaled over three hundred dollars, and he didn't have it. He didn't make a lot of money.

We were in a hell of a fix: winter in New Hampshire with no heat and no lights. Robbie was calm, but I knew what he must have been feeling inside.

Stephen came and jerry-rigged the gas, but he couldn't turn the lights on. They went to the store to get some candles. I felt so guilty and ashamed. All I could think about was to get out of Robbie's life for good; he deserved much better.

That seed was planted, and it grew and grew. I was also missing the kids, and I belonged with them. I couldn't think of anything positive. I saw no positiveness in me. I hated the thought of going back home, but it seemed like that was the only solution.

I began to think of Mildred too. Even though I had never met her, I believed in my heart she was the right kind of woman for Robbie.

My pain increased. For some reason, I could not think of a Scripture passage that might help me clear my thoughts, or even pick up my little New Testament and just read one. I concluded if I was out of Robbie's life, he and Mildred would get together.

Love is never enough. Stability is needed. Unhealthy notions took root in my mind, and I made impetuous choices until I could no longer tolerate the torment.

I wished for Passy Kate, but she had moved out with Lesley. Besides, she was a bigger drunk than I was, so she couldn't help me either.

I concluded that going back home was the best solution to our problem. I made that decision, but I was not pleased with it at all. Something else was pounding away, trying to convince me that I was wrong. But I wouldn't listen. I went with what my mind was saying, unstable as it was.

I had to tell somebody. Passy Kate was the only person I could think of. I went around some places she might be on her off day, but no one had seen her. I went to Lesley's house, and that was where I found her.

The place was a real dump. I wanted to cry, except I had no tears left. I told Kate of my decision. She was not thrilled at all about it. She even promised to come back to my apartment if I stayed, but I couldn't.

I didn't stay long, just long enough to inform her of my plans. She had been drinking, and I recall how she looked up at me and said, "Don't go."

I didn't want to, but a strong force compelled me to leave. I could feel the pressure on my brain, draining me of the little strength I had left.

I left, hoping I would get back home before Robbie did. But he was there when I arrived. He had already started making dinner for us.

I took off my coat and went into the kitchen. I just looked on as he stood in as chef for the evening. I couldn't believe what my eyes were showing me: how considerate, charming, and kind this man was. I didn't want to lose him, but something inside me was pushing me to run.

He turned and saw me standing there in the candlelight. He took me into his arms, and the warmth of that hug was strong enough to last me forever. Regardless how badly I behaved or the embarrassment I caused him, his true feelings never changed. Each time he looked at me, the love shone all over his face.

I knew what was going on in my head was nothing like what I felt in my heart. I made myself believe it was better for me to go back, join my girls, and live in a town mired in evil. I was only fooling myself when I came back to New Hampshire, hoping to make it work with Robbie. And then having to give it up was like slow death inside.

I waited until after we finished dinner. As we sat comfortablely on the sofa, I looked him up and down. He was so handsome to me. He was all I wanted. But I knew the time had come; the dream was over, and I was awake.

"Robbie, I made a decision," I said sorrowfully.

"Let's hear it."

They were the hardest words I believe I ever had to speak. "I've decided to go back home."

Shocked, he stared at me. "You mean go back down South."

"Yes."

"You decided to git the kids? Well, good. I've been waitin for you to tell me when you were bringin the kids home."

"No, honey. I mean to stay. I've decided to go back home to stay."

"Stay for good," he repeated, half like a question. He loosened his shoulders and sat silently. After a moment, he said, "You're serious, ain't you."

The expression on his face and the look in his eyes just convinced me more to get out of his life. I nodded. A part of me really wanted to explain, but there wasn't any good explanation.

I couldn't bear looking at him any longer. I dashed into the bedroom and poured every tear into the pillow. He rushed after me, begging for a reason. The only reason I had for him was, "I miss my babies." He knew there was another reason, but he would not find out.

We spent our last night together, and I moved in with my sister Tise. Cora invited me to spend the last few days with her, but I declined.

I stayed away from Robbie. He called me every day, imploring me to change my mind, but my mind was made up. I couldn't bear to humiliate him anymore. I knew if I stayed on, eventually he would hate me. I couldn't tolerate that. Freeing him was the only solution.

I had Tise tell him I was out, visiting with Cora. He believed her. An a hour later, he called back. She told him I hadn't gotten back. Twenty minutes later, he as at the door. I was sitting at the dining room table when Buster opened the door. Robbie saw me before I could move. He looked so hurt and tired, all because of me. His pain and my pain were more than either of us could endure.

He came in and sat, exchanging a few words with Buster. The entire time, his eyes stayed on me. Tise came out of the kitchen, smiling. "Hey, Robbie, how everythin goin with you?"

"I can't complain, Tise. How bout yourself?"

"Ah, so-so."

She called me into the kitchen. "Haley, is anything wrong between you and Robbie?"

I explained a little to her, and she cried, "Haley, why?"

Tise was my favorite sister, and I couldn't even tell her my reasons. She tried to convince me to stay on until after Thanksgiving. It was only five days away, but I intended to be home with my kids by then.

***

The time came for me to leave. Buster drove me to the bus station. Robbie was there, waiting for me. I purchased my ticket. When the bus came, Robbie helped me get situated. He kissed me hard. "Regardless what happens or where you go, I will never forgit you, Haley," he said.

The bus drove slowly off. For as long as I could see him, he watched me steadily. I cried until I was tearless.

***

I hadn't seen Aunt Lorena for years. I arrived at the bus station at eight-forty on Wednesday morning. I got off the bus and went directly to the washroom. I looked in the mirror, and I looked terrible. The tearstains had dried on my face, and my eyes was bloodshot. My hair looked as if a chicken had been scratching through it.

I washed my face and put on fresh makeup. I combed my hair and tried to make myself presentable before calling Aunt Lorena. No matter how I managed to make myself look, there was a stain that I could not remove, the hurt stain in my heart.

I went to the phone booth and dialed Aunt Lorena's number. "Hello?" a man answered.

"Hello, may I speak to Lorena Bollen?"

"Yes, you may." I heard him cover the receiver, then call out, "Lorena, honey, you have a call."

"Find out who it is. I'm taking a bath, and I'll git back with them," she said.

"Hello, may I ask who's calling?" the man said to me.

"Dis is her niece Haley. Is dis Uncle Bollen?"

"Yes! Yes, it is. Where are you calling from? Aunt Lorena is taking a bath."

"I'm here at de Trailways bus station. Kin someone come pick me up?"

I heard Aunt Lorena in the background. "Is that my baby? Where is she?"

"She's at the Trailways bus station, and she wants someone to pick her up."

"Tell her Marilyn will be right there."

"Haley! Marilyn will be there for you in a few minutes. Wait there."

"All right, Uncle Bollen. I'll be waitin for er. Good-bye."

When I hung up, tears poured down my face. The joy in their voices about the surprise I had sprung upon showed this was a happy moment for them, but I couldn't be at all pleased about it.

I rushed back to the washroom and tried to pull myself together before Marilyn arrived. I was almost incoherent. After washing my face in ice-cold water, I began to feel a little better.

When I came out, I saw a woman who I thought looked like my cousin. She looked at me, then turned and walked outside. I convinced myself that wasn't her and sat down in the waiting room.

I saw the lady looking in through the window. She turned away, got into a car, and drove off. I realized that *had* been Marilyn coming for me, and we hadn't recognized each other.

I went to the phone booth and placed another call to Aunt Lorena, telling her, "I thought I recognized Marilyn, but by the time I realized it was her, she left."

"Wait, here she is, driving up now. Hold on a second. I'm gonna send her right back."

She came back to the phone and said, "You wait there, baby. Marilyn is on her way back. I shoulda know you wouldn't recognize my baby. I am so glad you're here, and I'll see you when you git to the house."

Her voice had such a soft, pleasant sound to it. I kept the thought of seeing her and the sound of her voice in my mind until Marilyn arrived.

This time I saw her as she drove into the parking lot. I hurried over to her as she opened the door to get out of the car. When we hugged each other, it was a warm and welcoming hug. I felt as if I'd always known her.

Aunt Lorena and Uncle Bollen were waiting at the house for me, along with Marilyn's twelve-year-old daughter Valerie. Everything seemed different. I couldn't quite figure out what it was.

I walked up on the porch. Aunt Lorena embraced me like we were never going to see each other again. "My baby," she said, over and over. "You sure is my brother's daughter. I just hate so much Mama didn't ever get a chance to see you."

We went into the house and sat around, talking about everything and everybody. I rather enjoyed our conversation. It kept my mind off of my problems.

"How long you gon stay?" Uncle Bollen asked.

"I don't know. I haven't really thought about it."

"Well, I'm sure you'll stay and have Thanksgivin wit us."

"Maybe I will. We'll just see. I think I want to change into something comfortable," I said hurriedly. That was the only excuse I could come up with to get out of the room. I couldn't think of having Thanksgiving with anyone except my kids. And I definitely didn't want any of them to know I was having problems.

I changed into a pair of comfortable slacks and a sweater. Neither Aunt Lorena nor Uncle Bollen were drinkers or smokers. I craved a drink. I speculated that if only I could get just one drink, it would help ease my aching heart.

I managed to get Marilyn off alone and suggested to her that I wanted to see Uncle Alex and Becca. Would she ask Aunt Lorena for the car so she could take me over there?

She informed me it would go over better if I asked her. I hesitated, then thought, *What the hell.*

"Aunt Lorena," I said, as persuasively as I could, "I'm planning on leaving tomorrow morning. I'd like to see Uncle Alex and Becca before I leave. Do you mind letting Marilyn drive me over there?"

"I'm surprised you gon leave on Thanksgiving Day," my aunt said sadly. "I was hoping you spend it with us. But if that's what you want to do, then I won't try to stop you. I understand how anxious you is to git home to your babies. Sure, Marilyn kin take you over there."

"Thanks, Aunt Lorena," I said gratefully.

I'd had no intention of leaving on Thanksgiving Day. It was an impulsive decision.

Marilyn drove me over to Uncle Alex's house, where we had a short visit—just long enough to see that he and his family were in the best of health, and to assure him that Daddy was the same. It broke my heart to see how well Daddy's family was doing and the lovely homes they were living in. His brother and brother-in-law were hard workers and good providers. It had made the difference for their families.

Leaving Uncle Alex, we went to Becca's house. She was highly intoxicated, but when we got out of the car, she recognized me immediately and started shouting, "Dat's Uncle Macky daughter dere, I'll know her anywhere!"

She hugged me, and I had to hold my breath. I could imagine how I must have smelled when I was feeling about like she was. Even the smell didn't turn off my wish for a drink, but when she offered me what she was drinking, that certainly did.

"Have a drink," she kept insisting.

"No, I can't drink dat brand," I declined.

"Well, come on, we'll buy you what kind you want."

"Naw, it's all right. Y'all drink. I really don't want anythin."

"I ain't gonna hear of it. You're Uncle Macky's daughter an all. I know he drink, so dis is a celebration."

She wouldn't accept no for an answer, so I gave in to her. We all crawled into Aunt Lorena's car and went to the package store. I had my choice of any brand of whiskey on the shelf, but I chose red wine instead. Somehow I couldn't stand the sight of whiskey.

When we got back to Becca's house, we sat gathered in her tidy living room. I watched them pour whiskey into their stomachs like I couldn't have believed if I hadn't sat and witnessed it for myself. I didn't want to feel odd, so I opened my bottle and poured a small amount into my glass.

As I sipped the wine, Becca's man Danny gave me a leering grin. I gave him one back and passed it off as drunkenness. I really did believe that's all it was, until every time I looked up, he was mummering and winking at me. I begin to feel very uncomfortable.

Everyone else seemed to be enjoying themselves rapturously. They were asking me questions and I was answering them as best I knew how. Our acquaintance came on instantaneously. Soon it was like I was at home.

I glanced over at Danny, slumped down in his chair, steadily winking and blinking at me. I looked back with contempt, hoping he would get the message that I didn't appreciate his attitude. He paid me no mind.

I had to get out of the room. I asked Becca where her bathroom was and pretended I had to use it. When I got up to pass him, the dirty rat tried to pat me on the rear.

And Becca saw him. "You low-down dirty sumbitch, you mean you sat on your ugly ass tryin to pat my cousin's ass, and I'm sittin here lookin at you?" she said, hurt and angry. A big argument intensified between them.

Danny reminded me of my father in the way he reviled Becca every way he could. I gathered from the argument that I was not the first woman he ever got fresh with. The violence got so bad that Marilyn and I separated them. I carried Becca outside to calm her down. Yes, she was a blood relative of my father's, all right.

As I comforted her, she told me how sorry she was and that she didn't blame me for any of it. Her description of Danny that evening showed he was a truly evil man, and her life was a living hell with him—just as my mother's was with my father. I believe that was one of the reasons why she and my mother were heavy drinkers. I inherited my drinking habits from them. Becca was short like me but swift like a fish, with no fear in any part of her body.

As Marilyn and I drove off, Becca sat on the porch, waving goodbye, looking like she had just lost her only friend. My heart was really touched, leaving me with a lot of unanswered questions.

Marilyn drove us along the avenues and pointed out different parts of the city, like where the Godfather of Soul grew up. It was fascinating to me. She realized she was out of cigarettes and pulled off to a corner store for a pack. She encountered two friends who were dirty, drunk, nappy-headed, and in terrible need of a shave. When she introduced me to them, I was strongly reminded of the type of folk Passy Kate socialized with, not to ever forget the ones we had grown up around. I sat patiently in the car as she chatted with them.

I knew Marilyn was a little intoxicated, but I didn't realize she was as intoxicated as she was until she went into the store and came out again. I thought she was coming back to drive, but instead she came to my window and said she'd be back shortly.

I waited in the car for at least another thirty minutes, and she still hadn't returned. I got impatient and got out of the car to see where she was. Lord knows I didn't know where I was. I kept a suspicious eye on the rough-looking Negroes who were hanging around the store, drinking beer, shooting dice, and cursing. I certainly was no stranger to that class of people.

I spotted Marilyn leaning up against another car, hugging and kissing on one of the men she had introduced me to. She was acting like she was madly in love. I cleared my throat and said, "Excuse me, Marilyn."

She said in shame, "I'm comin right now."

"We did tell Aunt Lorena we wouldn't be gone long."

"Right. Got you," she said.

She started toward our car, and I could see she was as drunk as can be. She managed to get behind the wheel. I asked her with concern, "You all right? Are you sure you kin drive?"

"Yes, Cousin Haley, you worry too much. I'm fine and I kin drive. Fasten your seat belt."

She backed the car out and drove smack into another car. Then she sped away. I shouted, "Marilyn, you just hit another car!"

"Yeah, I know. I don't think it's hurt."

"How kin you know when you didn't look to see?"

"I know."

"What about Aunt Lorena's car? Ain't you gonna check to see if her car been dented?"

"Oh my God! I hadn't thought about Mama's car."

"Slow down! Slow down an pull over to the side. I'll git out an check it for you."

She paid no attention. By then, her driving was frightening me. "Marilyn!" I shouted again. "Slow the car down! You're drivin fifty miles an hour in a twenty-five zone. Now slow the car down!"

Without any warning, she made a left-hand turn and parked. She got out about the same time I did. The left fender was bent in, and the brown paint was scratched. I couldn't help but wonder about the other car that was hit.

She got back into the car. Another car came up behind her, and at first I thought it was the police. But the car didn't have a light on the top. We got to Aunt Lorena's house and she drove up the driveway. I asked her if she was all right. She said she was, and she wanted me to promise I wouldn't tell Aunt Lorena, no matter what. Her voice trembled, and I knew she was in terrible trouble. I didn't know how I was going to keep that promise. I didn't want to get involved. "All right, Marilyn. Whatever you tell her is fine with me," I replied.

We got out of the car. I thought Marilyn was coming into the house with me. Instead, the car that had been behind us stopped in front of the house. She jumped in, and it drove off fast, leaving me standing.

I didn't know what to think. Aunt Lorena came to the door just as I commenced to go in, smiling just as happily as ever. I didn't know if she would notice her car. I didn't know what to tell her about Marilyn. I was in a confused state of mind.

"Hey, baby, y'all back," Aunt Lorena said.

"Yes, ma'am."

"I was wonderin when y'all was gonna git back, but I told Bollen y'all young folk probly was enjoin y'all selves."

"Yes, ma'am, we was."

"Where is Marilyn?" she asked.

I started into the house, hoping she'd follow me in. What could I tell her without betraying Marilyn's confidence in me?

"Haley? Where is Marilyn?"

"I think she ran down to the corner store."

She looked at me in disbelief and walked down the steps and over to the car, saying, "Let me see if she took the keys with her. Marilyn is always leaving my keys in the car."

As she passed to go to the driver's side, she saw the dent in the rear. Her face flickered. "Lord have mercy, what on earth happened to my car?"

I walked over and put my hand on her shoulder. She was infuriated. She just looked at me and I at her.

Then she called Uncle Bollen out. They both looked at the car. "I know you don't want to git involved, Haley, but Marilyn doesn't have a license. If you know what happened, please tell us. The only reason we let Marilyn drive is because you are here. We don't let her drive normally because she is irresponsible." She spoke gently and softly. Her kind generosity was too important to me to leave her in suspense, but I thought if I stalled for more time, maybe Marilyn would come back.

I stalled as long as I possibly could. But when she asked me if Marilyn had been drinking, my loyalty was to Aunt Lorena and I couldn't lie to her. "Yes, Aunt Lorena, she is had a few drinks. We were on our way back here when she had a slight accident. She was backing out from a store, and backed into a parked car."

"Did she damage the car any, baby?" she asked, frightened.

"I don't know. She didn't stop to see."

"You mean it was hit an run."

"Yes, ma'am, I guess it was."

"You see, Bollen? This is it. Marilyn has got to go," she exclaimed.

"Calm down, Lorena," he said, taking her in his arms and holding her close. I couldn't remember ever hearing my father say that many kind words to my mama.

I gathered from what Aunt Lorena was saying that Marilyn was a heavy drinker. She cried as if Marilyn had killed someone.

I took the seven forty-five bus for home on Thanksgiving morning. When we left Aunt Lorena's for the bus station, Marilyn still hadn't come home. Aunt Lorena tried to hide what she was feeling as she drove me to the station. Despite the little time I had spent with her, I knew when something was disturbing her. And I saw how upset she really was at Marilyn. Still, she laughed and waited with me until my bus departed.

When the time came for me to board, I dreaded doing so. Riding alone, my mind wandered. I began to think of the good times Robbie and I had shared together and the heartache I had caused him. It all hurt awful bad. It was the only thing I could think about—that, and the fact I was never going to see him again.

I was hoping for another way out of the life I found myself in. The dreams of the good life I wanted for me and my childrens were like dust in the wind. Blaming others for my mishaps wasn't cutting it, but doing something about the situation seemed impossible. I pondered my direction and concluded that maintaining a pure confession of faith was of the utmost importance.

Chapter 27: Back Home

On November 26 at seven thirty in the evening, I knocked on Mama's door. I heard Mama laugh out and say, "I know dat gal wsn't gon let them chilluns stay down here, Mack! You see she back already."

I opened the door and went into Mama's room and hugged her. Then I went directly to the children's room. The boys were asleep in one bed, and across from them, the girls were sound asleep in the other. I woke them up and held them for the longest time. I was so glad to see them, and I promised I would never leave them again.

They were tired and soon went back off to sleep. I didn't mind. I knew I would be there when they got up in the morning.

Mama's first question when I went back to their room was "Why you come back so soon?"

I laughed and said, "I came back to stay."

I filled Mama and Daddy in about my short visit with Daddy's relatives and all the fun we had together. Around two o'clock in the morning, Willa Max and Annie Dora came in. I didn't understand Mama and Daddy's motive for allowing them to stay out till all hours of the night. When I was their ages, I could barely go to a movie. Willa Max was only about twelve, and Snappy was just into her teens. An unlimited curfew was a bit premature.

***

I devoted all of my time to the kids. I couldn't achieve enough loving. I enjoyed every moment I spent with them, and I vowed never to leave my daughters with anyone ever again.

It was a cold and dreary day. I was basking beside the fire, wishing that things had been different in my life, wishing for another opportunity to return to school. That thought was constantly on my mind. When I mentioned it to Mama, she said it was my conscience wishing for something I could never have. There was no way I was going to accept that—no way!

Loneliness gained control of me. From all angles, I had nothing left except anguish.

In walked Willa Max and Snappy. Snappy was wheezing like every breath she took would be her last. Quickly I lost the focus on me and directed my attention on them. They were yelling and cursing at each other like strangers. I tried to compose them in every way possible, but neither of them listened. I tried insulting them, but my insults only insulted myself.

All the shouting woke Daddy up. He came through, demanding they stop the arguing instantly, but they were like two hungry bulls.

Finally Snappy stopped. I think her breath was about gone; she had to stop. But Willa Max continued.

They ended up out in the backyard, where all the noise brought neighbors out to investigate. Lila was one of the first faces I recognized. I was hysterical but still determined to hold on to Willa Max. Millie Mae joined the struggle. With the two of us coming between the two of them, they settled down.

***

I went out with Lila and her crew again. I was determined to drink enough to feel good, not stupid. As they drank down whiskey straight, I diluted my drink with water. "Drink, Haley!" Lila kept insisting, but the more she insisted, the more I diluted.

A guy named Rosco stood at the end of the counter staring at my mouth like there was something he desperately wanted to say to me but didn't quite know how. I remembered dancing with him in high school—Rosco Graham. Lila spoke for him: "Haley, Rosco wants you bad as hell!"

I acknowledged he was up to something. Even if it was true he wanted me, the only reason would be because the word was out that I was the first girl he was ever with. I guess the folk down there thought that way, that I was just that girl from Rat Row. I listened to him from the outside and felt nothing from the inside.

Little Freddy walked over, and we danced. He gave me the girls' Christmas money. I said thank you without another word exchanged and went back to my seat. Lila urged me to come to the bathroom with her.

I had no idea what she wanted, but there was only one way to find out.

"Haley, I got a message for you from somebody. He want to see you. Said it is urgent that he git together with you."

I looked at her, fully aware that this was what Lila always did. I played along with her with no intentions of doing anything with anybody she was trying to set me up with.

"What you want me to tell em?" she asked.

"First of all, who is it want to see me so bad?"

"I told you—Rosco."

"Rosco Graham! Oh, hell, naw, not that Negro. You're kiddin. He can't stand me. The man hate the ground I walk on, and frankly, I can't stand his red ass either. Hell naw."

"That's what you think. Take it from me. It's Christmas, and I know you ain't got to worry bout the past. I know he been eyein you for many years, and you know how you like to show who's up when dey cross you. Dem little gurls is your life. You better go for whatever it is he's offerin. Hurry! What you want me to tell em? I got to git back behind de counter fore Duke git back."

Yes, I knew the game so well. It was my time to play. "Tell him nothin."

From then on, Rosco followed me around. Everywhere I went, he was there, sending messages from Lila. He wouldn't take no for an answer. He looked stoned, and I concluded it was wise to take a rain check on him. His watching made me feel awfully uncomfortable.

I got up and walked over to Flappy Boots's café to get away from him. Doletha was parked in front with her two beautiful little girls. I stopped to say hello.

"Git in and sit down Haley," Doletha said. "Chat with me a while. I ain't seen you since you come back. So tell me, how is everything going?"

I got in the front seat with her. I played with the kids, and they rather enjoyed my company, just as I enjoyed sharing a happy moment with them. Doletha asked me if I had got all of my Christmas shopping done. I dared not tell her anything but yes.

She was her same old self, still the same boaster. Always wanting to be more then what she was. I listened to her brag of Ezekiel and what had happened to her. She literally bragged on the sordid pain.

As she was talking, I recalled it was Doletha who came between Rosco and me in the first place. I remembered all the mornings I walked into our classrooms and she was the first one to make fun of my clothes. The memories struck me hard in my heart. My conversation with Lila was still in my mind. The more I drank, the more I considered it, and the more it appealed to me. I decided to go for it.

***

I went downtown and got my girls their gifts and chatted with Pearly Mae for a few moments. That evening, I went out to the cafés. Rosco was there, and he didn't hesitate to make his feelings known. He sat down next to me. All eyes danced on us, especially Little Freddy's. He was looking so hard, I really thought he was going to come over. I could tell what each and every one of them was thinking.

Rosco asked me to dance. *What the hell*, I thought. *Why not make those Negroes eat their hearts out?*

We danced closely. He asked, "Did Lila tell you what I said?"

I pretended I didn't know what he was talking about.

He said, "You mean she didn't tell you what I said a few days ago?"

"Oh! I thought you meant recently."

"Have you considered my proposition?"

"Sure, I've considered, but I haven't decided anything yet. Like I told her, we'll have to talk later."

"How much later? Why not now?"

"Because now is not the right time," I said uncertainly.

Little Freddy was getting more wasted by the minute. I could always tell when he was up to no good, and the way he was pouring whiskey into his mouth, hell was building up. His eyes were saying it was ass-kicking time. I knew he would soon put on a show free of charge.

I told Rosco I had to go across the street and I would be back shortly. I walked over to Flappy Boots's café. His place was jam-packed. Everyone was dancing and having a magnificent time.

I saw Danny Major by the jukebox. I squeezed through to him. "Haley Keath, long time no see," he said.

"My goodness, it has been a long time, Danny."

"Come and meet my wife. She don't know anyone here. I'd like for you to show her around."

"Sure I will."

She was sitting on one of the bleachers up against the wall. She looked awfully apprehensive. It wasn't an unusual look for a person in a small town and strange place. Danny said, "Honey, meet an old classmate of mine, Haley Keath. Haley, this is my wife Ann."

We shook hands and a friendship began. He went back to his hole over by the jukebox, leaving us to get better acquainted.

"Haley, kin you show me where the restroom is?"

"Come, darling. The only restroom in this one-horse town is on the ground behind some bushes," I said, laughing. I led her out behind the café, where I met up with Little Freddy.

"I was just looking for you," he stated.

"Looking for me? For what?"

Pulling my arm almost out of the socket, he said angrily, "Don't try to git smart with me."

"You're hurting my arm, Little Freddy. Let go," I said, jerking away from him. "Ann, go right back and do what you have to. I'll watch for you." She walked off, leaving us alone. "All right, Little Freddy, what the hell you following me for now?"

"I have a question. You going with Rosco Graham now?"

"Are you asking me or telling me? Besides, it's none of your business. I've told you once and I'll tell you again: if you keep bothering me, I'll deal with you later."

I rushed off. My words immediately weighed heavily in my mind. I decided that night I was finished with Little Freddy.

***

During the New Year, I stayed close to home with the children. My life was a shambles and I knew it. I was in need of a job. I dreaded leaving home because I didn't want more lies told on me. I spoke to various people who came in and out of the house, buying whiskey, about some jobs possibilities, but nothing came along.

I was out in the backyard one day, hanging up clothes, and Lila called me. I knew deep down that she disliked me, but it didn't matter to me for some reason. I crossed the ditch and heard Annie Dora and Willa Max having a terrible fight. Annie Dora didn't stand a chance. Willa Max was all over her. I was certain Willa Max was gonna get hurt because she was close to her time to give birth to her first baby.

Daddy and I pulled them apart forcefully. Willa Max assured me she was fine. I asked her what they were fighting about, and she said, "A white lady named Mrs. Janice Whitney came lookin for you to work for her. Annie Dora talked to her an told her you'd gone back up north, but she, Annie Dora, was interested in de job."

Mrs. Whitney believed Snappy and hired her. My sister undermined me out of a job I desperately needed, knowing she was not well enough to keep it. In two days, she was finished, dragging in and barely able to breathe.

***

My little brother Billy came in and told me somebody wanted to see me. I stepped outside, and it was Rosco. He was more determined than ever to see me I thought it was as good a time as any to carry out my vendetta against Doletha and the rest.

***

It was midwinter. I was sitting in Lila's place, playing a game of tunk with her. Cindy came in and revealed to me that the Trapper School was accepting applications for new enrollments, and I could go and place one. I was accepted and started school in two weeks.

***

My first paycheck was thirty-five dollars. On the Tuesday I received it, I got home to find Willa Max had gone into labor. She didn't have any money to get a midwife. I told Daddy to get Mrs. Figgins, and I would pay for her to deliver my sister's baby.

I watched Willa Max suffer for hours, and she was only a baby herself—she had turned thirteen years old not two months before. Every pain she had, I felt that same pain, only mine were not labor pains. My mother wiped sweat from Willa Max's face and rubbed her stomach, just as she had done for me when I lay in labor so long for Rejetta.

At ten thirty, Willa Max gave birth to a beautiful eight-pound baby girl, and she gave me permission to name her. I named her Brenda Rejetta.

***

I was rather enjoying going to school every day, but awfully disappointed in how little I knew. However, I was very proud of learning subjects I could remember taking when I attended regular school. My strongest enemy whispered and wrote notes about me to Vassie Blackmon, just as Doletha used to do. I would ignore her like it never happened. She never knew Vassie gave me the notes to read, and I never gave Vassie away—until one day I was so fed up about a lying note that I went over and confronted her with one of my favorite threats. She knew I would carry it out. I dared her to write another one.

***

Two houses were available for rent in Brake's quarter. I took off early one day to inquire about renting one. The one I was really interested in had already been taken, so I had to settle for the only one left. It was the worst house in the quarter, and next door to Delta.

***

One cold, rainy night, Little Freddy and I had made plans. I waited home for him. The longer I waited, the more impatient I became. At eight o'clock, I was thinking of all the things that had happened in my life and the pain people had caused me, and I became very unreasonable. I went out in that pouring rain and walked to the café. I got a bottle and drank it.

Shortly after I arrived, Timothy Bird came in. I offered him two dollars to take me up to where they lived. I felt betrayed and deceived by Little Freddy, and I wasn't about to let him get away with it.

I had Timothy to wait for me. Lights were on in the house, and I could hear the TV playing. It was around twenty degrees and pouring down rain. I walked up on the porch and knocked on the door. She opened it and seemed struck with astonishment.

"Haley Keath! What in de world is you doin out in all of dis rain?" she asked.

Without being invited, I walked in ruthlessly. He was sitting cozy before the fire with his arms folded, watching TV.

"I saw y'all lights on and just stopped by to say hello. I'm so mad, I don't know what to do," I stated indignantly.

"What you so mad about?" she asked with concern. I glanced at him; he was putting his shoes on.

I said, "Men. They don't do nothin but lie. I been stood up."

"Haley! What happened? Little Freddy stood you up?"

"Yeah, you kin say dat! I won't stay, gurl. I was just in your neck of the woods an decided to pop in. Sorry about the intrudin. I'm goin back to Lila's place. I got a feelin he'll be dere when I git back."

***

I had signed up for a sewing class at the Trapper School. The class had been given the opportunity to make dresses for ourselves or any kids that we wanted to, so I made me and the girls dresses alike. I had finished theirs and was working on mine. I couldn't seem to get the zipper in correctly. Mrs. Wood, the instructor, was determined I was going to insert that zipper myself. I was getting more frustrated by degrees; every time I put it in, I had to take it back out. She had me watch her, and then for about the fifth time I had to take the zipper out of the dress. I tore the material a little. She looked at me with despair and murmured, "As you sew, sew shall you rip. Now keep sewing."

At last I got I got the zipper sewed in, and I became a seamstress on that day. I even enjoyed a sense of optimism about myself. I went home that evening feeling good about myself.

***

I met Mrs. Teekie down past the judge's house. As we passed each other, we both said, "Good evening," not at first noticing who we were speaking to.

She turned around. I looked back at her and couldn't think of any reason why she had turned around. She said, "Ain't you Ms. Jenny Rue's girl?" She looked as if I were a ghost. I stared at her as if she were the witch who captured Hansel and Gretel. But there was something in her eyes that told me she definitely was not a witch.

I answered, "Yes, ma'am, I am."

"Which one of her girls you is?"

"I'm Haley."

"Den you dat one wit dat Little Freddy dude."

"Oh? So dey say."

"Look, honey, I'm old nough to be your ma, an I won't tell you nothin wrong. Lord knows I don't tend to nobody's business, but I guess de good Lord want me to let you know dis: you be careful drinkin with dem girls, specially dat one name Lila. Stay out of her place, you hear me, girl?"

She waited for me to respond to her warning. I was for a minute unsure how to. I could see, deep in her eyes, that she was delivering a message from God. Our spirits connected. I said, "Yes, ma'am."

"Den you listen to me, and hear me real good. Mrs. Teekie is tellin you to stop. Stop drinkin with dem people and stay away from round dem folk. Dey don't like you, an I know what I'm talkin bout. Every time you drink with dem, you risk your life. Dey scare to fight ye fair cause dey know you gon put some on em. So dey git you in whiskey. You see, gurl? All dem dat hatin on you done been wit dat Freddy dude. I live up dere by dat Lila, de main one. I don't know what you done to her, but she hate your guts. See, I hear a lot of talk, what dey be sayin bout ye. It ain't good talk. You de one dey low-rate de worst."

I grunted, clutching my arms tightly, soaking in the bad news. I knew she was telling the truth. I heard every word that came from her mouth. I thanked her dearly for sharing with me what I already knew. It was like I was hypnotized in some way by what was going on with me. It all came back to this: "For the wages of sin is death, but the gift of God is eternal life through Christ Jesus our Lord" (Rom. 6:23 KJV). I saw no way. I knew no way. But in that moment, I knew Jesus was my way.

I thought of nothing but what Mrs. Teekie fed me that day. I could hardly digest it, but I knew it was filling.

It was thoughtful of her to warn me. I knew every false accusation being spread by them. It outraged me in such a way that it made me bawl. I felt there was much more to the story than she let on, but even what little she said made me open my eyes. Folk round there said she was crazy, but she certainly didn't sound crazy to me. She was polite and very sincere. I heard, I listened, and I took heed.

***

Bessie Neil had taken the house that I was going to rent, but somehow she and I ended up friends. We visited each other and took our children to church on Sundays. She, Rosco, and I did everything together. Whenever we went out, it was together. My relationship with Rosco escalated more than either of us had anticipated it would. He began to confide in me about his life.

I stopped going to the cafés altogether, just as Mrs. Teekie had suggested. Suddenly Delta started visiting me on a regular basis. All her conversation was stories. Bessie Neil warned me about Delta on several occasions. I would say, "Everybody knows how Delta is." I just looked over her and her statements, being very aware of her fishing and what she hoped to catch.

***

Months had gone by. I had stopped hanging out in the bottom, until one Sunday after church, Bessie Neil convinced me to go with her. We got the kids settled down, and we walked over that evening. Lila's place was jumping. Bessie Neil implored me to go there with her. I was determined not to, but her convincing was more than my declining. I ended up going in with her.

She got us a bottle and we took a seat in the back. The regulars were there. All eyes centered on me. The jukebox kicked off with "Down in the Valley" and "Beautiful Brown Eyes." My eyes were certainly big, brown, and beautiful.

After we had been in there for a while, someone told Bessie Neil that her parents were at her house to take the kids home with them. She insisted that I sit and wait until she came back. She promised she would come back.

I waited. People came and went. It seemed like the only record that was playing was "Down in the Valley."

I went to the bathroom and left my drink on the table. After returning from the restroom, I drank the drink down without giving it a second thought. Rosco came in, and I took one look at him and I couldn't stand the sight of him.

That was all I remembered until the next morning. I woke with my head hurting. Loud knocking was at the door. My stomach was turning a flip. Clothes was strewn all over the floor. My room looked as if a hurricane had come through it.

I got up, went to the door, and opened it. Bessie Neil came in, yelling, "Gurl! What was de matter wit you?"

"What was de matter wit me when?" I asked, holding both hands to my head.

"You don't know? I got back from seein my kids off, an you was de show."

"Bessie Neil, show what? What de hell are you talkin bout?"

"Gurl, when I got back to Lila's place, you was cursin everybody out. You was stoned like a ragin maniac."

I had no memory at all of what happened after she left me. I had been intoxicated for sure, but from what? I only recalled having two small drinks. How was it possible for me to lose my memory within twenty minutes?

***

I came home from school and sat warming by the fire, beating my head as I tried to remember what happened to me on Sunday. Rosco came by, and we discussed it. He told me pretty much the same thing Bessie Neil had told me. He comforted me with deepest concern. He reassured me that he cared deeply for me, and I believed he did.

***

Around ten o'clock one morning, I was about to take a bath when I heard a car pull up in front of my house. I opened the door and it was her. She had the most furious look on her face. I knew exactly what she was there for. "Come in," I invited.

She stormed in angrily. She didn't hesitate; she got directly to the point of her visit, which I already knew. She was enraged, and she had every right to be. Looking into her eyes, I hurt for her. I knew she was not at fault for any of her actions. How was I ever going to get over the hurt I caused?

I was left with pure guilt. It went to bed with me at night. It got up with me every morning. Everywhere I went, guilt followed me. I lived with it every day of my life. Being spiteful does not pay. It boomerangs back on us and becomes a constant reminder of what happens and to whom it happens. It is not worth the guilt, pain, or any other payment that comes with it.

Rosco came by that night. I debated whether to tell him about my visit. I was about to bring up the subject, when he said, "Somethin strange happened tonight when I got in from work."

"What?"

"Ernestine and Marlene kept mentionin your name. I didn't know what to make of it. However, I know dey like you a lot. When you been around or dey seen you somewhere, dey always mention your name until she make em go off to bed."

I was amazed. "Oh, dey would? Really?"

"Yeah, dey would."

"So now you want to know if dey seen me today."

"Not really; I just ain't heard em mention you for a while fore today."

"I wasn't gon say anythin, but dey did see me today. Dere mother paid me a visit, and she had em wit her."

"She did?"

"Yeah, she did. I'm surprised she didn't tell you."

"Naw, I didn't know nothin about it," he said.

***

One Monday night when he came by, he had a sad look about him. I knew something was wrong, but I didn't ask. He was tired. He sat down for a while before telling me she was gone. She had moved back to her mama's. I reflected on her and how she gave and what she was getting in return.

In the beginning I did gloat at the thought that after almost sixteen years of pain, she'd gotten it all back in one night. I had no sympathy for her. I didn't have sense enough to feel sorry for her or even to realize the damnation I had placed upon my own life. I didn't care. I didn't know the words, "Vengeance belongeth unto me, I will recompense, saith the Lord" (Heb. 10:30 KJV).

The revenge I plotted came back on me triple. Her hurt was the most hideous act I could have committed. It was something I terribly regretted.

***

I looked at her and showed her the door. I slammed it behind her, and in that instant, I realized the devil had used me again. I demanded he leave and go after her.

I lay down to take a quick snooze, but I lay awake, thinking of the pain she left with and I helped cause. I knew I was not a cruel person. I began to hate myself for the the role I had played in hurting the one person that I said I loved.

I made a decision, but I had no plan. I had to come up with a plan that would put them back together. In my heart I was convicted of my horrible sin.

He may have told her he wanted me, but I knew Rosco was not over his love for her. She was the mother of his children, whom he loved dearly. I was not going to play second anymore. They had kids, and for him to see his kids, he had to see her.

And I loved them both. Though they didn't know what I was doing, I had a guilty feeling for causing their pain. I felt more and more guilt each time I was with him. I knew I had to do something about it, and the most decent thing I could come up with was to get him out of my life. I could use Little Freddy to do it, make him my scapegoat.

***

When we got to school that Monday morning, we were hit by some disturbing news. We had already taken the high school equivalency test and had about six weeks to wait before we heard the results. But the school's funds had run out and classes were being discontinued. That was our last week.

I took the news rather hard. It was my only source of income. I didn't know what I was going to do.

I was sitting and considering plans. Unexpectedly, Millie Mae sat down beside me like we were the best of friends. I knew she was up to no good. I knew her better than she knew herself. I sat still, pretending she wasn't even there.

She slipped me a note. I took it, and it read, "*Haley, I talked to Little Freddy last night and he told me to tell you if I saw you today that he wanted you back. I'll be seeing him tonight. What you want me to tell him.*"

I wrote on the bottom of the paper, "*Nothing*," and I handed it back to her.

She wrote that he realized he'd made a terrible mistake by not making the relationship with me work. He knew Ruthella was just like her mama, laying with everybody she could.

That time, I didn't return the note. I just looked at her and smiled. I kept the note for evidence. I knew it would come back; if Little Freddy found anything out about Ruthella, Millie Mae would have something to do with it.

That night as I was bathing, I heard footsteps on my porch, then a soft tap. I thought it might be Rosco coming early, but I hadn't heard his car drive up. I asked, "Who is it?"

No one answered.

Thinking now that it was probably the wind I'd heard, I continued to bathe. The tap came again. "Who is it?" I asked.

"It's Little Freddy, Haley."

"Little Freddy, what do you want?"

I dried myself, put on my gown and robe, and opened the door. "Little Freddy, what do you want?" I asked again harshly.

"Let me come in out of de cold, and I'll tell you."

Unwillingly, I opened the door. He came in, pulled a chair up to the fire, and sat down, warming his hands and making himself comfortably at home. "Good God, Haley babe, it is cold out dere. Dis is a nice warm fire you got here, and it sure feels good. Where did you git dis wood from? It looks like some of de wood Rosco would be able to git workin out in dat puck wood."

"Matter of fact, he did git it for me. Anyhow, I know you didn't come here to talk bout my wood and where I got it from, now did you?"

"Naw, I didn't. I came to talk bout us."

"What bout us?"

"Bout you and I gittin back together."

"No dice, Little Freddy. Never." I laughed out because it was so funny to me, the big, bad womanizer wanting me back. It was only because I was with somebody else. What a joke!

"Tell me what you mean, no dice?"

"What I said is what I mean, so if dat's what you here for, you kin leave now," I stated seriously.

"But Haley babe, we can't stay away from each other. No matter who I go wit, we always end up back together."

"'Haley babe' nothin. Little Freddy, you don't want me no more dan I want you. Don't you think you gon start runnin back to me cause you got a dose of your own medicine. Now you got to leave fore my company come an catch you here."

His charming look that electrified me disappeared into a pensive one, and then to an embittered one. It was a look I was no longer afraid of. He'd used my relationship as a weapon. It was unbelievable that Little Freddy was all of a sudden so concerned about somebody else's marriage. He certainly was in no position to be a marriage counselor for anyone.

I was ready to carry out my plan, and he played it all the way for me. I ordered him to leave my house, but he refused. Then he accused me of not keeping the childrens with me because I didn't have time for them. His attitude was disgusting.

Arguing with him only stimulated the atrocious feud between us. I kept a low profile, knowing full well what he wanted. What better time to use him to get out of the relationship I was in? I knew when his anger was stirred up, his next stage was fighting. The only way I had to calm him down was profess that I did want him back and make him think he was the only man for me. Rosco was just my company. I needed some way to break things off with Rosco, and Little Freddy was that way.

Little Freddy insisted that I cease the relationship that night, but I felt I needed a little more time for my plan to work completely. I could not allow him to compel me to do something. I was so close to achieving my mission.

I was trying to convince Little Freddy to give me until the weekend, when Rosco drove up. I considered pretending not to be at home, but Little Freddy's car was parked in front of the house. So I just allowed Little Freddy to do what he did best: think he was the man.

I told Little Freddy to open the door. When he opened it, Rosco's face was red as the fire, and it wasn't from the cold. They spoke civilly to each other, and I sat back, scared out of my mind but putting on a brave face before them.

Then Little Freddy demanded I end my relationship with Rosco that instant. I refused. They began to exchange harsh words, and before I knew what was happening, Little Freddy threw the first punch.

It was a scary sight. I begged them to stop, but they fought hard. Little Freddy straddled Rosco across the bed and punched down on him. They both were strong, but Little Freddy was faster. I screamed for Little Freddy to please leave and let me do what I had to do in privacy. When he got up, I pushed him out of my door, promising him I would take him back. He left, warning me as he walked out that I had until the weekend.

***

It was all working out for the best, regardless as to the reason. I would put the outside lock on the door at night, pretending not to be home, because he wouldn't stop coming. It worked for a few nights. When it no longer did, I brought my kids over to stay with me at night, knowing he could not stay at my house while my children were present.

That worked until Little Freddy began pestering me about taking him back. I knew his game well, and I knew he was in between women. He always wanted what he couldn't have.

Enough damage had been done, and I couldn't get any of it out of my mind. I knew I had ruied every chance of ever having her as my friend again, and that hurt me more than any words could have said.

Out of the clear blue he came, wanting me to leave town with him. I was anxious to leave, but not with him.

When he left, I sat before the fire, fantasizing about what life could be with him. It would never work for us, no matter what state we relocated to.

Someone walked up on the porch and knocked. I asked, "Who is it?"

"It's Little Freddy, Haley. Open de door."

I could see anger in his eyes when he walked in. He was like a rattlesnake ready to strike. "Did you tell Rosco?" he asked angrily.

Praying he didn't cause another fight, I lied, "Yes, I did." I had learned how to lie to him as I was lied to—anything to make him think he was in control.

I didn't want either of those men, but it was a surety that I needed Jesus. I was filled with anger and deceit, and was living a dangerous life. I never blamed anyone for not trusting me. Hell, I didn't trust me either, although I admitted who I was.

What I had witnessed in my house between Rosco and Little Freddy was shameful. All I wanted was to get the hell out. I didn't care how; I wanted out. Too many people were getting hurt from all directions. I hit, and when I did, I hit fast and hard. I hurt people.

People always do to someone else what someone else has done to them, and no one is safe. Word to the wise: don't bother folk whom you don't know. Unsaved folk do unsaved things.

God is always setting us up for something. No matter how smart we think we are, nobody has been born who can make a fool out of God. Please stop trying.

***

He was so happy. We planned to leave in two weeks. I was to meet him at the bus station on my birthday.

The following weekend, I received a letter from Tise. She informed me that Robbie had been in a terrible accident, and he was in critical condition.

On Wednesday, Mama came to my house. When I heard her calling for me to open the door, I knew something was wrong. She was standing there crying. She had come home to find Willa Max had taken the baby and left. I hadn't seen Mama that hurt for quite some time. We sat down, and I comforted her in every way I could. But what she was feeling was beyond my consolation. It wasn't easy for her to accept Willa Max leaving home like the rest of us, for to Mama, Willa Max was still just a baby herself.

***

Rosco came through for me, just as he promised. It was time to get the kids and I out of that town. When he left, he didn't know that was my final good-bye. Annie Dora and I planned to leave that Sunday.

I began my packing. No one knew I was leaving town except Annie Dora, and I had to make sure she didn't say a word. I was so close to going back to New Hampshire, I could see myself there. I counted the hours until Snappy, the kids, and I boarded the bus at ten-forty on Sunday morning.

When the bus pulled away, I was free of that town but not the past issues it left with me.

Author Biography

Evangelist Hazel Singleton has lived an interesting life. As a girl growing up in Colquitt, Georgia, on Rat Row, she had two parents and a houseful of siblings. But within the nest, she witnessed instability, fear, uncertainty, danger, secrets, and hardships. and insecurities. She experienced incredible highs and inconceivable lows. In the end, she was able to find meaning, purpose, and solace in the Word of God, and became a messenger for Christ. Her experiences helped to shape not only this book, but her ministry for God. Today, she uses her unique story to inspire others with similar life experiences to build a relationship with Jesus Christ, forgive others, forgive the past, and help heal someone else.

Printed in the United States
By Bookmasters